KJV Standard LESSON COMMENTARY®

2005-2006

Large Print Edition

International Sunday School Lessons

Edited by

Ronald L. Nickelson

Published by
STANDARD PUBLISHING

Jonathan Underwood,
Senior Editor, Adult Ministry Resources

Fifty-third Annual Volume

©2005
STANDARD PUBLISHING
A division of STANDEX INTERNATIONAL Corporation
8121 Hamilton Avenue, Cincinnati, Ohio 45231
Printed in U. S. A.

In This Volume

Fall Quarter 2005 (page 1)
You Will Be My Witnesses
Writers
Lesson Development: ....James Lloyd (1-4), Dennis Gaertner (5-13)
Verbal Illustrations: ....Charles R. Boatman
Learning by Doing: ....Ronald G. Davis
Let's Talk It Over: ....A. Eugene Andrews

Winter Quarter 2005-2006 (page 113)
God's Commitment—Our Response
Writers
Lesson Development: ....Lloyd Pelfrey (1-4), Harvey Bream (5-9), Mark Krause (10-13)
Verbal Illustrations: ....A. Eugene Andrews (1-4, 10-13), James B. North (5-9)
Learning by Doing: ....Ronald G. Davis (1-9), Alan Weber (10-13)
Let's Talk It Over: ....Kenneth Beck (1-4), Richard Baynes (5-13)

Spring Quarter 2006 (page 225)
Living in and as God's Creation
Writers
Lesson Development: ....David Marvin (1-4), J. Michael Shannon (5-9), Mark Krause (10-13)
Verbal Illustrations: ....Charles R. Boatman
Learning by Doing: ....Richard A. Koffarnus (1-4, 10-13), Ronald G. Davis (5-9)
Let's Talk It Over: ....Kenneth Beck (1-4), Tom Lawson (5-9), Mark Moore (10-13)

Summer Quarter 2006 (page 337)
Called to Be a Christian Community
Writers
Lesson Development: ....Kenny Boles (1-4), Tom Thatcher (5-13)
Verbal Illustrations: ....A. Eugene Andrews (1-9), Terry Bowland (10-13)
Learning by Doing: ....Alan Weber (1-9), Ronald G. Davis (10-13)
Let's Talk It Over: ....Jeffrey Snell (1-9), Kenneth Goble (10-13)

Artists
Title Pages: James E. Seward

Cover design by DesignTeam

Lessons based on International Sunday School Lessons © 2003 by the Lesson Committee.

Index of Printed Texts, 2005-2006

The printed texts for 2005-2006 are arranged here in the order in which they appear in the Bible. Opposite each reference is the number of the page on which it appears in this volume.

REFERENCE	PAGE
Job 1:14-22	303
Job 3:1-3	303
Job 3:11	303
Job 14:1, 2	312
Job 14:11-17	312
Job 32:6	312
Job 32:8	312
Job 34:12	312
Job 37:14	312
Job 37:22	312
Job 38:1	321
Job 38:4	321
Job 38:16, 17	321
Job 42:1, 2	321
Job 42:5	321
Psalm 8:1-9	267
Psalm 104:1-13	276
Psalm 139:1-3	285
Psalm 139:7-14	285
Psalm 139:23, 24	285
Psalm 145:1-13	294
Proverbs 2:1-5	348
Proverbs 3:1-6	348
Proverbs 3:13-18	348
Proverbs 8:1-5	357
Proverbs 8:22-32	357
Proverbs 11:1-14	366
Proverbs 31:8-14	375
Proverbs 31:25-30	375
Ecclesiastes 1:1-9	330
Ecclesiastes 3:1-8	339
Ecclesiastes 3:14, 15	339
Isaiah 42:1-9	139
Isaiah 49:5, 6	148
Isaiah 50:4-11	148
Isaiah 53:1-3	157
Isaiah 61:1, 2	166
Mark 16:1-14	321
Mark 16:20	321
Luke 1:46-55	157
Luke 2:8-20	166
John 20:19-23	330
Acts 2:1-8	11
Acts 2:36-42	11
Acts 2:43-47	20

REFERENCE	PAGE
Acts 3:1-16	29
Acts 4:1-4	38
Acts 4:23-31	38
Acts 4:32-35	20
Acts 6:8-15	47
Acts 7:54-60	47
Acts 8:4-17	56
Acts 8:26-38	65
Acts 9:3-18	92
Acts 10:1-20	74
Acts 12:1-16	83
Acts 16:6-15	101
Acts 16:40	101
Acts 18:1-4	110
Acts 18:18-21	110
Acts 18:24-28	110
Acts 20:17-28	119
Acts 20:36-38	119
1 Corinthians 1:10-17	395
1 Corinthians 2:1-16	404
1 Corinthians 3:1-15	413
1 Corinthians 4:1-13	422
1 Corinthians 7:1-15	431
1 Corinthians 8:1-13	440
1 Corinthians 9:24-27	449
1 Corinthians 10:1-13	449
1 Corinthians 12:1-13	458
1 Corinthians 13:1-13	467
2 Corinthians 2:5-11	476
2 Corinthians 7:2-15	476
2 Corinthians 8:1-15	485
2 Corinthians 9:3-15	494
2 Corinthians 12:1-10	503
1 Timothy 1:12-20	175
1 Timothy 2:1-8	184
1 Timothy 3:1-15	193
1 Timothy 4:1-16	202
1 Timothy 5:1-8	211
1 Timothy 5:17-25	211
2 Timothy 1:3-14	220
2 Timothy 2:14-26	229
2 Timothy 3:10-17	238
2 Timothy 4:1-8	238
Titus 2:1-15	247

Cumulative Index

A cumulative index for the Scripture passages used in the STANDARD LESSON COMMENTARY for the years September, 2004—August, 2006, is provided below.

REFERENCE	YEAR	PAGE
Genesis 2:4-7	2004-05	11
Genesis 2:15-25	2004-05	11
Genesis 6:5-8	2004-05	20
Genesis 6:13, 14	2004-05	20
Genesis 7:1-5	2004-05	20
Genesis 7:17	2004-05	20
Genesis 7:23	2004-05	20
Genesis 8:14-16	2004-05	20
Genesis 9:1	2004-05	20
Genesis 11:27-32	2004-05	139
Genesis 12:1-9	2004-05	139
Exodus 3:1-12	2004-05	29
Deuteronomy 29:1-15	2004-05	38
Ruth 1:3-9	2004-05	220
Ruth 1:14-18	2004-05	220
1 Samuel 16:1-13	2004-05	148
2 Samuel 7:18-29	2004-05	47
2 Kings 5:1-15a	2004-05	229
Job 1:14-22	2005-06	303
Job 3:1-3	2005-06	303
Job 3:11	2005-06	303
Job 14:1, 2	2005-06	312
Job 14:11-17	2005-06	312
Job 32:6	2005-06	312
Job 32:8	2005-06	312
Job 34:12	2005-06	312
Job 37:14	2005-06	312
Job 37:22	2005-06	312
Job 38:1	2005-06	321
Job 38:4	2005-06	321
Job 38:16, 17	2005-06	321
Job 42:1, 2	2005-06	321
Job 42:5	2005-06	321
Psalm 8:1-9	2005-06	267
Psalm 73:1-3	2004-05	83
Psalm 73:12, 13	2004-05	83
Psalm 73:16-18	2004-05	83
Psalm 73:21-26	2004-05	83
Psalm 104:1-13	2005-06	276
Psalm 139:1-3	2005-06	285
Psalm 139:7-14	2005-06	285
Psalm 139:23, 24	2005-06	285
Psalm 145:1-13	2005-06	294
Proverbs 2:1-5	2005-06	348
Proverbs 3:1-6	2005-06	348

REFERENCE	YEAR	PAGE
Proverbs 3:13-18	2005-06	348
Proverbs 8:1-5	2005-06	357
Proverbs 8:22-32	2005-06	357
Proverbs 11:1-14	2005-06	366
Proverbs 31:8-14	2005-06	375
Proverbs 31:25-30	2005-06	375
Ecclesiastes 1:1-9	2005-06	330
Ecclesiastes 3:1-8	2005-06	339
Ecclesiastes 3:14, 15	2005-06	339
Isaiah 42:1-9	2005-06	139
Isaiah 43:1-3a	2004-05	56
Isaiah 43:10-19	2004-05	56
Isaiah 49:5, 6	2005-06	148
Isaiah 50:4-11	2005-06	148
Isaiah 53:1-3	2005-06	157
Isaiah 61:1, 2	2005-06	166
Jeremiah 29:10-14	2004-05	65
Jeremiah 31:31-34	2004-05	65
Ezekiel 37:1-14	2004-05	74
Matthew 1:17-25	2004-05	157
Matthew 5:1-16	2004-05	431
Matthew 5:17, 18	2004-05	92
Matthew 5:21, 22	2004-05	92
Matthew 5:27, 28	2004-05	92
Matthew 5:31-35	2004-05	92
Matthew 5:38, 39	2004-05	92
Matthew 5:43-45	2004-05	92
Matthew 5:48	2004-05	92
Matthew 6:1-15	2004-05	440
Matthew 13:9-17	2004-05	449
Matthew 18:21-35	2004-05	458
Matthew 25:31-46	2004-05	467
Mark 1:4-13	2004-05	395
Mark 1:14-28	2004-05	175
Mark 2:1-12	2004-05	404
Mark 2:13-17	2004-05	184
Mark 3:13-19	2004-05	193
Mark 6:6b-13	2004-05	193
Mark 8:27-38	2004-05	202
Mark 10:32-45	2004-05	211
Mark 14:53-65	2004-05	413
Mark 15:1-3	2004-05	413
Mark 16:1-14	2005-06	321
Mark 16:1-16	2004-05	422
Mark 16:20	2005-06	321

REFERENCE	YEAR	PAGE
Luke 1:46-55	2005-06	157
Luke 2:8-20	2005-06	166
Luke 2:22-38	2004-05	166
Luke 4:16-24	2004-05	476
Luke 4:28-30	2004-05	476
Luke 8:40-56	2004-05	485
Luke 10:25-37	2004-05	494
Luke 14:7-11	2004-05	503
Luke 14:15-27	2004-05	503
John 3:1-17	2004-05	238
John 4:7-10	2004-05	247
John 4:19-26	2004-05	247
John 20:1-10	2004-05	294
John 20:19-23	2005-06	330
Acts 2:1-8	2005-06	11
Acts 2:36-42	2005-06	11
Acts 2:43-47	2005-06	20
Acts 3:1-16	2005-06	29
Acts 4:1-4	2005-06	38
Acts 4:23-31	2005-06	38
Acts 4:32-35	2005-06	20
Acts 6:8-15	2005-06	47
Acts 7:54-60	2005-06	47
Acts 8:4-17	2005-06	56
Acts 8:26-38	2005-06	65
Acts 9:3-18	2005-06	92
Acts 10:1-20	2005-06	74
Acts 12:1-16	2005-06	83
Acts 16:6-15	2005-06	101
Acts 16:40	2005-06	101
Acts 18:1-4	2005-06	110
Acts 18:18-21	2005-06	110
Acts 18:24-28	2005-06	110
Acts 20:17-28	2005-06	119
Acts 20:36-38	2005-06	119
Romans 1:16-20	2004-05	267
Romans 2:1-16	2004-05	276
Romans 3:9-20	2004-05	267
Romans 5:1-11	2004-05	285
Romans 5:18-21	2004-05	285
Romans 6:1-14	2004-05	294
Romans 8:1-17	2004-05	303

REFERENCE	YEAR	PAGE
Romans 10:5-17	2004-05	312
Romans 12:1, 2	2004-05	321
Romans 12:9-21	2004-05	321
Romans 14:1-13	2004-05	330
Romans 15:5, 6	2004-05	330
1 Corinthians 1:10-17	2005-06	395
1 Corinthians 2:1-16	2005-06	404
1 Corinthians 3:1-15	2005-06	413
1 Corinthians 4:1-13	2005-06	422
1 Corinthians 7:1-15	2005-06	431
1 Corinthians 8:1-13	2005-06	440
1 Corinthians 9:24-27	2005-06	449
1 Corinthians 10:1-13	2005-06	449
1 Corinthians 12:1-13	2005-06	458
1 Corinthians 13:1-13	2005-06	467
1 Corinthians 15:42-57	2004-05	101
2 Corinthians 2:5-11	2005-06	476
2 Corinthians 5:11-21	2004-05	110
2 Corinthians 7:2-15	2005-06	476
2 Corinthians 8:1-15	2005-06	485
2 Corinthians 9:3-15	2005-06	494
2 Corinthians 12:1-10	2005-06	503
Galatians 1:1-12	2004-05	348
Galatians 2:15-21	2004-05	348
Galatians 3:1-5	2004-05	348
Galatians 3:19-29	2004-05	357
Galatians 4:4-7	2004-05	357
Galatians 5:1-15	2004-05	366
Galatians 5:22-26	2004-05	375
Galatians 6:1-10	2004-05	375
Ephesians 2:11-21	2004-05	119
1 Timothy 1:12-20	2005-06	175
1 Timothy 2:1-8	2005-06	184
1 Timothy 3:1-15	2005-06	193
1 Timothy 4:1-16	2005-06	202
1 Timothy 5:1-8	2005-06	211
1 Timothy 5:17-25	2005-06	211
2 Timothy 1:3-14	2005-06	220
2 Timothy 2:14-26	2005-06	229
2 Timothy 3:10-17	2005-06	238
2 Timothy 4:1-8	2005-06	238
Titus 2:1-15	2005-06	247

How to Say It

The following pages list some of the names and hard-to-pronounce words used in the lessons of this edition of the STANDARD LESSON COMMENTARY® along with a phonetic pronunciation guide for each. In each lesson is an abridged version of this list that includes only the words used in that lesson.

A

ABEDNEGO. Uh-*bed*-nee-go.
ACHAIA. Uh-*kay*-uh.
AEGEAN. A-*jee*-un.
AESOP. *Ee*-sup.
AGUR. *Ay*-gur.
AHAZ. *Ay*-haz.
ALEXANDRIANS. Al-ex-*an*-dree-unz.
AL-QAEDA. Al *Kai*-duh.
AMPHIPOLIS. Am-*fip*-o-liss.
ANANIAS. An-uh-*nye*-us.
ANNAS. *An*-nus.
ANTIOCH. *An*-tee-ock.
APOLLO. Uh-*pah*-low.
APOLLONIA. Ap-uh-*low*-nee-uh.
APOLLOS. Uh-*pahl*-us.
AQUILA. *Ack*-wih-luh.
AREOPAGUS. Air-ee-*op*-uh-gus.
ARISTOBULUS. Uh-*ris*-toe-*bu*-lus (strong accent on *bu*).
ASSYRIA. Uh-*sear*-ee-uh.
AZOTUS. Uh-*zo*-tus.

B

BAAL PEOR. Bay-al-*pe*-or.
BABYLON. *Bab*-uh-lun.
BABYLONIANS. Bab-ih-*low*-nee-unz.
BARACHEL. *Bar*-uh-kel.
BATHSHEBA. Bath-*she*-buh.
BEREA. Buh-*ree*-uh.
BILDAD. *Bill*-dad.
BITHYNIA. Bih-*thin*-ee-uh.
BLASPHEMOUS. *blas*-fuh-mus.
BUZITE. *Bew*-zyet.

C

CAESAREA MARITIMA. Sess-uh-*ree*-uh Mar-uh-*tee*-muh.
CAIAPHAS. *Kay*-uh-fus or *Kye*-uh-fus.
CALIGULA. Kuh-*lig*-you-luh.
CANDACE. *Can*-duh-see.
CAPERNAUM. Kuh-*per*-nay-um.
CARTHAGE. *Car*-thij.
CASSINI-HUYGENS. Kuh-*see*-nee *Hoi*-genz.
CAVEAT EMPTOR (Latin). *ka*-vee-at *emp*-ter.
CENCHREAE. *Sen*-kree-uh.
CEPHAS. *See*-fus.
CHLOE. *Klo*-ee.
CILICIA. Sih-*lish*-i-uh.
CLAUDIUS CAESAR. *Claw*-dee-us *See*-zur.
CLEOPAS. *Clee*-uh-pass.
CORINTHIANS. Ko-*rin*-thee-unz (*th* as in *thin*).
CORNELIUS. Cor-*neel*-yus.
CRETAN. *Cree*-tun.
CRISPUS. *Kris*-pus.
CYRENIANS. *Sigh*-ree-nee-unz.

D

DAMASCUS. Duh-*mass*-kus.
DELPHI. *Del*-fi.
DEUTERONOMY. Due-ter-*ahn*-uh-me.
DIETRICH BONHOEFFER. *Dee*-trick *Bon*-huh-fur.
DIONYSIUS. Die-oh-*nish*-ih-us.
DYNAMIS (Greek). *doo*-nuh-mis.

E

EDOMITES. *Ee*-dum-ites.
ELIHU. Ih-*lye*-hew.
ELIPHAZ. *El*-ih-faz.
ELISHA. E-*lye*-shuh.
ELYMAS. *El*-ih-mass.
EMMAUS. Em-*may*-us.
EPHESUS. *Ef*-uh-sus.
EPHESIANS. Ee-*fee*-zhunz.
EPIMENIDES. Ep-ih-*men*-ih-deez.
ETHIOPIAN. E-thee-*o*-pee-un (*th* as in *thin*).
EUNICE. U-*nye*-see or *U*-nis.
EUNUCH. *you*-nick.
EUTHANASIA. you-thuh-*nay*-zhuh.
EZEKIEL. Ee-*zeek*-ee-ul or Ee-*zeek*-yul.

G

GAIUS. *Gay*-us.
GALATIA. Guh-*lay*-shuh.
GALILEANS. Gal-uh-*lee*-unz.
GALLIO. *Gal*-ee-o.
GAMALIEL. Guh-*may*-lih-ul or Guh-*may*-lee-al.
GERIZIM. *Gair*-ih-zeem or Guh-*rye*-zim.
GNOSTICS. *Nahss*-ticks.
GOLIATH. Go-*lye*-uth.

H

HANNAH. *Han*-uh.
HEROD AGRIPPA. *Hair*-ud Uh-*grip*-puh.
HEROD ANTIPAS. *Hair*-ud *An*-tih-pus.
HEROD ARCHELAUS. *Hair*-ud Are-kuh-*lay*-us.
HERODIANS. Heh-*roe*-dee-unz.
HYMENEUS. Hi-meh-*nee*-us.

I

ICONIUM. Eye-*ko*-nee-um.
IMMANUEL. Ih-*man*-you-el.
ISTHMIAN. *Is*-me-unh.

J

JOCHEBED. *Jock*-eh-bed.
JOSEPHUS. Jo-*see*-fus.
JOSES. *Jo*-sez.
JUDAISM. *Joo*-duh-izz-um or *Joo*-day-izz-um.
JUDAS ISCARIOT. *Joo*-dus Iss-*care*-ee-ut.
JUDEA. Joo-*dee*-uh.

K

KOINONIA (Greek). koy-no-*nee*-uh.
KORAH. *Ko*-rah.

L

LECHAEUM. Lek-uh-*ee*-um.
LEMUEL. *Lem*-you-el.
LIBERTINES. *Lib*-er-teens.
LUCIUS ANNAEUS SENECA. *Loo*-shuss Uh-*nee*-us *Sen*-uh-kuh.
LYDIA. *Lid*-ee-uh.
LYSTRA. *Liss*-truh.

M

MACEDONIA. Mass-eh-*doe*-nee-uh.
MACHIAVELLI. *Ma*-key-uh-*veh*-lee (strong accent on *Ma*).
MAGDALENE. *Mag*-duh-leen or Mag-duh-*lee*-nee.
MAGNIFICAT. Mag-*nif*-ih-cot.
MAO TSE-TUNG. Mau dzuh-*dung*.
MESHACH. *Me*-shack.
MESSIAH. Meh-*sigh*-uh.
MILETUS. My-*lee*-tus.
MOABITE. *Mo*-ub-ite.
MOSAIC. Mo-*zay*-ik.
MYSIA. *Mish*-ee-uh.

N

NABATAEN. *Nab*-uh-*tee*-un (strong accent on *tee*).
NAPOLEON BONAPARTE. Nuh-*pol*-yuhn *Bo*-nuh-*part* (strong accent on *part*).
NAZARETH. *Naz*-uh-reth.
NAZARITE. *Naz*-uh-rite.
NEAPOLIS. Nee-*ap*-o-lis.
NEBUCHADNEZZAR. *Neb*-yuh-kud-*nez*-er (strong accent on *nez*).
NICODEMUS. Nick-uh-*dee*-mus (strong accent on *dee*).
NIEBUHR. *Nee*-burr.

O

ONESIMUS. O-*ness*-ih-muss.

P

PAMPHYLIA. Pam-*fill*-ee-uh.
PENTECOST. *Pent*-ih-kost.
PHARAOH AKHENATON. *Fair*-o (or *Fay*-roe) Ock-*naw*-tun.
PHARISEES. *Fair*-ih-seez.
PHILETUS. Fuh-*lee*-tus.
PHILIPPI. Fih-*lip*-pie or *Fil*-ih-pie.
PHRYGIA. *Frij*-e-uh.
PILATE. *Pie*-lut.
PISIDIA. Pih-*sid*-ee-uh.
PONTUS. *Pon*-tuss.
POTIPHAR. *Pot*-ih-far.
PROSELYTES. *prahss*-uh-lights.

Q

QUATERNIONS. kwa-*ter*-nee-unz.

S

SABEANS. Suh-*be*-unz.
SADDUCEES. *Sad*-you-seez.
SALOME. Suh-*lo*-me.
SAMARITAN. Suh-*mare*-uh-tun.
SAMOTHRACIA. Sam-o-*thray*-shuh.
SANHEDRIN. *San*-huh-drun or San-*heed*-run.
SEBASTE. Seh-*bas*-tee.
SEPTUAGINT. Sep-*too*-ih-jent.
SHADRACH. *Shay*-drack or *Shad*-rack.
SHALOM (Hebrew). shah-*lome*.
SHEBA. *She*-buh.
SHECHEM. *Shee*-kem or *Shek*-em.
SHEKEL. *sheh*-kul.
SIMEON. *Sim*-ee-un.
SØREN KIERKEGAARD. So-ren *Kir*-kuh-gard.
STEPHANAS. *Stef*-uh-nass.
SUETONIUS. Soo-*toe*-nee-us.
SYCHAR. *Sigh*-kar.

T

TARSUS. *Tar*-sus.
TERTULLIAN. Tur-*tull*-yun.
THYATIRA. *Thy*-uh-*tie*-ruh (strong accent on *tie*; *th* as in *thin*).
TROAS. *Tro*-az.
TROPHIMUS. *Troff*-ih-muss.
TYRANNUS. Ty-*ran*-nus.
TYRE. Tire.

Z

ZACCHEUS. Zack-*key*-us.
ZAREPHATH. *Zair*-uh-fath.
ZEBEDEE. *Zeb*-eh-dee.
ZEUS. Zoose.
ZOPHAR. *Zo*-far.

Introduction to the Large Print Standard Lesson Commentary®

For more than one hundred years Standard Publishing has been producing materials for adult Sunday school classes. One of the most popular offerings in our line is the quarterly *Bible Teacher and Leader* and the annual STANDARD LESSON COMMENTARY® (an edition of the same material). The book you now hold is the latest addition to that line. We introduced a large print quarterly manual in 1998, coinciding with the beginning of the previous six-year cycle in the International Sunday School Lessons series. (See page 3.) Now we are combining those quarterly materials into an annual large print STANDARD LESSON COMMENTARY.®

Special Teacher Features

In the introductory pages to each quarter you will find study helps designed to give you a better handle on the people, places, and events covered in the quarter. Features that users of our STANDARD LESSON COMMENTARY® have come to appreciate remain in the large print edition. For example, the quarterly quiz appears within the introductory pages for each quarter. The quarterly quiz can be used as a preview of the quarter, as a review at the end of the quarter, or as a review after each lesson. The quiz may be copied and distributed to students. There is also a map in nearly every quarter and a chart—often a chronological summary—that appears on the backside of the same page. The map and chart can then be removed together and saved for future use.

The first page of each lesson includes the Scripture text. What follows is an outline and verse-by-verse commentary on the lesson text. This is the heart of the STANDARD LESSON COMMENTARY,® both the regular print edition and the new large print version. The "Learning by Doing" portion of the lesson treatment suggests various learning activities for the teacher to use, and the "Let's Talk It Over" page includes questions and answers designed to encourage your students' consideration of key issues.

Some Changes to Keep in Mind

Please be aware as you use the large print teacher book that the process of enlarging the print has necessitated some slight changes from how certain features appear. The large print STANDARD LESSON COMMENTARY® is not simply a photographic enlargement of the regular print version. That would have resulted in a large and cumbersome volume. Instead, pages were added to accommodate the one-third larger type. The most obvious impact of this procedure is that the one-page "Let's Talk It Over" feature had to be condensed slightly to keep it on one page in the large print edition. For the same reason, some of the questions that appear in the quarterly quizzes in the regular print edition were taken out of the large print edition.

The expansion left us with more space in the introductory section in the large print edition, so we have added some new features. The pronunciation guide known as "How to Say It," included in each lesson, is also included with all the words for the quarter grouped together. In addition, each quarter includes a "Quarter Review" at the end of the quarter.

Our Unchanging Purpose

Having called attention to some of the changes in the large print STANDARD LESSON COMMENTARY,® we want to conclude by emphasizing what has *not* changed in this manual—the faithful treatment of each week's lesson text in a manner that honors the Bible as God's holy and unchanging Word. We believe that such careful treatment of the Scripture has always been the primary strength of our Commentary.

You may have heard the oft-quoted maxim: "Methods are many, principles are few; methods may change, principles never do." This large print edition of the STANDARD LESSON COMMENTARY® is meant to serve as a new method to use in teaching the abiding principles of God's Word. We hope it helps you to achieve this most worthy goal.

Fall Quarter 2005

Special Features

You Will Be My Witnesses
(Acts)

	Page
Times Such As These	2
Christ for All! .... Ronald L. Nickelson	3
The Gospel Spreads to Jerusalem, Judea, and Samaria (Map Feature)	5
The Gospel Spreads to the Rest of the World (Map Feature)	6
When God Talks to Us .... A. Eugene Andrews	7
Quarterly Quiz	8
How to Say It	9
Lesson Planning Page	10
Quarterly Review	128

Lessons

Unit 1: In Jerusalem

September				
	4	The Spirit Comes	Acts 2:1-8, 36-42	11
	11	The Believers Share	Acts 2:43-47; 4:32-35	20
	18	Peter and John Heal a Lame Man	Acts 3:1-16	29
	25	The Church Is Bold	Acts 4:1-4, 23-31	38

Unit 2: In All Judea and Samaria

October				
	2	Stephen Is Faithful to the End	Acts 6:8-15; 7:54-60	47
	9	Philip Preaches in Samaria	Acts 8:4-17	56
	16	Philip Teaches an Ethiopian	Acts 8:26-38	65
	23	God Welcomes Gentiles	Acts 10:1-20	74
	30	Peter Escapes Prison	Acts 12:1-16	83

Unit 3: Unto the Uttermost Part of the Earth

November				
	6	Paul Meets the Lord	Acts 9:3-18	92
	13	Lydia Demonstrates Faithfulness	Acts 16:6-15, 40	101
	20	Priscilla and Aquila Serve Together	Acts 18:1-4, 18-21, 24-28	110
	27	Paul Says Good-Bye	Acts 20:17-28, 36-38	119

About These Lessons

"Ripples in a pond" is a good analogy for this quarter's lessons. On the Day of Pentecost, the church was born and began to spread outward from Jerusalem. Those ripples travel across both geography and time to reach us now. We not only experience those ripples personally, we help send them on!

Times Such As These

WE KNOW THAT WE are in the early part of the twenty-first century, but no one seems to have figured out what to call this particular decade. The 1990s were known as "the nineties," the 1980s were "the eighties," and so forth. But to call our current decade "the zeroes" just doesn't sound quite right! "The nulls" sounds even worse.

Yet every decade, whatever we eventually call it, should be known as a time of growth for God's people—both spiritually for the individual Christian and numerically for the church as a whole. This is the will of God. It has been His will for centuries. It shall continue to be His will until Jesus returns. It is stressed in this year's lessons.

Our lessons for the fall quarter sketch the rapid growth of the first-century church. Energized by the power of the Holy Spirit, the church expanded from a number of about 120 in Jerusalem (Acts 1:15) to countless thousands across the Roman Empire in about 30 years. Jesus wants His church to grow just as rapidly today. Allowing Him to empower us for this work is a key.

The winter lessons begin by showing us the foundation for the later growth of the church: the coming of Christ, as predicted by the ancient prophets. Following our Christmas lessons, we move to what are called the Pastoral Epistles to focus on personal spiritual growth. We will certainly see some of our spiritual shortcomings as we study these lessons. Allowing the Holy Spirit to correct these is a continuous challenge.

The spring lessons take us to the Wisdom Literature of the Old Testament. Our spiritual growth depends on understanding how God expects us to think and act. Learning from the Old Testament saints in this regard will help to keep us from repeating their mistakes.

Summer will find us back in the New Testament, specifically in the two letters written to the church at Corinth. The letters 1 and 2 Corinthians are painful to read, for they were written to correct a church in big trouble. But personal spiritual growth and the numerical growth of today's church depends on being able to address serious problems in a Christ-honoring way. These two letters have much to teach us still.

Times such as these—meaning the years we're living in right now and the problems they carry with them—demand such lessons, don't they?

International Sunday School Lesson Cycle
September, 2004—August, 2007

YEAR	FALL QUARTER (Sept., Oct., Nov.)	WINTER QUARTER (Dec., Jan., Feb.)	SPRING QUARTER (Mar., Apr., May)	SUMMER QUARTER (June, July, Aug.)
2004-2005	The God of Continuing Creation (Bible Survey)	Called to Be God's People (Bible Survey)	God's Project: Effective Christians (Romans, Galatians)	Jesus' Life, Teachings, and Ministry (Matthew, Mark, Luke)
2005-2006	"You Will Be My Witnesses" (Acts)	God's Commitment— Our Response (Isaiah; 1 and 2 Timothy)	Living in and as God's Creation (Psalms, Job, Ecclesiastes, Proverbs)	Called to Be a Christian Community (1 and 2 Corinthians)
2006-2007	God's Living Covenant (Old Testament Survey)	Jesus Christ: A Portrait of God (John, Philippians, Colossians, Hebrews, 1 John)	Our Community Now and in God's Future (1 John, Revelation)	Committed to Doing Right (Various Prophets, 2 Kings, 2 Chronicles)

Christ for All!

by Ronald L. Nickelson

WHAT "TYPE" OF CHRISTIANITY do you believe in? There seem to be three choices that are proposed these days. Many people believe in an *exclusive* Christianity. Under this idea, salvation is exclusively for those who make a confession of faith in Jesus Christ as they follow the biblical plan of salvation.

Others find that idea much too rigid. They propose instead an *inclusive* Christianity. Their idea is that people can be saved by Christ without placing faith in Him or without ever even hearing of Him. Such people can still be saved by Christ and only by Christ (so the theory goes) as long as they respond positively to whatever light of God's revelation that they are aware of.

Others hold a *pluralistic* view. They say Christianity may be "right for me," but other religions are equally "right for others." We can be saved by Christ, but (so the theory goes) others can be saved by Muhammad or Buddha just as well.

This quarter's lessons should leave no doubt: the Christianity that the Holy Spirit established on Pentecost is an *exclusive* Christianity. Those who spread the gospel of Jesus Christ in the first century "in Jerusalem, and in all Judea, and in Samaria, and unto the uttermost part of the earth" (Acts 1:8) lived and died for this belief. Peter, John, Stephen, Paul, Philip, Priscilla, and Aquila are New Testament names familiar to many of us. As we see them labor for the gospel this quarter, we will see no hint that they think that faith in Jesus is one option among many!

Unit 1. September: In Jerusalem

Lesson 1: The Spirit Comes. "Well begun is half done," so the old saying goes. Talk about a great beginning! An international crowd is on hand in Jerusalem on the Day of Pentecost when the Holy Spirit comes to mark the beginning of the church. A vital part of the message that day is that Jesus is "both Lord and Christ." This lesson's Golden Text of Acts 2:38 will come to fruition time and again throughout the book of Acts.

Lesson 2: The Believers Share. Many people recognize that *true community* is an important foundation for their lives. The most important community in the world is the church. The fellowship of believers was a marvel to behold, as they "had all things common." What a marvelous example for us! Having "all things common" begins with having a common Savior: Jesus Christ.

Lesson 3: Peter and John Heal a Lame Man. The healing of the man in Acts 3 is the first healing miracle recorded in that great book. This valuable lesson enriches us when we allow it to point us to something far more valuable than physical healing—the spiritual wholeness that comes only through God's Son.

Lesson 4: The Church Is Bold. Courage and conviction are human traits that seem to go in and out of style with the passing of time. Sometimes those traits are sadly misdirected, as in the cases of violent religious extremism today. Peter and John show us the right kind of boldness. It is a boldness that pushes the gospel forward in a way that honors God. The Holy Spirit stands ready to give boldness to us as well.

Unit 2. October: In All Judea and Samaria

Lesson 5: Stephen Is Faithful to the End. The pages of history are stained with the blood of Christian martyrs. After Pentecost the first recorded martyr was Stephen. Honoring God can exact a very high price! Yet Stephen and others died for their conviction of truth: Jesus is the Christ, the Son of the living God.

Lesson 6: Philip Preaches in Samaria. The stoning of Stephen marked the outbreak of persecution against the church. But God turned that evil into victory as "they that were scattered abroad went every where preaching the word" (Acts 8:4). In so doing, evangelists such as Philip crossed racial and cultural barriers with the gospel.

Lesson 7: Philip Teaches an Ethiopian. Although many longtime Christians "ought to be teachers" by now, they have yet to progress beyond the "milk" to the "meat" of God's Word (Hebrews 5:12). Philip was not one of those. When someone needed an explanation of Scripture, he was ready. With the eternal destinies of others at stake, how can we not be ready as well?

Lesson 8: God Welcomes Gentiles. Cornelius, a Gentile, was a man who knew something about God. Cornelius apparently realized the importance of prayer and helping the poor. He understood this without ever having heard the gospel. But that knowledge and practice wasn't enough. Cornelius still needed Christ.

Lesson 9: Peter Escapes Prison. Peter was in prison, awaiting execution for preaching the gospel. His fellow Christians were somewhere outside the prison gates. He was surrounded by pagan soldiers guarding him. And yet Peter was not abandoned. God was always with him. God is always with us, too. We are never alone.

Unit 3. November:
Unto the Uttermost Part of the Earth

Lesson 10: Paul Meets the Lord. Jesus Christ has the power to transform lives. Nowhere is this more evident than in the life of Saul of Tarsus (renamed Paul). It is unlikely that any of us will have a "Damascus Road experience" as he had. That will be God's choice, not ours. Jesus certainly has the power to change lives in other ways. For instance, He may very well change our lives by opening our hearts to the printed account of Paul's shocking experience.

Lesson 11: Lydia Demonstrates Faithfulness. The gospel expands fastest when believers are committed to serving in any way they can. This can mean inconvenience. Before we complain too much about our inconveniences, however, remember one thing: it was quite inconvenient for Jesus to come to earth and die on a cross! May God give each of us the heart of Lydia as we serve in the manner we are gifted.

Lesson 12: Priscilla and Aquila Serve Together. Sometimes Christians work alone to spread the gospel. One example occurred when Philip taught the Ethiopian. More often it is teamwork that wins the day. A shining example of how much a good team can accomplish is the combination of Priscilla and Aquila. May this couple always be a model to us.

Lesson 13: Paul Says Good-Bye. The Christian life has its "downs" as well as its "ups." Sad good-byes are part of our earthly sojourn. Yet we draw strength from fellow believers in such times. Sad good-byes challenge us to lift our thoughts to when all Christians will be together for eternity, never to be parted again.

Christ for All, and Christ Exclusively

This quarter's lessons offer us one example after another of the nature of the gospel message and how it spread. Behind the convictions of the first-century believers lie some powerful truths. Consider the following:

Matthew 7:14: "Strait is the gate, and narrow is the way, which leadeth unto life, and few there be that find it."

John 14:6: "I am the way, the truth, and the life: no man cometh unto the Father, but by me."

Acts 4:12: "Neither is there salvation in any other: for there is none other name under heaven given among men, whereby we must be saved."

The first two of these three passages are from the lips of Jesus during His earthly ministry. The third was spoken by Peter as he was filled with the Holy Spirit in the presence of the men who had sentenced Jesus to death (part of the context of lesson 4). When we place these three texts alongside the options of *exclusive* Christianity, *inclusive* Christianity, and *pluralistic* Christianity that we mentioned at the outset, which of the three options appears to be correct?

Only *exclusive Christianity* can be correct! Jesus Christ came to redeem all humanity from sin, but we must place our faith specifically in Him and in Him alone. Matthew 7:14; John 14:6; Acts 4:12 and a host of other texts require this. Our 13 lessons for the quarter demonstrate time and again the beliefs and actions of earliest Christians in this regard. They did not waver, and neither should we.

Answers to Quarterly Quiz on page 8

Lesson 1—1. They spoke with other tongues. 2. repent, baptized. **Lesson 2**—1. to help those who were in need. 2. resurrection. **Lesson 3**—1. true. 2. walking, leaping, praising God. **Lesson 4**—1. false; because they preached resurrection through Jesus. 2. David. **Lesson 5**—1. He had the face of an angel. 2. glory, standing. **Lesson 6**—1. false. 2. laid hands. **Lesson 7**—1. to worship. 2. true. **Lesson 8**—1. feared, alms, prayed. 2. a sheet full of unclean animals. 3. the Spirit. **Lesson 9**—1. false; it was James, the brother of John. 2. after the angel left. **Lesson 10**—1. Jesus. 2. suffer. **Lesson 11**—1. Macedonia. 2. hospitality. **Lesson 12**—1. tentmaking. 2. true. **Lesson 13**—1. bonds, affliction. 2. sorrow.

The Gospel Spreads to Jerusalem, Judea, and Samaria

- Tarsus

SYRIA

MEDITERRANEAN SEA

- Damascus

GALILEE

- Caesarea
- Samaria

JUDEA

- Jerusalem
- Gaza

The Gospel Spreads to the Rest of the World

When God Talks to Us

by A. Eugene Andrews

WOULDN'T IT BE GREAT if we could pick up a phone, give God a call, and ask Him what we should do? Even if we could, we probably would still get things fouled up, hearing only what we want to hear. That's often the way we treat the Bible, God's message to us.

The conversation could go something like this. "God, I was listening to what You said but I think we must have had a bad connection. It sounded like You said, 'He who would be greatest must be servant of all.' But that couldn't have been right. Probably what You said was, 'He who would be great must be served by all.' Right?"

Or perhaps it would go like this: "God, I was listening but I must have misunderstood. It sounded like You said if anyone would come after You, he must deny himself. But that can't be right. I'm sure what You said was, 'If anyone would come after me he must satisfy himself.'"

There are many who seek a personalized message from God but forsake the way God has said He will speak to us. God speaks first and foremost through the Bible. If we refuse to hear God speak in this way, it is unlikely we will properly hear God were He to speak to us personally.

Sometimes we want a graduate degree in understanding God when we've not successfully made it through kindergarten. We become like the first-time golfer who wants to score pars and birdies. Or we are like the beginning music student who wants to play like a concert musician without the years of practice.

It is difficult sometimes to discern specific things God may want to communicate to us for our personal life and specific decisions we are trying to make. Yet there are some general things God is saying to all of us. If we begin to listen to these things, we will find it much easier to understand God's guidance in the specifics.

One thing God wants to say to us is, "I want to turn your troubles into triumph." God always has been a master at this. Think of the Israelites as they stood on the shore of the Red Sea with the Egyptian army closing in behind them. Or think of David as he stood opposite Goliath. Another example is Paul, whose life was in jeopardy many times, whether from the Jewish authorities, in a shipwreck, or from the hatred of the Judaizers. In each of these times of trouble, God gave triumph.

A second message God wants to speak to us is, "I want to turn your problems into possibilities." First we have to admit that we have problems. Often we like to think, or have others think, that we've "got it all together." But we all have problems, and the first thing we have to do is admit it. Then we can allow God to do His work, to speak to us in the midst of the problem, and hear what He has to say about problems.

The apostle Paul learned this lesson. He prayed for his "thorn in the flesh" to be removed on three different occasions. God's answer was that it would not be removed, but rather, "My grace is sufficient for thee" (2 Corinthians 12:9).

God also wants to say to us, "I want to turn the unimaginable into reality." But what God has in mind is not the type of reality we see on so-called "reality TV shows"! Real life is living daily in the real world of pain, pressure, heartache, and sickness. It is in these seemingly impossible situations that God speaks to us words of hope and comfort. Often we can't imagine making it through difficult times; yet God is saying that with His help we can (see Ephesians 3:20).

A. W. Tozer wrote, "There are Christians among us today who seem to feel that their spiritual lives would have been greatly helped if they could have had voice-to-voice and person-to-person counsel from our Lord. I know it is fair to say that if one of the apostles . . . could return to the world from . . . yesteryear, there would not be room to contain the crowds that would rush in."

Recognizing that impossibility, Tozer goes on to declare, "However, there is good news for those who are anxious to hear a word from the Lord! If we have a mind to listen, we may still hear the voice of an apostle" (*A Treasury of A. W. Tozer*, pages 190, 191).

We hear the voices of the apostles when we allow God to speak to us through His holy Word. In seeking messages from God, we must look there first. As we sense God leading us in certain ways, we always check that impression against the written Word. We hear God when we not only look in the Bible first, but when we look there last.

Quarterly Quiz

This quiz can be used to preview the lessons, to review at the end of the quarter, or as a review after each lesson. The quiz may be copied and distributed to students. **The answers are on page 4.**

Lesson 1
1. On the day of Pentecost what special ability was given to those who were filled with the Holy Ghost? *Acts 2:1, 4*
2. When the convicted crowd asked the apostles, "What shall we do?" Peter said, "____, and be ____." *Acts 2:38*

Lesson 2
1. Why did the believers sell their possessions? *Acts 2:44, 45*
2. The apostles witnessed with great power about Jesus' ____. *Acts 4:33*

Lesson 3
1. The man who was healed by the gate of the temple had been lame all his life. T/F *Acts 3:2*
2. State the three things the healed man was doing as he entered the temple: ____, ____, and ____. *Acts 3:8*

Lesson 4
1. The Sadducees and the other Jewish leaders were upset with the apostles because they were doing miracles. T/F *Acts 4:1, 2*
2. Which Old Testament character did the apostles quote in their prayer of praise to God? (David, Solomon, Isaiah?) *Acts 4:25*

Lesson 5
1. When the council stared at Stephen, what did they notice about his appearance? *Acts 6:15*
2. As Stephen looked up into Heaven, he saw the ____ of God, and Jesus ____ at the right hand of God. *Acts 7:55*

Lesson 6
1. Philip was unable to perform miracles in Samaria, he because of unbelief. T/F *Acts 8:5-7*
2. When Peter and John came to Samaria, they prayed for the believers and ____ ____ on them. *Acts 8:14-17*

Lesson 7
1. Why had the Ethiopian eunuch gone to Jerusalem? (on business for his queen, to visit family, to worship?) *Acts 8:27*
2. Philip used a passage from Isaiah to preach about Jesus. T/F *Acts 8:30, 35*

Lesson 8
1. Cornelius the centurion was a devout man who ____ God, gave many ____, and always ____ to God. *Acts 10:1, 2*
2. What did Peter see in his vision? (the glory of God, a sheet full of unclean animals, a tree full of fruit?) *Acts 10:11, 12*
3. Who told Peter to go with the men who came to see him? *Acts 10:19, 20*

Lesson 9
1. James, the half-brother of Jesus, was the first apostle martyred for his faith. T/F *Acts 12:1, 2*
2. When did Peter know he was being delivered and not just dreaming? (when the angel awoke him, when he walked past the guards, after the angel left?) *Acts 12:8-11*

Lesson 10
1. Who spoke to Saul when he was on the way to Damascus? *Acts 9:3-5*
2. The Lord told Ananias, "I will show [Saul] how great things he must ____ for my name's sake." *Acts 9:16*

Lesson 11
1. Where did the man in Paul's vision invite him to come? *Acts 16:9*
2. What trait did Lydia demonstrate after her baptism? (prophecy, hospitality, mercy?) *Acts 16:15*

Lesson 12
1. Which craft did Aquila and Priscilla use to support themselves? *Acts 18:2, 3*
2. After being taught, Apollos became a powerful preacher who used Scripture to prove Jesus was the Christ. T/F *Acts 18:26, 28*

Lesson 13
1. As Paul headed for Jerusalem, he expected to experience ____ and ____. *Acts 20:23*
2. What emotion did the elders express after hearing Paul's speech to them? (joy, fear, sorrow?) *Acts 20:36-38*

How to Say It

Use this list to help you pronounce the names and hard to pronounce words in the lessons of the fall quarter.

A

ABEDNEGO. Uh-*bed*-nee-go.
ACHAIA. Uh-*kay*-uh.
AEGEAN. A-*jee*-un.
ALEXANDRIAN. Al-ex-*an*-dree-un.
AMPHIPOLIS. Am-*fip*-o-liss.
ANANIAS. An-uh-*nye*-us.
ANTIOCH. *An*-tee-ock.
APOLLONIA. Ap-uh-*low*-nee-uh.
APOLLOS. Uh-*pahl*-us.
AQUILA. *Ack*-wih-luh.
AREOPAGUS. Air-ee-*op*-uh-gus.
ARISTOBULUS. Uh-*ris*-toe-*bu*-lus (strong accent on *bu*).
ASSYRIANS. Uh-*sear*-e-unz.
AZOTUS. Uh-*zo*-tus.

B

BABYLONIAN. Bab-ih-*low*-nee-uhn.
BARABBAS. Buh-*rab*-us.
BARNABAS. *Bar*-nuh-bus.
BATHSHEBA. Bath-*she*-buh.
BEREA. Buh-*ree*-uh.
BITHYNIA. Bih-*thin*-ee-uh.
BLASPHEMOUS. *blas*-fuh-mus.

C

CAESAREA MARITIMA. Sess-uh-*ree*-uh Mar-uh-*tee*-muh.
CAESAREA PHILIPPI. Sess-uh-*ree*-uh Fih-*lip*-pie or *Fil*-ih-pie.
CAIAPHAS. *Kay*-uh-fus or *Kye*-uh-fus.
CALIGULA. Kuh-*lig*-you-luh.
CANDACE. *Can*-duh-see.
CENCHREAE. *Sen*-kree-uh.
CEPHAS. *See*-fus.
CILICIA. Sih-*lish*-i-uh.
CLAUDIUS. *Claw*-dee-us.
CORNELIUS. Cor-*neel*-yus.
CYPRUS. *Sigh*-prus.
CYRENIANS. *Sigh*-ree-nee-unz.

D

DAMASCUS. Duh-*mass*-kus.
DYNAMIS (Greek). *doo*-nuh-mis.

E

ELYMAS. *El*-ih-mass.
EPHESUS. *Ef*-uh-sus.
EUNUCH. *you*-nick.

G

GAIUS. *Gay*-us.
GALATIA. Guh-*lay*-shuh.
GALILEANS. Gal-uh-*lee*-unz.
GALLIO. *Gal*-ee-o.
GENTILES. *Jen*-tiles.
GERIZIM. *Gair*-ih-zeem or Guh-*rye*-zim.
GOLIATH. Go-*lye*-uth.

H

HEROD AGRIPPA. *Hair*-ud Uh-*grip*-puh.
HEROD ANTIPAS. *Hair*-ud *An*-tih-pus.
HEROD ARCHELAUS. *Hair*-ud Are-kuh-*lay*-us.
HERODIANS. Heh-*roe*-dee-unz.

J

JOSEPHUS. Jo-*see*-fus.
JUDAISM. *Joo*-duh-izz-um or *Joo*-day-izz-um.
JUDAS ISCARIOT. *Joo*-dus Iss-*care*-ee-ut.
JUDEA. Joo-*dee*-uh.

L

LECHAEUM. Lek-uh-*ee*-um.
LIBERTINES. *Lib*-er-teens.
LYDIA. *Lid*-ee-uh.
LYSTRA. *Liss*-truh.

M

MACEDONIA. Mass-eh-*doe*-nee-uh.
MEDITERRANEAN. Med-uh-tuh-*ray*-nee-un (strong accent on *ray*).
MESHACH. *Me*-shack.
MESSIAH. Meh-*sigh*-uh.
MILETUS. My-*lee*-tus.
MYSIA. *Mish*-ee-uh.

N

NABATAEN. *Nab*-uh-*tee*-un (strong accent on *tee*).
NAZARITE. *Naz*-uh-rite.
NEAPOLIS. Nee-*ap*-o-lis.
PAMPHYLIA. Pam-*fill*-ee-uh.
PENTECOST. *Pent*-ih-kost.
PHARAOH. *Fair*-o or *Fay*-roe.
PHARISEES. *Fair*-ih-seez.
PHILIPPIAN. Fih-*lip*-ee-un.
PHRYGIA. *Frij*-e-uh.
PILATE. *Pie*-lut.
PISIDIA. Pih-*sid*-ee-uh.
PONTUS. *Pon*-tuss.
PROSELYTES. *prahss*-uh-lights.

Q

QUATERNIONS. kwa-*ter*-nee-unz.

S

SADDUCEES. *Sad*-you-seez.
SAMARIA. Suh-*mare*-ee-uh.
SAMARITANS. Suh-*mare*-uh-tunz.
SAMOTHRACIA. Sam-o-*thray*-shuh.
SANHEDRIN. *San*-huh-drun or San-*heed*-run.
SEBASTE. Seh-*bas*-tee.
SEPTUAGINT. Sep-*too*-ih-jent.
SHADRACH. *Shay*-drack or *Shad*-rack.
SHECHEM. *Shee*-kem or *Shek*-em.
SILAS. *Sigh*-luss.
SUETONIUS. Soo-*toe*-nee-us.
SYCHAR. *Sigh*-kar.
SYNAGOGUE. *sin*-uh-gog.
SYRIAN. *Sear*-ee-un.

T

TARSUS. *Tar*-sus.
TERTULLIAN. Tur-*tull*-yun.
THESSALONICA. *Thess*-uh-lo-*nye*-kuh (strong accent on *nye*; *th* as in *thin*).
THYATIRA. *Thy*-uh-*tie*-ruh (strong accent on *tie*; *th* as in *thin*).
TYRANNUS. Ty-*ran*-nus.

Lesson Planning Page

Reproduce this outline and then fill it in each week to plan your lesson.

Lesson Aims

List the aims here, either directly from the lesson or revised to suit your individual needs.

Getting Started

Begin with an illustration from the beginning of the lesson, the "Into the Lesson" activity from the Learning by Doing section, a discussion question, or some other appropriate opener.

Lesson Development

List in order the activities you will use. These include key points from the commentary section, discussion questions, and activities from the Learning by Doing section.

I.

II.

III.

Conclusion & Application

How will you bring the lesson to a climax, stressing the key point and desired action steps?

Closing Activity

Dismiss the class with an activity that reinforces the Bible lesson.

Copyright © 2004. STANDARD PUBLISHING, Cincinnati, Ohio. Permission is granted to reproduce this page for ministry purposes only. Not for resale.

The Spirit Comes

September 4
Lesson 1

DEVOTIONAL READING: Psalm 16.

BACKGROUND SCRIPTURE: Acts 2.

PRINTED TEXT: Acts 2:1-8, 36-42.

Acts 2:1-8, 36-42

1 And when the day of Pentecost was fully come, they were all with one accord in one place.

2 And suddenly there came a sound from heaven as of a rushing mighty wind, and it filled all the house where they were sitting.

3 And there appeared unto them cloven tongues like as of fire, and it sat upon each of them.

4 And they were all filled with the Holy Ghost, and began to speak with other tongues, as the Spirit gave them utterance.

5 And there were dwelling at Jerusalem Jews, devout men, out of every nation under heaven.

6 Now when this was noised abroad, the multitude came together, and were confounded, because that every man heard them speak in his own language.

7 And they were all amazed and marveled, saying one to another, Behold, are not all these which speak Galileans?

8 And how hear we every man in our own tongue, wherein we were born?

. . . .

36 Therefore let all the house of Israel know assuredly, that God hath made that same Jesus, whom ye have crucified, both Lord and Christ.

37 Now when they heard this, they were pricked in their heart, and said unto Peter and to the rest of the apostles, Men and brethren, what shall we do?

38 Then Peter said unto them, Repent, and be baptized every one of you in the name of Jesus Christ for the remission of sins, and ye shall receive the gift of the Holy Ghost.

39 For the promise is unto you, and to your children, and to all that are afar off, even as many as the Lord our God shall call.

40 And with many other words did he testify and exhort, saying, Save yourselves from this untoward generation.

41 Then they that gladly received his word were baptized: and the same day there were added unto them about three thousand souls.

42 And they continued steadfastly in the apostles' doctrine and fellowship, and in breaking of bread, and in prayers.

GOLDEN TEXT: Peter said unto them, Repent, and be baptized every one of you in the name of Jesus Christ for the remission of sins, and ye shall receive the gift of the Holy Ghost.—Acts 2:38.

SEPTEMBER 4

THE SPIRIT COMES

> *You Will Be My Witnesses*
> Unit 1: In Jerusalem
> (Lessons 1-4)

Lesson Aims

After this lesson each student will be able to:
1. Recount the events of the Day of Pentecost that accompanied the birth of the church.
2. Explain how the power of the Holy Spirit helped bring the church into being.
3. Identify one way of helping his or her church remember its first-century origins.

Lesson Outline

INTRODUCTION
   A. Birthday Celebrations
   B. Lesson Background
I. EARTH-SHAKING EVENT (Acts 2:1-8)
   A. Pentecost Gathering (v. 1)
   B. Holy Spirit Power (vv. 2-4a)
   C. Holy Spirit Miracle (vv. 4b-8)
II. LIFE-CHANGING MESSAGE (Acts 2:36-42)
   A. Message Centers on Jesus (v. 36)
   B. Message Cuts to Hearts (v. 37)
     A Place Without Hope
   C. Message Offers Forgiveness (vv. 38, 39)
   D. Message Urges Resistance of Evil (v. 40)
   E. Message Produces the Church (vv. 41, 42)
     A Portable Church
CONCLUSION
   A. Our Relationship with the Spirit
   B. Prayer
   C. Thought to Remember

Introduction

Some churches possess the following cornerstone: *Founded in Jerusalem A.D. 30*. Wherever a church is located and regardless of when its building was constructed, it is good that its people remember the very first church. Today's lesson describes that wonderful day when the church was born. It was a day of miracles that changed history.

A. Birthday Celebrations

Pharaoh celebrated his birthday with a great feast for his officials (Genesis 40:20). Herod celebrated his the same way, but on that dark day he gave his own gift—the head of John the Baptist (Mark 6:21-29). People from all walks of life love to celebrate birthdays. Europeans and Americans celebrate birthdays with family dinners and parties where presents are given. Christians celebrate Jesus' birth by giving to others. Christians remember Pentecost as the birthday of the church.

B. Lesson Background

The Old Testament predicted deliverance in terms of people flocking together as sheep in a pen (Micah 2:12, 13). The prophet Joel, though, gave the greatest of all prophecies of Christ's church. Joel saw Judah devastated by a terrifying locust plague (Joel 2:1-11). Yet God promised to remove the plague and pour out His blessings if the people repented (Joel 2:12-27). But as he looked into the distant future, Joel said that God planned to do more than restore crops. He also promised to pour out His Spirit (Joel 2:28, 29).

Centuries later, just before He returned to Heaven, Jesus told His disciples that He would send them the promised Holy Spirit. They were to remain in Jerusalem until they were clothed with power from on high (Luke 24:49). Shortly thereafter, God fulfilled His promise and poured out His Spirit. Peter explained, "This is that which was spoken by the prophet Joel" (Acts 2:16).

I. Earth-Shaking Event (Acts 2:1-8)

Earthquakes are frightening beyond words. They can kill tens of thousands and wipe entire cities off the map. For example, one of the deadliest earthquakes of the twentieth century obliterated the sleeping city of Tangshan, China, in 1976, killing more than 240,000 people. But some events, especially the one in our lesson today, shake the earth in a good way.

A. Pentecost Gathering (v. 1)

1. And when the day of Pentecost was fully come, they were all with one accord in one place.

God wants His people to gather in public worship. The Day of Pentecost was one of the special days in Old Testament times that reminded Israel how God had blessed them (see Exodus 23:14-17). Feast days helped sweep away differences as the tribes gathered to praise God and offer sacrifice for sin.

Pentecost, also called The Feast of Weeks (Exodus 34:22; Deuteronomy 16:9-11), was held seven weeks and a day (fifty days) after the Passover Sabbath (Leviticus 23:15, 16). It marked the completion of the barley harvest. Two loaves were waved symbolically before the Lord, while animal sacrifices were presented as sin and peace offerings (Leviticus 23:17-20). It was a single day of joy for the blessings of the harvest.

What a wonderfully symbolic day for the birth of the church! Jesus compared God's Word with seed (Matthew 13:1-23). As a farmer scatters seed and later harvests a crop, so also the seed of God's Word grows in human hearts and produces an abundant harvest of souls. Jesus indicated that what we may call "fields of people" are just waiting to be harvested (John 4:35). As the Day of Pentecost dawns in A.D. 30, thousands of souls are about to be gathered in from those fields. This Pentecost will be a day of great spiritual harvest. [See question #1, page 19.]

When the text says *they were all with one accord in one place,* we may wonder exactly who *they* are. Some say that it is the 120 believers mentioned in Acts 1:15. It is more likely, though, that this refers only to the apostles, since that group was just mentioned in Acts 1:26. Jesus promised that this baptism of the Spirit was to be upon them (Acts 1:5).

B. Holy Spirit Power (vv. 2-4a)

2-4a. And suddenly there came a sound from heaven as of a rushing mighty wind, and it filled all the house where they were sitting. And there appeared unto them cloven tongues like as of fire, and it sat upon each of them. And they were all filled with the Holy Ghost.

The Old Testament pictured God's Spirit as a mighty force that caused people to walk in God's laws (Ezekiel 36:27), brought new life (Ezekiel 37:14), empowered leaders (Judges 3:10), and inspired prophets (Micah 3:8). Now God's Spirit is about to be poured out in an new way.

Two symbols describe this outpouring of the Spirit: *wind* and *fire.* The original word for spirit could mean "breath" or "wind," depending on context. God's presence is like a great wind (2 Samuel 22:16). Scripture does not say that those present feel a physical wind. Rather, it says they hear a *sound* like a *rushing mighty wind* that comes *from heaven* and fills the entire *house.*

Fire is also used as a symbol of God's presence (see Exodus 19:18). As the Holy Spirit fills the apostles, it appears as if *tongues like as of fire* rest over them. The fire is *cloven,* that is, divided into separate flames. [See question #2, page 19.]

The word *filled* is used when the Spirit empowers God's people for service (Acts 9:17) and inspires people with important messages (Acts 4:8). This is why Luke, the author of Acts, uses *filled* and why *tongues* are manifested. God is about to give an important message. See also Luke 24:49.

C. Holy Spirit Miracle (vv. 4b-8)

4b-8. And began to speak with other tongues, as the Spirit gave them utterance. And there were dwelling at Jerusalem Jews, devout men, out of every nation under heaven. Now when this was noised abroad, the multitude came together, and were confounded, because that every man heard them speak in his own language. And they were all amazed and marveled, saying one to another, Behold, are not all these which speak Galileans? And how hear we every man in our own tongue, wherein we were born?

A great number of people are in *Jerusalem* at Pentecost. Thousands come from all over the world. Acts 2:9-12 lists 15 countries. These are described as *every nation under heaven.* This sweeping language is often used to describe the

---

Home Daily Bible Readings

Monday, Aug. 29—God's Spirit Will Be Poured Out (Joel 2:23-29)
Tuesday, Aug. 30—God Is Always with Us (Psalm 16:5-11)
Wednesday, Aug. 31—The Holy Spirit Comes (Acts 2:1-13)
Thursday, Sept. 1—Peter Speaks to the Crowd (Acts 2:14-21)
Friday, Sept. 2—Peter Speaks About the Crucified Jesus (Acts 2:22-28)
Saturday, Sept. 3—Peter Speaks About the Risen Christ (Acts 2:29-36)
Sunday, Sept. 4—Three Thousand Are Baptized (Acts 2:1-8, 37-42)

known world of the day or the territory of Earth's leading empire (in this case the Roman Empire).

The people hear the message in their native languages. They are amazed because the apostles are simple *Galileans* and are not from a metropolitan area where they might have greater opportunity to learn other languages. The crowd perhaps recognizes the speakers as Galileans by their unique accent or dialect (compare Matthew 26:73).

Most of the crowd this day could understand the apostles if they had spoken in Greek. But the Spirit empowers the apostles to speak in the peoples' native languages for a reason: God wants to show everyone that the apostles speak for God and that their message is true. This miracle also makes it clear that their message is for all nations. The Holy Spirit will continue to empower the early church with the ability to speak in tongues and do other amazing things (1 Corinthians 12:1-11). [See question #3, page 19.]

II. Life-Changing Message (Acts 2:36-42)

Peter began his sermon by noting that the prophet Joel had predicted this great event (Acts 2:14-22). He reminded the crowd that although God worked great miracles through Jesus, they handed Jesus over to wicked men who crucified Him. God reversed their decision by raising Jesus from the dead just as the Scriptures had predicted (Acts 2:23-35). The apostles are witnesses. They had seen Jesus alive and had watched Him ascend to Heaven to sit at God's right hand. Peter now proclaims Jesus' death and resurrection.

A. Message Centers on Jesus (v. 36)

36. Therefore let all the house of Israel know assuredly, that God hath made that same Jesus, whom ye have crucified, both Lord and Christ.

VISUALS FOR THESE LESSONS

The small visual pictured in each lesson (e. g., page 15) is a small reproduction of a large, full-color poster included in the *Adult Resources* packet for the Fall Quarter. The packet is available from your supplier. Order No. 192.

This is the end of Peter's great sermon. Seven weeks earlier, Peter denied even knowing Jesus (Mark 14:66-72). Jesus forgave him and put him back to work (John 21:15-19). Peter is now a different man, filled with courage and power.

This message is often called the first complete gospel sermon because it is the first public announcement of the significance of Jesus' death, burial, resurrection, and ascension. By these things God made Jesus *both Lord and Christ.* The Scriptures had predicted that the Messiah would do all these things (Psalms 2, 16, 22; Isaiah 53). The word *Lord* indicates the one having authority and sovereign power. The word *Christ* means "anointed one, the one chosen by God."

B. Message Cuts to Hearts (v. 37)

37. Now when they heard this, they were pricked in their heart, and said unto Peter and to the rest of the apostles, Men and brethren, what shall we do?

This gospel message penetrates the soul like a sword (Hebrews 4:12). This sword of the Spirit (Ephesians 6:17) is designed to stab the old man of sin and bring about godly sorrow. In this case the people are *pricked* or "pierced" to the very core of their being. People in the crowd are sorry that they had rejected Jesus. Even though they had not driven the nails into His hands and feet, they had either agreed with those who did (Luke 23:21) or else they had approved of the crucifixion by their silence. They are sorry, but they know that this is not enough. So they ask the apostles what they must *do.* [See question #4, page 19.]

A Place Without Hope

Jason Roemer gives us this interesting insight into his childhood. He says, "I can remember my grandmother warning me when I was up to no good. . . . 'You don't want to end up on Alcatraz, do you?'"

From 1934 to 1963, Alcatraz was the end of the line for the worst of America's convicted felons. If the U.S. federal prison system could keep them nowhere else, they went to Alcatraz—"the Rock." George "Machine Gun" Kelly and Al Capone were among its infamous residents. Located in San Francisco Bay, Alcatraz offered tantalizing views of "the outside world" just over a mile away. Alcatraz was maximum security, and the 50-degree (Fahrenheit) water added to the idea that escape attempts were futile. This imprisonment was not only physical but psychological as well!

Many in Peter's audience on Pentecost may have felt their actions had committed them to a "spiritual Alcatraz." The message had convicted them of murdering God's Son—the promised Messiah! With all hope seemingly gone, how could they ever break out of this spiritual prison? This terrible dilemma was expressed in their hopelessly pained question, "What shall we do?"

All of us have put ourselves in a similar position—our sins have locked us into a prison of alienation from God. There is no escape from this prison by our own effort. But the message of the gospel is that there *is* hope! Jesus said, "I am alive for evermore, Amen; and have the keys of hell and of death" (Revelation 1:18).   —C. R. B.

C. Message Offers Forgiveness (vv. 38, 39)

38, 39. Then Peter said unto them, Repent, and be baptized every one of you in the name of Jesus Christ for the remission of sins, and ye shall receive the gift of the Holy Ghost. For the promise is unto you, and to your children, and to all that are afar off, even as many as the Lord our God shall call.

The word *repent* means "a change of mind that leads to a change of life." Instead of denying, excusing, or justifying their sins, the people must turn from them. [See question #5, page 19.] Peter also appeals for submission to baptism. Several important New Testament texts discuss the meaning of baptism. Romans 6:4 says, "Therefore we are buried with him by baptism into death." (See also Colossians 2:12; Galatians 3:27; and 1 Peter 3:21 [among others].) In the text at hand, baptism is closely connected with repentance.

The Bible also makes it clear that the Holy Spirit is at work when people are converted to Christ (see Titus 3:5, 6). God's Spirit renews us as we are washed and raised to newness of life. Ananias told Saul, "Why tarriest thou? arise, and be baptized, and wash away thy sins, calling on the name of the Lord" (Acts 22:16).

Peter indicates that when people turn to Jesus Christ and away from sin, God promises forgiveness of sins and the gift of the Holy Spirit. *Remission* simply means "forgiveness." The most important thing that people can do once they reach the age where they know that they have sinned against God is to have those sins forgiven.

Keep this map posted throughout Lessons 1 through 9 to set a framework for your students.

Visual for lesson 1

The wonderful thing is that God is not only willing to forgive sins, He is also willing to help us deal with sin in our lives. So the Holy Spirit, among other things, gives life from the dead and empowers us to overcome sin each day. This is *the gift* of the Holy Spirit.

The Holy Spirit also gives spiritual gifts (1 Corinthians 12:11). The apostle Paul indicates that not everyone has the gift of speaking in tongues or other miraculous gifts (1 Corinthians 12:29-31). But all Christians have the gift of the Holy Spirit promised by Peter. The wonderful gift of the Holy Spirit empowers God's people to live lives that please Him. With the gift of the Spirit, Christians have the power to put off the works of the flesh and to bear the fruit of the Spirit (Galatians 5:22-25).

D. Message Urges Resistance of Evil (v. 40)

40. And with many other words did he testify and exhort, saying, Save yourselves from this untoward generation.

The word *untoward* means "perverse and rebellious." The Israelites who rebelled against God were called "a perverse . . . generation" (Deuteronomy 32:5). Christians must shine like stars in a world darkened by sin and keep themselves "unspotted from the world" (James 1:27).

E. Message Produces the Church (vv. 41, 42)

41, 42. Then they that gladly received his word were baptized: and the same day there were added unto them about three thousand souls. And they continued steadfastly in the apostles' doctrine and fellowship, and in breaking of bread, and in prayers.

Sorrow over sin now turns to gladness as people find God's grace. What a moment! Three thousand people are *baptized!* Their decision changes their lives—and their eternity. They now *steadfastly* do things that they had not done before.

For one thing, they heed the apostles' teaching (or *doctrine*). Jesus had promised that the Holy Spirit would guide the apostles "into all truth" (John 16:13). The apostles now pass some of those truths along as they teach about Jesus' dying for sins and rising from the dead (compare 1 Corinthians 15:3-8). Only Jesus brings forgiveness of sins and eternal life. They teach people to seek salvation through Him, who will judge the world. That life-changing message, preserved in the pages of the New Testament, is the very center of the Christian faith. Pure doctrine is important!

Those who are *added unto them* also remain steadfast in *fellowship.* Christians share in the privilege of belonging to the greatest family on earth and working together to spread the good news. When Christians pool their money, time, and energy to this great task, we can say they are "fellowshiping" in the gospel (Romans 15:26; 2 Corinthians 8:4; 1 John 1:7). Christians also have a fellowship of suffering with Christ (Philippians 3:10).

In this passage, the *breaking of bread* could refer either to an ordinary meal or to the Lord's Supper (compare 1 Corinthians 10:16; 11:24). Just which idea the author has in mind here is a matter of some debate. At the very least, we should think that these meals are to involve some kind of close Christian fellowship since fellowship has just been discussed. (See also Acts 2:46 in next week's lesson.)

The new converts also remain steadfast *in prayer.* Whether it be individual prayers or prayers of Christians who join their hearts together when making requests to God, these Christians realize just how important prayer is to their new relationship with God. Great churches today are the ones, whether large or small, that continue to remain steadfast in these same areas.

A Portable Church

Many of us have become numb to news of religious structures around the world being blown up by radicals. So it was a welcome bit of news a couple of years ago when British designer Michael Gill announced a way to "blow up" churches in a constructive way: he has developed a vinyl minicathedral that can be inflated in just three hours!

Gill's Web site www.inflatablechurch.com shows the details. The inflatable "building" stands 47 feet high at the peak of the steeple, and there are fake stained-glass windows in its gothic arches. The designer says one of the advantages of the inflatable church building is that it can be taken wherever there are people who want a church service. He hopes his invention will restore interest in the church in England—a nation where church attendance has been falling off for many years.

We don't know whether Peter's sermon took more or less than three hours on the Day of Pentecost, but the power of the Spirit built a church in short order on that day. Three thousand people responded to a message that offered hope to those who so recently had given assent to the execution of the Messiah. The church that resulted was a "portable church." The new Christians had come to Jerusalem from all over the Roman world, and they would soon be taking their faith—and the church—with them wherever they went. Shouldn't we be doing the same?
—C. R. B.

Conclusion

What a beginning the church had! And the Holy Spirit continues to work in mighty ways yet today. Let us never forget our relationship with the Holy Spirit.

A. Our Relationship with the Spirit

The Spirit inspired God's Word, so we must obey it without hesitation (2 Peter 1:21).

Our bodies are the temple of the Holy Spirit, so we must not gratify the desires of the flesh (1 Corinthians 6:19; Galatians 5:16).

How to Say It

CORINTHIANS. Ko-*rin*-thee-unz (*th* as in *thin*).
DEUTERONOMY. Due-ter-*ahn*-uh-me.
EPHESIANS. Ee-*fee*-zhunz.
EZEKIEL. Ee-*zeek*-ee-ul or Ee-*zeek*-yul.
GALILEANS. Gal-uh-*lee*-unz.
JERUSALEM. Juh-*roo*-suh-lem.
LEVITICUS. Leh-*vit*-ih-kus.
MICAH. *My*-kuh.
PENTECOST. *Pent*-ih-kost.
PHARAOH. *Fair*-o or *Fay*-roe.

The Spirit gives us the most personal of relationships with God, so we must trust God with a childlike faith (Galatians 4:6).

The Spirit seals us for "the day of redemption," so we must not grieve the Spirit (Ephesians 4:30).

The Spirit makes people alive from the dead, so we must walk in newness of life and put to death the waywardness of the body (Romans 8:13; Titus 3:5).

The Spirit helps us to bear the fruit of the Spirit, so we need to walk with the Spirit (Galatians 5:22-25).

The Spirit helps us with our prayers, so we must pray in faith without wavering (Romans 8:26; James 1:6).

The Spirit raised Jesus from the dead and will resurrect us, so we must live in hope (Romans 8:11).

The Holy Spirit inspired Peter with the gospel message. That message is still just as powerful as ever and still changes lives. The church, born by the Spirit's power, still moves throughout the world for good. Have you let God's Spirit transform your life?

B. Prayer

Father, thank You for Jesus whom You have made both Lord and Christ. Thank You for the Holy Spirit, who empowers us to bear the fruit of the Spirit. Thank You for Your church that continues to be such a powerful force. May Your Spirit work in our lives and in our church so that Your will shall be done. In Jesus' name, amen.

C. Thought to Remember

"Not by might, nor by power, but by my Spirit, saith the Lord of hosts" (Zechariah 4:6).

Learning by Doing

This page contains an alternate lesson plan emphasizing learning activities. Classes desiring such student involvement will find these suggestions helpful.

Learning Goals

After participating in this lesson, each student will be able to:

1. Recount the events of the Day of Pentecost that accompanied the birth of the church.
2. Explain how the power of the Holy Spirit helped bring the church into being.
3. Identify one way of helping his or her church remember its first-century origins.

Into the Lesson

Decorate your class's assembly space with birthday items: balloons, streamers, a "Happy Birthday" banner, and perhaps a cupcake with a candle for each learner. If your personal budget allows, get half-dollars from your bank to give to each arriving student; perhaps put a small stick-on bow on each half-dollar and say, "Happy Birthday" as you distribute the coins. Once every one arrives and someone asks, "Whose birthday is it?" or something similar, say, "The Church! Today's study is of the founding of Christ's church in Jerusalem in the first century." If no one says so, tell the group that the half-dollar represents the 50 days when Pentecost follows Passover.

Into the Word

Either hand out birthday party invitations or let your class fold a piece of paper to be filled in as if it were a party invitation. Tell them you want the class to look at today's text and suggest elements of an invitation that God could have sent for the birthday of Christ's church. Suggest they consider such things as the actual event being celebrated, time, place, appropriateness of gifts, whether to R.S.V.P., special events at the party, special guests to be expected, special dress/costumes. Give an example or two of what they could include, such as "R.S.V.P.," with an asterisk explained as, "*Repent* if you please"; "Baptismal clothes recommended"; "No gifts, please; gifts will be distributed."

After a few minutes, ask for volunteers to say what they have included. Ask for clarification for any entry that needs it.

Into Life

If you distributed half-dollars at the beginning of class, you may want to suggest that students pass these along to others during the week with an explanation of their significance.

If your congregation has a badge maker, prepare one for each learner with this design: a cross separating the circle into four parts, a *1* in the upper left segment, a *21* in the lower right. Distribute these and give this explanation:

> I want to be a first-century Christian in the twenty-first-century culture. I look to the first-century New Testament for twenty-first-century direction.

Suggest that students be prepared to give a similar explanation to anyone who asks about the significance of the badge as it is worn.

The lesson writer's "Conclusion" is a "So what?" list of the important roles the Holy Spirit continues to offer in our lives. Prepare a three-column work sheet ahead of time for distribution to your students. (If you use the student book, this is included there.)

Put the following entries in column one, which is headed "The Holy Spirit at Work": (1) The Spirit inspired God's Word; (2) Our bodies are the temple of the Holy Spirit, who is within us; (3) The Spirit gives us the most personal of relationships with God; (4) The Spirit seals us for the day of redemption; (5) The Spirit makes people alive from the dead; (6) The Spirit helps us to bear the fruit of the Spirit; (7) The Spirit helps us with our prayers; (8) The Spirit raised Jesus from the dead.

Column two, headed "So We Must," will have these entries: (A) Flee sexual sin; (B) Live in hope; (C) Grieve not the Spirit; (D) Obey the Spirit without hesitation; (E) Pray in faith, nothing wavering; (F) Trust God with a childlike faith; (G) Walk with the Spirit; (H) Walk in newness of life and put to death the misdeeds of the body.

Third column, headed "Scripture Affirmation," will have these entries: (I) Romans 8:11; (II) Romans 8:26; (III) 1 Corinthians 6:19; Galatians 5:16; (IV) Galatians 4:6; (V) Galatians 5:22-25; (VI) Ephesians 4:30; (VII) Romans 8:13; Titus 3:5; (VIII) 2 Peter 1:21.

Direct students to connect affirmations in column one with consequences in column two and with Scripture in column three. Discuss correct connections, per the lesson writer's conclusion.

Let's Talk It Over

These questions are designed to promote discussion of the lesson. The answers here are only discussion starters. Let your class talk it over from there.

1. God is a God of purpose, and He definitely had a purpose for selecting Pentecost as the day on which the church began. What principles can the church learn from this today?

On the Day of Pentecost many devout Jews would gather in Jerusalem to observe the feast. This event provided not only a chance to begin with a large crowd on hand, but also guaranteed that the news of what took place would permeate the Mediterranean world as people returned home. For the church today, it is important to use special times and seasons of the year to make the most effective impact on the culture in which we live. With care, even secular holidays can be used as tools to reach others for Christ.

2. The two manifestations of the Spirit's coming (wind and fire) provide great symbolism for the church. How can the church "carry on" these significant symbols today without being "carried away" by fanciful applications?

The way you know wind is present is in the effect it has. Whether it is the feel of the wind upon your face, the swaying of trees in the breeze, or even the devastation of hurricane force winds, the presence of wind is recognizable. Like wind, the church can provide a strong presence in the world, gently touching lives and even changing the "landscape" of the world.

One well-known significance of fire is its role as a purifying agent. A sinful world needs the purity the church can provide.

3. The Day of Pentecost was a day when the gospel was presented in many languages. In what ways is this and is this not a model for proclaiming the gospel today?

Most of those present on the Day of Pentecost were probably at least bilingual: they would have been able to speak Greek (the common language) plus their own, native tongues. Thus it wasn't strictly necessary for the gospel to be preached in any language except Greek on that day. (Notice in Acts 2:7-12 that the people from various places were able to converse with one another.) But to hear the gospel preached in one's native language—how powerful this can be!

Jesus has told us to take the gospel into all the world (Matthew 28:19, 20). This means being able to communicate in native languages. We should not automatically assume that God will enable His modern-day messengers to preach miraculously in languages that they have not studied in a repeat of Pentecost. That's why organizations exist to train missionaries to speak foreign languages. Other groups have as their goal the translation of Scripture into various languages and dialects. Such groups need our support.

4. Simon Peter's presentation of the gospel was a long way from where he had been just five weeks earlier when he denied Jesus. What a tremendous change! In what ways do you see God continuing to make significant changes in people's lives today? In what ways can you and your church become a source of transformation for those in your sphere of influence?

Today we continue to see the life-changing power of the Spirit of God as broken families are healed, alcoholics are rescued, and those in prison for committing crimes are brought to Christ. Cultures are transformed as missionary efforts extend into dark places in the world. Churches that once were struggling for survival are now having a tremendous impact in their communities. Churches and Christians today can keep an outward focus to determine areas where the light of the gospel is needed. God calls the church to walk boldly by faith into such arenas.

5. One school of thought says that it is not necessary for one to repent or change one's way because this involves human effort, and we are not saved by human effort. What would you say to someone who claimed to be a Christian but had obviously not repented of sin?

Jesus came not only to be our Savior but also to be our Lord. Holding on to sin is a failure to allow the way of Christ to be the guiding force of living. Holding on to sinful ways means making oneself into his or her own "lord"; this says to the world that Christianity is nothing distinct, even though God has called His people to be distinct, to be holy, to be set apart (see 1 Peter 1:15, 16).

September 11
Lesson 2

The Believers Share

Devotional Reading: Romans 8:9-17.

Background Scripture: Acts 2:41-47; 4:32-37.

Printed Text: Acts 2:43-47; 4:32-35.

Acts 2:43-47; 4:32-35

43 And fear came upon every soul: and many wonders and signs were done by the apostles.

44 And all that believed were together, and had all things common;

45 And sold their possessions and goods, and parted them to all men, as every man had need.

46 And they, continuing daily with one accord in the temple, and breaking bread from house to house, did eat their meat with gladness and singleness of heart,

47 Praising God, and having favor with all the people. And the Lord added to the church daily such as should be saved.

. . . .

32 And the multitude of them that believed were of one heart and of one soul: neither said any of them that aught of the things which he possessed was his own; but they had all things common.

33 And with great power gave the apostles witness of the resurrection of the Lord Jesus: and great grace was upon them all.

34 Neither was there any among them that lacked: for as many as were possessors of lands or houses sold them, and brought the prices of the things that were sold,

35 And laid them down at the apostles' feet: and distribution was made unto every man according as he had need.

Golden Text: All that believed were together, and had all things common.—Acts 2:44.

LESSON 2   SEPTEMBER 11

You Will Be My Witnesses
Unit 1: In Jerusalem
(Lessons 1-4)

Lesson Aims

After this lesson each student will be able to:
1. Describe the various ways the earliest Christians shared their lives with each other.
2. Explain how God's Word, Christian love, and corporate worship give the church a strong foundation.
3. Plan a class project to help a needy family in the church.

Lesson Outline

INTRODUCTION
    A. Division and Unity
    B. Lesson Background
  I. EMPOWERED CHURCH (Acts 2:43-47)
    A. Miracles and Awe (v. 43)
    B. Giving and Receiving (vv. 44, 45)
      Utopia?
    C. Fellowship and Worship (vv. 46, 47a)
      Enthusiastic Fellowship
    D. Growth and Blessing (v. 47b)
 II. SUCCESSFUL CHURCH (Acts 4:32-35)
    A. Great Unity Achieved (v. 32)
    B. Great Message Proclaimed (v. 33)
    C. Great Love Shown (vv. 34, 35)
CONCLUSION
    A. Strength Through Love and Unity
    B. Prayer
    C. Thought to Remember

Introduction

A. Division and Unity

Saber-toothed cats roamed North America during the Ice Age. Their seven-inch-long canine teeth made them feared predators. An article in *National Geographic* included a photograph of the remains of two such cats that died while locked in mortal combat. One had bitten into the leg of the other so hard that his teeth became locked in the leg bone, thus dooming both.

One cannot help but wonder how humanity avoids extinction when it is so divided by hatred, prejudice, lust for power, and fear. The world is divided sharply by race, religion, and social standing. These differences are so intense that solutions seem impossible.

Many attempts have been made to unify the human race. Various empires have attempted it through military might. The atheist Robert Owen (1771–1858) tried to create a more perfect society through education and the abolition of social classes and personal wealth. Jim Jones's attempt to create a perfect society in Guyana ended with deception, murder, and mass suicide in 1978. All of these attempts missed the real problem: sin.

The human race has a sin problem that we simply cannot solve or circumvent on our own. That is why all human attempts to unite people end in failure sooner or later. But God can do what we cannot. God can solve the deepest problems of the human race, beginning with the sin problem. Revelation 7:9 indicates that Heaven will be enjoyed by people from all families, tribes, languages, and nations. The message of Christ breaks down barriers and unites people regardless of their many differences. Christ destroyed the barrier between Jew and Gentile and united them under a common Savior within His church (Ephesians 2:11-18). If God can unite groups once marked with such hostility, He can overcome any barrier that divides humanity.

B. Lesson Background

The book of Acts covers a span of about 30 years, beginning in A.D. 30. Today's lesson (as last week's) takes us into the earliest part of that time span. We will see the great unity enjoyed by the very first church. This will be a lesson in how we can succeed as they did.

I. Empowered Church
(Acts 2:43-47)

A. Miracles and Awe (v. 43)

43. And fear came upon every soul: and many wonders and signs were done by the apostles.

After communities are devastated by a tornado or an earthquake, people often walk around dazed, not knowing what to do next. The great outpouring of the Spirit, the powerful message of salvation by Peter, and the overwhelming number of conversions in a single day shakes Jerusalem to its foundations. But what happened on the Day of Pentecost was only the beginning. Jerusalem continues to be rocked by aftershocks that bring fear and awe *upon every soul*.

While some shake with fear as they realize that they had rejected and killed the Messiah, the fear that is mentioned here is that of respect, reverence, and awe. God continues to shake Jerusalem by empowering the apostles to do great miracles. The miracles are *wonders* because those who witness them are filled with great amazement. They are *signs* because they point people to the truth about Jesus (compare John 14:11). Peter had made the bold statement that God made Jesus "both Lord and Christ" (Acts 2:36). Now the apostles prove the truth about Jesus by miracles. Many of these undoubtedly include the same kinds of healing miracles that Jesus had performed while on Earth (example: Matthew 4:23).

It is a good thing to have godly fear (see Proverbs 1:7). Reverent awe of God is appropriate for Christians (compare Luke 5:26; 7:16). If the church had more people who feared the Lord, the church would be morally and spiritually stronger.

B. Giving and Receiving (vv. 44, 45)

44, 45. And all that believed were together, and had all things common; and sold their possessions and goods, and parted them to all men, as every man had need.

These verses have been used as a basis by communal groups and certain cults to encourage people to bring all of their possessions together in one place where everyone can live together and share one another's belongings equally. These two verses also have served as the basis for the belief of some that the first-century Christians practiced an early form of communism or socialism. But such ideas miss the point. Passages such as Acts 2:46 and 1 Corinthians 11:22 indicate that those Christians still had individual homes. It would be physically impossible for thousands of people suddenly to start living in one location in Jerusalem.

The fact that these earliest Christians have *all things common* indicates that they share their possessions by going so far as to sell property and give as everyone has *need*. This is well illustrated in Acts 4:32-37. There we read of Barnabas voluntarily selling a field and bringing the proceeds to give to the apostles. This allows the apostles to distribute the money as appropriate.

This is the generosity that marks the early church. It is not mandatory, however. Peter makes it clear to Ananias in Acts 5:4 that the property he owned was his to do with as he pleased. Today, various forms of government require that people give up some (or all) of what they have so that the state can redistribute it. The early Christians love one another so much that they want to help those in need. No sacrifice is too great for this.

God helps the needy, and Christians must be like-minded (1 John 3:17). This is one of the first lessons that the early Christians learn, and they learn it quite well. They really do love one another! [See question #1, page 28.]

UTOPIA?

In introducing today's lesson, we mentioned Robert Owen, a famous nineteenth-century atheist. (He debated Alexander Campbell in 1829 on the legitimacy of Christianity.) Although Owen's theology was flawed, his concern for the poor and needy was not. In England he proposed limiting common laborers to a 48-hour, 6-day work week, with no decrease in pay. Neither political nor industrial leaders were ready for this.

In America he bought the whole town of Harmony, Indiana, to give life to his dreams. In this town—renamed New Harmony—there would be a community of goods, no religious activities, and no competition in the production of goods. It was assumed that everyone would contribute mutually for the good of all. But within a year, this would-be utopia began to fail. It had no spiritual base for its founder's reforms.

Robert Owen found what all such social reformers from ancient times to modern Marxists have discovered: without the change of heart

Visual for lesson 2

God calls us to meet needs. In this regard, use this visual to reinforce the importance of question #1 on page 28.

> **How to Say It**
>
> ANANIAS. An-uh-*nye*-us.
> BARNABAS. *Bar*-nuh-bus.
> CEPHAS. *See*-fus.
> DYNAMIS (Greek). *doo*-nuh-mis.
> EPHESUS. *Ef*-uh-sus.
> JERUSALEM. Juh-*roo*-suh-lem.
> MESSIAH. Meh-*sigh*-uh.
> PENTECOST. *Pent*-ih-kost.

that faith brings, there will never be a utopia. On the other hand, the fledgling church of Christ proved that social change can occur when the transforming power of the gospel renews the human heart. Their example stands as a challenge to us of what love can do.

—C. R. B.

C. Fellowship and Worship (vv. 46, 47a)

46a. And they, continuing daily with one accord in the temple.

These early Christians are so excited about their newfound faith that they cannot stay apart from one another. They are motivated by love to come together each day for worship and fellowship. Three thousand people will find it difficult to meet anywhere else but on the grounds of the temple complex. Acts 3:11; 5:12 indicate that they may be gathering in Solomon's colonnade, which runs along the east side of the outer court.

Sadly, people sometimes let the things of this world and the responsibilities of life crowd worship and fellowship from their schedules. They lose that excitement that they had when they first became Christians. They feel no great loss when they skip church, having lost the wonder and joy of Christianity. In his book *Recapture the Wonder*, Ravi Zacharias notes that, "Wonder enriches you when you take time to reflect and ponder the greatness of our faith in Jesus Christ" and that "Wonder is retained by pondering." Unfortunately, he observes, "Thinking is a dying discipline in a society that throbs with activity."

Deliberately scheduling Bible study—the kind that really makes us think—helps us recapture the wonder of those feelings we had when we first came to Christ. In addition to Sunday (Lord's Day) Bible enrichment programs, some churches offer small-group studies during the week. Christians can value these opportunities.

46b. And breaking bread from house to house, did eat their meat with gladness and singleness of heart.

Many churches today enjoy fellowship meals. But fellowship is not limited to such activities. Here we see how the early Christians meet in one another's homes. There they share meals and enjoy one another's company. They enjoy that "singleness of heart" that sets them apart from the rest of the world. (See also Acts 5:42; 20:7.) This is not the kind of thing that can be "forced." It just happens as a natural outflowing of love. [See question #2, page 28.]

Christians are part of the greatest family in the world. It seems as natural as breathing for people who love one another—people who enjoy a common faith and a common salvation—to invite each other to their homes for food and fellowship. It helps bind together those of "like precious faith" (2 Peter 1:1). In modern society, people are often too busy with worldly activities to engage in this kind of fellowship. People get home after work, shut the garage door with an electric opener, and "cocoon" for the rest of the evening. Year after year they miss out on one of the real pleasures of the Christian life, opportunities that bind the church together.

ENTHUSIASTIC FELLOWSHIP

"Mr. and Mrs. Smith" were a Christian couple who had been active members for several years in an old, declining church. This church had lost its vision. It was content to keep doing what it had always done until it died. Mrs. Smith herself had been plagued for years with debilitating health problems that robbed her of her vitality and crushed her formerly lively spirit.

Then the Smiths moved to a new community. There they found fellowship in a congregation with a willingness to try new ways to reach the lost. This church had a program of enthusiastic missionary outreach and an abundance of small-group Bible studies. Other fellowship groups opened their homes for meals together. The congregation swept up the Smiths into its open arms.

A strange thing began to happen: Mrs. Smith's health problems got no better, but her spirits began to lift. As the vitality of the new congregation found its way into her life, the clinical depression she had fought for years no longer held her in its death grip. Although she felt no better

> **Home Daily Bible Readings**
>
> **Monday, Sept. 5**—Share with Those in Need (Deuteronomy 15:4-8)
> **Tuesday, Sept. 6**—Come to an Abundant Life (Isaiah 55:1-7)
> **Wednesday, Sept. 7**—The Parable of the Rich Fool (Luke 12:13-21)
> **Thursday, Sept. 8**—Do Not Worry (Luke 12:22-34)
> **Friday, Sept. 9**—The Believers Grow in Faith Together (Acts 2:43-47)
> **Saturday, Sept. 10**—The Believers Share Their Possessions (Acts 4:32-37)
> **Sunday, Sept. 11**—Many Sick People Are Healed (Acts 5:12-16)

physically, she got involved in a way she had not been for many years. Enthusiastic concern of others for her as well as her newfound opportunities for service changed her life.

Timeless principles that made the Jerusalem church so alive still work. When God's people respond to the gospel with enthusiasm, He works to change lives! —C. R. B.

47a. Praising God, and having favor with all the people.

The old saying "You can't please everyone" is true, but these Christians impress their community as a whole. It will be clear in the next two chapters, however, that not everyone is truly pleased with them. The religious leaders will arrest Peter and John and threaten them. However, when people are helping, sharing, loving, and caring for one another, even the hardest sinners in the community have to take notice and be impressed. This favor with *all the people* must make many unbelievers listen again to the gospel message as more and more respond to it.

D. Growth and Blessing (v. 47b)

47b. And the Lord added to the church daily such as should be saved.

So *the church* continues to grow *daily*. Many churches today have a tradition of making people wait until some future time before they can be baptized. But the earliest Christians proclaim the message of salvation each day and baptize without delay (compare Acts 8:36-38; 16:33). The earliest Christians see opportunities to bring people to salvation each day. [See question #3, page 28.]

Not only do they succeed by making a strong witness to the community, they also are successful in God's eyes. The Lord, after all, is the one who ultimately saves. Titus 3:5 says, "According to his mercy he saved us, by the washing of regeneration, and renewing of the Holy Ghost." God places the names of the saved in the Lamb's book of life (Revelation 21:27).

The translation *such as should be saved* is perhaps a bit difficult for modern ears to understand. Some will find the phrase, "those who were being saved" to be a little easier.

II. Successful Church
(Acts 4:32-35)
A. Great Unity Achieved (v. 32)

32. And the multitude of them that believed were of one heart and of one soul: neither said any of them that aught of the things which he possessed was his own; but they had all things common.

The wonderful unity that these early Christians enjoy is nothing short of remarkable. We know that it is impossible to force people to love one another. True love is something that flows naturally because of the relationship people have with God—a relationship that affects all other relationships of life.

This attitude should always be present among Christians (see Galatians 6:10). God places before us each day opportunities to do good. The trouble is that many people do not keep their eyes open for such opportunities, or else they ignore them when they see them. Christians are a part of a wonderful household of faith. When each looks out for ways to do good, a marvelous unity is enjoyed, a unity that serves as a solid foundation for everything else that happens in the church.

But Christ expects even more than this. "Let nothing be done through strife or vainglory; but in lowliness of mind let each esteem other better than themselves" (Philippians 2:3). Christ thought of us more than He thought of himself. If that were not the case, He would never have gone to the cross. But He did. Christians who consider other people's needs to be more important than their own have reached a stage of spiritual maturity that pleases God greatly.

B. Great Message Proclaimed (v. 33)

33. And with great power gave the apostles witness of the resurrection of the Lord Jesus: and great grace was upon them all.

Christians watch out for the physical needs of one another, but the church's primary mission is to provide witness to *the resurrection of the Lord Jesus* to the world. "For I delivered unto you first of all that which I also received, how that Christ died for our sins according to the Scriptures; and that he was buried, and that he rose again the third day according to the Scriptures: and that he was seen of Cephas, then of the twelve: after that, he was seen of above five hundred brethren at once" (1 Corinthians 15:3-6a).

Paul calls the gospel "the power of God unto salvation" (Romans 1:16). Preachers are fond of pointing out that the word *power* both in that passage and in the text before us is the Greek word *dynamis* from which we derive the English word *dynamite*. But that connection is only surface deep. Dynamite is destructive, while the power of God's *great grace* is a healing force. Everyone in the city of Jerusalem in A.D. 30 knows that Jesus had been crucified. But when God raised Jesus from the dead, God proved "with power" that Jesus is His Son (Romans 1:4). The message of the resurrection is proclaimed with great power by the apostles. Thousands find this eyewitness testimony irresistible. As a result, their lives are changed for all eternity. [See question #4, page 28.]

Surely God's great grace is poured out upon the church! God's continuing blessing is seen in the way the first-century church grows numerically, in the way that He answers prayers, and in the way that Christians grow spiritually in the grace and knowledge of the Lord Jesus. Churches that fulfill the royal law of loving one another (James 2:8) will find God blessing them with the riches of His grace.

C. Great Love Shown (vv. 34, 35)

34, 35. Neither was there any among them that lacked: for as many as were possessors of lands or houses sold them, and brought the prices of the things that were sold, and laid them down at the apostles' feet: and distribution was made unto every man according as he had need.

Again, Luke (the author of the book of Acts) refers to great acts of generosity. Two new things are here mentioned. First, no Christian lacks for the necessities of life. No member of this great congregation of believers can tolerate seeing a fellow believer lack food, clothes, or shelter.

Again, this does not mean that the Christians are selling absolutely all that they own because of the simple fact that they are still meeting in their homes and breaking bread from house to house. God expects people to take care of their own households. So God would not expect a person to move his own family out onto the street. In fact, Paul writes that anyone who does not take care of his immediate family has "denied the faith" (see 1 Timothy 5:8). So we see a balance by combining these ideas. Immediate family comes first, but not to the point that our own selfishness means that others lack basic necessities. (The rich young ruler was told to "sell all" in Luke 18:22 because of a problem that was specific to him.)

The other thing we learn is that when people sell property and give the proceeds to the church, they allow the leadership to make distribution to the ones in need. As the church grows, other people will be selected to oversee this task and accomplish it efficiently (Acts 6:1-6). [See question #5, page 28.] The Scriptures also tell us that the first-century church maintains a list of widows to help (1 Timothy 5:9, 10). God expects His people to take care of their own family members first. But when someone has no family, or when a family is destitute or has some special need, then Christians will do what they can to assist.

Many Christians today miss out on an important way of glorifying God when they believe that the government will always step in to help. Have we Christians lost our powerful witness to the community by failing to help others? Have Christians forgotten that the Lord taught that "it is more blessed to give than to receive"? (See Acts 20:35.) Think what an impact the church would have on the world if it sought to recapture this spirit of love and unity that permeated the earliest church!

Conclusion

A. Strength Through Love and Unity

Reproducing the doctrine and message of the first-century church in the twenty-first century is a worthy goal. Many congregations strive to restore the worship and teaching of those early believers. While that is good, such efforts fall short if Christians do not reproduce the heart and love of those early Christians as well. Unfortunately, the congregations of the first century would find themselves challenged in this regard all too soon (e.g., 1 Corinthians 1:10; 11:17-22; Galatians 5:15; Titus 3:10).

The case of the church at Ephesus proves that resisting false doctrine isn't enough (see Revelation 2:1-7). Jesus prayed for the unity of believers (John 17). The apostles encouraged it (Ephesians 4:3). The first-century church at Jerusalem lived it. A key to this unity is mutual love expressed through action (1 John 3:16-18). No wonder the earliest church was a thing of great power that brought new life to an entire city! Churches today must realize that such unity will continue to empower the church and will cause it to enjoy the favor of God.

B. Prayer

Father, thank You for the church founded by Your Son. Please keep our hearts filled with love for one another. Bind us together in a spirit of great unity. Melt away those sinful attitudes that often tear us apart. May Your church today be a powerful witness of Your love and mercy and grace. In Jesus' name, amen.

C. Thought to Remember

"Hereby perceive we the love of God, because he laid down his life for us: and we ought to lay down our lives for the brethren" (1 John 3:16).

Learning by Doing

This page contains an alternate lesson plan emphasizing learning activities. Classes desiring such student involvement will find these suggestions helpful.

Learning Goals

After participating in this lesson, each student will be able to:

1. Describe the various ways the earliest Christians shared their lives with each other.
2. Explain how God's Word, Christian love, and corporate worship give the church a strong foundation.
3. Plan a class project to help a needy family in the church.

Into the Lesson

As students arrive, divide them into two groups with separate seating. Use some artificial criterion, such as those wearing black shoes from those wearing shoes of color or those carrying something from those empty-handed.

Have an artistic member of the class draw a simple outline of an "old-fashioned" church building from the perspective of looking at it toward the front entrance. A simple steeple with a cross atop it and arched windows will help the image convey "church." For the gable, use double lines to mark it off, then divide it into ten parts. Across the foundation have a similar double-lined section divided into nine spaces.

Say, "The lesson writer uses two key words in his outline for today's study. Guess a letter included in either of these two words—one has ten letters, one has nine—and I will write it in appropriately. As soon as you think you know either of the words, say it, and I will write it in." The word to be written into the ten gable spaces is *successful*. The word for the nine foundation spaces is *empowered*. Once both words are identified say, "The successful church is an empowered church—empowered by God with love, through worship and fellowship."

Next, say, "I am going to give you two minutes to write down factors that make us different from one another." If they need help getting started, suggest answers such as age, birthplace, and different learning styles. At the end of the two minutes, have the student who has the most entries read his or her list. Afterward, ask others to tell items on their lists that went unnamed. Comment simply, "Many things differentiate us. Today's text and study highlights the factors that unify us in the church."

Into the Word

Give each learner the following list of six unifying factors for a group: Common Emotions, Common Beliefs, Common Assets, Common Worship, Common Sense of Grace, and Common Leadership. (This list is included in the student book.) Ask students to put verse numbers from today's text next to each unifying factor to show which factor is illustrated in that passage. For example, Acts 2:43 (fear/awe unifies them, and they all looked to the apostles as leaders), would be cited with the Common Emotions factor.

Give students time to work their way through the text and make their decisions, and then go through them unifying factor by unifying factor and ask for verse notations. If students differ, have them explain their choices. Though a variety of possibilities exist, here is one printed text choice for each of the common factors: Emotions, 4:34 (love); Beliefs, 4:33 (Jesus' resurrection); Assets, 2:44 ("all things"); Worship, 2:47 ("praising God"); Sense of Grace, 4:33 (great grace upon all); Leadership, 4:35 (money turned over to the apostles). Ask the class if they can identify other unifying factors for a functioning group.

Acts 2:44 is an excellent summary of the thrust of today's study. Go around your group and have each person say that verse: "All that believed were together, and had all things common." Hearing it over and over should fix the idea in their memories. At the end say, "The church's togetherness (unity) and its commonality (fellowship) are always the secret of a successful church."

Into Life

In the early days of the Jerusalem church, members were willing to sell some of their possessions in order to fund the needs of others. Discuss the possibility and logistics of a "class garage sale" with the income to be given to the congregation's benevolence fund or to a needy family of the class's choice. It may be preferable to suggest individual families have their own garage sales and make anonymous contributions.

Consider also organizing a work crew of volunteer class members to go into homes of the less fortunate or physically limited for home repairs and maintenance. Projects can be as simple as painting a room.

Let's Talk It Over

These questions are designed to promote discussion of the lesson. The answers here are only discussion starters. Let your class talk it over from there.

1. One of the marks of the Lord's church is concern for one another, especially those in need. How can we more effectively meet needs of other believers in church and in our area?

One of the most effective things a church can do is simply to keep its eyes and ears open to signs of those who are hurting and in need. Establishing a functioning benevolence committee that oversees this task can be beneficial.

Food pantries and clothes closets, where such items are gathered and held for specific needs, make the church ready to respond in times of crisis. As God has blessed us with homes and automobiles, we can use these to minister to others by providing housing to those in times of devastation or transportation to those who are not able to drive. What we do in the name of Jesus shows others His love.

2. Jesus prayed for the unity of His followers in John 17:20, 21. In Ephesians 4:3, Paul encourages Christians to make every effort to maintain unity. How can the church continually maintain the unity Paul commanded and for which Christ prayed?

At least one key ingredient for maintaining unity is to realize that *unity* is not the same as *uniformity*. Being one in heart and mind in putting Christ first does not require us all to think exactly alike on every issue, which would be uniformity. We need not carry a burden of guilt for not agreeing on matters of expediency. Yet when we do disagree, we can do so without being disagreeable. A principle much espoused is that, "Methods are many, principles are few; methods change, principles never do." Understanding the difference between methods and principles will help in maintaining unity without expecting uniformity.

The church holds all things in common by first realizing that God owns all and grants all blessings. As stewards we recognize that what God has blessed us with is not for our use only, but also for the benefit of others, especially those who are part of the family of faith (again, see Galatians 6:10). What a vital part of our unity this is!

3. Why is it significant to understand that it is the Lord who adds to the church? How should this fact affect the life of the church?

People have a tendency to look on the outward aspects of others to determine who is (or who should be) part of the church. But God looks inward; see 1 Samuel 16:7. Whereas we may look on the fulfillment of certain rituals as making a person part of the church, the Lord knows the heart. It is God's grace, not human work, that saves and adds people to the church.

Since it is God's church, and He is the one who does the adding, this means that there is no place for judgmental attitudes and feelings of superiority in the life of the church. (See Romans 14.) This is all the more true when we think of how Jesus emptied himself, even to death on a cross.

4. How can the power of the gospel most forcibly be made known in the church and world today? How well is our church doing?

Paul sought to know Christ "and the power of his resurrection" (Philippians 3:10). The church will continue to be a force as that fact is preached and taught.

Churches that get sidetracked by various other issues can become powerless. The seven churches of Revelation 2 and 3 had problems, to varying degrees, in this regard. In those two chapters, God challenges the churches to focus on the big picture. The challenge comes with some dire warnings, too! In one instance, the warning is that God will "remove thy candlestick out of his place" if corrective action isn't taken (Revelation 2:5).

5. Gifts from those in the church were brought and laid at the feet of the apostles. Why is it a good idea that gifts are brought to those in positions of authority in the church?

Giving to meet needs through the church, and not individually, gives the glory to Christ's church and not to the individual giving the gift. A practical reason for giving in this manner is that the leaders of the church may have some insights into a particular request for help that an individual may not have.

Peter and John Heal a Lame Man

September 18
Lesson 3

DEVOTIONAL READING: Luke 7:18-23.

BACKGROUND SCRIPTURE: Acts 3.

PRINTED TEXT: Acts 3:1-16.

Acts 3:1-16

1 Now Peter and John went up together into the temple at the hour of prayer, being the ninth hour.

2 And a certain man lame from his mother's womb was carried, whom they laid daily at the gate of the temple which is called Beautiful, to ask alms of them that entered into the temple;

3 Who, seeing Peter and John about to go into the temple, asked an alms.

4 And Peter, fastening his eyes upon him with John, said, Look on us.

5 And he gave heed unto them, expecting to receive something of them.

6 Then Peter said, Silver and gold have I none; but such as I have give I thee: In the name of Jesus Christ of Nazareth rise up and walk.

7 And he took him by the right hand, and lifted him up: and immediately his feet and ankle bones received strength.

8 And he leaping up stood, and walked, and entered with them into the temple, walking, and leaping, and praising God.

9 And all the people saw him walking and praising God:

10 And they knew that it was he which sat for alms at the Beautiful gate of the temple: and they were filled with wonder and amazement at that which had happened unto him.

11 And as the lame man which was healed held Peter and John, all the people ran together unto them in the porch that is called Solomon's, greatly wondering.

12 And when Peter saw it, he answered unto the people, Ye men of Israel, why marvel ye at this? or why look ye so earnestly on us, as though by our own power or holiness we had made this man to walk?

13 The God of Abraham, and of Isaac, and of Jacob, the God of our fathers, hath glorified his Son Jesus; whom ye delivered up, and denied him in the presence of Pilate, when he was determined to let him go.

14 But ye denied the Holy One and the Just, and desired a murderer to be granted unto you;

15 And killed the Prince of life, whom God hath raised from the dead; whereof we are witnesses.

16 And his name, through faith in his name, hath made this man strong, whom ye see and know: yea, the faith which is by him hath given him this perfect soundness in the presence of you all.

GOLDEN TEXT: His name, through faith in his name, hath made this man strong, whom ye see and know.—Acts 3:16a.

SEPTEMBER 18 — 30 — PETER AND JOHN HEAL A LAME MAN

> *You Will Be My Witnesses*
> Unit 1: In Jerusalem
> (Lessons 1-4)

Lesson Aims

After participating in this lesson, each student will be able to:

1. Retell the story of Peter and John's healing of the man who was crippled.
2. Summarize Peter's claim that Jesus deserves the glory for healing.
3. Participate in a time of prayer for people to be healed physically and spiritually in Jesus' name.

Lesson Outline

INTRODUCTION
    A. Problems Without Human Solutions
    B. Lesson Background
  I. INCIDENTAL MEETING (Acts 3:1-3)
    A. Two Men Going to Pray (v. 1)
    B. One Man in Desperate Need (vv. 2, 3)
 II. UNEXPECTED ANSWER (Acts 3:4-6)
    A. Ordinary Expectation (vv. 4, 5)
    B. Extraordinary Gift (v. 6)
      Better Than Expected
III. AMAZING MIRACLE (Acts 3:7-10)
    A. Healing and Standing (v. 7)
    B. Walking, Leaping, and Praising (v. 8)
    C. Recognition and Amazement (vv. 9, 10)
      It's Catching!
IV. POINTED SERMON (Acts 3:11-16)
    A. Large Crowd Gathers (v. 11)
    B. God Gets the Credit (vv. 12, 13a)
    C. People Are Accused (vv. 13b-15)
    D. Jesus Granted the Healing (v. 16)
CONCLUSION
    A. The Worst Problems of Life
    B. Prayer
    C. Thought to Remember

Introduction

A. Problems Without Human Solutions

This world is frightening because of its many problems that appear to have no solution. According to the World Health Organization, malnutrition affects close to 800 million people. Hunger plays a major role in the deaths of 14,000 children every day. Access to health care is a major concern for many. Terrorism continues to threaten world security. Even the best diplomats lack long-term solutions. So many problems!

The story is told of a captain who ran from the battlefield. "General, the enemy is too numerous. We cannot hope to win!" he exclaimed. But the general responded, "Captain, we are not here to count the enemy but conquer them. And conquer them we must." God expects the same thing, and He provides the power to do so. No problem is so big that God cannot handle it. Human wisdom and strength cannot win the day, but God can help His people win even the most difficult battles of life.

B. Lesson Background

Today's lesson demonstrates that God's power can solve problems that seem to have no solution. The power to change the world rests not in human ingenuity. Rather, it rests in God and in His message.

That message can change the world one life at a time. Some changes are instantaneous and miraculous while others take much longer to unfold. We see both categories in the pages of Scripture. But God, on His own timetable, wins the victory. We're now only three lessons into our study in Acts, but already we have seen God's power and His victories time and again. Today it's time to see one more. A great miracle is about to prove the truth of Christianity yet again. It all begins with a meeting that no one planned and was on no one's daily schedule.

I. Incidental Meeting
(Acts 3:1-3)

A. Two Men Going to Pray (v. 1)

1. Now Peter and John went up together into the temple at the hour of prayer, being the ninth hour.

Perhaps *Peter and John* had been preaching earlier in the day. They now walk together to *the temple* to pray at *the ninth hour*. Many Jews consider 6:00 A.M. (sunrise) to be the beginning of the day, so the ninth hour is equivalent to 3:00 P.M. The rhythm of temple practice revolves around sacrifice and prayer at set times (see Exodus 29:38, 39; Numbers 28:4, 8; Psalm 141:2; Ezekiel 46:13-15). Jesus' death made animal sacrifices obsolete (Hebrews 9:11-15; 10:1-12), but it is still appropriate for Peter and John to pray. They may have opportunity to share Christ with others who are there.

Christians still need regular times of prayer. Daniel was an extremely busy man, but he was not too busy to pray (see Daniel 6:10). Modern Christians tend to allow busy schedules and entertainment opportunities to crowd out prayer time. Christians can learn much from Peter and John who, in spite of being very busy teaching thousands of Christians who are new in the faith, still understand their deep need for prayer. [See question #1, page 37.]

B. One Man in Desperate Need (vv. 2, 3)

2, 3. And a certain man lame from his mother's womb was carried, whom they laid daily at the gate of the temple which is called Beautiful, to ask alms of them that entered into the temple; who, seeing Peter and John about to go into the temple, asked an alms.

Peter and John arrive at one of the gates of the temple complex. Modern scholars have tried to determine exactly which gate *is called Beautiful*, but this is very difficult. The Jewish historian Josephus suggests that it is made of Corinthian bronze. He describes it as a thing of exquisite workmanship, being of greater value than the gates plated with silver and set in gold.

As *Peter and John* prepare to enter the temple, *a certain man* crippled from birth asks them for money. He is over 40 years old (Acts 4:22). It is hard for many to imagine what it would be like to deal with such a long-term problem. Perhaps he was taught to beg even as a little child.

One cannot help but wonder if this man is now all alone in the world. Perhaps his parents are dead. If he has brothers and sisters, they may consider him to be too much of a burden. Perhaps all he has are two or three people who pity him enough to help him to the temple where he can beg for money. One of the entrances to the temple is an ideal location for this.

Those who are challenged physically sometimes feel isolated, lack self-respect, and are unable to enjoy life. They even find themselves rejected by their own family members, who consider them a burden or do not know how to help them. On the other hand, people find it difficult to know what to do when they meet those who ask for money. Most people want to be generous and help those in need, but many are reluctant to give because they know that some misrepresent themselves and their need. Many find such moments uncomfortable, but Peter sees this an opportunity to help this man.

II. Unexpected Answer
(Acts 3:4-6)
A. Ordinary Expectation (vv. 4, 5)

4, 5. And Peter, fastening his eyes upon him with John, said, Look on us. And he gave heed unto them, expecting to receive something of them.

The beggar asks *Peter* and *John* for money in the same way that he has asked countless others. The man evidently has begged for so long that it has become a routine. Perhaps he has his head down, feeling embarrassed or ashamed to beg for a living.

Some probably give him coins without pausing even for a moment to offer a kind word. Others perhaps hurry right on by, neither wanting to be bothered nor wanting others to notice their stinginess. Some even may have seen this man so often that he just blends into the background and goes unnoticed. But Peter and John stop and tell the man to *Look on us.* So he looks up, hoping for a gift.

B. Extraordinary Gift (v. 6)

6. Then Peter said, Silver and gold have I none; but such as I have give I thee: In the name of Jesus Christ of Nazareth rise up and walk.

What comes next is startling, to say the least! For that one instant, the man's face must fall with disappointment when he hears that they have no money. After all, he needs *silver and gold* to buy his next meal. But Peter wants to give him something better: the ability to *walk* by the power *of Jesus Christ of Nazareth.* As the Son of God, He was chosen by the Father to be

---

How to Say It

BARABBAS. Buh-*rab*-us.
BARNABAS. *Bar*-nuh-bus.
CORINTHIANS. Ko-*rin*-thee-unz (*th* as in *thin*).
ISAIAH. Eye-*zay*-uh.
JOSEPHUS. Jo-*see*-fus.
NAZARETH. *Naz*-uh-reth.
PILATE. *Pie*-lut.

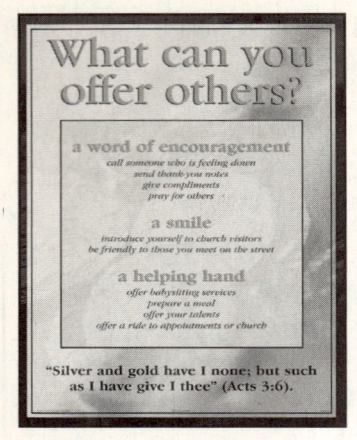

Use the question on this poster to challenge your students to think beyond themselves.

Visual for lesson 3

the Savior of the world. His power can make the lame to walk.

Many of us today cannot say *silver and gold have I none* because we do indeed have money. Christians with financial resources have an obligation to be generous and share with others in need (see 1 John 3:17, 18).

But even if a person has no money, people still have so much to give. How much does it cost to pray for someone who is in desperate need? How much does it cost to bring a word of comfort to a neighbor who has lost a family member? How much does it cost to share the good news of God's grace to someone who is lost? So much can be done that costs nothing. A "cup of cold water" can be a powerful help at times (Matthew 10:42). God blesses all Christians so that each may bless others who are faced with seemingly impossible problems. When we help others *in the name of Jesus,* God will bless (compare Acts 3:16; 4:10).

BETTER THAN EXPECTED

At the turn of the millennium just a few years ago, the African nation of Congo was in a war that would go on for years with a steadily rising death toll. Some authorities say only 10 percent of the victims were killed in battle; the rest died from starvation and disease. Adding to the tragedy is the case of the people who died at the hands of their priest!

In late 2003 in the small town of Bosobe, a priest promised his congregation that he would give them salvation. Marauding militias used terror, rape, and murder as the means to maintain power in that war-torn country. So one can understand the desire for salvation, whether temporal or eternal. The priest promised his people they would find salvation by drinking a potion he gave them. Of the 100 who drank it, 64 died from the poison it contained. What they got was far from what they expected!

What a different situation for the man in today's text. He didn't expect salvation, only money to help maintain his misery-filled life. What he got instead was healing and wholeness. God will judge the priest in the Congo for what he did to those who trusted him. But we can be sure of God's pleasure in what Peter and John did for the man who was crippled. We may not be able to perform miracles, but we can offer the gospel, which is the most important thing. One measure of our Christian lives is that we offer to those who need our help something more and better than what they expect.
—C. R. B.

III. Amazing Miracle
(Acts 3:7-10)
A. Healing and Standing (v. 7)

7. And he took him by the right hand, and lifted him up: and immediately his feet and ankle bones received strength.

Notice that the man doesn't initially stand on his own. Instead, Peter takes the man's *right hand* and lifts *him up*. This perhaps helps the man overcome a moment of uncertainty. Peter's command to rise up and walk undoubtedly seems incredible. He has never once taken a step, so Peter helps him up.

This is a true miracle that goes far beyond everyone's imagination. The healing is instantaneous and complete. This man immediately receives strength in his *feet* and ankles, so he rises to walk. After 40 years of atrophy, the deteriorated muscles suddenly come alive.

Not to be overlooked is the fact that this man has no experience in walking. A toddler has to learn to keep balance, falling many times while taking those first steps. But this man immediately walks—and more (see next). [See question #2, page 37.]

B. Walking, Leaping, and Praising (v. 8)

8. And he leaping up stood, and walked, and entered with them into the temple, walking, and leaping, and praising God.

Isaiah 35:6 describes the joys of the redeemed by predicting how the lame would leap as a hart (or deer). Has this man become so discouraged that he thinks he has no reason to go *into the temple* and thank God? (Compare Leviticus 21:16-23.) After all, he sat begging while others entered to pray. Now he also goes inside. This somber time of prayer is interrupted by a man who is jumping into the air and shouting praise to God for a great blessing!

C. Recognition and Amazement (vv. 9, 10)

9, 10. And all the people saw him walking and praising God: and they knew that it was he which sat for alms at the Beautiful gate of the temple: and they were filled with wonder and amazement at that which had happened unto him.

Now people react quite differently toward this man. He no longer blends into his surroundings. They can ignore him no longer. He is a *walking* and talking testimony to the power of Almighty *God.* No one doubts his identity or the miracle that has taken place. The joy and praise is contagious and spreads quickly through the crowd. [See question #3, page 37.]

It's Catching!

Have you noticed you can make yourself yawn just by thinking about it? At some time, someone probably has said to you, "Stop that yawning! You're making me do it, too." What is there about yawning that seems to be so contagious?

People even from the time of Aristotle (who lived more than three hundred years before Christ) were aware of the contagious nature of yawns. As you would expect, modern psychologists have studied the phenomenon also. Although babies yawn even in the womb, yawning apparently doesn't become contagious until about age two, when a child begins to recognize himself in a mirror. Some believe yawning has something to do with our self-perception and how we relate to others. It may be a subconscious way for us to show empathy for others.

Now think about how other behaviors affect us. It is hard not to feel some excitement when someone else is demonstrating ecstatic joy or enthusiasm, whether it is over their football team scoring a touchdown or as they are telling us some good personal news they have just received. This is what was taking place with the man who had just been healed of his lameness. As he jumped for joy and praised God for what had happened to him, the crowd who saw him was also caught up in a spirit of wonder and excitement. Does anyone ever get amazed and excited because of how *we* rejoice in God's blessings?

—C. R. B.

IV. Pointed Sermon
(Acts 3:11-16)

A. Large Crowd Gathers (v. 11)

11. And as the lame man which was healed held Peter and John, all the people ran together unto them in the porch that is called Solomon's, greatly wondering.

The porch that is called Solomon's is a covered colonnade on the east side of the temple. This was a familiar area to Jesus (see John 10:23), and it will remain a popular meeting place for the earliest Christians (Acts 5:12). *People* run to this area as the man who had been lame holds tight to *Peter and John.*

B. God Gets the Credit (vv. 12, 13a)

12, 13a. And when Peter saw it, he answered unto the people, Ye men of Israel, why marvel ye at this? or why look ye so earnestly on us, as though by our own power or holiness we had made this man to walk? The God of Abraham, and of Isaac, and of Jacob, the God of our fathers, hath glorified his Son Jesus.

The first time that this lesson writer had contact with a homeless person, money was given along with an invitation to go to church. The man's reply was startling: "What has God ever done to make me thankful?" Nothing seemed to reach that man. This sermon by Peter, though, has far greater success.

Home Daily Bible Readings

Monday, Sept. 12—Jesus Tells of His Healing Power (Luke 7:18-23)

Tuesday, Sept. 13—The Twelve Receive Power to Heal (Luke 9:1-6)

Wednesday, Sept. 14—Jesus Rebukes a Demon (Luke 4:31-37)

Thursday, Sept. 15—A Beggar Asks for Alms (Acts 3:1-5)

Friday, Sept. 16—A Man Is Healed (Acts 3:6-10)

Saturday, Sept. 17—Peter Speaks to the People (Acts 3:11-16)

Sunday, Sept. 18—Peter Tells the People to Repent (Acts 3:17-26)

Peter undoubtedly sees utter amazement in the eyes of those who gather around him and the man who had been lame. People are often drawn to charismatic persons who claim to have God's power or who seem to be spiritual giants. Paul and Barnabas will have to deal with this later while performing an identical miracle (Acts 14:8-13). But the apostles refuse to take credit for the miracles. Peter immediately points people to *God* and to *his Son Jesus*. [See question #4, page 37.]

Notice that Peter calls God *the God of Abraham, and of Isaac, and of Jacob, the God of our fathers*. This reminds the people of the covenant God made with Abraham and his descendants. The apostles proclaim that Jesus fulfills these promises. "If ye [whether Jew or Gentile] be Christ's, then are ye Abraham's seed, and heirs according to the promise" (Galatians 3:29). In fact, each of the following blessings is said specifically to be a fulfillment of the promise God made to Abraham and the fathers: Jesus' birth (Luke 1:68-75); His resurrection (Acts 13:32, 33); the conversion of sinners (Acts 3:24-26); justification through faith (Galatians 3:8; Romans 4:16-18); the gift of the Holy Spirit (Galatians 3:14); and the plan to bring people to Christ (Galatians 3:26-29).

C. People Are Accused (vv. 13b-15)

13b-15. Whom ye delivered up, and denied him in the presence of Pilate, when he was determined to let him go. But ye denied the Holy One and the Just, and desired a murderer to be granted unto you; and killed the Prince of life, whom God hath raised from the dead; whereof we are witnesses.

Peter now reminds the people of their guilt regarding the death of Jesus. Surely their memories are still fresh with regard to those horrible events of just several weeks previous! *Pilate*, the Roman governor, knew that the religious leaders were jealous of Jesus' popularity (Matthew 27:18). His custom was to release a prisoner during Passover, so he planned to release Jesus. But the leaders and their supporters demanded that he release Barabbas, who had committed murder in an uprising against Rome (Mark 15:7). Peter sees irony in the fact that they chose *a murderer* over the prince of life—someone who takes life rather than gives it.

Peter also makes it clear that God can reverse even the most horrible decisions people can make. Daniel had been thrown into the lions' den, but God reversed the decision by stopping the mouths of the lions. Daniel was rewarded instead of being eaten alive (Daniel 6). Joseph was sold as a slave by his own brothers, but God reversed their decision and Joseph became a great man in Egypt (Genesis 41:41). But the greatest example is the one in our text. Humanity's sin problem was so great that people even murdered God's Son, who came to give abundant *life*. God reversed that decision by raising Jesus *from the dead*. God brought about His greater plan by working through human weakness.

Peter uses two arguments to convince the crowd about Jesus. First, he makes it clear that eyewitnesses of Jesus' resurrection are present. Peter and John saw Jesus alive after being crucified (John 20:19, 20; 21:1). The second reason is given next.

D. Jesus Granted the Healing (v. 16)

16. And his name, through faith in his name, hath made this man strong, whom ye see and know: yea, the faith which is by him hath given him this perfect soundness in the presence of you all.

Peter also states that the *man* who had been lame is living proof that Jesus is alive because he was healed in Jesus' *name*. This miracle proves everything Peter has to say about Jesus.

Peter shows great boldness by proclaiming Jesus to the very ones who had been instruments of His death. A few weeks earlier, Peter's fear had caused him to stay behind locked doors (again, John 20:19). Now he boldly lifts Jesus up to this crowd because he wants them to know that the greatest problem of the human race is not physical pain or suffering (see Acts 3:17-26, not in today's text). The greatest problem is sin.

Sin cripples every soul. Those without Jesus are even worse off than the man who was crippled had been. But all can be healed by God's power and can receive joy, peace, forgiveness of sins, and eternal life by the one who is the prince of life. [See question #5, page 37.]

Conclusion

A. The Worst Problems of Life

The world is filled with people whose situations seem hopeless. Bill and Gloria Gaither, the authors of many wonderful Christian songs, had gone through some difficult times. Bill had been seriously ill. Gloria sat in a dark room experiencing torment and fear and thinking about what an awful world this is. They were expecting a baby, but she wondered, "Who in their right minds would bring a child into a world like this?"

Then something happened. The panic and fear turned to calm and assurance as she remembered the empty tomb of Jesus. She knew she could have that baby and face the future with optimism and trust because Jesus lives. As a result, she wrote that marvelous song, "Because He Lives." It speaks of facing the future without fear.

The world is filled with seemingly insurmountable problems, but none are so great that God cannot help us to face them all. The facts of Jesus' resurrection and the indwelling Holy Spirit help deal with grief, discouragement, temptation, suffering, pain, and loss as we look to eternity.

B. Prayer

Father, may we never hinder Jesus, the prince of life, from bringing new life to our souls. May we know that His great power can heal, give eternal life, and bless abundantly. In Jesus' name, amen!

C. Thought to Remember

The living Jesus still heals.

Learning by Doing

This page contains an alternate lesson plan emphasizing learning activities. Classes desiring such student involvement will find these suggestions helpful.

Learning Goals

After participating in this lesson, each student will be able to:

1. Retell the story of Peter and John's healing of the man who was crippled.
2. Summarize Peter's claim that Jesus deserves the glory for healing.
3. Participate in a time of prayer for people to be healed physically and spiritually in Jesus' name.

Into the Lesson

Begin class with a time of prayer, but recruit a class member to interrupt the prayer soon after you have begun by jumping up and shouting, "Praise the Lord! He's a mighty God!" repeatedly as he or she leaps about the room. As students react, say, "This is exactly what happened in the events described in Acts 3. At a reverent, quiet hour of prayer in a worship assembly, someone dared interrupt with shouts and dances. Let's take a closer look at that marvelous and interesting story."

Into the Word

Display the following words as a list: *a, about, and, and, heal, Jesus, John, lame, man, Peter, preach, then, who, was.* Say to your class, "If you reorganize these 14 words correctly, you will have a one-sentence summary of the story told in Acts 3." Give students some time to think. If they need a clue, say, *"Peter* is the first word." If they need more help, say, *"Jesus* is the last word—in more ways than one!" The complete sentence is "Peter and John heal a man who was lame and then preach about Jesus."

Label this next activity, "Peter Did It." Give your students the following list of sentences (here alphabetized by the second word in each). Ask students to put them in chronological order *(Verse answers are provided in parentheses—do not give those.)* Peter accompanied a friend to the temple *(1)*; Peter accused his audience, without hesitation *(14)*; Peter admitted he had no money *(6)*; Peter affirmed the resurrection of Jesus and claimed to be a witness *(15)*; Peter asked for the beggar's attention *(4)*; Peter assumed that some of his audience were at the early morning "trial" of Jesus before Pilate *(13)*; Peter corrected the view that the healing power was his and John's *(12)*; Peter credits the God of the Old Testament for working this miracle to honor Jesus *(13)*; Peter expressed his surprise that such a miracle would create marvel *(12)*; Peter helped the man to stand *(7)*; Peter indicated the great power in Jesus' name and faith in Jesus *(16)*; Peter invoked the name of Jesus to heal the man *(6)*; Peter reached the Solomon's porch area of the temple *(11)*; Peter heard a request for a monetary gift *(3)*.

Into Life

Say to your class, "Medications are a major factor in the life of many adults. Though the curse of sin and death remains on the earth, God's grace has allowed mankind to discover a wealth of pharmaceutical realities He created in the beginning. Make a list of what you think are the greatest medicinal discoveries." After a list is compiled, invite the class to join you saying in unison, "Praise God for _____," filling in each entry on your list in turn. Comment that, "All too often we take for granted the marvelous blessings God has given us."

Nearly everyone has a physician who has helped him or her with disease and pain. But doctors, like most professionals, seldom receive words of encouragement from their patients. Hand out blank thank-you cards and recommend that students jot their doctor a quick note to the effect, "I thank God that you dedicated yourself to the healing art. May He strengthen you for your service. May His wisdom aid yours each day." If students seem a bit hesitant, indicate that sending the note anonymously could work as well as signing it.

Say, "Though physical healing is much to be valued and prayed for, spiritual healing is all the more critical." Close the class time with a group prayer asking for God's grace to be with those in your class, your congregation, and beyond who are afflicted with physical and spiritual disease.

After naming those in need, use these words to close the prayer: "God, we know that all die *because of* sin, so we are coming to pray for those who are still dead *in* sin. Heal them by Your gospel. Provide that Christian 'physician' who can prescribe salvation. In the name of the great physician, amen."

Let's Talk It Over

These questions are designed to promote discussion of the lesson. The answers here are only discussion starters. Let your class talk it over from there.

1. Judaism had designated times for prayer. This is still true in many world religions today. Christianity does not have standardized times for prayer, but rather we are encouraged to pray continually (1 Thessalonians 5:17). In addition to that, do you think it is a good idea to have set times for concentrated prayer? Why, or why not?

Establishing personal prayer time should not be done in a legalistic manner. Certain leaders may state personal preferences for specific prayer times, but they are just that—personal preferences. Perhaps each Christian should do a spiritual self-examination to determine the ebb and flow of life in his or her regular schedule.

For some, regular prayer may mean getting up earlier. For others, it may mean staying up a little later. Others may need to give up or cut back on some habits or hobbies that take time away from personal time with God. This may mean less TV, fewer shopping trips, or a more limited participation in a favorite recreational activity.

2. The full and instantaneous healing of the man who was disabled brings us joy when we read of it. But this account may have a different effect on someone who prays for healing but does not receive it. How should one respond when the healing sought does not come?

It is important to understand that God does not promise healing for every disease and infirmity in this life. Paul himself even prayed for his "thorn in the flesh" to be removed, but it was not (2 Corinthians 12:7-9). We also remember God's promise to Paul that His grace would be sufficient to help him deal with his difficulty. Accepting God's grace and glorifying God as Lord even in the midst of an illness, disability, or disappointment could be the very thing that God will use to draw a person closer to Him.

We also do well to remember that any healing that does come will be temporary because our bodies are temporary. This means that we should seek spiritual healing above all else.

3. When God works, praise follows. How can we praise God for His mighty works? Why should we do so?

Praise doesn't have to take the form of loud "amens" or "halleujahs." Simply acknowledging God's goodness and giving Him the glory for all good gifts is also praise. Another way to praise is to be available to share with others how God has worked so they will know that God can do the same for them. Expect your students to have a long and diverse list of ways to praise God.

4. Servants of God are often given praise for the good things they do. When this happened to Peter, he immediately deflected the attention away from himself and pointed to God. What cautions should we take to be sure all the glory goes to God?

As Herod found out in Acts 12:21-23, accepting praise that belongs to God can be deadly! While it is not wrong to express appreciation to another or receive words of appreciation, we must be careful to not allow sinful pride to creep in. If someone commends a lesson we teach, it may be good to ask what was especially helpful for him or her in the lesson rather than merely basking in the praise.

Asking God for help in practicing humility can be an important part of the prayer life of the servant of God. But beware: having a humility that you're proud of will be a contradiction in terms!

5. God can take the worst of situations and bring good from them. He promises His people that He will do so (Romans 8:28). How has God demonstrated His power to bring good out of a bad situation in your life? in your church?

Expect some very personal and diverse answers. The wide variety of answers can include coming back to spiritual wholeness after a divorce, leaning on God's help in dealing with a rebellious child, knowing of God's care during severe financial trials, "waiting on the Lord" while sitting in a prison cell, and having a greater concern for the lost after a church split.

Stress that God's power of healing is a way in which He often brings victory from seeming defeat. God has taken some churches that have lost their way and turned them around into mighty instruments for His glory.

September 25
Lesson 4

The Church Is Bold

DEVOTIONAL READING: Ephesians 6:10-20.

BACKGROUND SCRIPTURE: Acts 4:1-31.

PRINTED TEXT: Acts 4:1-4, 23-31.

Acts 4:1-4, 23-31

1 And as they spake unto the people, the priests, and the captain of the temple, and the Sadducees, came upon them,

2 Being grieved that they taught the people, and preached through Jesus the resurrection from the dead.

3 And they laid hands on them, and put them in hold unto the next day: for it was now eventide.

4 Howbeit many of them which heard the word believed; and the number of the men was about five thousand.

. . . .

23 And being let go, they went to their own company, and reported all that the chief priests and elders had said unto them.

24 And when they heard that, they lifted up their voice to God with one accord, and said, Lord, thou art God, which hast made heaven, and earth, and the sea, and all that in them is;

25 Who by the mouth of thy servant David hast said, Why did the heathen rage, and the people imagine vain things?

26 The kings of the earth stood up, and the rulers were gathered together against the Lord, and against his Christ.

27 For of a truth against thy holy child Jesus, whom thou hast anointed, both Herod, and Pontius Pilate, with the Gentiles, and the people of Israel, were gathered together,

28 For to do whatsoever thy hand and thy counsel determined before to be done.

29 And now, Lord, behold their threatenings: and grant unto thy servants, that with all boldness they may speak thy word,

30 By stretching forth thine hand to heal; and that signs and wonders may be done by the name of thy holy child Jesus.

31 And when they had prayed, the place was shaken where they were assembled together; and they were all filled with the Holy Ghost, and they spake the word of God with boldness.

GOLDEN TEXT: Lord, behold their threatenings: and grant unto thy servants, that with all boldness they may speak thy word.—Acts 4:29.

> *You Will Be My Witnesses*
> Unit 1: In Jerusalem
> (Lessons 1-4)

Lesson Aims

After participating in this lesson, each student will be able to:

1. Retell Peter and John's bold proclamation of the gospel in spite of persecution.
2. Discuss the depth of the apostles' faith in relation to their boldness.
3. Write a prayer asking God for boldness in witnessing for Jesus.

Lesson Outline

INTRODUCTION
    A. Sobering Persecution
    B. Lesson Background
I. BOLD WITNESS (Acts 4:1-4)
    A. Confrontation (v. 1)
    B. Message (v. 2)
    C. Imprisonment (v. 3)
    D. Result (v. 4)
II. CONFIDENT ATTITUDE (Acts 4:23-28)
    A. God's Power (vv. 23, 24)
    B. God's Word (vv. 25, 26)
    C. God's Purpose (vv. 27, 28)
        The Power of Confidence
III. FEARLESS DETERMINATION (Acts 4:29-31)
    A. Determined in Spite of Threats (v. 29)
    B. Determined to Show God's Power (v. 30)
    C. Determined to Preach God's Word (v. 31)
        Shaking the House
CONCLUSION
    A. God, Please Make Us Bold!
    B. Prayer
    C. Thought to Remember

Introduction

A. Sobering Persecution

In *The World Christian Encyclopedia,* David Barrett estimates that just under 70 million Christians have died for their faith during the first 2,000 years of church history. But of that number, 45 million (almost two-thirds) were killed during the twentieth century alone. Barrett includes a map that indicates that a significant portion of the world remains "highly dangerous" to Christians.

As frightening as that may be, it does not even take into account the many Christians who have been persecuted without being killed. Some countries forbid Christian literature. Others deny employment to Christians. Many Chinese Christians have to worship secretly. Even in America some parents refuse to allow their children to be baptized or to enter Christian service. Not to be forgotten are those who are forbidden to read a Bible or pray in a public place or are harassed because of their faith. Paradoxically, it seems that the more "tolerant" society becomes, the more intolerant it is to Christians.

B. Lesson Background

Last week we saw Peter and John on their way to pray when they were interrupted by an opportunity to heal a man who was crippled. As we will see today, Peter and John would never make it to their intended time of prayer. Jesus warned His disciples that they would be hated and persecuted as their master had been (Matthew 10:22). Today's lesson records the first known persecution against the church after its birth on the Day of Pentecost. Peter and John had healed a man in Jesus' name. The crowds were amazed and listened as they proclaimed the resurrection of Jesus. Those in authority opposed their message, but the apostles overcame fear. The boldness of Peter and John presents a strong example for Christians yet today.

I. Bold Witness
(Acts 4:1-4)

A. Confrontation (v. 1)

1. And as they spake unto the people, the priests, and the captain of the temple, and the Sadducees, came upon them.

They refers to Peter and John. These two now face opposition at the hands of some of the very men who had crucified Jesus only a short time earlier. Many *priests* serve in the temple. The *captain of the temple* guard commands what may be thought of as a temple police force. Judas Iscariot had betrayed Jesus into the hands of "the chief priests and captains" of the temple (Luke 22:4). It was they who had arrested the Lord (Luke 22:52).

The Sadducees also opposed Jesus. They had been relentless in their attempts to undermine His ministry. They joined with the Pharisees in testing Jesus by asking for a sign from Heaven when He already had performed numerous signs (Matthew 16:1). They had asked questions, hoping to use Jesus' words against Him (Mark 12:18-27). The Sadducees deny the resurrection of the body (Matthew 22:23; Acts 23:8), so when they hear Peter and John teaching the truth of this doctrine (Acts 3:15), they are alarmed.

This particular Jewish party originated sometime after the Jews returned from the Babylonian captivity (536 B.C.). The Jewish historian Josephus tells us they are aristocratic and that most of their supporters are wealthy. People in general do not follow them, but they exercise great authority.

The phrase *came upon them* seems harmless at first glance. But as the story unfolds we will see the true intent. The captain of the temple may think that the apostles are inciting a riot. But the fact that the priests and Sadducees come with them indicates that the temple leaders are upset mostly at the apostles' teaching. [See question #1, page 46.]

B. Message (v. 2)

2. Being grieved that they taught the people, and preached through Jesus the resurrection from the dead.

We noted in our previous discussion that the Sadducees deny *the resurrection* of the body. The apostles proclaim that the healing had been done in Jesus' name, the same Jesus they had crucified, but whom God had raised from the dead (Acts 3:15, 26). The miracle and the message of resurrection now threaten the very existence of the Sadducees. If God had raised Jesus' dead body from the grave, then the Sadducees' teaching is in error. Thus they have to exercise their authority quickly and show the people "who's boss." If they fail, they could lose control of the masses.

It is essential to remember that the resurrection of Jesus is central to the message of the early church. It is impossible to explain the great success of the early church without the truth of the resurrection of Christ. But this message of resurrection is the very thing that the enemies of the church resist (Matthew 28:11-15). They have to know that Jesus' resurrection is the one element that either proves or disproves the apostles' message. If Jesus is still in the tomb, then all of this is for nothing (1 Corinthians 15:4, 12-19). But if Jesus is alive, then everything He ever taught is true, and all that the apostles are teaching is also true.

C. Imprisonment (v. 3)

3. And they laid hands on them, and put them in hold unto the next day: for it was now eventide.

Peter and John are arrested. The fact that the opponents in verse 1 *laid hands on them* seems to indicate that these two are manhandled as they are put in jail. In spite of all of the good that they have accomplished, they are treated as common criminals (compare Luke 22:52). [See question #2, page 46.]

Eventide means that it is about sunset, or roughly 6:00 P.M. Since Peter and John had arrived at the temple at about 3:00 P.M. and the miracle took place right away, these two must have preached to the crowd for the better part of three hours. Thus it takes some time for the authorities to move against them. The authorities spend the night preparing charges and planning their next move once they have these two in jail.

Comparing and contrasting the arrest of these two apostles with the arrest of Jesus is interesting. Peter and John are arrested in broad daylight, surrounded by hundreds of people. The people know what happened, so the authorities proceed with discretion. Jesus, on the other hand, was arrested in a remote location in the middle of the night. He was given a hasty, nighttime trial that probably was illegal in its format.

Home Daily Bible Readings

Monday, Sept. 19—Be Strong in the Lord (Ephesians 6:10-20)

Tuesday, Sept. 20—Paul Preaches the Gospel Courageously (1 Thessalonians 2:1-8)

Wednesday, Sept. 21—Peter and John Are Arrested (Acts 4:1-7)

Thursday, Sept. 22—Peter Speaks About Jesus Christ (Acts 4:8-12)

Friday, Sept. 23—Peter and John Are Warned (Acts 4:13-17)

Saturday, Sept. 24—Peter and John Refuse to Stop (Acts 4:18-22)

Sunday, Sept. 25—The Believers Pray for Boldness (Acts 4:23-31)

D. Result (v. 4)

4. Howbeit many of them which heard the word believed; and the number of the men was about five thousand.

Some will always oppose the gospel and deny the truth of God's Word. But that does not stop the message of Christ from changing people's lives. Through the power of the Holy Spirit, the church cannot but succeed when the message of Jesus is proclaimed to a lost world. And it will succeed even in the midst of opposition.

The authorities can throw Peter and John in prison, but they cannot stop their message. It is the custom in that part of the world to count only the *men* (compare Matthew 14:21; 15:38). What that means is that the church is much larger than *five thousand*. It is now possibly no more than two or three months after the Day of Pentecost, when the number of believers in the Jerusalem area swelled from 120 (Acts 1:15) to three thousand (Acts 2:41). Thus the number five thousand shows how rapidly the church is growing and how it succeeds, even in the midst of persecution. [See question #3, page 46.]

II. Confident Attitude
(Acts 4:23-28)
A. God's Power (vv. 23, 24)

23, 24. And being let go, they went to their own company, and reported all that the chief priests and elders had said unto them. And when they heard that, they lifted up their voice to God with one accord, and said, Lord, thou art God, which hast made heaven, and earth, and the sea, and all that in them is.

Some interesting things happen in Acts 4:5-22 (not in today's text). Peter and John are released, but not before they were brought before the Jewish Supreme Court, the Sanhedrin (Acts 4:15). *The elders*, rulers, and teachers of the law assembled for the trial. Even Annas and Caiaphas, the high priests who had condemned Jesus, were present (Acts 4:5; compare John 18:12-14).

These two had demanded that Peter and John tell them, "By what power, or what name, have you done this?" (Acts 4:7). In no uncertain words, Peter replied that this miracle had been done in the name of Jesus Christ of Nazareth. Peter reminded those religious leaders that they had crucified Him, but God had raised Him from the dead (Acts 4:10).

How to Say It

ABEDNEGO. Uh-*bed*-nee-go.
ANNAS. *An*-nus.
BABYLONIAN. Bab-ih-*low*-nee-uhn.
CAIAPHAS. *Kay*-uh-fus or *Kye*-uh-fus.
GOLIATH. Go-*lye*-uth.
JOSEPHUS. Jo-*see*-fus.
JUDAS ISCARIOT. *Joo*-dus Iss-*care*-ee-ut.
MESHACH. *Me*-shack.
NAZARETH. *Naz*-uh-reth.
PENTECOST. *Pent*-ih-kost.
PHARISEES. *Fair*-ih-seez.
SADDUCEES. *Sad*-you-seez.
SHADRACH. *Shay*-drack or *Shad*-rack.
TERTULLIAN. Tur-*tull*-yun.

Peter went on to proclaim that salvation is found in Jesus alone (Acts 4:12). Their enemies noted the courage of the two (Acts 4:13), but could not deny what they said because of the great miracle they had performed. Instead of being changed by the truth as thousands already had been, they simply admitted that they could not deny that a miracle had happened—but they refused to believe that it had anything to do with Jesus (Acts 4:14-16). They were determined to stop the apostles from speaking further in that name (Acts 4:17).

The apostles, though, said that they would never stop speaking about what they had witnessed (Acts 4:20). This caused a dilemma for the authorities. They wanted to punish them, but they were afraid of the people. Unable to agree on the form of punishment, they tried to frighten them with threats before releasing them (Acts 4:21).

As soon as they are released, the two men report to their fellow believers *(their own company)* what had happened. The most appropriate thing that they can do at this point is to pray, which they do *with one accord*. They begin by acknowledging *God* as the one who is the great creator of the universe (Genesis 1:1). In the midst of persecution it is important to remember that God is the one with supreme power and authority.

B. God's Word (vv. 25, 26)

25, 26. Who by the mouth of thy servant David hast said, Why did the heathen rage, and the people imagine vain things? The kings of

the earth stood up, and the rulers were gathered together against the Lord, and against his Christ.

The first two verses of Psalm 2, written by *David,* are quoted. Earlier, Peter had referred to David as a prophet who predicted Jesus' resurrection (Acts 2:25-31). The second psalm is one of the most important prophecies of the messianic work of Jesus because it predicts His persecution, resurrection, and glorification. The early church often referred to this psalm (see Acts 13:32, 33; Hebrews 1:5; 5:5; Revelation 2:27).

The phrase *stood up* brings to mind how Goliath stood to defy God's people (1 Samuel 17:8). He learned the hard way that God does not take such insolence lightly.

C. God's Purpose (vv. 27, 28)

27, 28. For of a truth against thy holy child Jesus, whom thou hast anointed, both Herod, and Pontius Pilate, with the Gentiles, and the people of Israel, were gathered together, for to do whatsoever thy hand and thy counsel determined before to be done.

The identity of those mentioned in verses 25 and 26 is now revealed. The "heathen" are *Gentiles.* Their rulers include the Roman governor *Pilate,* under whose orders Jesus was tortured and crucified mercilessly. "The people" of verse 26 undoubtedly include Israelites, led by King *Herod,* who shared in the responsibility for Jesus' death. They had dared to do these things to God's *holy child Jesus.*

Nothing is outside God's knowledge or authority. God had already revealed the suffering of the Messiah by David one thousand years before it happened. God also revealed it by other prophets such as Isaiah, who prophesied over seven centuries before Jesus' death. It was God's predetermined *counsel* that the Messiah must suffer (Luke 9:22). Jesus could not save humanity from sin unless He took the punishment of sins upon himself. His suffering paid the price that God had set for sin's punishment. This is what purchases our salvation for eternity.

THE POWER OF CONFIDENCE

Several Hollywood personalities have proclaimed boldly their faith in Scientology. On the other hand, few show-business personalities are known for their faith in Christ. For many, God simply is not part of their lives. This fact was indicated clearly in a recent article in the *Los Angeles Times Magazine.* One "romantic leading man" said, "I don't know if I believe in God." A well-known character actor said (somewhat wistfully, it would seem), "I don't believe in God now. I can still work up an envy for someone who has faith. I can see how that could be a deeply soothing experience."

Further, an actress famed for her role in *Star Wars* (her Web site unabashedly labels her "a cultural icon") said, "I love the idea of God, but it's not stylistically the way I function." Another leading lady puts it this way: "I like all religions, but only parts of them."

Does anyone see a common denominator in these statements? Could it be that when people are idolized by the public, they begin to believe their press notices and thus have no room in their lives for the *real* God? Think of how different Peter and John were: they had seen God at work in Christ and in their lives. As a result, they had absolute confidence in God's ability to protect them in the present and to shape their future. This kind of confidence gives hope! —C. R. B.

III. Fearless Determination
(Acts 4:29-31)

A. Determined in Spite of Threats (v. 29)

29. And now, Lord, behold their threatenings: and grant unto thy servants, that with all boldness they may speak thy word.

The apostles are determined now more than ever to continue preaching the good news of Jesus Christ. One of the remarkable parts of this story is how the apostles do not pray that persecution might end. They realize that persecution can end only if God's people end their witness. Only when the church no longer presents Jesus as Savior will the church cease to be persecuted.

The apostles know that they must continue preaching the gospel, so they ask that God would make them bold. Peter has no desire to cower in fear as he once did when he denied even knowing Jesus (Matthew 26:69-75; John 20:19). The apostles leave the persecutors in God's hands. The apostles intend to continue doing God's will. [See question #4, page 46.]

B. Determined to Show God's Power (v. 30)

30. By stretching forth thine hand to heal; and that signs and wonders may be done by the name of thy holy child Jesus.

Refer to this photograph as you introduce question #4 on page 46.

Visual for lesson 4

The apostles also request that God's mighty *hand* continue to work through them. This again acknowledges that the power does not come from themselves. If miracles are accomplished, it is God at work. They pray that other miracles may be performed as *signs* pointing people to Jesus and as *wonders* causing people to be amazed at the power of His name. These miracles are not mere acts of kindness to people who need physical healing. These miracles have a much larger purpose: they establish the truth of the gospel.

C. Determined to Preach God's Word (v. 31)

31. And when they had prayed, the place was shaken where they were assembled together; and they were all filled with the Holy Ghost, and they spake the word of God with boldness.

God responds to the prayer in a mighty way when the house shakes as though moved by an earthquake (compare Exodus 19:18; Isaiah 6:4). Those present are again *filled with the Holy Ghost* as on the Day of Pentecost. The Holy Spirit manifests himself in such a way that the apostles are assured that God loves them and wants to help them. [See question #5, page 46.] This causes them to go out into the world with renewed confidence. It is God who gives them the *boldness* that they requested in verse 29.

SHAKING THE HOUSE

The United States of America of the early 1800s was an irreligious nation in certain ways. Christians found themselves disenchanted with the rigid control of the faith by professional clergy and how the church had divided into warring sects. But a movement was under way that would shake the house of American religious expression. Its effects are seen to this very day. It was called the Second Great Awakening, lasting from the 1790s to the 1840s.

The tone of the change that was underway was set a half-century earlier by Samuel Davies in the original Great Awakening, perhaps dated from the 1730s to the 1770s. In one sermon Davies called Christians to unity: "My brethren, I would now warn you against this wretched, mischievous spirit of party. . . . A Christian! A Christian! Let that be your highest distinction!"

As in apostolic times, when the followers of Christ have followed courageously, prayed fervently, and spoken boldly, God has "shaken the house" and changed the world. We must pray that God will do it again . . . and again!

—C. R. B.

Conclusion

A. God, Please Make Us Bold!

God's people must be bold. God told Joshua to be strong and courageous as a leader of God's people (Joshua 1:6, 7). Shadrach, Meshach, and Abednego, Daniel's friends, courageously obeyed God's Word even though it meant being thrown alive into a furnace of fire (Daniel 3). David testified that even if an army attacked him he would not fear (Psalm 27:3).

Christians must be courageous in this world. The Word of God encourages us not to be frightened by those who oppose us, but to stand united in defense of the faith (Philippians 1:27, 28).

The apostle Peter is the one we see speaking in today's lesson. He will come to experience much persecution over several decades of ministry. Toward the end of his life, he can still challenge us to refuse to conform to the evil desires of the world and to fear no one but God. The world may think it strange that we do not live immoral lives as they do. They may even heap abuse on us, but we still courageously live lives that please God (1 Peter 1:13-16; 4:2-5).

The Word of God encourages us to live boldly as strangers in this world, living such good lives among the pagans that they will see our good deeds and glorify God (1 Peter 2:9-12). We remember that even if we suffer for doing what is good, we must not be afraid because God will bless us (1 Peter 3:13-15).

We also remember the bold example of Jesus, who refused to speak evil of those who mistreated Him (1 Peter 2:21-23). We can rejoice when we are insulted because of the name of Christ. God is pleased when we face persecution boldly and continue to do good (1 Peter 4:12-19).

The apostle John was Peter's companion before the Sanhedrin. While exiled on Patmos years later, he encouraged the church not to fear suffering (Revelation 2:10). Yes, persecution is real to every believer. No one knew this better than Paul: "All that will live godly in Christ Jesus shall suffer persecution" (2 Timothy 3:12). Jesus warned, "If they have persecuted me, they will also persecute you" (John 15:20). But let us never forget that like the apostles we can, "come boldly unto the throne of grace, that we may obtain mercy, and find grace to help in time of need" (Hebrews 4:16). Let us pray for boldness that Jesus Christ will be exalted.

B. Prayer

Father, many are lost and are dead in sin. Make us bold so that we will proclaim Your Son as the Savior of the world. May our friends and neighbors know of the power in Jesus' name to forgive and to save and to give hope. Give *[list a specific name]*, who serves in a dangerous area of the world, boldness to preach Jesus. In Jesus' powerful name, amen!

C. Thought to Remember

"I have chosen you out of the world, therefore the world hateth you" (John 15:19).

Learning by Doing

This page contains an alternate lesson plan emphasizing learning activities. Classes desiring such student involvement will find these suggestions helpful.

Learning Goals

After participating in this lesson, each student will be able to:

1. Retell Peter and John's bold proclamation of the gospel in spite of persecution.
2. Discuss the depth of the apostles' faith in relation to their boldness.
3. Write a prayer asking God for boldness in witnessing for Jesus.

Into the Lesson

Display the following on the board as class begins. Use a two-column format: Key Words and Verses. Under the Key Words heading have these three scrambled words: *bdlo, aeeflrss,* and *cdefinnoti;* under the Verses heading, have Acts 4:1-4; Acts 4:23-28; and Acts 4:29-31. After the words are deciphered *(bold, fearless,* and *confident)*, ask, "Is this the order in which these three characteristics arise? Or should the order be different? That is, does boldness precede confidence and confidence precede fearlessness? Or is another sequence more accurate?"

Let your class discuss and decide. You may want to add the other words the lesson writer uses in his outline: bold *witness,* confident *attitude,* and fearless *determination*.

Into the Word

Form three discussion groups and give them the following directions.

Group One: Read Acts 4:1-4 and answer the following questions: Acts 2 describes a large assembly in the temple area in which Jesus was preached as the Christ without opposition; why would the religious leaders react so swiftly and violently on the occasion in Acts 4? How do you suppose the witnesses of Peter and John's arrests reacted? Why would the temple leaders put Peter and John in prison and delay a trial simply because it was late in the day? Didn't they try Jesus at night?

Group Two: Quickly skim through Acts 4:5-22, which is not part of today's printed text. Answer the following questions: What was the gist of Peter's address to the Jewish leaders? Why did the Jewish leaders put Peter and John and the healed man out of the assembly before they deliberated? Why did they let Peter and John go?

Group Three: Read Acts 4:23-31 and answer the following questions. Why would the Christians recite the story of Jesus' arrest and condemnation in their prayer? What elements of their prayer do you find worthy of imitation in contemporary Christians' prayers?

Allow the groups have time for reading and discussion. Then ask group representatives to answer their questions for the whole class.

Say to your class, "The incident in Acts 4 notes things that still are opposed strongly around the world. What 'controversial' issues are included in the text that even today are considered 'fighting words'?"

If the class is slow to respond, ask, "What is there in verse 2 that continues to elicit denials and even anger?" *(The answer is that in Jesus there is resurrection from the dead.)* If the group needs further help, ask, "What is it in verse 27 that stirs anger, and even violence, as seen in Mel Gibson's film on the death of Christ?" *(The answer deals with who were responsible for having Jesus killed. Verse 27 rightly includes all who are a party to the sin.)* Your class may well see and highlight other doctrines that face almost immediate and constant attack.

Into Life

Note that one secret of the early church's success in prayer was that they "lifted up their voice to God with one accord" (v. 24). The unity of purpose and desire is critical. Have your class stand around the room in a circle holding hands as a reflection of the unity you have in Christ. Distribute to volunteers the following short, single-sentence prayers, to be said aloud in any order: "Make us one, Lord"; "Give us boldness, Lord"; "You are God, O Lord"; "See our enemies, Lord"; "Help us speak, Lord"; "Shake us, Lord, from lethargy"; "Fill us with the Spirit, Lord"; "Take our fears, Lord"; "Deepen our faith, Lord."

Give your students a copy of the following self-rating scale that uses the lesson writer's outline. (This in included in the student book.) Indicate to learners that they should respond to each statement with *always, usually, most of the time, occasionally,* or *never.* "In matters of my faith in Jesus Christ, (1) I make a bold witness; (2) I have a confident attitude; (3) I have fearless determination."

Let's Talk It Over

These questions are designed to promote discussion of the lesson. The answers here are only discussion starters. Let your class talk it over from there.

1. The apostles were confronted by many enemies of the gospel. How do we tell the difference between an enemy who is not interested in truth and an enemy who may be won over by the truth?

There is much value in the old saying, "Follow the money." Sometimes opposition may arise from those whose sinful livelihood is threatened by the church's influence (owners of various types of businesses, for example). Such people are often very uninterested in truth.

At other times the opposition is from other believers and other churches. This may be the result of jealousy toward a growing church or disagreement on some method the church may be using. Such folks can be very receptive to working through differences in a biblical way.

2. Persecution is often the result of prejudice. In what ways are prejudice and bias against Christianity still evident in today's culture? How should we respond?

Sometimes the enemies of the gospel use the idea of separation of church and state to try to silence Christians from speaking of their faith. We also may see bias when a college student is denied the financial assistance available to others because he or she is taking theological studies. In some communities, churches are hindered by stiff zoning regulations or use of property. These are just a few possibilities!

Our response will be tailored to the situation. In Mark 11:15 Jesus reacted to a situation with active indignation; in Mark 15:3-5 He responded to another situation with quiet dignity. We must prayerfully balance Peter's declaration, "We ought to obey God rather than men" (Acts 5:29), with Paul's admonition to be subject to governing authorities (Romans 13:5). This is a difficult balance, but the Holy Spirit will strengthen us.

3. In about A.D. 197, Tertullian said, "the blood of martyrs is the seed of [the church]." When persecution comes, the church characteristically moves forward with growth and effectiveness. In what ways have you seen opposition result in the growth of the church?

People are looking for something that has a strong impact upon life. Many are not content with just going through routines, but rather are seeking something that adds value to life. When people see Christians willing to sacrifice for their faith, they are often drawn to it. Also, we cannot overlook the fact that God blesses those who are faithful to Him in the face of opposition.

4. Boldness was a mark of the first-century church. In what ways will our boldness be similar to and different from the boldness of first-century believers? What is the difference between boldness and foolhardiness?

Our boldness, like that of the first-century Christians, begins with accepting the truth of the gospel. If we doubt, it will be hard to speak boldly. Boldness and effectiveness take root in the support and encouragement of fellow Christians. As with the earliest Christians, we must not neglect prayer in instilling faith and boldness.

For those of us who live in western democracies, it is unlikely that we will be challenged to witness "before kings and rulers" as the earliest Christians were (Luke 21:12). Perhaps we will show our boldness through writing letters to the editor, in opposing anti-Christian agendas in school systems, or in learning how to give (and live) a Christian response to those who are infected with a postmodern mind-set. Boldness is tested when we risk losing something because of our Christian witness. Foolhardiness involves rashness and lack of godly discretion.

5. The role of the Holy Spirit is much debated today. How should we express our understanding of the Word of God in this regard? When do our attempts at dialogue on the role of the Holy Spirit do more harm than good?

Good dialogue begins with good listening. When in the midst of a dialogue, are you really listening to what the other person is saying, or do you find yourself merely waiting for him or her to stop talking so you can give your rebuttal? When a dialogue begins to shed more "heat" than "light," that is the time to think about graciously excusing oneself from the discussion.

Stephen Is Faithful to the End

October 2
Lesson 5

DEVOTIONAL READING: Isaiah 6:1-8.

BACKGROUND SCRIPTURE: Acts 6:8–7:60.

PRINTED TEXT: Acts 6:8-15; 7:54-60.

Acts 6:8-15; 7:54-60

8 And Stephen, full of faith and power, did great wonders and miracles among the people.

9 Then there arose certain of the synagogue, which is called the synagogue of the Libertines, and Cyrenians, and Alexandrians, and of them of Cilicia and of Asia, disputing with Stephen.

10 And they were not able to resist the wisdom and the spirit by which he spake.

11 Then they suborned men, which said, We have heard him speak blasphemous words against Moses, and against God.

12 And they stirred up the people, and the elders, and the scribes, and came upon him, and caught him, and brought him to the council,

13 And set up false witnesses, which said, This man ceaseth not to speak blasphemous words against this holy place, and the law:

14 For we have heard him say, that this Jesus of Nazareth shall destroy this place, and shall change the customs which Moses delivered us.

15 And all that sat in the council, looking steadfastly on him, saw his face as it had been the face of an angel.

. . . .

54 When they heard these things, they were cut to the heart, and they gnashed on him with their teeth.

55 But he, being full of the Holy Ghost, looked up steadfastly into heaven, and saw the glory of God, and Jesus standing on the right hand of God,

56 And said, Behold, I see the heavens opened, and the Son of man standing on the right hand of God.

57 Then they cried out with a loud voice, and stopped their ears, and ran upon him with one accord,

58 And cast him out of the city, and stoned him: and the witnesses laid down their clothes at a young man's feet, whose name was Saul.

59 And they stoned Stephen, calling upon God, and saying, Lord Jesus, receive my spirit.

60 And he kneeled down, and cried with a loud voice, Lord, lay not this sin to their charge. And when he had said this, he fell asleep.

GOLDEN TEXT: Stephen, full of faith and power, did great wonders and miracles among the people.—Acts 6:8.

OCTOBER 2   48   STEPHEN IS FAITHFUL TO THE END

> *You Will Be My Witnesses*
> Unit 2: In All Judea and Samaria
> (Lessons 5-9)

Lesson Aims

After participating in this lesson, each student will be able to:

1. Describe the stoning of Stephen and the events that led up to it.
2. Contrast the fearful retreat of some Christians with the courageous leadership of Stephen.
3. Write a eulogy for Stephen based on the text.

Lesson Outline

INTRODUCTION
   A. Handling the Hardships
   B. Lesson Background
I. POWER AND OPPOSITION (Acts 6:8-15)
   A. Ministry of Power (v. 8)
   B. Source of Opposition (vv. 9, 10)
   C. Charge of Blasphemy (vv. 11-14)
   D. Demeanor of an Angel (v. 15)
II. TESTIMONY AND TORMENT (Acts 7:54-58)
   A. Fury of the Sanhedrin (v. 54)
   B. Vision of Glory (vv. 55, 56)
   C. Action of Mob (vv. 57, 58)
   When the Truth Hurts
III. PRAYER AND DEATH (Acts 7:59, 60)
   A. Appeal to Jesus, Part 1 (v. 59)
   B. Appeal to Jesus, Part 2 (v. 60)
   "Framing" One's Response
CONCLUSION
   A. Suffering for Jesus
   B. Prayer
   C. Thought to Remember

Introduction

A. Handling the Hardships

Stories abound of people who face hardships in life. Sometimes we wonder how we would hold up if life delivered some of the catastrophic blows that some people must handle. We eagerly listen to some hint of the source of their strength, and then ask whether we have developed this in ourselves.

Max Cleland led a typical all-American life in high school, starring in sports and receiving the title of most outstanding senior. At the age of 24 he volunteered for combat duty in Vietnam, where he became a first lieutenant in the Army. Just one month before returning home, Cleland discovered a grenade that had been dropped accidentally. Moving quickly to snatch it away, he was thrown backward by its explosion. He looked down to find his right hand and right leg missing and his left leg badly mangled. Though not expected to survive, Cleland recovered from his triple amputation, and he recalled two things: the apostle Paul had said that hope "maketh not ashamed" (Romans 5:5), and General George S. Patton, Jr. had said, "Success is how high you bounce when you hit bottom."

So when Cleland returned to civilian life, he entered politics, learned to drive a car specially equipped for him, and traveled extensively to mobilize support for veterans' causes. At age 34 he became the youngest man ever to head the Veterans Administration. Later he was elected to be a senator from Georgia. Max Cleland summarizes his experience this way: "Life doesn't revolve around an arm and a leg. People look at you the way you look at yourself."

Today's lesson presents a servant of God who faced a catastrophic blow as well. It was a blow that led directly to his death. The story of God's servants is stained with the blood of prophets and apostles who paid the price for speaking the truth, and today's lesson presents this reality in especially vivid detail. The story is not a pretty one, but one that Bible students need to face squarely because the days of persecution for believers are not over.

B. Lesson Background

The book of Acts begins the story of the earliest church by focusing on developments within Jerusalem. The theme of "witnesses" in Jerusalem, in all Judea and Samaria, and to the ends of the earth (Acts 1:8) demands that this book present a sketch of the activities of the Jerusalem church. So the narrative begins with events that occurred on the Day of Pentecost (Acts 2:1-41), providing plenty of information regarding the power behind this dynamic Jerusalem fellowship.

Then in chapters 3 through 5 of Acts come snapshots of the ministry of the Jerusalem church. These focus especially on the powerful actions of God and the way the apostles used those events to proclaim Christ.

Acts 6 begins with a description of the necessity of choosing those of Greek background to serve in the Jerusalem church (Acts 6:1-7). In the process we see two dynamic preachers of the gospel whose ministries Luke (the author of the book of Acts) describes in some detail. These preachers are Stephen (6:8–8:3) and Philip (8:4-40). Stephen's preaching leads to his execution at the hands of the Sanhedrin, establishing him as the first martyr for Christ on record. Philip's willingness to preach the gospel leads him to great success among the Samaritans and to the inquisitive traveler from Ethiopia (next two lessons).

In the book of Acts, the inspired author carefully documents how the first preachers of the gospel, whether apostles or servants in the Jerusalem church, faced their opponents and problems with courage. They refused to compromise the truth about Jesus Christ.

I. Power and Opposition (Acts 6:8-15)

The book of Acts introduced Stephen in 6:3, 5 as one chosen by the Jerusalem church to "serve tables." Acts now continues the focus on Stephen by describing his ministry as a preacher of the gospel.

A. Ministry of Power (v. 8)

8. And Stephen, full of faith and power, did great wonders and miracles among the people.

Home Daily Bible Readings

Monday, Sept. 26—Stephen Is Arrested (Acts 6:8-15)

Tuesday, Sept. 27—Stephen Speaks to the Council (Acts 7:1-8)

Wednesday, Sept. 28—Stephen Tells the Joseph Story (Acts 7:9-16)

Thursday, Sept. 29—Stephen Tells Moses' Early Story (Acts 7:17-29)

Friday, Sept. 30—Stephen Tells of Moses, the Liberator (Acts 7:30-43)

Saturday, Oct. 1—Stephen Challenges His Hearers (Acts 7:44-53)

Sunday, Oct. 2—Stephen Is Stoned to Death (Acts 7:54-60)

Stephen is obviously a man who has God's full approval. For the first time in the book of Acts, we see *miracles* performed by someone who is not an apostle. The miracles probably consist of healing and exorcisms (see Acts 3:1-10; 5:14-16). Perhaps the laying on of the apostles' hands conveys this *power* (see Acts 6:6). Stephen's miraculous ministry is not one of self-promotion. Rather, Hebrews 2:3, 4 notes that miracles were performed by the apostles and earliest Christian preachers as a way of confirming the truth of the gospel. Modern examples of healers or miracle workers who seem to seek personal profit from their "power" demonstrate that they do not understand a ministry like Stephen's.

B. Source of Opposition (vv. 9, 10)

9. Then there arose certain of the synagogue, which is called the synagogue of the Libertines, and Cyrenians, and Alexandrians, and of them of Cilicia and of Asia, disputing with Stephen.

Now for the first time in the book of Acts we see opposition to the gospel coming from a source other than the Sanhedrin, though the source is still a Jewish one. *The synagogue of the Libertines* describes a Jewish house of worship composed of former slaves, or descendants of slaves, who had been liberated from their bondage. Freedmen are plentiful in the Roman world, and they come from every nationality. These freedmen are Jews who had once lived in Cyrene or Alexandria in northern Africa, as well as the provinces of *Cilicia* and *Asia*. The apostle Paul himself could have participated in this synagogue because he was a Jew from Cilicia (Acts 22:3).

Whether more than one synagogue is in view here is a matter of some debate. In any case, the dispute *with Stephen* may have started with the point that his ministry is being conducted in the name of Jesus Christ. The Jewish leadership in Jerusalem does not want the believers teaching or speaking in that name (see Acts 4:17).

10. And they were not able to resist the wisdom and the spirit by which he spake.

Stephen was recognized previously in Acts 6:3 as one "full of the Holy Ghost and wisdom." Whatever arguments Stephen's critics try, they are unable to dislodge him from the truth of Christ. This is true both in terms of his accuracy in using Old Testament reflections on the Messiah as well as in the power of his words, as will be seen in Acts 7. Truth is its own defense. Believers who exemplify Christ in their lives and speak the truth accurately will be powerful witnesses for the Lord. [See question #1, page 55.]

C. Charge of Blasphemy (vv. 11-14)

11. Then they suborned men, which said, We have heard him speak blasphemous words against Moses, and against God.

When Stephen's antagonists cannot overturn his arguments, they resort to falsehoods. The foundational accusation is that Stephen's words contradict both *Moses* and *God*. Since the Law of Moses was given by God, these charges easily could have centered on Jewish institutions sanctioned in the Law of Moses and, therefore, inspired by God. The word *blasphemy* in a Jewish context makes the guilty person worthy of death (compare Leviticus 24:16; Matthew 26:62-66). Yet Stephen continues to perform his ministry without flinching, knowing that the critics are accusing him of speaking *against God*. [See question #2, page 55.]

12. And they stirred up the people, and the elders, and the scribes, and came upon him, and caught him, and brought him to the council.

The *council* refers to the Jewish Sanhedrin, composed of 71 members, representing both the Sadducees and the Pharisees, two major parties within Judaism. Jerusalem is the council's seat of power, not only in religious matters but also in civil affairs. The council exercises its power under the watchful eye of Rome. Some of the members of the Sanhedrin hearing the case against Stephen undoubtedly were also present at the hearing of Jesus.

13. And set up false witnesses, which said, This man ceaseth not to speak blasphemous words against this holy place, and the law.

False witnesses are set forward in order to seal Stephen's condemnation. Just as in the trial of Jesus, those witnesses who testify against him are interested primarily in twisting his words rather than quoting him fairly (see Matthew 26:60). Now their charges take on a more specific reference than in Acts 6:11. The phrase *this holy place* is a reference to the place where they are hearing the charges. The Sanhedrin meets in court session in the temple complex, so this charge from the false witnesses involves accusations that Stephen is speaking against the temple of God.

Threats against sacred sites can draw the death penalty in the Greco-Roman world. This was equally true for the Jews of Old Testament times (see Jeremiah 26:1-11). In addition, the Old Testament law of God provided for animal sacrifices, so anything Stephen said about Christ as the perfect sacrifice (compare Hebrews 9:13-28) could be twisted to mean that Stephen is undermining God's law.

14. For we have heard him say, that this Jesus of Nazareth shall destroy this place, and shall change the customs which Moses delivered us.

The Sanhedrin protects the temple, and the party of the Sadducees provides most of the leadership that operates that facility. To do away with the temple would mean doing away with their professions. In John 11:48 we heard the Sanhedrin members say of Jesus, "If we let him thus alone, . . . the Romans shall come and take away both our place and nation." In that passage, *place* can refer to the temple. The temple is the engine that drives the economy of Judea. It supplies jobs for thousands of construction workers, priests, and attendants. Thus the misguided Sanhedrin probably is not trying to protect the religion of Israel as much as it is protecting its own economic security. The charge of changing *the customs which Moses delivered us* is similar to the accusation against Paul in Acts 21:21.

D. Demeanor of an Angel (v. 15)

15. And all that sat in the council, looking steadfastly on him, saw his face as it had been the face of an angel.

How to Say It

ALEXANDRIANS. Al-ex-*an*-dree-unz.
BLASPHEMOUS. *blas*-fuh-mus.
CILICIA. Sih-*lish*-i-uh.
CYRENIANS. Sigh-*ree*-nee-unz.
ETHIOPIA. E-thee-*o*-pee-uh (*th* as in *thin*).
JERUSALEM. Juh-*roo*-suh-lem.
LEVITICUS. Leh-*vit*-ih-kus.
LIBERTINES. *Lib*-er-teens.
PENTECOST. *Pent*-ih-kost.
PHARISEES. *Fair*-ih-seez.
SADDUCEES. *Sad*-you-seez.
SAMARITANS. Suh-*mare*-uh-tunz.
SANHEDRIN. *San*-huh-drun or San-*heed*-run.
SYNAGOGUE. *sin*-uh-gog.

Stephen's fearless *face* exhibits something like one who had been in the presence of God—as in the case of angels. Without a doubt, this servant of God demonstrates a courage that would be impossible without help from the Lord. God is powerful in this man's life, and his fortitude before the authorities proves it.

How many modern "heroes of the faith" can we name today? How many believers are standing courageously against those who want to stop the preaching of the gospel? We hear stories about persecuted Christians in a variety of countries around the world. Even in our own culture there are those who suffer for their testimony. This reality will be with us as long as people walk in the darkness and do not want to hear the truth because their deeds are evil (John 3:19).

II. Testimony and Torment (Acts 7:54-58)

Acts 7:1-53 (not in our text for today) describes in detail Stephen's lengthy address to the Sanhedrin. In his review of Old Testament history, Stephen does not introduce any new facts. But in selecting the accounts that he does, he demonstrates a long history of Jewish rebellion against the will of God. He also demonstrates the important point that God does not require a sacred place, like the temple, for relating to His people (Acts 7:48).

A. Fury of the Sanhedrin (v. 54)

54. When they heard these things, they were cut to the heart, and they gnashed on him with their teeth.

This Sanhedrin might be called a particularly bloodthirsty one. Not only had they crucified Jesus, they had also punished the apostles (Acts 5:17-40). Now this same body is ready to deal a crushing blow to the ministry of Stephen. The members of the Sanhedrin are *cut to the heart*, or enraged, and they demonstrate this with *their teeth*—perhaps by grinding them together in some visible way. Compare Psalm 37:12. [See question #3, page 55.]

B. Vision of Glory (vv. 55, 56)

55, 56. But he, being full of the Holy Ghost, looked up steadfastly into heaven, and saw the glory of God, and Jesus standing on the right hand of God, and said, Behold, I see the heavens opened, and the Son of man standing on the right hand of God.

Stephen does not throw insults at his accusers, but turns his gaze heavenward. [See question #4, page 55.] As he does, he catches a heavenly vision of the Lord *Jesus* Christ. He is not sitting at the right hand of God, as is usually the description (see Matthew 26:64; Mark 16:19; Luke 22:69), but is *standing* at *the right hand of God*. Perhaps He is standing to welcome the first Christian martyr. Perhaps He is standing to fulfill the image in Daniel 7:9-16 of the one standing in the presence of the Ancient of Days.

Whatever the case, this is a heavenly vision brought to Stephen at the very moment of his fatal torment. It echoes the heavenly encouragement often delivered to saints at the moment of their trials (see Acts 4:31; 22:17-21; 23:11; 27:23-26). As Peter's confession of Christ was revealed to him by the Father (Matthew 16:16, 17), so Stephen confesses because of what is revealed to him. He can do so because he is *full of the Holy Ghost*, while those who torment him are full of the rage of the evil one.

This statement of Stephen serves as a confession of faith. In seeing Jesus standing at the right hand of God, Stephen uses the words *Son of man* to describe Him. This is the same phrase Jesus used to describe himself so often (example: Mark 8:31). It is a title that can be traced to Daniel 7:13, 14. Note also that in Acts 7:59 (below), Stephen identifies the Lord as Jesus.

C. Action of Mob (vv. 57, 58)

57, 58. Then they cried out with a loud voice, and stopped their ears, and ran upon him with one accord, and cast him out of the city, and stoned him: and the witnesses laid down their clothes at a young man's feet, whose name was Saul.

The sentence of death is passed upon Stephen without the benefit of a fair trial. The Sanhedrin takes into their own hands the administration of capital punishment, a penalty that is reserved for the Romans to carry out (compare John 18:31). In the case of Stephen, the council members are too furious to worry about the rule of law. They are in "lynching mode" now. Luke (the author of the book of Acts) is careful to note the presence of *Saul*, a fact that Saul himself (renamed Paul) will point out as he speaks to a crowd in Acts 22:20.

WHEN THE TRUTH HURTS

For more than a half-century, critics of the Roman Catholic church have claimed that the pope and the church aided the Nazi extermination of six million Jews during World War II. That church has denied vociferously those claims. However, the Roman Catholic church backtracked somewhat in 1998 when the Vatican published a document entitled, "We Remember: A Reflection on the Shoah." (The word *Shoah* means "horror" and is the Hebrew word for the Holocaust.)

The Vatican admitted that the document was an "act of repentance." It confessed "the errors and failures of . . . sons and daughters of the Church" that contributed to the Holocaust. Although expressing the church's "deep sorrow for the failures of her sons and daughters in every age," the paper stopped short of criticizing the actions (or inactions) of church officials.

Of course, it is always easy to look back and say, "This is what should have happened." But it is hard to admit one's sins, and the frequent reaction to unsettling truth is equivocation or even outright denial. The knife-edge of truth cut Stephen's persecutors to their hearts and enraged them to the point of murder. How do we react when the truth "finds us out"? —C. R. B.

III. Prayer and Death
(Acts 7:59, 60)

With his last words, Stephen does not accuse his tormentors. Instead, he prays for them.

A. Appeal to Jesus, Part 1 (v. 59)

59. And they stoned Stephen, calling upon God, and saying, Lord Jesus, receive my spirit.

This is a prayer of faith, uttered with Stephen's dying breath. Even as the stones are crushing the life from him, he places his destiny in the hands of God. As he does, he prays just as Jesus did from the cross—that God would *receive* his *spirit* (Luke 23:46).

B. Appeal to Jesus, Part 2 (v. 60)

60. And he kneeled down, and cried with a loud voice, Lord, lay not this sin to their charge. And when he had said this, he fell asleep.

Stephen's final words are for his tormentors, just as was true of Jesus, who asked His Father to forgive those who were crucifying Him (Luke

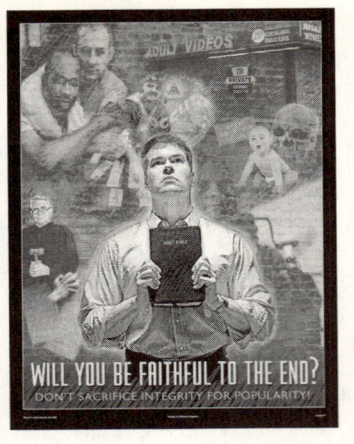

This collage can be a discussion starter on things that challenge our faithfulness.

Visual for lesson 5

23:34). The courage to suffer such persecution without becoming angry toward those who are bringing the suffering is quite amazing. Think about how often we have turned to vengeance for lesser offenses!

When Stephen refuses to condemn his enemies, he demonstrates a heart filled with the grace of God. It is a heart driven by faithfulness to God's cause. The book of Acts describes his death in the same way that other New Testament verses describe death for the Christian—like falling *asleep* (see 1 Thessalonians 4:13-18). Like sleep, it is temporary. Stephen knows where his eternal home is.

"FRAMING" ONE'S RESPONSE

An original, early 1900s gilded picture frame by Herman Dudley Murphy is worth more than $250,000—for a picture frame measuring only 3 by 4 feet! A simple nineteenth-century frame of 5 by 5 *inches* recently sold for $1,500. Edouard Manet (ed-WARD mah-NAY), the nineteenth-century French impressionist painter, once said, "Without the proper frame, the artist loses 100 percent." He was saying that even a *great* painting is diminished significantly if it is not viewed in the context of the proper frame. To make the point, an expert on the *Antiques Roadshow* TV program described putting an 1890s portrait in a 1960s-era frame "like dressing up a pig in a tutu."

Think of the "spiritual frame" in which Stephen places his death as the first Christian martyr. Where have we previously heard the sentiments of his dying prayer? Faced with the worst his tormentors could do to him, Stephen "framed" his response to their evil actions in the dying words of his Lord.

His thoughts are in keeping with Jesus' instructions in the Sermon on the Mount: rather than returning "an eye for an eye," demonstrate the presence of God in your heart by an attitude of forgiveness. Stephen's example shows us how to put a frame of Christlikeness around our lives and thus increase the value or our witness immensely!
—C. R. B.

Conclusion

A. Suffering for Jesus

Like Stephen, there are courageous servants of God today who stand up and speak the truth even when the pressure is against them. In some countries Christians are targeted because they are not in the majority, and they pay a heavy price for their faith. In other cultures there are believers who take courageous positions for Christ at work and in the home. Let us be sure to honor those whose testimonies for Christ cost them so much. [See question #5, page 55.]

B. Prayer

Lord, help us to demonstrate that there are some things worth dying for, and that truth about Jesus is the most important of these. Strengthen us through Christ. In His name, amen.

C. Thought to Remember

Taking up the cross is more than wearing a type of expensive jewelry. It is a willingness to serve Christ even when it hurts.

Learning by Doing

This page contains an alternate lesson plan emphasizing learning activities. Classes desiring such student involvement will find these suggestions helpful.

Learning Goals

After participating in this lesson, each student will be able to:

1. Describe the stoning of Stephen and the events that led up to it.
2. Contrast the fearful retreat of some Christians with the courageous leadership of Stephen.
3. Write a eulogy for Stephen based on the text.

Into the Lesson

As students arrive, hand them each a small rock. As class begins, ask this simple question: "What can you do with a rock?" Expect such answers as "Build with it"; "Throw it into a stream to splash"; "Use it as decoration in a flower bed"; "Put it in a fish tank"; "Pave a dirt road or path with it"; "Mix it with other materials to make concrete." If no one suggests, "Stone someone with it," then bridge to today's study by saying, "There is one other use for a rock prescribed in the Old Testament: stone someone to death with it. That is the use we see in today's text when Stephen is martyred by angry listeners."

Into the Word

Because this is a lesson in which truth meets opposition and lies, use the following true-false quiz (included in the student book) to draw attention to the printed text. Answers and explanations are in parentheses.

1. Until the incident in today's text, Stephen had had a quiet ministry among the Christians. *(False; he was busy doing "great wonders and miracles.")*

2. Stephen's initial opposition came from the temple leaders. *(False; his disputers and accusers were from a particular synagogue, the Libertines.)*

3. Unable to resist the wisdom of his words, Stephen's accusers had to agree they were true. *(False; they were not able to dissuade him by argument, but they refused to believe his affirmations about Jesus.)*

4. The men from the synagogue decided to find false witnesses to indict Stephen. *(True; v. 11.)*

5. Stephen's accusers charged him with blasphemy against Moses, against God, against the temple, and against the Law. *(True; vv. 11, 13.)*

6. Stephen was hunted down, manhandled, and dragged off to the Sanhedrin. *(True; after*

hearing Stephen, the men from the synagogue stirred up common people, the Jewish elders, and the teachers of the law—they forced him to appear before the Sanhedrin. See v. 12.)

7. For a second time, Stephen's accusers used false witnesses against him. *(True; the first time was in v. 11 before Stephen was arrested. The second time was in v. 13 before the Jewish council.)*

8. The foundational accusation against Stephen was that he was claiming Jesus was the Christ. *(False; their charge reflects the false indictment of Jesus that He would destroy the temple [see Matthew 26:61] and that He was going to change Moses' Law.)*

9. Stephen's face glowed, as did Moses' face after Sinai as recorded in Exodus 34:29-35. *(True, although there is no such comparison in the text: Stephen's face glowed like "an angel"; Moses' face reflected the glory of God himself.)*

10. The decision to kill Stephen was purely a logical and legal one: blasphemers were to be killed. *(False; the decision appears to have been made in a jealous and emotional rage [see v. 54], although Leviticus 24:11-16 did prescribe stoning for blasphemy.)*

11. Stephen is the only person in the Bible said to have been able to look into Heaven itself. *(False; see Isaiah 6 and Revelation 1 for two other examples.)*

12. Without approval of the Roman authorities, the Jewish leaders pushed Stephen violently outside the temple and city and stoned him. *(True; Stephen's murder was done in a blind rage, so no thought of proper authority was even considered.)*

13. Stephen died in anticipation of being with Jesus and with forgiveness on his lips. *(True; see vv. 59, 60. This is a model for any who serve Jesus.)*

Into Life

See if your church office or local Christian bookstore can provide you bulletins designed for a funeral. Give each learner one (or simply a piece of paper folded) and give this direction: "You have been asked to deliver the eulogy for Stephen's funeral as held by the Jerusalem Christians. Put your notes of what you want to say into this memorial bulletin." After a bit of time, ask class members to read their eulogies.

Let's Talk It Over

These questions are designed to promote discussion of the lesson. The answers here are only discussion starters. Let your class talk it over from there.

1. Stephen's testimony was one that could not be refuted. How can we witness in such a way today? Why is it important to do so?

Stephen had something going for him that we often don't: he and his opponents shared what may be called a "common basis" in their mutual recognition of the Old Testament as God's Word. What Stephen and his opponents did not share, of course, was Stephen's acknowledgement that Jesus is the one who fulfills Old Testament predictions of Messiah.

Today we often struggle to find a common basis from which to begin! Grounding our message on certain facts of history—that there really was someone named Jesus, for example—may be a good starting point. In a postmodern culture, however, many believe that truth is what each person thinks is true for himself or herself. Witnessing for Jesus can be very difficult in such cases. A good starting point here is to be sure that our actions match our words. When there is a difference between what one says and what one does, people usually will follow the action rather than the words.

2. The first-century enemies of the gospel did all they could to undermine the integrity of the people of God. In what ways have you seen people discredited today? Why is this done?

It's an old trick: if you don't like *the message*, try to discredit *the messenger*. A misrepresentation of the facts is one way this is done. For example, the world cannot understand the concept of loving the sinner while hating the sin. Thus those who would seek to uphold the principles of God are labeled intolerant, homophobic, or bigoted. The method of personal attack is used when attacks against the principles become fruitless. It is often a sign of desperation.

3. What is it about being confronted with truth that causes people to become "riled up"? Is it always possible to witness for Christ without angering people? Why, or why not?

In a postmodern culture where tolerance has been defined as acceptance of all values and where all "truths" are considered equal, people may not accept anyone else's ideas of what is right and wrong. We truly live in an age when people justify their actions because what they do is correct in their own eyes (cf. Judges 21:25).

We should never set out to make people angry simply for the sake of doing so. But even when our witness is thoroughly "with grace, seasoned with salt" (Colossians 4:6), people can react unpredictably. As with question 1 above, a foundational concern we should have is to make sure our actions match our words.

4. Stephen did not fight back or vow to get even. Why is it important that Christians not respond in vindictive anger when facing opposition? How can we prepare ourselves to respond in a proper way?

Anger in and of itself is not condemned in Scripture (compare Ephesians 4:26), but it is to be kept in check spiritually. Much of what we like to call proper anger, or righteous indignation, is based in pride. To respond without vindictive anger is to be like Jesus at His trials. Though He occasionally became angry, it was anger on behalf of the name and kingdom of God. Anger channeled appropriately seeks to point out error and bring about the advancing of God's kingdom, not a personal agenda. James 1:20 tells us that what we might call unrighteous anger "worketh not the righteousness of God."

5. Many have suffered for Christ throughout the history of the church. How do we tell the difference between true suffering and mere inconvenience? Why is this distinction important?

While there is certainly true persecution in the world today, much of what we may call "suffering for the faith" is little more than minor impositions on our routines. Teaching a class of junior high boys in Sunday school may have its challenges, but it is not suffering persecution. Foregoing a meal at a nice restaurant so that you may have a little more to give to a faith-promise campaign is not suffering in the truest sense. Recognizing minor inconveniences for what they are will help keep us from having a "look how much I've suffered" mentality.

October 9
Lesson 6

Philip Preaches in Samaria

DEVOTIONAL READING: Acts 19:1-10.

BACKGROUND SCRIPTURE: Acts 8:4-25.

PRINTED TEXT: Acts 8:4-17.

Acts 8:4-17

4 Therefore they that were scattered abroad went every where preaching the word.

5 Then Philip went down to the city of Samaria, and preached Christ unto them.

6 And the people with one accord gave heed unto those things which Philip spake, hearing and seeing the miracles which he did.

7 For unclean spirits, crying with loud voice, came out of many that were possessed with them: and many taken with palsies, and that were lame, were healed.

8 And there was great joy in that city.

9 But there was a certain man, called Simon, which beforetime in the same city used sorcery, and bewitched the people of Samaria, giving out that himself was some great one:

10 To whom they all gave heed, from the least to the greatest, saying, This man is the great power of God.

11 And to him they had regard, because that of long time he had bewitched them with sorceries.

12 But when they believed Philip preaching the things concerning the kingdom of God, and the name of Jesus Christ, they were baptized, both men and women.

13 Then Simon himself believed also: and when he was baptized, he continued with Philip, and wondered, beholding the miracles and signs which were done.

14 Now when the apostles which were at Jerusalem heard that Samaria had received the word of God, they sent unto them Peter and John:

15 Who, when they were come down, prayed for them, that they might receive the Holy Ghost:

16 (For as yet he was fallen upon none of them: only they were baptized in the name of the Lord Jesus.)

17 Then laid they their hands on them, and they received the Holy Ghost.

GOLDEN TEXT: Now when the apostles which were at Jerusalem heard that Samaria had received the word of God, they sent unto them Peter and John.—Acts 8:14.

LESSON 6   57   OCTOBER 9

> *You Will Be My Witnesses*
> Unit 2: In All Judea and Samaria
> (Lessons 5-9)

Lesson Aims

After participating in this lesson, each student will be able to:

1. Summarize Philip's ministry in Samaria.
2. Explain how Philip helped break down cultural barriers by preaching to the Samaritans.
3. Support his or her church's efforts at cross-cultural evangelism.

Lesson Outline

INTRODUCTION
    A. Taking Christ Where People Are
    B. Lesson Background
  I. MINISTRY OF PHILIP (Acts 8:4-8)
    A. Proclamation (vv. 4, 5)
      A Church on the Move
    B. Result (vv. 6-8)
 II. CONVERSION OF SIMON (Acts 8:9-13)
    A. Simon's Reputation (vv. 9-11)
    B. Simon Abandoned (v. 12)
    C. Simon Believes (v. 13)
III. MINISTRY OF PETER AND JOHN (Acts 8:14-17)
    A. News Spreads (v. 14)
    B. Prayer Offered (vv. 15, 16)
    C. Holy Spirit Received (v. 17)
      "Say the Magic Word"
CONCLUSION
    A. Mission Successes, Mission Problems
    B. Prayer
    C. Thought to Remember

Introduction

A. Taking Christ Where People Are

An astute observation (attributed to George MacLeod) puts a lot of things in perspective: "I simply argue that the cross be raised again at the center of the marketplace as well as on the steeple of the church. I am recovering the claim that Jesus was not crucified in a cathedral between two candles, but on a cross between two thieves; on the town garbage heap; at a crossroad so cosmopolitan that they had to write his title in Hebrew and in Latin and in Greek . . . and at the kind of place where cynics talk smut, and thieves curse, and soldiers gamble. Because that is where He died. And that is what He died about. And that is where churchmen ought to be, and what churchmen ought to be about."

What this writer says reminds us that we have work to do for Christ. This is a work that emphasizes content over cosmetics and Christ over self. It is a work that takes the gospel beyond the church walls rather than simply being contained within them. It is a work that may be uncomfortable. In today's lesson Philip shows us that we should take up this work regardless of how uncomfortable it may be.

B. Lesson Background

Last week we studied the martyrdom of Stephen. That event unleashed a tidal wave of persecution upon the Jerusalem church (Acts 8:1). Jerusalem believers were scattered everywhere like seed borne on the wind, many of them traveling north to cities such as Tyre, Damascus, and Antioch. Those Christians were not safe anywhere they went, because Saul began tearing the church apart. Distant cities were within his reach (Acts 8:3).

Nevertheless, the book of Acts makes clear that these believers left their homes, carrying the gospel wherever they went. As a result, the areas north of Jerusalem began to hear the gospel. New converts began showing up in every city.

I. Ministry of Philip
(Acts 8:4-8)

A. Proclamation (vv. 4, 5)

4. Therefore they that were scattered abroad went every where preaching the word.

Stephen's ministry continued the theme of "witnesses . . . in Jerusalem" (Acts 1:8). Now Luke (the author of the book of Acts) shows us how the gospel begins to spread like ripples in a pond. Jesus' command to be witnesses "in all Judea, and in Samaria" (again, 1:8) is thus being fulfilled. [See question #1, page 64.]

The word is a reference to the gospel of Jesus Christ (see Acts 6:4; 16:6; 2 Corinthians 4:2). In a Jewish context, the idea is one of explaining from the Old Testament Scriptures that the Christ had to suffer and rise from the dead (compare Acts 17:3).

> **How to Say It**
> ANTIOCH. *An*-tee-ock.
> ASSYRIANS. Uh-*sear*-e-unz.
> DAMASCUS. Duh-*mass*-kus.
> ELYMAS. *El*-ih-mass.
> GERIZIM. *Gair*-ih-zeem or Guh-*rye*-zim.
> SAMARITANS. Suh-*mare*-uh-tunz.
> SEBASTE. Seh-*bas*-tee.
> SHECHEM. *Shee*-kem or *Shek*-em.
> SYCHAR. *Sigh*-kar.
> TYRE. Tire.

Philip has been mentioned already in Acts 6:5. His *preaching* enables the Samaritans to understand *Christ* as sent by God in fulfillment of Old Testament prophecies. As the believers scatter outward from Jerusalem, they take with them this good news about Jesus Christ to whomever will listen.

A CHURCH ON THE MOVE

The first European settlers in North America could have dreamed neither of how vast the continent was nor of how their descendants would move ever westward. The U.S. Census Bureau keeps track of this migration in America, and every 10 years announces the hypothetical "human center of gravity" of the nation.

In 1790 that population center was Chestertown, Maryland. The center has been moving in a westerly direction ever since. By 1890 the center was Greensburg, Indiana. By 2000 it was in Edgar Springs, Missouri, about 100 miles southwest of St. Louis, where the Jefferson National Expansion Memorial commemorates the historic migration. The memorial and its Gateway Arch symbolize the city's role as "Gateway to the West" in the days following the Louisiana Purchase during Thomas Jefferson's presidency.

The first Christians could not have known it at the time, but Philip's mission to Samaria would start a massive shift in the church's "population center." Lacking perspective, some probably took a dim view of extending the gospel to Samaritans and Gentiles. Others, however, rejoiced. Today, Christianity's population center is shifting from the northern hemisphere to the southern, where eager ears are hearing the gospel gladly. God moves to where people seek Him. Like those first Christians, we can resist or we can rejoice. Which will it be? —C. R. B.

5. Then Philip went down to the city of Samaria, and preached Christ unto them.

Philip conducts his ministry outward from Jerusalem. The land where the Samaritans live originally had rested squarely in the middle of the tribes of Israel in Old Testament times. When the Assyrians invaded and took captive great portions of the Israelite population in 722 B.C., Samaria was left desolate. The few Jews who were left behind in Samaria struggled against the pressures to blend with their neighbors. Ultimately, intermarriage diminished the distinctive Jewish identity of much of this population (2 Kings 17). Beyond this, the Samaritans constructed their own rival temple at Mount Gerizim (see John 4:20).

The Jewish religious leadership in Jerusalem accused the Samaritans of losing their faith, and, as a result, a level of hatred grew. This hatred sometimes moved Samaritans and Judean Jews to separate themselves from one another (see John 4:9). It is to these despised neighbors to the north that Philip travels to preach the gospel.

We aren't really certain which *city of Samaria* is in mind here. Some possibilities include Sebaste, Gitta, Sychar, or the old capital city of Shechem. No one knows for sure. In any case, Philip's ministry takes him to a territory and a people despised by the Jews in Jerusalem.

Today's lesson finds in Philip's ministry to the Samaritans an example of how we are to share the gospel beyond our own borders. His willingness to travel to Samaria with the gospel of Christ inspires us to carry the same gospel to parts of our world that we may find uncomfortable. How will we answer the call of Christ to be witnesses to the Samaritans in our world?

B. Result (vv. 6-8)

6. And the people with one accord gave heed unto those things which Philip spake, hearing and seeing the miracles which he did.

Here the book of Acts speaks of *miracles* and preaching in a way that reveals the connection between them. Miracles are intended to draw attention to the message of Christ (compare John 14:11). The Samaritans see the miracles in Philip's ministry, and this causes them to take seriously his preaching. The wording indicates their authentic response to the truth of Christ, as they give *heed* to what they hear. Their response to the Word is more than just a passing, superficial attention, such as may be true of mere entertainment. They are serious in attending to the demands of Philip's message. [See question #2, page 64.]

7. For unclean spirits, crying with loud voice, came out of many that were possessed with them: and many taken with palsies, and that were lame, were healed.

The powerful miracles consist of healings and exorcisms, as is true elsewhere in Acts (see 5:16; 19:11-19). The presence of evil *spirits* is mentioned frequently in the Gospels and Acts, and the reality of the spirit world should not surprise us. Paul writes that our struggle is "not against flesh and blood, but against principalities, against powers, against the rulers of the darkness of this world" (Ephesians 6:12). Modern Christians must deal with the reality of Satan and his power, whether this power is demonstrated in overt demonic activity or in more subtle forms of temptation to sin.

8. And there was great joy in that city.

This *joy* is the outcome of the acceptance by the Samaritans of the Word of Christ brought by Philip. The book of Acts frequently notes the joy and gladness that come with salvation through Christ (see 2:46; 8:39; 13:48). Sharing the good news means sharing a joy that will never fade away. [See question #3, page 64.]

II. Conversion of Simon
(Acts 8:9-13)
A. Simon's Reputation (vv. 9-11)

9, 10. But there was a certain man, called Simon, which beforetime in the same city used sorcery, and bewitched the people of Samaria, giving out that himself was some great one: to whom they all they all gave heed, from the least to the greatest, saying, This man is the great power of God.

This *certain man, called Simon* is a person who uses some kind of magic, or *sorcery,* to boost his own reputation. He is at the point where people refer to him as *some great one* or even a divine *power.* And he obviously welcomes the adulation.

In the ancient world, sorcerers usually employ various magical arts such as astrology, divination, incantations, and potions for practicing their "profession." In the Old Testament, God expressly forbade such practices (see Leviticus 19:26; Deuteronomy 18:10, 14; 2 Kings 17:17; 21:6). Even so, sorcery was common among pagans (see Exodus 7:11; Daniel 2:2). Later in Acts will come a reference to another magician named Bar-Jesus or Elymas (Acts 13:6-12), but unlike here that case is cast in a negative light.

11. And to him they had regard, because that of long time he had bewitched them with sorceries.

It seems that Simon has retained sole possession of the stage in Samaria for quite some *time.* His impact is probably felt at all levels of that society. So the book of Acts records the face-off between the ministry of Philip and the influence of Simon. What happens when the gospel is carried to cultures where lesser religious powers are served? Will the Samaritan people stick with Simon, or will they now follow Christ?

B. Simon Abandoned (v. 12)

12. But when they believed Philip preaching the things concerning the kingdom of God, and the name of Jesus Christ, they were baptized both men and women.

Philip's preaching reaches through the haze of Simon's deception. As a result, *both men and women* believe the message of Christ and accept the invitation to be *baptized.* This statement demonstrates that the gospel of Jesus Christ conquers the powers of evil and falsehood when it is preached truthfully. Acts 19:14-16 will show, on the other hand, what can happen when the gospel is preached falsely. Our text shows clearly that the Samaritans respond with authentic faith when they hear the news of Jesus Christ. This point is important for what follows.

C. Simon Believes (v. 13)

13. Then Simon himself believed also: and when he was baptized, he continued with

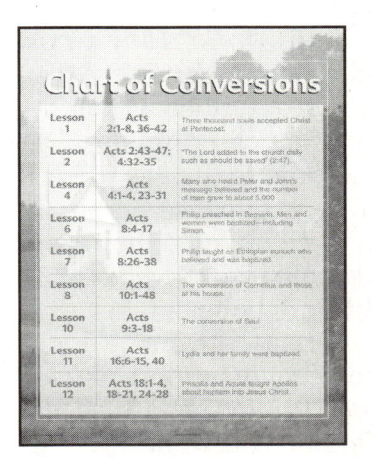

Use this chart to demonstrate that the book of Acts is a book about conversions.

Visual for lesson 6

Philip, and wondered, beholding the miracles and signs which were done.

The ultimate victory comes when *Simon himself* accepts the gospel message and submits to baptism. Luke (the author of Acts) uses the same language of conversion that is seen elsewhere. On the Day of Pentecost, for example, Peter told the audience to repent and be baptized, and the text follows with the news that about 3,000 were indeed baptized (Acts 2:38-41). In the same way, Simon *believed* and *was baptized;* his new faith then moves him to support the ministry of *Philip.* [See question #4, page 64.] There apparently is no such thing as an "unbaptized Christian" in the first-century church.

III. Ministry of Peter and John (Acts 8:14-17)

A. News Spreads (v. 14)

14. Now when the apostles which were at Jerusalem heard that Samaria had received the word of God, they sent unto them Peter and John.

Reports of conversions in *Samaria* come as wonderful news. This story would make headlines today. In *Jerusalem* there must be amazement and perhaps even some skepticism. So *the apostles* in Jerusalem respond immediately. Their decision is to send *Peter and John* northward to see the situation with their own eyes.

B. Prayer Offered (vv. 15, 16)

15. Who, when they were come down, prayed for them, that they might receive the Holy Ghost.

The apostles' first action upon arrival is prayer. They need to make sure that the new believers receive the same gift of *the Holy Ghost* that was bestowed on the Day of Pentecost. The journey of Peter and John is described as coming *down* because of the elevation of Jerusalem.

This language about receiving the Holy Spirit is surprising on the surface because earlier in Acts the preaching of Peter connects the reception of the Holy Spirit with baptism (Acts 2:38). The Samaritans had not only believed, but they also had been baptized. Their conversion looks authentic in light of the language of Acts (see comments above at 8:6), so why have they not yet received the Holy Spirit? And what does this account imply about the reception of the Holy Spirit today? One thing that should be noticed immediately is that the reception of the Spirit is connected here with prayer. Prayer is linked elsewhere with the authentic conversion of a person to Christ (see Acts 9:11; 10:2).

16. (For as yet he was fallen upon none of them: only they were baptized in the name of the Lord Jesus.)

This parenthetical verse begins to offer an explanation for the absence of the Holy Spirit with regard to the Samaritans after their baptism. To take this verse to mean that they were *baptized* improperly creates a problem since the baptism of the Samaritans *in the name of the Lord Jesus* matches the plea "be baptized . . . in the name of Jesus Christ" in Acts 2:38. We must read the next verse to move toward a solution.

C. Holy Spirit Received (v. 17)

17. Then laid they their hands on them, and they received the Holy Ghost.

The Samaritans had not *received the Holy Ghost* because they simply had been baptized, rather than being baptized and having the apostles' *hands* laid on them. When this is accomplished, they do indeed receive the Holy Spirit.

But this verse raises an important question: Why is the laying on of the apostles' hands required for receiving the Holy Spirit in this case while there is no mention of the same thing on the Day of Pentecost? This is a difficult question and several answers have been proposed. Some argue that the Holy Spirit's coming is unpredictable and that in the case of the Samaritans (and later the Ephesian believers—see Acts 19:1-6), the laying on of an apostle's hands is necessary for unknown reasons.

Another theory proposes that the laying on of the apostles' hands isn't for the indwelling of the Holy Spirit that all Christians receive, but is for bestowal of certain spiritual gifts, such as speaking in tongues. This theory is tied in with what Simon sees and how he reacts in Acts 8:18-24. When he sees the result of the laying on of the apostles' hands, he is impressed sufficiently that he wants to pay money to have the same power (v. 18). It's not that he wants the Holy Spirit to dwell within him (so the theory goes), but rather he wants the ability to lay hands on people and have them receive the visible signs of the Spirit's presence in terms of miraculous spiritual gifts. Thus when the text comments that the Samaritans only had been baptized (v. 16), the meaning under this theory is that without the laying on of the apostles' hands they could not receive the miraculous gifts from the Spirit.

Yet another idea says that the key lies in the religious and cultural differences between Samaritans and Jews. Perhaps the Samaritans were willing to give Philip a fair hearing because he was a Grecian Jew (see Acts 6:1, 5) rather one of the "pure blood" Jews that the Samaritans despise. Under this theory, the Samaritans are thus willing to accept Philip's message, but they also need to see that "salvation is of the Jews" (John 4:22); this requires Peter and John—two "pure blood" Jews—to come and lay hands for receiving the Holy Spirit. Thus God in His wisdom provides both (1) a messenger whom the Samaritans will listen to (meaning Philip) and (2) a way for the Samaritans to see where salvation truly lies. One happy result should be that racial and cultural antagonism between Jewish Christians and Samaritan Christians would then disappear.

Whichever theory is best (even if it's a theory not mentioned here), our text highlights the unique role of the apostles. While they are alive, their function as representatives of Christ is crucial in many settings.

"Say the Magic Word"

Parents often find they have difficulty getting their children to be polite. The basic niceties of society do not seem to come naturally to children. They must be coerced, instructed, and sometimes begged into doing and saying what will later be expected of them as civilized adults. "Please" and "thank you" are two phrases that most of us have found to be helpful in smoothing the occasionally rough waters of social discourse.

Some parents have found that getting a child to say "please" when asking for something comes easier when it is called a "magic word." So the phrase "say the magic word" becomes a frequent parental refrain until the "magic word" becomes a natural part of the child's vocabulary. Of course, the parent is speaking figuratively rather than of magic as we may normally think of it. Most children realize this, too.

But curiously, some Christians have fallen into the trap of thinking in terms of "magic words" when trying to solve the interpretation difficulty of verses 16 and 17, as noted above. Some Christians speculate that the new believers in Samaria had not been baptized "properly"—that is, without the "right words" having been said over them. Acts 2:38 calls for baptism *in the name of Jesus Christ*, and Matthew 28:19 calls for baptism *in the name of the Father, and of the Son, and of the Holy Ghost*. Quibbling about such variations in the words said at baptism misses the point. Paul does not say in Romans 6 that baptism's power lies in "saying the magic words," but in uniting our wills and spirits with the death and resurrection of Christ. No magic here! It is the power of God.

—C. R. B.

Conclusion

A. Mission Successes, Mission Problems

Philip's courageous trip to preach to the Samaritans opened doors for God's grace. When modern believers determine to preach the gospel beyond their own cultural borders, God is honored. Surprising results can come, as missionaries will attest. What mission fields are waiting for us to respond to today?

Whatever mission field God calls us to—whether it be a far-off land or our own places of work—we should not be surprised at setbacks. We see a setback in Acts 8:18-23, just after the close of today's text. There Simon was so impressed by what he saw that he wanted to pay money for the same power.

Simon's offer can be connected easily with his former profession as a sorcerer. His wish to captivate an audience surfaced again, and he could think of no better way to acquire the ability of

---

Home Daily Bible Readings

Monday, Oct. 3—Jesus Teaches in Judea (Matthew 19:1-12)

Tuesday, Oct. 4—Healing in Jericho (Matthew 20:29-34)

Wednesday, Oct. 5—Zaccheus Welcomes Jesus (Luke 19:1-10)

Thursday, Oct. 6—Jesus Meets a Samaritan Woman (John 4:1-10)

Friday, Oct. 7—Water Gushing Up to Eternal Life (John 4:11-15)

Saturday, Oct. 8—Philip Preaches in Samaria (Acts 8:4-13)

Sunday, Oct. 9—Peter and John Preach in Samaria (Acts 8:14-25)

Peter and John than to pay for it. The reception of the Spirit by his fellow Samaritans was connected with power. Thus Simon was moved somehow to make his unseemly offer.

Simon may have thought that he could pay for a trade secret, but the apostle Peter was not amused. Peter's subsequent curse on both Simon and his money amounts to some of the harshest words in Scripture: "Thy money perish with thee, because thou hast thought that the gift of God may be purchased with money" (Acts 8:20).

Without flinching, Peter then went on to cite the source of the problem: "thy heart is not right in the sight of God" (v. 21). The problem of sin starts, as always, with the condition of the heart. It is an issue of standing in a right relationship with God. [See question #5, page 64.]

B. Prayer

Lord of the nations, help us to remember that there are people of every race and culture who are ready to become Your children. But they can do so only if we will take the gospel of salvation to them. We confess that we have not always had the heart to do this as we ought. May the Spirit give us such a heart today. We pray through Christ, amen.

C. Thought to Remember

The gospel is meant for all the world, including those parts that do not look just like home.

Learning by Doing

This page contains an alternate lesson plan emphasizing learning activities. Classes desiring such student involvement will find these suggestions helpful.

Learning Goals

After this lesson each student will be able to:
1. Summarize Philip's ministry in Samaria.
2. Explain how Philip helped break down cultural barriers by preaching to the Samaritans.
3. Support his or her church's efforts at cross-cultural evangelism.

Into the Lesson

Display five concentric circles labeled simply, "Moving Out." As class begins, write in each circle (beginning in the middle) one of the following words: *community, state, nation, continent,* and *world.* Ask the class to name a missionary or missions organization working in each of the places designated. Write in responses. When completed, say, "Today's text is a record of the church moving out just as Jesus had directed. The spread of the gospel had started in Jerusalem and Judea; now it's time for it to move out—out to Samaria."

A good map of New Testament Palestine will be very useful in this lesson. Display one, if available.

Into the Word

Copy the following script for an "Interview with Simon of Samaria." Prior to today's class, recruit a volunteer to read the part of Simon. Ask the class to follow along in the text to distinguish which details are recorded in the biblical account and which ones are literary license.

TEACHER (*T* in following): Simon, what was there about Philip's preaching of Christ the man that so appealed to you?

SIMON (*S* in following): I must admit, the words kind of came and went, but when I saw the miracles he did—*wow!* They were the real deal.

T: Which miracles impressed you the most?
S: Well, compared with my tricks, all of them. But when I saw evil spirits running away and cursing, and when I saw people who couldn't walk made whole, I struggled to believe it. I am familiar with trickery, you know.

T: What was the general mood in your city?
S: Ever since the Romans had arrived, there was a dark pall over the town. But Philip brought a sunshine of the Spirit. Joy filled the air.

T: Did you really have the people fooled?
S: Fooled? Oh, yes. They all thought I was someone great. They believed anything I said.

T: Why were you baptized, Simon?

S: Philip's message promised a new life. Honestly, I was tired of my old one—a life of deceit.

T: What was your impression of Peter and John when they arrived from Jerusalem?

S: They looked ordinary—Galileans, if my ear was correct. But they were far from ordinary. And their prayer was simple—a simple request for us to receive the Holy Spirit. God honored them. With a light touch of the hand, the Holy Spirit was given. What a gift! What a sensation!

[Optional: create additional script here for Acts 8:18-23, not in today's lesson text.]

T: It is good to see you today, Simon.

S: Let me ask your believers *(turning to class)* to pray for one another. All of us have sin in our hearts. We need one another.

Into Life

Have a general class discussion about "sorcerers today." Ask these questions: (1) Who are individuals you would call "sorcerers of modern culture"? Why would you label them this way? (2) How do you explain the apparent abilities to act as spiritual mediums? (3) In what sense could these modern-day sorcerers be considered "seekers of truth"? How could such a person be approached with the truth of the gospel?

Ask the class to respond to the following characteristics to see if they are "Like Simon." (This activity is also in the student book.) Say, "Most of us resemble Simon of Samaria at different points in our lives. As a self-evaluation, respond to the following characteristics: pretending to be more than we are; accepting praise unworthily; using sin to get attention; hanging around with the 'popular crowd'; (the next three are optional) expecting money to buy the most valuable things; being publicly humiliated by appropriate correction; hypocritically expressing faith; thoughtlessly jumping after the 'next new thing.'"

Return to the concentric circles idea used at the beginning of the lesson. Go back and write in names of Christians whom your congregation or class supports who are working in each area. Ask volunteers to pray for each as they are written in.

Let's Talk It Over

These questions are designed to promote discussion of the lesson. The answers here are only discussion starters. Let your class talk it over from there.

1. Being "scattered abroad" means that the Christians of the early church were willing to suffer persecution for their faith to continue to proclaim the gospel. What does this say about the trustworthiness of the gospel? How should this affect our stand for the gospel today?

Some of the earliest Christians were eyewitnesses of the work of Christ. Convinced of the truthfulness of the gospel, they responded by upholding it in dire circumstances. If the eyewitnesses knew that their own testimonies were fabricated, they certainly would have renounced their faith when faced with deadly persecution. A rational person is not willing to die for a lie that he or she knows is a lie.

The suffering that the first-century Christians endured for their faith is thus a testimony to the truth of the gospel message. Today we build upon the faith foundation of these first-century saints. If we should doubt the testimony of the Word itself, we need but look at their faith and commitment to be challenged to maintain our own walk with Christ.

2. Though we may not perform miracles to gain a hearing, what are some things that Christians can do today to be an influence?

One key element to reach others effectively with the gospel message is to be sure that our lives match up with the words we share. People do not just want to know if what we say is true, they want to know if we are living out that truth ourselves. If we are teaching about a Lord who calms our fears yet we live in a visible state of anxiety, then our actions belie the words we speak. As a result, people will refuse to believe.

We also gain a hearing by responding appropriately to one another in the church. To proclaim a gospel of love and peace while allowing strife and discord to fill our churches undermines the validity of the gospel message.

3. Where the work of God is done and the Word is proclaimed, joy results. How is the joy in your church? How is the joy in your life?

In many churches, and in the lives of many Christians, joy is a missing ingredient. The singing is lethargic, the prayers repetitive, the giving abysmal. Relationships are strained, and outreach is too often nonexistent.

One reason for a lack of joy is that we have become consumers of the message and of what the church "can do for us." Greater joy may be found instead by seeing ourselves as recipients of God's grace and sharers of that message. When that happens, gratitude grows. When gratitude grows, so will joy. As a result, we will give of ourselves more deeply in kingdom work. We will not then be surprised to see new souls coming to Christ.

4. Those won to the gospel in the New Testament era often came out of very pagan backgrounds. How can the church today affect a pagan culture for Christ? Which things are primary, and which are secondary? Why?

First and foremost, Christ must be preached. Only Christ can change the heart of an unbeliever. Second, a renewal of a powerful prayer ministry must occur in the life of the church. Prayer is one of those things we often pay lip service to, but fail to practice with intensity.

Combined with this preaching and prayer should be the planting of churches in areas where there is a strong influence of paganism. Entertainment centers, cities of tremendous commercial or political power, as well as areas with large and prestigious educational institutions often are neglected in our church-planting efforts. New church plants will help stem the tide of ungodly influences from such locations.

5. What signs can indicate that someone in the church is seeking personal glory instead of God's glory? How do we keep from falling into this trap?

A leader's emphasis on hurrying people to make decisions for Christ instead of helping people to become disciples of Christ may indicate the desire to build numbers for personal glory. If we see such a leader obsessed with reporting or publishing "the numbers," then we should be alert to the possibility that we may have a problem on our hands. Emphasizing money over ministry is also an indicator.

Philip Teaches an Ethiopian

October 16
Lesson 7

DEVOTIONAL READING: Acts 11:19-26.

BACKGROUND SCRIPTURE: Acts 8:26-40.

PRINTED TEXT: Acts 8:26-38.

Acts 8:26-38

26 And the angel of the Lord spake unto Philip, saying, Arise, and go toward the south, unto the way that goeth down from Jerusalem unto Gaza, which is desert.

27 And he arose and went: and, behold, a man of Ethiopia, a eunuch of great authority under Candace queen of the Ethiopians, who had the charge of all her treasure, and had come to Jerusalem for to worship,

28 Was returning, and sitting in his chariot read Isaiah the prophet.

29 Then the Spirit said unto Philip, Go near, and join thyself to this chariot.

30 And Philip ran thither to him, and heard him read the prophet Isaiah, and said, Understandest thou what thou readest?

31 And he said, How can I, except some man should guide me? And he desired Philip that he would come up and sit with him.

32 The place of the Scripture which he read was this, He was led as a sheep to the slaughter; and like a lamb dumb before his shearer, so opened he not his mouth:

33 In his humiliation his judgment was taken away: and who shall declare his generation? for his life is taken from the earth.

34 And the eunuch answered Philip, and said, I pray thee, of whom speaketh the prophet this? of himself, or of some other man?

35 Then Philip opened his mouth, and began at the same Scripture, and preached unto him Jesus.

36 And as they went on their way, they came unto a certain water: and the eunuch said, See, here is water; what doth hinder me to be baptized?

37 And Philip said, If thou believest with all thine heart, thou mayest. And he answered and said, I believe that Jesus Christ is the Son of God.

38 And he commanded the chariot to stand still: and they went down both into the water, both Philip and the eunuch; and he baptized him.

GOLDEN TEXT: Philip opened his mouth, and began at the same Scripture, and preached unto him Jesus.—Acts 8:35.

> *You Will Be My Witnesses*
> Unit 2: In All Judea and Samaria
> (Lessons 5-9)

Lesson Aims

After participating in this lesson, each student will be able to:

1. Retell how Philip used Scripture to teach the Ethiopian about Jesus.
2. Explain how Philip's use of the Old Testament is a model for us today.
3. List Scriptures that can be used to help someone make a decision for Christ.

Lesson Outline

INTRODUCTION
   A. Perfectly Quoted Scripture
   B. Lesson Background
I. PREACHING TO THE ETHIOPIAN (Acts 8:26-29)
   A. Angelic Directive (v. 26)
   B. Ethiopian Traveling (vv. 27, 28)
   C. Spirit's Command (v. 29)
II. ANSWERING BIBLE QUESTIONS (Acts 8:30-35)
   A. Philip's Question (v. 30)
   B. Ethiopian's Invitation (v. 31)
   C. Isaiah's Prediction (vv. 32, 33)
   D. Ethiopian's Question (v. 34)
   E. Philip's Response (v. 35)
     Do You Understand?
III. RESPONDING TO THE GOSPEL (Acts 8:36-38)
   A. Question About Baptism (v. 36)
   B. Submitting to Baptism (vv. 37, 38)
     Expected Response, Expected Submission
CONCLUSION
   A. Helping Others Find the Way
   B. Prayer
   C. Thought to Remember

Introduction

A. Perfectly Quoted Scripture

Dave Veerman describes how his family determined to learn the Bible by memorizing one verse each week. His daughters were ages ten and six, so this pace seemed about right. Dave and his wife, Gail, kept the verses on cards where they could be easily seen, recited, and discussed. While at home one evening, the parents heard the girls fighting. One yelled, "I hate you!" and the other responded in a similar manner.

Dave relates that he did not wish to jump headlong into the fray, so he called one of his daughters by name and asked her what the verse was for the week. He hoped that the recitation of the verse in question would serve to quiet the fight by its implication.

Dave heard his daughter Kara promptly quote 1 John 4:11, which speaks of the importance of loving one another, but then the girls went right back to fighting. So Dave tried the same tactic with the other daughter, Dana. The results were the same. Before intervening personally, Dave and Gail couldn't help but laugh.

Human nature is fascinating, isn't it? The religious leaders of the first century A.D. knew the Old Testament Scripture inside out. They could quote it word for word and with passion. They believed it. Yet they were somehow unable to apply it as God intended. They didn't see how it applied to Jesus. As a result, those leaders killed Jesus and launched a persecution of the church. Yet God knows how to bring about the spread of the gospel in the midst of such an evil plan.

B. Lesson Background

In Acts 6–8 the theme of witnesses in Jerusalem transforms into the theme of witnesses in all Judea and Samaria as the persecution breaks out (compare Acts 6:7 with 8:1). Stephen and Philip, two chosen in Acts 6:1-6 to serve, become key figures. Luke (the author of the book of Acts) depicts Stephen's ministry as resulting in a hearing before the Sanhedrin that leads to his martyrdom (6:8–8:1). Philip's ministry follows that tragedy and involves the conversion of the Samaritans (8:4-25). His witness to the Ethiopian official comes next (today's lesson).

Both Stephen and Philip faithfully proclaimed Christ wherever they went. Stephen's faithfulness ended in execution. Philip's faithfulness took him to witness to people of different cultures. God was glorified in both cases.

In this part of the record of Acts, events reveal a theme not reflected in the longer title *The Acts of the Apostles*. Stephen and Philip were not apostles at all. The Bible thus presents the diligent work of believers other than the apostles. As a matter of fact, the growth of the earliest church depended very much on nonapostles who took seriously their duty to preach Christ.

Today's lesson reminds us that we are the ones God desires to use for helping people come to understand salvation. Philip's example demonstrates that modern believers should be ready with answers to the questions that lead to salvation.

I. Preaching to the Ethiopian (Acts 8:26-29)

A. Angelic Directive (v. 26)

26. And the angel of the Lord spake unto Philip, saying, Arise, and go toward the south, unto the way that goeth down from Jerusalem unto Gaza, which is desert.

God clearly blessed Philip's preaching to the Samaritans (Acts 8:6). But *Philip* has more work to do as *the angel of the Lord* commands a journey southward. [See question #1, page 73.] The road that leads to *Gaza* is not necessarily a *desert* road in the sense that it runs through sand dunes and sagebrush. The term speaks of the fact that the area is uninhabited.

B. Ethiopian Traveling (vv. 27, 28)

27, 28. And he arose and went: and, behold, a man of Ethiopia, a eunuch of great authority under Candace queen of the Ethiopians, who had the charge of all her treasure, and had come to Jerusalem for to worship, was returning, and sitting in his chariot read Isaiah the prophet.

Philip's quick reaction to the divine commission is seen in the phrase *arose and went.* Acts indicates more than once this kind of obedience to an opening for preaching (see 9:20; 16:10). This is as it should be. The response of any believer to the command of God to go and tell someone of Christ should be immediate and decisive. Even so, the Bible records instances of God's people hesitating at times (examples: Exodus 4:13; Acts 9:13, 14). [See question #2, page 73.]

The person that Philip meets on the road is *a man of Ethiopia.* This location is in Africa, just south of Egypt, where there are large Jewish communities. It is not unreasonable to think of this man as being Jewish, *returning* to Ethiopia from *Jerusalem,* where he had worshiped at the temple. Eunuchs in the time of the apostles are officials in the palaces of kings and queens. Because most kings possess harems, male servants often were emasculated to prevent them from molesting the women in the royal entourage. In some situations, however, the term *eunuch* applies to officials regardless of their physical condition. If the term *eunuch* here indicates that this man carries the physical disability of his position when he travels to Jerusalem, then his condition carries with it some noticeable social barriers (see Deuteronomy 23:1). His role in the palace is under Queen *Candace,* a dynasty name that is transferred to several women who occupy the Ethiopian throne.

This man's reading material that day is the Bible, and he has zeroed in on a passage from the book of *Isaiah.* Most likely this document is in scroll form. Since such scrolls are always copied laboriously by hand, they are expensive. Thus this Ethiopian is a man of some means.

C. Spirit's Command (v. 29)

29. Then the Spirit said unto Philip, Go near, and join thyself to this chariot.

Philip receives guidance from God each step along the way, whether by the angel of the Lord or by the Holy *Spirit.* God's plan in evangelism is to bring the believer together with the unbeliever so that the gospel can be shared. Philip's role, as seen in the verses that follow, is to preach and teach Christ. And that is the role for believers today.

How to Say It

AZOTUS. Uh-*zo*-tus.
CAESAREA. Sess-uh-*ree*-uh.
CANDACE. *Can*-duh-see.
ETHIOPIAN. E-thee-*o*-pee-un (*th* as in *thin*).
EUNUCH. *you*-nick.
ISAIAH. Eye-*zay*-uh.
JUDEA. Joo-*dee*-uh.
MEDITERRANEAN. *Med*-uh-tuh-*ray*-nee-un (strong accent on *ray*).
PHILIPPIAN. Fih-*lip*-ee-un.
PILATE. *Pie*-lut.
SAMARIA. Suh-*mare*-ee-uh.
SAMARITANS. Suh-*mare*-uh-tunz.
SANHEDRIN. San-huh-drun or San-*heed*-run.
SEPTUAGINT. Sep-*too*-ih-jent.
THESSALONIANS. *Thess*-uh-*lo*-nee-unz (strong accent on *lo; th* as in *thin*).

II. Answering Bible Questions (Acts 8:30-35)

A. Philip's Question (v. 30)

30. And Philip ran thither to him, and heard him read the prophet Isaiah, and said, Understandest thou what thou readest?

Philip's obedience to the command of God is evident again as he runs to the side of the Ethiopian. It is rare for a Jewish man to display such a lack of dignity, but nevertheless it is mentioned a few times in the Bible (see Luke 15:20; 19:4; 24:12). The Ethiopian is reading *the prophet Isaiah* with great interest. So Philip starts the conversation by asking him what he is reading. What a perfect opening for sharing Christ!

Philip raises the same question that can be raised whenever we have the chance. A lot of people have Bible questions. Philip opens the conversation by asking if the Ethiopian understands what he is reading from Isaiah, a Bible book that can produce plenty of questions!

B. Ethiopian's Invitation (v. 31)

31. And he said, How can I, except some man should guide me? And he desired Philip that he would come up and sit with him.

The Ethiopian official is puzzled about what he is reading and he is ready for answers. Philip's question results in an invitation to *come* closer for a dialogue. Believers should prepare themselves for opportunities such as this one (see 1 Peter 3:15). Why should such a chance be missed because we are not ready? [See question #3, page 73.]

C. Isaiah's Prediction (vv. 32, 33)

32, 33. The place of the Scripture which he read was this, He was led as a sheep to the slaughter; and like a lamb dumb before his shearer, so opened he not his mouth: in his humiliation his judgment was taken away: and who shall declare his generation? for his life is taken from the earth.

At this point in the record of Acts, we learn exactly which passage from Isaiah is creating the questions for the Ethiopian. This quotation comes from Isaiah 53:7, 8 as found in the *Septuagint* (which is the Greek translation of the Hebrew Bible as produced in the two centuries preceding the birth of Christ).

This section of Isaiah is part of the Servant Songs. Isaiah contains four of these songs in which the prophet describes a coming "servant of the Lord" who will represent the living God, but will be tormented for doing so. They are found in Isaiah 42:1-9; 49:1-13; 50:4-11; and 52:13–53:12.

The question that had intrigued godly people for centuries was the identity of the servant in these songs. Even among the ancient Jews there was a belief that these verses appear to describe the coming Messiah, although few could comprehend the idea of God's chosen One having to suffer. So the question of the Ethiopian is not surprising. The phrase *declare his generation* has to do with Jesus' premature death.

D. Ethiopian's Question (v. 34)

34. And the eunuch answered Philip, and said, I pray thee, of whom speaketh the prophet this? of himself, or of some other man?

The Ethiopian wants to know what nearly every Bible scholar wants to know: Is Isaiah describing *himself* in his ministry as a *prophet* of the Lord? Is he describing the nation of Israel, which is sometimes referred to as the Lord's servant (example: Isaiah 49:3)? Or is Isaiah describing the coming ministry of the Messiah?

The Ethiopian's request *I pray thee* conveys a certain intensity. *Philip* now has the perfect opportunity to speak the truth of God.

E. Philip's Response (v. 35)

35. Then Philip opened his mouth, and began at the same Scripture, and preached unto him Jesus.

Philip's answer to the Ethiopian's question is to instruct about *Jesus*. This, of course, tips off modern readers as to the identity of the servant in this passage from Isaiah. Philip's instruction

Use this artwork to remind your students of the church's main task.

Visual for lesson 7

undoubtedly informs the Ethiopian about the facts of Jesus' life, crucifixion, and resurrection. Judging from the other passages in Acts, the discussion probably includes details about Jesus' miracles, His innocence of wrongdoing, His hearings before the Sanhedrin and before Pilate, and His resurrection appearances (see Acts 2:22-33; 13:23-31).

These are the facts about the gospel of Christ that should be close to the heart and on the tip of the tongue of every Christian. These are the things we believe about Jesus, and because we believe we find salvation through Him. How can we ever justify ourselves if we cannot inform people of at least this much when they ask us questions about the Bible? [See question #4, page 73.]

Do You Understand?

The National Institute for Literacy says that America has a higher percentage of illiterate adults than either Canada or several nations of Europe. More than 20 percent of American adults cannot read well enough to apply for a good job (or keep it if they get hired). These 45 million-or-so Americans are unable to read a children's story or help with their children's education.

As troubling as these statistics are, they pale in comparison with the problem of biblical illiteracy. A little over a year ago, a candidate for the U.S. presidency did what politicians often do: he tried to make voters think he was more religious than his off-the-campaign-trail behavior indicated. To validate his profession of "being religious," he named the book of Job as his favorite book in the New Testament! Perhaps he simply misspoke, but his gaffe is symptomatic of a problem in modern culture. This problem is particularly troubling within the church itself. What some politely call a "diversity" in doctrinal viewpoints among Christians is described more accurately as "a crisis of biblical illiteracy" (Barna Research, "Religious Beliefs Vary Widely by Denomination," June 25, 2001).

The Ethiopian's problem was not really one of illiteracy—scriptural or otherwise. As a Jew, he could read, and he knew the Scriptures to a point. What he needed was someone to help him understand the Scriptures beyond the confines of the Old Testament. Specifically, he needed to be able to identify himself with Israel's hope—the Messiah. Would you have been biblically literate enough to lead that man to Christ as Philip did? —C. R. B.

III. Responding to the Gospel (Acts 8:36-38)

A. Question About Baptism (v. 36)

36. And as they went on their way, they came unto a certain water: and the eunuch said, See, here is water; what doth hinder me to be baptized?

This verse surely implies that the instruction about Jesus to this point has included teaching about baptism as a response to the gospel message (see Acts 2:38; 22:16). Archaeologists have located a couple of places along this route where springs of water can be found. Thus it would not have been difficult for the eunuch to notice one of these and pose this question to Philip.

B. Submitting to Baptism (vv. 37, 38)

37. And Philip said, If thou believest with all thine heart, thou mayest. And he answered and said, I believe that Jesus Christ is the Son of God.

This verse does not appear in the earliest manuscripts. Perhaps your edition of the *King James Version* has an asterisk (*) to note this fact. Nevertheless, it is safe to assume that Philip's preaching emphasizes the need for the Ethiopian to put his faith in Christ, just as is true in Paul's preaching (see Acts 16:31; 18:8).

38. And he commanded the chariot to stand still: and they went down both into the water,

---

Home Daily Bible Readings

Monday, Oct. 10—Jesus Teaches About Responding to Others (Matthew 5:38-42)

Tuesday, Oct. 11—Jesus Teaches About Signs (Matthew 12:36-42)

Wednesday, Oct. 12—Jesus Teaches Nicodemus About Rebirth (John 3:1-15)

Thursday, Oct. 13—Jesus Rebukes the Pharisees and Scribes (Matthew 15:1-9)

Friday, Oct. 14—Jesus Asks the Pharisees a Question (Matthew 22:41-46)

Saturday, Oct. 15—Philip Meets the Ethiopian Official (Acts 8:26-31)

Sunday, Oct. 16—Philip Proclaims the Good News (Acts 8:32-40)

both Philip and the eunuch; and he baptized him.

The language of the baptism implies immersion as the mode, since there would be no reason to go down *into the water* unless an immersion is intended. We should notice that baptism is presented here as elsewhere in the New Testament: it accompanies the faith of a person who has accepted the claims of Christ as being true. Notice that there is no hint of the need for a probationary period in which the believer is tested or trained prior to the baptism. Just as in the case of the Philippian jailer (Acts 16:33), the Ethiopian can be baptized immediately on the basis of his faith in Christ.

Every modern believer has the tools for witnessing as Philip does in this situation. The Bible offers all of the information about the ministry of Christ, how He suffered and died but rose on the third day to bring the hope of everlasting life. The Bible also provides the information needed for becoming a Christian. There is no reason for modern believers not to be as prepared as Philip when the opportunity comes to lead someone to Christ.

EXPECTED RESPONSE, EXPECTED SUBMISSION

What do we see while we stand in the checkout lane of our local grocery store? Racks of tabloids picturing the latest antics of the world's celebrities! On TV we see their fans follow them nearly everywhere, screaming and shrieking when they see their idols. It *does* seem almost idolatrous, doesn't it? Some may think this kind of attitude toward celebrities began with the fans of the Beatles or Elvis. Yet some of us remember when teenaged "bobby-soxers" swooned at the sight of the young Frank Sinatra!

Regardless of when the phenomenon began, it is now what we expect to see. For example, when a popular entertainer appeared in court a couple of years ago to enter his plea on a criminal charge, thousands of his fans gathered outside the courthouse. Some had been up all night in a bus convoy to be there for the occasion; others had even flown in from Japan and Europe! He did not disappoint them: after the hearing, he climbed atop his limousine and invited the screaming multitude to his nearby mansion for a celebration.

We worship the God of the universe, not entertainers. And yet the expected response to hearing the gospel is both calmer and more thoughtful. The book of Acts tells us of convert after convert who entered the waters of baptism in humble submission as God was working in their hearts. This is still the response that God expects of those who come to Him in faith.

—C. R. B.

Conclusion
A. Helping Others Find the Way

As is true at the beginning of this narrative, the event closes with divine guidance: the baptism of the Ethiopian was followed by Philip being *caught away* (Acts 8:39). Philip disappeared from sight.

The phrase *caught away* implies a supernatural action that removed Philip from the spot of the baptism. The Greek word for *caught away* is the same word as found in 1 Thessalonians 4:17, where Paul writes that at the appearance of Christ the believers who are alive will be *caught up* together to meet the Lord in the air. In Philip's case, this is not some kind of "rapture," of course. But the snatching away was both sudden and miraculous. Perhaps the Ethiopian searched behind a sand dune or two, but Philip was gone just as suddenly as he had arrived.

Even so, the Ethiopian went on his way rejoicing (v. 39). This notation is the way that Acts refers to the commitment after the baptism. When people are converted to Christ, the book of Acts usually does not merely describe belief and baptism. A statement usually is supplied to show readiness to follow Christ after the baptism. In the case of the Ethiopian it is going his way rejoicing. [See question #5, page 73.] In the case of the converts on the Day of Pentecost, "they continued steadfastly in the apostles' doctrine and fellowship, and in breaking of bread, and in prayers" (Acts 2:42). After Simon was converted to Christ, "he continued with Philip, and wondered, beholding the miracles and signs which were done" (Acts 8:13). After Lydia was converted to Christ, she invited the apostles to her home (Acts 16:15).

But the account before us also testifies to the fact that God was not finished with Philip's ministry. After disappearing from the side of the Ethiopian, Philip appeared at Azotus on the Mediterranean coast and then at Caesarea by the sea, King Herod's lavish city. Philip will not be mentioned again until Acts 21:8, some 20 years later, in the same city of Caesarea.

Philip's ministry gives modern Christians a reason to ask whether we have prepared ourselves for moments such as Philip faced. Have we learned enough about the life and ministry of Jesus that we could help lead someone to salvation? Are we prepared to speak to someone about how Jesus died on the cross, was buried in the tomb, and rose on the third day?

Safety officials often warn us that every family should prepare an exit strategy from their homes before a catastrophe occurs, because it is much too late to react when the crisis comes. By the same token, every believer should prepare a witnessing strategy for answering questions that may lead to salvation. We should learn what God's will is for sinners who ask, "what shall we do?" as was asked on the Day of Pentecost (Acts 2:37). We should be prepared to answer as the apostles answered such questions.

B. Prayer

God of truth, make us bolder, we pray, to share the truth of salvation. You have revealed that truth to us, and we must share it. We pray in the name of the one who brought truth to light for all of us. In Jesus' name, amen.

C. Thought to Remember

God will use you in His service to the extent that you have prepared yourself to be used.

Learning by Doing

This page contains an alternate lesson plan emphasizing learning activities. Classes desiring such student involvement will find these suggestions helpful.

Learning Goals

After participating in this lesson, each student will be able to:

1. Retell how Philip used Scripture to teach the Ethiopian about Jesus.
2. Explain how Philip's use of the Old Testament is a model for us today.
3. List Scriptures that can be used to help someone make a decision for Christ.

Into the Lesson

Display a toy rubber duck sitting beside a clear glass bowl of water. As class begins, ask, "What old saying does this scene represent?" When someone suggests, "like a duck out of water," say, "Certain things belong together. A duck in the water is as happy as . . . well, a duck in the water. God knew that a traveling Ethiopian official and a certain Christian evangelist belonged together. He made the arrangements. Let's see the story in today's text in Acts 8."

Into the Word

Call this activity, "Surprise or No Surprise." Give each learner a copy of the 11 statements below (which also appear in the student book) and ask them to decide if the truth in these statements is in any way surprising. Direct them to put *surprise* or *no surprise* before each statement and be prepared to give a rationale for their choices. (Some brief explanatory notes are given in parentheses after each statement.)

1. God knows the precise location of the Ethiopian official—in the desert. (*No surprise,* for God is all-knowing.)
2. An Ethiopian has been to Jerusalem to worship. (*No surprise,* for many Jews lived in North Africa, and perhaps this man was a convert.)
3. An Ethiopian has a scroll of the book of Isaiah. (*Surprise,* because such scrolls were rare and valuable. He may have purchased it for his queen.)
4. A treasurer for the queen of Ethiopia can read the language of the scroll. (*No surprise;* this was a Greek version of the Old Testament, and Greek was a nearly universal language among the educated.)
5. A Jewish man runs to catch up with a traveler. (*Surprise,* in that Jewish men generally would not run, considering it undignified; but *no surprise* in that Philip was obeying God's specific command.)
6. The Ethiopian official does not understand fully what he is reading. (*No surprise,* for even Old Testament scholars debated the messianic passages—and still do!)

7. Philip recognized what the man was reading as coming from the book of Isaiah. (*No surprise*, for a devout Jew would be on very familiar terms with the writings of the Old Testament.)

8. Isaiah pictured a Messiah who did not defend himself with power. (*No surprise* to those of us who understand the nature of the Messiah from this side of the cross, but perhaps a big *surprise* to a Jew of the earlier era.)

9. The travelers find water in a desert. (*No surprise;* this desert place simply means uninhabited, and several seasonal streams flow from the hill country to the sea.)

10. The official asks to be baptized. (*No surprise*, for baptism is part of the gospel presentation in the book of Acts.)

11. Philip baptizes the Ethiopian. (*No surprise*, for that is part of what he was sent to do.)

[Of course, students may have a different view on some of these; let them express their views and give their rationale.]

Into Life

Establish two discussion groups and give each group one of the following two case studies to analyze.

Case #1. A stylist working on your hair has on the counter a book about angels. As she works, she says, "I'm just not sure whether that book is right about angels or not. Some of it is pretty weird stuff." What Bible texts and occasions would you suggest to identify revelation about angels and their ministry?

Case #2. A rider gets on the bus and seats himself beside you. He is reading one of the contemporary bestsellers on the end times. After you comment, he says, "This stuff is so strange—I wonder if any of it is true." What Bible texts do you refer to in response?

Allow time for groups to discuss their scenarios. Then ask each to read its case to the whole class and list their answers.

Let's Talk It Over

These questions are designed to promote discussion of the lesson. The answers here are only discussion starters. Let your class talk it over from there.

1. Whether it is Abraham, Jonah, or Philip, God is in the business of calling His people to arise and go. In what ways is God calling you as an individual to take His message into the world? How is God calling your church?

In the circle of influence of all Christians, there are people who do not know Christ as Lord and Savior—neighbors, family members, coworkers. Living a lifestyle consistent with the teaching of Scripture is an important part of being a light in the darkness. But that, by itself, isn't enough since "faith cometh by hearing, and hearing by the word of God" (Romans 10:17). God calls each of us to be ready always to give an answer for the hope that we have (1 Peter 3:15).

Churches can be involved in the task by encouraging Christians to enter into cross-cultural ministry. Also important is support for Bible colleges in the task of training workers to take the gospel worldwide. But support for others should never be used as an excuse for failing to share personally one's faith with another and to pray for unsaved people specifically by name.

2. Philip's response to God's command was immediate obedience. Often we fail to obey at once. Why are we often reluctant to go when God's call is clear?

A primary reason we often fail to go is a mistaken idea of what it means *to go*. "To go with the gospel" can conjure up images of selling all we have and moving overseas or entering into a full-time Christian vocation. But the command *go* undoubtedly includes modeling the life of a Christian anywhere and everywhere.

A second reason for the reluctance is fear. If God is calling us to go to a family member, our fear is that we will be accused of judging. If it is a friend, we fear the person will stop being our friend. If it is a coworker, we fear friction in the workplace should the person not like the message we share. If we are called to go to a stranger, there is a fear of meeting with hostility.

In such cases we remember that "God hath not given us the spirit of fear; but of power, and of love, and of a sound mind" (2 Timothy 1:7). With God behind us, how can the enemy prevail?

3. Being sent by God obviously requires some level of knowledge of the Word of God. What things should we know? Why?

People to whom we go have questions just as the Ethiopian had. Salvation comes when a person accepts Jesus according to the New Testament plan of salvation, but certain facts about Jesus and His salvation also must be accepted. Knowing the truth about grace and its relationship to faith and works is vital. Being aware of errors that are taught about these things so that we can provide effective answers will improve our witness.

4. How can we be effective instruments of God as Philip was?

The first thing Philip sought to do was gain an understanding of the knowledge the Ethiopian possessed. In verse 30 we see the first thing Philip did was ask the man if he understood what he was reading. To help others understand about Jesus, we can first try to determine what they already grasp.

After letting the person share his or her level of knowledge, we then begin at that point to teach about Jesus, just as Philip did. This means that it is necessary to take time to get to know those with whom we are working. A canned approach to evangelism rarely is effective because of differences in people's knowledge and attitudes.

5. After his baptism, the Ethiopian rejoiced (v. 39). Unfortunately, some Christians lose that initial joy of salvation. How can we maintain our joy?

The Word of God is the food that nourishes our senses of gratitude, wonder, and joy. Continual study of Scripture keeps joy alive. As Ravi Zacharias puts it, "Wonder is retained by wise pondering" (*Recapture the Wonder*, 2003). The anticipation of Heaven and participation in corporate worship help maintain our joy. Financial giving is a source of joy for the spiritually mature.

The ultimate joy for a Christian is seeing someone else come to Christ. When we take time to share our faith, we have the joy of seeing a new soul come to Christ.

October 23
Lesson 8

God Welcomes Gentiles

DEVOTIONAL READING: Acts 13:44-49.

BACKGROUND SCRIPTURE: Acts 10:1-48.

PRINTED TEXT: Acts 10:1-20.

Acts 10:1-20

1 There was a certain man in Caesarea called Cornelius, a centurion of the band called the Italian band,

2 A devout man, and one that feared God with all his house, which gave much alms to the people, and prayed to God always.

3 He saw in a vision evidently, about the ninth hour of the day, an angel of God coming in to him, and saying unto him, Cornelius.

4 And when he looked on him, he was afraid, and said, What is it, Lord? And he said unto him, Thy prayers and thine alms are come up for a memorial before God.

5 And now send men to Joppa, and call for one Simon, whose surname is Peter:

6 He lodgeth with one Simon a tanner, whose house is by the sea side: he shall tell thee what thou oughtest to do.

7 And when the angel which spake unto Cornelius was departed, he called two of his household servants, and a devout soldier of them that waited on him continually;

8 And when he had declared all these things unto them, he sent them to Joppa.

9 On the morrow, as they went on their journey, and drew nigh unto the city, Peter went up upon the housetop to pray about the sixth hour:

10 And he became very hungry, and would have eaten: but while they made ready, he fell into a trance,

11 And saw heaven opened, and a certain vessel descending unto him, as it had been a great sheet knit at the four corners, and let down to the earth:

12 Wherein were all manner of fourfooted beasts of the earth, and wild beasts, and creeping things, and fowls of the air.

13 And there came a voice to him, Rise, Peter; kill, and eat.

14 But Peter said, Not so, Lord; for I have never eaten any thing that is common or unclean.

15 And the voice spake unto him again the second time, What God hath cleansed, that call not thou common.

16 This was done thrice: and the vessel was received up again into heaven.

17 Now while Peter doubted in himself what this vision which he had seen should mean, behold, the men which were sent from Cornelius had made inquiry for Simon's house, and stood before the gate,

18 And called, and asked whether Simon, which was surnamed Peter, were lodged there.

19 While Peter thought on the vision, the Spirit said unto him, Behold, three men seek thee.

20 Arise therefore, and get thee down, and go with them, doubting nothing: for I have sent them.

GOLDEN TEXT: While Peter thought on the vision, the Spirit said unto him, Behold, three men seek thee. Arise therefore, and get thee down, and go with them, doubting nothing: for I have sent them.—Acts 10:19, 20.

LESSON 8 75 OCTOBER 23

> *You Will Be My Witnesses*
> Unit 2: In All Judea and Samaria
> (Lessons 5-9)

Lesson Aims

After participating in this lesson, each student will be able to:

1. List the events leading up to Peter's visit with Cornelius.
2. Discuss the prejudices that Peter and Cornelius had to overcome.
3. Acknowledge a personal struggle with prejudice and determine one way to overcome it.

Lesson Outline

INTRODUCTION
    A. Hearts Full of Prejudice
    B. Lesson Background
I. VISION OF CORNELIUS (Acts 10:1-8)
    A. Devout Cornelius (vv. 1, 2)
    B. Heavenly Visitor (vv. 3-6)
       Hearing Voices
    C. Relayed Message (vv. 7, 8)
II. VISION OF PETER (Acts 10:9-16)
    A. Prayer, Hunger, Trance (vv. 9, 10)
    B. Animals, Reptiles, Birds (vv. 11, 12)
    C. Command, Reply, Rebuke (vv. 13-16)
III. COMMISSION FOR PETER (Acts 10:17-20)
    A. Men Inquire (vv. 17, 18)
    B. Spirit Directs (vv. 19, 20)
       Breaking Tradition
CONCLUSION
    A. Go into *All* the World
    B. Prayer
    C. Thought to Remember

Introduction

A. Hearts Full of Prejudice

Daniel "Chappie" James, Jr. (1920–1978) was the first African-American to attain the rank of four-star general in the U.S. armed forces. There were many bumps along the way. At a speech given in Philadelphia in 1976, General James recalled a certain incident of racism in his life. After being promoted to full colonel, he was wearing his military uniform with pride as he walked down a sidewalk in his hometown one day. Suddenly, two men confronted him and ripped the rank insignia from his shoulders. The men heaped verbal abuse on James, saying insulting and racist things. They told him that no person of his race could possibly be a colonel in the U.S. Air Force.

But America had looked past skin color in promoting James ever higher in rank. The fact is, James had done a superb job in position after position. He deserved his promotions on merit.

Many in our world still struggle to look past racial, ethnic, and cultural dividing lines. But God has no such difficulty. His impartiality is not based on our merit but is based on the fact that all humans are created in His image. Today's lesson shows how God sent the apostle Peter to offer salvation across the dividing line between Jew and Gentile—an unbridgeable chasm to the thinking of many in the first century. The courage of Peter's actions in preaching to Cornelius should guide us to consider our own behavior toward people of other cultural or racial backgrounds. [See question #1, page 82.]

B. Lesson Background

Jesus commissioned the apostles to be His witnesses "in Jerusalem, and in all Judea, and in Samaria, and unto the uttermost part of the earth" (Acts 1:8). The first seven chapters of Acts describe the way that witness was presented in Jerusalem from events on the Day of Pentecost (chapter 2), to the healing of the man who was lame (chapter 3), to the ministries of Stephen (6:8–8:1) and Philip (8:4-40).

After the martyrdom of Stephen, the believers were scattered from Jerusalem, preaching the gospel wherever they went. Conversions of people to Christ are presented from both the Jerusalem period before the death of Stephen and the period afterward in which the witnesses go to all Judea and Samaria. The succession of converts includes people such as the Samaritans (8:4-25), the Ethiopian (8:26-40), and Saul of Tarsus (9:1-31). Human logic tells us that at least some of those included would be unlikely believers in Christ. But Acts 10 presents a convert much more unexpected.

Jews and Gentiles in the Roman world looked at each other with much suspicion. Gentiles found Jewish beliefs and customs to be confusing and narrow-minded, while Jews thought of Gentiles as pagan and immoral. Some Gentiles, however, became convinced that the God of the

Visual for lesson 8

Start a discussion by turning this statement into a question: "Is our church open to all?"

Jews was good and true. In some cases, these Gentiles converted to Judaism, becoming what was known as *proselytes.* The book of Acts mentions that the worshipers on the Day of Pentecost included such proselytes (2:10).

In other cases, Gentiles did not convert fully to Judaism, but engaged in worship with Jews and lived by many of the requirements of the Law of Moses. These worshipers were referred to as *God-fearers* and are also mentioned in Acts. When Paul stood to speak in the synagogue at Antioch of Pisidia, he directed his words to the "Men of Israel, and ye that fear God" (13:16); by the latter he meant godly Gentiles. When the missionary speakers began proclaiming the gospel of Christ, such synagogue worshipers were ripe for conversion to Christ.

One other factor that is essential for understanding the account about Cornelius is the political situation in Palestine. Rome ruled the Mediterranean area, but they did not consider Jerusalem to be the capital city of Judea. Instead, Caesarea Maritima (or "Caesarea by the sea") was where Roman rule was established, some sixty miles northwest of Jerusalem. (Note: This Caesarea is different from Caesarea Philippi, so don't get the two confused.)

I. Vision of Cornelius
(Acts 10:1-8)
A. Devout Cornelius (vv. 1, 2)

1. There was a certain man in Caesarea called Cornelius, a centurion of the band called the Italian band.

Cornelius has not been mentioned to this point in the book of Acts. Though nothing about the name itself is revealing, the mention of his home *in Caesarea* and his position as *a centurion* communicates to us that this man is a Gentile. Caesarea, a beautiful Gentile city, was rebuilt by Herod the Great from about 22 to 10 B.C. to honor Caesar Augustus.

A centurion commands a cohort, which is a subunit of a Roman legion. Legions consist of about 6,000 troops, and each centurion commands between 80 and 100 men. *The Italian band* is a name that the soldiers use to describe this particular cohort, a practice not uncommon for Roman soldiers. Centurions are respected for their dedication to their responsibilities.

2. A devout man, and one that feared God with all his house, which gave much alms to the people, and prayed to God always.

The description of Cornelius now includes matters related to his spiritual life. Being *devout* and one who fears *God* suggests that he lives in a way that is consistent with the Law of Moses, even though he is not a full proselyte or convert. His charitable gifts *(alms)* and his prayer life show where his heart truly lies. [See question #2, page 82.] His faith in God is not a selfish faith. Luke (the author of the book of Acts) describes other Gentiles in somewhat similar ways in Acts 13:50; 16:14; 17:4, 17; and 18:7.

B. Heavenly Visitor (vv. 3-6)

3. He saw in a vision evidently, about the ninth hour of the day, an angel of God coming in to him, and saying unto him, Cornelius.

Cornelius now experiences *a vision* from the Lord similar to such visions elsewhere in the Bible. The surprise in this, of course, is that Cornelius is a Gentile. The word *evidently* (which can also be translated "in an evident way") describes how distinct the vision is when Cornelius experiences it. *The angel of God* is evident enough that Cornelius cannot miss him.

The ninth hour of the day is 3:00 P.M. The mention of this time is important. It is at this same time that Peter and John were going to the temple in Acts 3:1, one of the three times of prayer in the temple: early morning, afternoon, and sunset. So Cornelius, the Gentile God-fearer, stands in God's presence in prayer (see Acts 10:30) at the same time of day that dedicated Jewish worshipers are in prayer as well.

4. And when he looked on him, he was afraid, and said, What is it, Lord? And he said unto him, Thy prayers and thine alms are come up for a memorial before God.

Who cannot sympathize with Cornelius in his reaction of fear in seeing the angel? Fear is the reaction to an appearance of the heavenly visitors in several places in the Bible (examples: Matthew 28:5, 8; Luke 1:11, 12; 2:9).

In the midst of his fear, Cornelius expresses awareness that this is indeed no ordinary visitor. The angel himself confirms this in responding that God has taken note of Cornelius's *prayers* and *alms*. The idea of *a memorial before God* is somewhat similar to wording in Leviticus 2:2 and Philippians 4:18. The sincere acts of devout truth-seekers such as Cornelius are not ignored in Heaven. His acts of faithfulness have found acceptance with God, who looks at the heart. Even with all of Cornelius's devotion, however, he still needs the salvation that only Christ can bring.

5, 6. And now send men to Joppa, and call for one Simon, whose surname is Peter: he lodgeth with one Simon a tanner, whose house is by the sea side: he shall tell thee what thou oughtest to do.

Joppa is another coastline city, located about 30 miles to the south of Caesarea. Acts prepares us for this command from the angel by reporting at the end of Acts 9 that *Peter* had decided to stay with *Simon*, who is *a tanner* (9:43). A tanner works with animal skins for a living, so having a *house* by the *sea* serves as a help to the tanning process because of the water needed. Thus Peter is staying in a house where there will be constant exposure to the dead carcasses that Jews know will bring defilement (see Leviticus 11). Perhaps this environment helps to explain the content of the vision that God brings to Peter (see below).

The angel's words to Cornelius include in them the purpose for summoning Peter: he is coming to *tell thee what thou oughtest to do*. When Peter retells this story later in Acts, he summarizes the words of the angel as telling Cornelius that Peter would bring "words, whereby thou and all thy house shall be saved" (Acts 11:14). As is true in the account of Philip and the Ethiopian (Acts 8:26-40), God's way of evangelism is to bring a human messenger into contact with the one who needs the message. Thus the angel, instead of bringing the message of salvation directly to Cornelius, commands him to send for Peter, who will bring the gospel message.

This principle should guide our thinking today when it comes to evangelism. The church's mission should focus on sending messengers with the gospel, even to people of other races and cultures. See Matthew 28:19, 20.

HEARING VOICES

What are some of the symptoms of insanity? If you said "hearing voices," you have given a typical answer. "Hearing voices" is sometimes used as a defense in criminal cases in which the defendant claims to have heard a voice telling him or her to kill someone else.

Now a new invention can make us hear real voices in a unique way. It is an ultrasound device, able to send a focused beam of sound to a single person hundreds of feet away. The marketing industry is already rejoicing over the sales potential of the invention. A large discount store chain and a popular fast food outlet have begun testing the device. So if you hear a tiny voice whispering in your ear, "Buy Brand X coffee" or "Supersize your order," and no one around you hears it, relax. You are *not* going crazy!

Peter and Cornelius were neither insane nor "hearing voices." God sent a messenger to each of them so both sight and sound could confirm the message. Each of them saw, heard, and responded positively. We may never get a message in that same way, but God still speaks to us through His Word. When we open its pages and read, our response should be as positive and immediate as theirs.
—C. R. B.

How to Say It

ANTIOCH. *An*-tee-ock.
CAESAREA MARITIMA. Sess-uh-*ree*-uh Mar-uh-*tee*-muh.
CAESAREA PHILIPPI. Sess-uh-*ree*-uh Fih-*lip*-pie or *Fil*-ih-pie.
CORNELIUS. Cor-*neel*-yus.
ETHIOPIAN. E-thee-*o*-pee-un (*th* as in *thin*).
GENTILES. *Jen*-tiles.
JERUSALEM. Juh-*roo*-suh-lem.
LEVITICUS. Leh-*vit*-ih-kus.
MEDITERRANEAN. *Med*-uh-tuh-*ray*-nee-un (strong accent on *ray*).
PHILIPPIANS. Fih-*lip*-ee-unz.
PISIDIA. Pih-*sid*-ee-uh.
PROSELYTES. *prahss*-uh-lights.
SAMARITANS. Suh-*mare*-uh-tunz.
SYNAGOGUE. *sin*-uh-gog.
TARSUS. *Tar*-sus.
TYRE. Tire.

C. Relayed Message (vv. 7, 8)

7, 8. And when the angel which spake unto Cornelius was departed, he called two of his household servants, and a devout soldier of them that waited on him continually; and when he had declared all these things unto them, he sent them to Joppa.

And so the drama continues to unfold! For reasons unknown to us, the angel did not tell *Cornelius* to go to *Joppa* personally. Rather, Cornelius is to "send men" (v. 5), so that's exactly what he does.

II. Vision of Peter
(Acts 10:9-16)
A. Prayer, Hunger, Trance (vv. 9, 10)

9, 10. On the morrow, as they went on their journey, and drew nigh unto the city, Peter went up upon the housetop to pray about the sixth hour: and he became very hungry, and would have eaten: but while they made ready, he fell into a trance.

As the messengers from Cornelius travel on their day-long journey, Peter is exercising his faith just as Cornelius had. *The sixth hour* is noon. This time of day is not a "normal" hour for prayer for Jews, but it shows us that Peter isn't locked into a ritualistic pattern for prayer. [See question #3, page 82.]

Peter's choice of the rooftop for prayer reminds us of the flat-roofed structures of homes in that area. This place allows Peter to pray quietly with the benefit of cool breezes from the sea. But while waiting for the meal to be prepared, Peter falls *into a trance*. Thus the experience of Peter parallels that of Cornelius (see Acts 10:3, above). The will of God is to be once again revealed through a trance or a vision. Peter is about to be enlightened with regard to God's plan for Gentiles.

B. Animals, Reptiles, Birds (vv. 11, 12)

11. And saw heaven opened, and a certain vessel descending unto him, as it had been a great sheet knit at the four corners, and let down to the earth.

Peter's vision begins with the opening of *heaven*, an indication that the point of the trance will be a message from God. This point is emphasized in the direction from which the *great sheet* is coming, that is, down from Heaven *to the earth*.

12. Wherein were all manner of fourfooted beasts of the earth, and wild beasts, and creeping things, and fowls of the air.

On the sheet is a multitude of various animals. They represent food to a hungry man. The designations *wild beasts, and creeping things, and fowls of the air* matches rather closely a similar description in Genesis 6:20.

C. Command, Reply, Rebuke (vv. 13-16)

13. And there came a voice to him, Rise, Peter; kill, and eat.

There is no mystery about the source of the *voice*. The opened heavens and direction of the sheet make clear that the *voice* is from the Lord. His voice comes to *Peter* as a command to *kill* one of these animals and prepare a meal.

14. But Peter said, Not so, Lord; for I have never eaten any thing that is common or unclean.

Peter knows he is addressing the *Lord,* and his first words are a reaction to the thought of eating *unclean* animals. The Law of Moses divided animals into the categories of "clean" and "unclean." Leviticus 11 presents details about the distinction between these animals. That passage closes with the divine command that the people of God should not defile themselves with any of the unclean animals (11:43). Clean animals, as defined in that passage, are acceptable for eating and offering sacrifices to the Lord. This issue has nothing to do with hygiene. To eat unclean animals is to reject the authority of God and to make oneself defiled before Him.

Peter's reaction is an honest one. He is horrified at the thought of making himself unclean before the Lord. He refuses to eat anything *common* in this regard. This reaction should be remembered not only in terms of Peter's sense of defiling himself, however, but also in Peter's sense of what Gentiles are doing to themselves when they eat unclean animals.

15, 16. And the voice spake unto him again the second time, What God hath cleansed, that call not thou common. This was done thrice: and the vessel was received up again into heaven.

With the *second* and third sound of the Lord's voice comes not only an emphasis of the original point, but an additional principle. This principle relates to food, but applies directly to Peter's views about Gentiles. God has *cleansed* animals, so Peter should stop thinking of them as unclean or unholy. This same principle surfaces in Mark's Gospel. After Jesus declared all foods clean, the next event in Mark is the visit of Jesus to a Gentile woman in the vicinity of Tyre (Mark 7:19, 24-30). [See question #4, page 82.]

Once the vision is completed, the sheet is taken *up again into heaven,* and this part of Peter's lesson is over. As events unfold, however, the point that the vision makes will not be lost on Peter. Later, in the home of Cornelius, Peter will say that he learned from the vision that he should not avoid contact with Gentiles because God does not show favoritism (Acts 10:34, 35).

III. Commission for Peter
(Acts 10:17-20)
A. Men Inquire (vv. 17, 18)

17, 18. Now while Peter doubted in himself what this vision which he had seen should mean, behold, the men which were sent from Cornelius had made inquiry for Simon's house, and stood before the gate, and called, and asked whether Simon, which was surnamed Peter, were lodged there.

Full understanding does not come instantly for *Peter.* But notice how God has arranged the timing of things: He begins to provide the answer in the form of visitors *from Cornelius* at the very time when Peter is trying to comprehend the *vision.* The note that they are standing *before the gate* indicates a typical first-century courtyard.

B. Spirit Directs (vv. 19, 20)

19, 20. While Peter thought on the vision, the Spirit said unto him, Behold, three men seek thee. Arise therefore, and get thee down, and go with them, doubting nothing: for I have sent them.

Peter is still on the roof considering the meaning of *the vision* when the Lord steps in again. This time it is the voice of the Holy *Spirit* that tells Peter that the visitors are part of the divine plan. He is to *go with them* without question. To do so will mean that Peter is setting aside some of the ancient Jewish prohibitions against contact with Gentiles, as God intends. To go to Caesarea with these strangers will mean lodging in a Gentile home, and perhaps sitting down to a meal with Gentiles. Neither idea is appealing to a Jew who seeks to live according to the Law of Moses.

So it is that the voice of the Spirit interrupts Peter's thought process to send him to a destination where the gospel of Christ is needed. Peter needs to know that the journey ahead will come in connection with the mission of Christ. As is true in so many places in Acts, God directs His servant so that he comes into contact with those who need salvation (see Acts 8:26; 13:1-3; 16:9). [See question #5, page 82.]

Breaking Tradition

What comes to mind when I say, "traditional wedding"? This will depend on one's culture. For most western Christians, at least, it means a church wedding. Traditional weddings may also include a white bridal gown, a few attendants, and a reception featuring a multitiered wedding cake (again, depending on culture).

One of the strangest nontraditional weddings ever was held on August 10, 2003. The bride, Ekaterina Dmitriev, said her vows while looking at a television screen in Houston's Johnson Space Center. The groom, Yuri Malenchenko, was wearing a bow tie with his space suit while orbiting 240 miles overhead in the international space station. The groom's mother cried—that's traditional—but it was because she thought the whole thing was unnecessary sensationalism!

When Peter answered God's call, he was, in a sense, officiating at a nontraditional wedding. Cornelius, a Gentile, was becoming part of the church, the bride of Christ. This was contrary to the traditions Peter had known all his life. In a changing world, we sometimes must be willing to give up our traditions in order to reach

---

Home Daily Bible Readings

Monday, Oct. 17—Cornelius Has a Vision (Acts 10:1-8)

Tuesday, Oct. 18—Peter Has a Vision (Acts 10:9-16)

Wednesday, Oct. 19—Cornelius's Men Call on Peter (Acts 10:17-22)

Thursday, Oct. 20—Peter Visits Cornelius (Acts 10:23-33)

Friday, Oct. 21—Peter Shares the Good News (Acts 10:34-43)

Saturday, Oct. 22—Gentiles Receive the Holy Spirit (Acts 10:44-48)

Sunday, Oct. 23—Peter Explains How Gentiles Also Believed (Acts 11:1-15)

the lost. So we must ask: Which of *our* traditions stand in the way of others who need Christ? —C. R. B.

Conclusion

A. Go into *All* the World

Peter's trip to see Cornelius was not without controversy. Peter's actions will bring criticism upon himself when, in Acts 11:1-18, he is called upon to answer to the charge of entering the home of a Gentile. Peter ably defends himself, and all agree that he did the right thing.

For too long believers have permitted the "Gentiles" of modern culture to remain those who are untouched with the gospel. Peter's vision tells us today that God disapproves when we pick and choose those members of society whom we think deserve the kingdom of God. All races and ethnic groups should hear the gospel. The Spirit is sending us to our own "Gentile city." How will we answer that call?

B. Prayer

God of love and mercy, help us to reach those of every nation who need Your saving grace. Encourage us to be ready for them with the gospel of Christ. Through Christ we pray, amen.

C. Thought to Remember

We have no right to build smaller doors for the kingdom than God originally designed.

Learning by Doing

This page contains an alternate lesson plan emphasizing learning activities. Classes desiring such student involvement will find these suggestions helpful.

Learning Goals

After participating in this lesson, each student will be able to:

1. List the events leading up to Peter's visit with Cornelius.
2. Discuss the prejudices that Peter and Cornelius had to overcome.
3. Acknowledge a personal struggle with prejudice and determine one way to overcome it.

Into the Lesson

Decorate your classroom with flags of various nations to represent the church's move to incorporate the Gentiles. Also display a large, face-shaped oval on the board. Label it, "The Ugly Face of Prejudice." Ask the class to suggest features on such a face. To get them started, sketch an eye and say, "an eye that looks down on others." Other possibilities include, "an ear that hears selectively," "an ear that hears only one tongue or dialect," "a mouth filled with criticism," and "an upturned nose of snobbery." Conclude by saying, "It is truly an ugly face."

Into the Word

Collect the following objects: Italian flag, toy sword, bag of coins, a clock set to 3:00, a leather object, a fancy dinner napkin, stuffed animals (two or three), a dirty rag, and a math flashcard bearing "3 x 1." Randomly display the items.

Then say to the class, "Before we read today's text, I want you to see some objects I have brought. After the reading, we will come back to them." Have a good oral reader read the text, and then ask, "How can you relate each of these objects to things in the text?"

Let the class make suggestions. One possible relationship for each is given here: the flag represents Cornelius's home and army band; the sword represents his rank as centurion; coins represent his generosity; the clock represents the "ninth hour," 3:00 P.M.; the leather object represents Simon the tanner; the napkin represents Peter's hunger; the stuffed animals represent the contents of the sheet from Heaven; the dirty rag represents the concept of unclean; the math flashcard represents the three times God gave the same message.

Prepare flashcards for the following words: *name, nationality, vocation, location, diet, piety, family, generosity, prayer, revelation, worship, sanctification*. Show these words one at a time and then say, "Some of these words are things that sometimes create prejudice while some are things that should eliminate prejudice. Let's separate these words into the two groups. Help me decide which words often are associated with prejudice and which words are likely to alleviate prejudice."

The first five words are factors often accompanying prejudice; the other seven are matters that should help alleviate or eliminate prejudice. Ask the class, "In what verse(s) do you see these words or ideas represented?"

Though a variety of responses may be accepted, here is a possibility for each: *name* and the fact that Latin, Greek, and Hebrew names are all included in the text; *nationality* and Cornelius being an Italian (Roman); *vocation* regarding the occupations of Cornelius and Simon; *location* and the prejudices that accompany country/continent differences; *diet* and the Jewish dietary law; *piety* and Cornelius's devoutness; *family* and the fact Cornelius's whole house followed his example; *generosity* and the willingness to give money to the needy; *prayer* and the submission to God that bespeaks equality; *revelation* and the need of both Cornelius and Peter for God to speak; *worship* and the fact that Cornelius's prayers and alms received God's commendation; *sanctification* and the fact that God can make clean in the manner that He chooses. (A similar activity is included in the student book.)

Into Life

Say, "Because of our life experiences, most of us carry some intrinsic prejudices that we have not allowed the Spirit to remove. I want us to have a time of silent prayer in which I will suggest areas of possible prejudice. If one of these areas is a hidden issue within you, stop and pray that God's Spirit will be given free rein as you seek to leave that prejudice behind. Let us pray."

In your prayer list various factors that result in prejudice. End with this prayer: "God, we know that You are the creator of all people and that all have eternal value to You. Help us by Your Spirit to value all people redemptively, as You do. In the name of the one who died for us all, even Jesus, amen."

Let's Talk It Over

These questions are designed to promote discussion of the lesson. The answers here are only discussion starters. Let your class talk it over from there.

1. Prejudice has been a scar on society from the earliest of times. Why is prejudice so prevalent? What are some forms of prejudice that we need to be aware of?

Prejudice is often ingrained into our lives from early childhood. The prejudices of one generation carry over to the next. Prejudice is often based upon pride. This pride considers those who are "like me" as being of most significance, with all others being inferior. Prejudice, a sin that appears in many forms, exists because of ignorance (or willful disregard) of the facts.

Prejudice may be racial or regional. Cultural differences, instead of being appreciated, are often a source of division and distrust. The sin of prejudice raises its ugly head along gender and economic lines as well. Further, those who have achieved a high educational level often look with disdain on those who are not as well educated. In turn, the less educated look with suspicion on those having college degrees. Often in the church we see prejudice concerning the denominational background someone comes from, the style of music someone prefers, or how people dress. Preachers themselves have experienced prejudice with regard to what school they attended.

2. Does God hear the prayers of lost (unsaved) people? Why, or why not? How can this text be used to help answer this question?

Cornelius, a man who had not been saved by the blood of Christ, was a praying man—and God was very much aware of his prayers. God, who knows all things, is certainly aware of the prayers of saved and unsaved alike.

We should note, however, that although God undoubtedly is *aware of* all prayers, that doesn't mean He *attends to* all prayers with equal interest (see Lamentations 3:44 and 1 Peter 3:7). God probably ignores prayers offered with wrong motives (see James 4:3). Cornelius was a man who prayed with right motives.

3. In ancient times as now, various religions of the world have specific times set aside for prayer. Is this important for modern Christians? Why, or why not?

These days we often like to talk about the personal nature of Christianity and our relationship to Christ. We abhor legalism and consider the idea of "specific prayer times" to be just that. This especially is true if such prayer times are decided by another.

So perhaps we take it a step further by not even setting aside personal time for prayer. This may be due to a fear of legalism, but it may also be due to simple laziness, busyness, or lack of appreciation for the power and purpose of prayer. We are sidetracked so easily by the activities of the day that we often forget to pray. A regular time for prayer, carved into our daily schedules, would keep us from forgetting. It would remind us constantly of our need to rely on God.

4. Even today there can be a tendency to hold to legalistic righteousness. Why is there often a preference to hold to legalistic requirements instead of to the freedom found in Christ?

Modern culture is steeped in what is called performance-based or outcomes-based assessment. But if this thinking is allowed to determine how we relate to God, it will mean that what we do is more important than what God has done in Christ. As a result, we may end up developing mental checklists of things (works) that we think we should do to get right (or stay right) with God. This gives us a feeling of control. But there is great freedom in knowing that Christ is in control (Galatians 5:1).

5. As God called on Peter to lay aside his prejudices or biases, He calls upon all of us to do so as well. In what ways might God be calling on you to overcome your prejudices or biases today?

A key way to lay aside prejudice is to learn to accept people as being created in the image of God. We show this in our churches as we make specific attempts to reach across those lines of prejudice that we may hold in order to fulfill the Great Commission (Matthew 28:19, 20). It may also mean reshaping our worship traditions, times of meeting, or programs to better reach another culture or generation.

Peter Escapes Prison

October 30
Lesson 9

DEVOTIONAL READING: Psalm 46.

BACKGROUND SCRIPTURE: Acts 12:1-17.

PRINTED TEXT: Acts 12:1-16.

Acts 12:1-16

1 Now about that time Herod the king stretched forth his hands to vex certain of the church.

2 And he killed James the brother of John with the sword.

3 And because he saw it pleased the Jews, he proceeded further to take Peter also. (Then were the days of unleavened bread.)

4 And when he had apprehended him, he put him in prison, and delivered him to four quaternions of soldiers to keep him; intending after Easter to bring him forth to the people.

5 Peter therefore was kept in prison: but prayer was made without ceasing of the church unto God for him.

6 And when Herod would have brought him forth, the same night Peter was sleeping between two soldiers, bound with two chains: and the keepers before the door kept the prison.

7 And, behold, the angel of the Lord came upon him, and a light shined in the prison: and he smote Peter on the side, and raised him up, saying, Arise up quickly. And his chains fell off from his hands.

8 And the angel said unto him, Gird thyself, and bind on thy sandals. And so he did. And he saith unto him, Cast thy garment about thee, and follow me.

9 And he went out, and followed him; and wist not that it was true which was done by the angel; but thought he saw a vision.

10 When they were past the first and the second ward, they came unto the iron gate that leadeth unto the city; which opened to them of his own accord: and they went out, and passed on through one street; and forthwith the angel departed from him.

11 And when Peter was come to himself, he said, Now I know of a surety, that the Lord hath sent his angel, and hath delivered me out of the hand of Herod, and from all the expectation of the people of the Jews.

12 And when he had considered the thing, he came to the house of Mary the mother of John, whose surname was Mark; where many were gathered together praying.

13 And as Peter knocked at the door of the gate, a damsel came to hearken, named Rhoda.

14 And when she knew Peter's voice, she opened not the gate for gladness, but ran in, and told how Peter stood before the gate.

15 And they said unto her, Thou art mad. But she constantly affirmed that it was even so. Then said they, It is his angel.

16 But Peter continued knocking: and when they had opened the door, and saw him, they were astonished.

GOLDEN TEXT: Behold, the angel of the Lord came upon him, and a light shined in the prison: and he smote Peter on the side, and raised him up, saying, Arise up quickly. And his chains fell off from his hands.—Acts 12:7.

> *You Will Be My Witnesses*
> Unit 2: In All Judea and Samaria
> (Lessons 5-9)

Lesson Aims

After participating in this lesson, each student will be able to:

1. Relate the sequence of events of Peter's imprisonment and escape.
2. Explain how prayer can lead to God providing escape from a seemingly impossible situation.
3. Identify a Christian in another country—perhaps a missionary supported by the church—who is in prison for preaching the gospel and pray together for God's intervention.

Lesson Outline

INTRODUCTION
    A. Facing Dangers
    B. Lesson Background
I. PETER'S ARREST (Acts 12:1-4)
    A. Herod's Persecution (vv. 1, 2)
    B. Herod's Plans (vv. 3, 4)
    History Repeating Itself
II. PETER'S ESCAPE (Acts 12:5-11)
    A. Appearance of the Angel (vv. 5-7)
    B. Instructions from the Angel (vv. 8-11)
III. PETER'S RETURN (Acts 12:12-16)
    A. Arrival and Prayer (v. 12)
    B. Knock and Answer (vv. 13, 14)
    C. Criticism and Amazement (vv. 15, 16)
    More Than One Kind of Prison
CONCLUSION
    A. Victory over Evil
    B. Prayer
    C. Thought to Remember

Introduction

A. Facing Dangers

We usually feel quite secure as we fly, don't we? But back in the 1930s it may not have been so safe. In *A Treasury of Humor*, Eric Johnson relates the following set of instructions from one of the first manuals for stewardesses—now called flight attendants: (1) Keep the clock and altimeter wound up. (2) Carry a railroad timetable in case the plane is grounded. (3) Warn the passengers against throwing their cigars and cigarettes out the windows. (4) Keep an eye on passengers when they go to the lavatory to be sure they don't mistakenly go out the emergency exit.

The dangers that these instructions guard against no longer exist, thankfully! But that doesn't mean that there are no longer any dangers associated with flying. Today we're always on the alert for terrorist attacks, for example. This kind of threat was virtually unknown in the 1930s. So one set of dangers has been replaced by another.

Today's lesson lets us observe how the first-century Christians faced certain dangers. The dangers we face as twenty-first-century Christians may be somewhat different, but the question is the same: How courageous are we when opponents spring up to hinder our witness for Christ? The example of the apostle Peter presses us to answer that question honestly and to take stock of our faith in God's ability to protect us.

B. Lesson Background

The apostles were natural targets as soon as the persecution of believers began. Luke (the author of the book of Acts) reports that they stayed in Jerusalem in spite of the pressure against the Christians (see Acts 8:1). Life could not have been easy for this hardy band. The martyrdom of Stephen brought a strong initiative from Jewish authorities to stamp out this group known as "the way" (see Acts 24:14). Jesus had called them to be His witnesses (Acts 1:8), but He never promised them that they would not suffer. Acts is a record of how the witness of the gospel spread throughout Jerusalem, then through Judea and Samaria, and to the world. In telling this story, Acts also relates some of the ways that the gospel was opposed, especially by Jewish authorities.

Today's lesson is a good time to remember that Palestine in the days of the apostles was still dominated by Roman rule. At times the Romans governed Palestine with proconsuls, or governors. At other times they used client-kings. (Sometimes they used both at once.) A client-king had authority only as Rome dictated. But if the king was governing efficiently in the eyes of Rome, then he had freedom to govern as he wished.

The Herodians were client-kings. Herod the Great (of Matthew 2:1-12) was shrewd in his political maneuvers. This gave him a prominent role as king in Palestine (37 B.C. to 4 B.C.). His sons, Herod Archelaus (see Matthew 2:22), Herod Philip (Luke 3:1), and Herod Antipas (Matthew 14:1, 2), each shared in rule over Palestine after the death of their father. The following generation of Herodians produced Herod Agrippa I, the Herod in today's lesson.

I. Peter's Arrest
(Acts 12:1-4)
A. Herod's Persecution (vv. 1, 2)

1. Now about that time Herod the king stretched forth his hands to vex certain of the church.

This particular *Herod the king* is Herod Agrippa I, the son of Aristobulus, who was a son of Herod the Great. The latter years of Herod the Great's reign were marked by jealousy, suspicion, and intrigue concerning potential rivals to his throne. So he had his son Aristobulus (among others) executed.

But the son of Aristobulus survived and was reared and educated in Rome. There he came into contact with Romans such as Claudius and his nephew Gaius, later to become emperors. Gaius (that is, Emperor Caligula) granted him this kingship in Palestine in about A.D. 37. When Claudius comes to power after Gaius (Caligula) is assassinated, he extends the authority of Herod Agrippa even further.

How to Say It

ARISTOBULUS. Uh-*ris*-toe-*bu*-lus (strong accent on *bu*).
CALIGULA. Kuh-*lig*-you-luh.
CLAUDIUS. *Claw*-dee-us.
DEUTERONOMY. Due-ter-*ahn*-uh-me.
GAIUS. *Gay*-us.
HEROD AGRIPPA. *Hair*-ud Uh-*grip*-puh.
HEROD ANTIPAS. *Hair*-ud *An*-tih-pus.
HEROD ARCHELAUS. *Hair*-ud Are-kuh-*lay*-us.
HERODIANS. Heh-*roe*-dee-unz.
JUDEA. Joo-*dee*-uh.
NABATAEN. *Nab*-uh-*tee*-un (strong accent on *tee*).
QUATERNIONS. kwa-*ter*-nee-unz.
SAMARIA. Suh-*mare*-ee-uh.

The phrase *stretched forth his hands* implies violence. Herod Agrippa I, like all the Herods, certainly is capable of ruling with blood on his hands. His reasons for attacking *the church* are not given in detail, but verse 3 (below) offers one of the motives for this violence.

2. And he killed James the brother of John with the sword.

This *James*, son of Zebedee, is the one frequently mentioned in the Gospels in company with Peter and *John* (see Matthew 4:21). This is not the James who is a half-brother of Jesus and important to the leadership of the church later (see Acts 15:13-21; Galatians 1:19; 2:9).

The death of the James mentioned here is the first martyrdom of the Twelve, since Stephen was not an apostle. The use of *the sword* represents death by beheading. The authority of Herod to administer capital punishment comes with his status as client-king under Roman dominion. This one-sentence notation about James lacks so many details that we would find interesting. How do the apostles handle this frightening new persecution? How does the family of James deal with it? What impact does it have on the church in Jerusalem? [See question #1, page 91.]

B. Herod's Plans (vv. 3, 4)

3. And because he saw it pleased the Jews, he proceeded further to take Peter also. (Then were the days of unleavened bread.)

The Herods are not respected in Jerusalem because they are of Nabataen, rather than Jewish, heritage. For this reason they spend much of their time considering how to deal with a sometimes hostile Jewish populace. In this case, King Herod perceives the Jewish approval of the execution of James and determines that executing *Peter* will also gain approval. [See question #2, page 91.]

The time of year, noted as *the days of unleavened bread*, corresponds with March–April. This seven-day event connects with the Passover feast (Exodus 23:15; 34:18; Deuteronomy 16:1-8; Luke 22:1). Since we know from sources outside the Bible that this King Herod dies in A.D. 44—an event that is described in Acts 12:23—we can assume that the arrest of Peter occurs around A.D. 43.

This arrest shows us the motivation for Herod's further action as one of seeking Jewish approval as it is timed with this feast. It is possible that

> **Home Daily Bible Readings**
>
> **Monday, Oct. 24**—Peter Heals One and Revives Another (Acts 9:32-42)
> **Tuesday, Oct. 25**—Jesus Is Tempted (Luke 4:1-13)
> **Wednesday, Oct. 26**—Jesus Prays in Gethsemane (Matthew 26:36-46)
> **Thursday, Oct. 27**—Jesus Dies on the Cross (Mark 15:33-37)
> **Friday, Oct. 28**—James Is Killed and Peter Imprisoned (Acts 12:1-5)
> **Saturday, Oct. 29**—An Angel Frees Peter from Prison (Acts 12:6-11)
> **Sunday, Oct. 30**—Peter Tells the Others What Happened (Acts 12:12-17)

Herod selects this timing to be parallel to the time of Jesus' own trials and crucifixion some 13 or 14 years previously, but this is just a guess.

4. And when he had apprehended him, he put him in prison, and delivered him to four quaternions of soldiers to keep him; intending after Easter to bring him forth to the people.

The *quaternions* are squads of four *soldiers,* so Peter is guarded by four squads with four soldiers in each squad—a total of 16. This number of squads corresponds to the four watches of the night and is an indication that Peter's guard is a full-time one. The use of *Easter* here in the *King James Version* does not imply that King Herod celebrates the resurrection of Christ. Rather, it is a way of speaking about the conclusion of the Passover feast, marked by Christians as Easter Sunday. The intent to bring Peter *forth to the people* speaks of an impending public trial.

History Repeating Itself

George Santayana (1863–1952) wrote, "Those who cannot remember the past are condemned to repeat it." His statement is understood more clearly in its popularized form, "Those who will not *learn* from the past . . . " History proves this truth. The war once called "the war to end all wars" is now known simply as World War I. In the 90 years since that war, World War II and many smaller wars have followed because political leaders are still sinful and humanity hasn't yet learned how to deal with the problem. So we keep repeating the past.

The Herods didn't learn the lesson either. As is the case with so many others, their perverted ambition got in the way. Agrippa probably looked back at the popular support that Herod Antipas enjoyed when he agreed with Pilate's execution of Jesus. Ignoring the fact of Jesus' resurrection, Agrippa may have thought Jesus' death at Passover made it an auspicious time to kill James. When he saw the public favor he gained by that evil act, he thought to do the same with Peter. But he wasn't counting on God's intervention. Evildoers ignore the lessons of the past.

Christians should remember the other side of the equation: If we learn the lessons of biblical history, we will find that righteousness eventually prevails and those who practice it are blessed. It may not happen immediately, but God always keeps His promises. —C. R. B.

II. Peter's Escape
(Acts 12:5-11)
A. Appearance of the Angel (vv. 5-7)

5. Peter therefore was kept in prison: but prayer was made without ceasing of the church unto God for him.

Imprisonment in the Roman world usually means that the prisoner is condemned to die already or that hearings are scheduled. Unlike modern systems, prisoners generally are not held for long periods of time.

The book of Acts presents an interesting contrast: while Peter is locked up in prison, *the church* is praying. Note that nothing is said about the content of their prayers. It does not say, for example, that the church is praying for Peter's release. Perhaps they are, perhaps not. With the martyrdom of Stephen and James on their minds, their prayers most likely include a request for Peter to have courage to face the persecution coming against him. In fact, it is an act of courage for the church to assemble under these circumstances. [See question #3, page 91.]

6. And when Herod would have brought him forth, the same night Peter was sleeping between two soldiers, bound with two chains: and the keepers before the door kept the prison.

Peter's faith is obvious: on the very night before his probable execution he is *sleeping* peacefully while surrounded by guards! [See question #4, page 91.] The *two soldiers* mentioned are the ones to whom Peter is chained. The other two soldiers (from this particular shift of four soldiers) stand guard at *the door.*

7. And, behold, the angel of the Lord came upon him, and a light shined in the prison: and he smote Peter on the side, and raised him up, saying, Arise up quickly. And his chains fell off from his hands.

Our text now describes a *prison* escape like no other! The fact that the initiative is from God and not from *Peter* is emphasized. *The angel of the Lord* arrives in the cell and the *light* shines, perhaps similar to the night of Jesus' birth when the glory of the Lord shone around the shepherds (Luke 2:9). Peter's sleepiness is another emphasis in the account. He is far too sleepy to engineer his own escape, and the angel even has to tell him how to get dressed (next verse).

B. Instructions from the Angel (vv. 8-11)

8. And the angel said unto him, Gird thyself, and bind on thy sandals. And so he did. And he saith unto him, Cast thy garment about thee, and follow me.

The angel's instructions to Peter about getting dressed are a reminder of the clothing styles of the day. To *gird* means that Peter will wrap around his waist a wide cloth belt. Binding up the *sandals* consists of wrapping the long leather straps around the calf. Peter has dressed himself countless times before, of course, so the fact that the angel must give instructions indicates how sleepy Peter is. He certainly is too sleepy to mastermind his own escape!

9. And he went out, and followed him; and wist not that it was true which was done by the angel; but thought he saw a vision.

Peter is sure that his senses are fooling him. "I must be dreaming," he undoubtedly thinks. His groggy condition does not allow him to consider any of this as real. Nevertheless, he obeys the instructions of *the angel* and walks out of the cell.

10. When they were past the first and the second ward, they came unto the iron gate that leadeth unto the city; which opened to them of his own accord: and they went out, and passed on through one street; and forthwith the angel departed from him.

The guards are apparently in a deep sleep, perhaps brought on by the Lord (compare Matthew 28:4). Of course, all of this is done by the power of God alone. The entire episode is more properly thought of as a "release" than an "escape," because Peter could do none of it himself. *The angel* eventually disappears, his task finished.

11. And when Peter was come to himself, he said, Now I know of a surety, that the Lord hath sent his angel, and hath delivered me out of the hand of Herod, and from all the expectation of the people of the Jews.

Now, for the first time, *Peter* realizes for sure that this is reality and not a dream. His rescue is from *Herod,* who exercised authority in executing James. Peter also is rescued from *the Jews* because it is the Jewish leadership who approved that execution (see 12:3, above). In the book of Acts, frequently there are Jewish voices behind the decision of a ruler under Roman dominion who passes judgment or makes a decision concerning believers. See Acts 18:12; 19:32-41; 24:1-4; 25:1-5.

III. Peter's Return
(Acts 12:12-16)
A. Arrival and Prayer (v. 12)

12. And when he had considered the thing, he came to the house of Mary the mother of John, whose surname was Mark; where many were gathered together praying.

In verse 5 we saw that the church was *praying.* Now we learn one of the locations for this prayer. The mention of *John, whose surname was Mark* introduces a personality who will appear as a missionary traveler with Paul (Acts 13:5). Here we learn that his *mother* is a certain *Mary,* and that she owns a *house* in Jerusalem large enough for the believers to meet for prayer. Most people in the ancient world do not venture from their homes at night, so these believers are demonstrating dedication in being absent from their own homes to attend this prayer meeting.

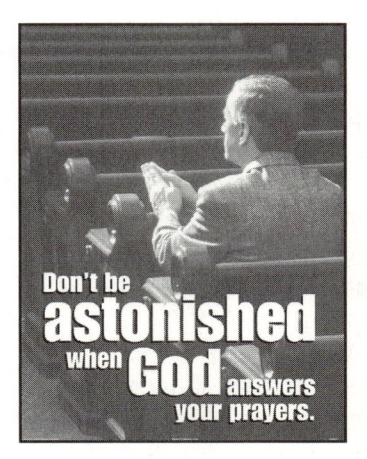

Use this visual as you discuss the astonishment mentioned in verse 16.

Visual for lesson 9

B. Knock and Answer (vv. 13, 14)

13, 14. And as Peter knocked at the door of the gate, a damsel came to hearken, named Rhoda. And when she knew Peter's voice, she opened not the gate for gladness, but ran in, and told how Peter stood before the gate.

Peter's knocking, which perhaps goes on for several minutes, endangers him further. The soldiers might be close behind. This house is a large one, since an outer *gate* is mentioned. *Rhoda,* probably a servant girl, answers the knock. Her reaction is somewhat amusing. She cannot believe this is really Peter even though she personally hears his *voice.* She is so stunned that she dashes back inside without even letting Peter in!

C. Criticism and Amazement (vv. 15, 16)

15. And they said unto her, Thou art mad. But she constantly affirmed that it was even so. Then said they, It is his angel.

This verse often brings forth the criticism that the church in Jerusalem does not have enough faith. This criticism says that here they are praying for Peter's release, and when he is released they do not believe it. In other words, they cannot accept the answer to their own prayers.

The problem is that Acts does not say they were praying for Peter's release. Their reaction to the news that *Peter* is standing at *the gate* is more consistent with the notion that they fully expect Peter's execution, and that they are praying that he will meet the trial with faith. Thus the theory of those present that this is Peter's *angel.*

16. But Peter continued knocking: and when they had opened the door, and saw him, they were astonished.

Luke (the author of the book of Acts) heightens the drama of Peter's release by reporting Peter's *continued knocking* at the gate. All this noise out on the street does nothing at all to contribute to Peter's safety! Nevertheless, Peter's release is secured by a power greater than all of Herod's forces. [See question #5, page 91.]

When believers place their trust in the Lord to face dangerous times, the will of God always wins out. This is not to guarantee that every believer will escape the sword. We could ask the family of the apostle James about that! But whether saints are spared paying the ultimate price or are forced to yield up this earthly existence at the hands of some evil power such as Herod, the promise of Acts is that the Word of God will run free.

This victory of God's truth will come no matter what attempts are made to silence the messengers of Christ. In fact before chapter 12 of Acts closes, the evil king who murdered the apostle James and tried to eliminate the voice of the apostle Peter must accept death himself. He can find no escape because his death is brought on by the same Lord who opened the prison doors for the apostle Peter (see again Acts 12:23).

By this point, the believers understand that this is indeed *Peter* and not an angel. Now they recognize that God has performed a miraculous work, and they are as *astonished* as at any time when powerful deeds of God are seen. This reaction is exactly the one that is recorded so often in the Gospels when people witnessed the miracles of Jesus (Luke 7:16; 9:43; etc.).

More Than One Kind of Prison

How to Break Out of Prison is the cleverly misleading title of John Wareham's recent book. One day a week, the author goes to Rikers Island prison in New York to teach a class of inmates how to change the negative thinking that put them there. Wareham has discovered that executives of large corporations sometimes use those same kinds of negative thinking patterns! The result is that they short-circuit their careers and destroy their family lives.

Although written for corporate executives, the book's principles apply to the lives of us all. Wareham discusses the ways we can get stuck in doing things one way. It may never occur to us that new ways of performing a given task might allow us to work more productively. Ironically, we may even strongly resist when someone suggests a different approach! (It even happens in churches, doesn't it?) Wareham calls this a "mental prison" that can confine our lives and restrain our potential as surely as stone walls and steel bars.

The church's amazement at Peter's escape surprises us at first. Was this what they were praying for or not? Their disheartenment had become a prison! But as we think about it, we begin to realize that prisons of stone and steel (or of doubt and discouragement) cannot confine God. Has *our* church ever tried to limit God in the prison of our negative thinking? —C. R. B.

Conclusion

A. Victory over Evil

Today's passage does not guarantee that all believers will escape the hands of their tormentors. Church tradition holds that Peter eventually will embrace his own martyrdom in Rome. If victory means expecting to escape the trials that come against us, then modern Christians will be sadly disappointed. What is guaranteed is that even though all earthly forces may assemble against the Word of God, they cannot prevail. Victory for God's truth is assured. Evil kings can try to silence God's messengers, but the Lord will break the chains and spring open the doors so that the truth can run free.

Our role as witnesses gives us the privilege of participating in this universal victory over the evil one. So when God chooses to intervene on our behalf and snap the chains or spring open the doors, we should never accept these actions selfishly. It is not because we have attained a special holiness that God moves on our behalf. But because we serve faithfully as His messengers, we gain the joy of experiencing the victories that come.

B. Prayer

Almighty God, we trust this day in You, because Your power is superior to all the forces on earth that want to harm Christians. We ask for the courage of Jesus who made the good confession before Pontius Pilate and faithfully spoke Your truth. In Jesus' name, amen.

C. Thought to Remember

God lets us participate in His victories, and the evil one is reminded constantly that his days are numbered.

Learning by Doing

This page contains an alternate lesson plan emphasizing learning activities. Classes desiring such student involvement will find these suggestions helpful.

Learning Goals

After participating in this lesson, each student will be able to:

1. Relate the sequence of events of Peter's imprisonment and escape.
2. Explain how prayer can lead to God providing escape from a seemingly impossible situation.
3. Identify a Christian in another country—perhaps a missionary supported by the church—who is in prison for preaching the gospel and pray together for God's intervention.

Into the Lesson

Say, "Today's text introduces one of the Bible's bad guys. Listen to the following statements and identify which 'Bible bad guy' is in mind."

1. "I had a wonderful world to live in, but I killed my brother in a fit of anger." *(Cain)*
2. "I was God's choice to lead His people as their first king, but my own will negated His choice." *(King Saul)*
3. "Gifted by God, I let my lusts and pride overcome me. I ended up blinded, then dead." *(Samson)*
4. "I had such an egocentric view that God caused me to go mad and live like an animal, eating grass." *(Nebuchadnezzar)*
5. "Hearing about someone being born to become king was enough for me to act. Young boys had to die!" *(Herod the Great)*
6. "I acted just like my grandfather. I would do almost anything to appease the Jews I ruled over." *(Herod Agrippa I)* If no one guesses number six, identify him as the bad guy in today's text.

Into the Word

Distribute paper and pens. Say, "I want you to do something you probably haven't done since first grade. I want you to trace an outline of your hand." Let them do so.

Next, say, "Now as I read our text a verse at a time, listen and write something a person either does with his or her hand or a use of the hand in the text that could be inferred." Read verse 1 and give them an example: use the hand to attack another person. Here are other examples from today's text: use a weapon to kill another (v. 2); eat ceremonial foods such as Passover and communion (v. 3); keep a person confined (v. 4); lift them up in prayer (v. 5); hold restraints such as chains or handcuffs (v. 6); touch or shake another person (v. 7); put on clothes and shoes (v. 8); open doors or gates (v. 10); knock on a door (v. 13); gesture dramatically, trying to convince someone you are telling the truth (v. 15); point (to where Peter was at the door; v. 14).

Class members may suggest other uses. If they need help, ask them a question such as, "What did the angel do to Peter, as verse 7 records?"

As an alternative way to get students to look at the text, say, "Because the stories in Acts are of real people in real history, we see the full range of human emotions. Look at today's text, Acts 12:1-16, and identify a verse number wherein each of the following emotions and behaviors (given in alphabetical order) are shown or implied": astonishment (v. 16); curiosity (v. 9); faith (v. 11); fear (generally); gladness (v. 14); grief (v. 2); hope (v. 5); hostility (v. 1); irritation (v. 15); patience (v. 5); persistence (v. 16); pleasure (v. 3); shock (v. 7); surprise (v. 7); unity of purpose (v. 12).

Your students may suggest other possibilities. (A related activity is included in the student book; however, the words are scrambled.)

Into Life

As a group, make a short list of Christians who struggle with difficult life circumstances. After a list of four or five is made, ask for that same number of volunteers to invite several class members into their homes for a short prayer meeting to pray for one of those specific situations during the coming week. Before closing, give volunteers time to arrange such a meeting with others. Use the following words as a reminder: "Assembling in someone's home for the purpose of praying for someone in distress is simply part of following the example of the first-century church, as in today's text."

If time permits, make a list of elements that would be appropriate for such prayers: the faith of the person in distress, the comfort of that person's family, the opportunity of that person to witness to the gospel, a growing sense of compassion and concern within the praying group, etc.

Let's Talk It Over

These questions are designed to promote discussion of the lesson. The answers here are only discussion starters. Let your class talk it over from there.

1. Persecution of Christians is still prevalent in our world, though not much is heard about it in the media. Why are modern Christians often apathetic or ignorant of this? What can be done to raise the awareness of this tragic practice?

"Out of sight, out of mind" may be the problem. Yet simple Internet searches can reveal the sobering statistics about the persecution of Christians. The Web site www.persecutedchurch.org is excellent. It gives information regarding an International Day of Prayer to be held on behalf of the persecuted church. Participation in this event can expose your congregation to the worldwide plight of persecuted Christians. Often we get so wrapped up in what is happening locally that we lose sight of the global picture of the church.

2. For every tyrant who falls there seem to be two to take his place. They thrive by oppressing others. How should the church respond?

First, we should recognize that oppressive situations do exist. The church can ask God to show it how to respond—prayer comes first. Though the church may not have the political influence to remove tyrants, Christians can support the government in its efforts to rid the world of evil leaders.

But the church's greatest contribution to stopping evil in the world is the presentation of the good news of Christ. It does little good to remove a tyrant from power if the power vacuum that results simply means that more evil will come in from a different direction (compare Luke 11:24-26).

3. Ephesians 6:18 and 1 Thessalonians 5:17 encourage prayer at all times and in all situations. How can your church improve its prayer life for the work of God's kingdom?

We often hear the humorous line, "When all else fails, read the directions." Sometimes the church and Christians live by the principle, "When all else fails, pray." The idea is that we do all we can first, then we ask God to take over only after our efforts fall flat.

A more Biblical principle is to pray at all times—before, during, and after our efforts for Him. The restoration of prayer meetings is a vital need in the church. Time focused on prayer is not wasted time. These times of prayer should include *specific* concerns, with spiritual issues predominating. Often our prayer time amounts to little more than a listing of the names of those who are sick. Sometimes we also throw in vague, general prayers for "those who need Christ."

Specific prayers for specific needs are so much better! Regularly sharing prayer concerns and updating prayer lists for the church is another way to be sure that the importance of prayer is foremost in our minds. Many churches take advantage of e-mail and Web sites in this regard.

4. We may find it amazing that Peter was able to sleep in a situation such as this! How can someone be at peace when his or her life seems to be crumbling all around?

For the Christian, this feeling of peace is rooted in a faith for the future that is based on the evidence of God's promises kept in the past. It is in this regard that faith provides for us the "substance of things hoped for" (Hebrews 11:1).

Coupled with our faith are the shining examples of Christians who have endured tough times—even martyrdom. We also remember that in Christ we can't lose. The worst that the world can do to us is to kill our earthly bodies, which are temporary anyway. Even if our lives are required of us, we know that, "to live is Christ, and to die is gain" (Philippians 1:21).

5. God delivered Peter from jail, and God is still in "the delivery business." How have you experienced God's deliverance in your life? How can you tell the difference between God's deliverance and the successes that we have by our own power?

Answers will, of course, be highly personal. God has provided relief and deliverance from sickness for many. For others, financial struggles seemed to have won the day, but God provided a way out. Marriages that appeared to be beyond hope have been restored by the power of God. And the greatest deliverance of all is that God delivers us from death to life, from the hopelessness of Hell to the gates of Heaven—through the cross and resurrection of Jesus Christ.

November 6
Lesson 10

Paul Meets the Lord

DEVOTIONAL READING: Acts 9:23-31.

BACKGROUND SCRIPTURE: Acts 9:1-31.

PRINTED TEXT: Acts 9:3-18.

Acts 9:3-18

3 And as he journeyed, he came near Damascus: and suddenly there shined round about him a light from heaven:

4 And he fell to the earth, and heard a voice saying unto him, Saul, Saul, why persecutest thou me?

5 And he said, Who art thou, Lord? And the Lord said, I am Jesus whom thou persecutest: it is hard for thee to kick against the pricks.

6 And he trembling and astonished said, Lord, what wilt thou have me to do? And the Lord said unto him, Arise, and go into the city, and it shall be told thee what thou must do.

7 And the men which journeyed with him stood speechless, hearing a voice, but seeing no man.

8 And Saul arose from the earth; and when his eyes were opened, he saw no man: but they led him by the hand, and brought him into Damascus.

9 And he was three days without sight, and neither did eat nor drink.

10 And there was a certain disciple at Damascus, named Ananias; and to him said the Lord in a vision, Ananias. And he said, Behold, I am here, Lord.

11 And the Lord said unto him, Arise, and go into the street which is called Straight, and inquire in the house of Judas for one called Saul, of Tarsus: for, behold, he prayeth,

12 And hath seen in a vision a man named Ananias coming in, and putting his hand on him, that he might receive his sight.

13 Then Ananias answered, Lord, I have heard by many of this man, how much evil he hath done to thy saints at Jerusalem:

14 And here he hath authority from the chief priests to bind all that call on thy name.

15 But the Lord said unto him, Go thy way: for he is a chosen vessel unto me, to bear my name before the Gentiles, and kings, and the children of Israel:

16 For I will show him how great things he must suffer for my name's sake.

17 And Ananias went his way, and entered into the house; and putting his hands on him said, Brother Saul, the Lord, even Jesus, that appeared unto thee in the way as thou camest, hath sent me, that thou mightest receive thy sight, and be filled with the Holy Ghost.

18 And immediately there fell from his eyes as it had been scales: and he received sight forthwith, and arose, and was baptized.

GOLDEN TEXT: Immediately there fell from his eyes as it had been scales: and he received sight forthwith, and arose, and was baptized.—Acts 9:18.

LESSON 10 93 NOVEMBER 6

> *You Will Be My Witnesses*
> Unit 3: Unto the Uttermost Part of the Earth
> (Lessons 10-13)

Lesson Aims

After participating in this lesson, each student will be able to:
1. Summarize Saul's conversion experience.
2. Explain the significance of Saul's conversion.
3. Praise God for one specific way his or her life has been changed by knowing God.

Lesson Outline

INTRODUCTION
    A. Zero Tolerance
    B. Lesson Background
 I. HEAVENLY VOICE (Acts 9:3-9)
    A. Light from Heaven (v. 3)
    B. Voice from the Lord (vv. 4-6)
    C. Surprise of Saul's Companions (vv. 7-9)
 II. FAITHFUL MESSENGER (Acts 9:10-16)
    A. Command to Ananias (vv. 10-12)
    B. Concerns of Ananias (vv. 13, 14)
        The Meanest Man Alive
    C. Answer for Ananias (vv. 15, 16)
 III. CONVERTED TORMENTOR (Acts 9:17, 18)
    A. Visit from Ananias (v. 17)
    B. Baptism of Saul (v. 18)
        A New Way of Seeing
CONCLUSION
    A. Transforming Power
    B. Prayer
    C. Thought to Remember

Introduction

A. Zero Tolerance

College basketball fans know the name of Bobby Knight, the former coach of the Indiana University basketball team. His reputation was built not only on winning, but also on a manner of handling the press that was direct, and sometimes tactless. At times he also exhibited a red hot temper during games that he coached. When the university officials grew tired of repairing damage caused by Knight's outbursts, they established a zero-tolerance policy with him. He was not permitted one infraction that involved control of his temper or abuse of a student, a player, or a member of the media.

After the policy was announced, Knight soon violated it, and he was fired. Someone said afterward that it is good that God does not establish a zero-tolerance policy toward us, or who would be able to stand in the judgment?

Today's lesson about the conversion of Saul of Tarsus challenges us to remember that the gospel is more powerful than our sin. God's policy toward us does not rule us out after one slip. Instead, God confronts us with the gospel of grace.

B. Lesson Background

The book of Acts specializes in unlikely conversions. Philip preaches to a Samaritan sorcerer named Simon and converts him to Christ (Acts 8:4-13). Peter preaches the gospel in the home of the Gentile Cornelius and converts him to Christ (Acts 10:25-48). Paul preaches the gospel to some skeptical intellectuals in Athens and converts some of them to Christ (Acts 17:16-34).

What an impact the powerful gospel of Christ can have! A main theme of Acts is witnessing "unto the uttermost part of the earth" (Acts 1:8), and these preachers carried out that mission. Saul of Tarsus (later called Paul, beginning in Acts 13:9) is a vital part of this story. He began to persecute the church fiercely after the martyrdom of Stephen (Acts 8:1-3). We may say that the church was under a terrorist attack, and that the attack came from a tormentor who created a climate of fear (Acts 9:1).

Saul of Tarsus had participated in the execution of Stephen by guarding the coats of those who were throwing the stones (Acts 7:58–8:1; 22:20). Saul's authority to round up Christians in Damascus included letters from the high priest, who presided over the Sanhedrin (Acts 9:2). This authority has been called into question because the Sanhedrin, based in Jerusalem, normally did not exercise authority over synagogues as far away as Damascus. Acts does not, however, elaborate on the content of these letters from the high priest. They may not have been documents with legal authority, but letters recommending that the synagogues take action against believers in Jesus. Such recommendations would carry much weight for those who respected the temple leadership in Jerusalem.

Saul's conversion was a landmark event in the life of the church. [See question #1, page 100.] Acts highlights the event by presenting the full account three times—in Acts 9:1-19; 22:1-21; and 26:1-18—with some variation in details. Today's lesson explores the first of these accounts in Acts and examines the effects of the powerful gospel of God's grace on a sinful life.

I. Heavenly Voice
(Acts 9:3-9)
A. Light from Heaven (v. 3)

3. And as he journeyed, he came near Damascus: and suddenly there shined round about him a light from heaven.

Saul probably walks the 150 miles from Jerusalem to *Damascus.* This is a city of great historical significance, mentioned more than 40 times in the Old Testament. The journey takes about a week to complete, so there can be no doubt about Saul's commitment to arresting Christians.

The expression *light shined round about him* is similar to the description in Luke 2:9, which tells us of the appearance of the angels to the shepherds in the field on the night of Jesus' birth. There the light is specifically "the glory of the Lord." The brilliant light in the passage before us bathes Saul in its brightness. He is about to receive a message from the Lord.

B. Voice from the Lord (vv. 4-6)

4. And he fell to the earth, and heard a voice saying unto him, Saul, Saul, why persecutest thou me?

Saul's reaction to the blinding light is to fall to the ground. The voice is from Jesus (see v. 5, next). Calling *Saul* by name twice seems to emphasize that the words are meant for him alone. The question put to Saul involves his actions against the believers, but the words are personal: *Why persecutest thou me?* When Saul persecutes Christians, he is persecuting Jesus. Jesus makes the same point in His parable about the sheep and the goats when He says that God will announce at the judgment that what was done or not done for the brothers was, in fact, done or not done to Jesus himself (Matthew 25:31-46). Saul is about to learn that hurting Christians means hurting Jesus. [See question #2, page 100.]

5. And he said, Who art thou, Lord? And the Lord said, I am Jesus whom thou persecutest: it is hard for thee to kick against the pricks.

Saul's first reaction is to call very respectfully for the identity of the voice. The use of the word *Lord* in his question does not necessarily mean that he is confessing Jesus as Lord just yet. The term can also be translated *sir.*

The phrase *it is hard for thee to kick against the pricks* does not occur in the earliest Greek manuscripts of this particular verse. However, this phrase is also found in Acts 26:14, so we know for sure that this is what Saul heard. Jesus' figure of speech about animal prods *(pricks)* makes the point about Saul's tactics against the believers. Saul's persecution of Christians amounts to resisting God, much like an animal resists being moved, even though a sharp stick is being used to jab it in the side or hind quarters.

Jesus thus reveals how contrary to the will of God is Saul's campaign against the believers. Later in life the apostle will acknowledge this when he admits that he did not deserve to be called an apostle because he persecuted the church (1 Corinthians 15:9). Yet he will maintain that he persecuted believers because of ignorance and that he found forgiveness through the grace of the Lord (1 Timothy 1:12-14).

6. And he trembling and astonished said, Lord, what wilt thou have me to do? And the Lord said unto him, Arise, and go into the city, and it shall be told thee what thou must do.

The 20 words that come before *Arise* are not found in the earliest Greek manuscripts. However, Saul's question is very similar to what we see in Acts 22:10, part of a parallel account of this event. Thus accuracy is maintained as we

---

How to Say It

ANANIAS. An-uh-*nye*-us.
ATHENS. *Ath*-unz.
BATHSHEBA. Bath-*she*-buh.
CORNELIUS. Cor-*neel*-yus.
DAMASCUS. Duh-*mass*-kus.
GENTILE. *Jen*-tile.
ISAIAH. Eye-*zay*-uh.
JERUSALEM. Juh-*roo*-suh-lem.
MESSIAH. Meh-*sigh*-uh.
NEHEMIAH. *Nee*-huh-*my*-uh (strong accent on *my*).
SAMARITAN. Suh-*mare*-uh-tun.
SANHEDRIN. *San*-huh-drun or San-*heed*-run.
SYNAGOGUE. *sin*-uh-gog.
TARSUS. *Tar*-sus.

see the full force of the revelation hit Saul. His reaction resembles that of others who saw an appearance of God's glory. Isaiah saw the glory of the Lord in the temple and was humbled by his sin (Isaiah 6:1-7). Peter realized he was face to face with the Lord in the boat and reacted with similar humility (Luke 5:1-11).

Saul's question reveals a heart ready to do God's will. The Lord's instructions are to *go into the city* of Damascus, where Saul is headed anyway. The parallel account in Acts 26:16-18 includes instructions that describe the ministry that Saul will be called to fulfill (also in Acts 9:15, 16). Here the Lord's words include an allusion to the visit by Ananias (see 9:10-18, below).

C. Surprise of Saul's Companions (vv. 7-9)

7. And the men which journeyed with him stood speechless, hearing a voice, but seeing no man.

Saul's fellow travelers do not see the one speaking to Saul. They do not comprehend what is happening. Acts 22:9 offers us a similar description.

8, 9. And Saul arose from the earth; and when his eyes were opened, he saw no man: but they led him by the hand, and brought him into Damascus. And he was three days without sight, and neither did eat nor drink.

Saul's blindness reduces him to helplessness. But his refusal to *eat* or *drink* is an indication of his humiliation at hearing the words of Jesus on the road. He is humbled at the judgment pronounced by Jesus, because he now realizes that he has been persecuting the people of God. Fasting in the Bible is connected frequently with sorrow. David fasted after his sin with Bathsheba and the sickness of his son (2 Samuel 12:13-23). Nehemiah fasted because of his sorrow over the disgraceful condition of Jerusalem (Nehemiah 1:4). Saul's fasting probably indicates his sorrow for his own sin and his repentance before God.

Thus the book of Acts shows us the image of the fierce persecutor of the church brought to his knees before the Lord whom he persecuted. The powerful gospel reaches into Saul's heart. The knowledge that Jesus is really the Messiah will capture Saul completely. His transformation is about to begin.

Modern believers should not be surprised about the powerful impact of Christ on wayward sinners. We can all think of examples of people who came face to face with Christ, and the change was dramatic. The truth of Jesus Christ still operates with this power today. No wonder we are called to be witnesses of this truth (Acts 1:8)! [See question #3, page 100.]

II. Faithful Messenger
(Acts 9:10-16)
A. Command to Ananias (vv. 10-12)

10. And there was a certain disciple at Damascus, named Ananias; and to him said the Lord in a vision, Ananias. And he said, Behold, I am here, Lord.

Using the term *disciple* to describe *Ananias* reminds us that early Christians are often referred to by this term (see Acts 11:26, 29; 14:20, 28). Ananias is a follower of Christ because he has accepted the gospel as true and has identified himself with those who acknowledge Jesus as *Lord*.

Ananias's response to the voice of God is similar to what Eli instructed young Samuel to offer when he heard God's voice. The boy was told to respond with, "Speak; for thy servant heareth" (1 Samuel 3:10). When Isaiah heard the voice of the Lord in the vision in the temple, he responded with "Here am I; send me" (Isaiah 6:8). Ananias answers in a way that demonstrates his obedience.

11, 12. And the Lord said unto him, Arise, and go into the street which is called Straight, and inquire in the house of Judas for one called Saul, of Tarsus: for, behold, he prayeth, and hath seen in a vision a man named Ananias

---

Home Daily Bible Readings

Monday, Oct. 31—Jesus Calls Disciples and Changes Lives (Luke 5:4-11)

Tuesday, Nov. 1—Peter Responds to Criticism from Believers (Acts 11:1-10)

Wednesday, Nov. 2—The Believers in Jerusalem Praise God (Acts 11:11-18)

Thursday, Nov. 3—Saul Sees the Glorified Christ (Acts 9:1-9)

Friday, Nov. 4—Ananias Receives Instructions in a Vision (Acts 9:10-16)

Saturday, Nov. 5—Saul Begins to Proclaim Jesus (Acts 9:17-22)

Sunday, Nov. 6—Saul Proclaims Jesus in Jerusalem (Acts 9:23-31)

coming in, and putting his hand on him, that he might receive his sight.

In the case of *Ananias,* the voice of *the Lord* speaks for the purpose of sending a disciple on a mission, as with Isaiah. This particular Ananias is not known elsewhere in the New Testament. He is not an apostle or a prophet, but apparently an "ordinary" believer who now receives an active role in the drama of Saul's conversion. Acts 22:12 describes Ananias as a Jew devoted to following the Law of Moses and highly respected among other Jews in the city. [See question #4, page 100.]

Even the address for finding *Saul* is included. The description of Saul being in prayer implies that his heart is ready for receiving the Word of the Lord. The vision presents a summary of what Ananias is to do when he comes to see Saul. Ananias will say and do even more than what is noted briefly here, as the book of Acts makes clear.

The street which is called Straight runs east and west through the city. This street is a colonnaded thoroughfare enclosed with gates at both ends. Of course, the irony that Saul of Tarsus is now ready to walk the "straight and narrow" pathway cannot be missed (compare Matthew 7:14). The disciple named *Judas* mentioned here is unknown elsewhere in the New Testament.

B. Concerns of Ananias (vv. 13, 14)

13, 14. Then Ananias answered, Lord, I have heard by many of this man, how much evil he hath done to thy saints at Jerusalem: and here he hath authority from the chief priests to bind all that call on thy name.

This fearful reaction from *Ananias* certainly is easy to understand, given the reputation of Saul for locking up Christians as prisoners (9:2). The letters carried by Saul from *the chief priests,* though not legally binding on the synagogues north of *Jerusalem,* would carry *authority* because of the high level of respect for the Jerusalem leadership. The words of Ananias seem to imply that he has heard reports about Saul, but has not been involved personally in the persecution in Jerusalem. Thus he is probably not one of those believers scattered from Jerusalem (Acts 8:1). His mention of *thy name* is a reference to the name of Jesus, as in verse 15 (below).

Ananias does not speak these words out of disrespect for the Lord's command, but as a natural reaction of fear. There are times in the service of the Lord that fear of those who will do bodily harm is a factor in deciding when and where to serve. Paul's preaching in several cases is adjusted according to the dangers of angry opponents (see Acts 13:51; 14:20; 19:30). [See question #5, page 100.]

THE MEANEST MAN ALIVE

George Foreman is best known today as a smiling pitchman for his line of barbecue grills. Yet there was a time when many considered him the meanest man alive. His brute strength and ugly disposition made him a greatly feared boxer, and he became heavyweight champion in 1973. Then on March 17, 1977, Foreman lost a fight he should have won easily. That night, in his despair, he turned to Christ and quit boxing. A boxing historian calls the event "one of the greatest turnarounds in history in terms of persona and likability."

Foreman returned to boxing ten years after his conversion because he needed money to support the recreational center he had started for poor urban youth. In one of the greatest comebacks in boxing history, he became heavyweight champion of the world in 1994 at age 45! Today he is a preacher at a small church in Houston, supported largely by the profits from his grill business.

It is hard not to see at least a faint parallel between the "before" and "after" pictures of George Foreman and Saul of Tarsus. Ruthlessness had characterized the earthly careers of both. Yet Christ is the one who can turn such lives around—for eternity. Christ works in the lives of sinful, mean, and surly people to remake them in His loving image. How much work does God still have to do in us?   —C. R. B.

C. Answer for Ananias (vv. 15, 16)

15, 16. But the Lord said unto him, Go thy way: for he is a chosen vessel unto me, to bear my name before the Gentiles, and kings, and the children of Israel: for I will show him how great things he must suffer for my name's sake.

The Lord speaks in order to ease the anxiety of Ananias. God's purposes for Saul are revealed so that Ananias can understand that there is a divine use for this life that had created such havoc for the church. Saul will be a *chosen vessel* (figuratively, a favorite water jug or a special vase) for the master in a way similar to Old Testament Israel as a cho-

Visual for lesson 10

Point to these two photos as you ask, "What was life like for you 'before' and 'after' you placed faith in Christ?"

sen possession (see Exodus 19:5; Deuteronomy 7:6; 26:18). Ananias cannot miss the point that the Lord has very important plans for Saul.

Bearing the name of the Lord *before the Gentiles and kings* foreshadows certain events, as seen in Acts 24 and 25. Then there will be times when Saul (later renamed Paul) stands before Jewish audiences, *the children of Israel,* as well (Acts 13:13-52). These accounts present specific instances of Paul's own sufferings for the gospel. The tormentor will become the tormented. This news convinces Ananias to risk his life to go and stand in the same room with Saul.

What a transformation the church is about to witness in the life of Saul of Tarsus! This should convince modern believers that the gospel has more power to transform lives than we can possibly imagine. Later Saul (Paul) will refer to himself as "chief" of sinners (1 Timothy 1:15). If God can transform the worst of sinners, how much more can we expect him to do so with the sinners we know? [See question #6, page 100.]

III. Converted Tormentor
(Acts 9:17, 18)
A. Visit from Ananias (v. 17)

17. And Ananias went his way, and entered into the house; and putting his hands on him said, Brother Saul, the Lord, even Jesus, that appeared unto thee in the way as thou camest, hath sent me, that thou mightest receive thy sight, and be filled with the Holy Ghost.

The laying on of hands is important in Acts (see Acts 8:17; 13:3; 19:6). The identification of *Jesus* as *Lord* here corresponds to a major truth in Acts: Jesus is both Lord and Christ (Messiah, or "anointed one"; Acts 2:36; 10:36; 11:17; 28:31). *Ananias* presents a truth to *Saul* that Saul already has come to accept because of his experience on the road to Damascus.

B. Baptism of Saul (v. 18)

18. And immediately there fell from his eyes as it had been scales: and he received sight forthwith, and arose, and was baptized.

In verse 17, Ananias stated that his reasons for coming were twofold. First, he came to Saul so that he could receive his *sight* back; this happens when something like *scales,* or a flaky layer of substance, falls from Saul's *eyes.* The second objective for Ananias is that Saul might receive the Holy Spirit; this is accomplished when Saul is *baptized.* Verses 17 and 18 demonstrate the connection between baptism and the reception of the Holy Spirit (compare Acts 2:38; Titus 3:5).

"The rest," we may say, "is history." Saul becomes a dynamo for Jesus because the power of the gospel turns him from a persecutor of Christ to a preacher of Christ.

A NEW WAY OF SEEING

Michael May was 3 years old when an accident left him blind in his left eye and barely able to see light in the right one. He describes that partial vision as "like looking through a windshield that's completely iced over." He worked at having as normal a life as possible. May even become an expert skier and helped to develop a Global Positioning System receiver that works with the Braille method. Four corneal transplant attempts were unsuccessful. Then, 43 years after the accident, donor stem cells from an adult cornea and a fifth transplant succeeded.

After regaining his vision, he found that the ability to see is almost as much in the brain as it is in the eye. Because the accident happened when May was so young, his adult brain had to train itself to recognize objects in a way the rest of us do automatically. He said, "I need to see something for the tenth time before it sinks in what it is. It's like learning a language. You have to build up the vocabulary."

Saul's experience was somewhat like this. But we're not talking about his loss and recovery of physical sight. The problem was long-term spiritual blindness. His temporary physical blindness in Damascus opened the eyes of his heart, and he began learning a whole new spiritual language. He didn't immediately become the person we know as the apostle Paul. It took several years for him to sort out what he began to see spiritually. In what ways are our experiences like Saul's? —C. R. B.

Conclusion

A. Transforming Power

Think of the believers you know of who could have been described as *the worst of sinners*. What differences do you now see? How do you explain these differences? Those who knew Saul of Tarsus were amazed at the difference after he met the Lord. When he began preaching in the synagogues after his baptism, those who heard about it could not believe the change (see Acts 9:21).

The gospel of Christ still has power to transform lives. That power has never dimmed. Our obligation is to reach out with this gospel to the worst of sinners. Who knows what surprises we will see!

B. Prayer

Lord of grace and mercy, we ask today that You remind us of the potential within each sinner we know. Help us to think of him or her as ready for the truth of Jesus Christ. Let us look upon each as a potential "Paul," and not as a "Saul." As we do, may we see ourselves the same way. We pray in Christ, amen.

C. Thought to Remember

The worst sinner is capable of becoming the best Christian.

Learning by Doing

This page contains an alternate lesson plan emphasizing learning activities. Classes desiring such student involvement will find these suggestions helpful.

Learning Goals

After participating in this lesson, each student will be able to:

1. Summarize Saul's conversion experience.
2. Explain the significance of Saul's conversion.
3. Praise God for one specific way his or her life has been changed by knowing God.

Into the Lesson

Recruit several class members—ideally spanning a wide age range—to recount their conversions to Christ. Suggest that they include details such as the people who influenced them, the specific occasion of confession and submission, the sudden changes in the way they behaved and how others behaved toward them, and other matters they consider significant.

At the end of their accounts say, "All of us have some vivid memories of the occasion when we first named Jesus as Lord. Today's study is of one whose life was turned around completely in a series of startling events."

Into the Word

Recruit three good readers to assist with this activity. Say, "Our text today records the occasion of Paul's call to faith and ministry. Two other times Paul recites the occasion when he was being challenged regarding his ministry: before the Jews in Jerusalem and before King Agrippa in Caesarea. Our readers are going to read the three texts in a comparison format. Listen for common elements; listen for variations." Prepare the following list in advance for your three readers. Instruct them to alternate reading to the class, as implied by the lists.

9:1, 2	22:4, 5	26:9-11
9:3, 4	22:6, 7	26:12-14
9:5, 6	22:8	26:15
9:7, 8	22:9-11	26:16
9:9-14, 17	22:12, 13	26:17, 18
9:15, 16, 18	22:14-16	[none]
9:19, 20	[none]	26:19, 20

As class members note variations, remind them that the three accounts were given with different purposes to different audiences. Note these purposes: the first account is God's general revelation of the events involved; the second account is Paul's defense and explanation of his ministry to angry Jews who had assumed Paul had brought Gentiles into the temple; the third account is Paul's defense of himself before a political ruler as to why he is under arrest and why he has appealed to Caesar's court.

An alternate activity for examining today's text is to "interview" three of the minor characters in the story: Judas of Straight Street, with whom Paul was staying upon his arrival in Damascus; the (hypothetical) wife of Ananias; and one of Paul's fellow travelers from Jerusalem to Damascus.

After a reading of the text, ask the class to develop questions they would like to have these three characters answer if they were available for an interview. Share the following examples: for Judas, "What did Saul tell you when he was brought in blind to your house?"; for the wife, "Had your husband ever gotten up and run out in such a way as he did on the occasion he went to Saul?"; for one of Saul's fellow travelers, "What exactly did you see and hear on the road when Saul fell to the ground?" As the questions are developed, ask what the questioner thinks the answer may be.

Say to your class, "Ananias is called *disciple* in verse 10 of our text. Which title do you prefer for your relationship to Christ: child of God, believer, Christian, disciple, saint? Why do you prefer that choice?" Give opportunity for various choices and explanations.

Into Life

Say, "God declared Saul to be His chosen vessel for a special purpose (Acts 9:15). When you look around our congregation, whom do you see who especially seems to be called for a specific purpose in God's kingdom?"

Collect several small ceramic vases, such as those sold in dollar stores. Provide one for each learner. Ask each to choose a name from the list the class compiled and write a short thank-you note. The note can be as simple as, "I thank God that He is using you as a chosen vessel for____." Roll the completed note and insert it into the small vase. Ask an older children's class to deliver the "vessels" to the people intended.

Let's Talk It Over

These questions are designed to promote discussion of the lesson. The answers here are only discussion starters. Let your class talk it over from there.

1. From a human perspective, some people seem too far from the truth to be reachable. Why are we often hesitant to take the gospel to those who seem so far from belief? What can your church do to correct this situation?

We have to stop deciding who is worthy of our efforts. Obeying the Great Commission (Matthew 28:19, 20) means going to all people groups and people at all stations of life. This is not optional.

Some of those we consider beyond the reach of the gospel are the influential, whether it is those of celebrity status or those with political influence. As a result we have been very slow at times to plant churches and make an effort to reach the places where such people live. Supporting church planting and other outreach efforts in these strategic centers is needed.

Remember that our task is planting and watering the seed—and trusting God for the increase (1 Corinthians 3:6). He has proven time and again that He is able to provide increase in situations that we think impossible.

2. How can we be guilty of persecuting Christ today? How do we avoid this?

In subtle and overt ways, we persecute Him by our attitude toward those who are part of the body of Christ. As Saul persecuted the people of God and thus persecuted Christ, so we do the same when we dishonor our fellow believers (compare Romans 14:4). We also may be guilty of persecuting Christ when we show a lack of respect with regard to the things of God, such as His Word, His church, and even His creation.

Growth in God's Word is a vital preventive measure (Hebrews 5:14). Discuss methods that will help your students grow in this regard.

3. How can you determine whether or not someone has had a real encounter with God—or is this even our prerogative? What are the results of coming into contact with God in a personal way?

Genuine encounters with God do not lead to pride, but rather to humility. A noticeable change in attitude and lifestyle results from such encounters. We see all this in the life of Paul. Some who claim to have had special encounters with God or messages from God try to parlay this into financial gain or personal prestige. Close encounters of a personal kind with God will result in honoring God, not self.

4. God does not always use the high-powered evangelist or gifted communicator to reach the lost. He wants to use all His people for this purpose. Who is God calling you to reach with the gospel right now? How will you do it?

This question can lead into a time of prayer for specific people. Within each of our circles of influence are those who need the Lord. It may be a family member, coworker, or neighbor. Remember: you have contact with that person when the "gifted" evangelist does not. God uses natural relationships to reach others. New Testament examples of this are found in John 1:40-42, 44-46; 4:28-30.

5. The "fear factor" is a major reason Christians fail to reach out to others with the gospel of Christ. How can this fear be overcome?

Each person must develop his or her own godly technique. But generally speaking, fear is overcome by faith. Trusting in our own power leads to fear because we know that we are not sufficient to do the work of God on our own. We must always remember God has put His Spirit within us. This Spirit produces in us a power to overcome fear (2 Timothy 1:7).

6. God used Saul, the "chief" of sinners, to do great things. Why may it seem that those who are saved from grievous sin such as Saul's become tremendous instruments in God's hands?

People who grow up in the church and have lived lives fairly consistent with the principles of God's Word can become complacent with their faith. Faith can be taken for granted. Someone who has been saved from seeming hopelessness may have a deeper appreciation for the magnitude of God's grace. The one who has been forgiven much realizes the depths from which he or she has been saved and therefore seeks to serve God out of a deep appreciation (compare Luke 7:47).

Lydia Demonstrates Faithfulness

November 13
Lesson 11

DEVOTIONAL READING: Acts 16:25-34.

BACKGROUND SCRIPTURE: Acts 16.

PRINTED TEXT: Acts 16:6-15, 40.

Acts 16:6-15, 40

6 Now when they had gone throughout Phrygia and the region of Galatia, and were forbidden of the Holy Ghost to preach the word in Asia,

7 After they were come to Mysia, they assayed to go into Bithynia: but the Spirit suffered them not.

8 And they passing by Mysia came down to Troas.

9 And a vision appeared to Paul in the night; There stood a man of Macedonia, and prayed him, saying, Come over into Macedonia, and help us.

10 And after he had seen the vision, immediately we endeavored to go into Macedonia, assuredly gathering that the Lord had called us for to preach the gospel unto them.

11 Therefore loosing from Troas, we came with a straight course to Samothracia, and the next day to Neapolis;

12 And from thence to Philippi, which is the chief city of that part of Macedonia, and a colony: and we were in that city abiding certain days.

13 And on the sabbath we went out of the city by a river side, where prayer was wont to be made; and we sat down, and spake unto the women which resorted thither.

14 And a certain woman named Lydia, a seller of purple, of the city of Thyatira, which worshipped God, heard us: whose heart the Lord opened, that she attended unto the things which were spoken of Paul.

15 And when she was baptized, and her household, she besought us, saying, If ye have judged me to be faithful to the Lord, come into my house, and abide there. And she constrained us.

. . . .

40 And they went out of the prison, and entered into the house of Lydia: and when they had seen the brethren, they comforted them, and departed.

GOLDEN TEXT: When she was baptized, and her household, she besought us, saying, If ye have judged me to be faithful to the Lord, come into my house, and abide there. And she constrained us.—Acts 16:15.

> *You Will Be My Witnesses*
> Unit 3: Unto the Uttermost Part of the Earth
> (Lessons 10-13)

Lesson Aims

After participating in this lesson, each student will be able to:

1. Retell the account of Lydia's conversion.
2. Compare and contrast the importance of hospitality in the ancient and modern worlds.
3. Plan two class hospitality events: one for believers and one for unbelievers.

Lesson Outline

INTRODUCTION
    A. Congress on Hospitality
    B. Lesson Background
  I. GUIDANCE FROM THE SPIRIT (Acts 16:6-10)
    A. Spirit's Prohibition (vv. 6, 7)
    B. Man from Macedonia (vv. 8-10)
    "If Only . . . "
 II. CONVERSION OF LYDIA (Acts 16:11-14)
    A. Arrival in Philippi (vv. 11, 12)
    B. Response of Lydia (vv. 13, 14)
III. HOSPITALITY OF LYDIA (Acts 16:15, 40)
    A. Baptism of Lydia's Household (v. 15)
    Unsung Heroes
    B. Paul's Farewell to Lydia (v. 40)
CONCLUSION
    A. Homes Used for God's Glory
    B. Prayer
    C. Thought to Remember

Introduction

A. Congress on Hospitality

A well-known professor has issued a challenge to the church that must be taken seriously. He was summoning the church to a national congress on hospitality. He says that it could be held in Minneapolis near the Betty Crocker® Kitchens, and could perhaps borrow the Pillsbury Doughboy® as its symbol. After all, he says, there is truth to the old slogan, "Nothing says lovin' like something from the oven."

His point is to remind believers that the world of Jesus was a world where hospitality meant "love of strangers." Yet he charges that too often people who visit our churches feel unwelcome. They are not greeted enthusiastically. They are not even noticed. It is as if we think a one-line greeting in the Sunday bulletin covers the need adequately.

But, says the professor, hospitality breaks down barriers and helps to build bridges. For those who are tempted to shrug off this call for a congress on hospitality because other evangelistic outreaches are planned, the professor points out that hospitality does not conflict with outreach, but rather complements it. To invite someone in for coffee, to offer to baby-sit, to take a meal to a sick mother—all of these show that Christians care. And people will listen to someone who cares. [See question #1, page 109.]

Then he concludes his remarks by saying that he withdraws his call for a congress on hospitality! Instead, he says we should invite a few lonely folks into our homes. There we can show them genuine Christian hospitality. This, too, is the love of Christ.

B. Lesson Background

By the time the reader of Acts meets Lydia, the preaching of the gospel has traveled from Jerusalem to all Judea and Samaria and onward to the Gentile world. Acts 1:8 predicted this. As the book of Acts unfolds, we see examples of conversions at each stage of the story. In Jerusalem there are conversions of people such as the audience at Pentecost (2:38-41) plus a large number of priests (6:7). Beyond the city limits of Jerusalem there are the conversions of the Samaritans (8:4-25), the Ethiopian (8:26-40), Saul of Tarsus (9:1-19), and Cornelius (chapter 10). Well outside the boundaries of Judea and Samaria, there are the conversions of the Philippian jailer (16:16-34), the Corinthians (18:7, 8), and more.

Beginning in Acts 13:1, the missionary travels of the apostle Paul are the focus of the book. The church in Antioch commissioned Paul and Barnabas to carry the gospel beyond that Syrian city to the regions of Cyprus (a large island), Pisidia, Pamphylia, and Galatia. We often refer to this as Paul's first missionary journey (Acts 13:1–14:28). On the next missionary journey (Acts 15:36–18:22), Paul and Silas visited the previous locations, but then pushed farther west toward Roman Asia.

It is at this point in the second missionary journey of Paul that we arrive at today's lesson. The example of the convert named Lydia challenges modern believers to think of hospitality as part of faithful obedience in service to Christ. The year is perhaps A.D. 50, and it has been some 16 years since Paul's conversion (last week's lesson).

I. Guidance from the Spirit
(Acts 16:6-10)
A. Spirit's Prohibition (vv. 6, 7)

6, 7. Now when they had gone throughout Phrygia and the region of Galatia, and were forbidden of the Holy Ghost to preach the word in Asia, after they were come to Mysia, they assayed to go into Bithynia: but the Spirit suffered them not.

The missionary journeys of Paul are usually aimed at the larger Roman cities. For this reason, cities like Antioch of Syria, Ephesus, and Corinth are prominent in the account of Paul's work. The regions of *Phrygia* and *Galatia* are locations in which Paul and Barnabas had established churches on the first missionary journey.

How to Say It

AEGEAN. A-*jee*-un.
AMPHIPOLIS. Am-*fip*-o-liss.
ANTIOCH. *An*-tee-ock.
APOLLONIA. Ap-uh-*low*-nee-uh.
ATHENS. *Ath*-unz.
BEREA. Buh-*ree*-uh.
BITHYNIA. Bih-*thin*-ee-uh.
CORNELIUS. Cor-*neel*-yus.
CYPRUS. *Sigh*-prus.
ETHIOPIAN. E-thee-*o*-pee-un (*th* as in *thin*).
GALATIA. Guh-*lay*-shuh.
LYDIA. *Lid*-ee-uh.
MACEDONIA. Mass-eh-*doe*-nee-uh.
MYSIA. *Mish*-ee-uh.
NEAPOLIS. Nee-*ap*-o-lis.
PAMPHYLIA. Pam-*fill*-ee-uh.
PHRYGIA. *Frij*-e-uh.
PISIDIA. Pih-*sid*-ee-uh.
SAMOTHRACIA. Sam-o-*thray*-shuh.
SYNAGOGUE. *sin*-uh-gog.
SYRIAN. *Sear*-ee-un.
THESSALONICA. Thess-uh-lo-*nye*-kuh (strong accent on *nye*; *th* as in *thin*).
THYATIRA. *Thy*-uh-*tie*-ruh (strong accent on *tie*; *th* as in *thin*).

Now Paul and Silas seek to spread the gospel beyond what was accomplished previously.

On the route that Paul and Silas are traveling, Asia is located to the west and Bithynia to the north. For reasons unknown, *the Spirit* communicates to the missionaries that these destinations are off limits. [See question #2, page 109.]

The travelers obey the direction they receive. Since traveling west or north is prohibited, they move in a northwesterly direction toward Troas and beyond.

B. Man from Macedonia (vv. 8-10)

8. And they passing by Mysia came down to Troas.

We can only wonder what the travelers think as they are led to restrain their preaching when *Mysia* is such a logical target. *Troas* is close to the ruins of the ancient city of Troy and is located on the eastern coastline of the Aegean Sea. This port city is an important link in the Mediterranean network of commercial activity. Finding a Roman sailing vessel headed for other destinations will not be difficult. Paul will revisit this important city at a later time (see Acts 20:5, 6; 2 Corinthians 2:12).

9. And a vision appeared to Paul in the night; There stood a man of Macedonia, and prayed him, saying, Come over into Macedonia, and help us.

Macedonia is a province brought under Roman control by 146 B.C. Made famous during the Greek period by Philip II, father of Alexander the Great, Macedonia contains well-known cities such as Philippi and Thessalonica. During *the night,* Paul sees what is often called the Macedonian *vision.* What distinguishes the *man* in Paul's vision as being from Macedonia is not specified, but the invitation is clear.

In saying *help us,* the assistance that the man calls for is to hear the gospel of Christ. When we send the gospel to people who have not heard it, we are offering the best possible help that we can give!

10. And after he had seen the vision, immediately we endeavored to go into Macedonia, assuredly gathering that the Lord had called us for to preach the gospel unto them.

The quick response of Paul to *the vision* reflects his readiness to obey the will of *the Lord.* We can wonder at the arrangements that Paul needs to make in going down to the docks, waiting for a Roman commercial vessel sailing in the

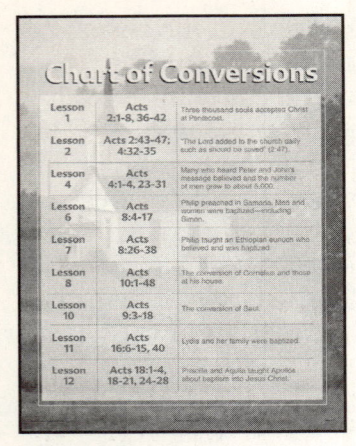

Use this chart to demonstrate that the book of Acts is a book about conversions.

Visual for lessons 6, 11

direction of *Macedonia,* and contacting the ship's captain in order to pay for passage. But the book of Acts skips over all of these details. What is primary is that Paul moves quickly to obey the call from God. [See question #3, page 109.]

The use of the term *we* in this verse is an example of sections in Acts where the narrative takes on a first-person perspective. These "we sections" are found in Acts 16:10-17; 20:5–21:18; and 27:1–28:16. Because the rest of Acts uses the third-person in speaking of what "he" did or "they" did, the use of *we* in these sections is best explained by concluding that the author (namely Luke, the companion of Paul) becomes a participant in these events.

"IF ONLY . . ."

"For of all sad words of tongue or pen, The saddest are these: 'It might have been.'" These words of John Greenleaf Whittier (1807–1892) have a pathetic ring to them that most of us can relate to. Who among us has not said, "If only I had done such and such, things might be better now"?

Sometimes the issues are larger than personal. When Prime Minister Neville Chamberlain returned from Germany after meeting with Adolf Hitler in September 1938, he informed the British nation that the recently signed accord represented "the desire of our two peoples never to go to war with one another again. . . . My good friends, this is the second time in our history that there has come back from Germany to Downing Street peace with honor. I believe it is peace in our time."

But less than two years later, Nazi Germany's air force had begun a lengthy bombardment of Britain. How many British citizens must have said, "If only we had not listened so naively to Mr. Chamberlain, we might have been spared the results of Nazi treachery!"

On the other hand, Christians in the Western world will never complain, "If only Paul had not followed the Spirit's leading, things would be better now." The hand of God was at work, and there is nothing to regret. Because Paul went where the Spirit led, Christianity became the dominant force in Western history for 2,000 years!

—C. R. B.

II. Conversion of Lydia
(Acts 16:11-14)
A. Arrival in Philippi (vv. 11, 12)

11. Therefore loosing from Troas, we came with a straight course to Samothracia, and the next day to Neapolis.

Samothracia (also spelled Samothrace) is a small island-city, rising about 5,500 feet above sea level, off the eastern coast of Macedonia. *Neapolis* serves as the port city for Philippi, which is located about ten miles inland. The sea voyage takes only a *day,* implying that the wind is favorable for the journey. Later, the same journey going in the opposite direction will take five days (Acts 20:6).

12. And from thence to Philippi, which is the chief city of that part of Macedonia, and a colony: and we were in that city abiding certain days.

Philippi is a major Roman *city* with a rich history. Named after Philip II, the city came under Roman control in 168 B.C. It is not the capital city of Macedonia, but rather is considered a leading city in one of the four districts into which Macedonia is divided. It became a *colony* (in 42 B.C.) because of its allegiance to Rome and its desire to be patterned after the Imperial City itself. Philippi is populated with retired Roman soldiers and not many Jews. The ministry lasts *certain days,* which may mean a stretch as short as a week.

B. Response of Lydia (vv. 13, 14)

13. And on the sabbath we went out of the city by a river side, where prayer was wont to be made; and we sat down, and spake unto the women which resorted thither.

Paul's usual pattern is first to go to the local synagogue when beginning a ministry in a new city (see Acts 13:14; 14:1; 18:4). In Philippi, however, the procedure is different as the travelers go to a place *by a river.* This may be a reference to the Gangites River, about a mile from town.

The gathering here of certain *women* for *prayer* on *the sabbath* probably indicates that there is no synagogue in Philippi. Speaking with the women from a seated position places Paul in the role of a rabbi teaching his audience (compare Luke 4:20, 21).

14. And a certain woman named Lydia, a seller of purple, of the city of Thyatira, which worshipped God, heard us: whose heart the Lord opened, that she attended unto the things which were spoken of Paul.

The description of *Lydia* as one who worships *God* means that she is Jewish, a convert to Judaism, or a God-fearing Gentile. Perhaps she and the others meet outside of the city because the city authorities consider her religion a threat. [See question #4, page 109.]

Her profession indicates status and wealth, since *purple* cloth frequently is sold to royalty in the ancient world. The trade is often associated with the city of *Thyatira* in the Roman province of Asia (compare Revelation 2:18). Verse 15 (next) substantiates her status and wealth because her house is large enough to provide lodging for the missionaries.

In spite of the independence and wealth of Lydia, her *heart* is ready for the message of Christ. Her heart is *opened* up by the *Lord* as Paul speaks the word of God; she responds to the gospel. The phrase that describes God's actions in the heart of Lydia is important. There are some Christians who believe that God alone determines who responds to the gospel. Their position is that God opens up hearts as He determines to do, and hearers have no responsibility in the matter. This doctrine, when carried to its logical end, amounts to salvation against one's free will.

Though this verse makes clear that the Lord takes action in Lydia's heart, it does not rule out Lydia's own freewill faith as important in the process. This verse does not say, for example, that the Lord gave Lydia faith and repentance.

Accepting Christ depends both on the action of God in revealing to us the truth and on our personal, freewill initiative in accepting that truth. Paul talks about how we should work out our own salvation, but at the same time it is God who works in us to act according to His will (Philippians 2:12, 13). The Bible makes clear that God holds people responsible for their beliefs and actions. The Lord opens Lydia's heart to respond, but she must still respond to the truth by her own volition.

How revealing is this event when it comes to our understanding of evangelism! When we pray for those who need to accept Christ, we are praying to the Lord who opens hearts. But people with open hearts still need to hear the gospel from someone who takes the time to proclaim it. This group of women welcome into their circle some visitors from a distant land, and, without knowing it, they are bringing into their circle the message of the Christ who came to offer salvation to all.

III. Hospitality of Lydia (Acts 16:15, 40)

A. Baptism of Lydia's Household (v. 15)

15. And when she was baptized, and her household, she besought us, saying, If ye have judged me to be faithful to the Lord, come into my house, and abide there. And she constrained us.

Paul's words to the women beside the river apparently include a discussion of the need to submit to baptism. Throughout the book of Acts, the story is the same with people who are converted to Christ. Typically, their faith and baptism are mentioned specifically. The Samaritans who listened to Philip's preaching believed and were baptized (8:12). The same is true of the

---

Home Daily Bible Readings

Monday, Nov. 7—Show Hospitality to Strangers (Hebrews 13:1-6)
Tuesday, Nov. 8—Mary and Martha Welcome Jesus (Luke 10:38-42)
Wednesday, Nov. 9—Serve One Another with Your Gifts (1 Peter 4:7-11)
Thursday, Nov. 10—Lydia Becomes a Faithful Follower (Acts 16:11-15)
Friday, Nov. 11—Paul and Silas Are Imprisoned (Acts 16:16-24)
Saturday, Nov. 12—The Converted Jailer Shows Hospitality (Acts 16:25-34)
Sunday, Nov. 13—Paul and Silas Are Freed (Acts 16:35-40)

Philippian jailer and his family (16:31-33). The Corinthians who listen to Paul's preaching also believe and are baptized (18:8). Lydia's conversion follows the same pattern.

After her baptism, Lydia makes a proposal that must not be overlooked. The book of Acts consistently offers a description of the heart of the person after baptism, and this is true with Lydia as well. In the case of the Ethiopian, he left rejoicing (Acts 8:39). The Philippian jailer is filled with joy, but also brings the missionaries into his house and prepares a meal for them (16:34). Part of Lydia's response after her baptism is her insistence that Paul and his companions come lodge at her house. [See question #5, page 109.]

This invitation should be understood in the proper context. It would not have been considered a moral issue because there are likely both men and women who already live in Lydia's house as servants. But it may be a dangerous arrangement for Lydia because of potential resistance from a community that may be opposed to the gospel. The fickle mob that opposes the progress of the gospel can be seen at Ephesus (Acts 19:28). Lydia can invite the missionaries to stay in her home, but she cannot guarantee what the reaction of the neighbors will be. Her invitation, more than just an inconvenience to her busy schedule, is an act of courage.

UNSUNG HEROES

Almost everyone knows the name Lance Armstrong. We also know about his courageous recovery from cancer several years ago and how he became a record-setting *Tour de France* bicyclist. But has anyone here ever heard of Floyd Landis? Landis was one of Armstrong's teammates for the 2003 *Tour de France* in which Armstrong won his fifth straight victory. Seven months before the race, Landis broke his hip in a training accident. He had hip surgery again just two months before the big race.

In the intricate strategy of bicycle racing, a champion's victory is due almost as much to his teammates' skills in protecting him from the challenges of other teams as it is to his own strength and stamina. This is where Landis came in. The determination of the "little guy" helped the champion to win the prize, while Landis finished in 77th place.

Lydia was also such a person. Paul's name appears 128 times in Acts (in the original Greek), while Lydia is named only twice. But she helped "the champion" succeed by her largely unsung contribution. True faith is demonstrated by a willingness to serve where needed even when others have the spotlight. Lydia's hospitality to Paul is an example of this. Her love for the cause of Christ prompted her quiet help to Paul in his ministry. How many of us practice this unobtrusive, but still vitally important, proof of our faith?
—C. R. B.

B. Paul's Farewell to Lydia (v. 40)

40. And they went out of the prison, and entered into the house of Lydia: and when they had seen the brethren, they comforted them, and departed.

The dangerous situation in Philippi erupted in persecution for Paul and Silas when the evil spirit was thrown out of the slave girl and her owners objected to the loss of their profit (Acts 16:19-21). Paul and Silas were beaten and thrown into jail as a result (16:22, 23).

Following the events of Acts 16:24-34, the city officials decided to release them and send them out of the city quietly (16:35, 36). The forthcoming travels will take the missionaries on to such places as Amphipolis, Apollonia, Thessalonica, Berea, Athens, and Corinth (chapters 17 and 18). Thus the gospel will spread despite persecution.

Before departing from Philippi, Paul and his companions feel compelled to stop again at the home of *Lydia*, whose generous hospitality has been so welcome. This also gives them a chance to see *the brethren*. This is a reference to the new church meeting at Philippi, probably in Lydia's home.

Once again the hospitality of Lydia steps to center stage. The chance for the missionary travelers to see their fellow Christians requires a place for the meeting. Lydia's home is not only open to the missionaries, but also to the entire church. This fact implies that she has a large home by first-century standards. Whatever the risk from her pagan neighbors, Lydia is devoted to helping those who travel to preach the gospel of Christ.

Conclusion

A. Homes Used for God's Glory

Lydia's example sets the pace for modern believers who want to use their resources in ways that advance the cause of Christ. One of the best resources a believer has is often his or her own home.

Using our homes for the work of the gospel means considering our homes as gifts given to us by the Lord. As with God's other gifts, it means dedicating our homes to the glory of God and then opening our doors to opportunities that arise. Perhaps these opportunities will come in the form of missionaries who need a place to stay while on furlough. Or perhaps the church will need a place for young people to gather. Or perhaps a troubled family will need some temporary shelter.

In all of these cases, believers in Christ can make their hospitality a witness for the gospel of Christ. This is the reason for commands such as Hebrews 13:2: "Be not forgetful to entertain strangers: for thereby some have entertained angels unawares." What an important way to demonstrate faithfulness!

B. Prayer

Lord, may the gospel of Christ open not only our eyes to the truth, but our doors to the cause of preaching the gospel. We pray this through Christ who opened His heart for us, amen.

C. Thought to Remember

Sometimes to open a door is the best way to open a heart.

Learning by Doing

This page contains an alternate lesson plan emphasizing learning activities. Classes desiring such student involvement will find these suggestions helpful.

Learning Goals

After participating in this lesson, each student will be able to:

1. Retell the account of Lydia's conversion.
2. Compare and contrast the importance of hospitality in the ancient and modern worlds.
3. Plan two class hospitality events: one for believers and one for unbelievers.

Into the Lesson

Prepare 11 index cards with the following sets of letters front and back respectively: H and E; O and V; S and A; P and N; I and G; T and E; A and L; L and I; I and S; T and M; Y and an exclamation point. Display the cards so that the word *hospitality* is spelled. (One way to display the cards would be to attach them to the wall with reusable adhesive).

Say, "Our study today is a lesson about hospitality and its results. But it is also a lesson about another Christian responsibility. Behind each of these cards is another letter. Try to guess the letters that will reveal the second Christian responsibility we will examine in today's lesson. As you correctly guess a letter, I will turn over the corresponding card." Allow students to suggest letters until someone correctly identifies the word *evangelism*. Then say, "Lydia's hospitality provided an excellent opportunity for evangelism. It always does."

Into the Word

Display a wall map or PowerPoint® computer image that highlights the geography of today's study. Seeing the important cities of the first-century Roman world will help students understand the culture as well as the geography.

Present the class the following quiz (also found in the student book) and direct them to answer each question with a verse number from today's text in Acts 16:6-15, 40. (Answers are given in parentheses.)

___ 1. What was Lydia's source of livelihood? *(v. 14)*

___ 2. Who comforted whom when Paul and Silas were finally released from imprisonment? *(v. 40)*

___ 3. Where did Jewish believers assemble in Philippi? *(v. 13)*

___ 4. Does the Spirit ever say no to good plans? *(vv. 6, 7)*

___ 5. What did Lydia and others in her household do when they accepted Jesus? *(v. 15)*

___ 6. Did anyone else in Paul's company have his same dream of a man in Macedonia? *(v. 10)*

___ 7. What kind of sailing weather did Paul encounter from Troas to Neapolis? *(v. 11)*
___ 8. The man of Macedonia called for help; what is the best help anyone can be given? *(vv. 9, 10)*

If your congregation has a woman who enjoys drama, recruit her to give the following monologue as Lydia. Be sure to give her a copy of the monologue early enough for advance preparation.

"When Paul and Silas were arrested, the news came back to me immediately. Philippi is not the kind of city where such an event escapes notice. Those rascals using that poor girl with a demon's voice would not lose their profit quietly, you understand. Paul and Silas were my honored houseguests. I first thought, *Lydia, you must rush down to the jail and see what you can do.* But Cleotus, my beloved servant, said, 'Mistress, to do so is dangerous. You must not go!' All we could do was pray and wait to see the outcome.

"My mind returned to that Saturday evening by the river. Devoted women from all over Philippi were there to pray and worship, for we had no synagogue hall. When strangers arrived, we were leery, but Paul's words clearly were from God.

"We were in the right place. When Paul pictured the death and resurrection of Christ, his instruction to be baptized brought no objections.

"I was exultant. Everything seemed so new. My house is large, but it had the lonely emptiness of business. So I invited Paul and his company to stay with us. What a blessed time we had!"

Into Life

Divide your class into two groups: the "Jailers" and the "Lydias." Note that both the jailer and Lydia hosted Paul in their homes at the time of their conversions. Ask the "Jailers" to plan an occasion for hosting a group of unbelievers for a kindness event (perhaps taking treats to a local fire station or the like). Ask the "Lydias" to plan an event for believers (perhaps taking Christian widows and widowers out for a luncheon).

Let's Talk It Over

These questions are designed to promote discussion of the lesson. The answers here are only discussion starters. Let your class talk it over from there.

1. How can your church become a "congress of hospitality"?

Every Christian should make a point to visit an unfamiliar church at least once per year; this will remind us of what it feels like to be a first-time visitor. Sadly, many churches are indifferent to the need to make guests feel welcome and at ease. Signs that point visitors to classrooms, rest rooms, and the auditorium are useful, but cannot replace the human touch. People must be willing to serve as personal guides to visitors.

Hospitality also can be offered through refreshment tables in an appropriate place to provide an opportunity for interaction. Important in this is that church members be taught how to engage strangers in conversation. It starts with deciding to make eye contact!

2. We often go forward with our plans when they may be against what the Holy Spirit desires. How does the Spirit say *no* to plans we make that are out of line with the will of God? How has the Spirit said *no* to some of our church's plans?

Taking time to seek the direction of the Spirit prior to making plans is vital. All plans are to be weighed against the teaching of the Bible to make sure we are not in violation of what God has already revealed to us. Plans also should be considered in light of the gifts God has given to the church; when no one who is gifted for a task comes forth to do that task, this may be the Spirit saying *no*. The Spirit also may say *no* by closing doors of opportunity.

3. Paul and his companions immediately followed the leading of the Spirit. But, like Gideon in Judges 6, we often want further confirmation before obeying. Why are we this way? How can we more readily follow the Spirit's leading?

Sometimes we fail to follow the Spirit's leading because we are not sure it is truly the direction of the Spirit we are sensing. Not wanting to be out of line with the will of God causes hesitation on our part. This is a good thing. We want to move forth by faith, not merely by feeling. Following what some sense as the direction of God because of a feeling has led to monumental blunders and failures in the work of God.

We can be more ready to sense and follow the Lord's leading by being sure we are being faithful in our daily walk with God. Being in a proper relationship with the Lord makes us more attune to His direction. Remember: the Spirit will never lead in a way that is contrary to the Word.

4. Many like Lydia believe God exists and thus they worship Him. How should the church respond to unchristian "God-fearers"? Who are the unsaved God-fearers in our community?

Even sincere God-fearers are lost apart from Christ (see Acts 4:12). God does not accept people into Heaven on the basis of good works or mere sincerity, but on acceptance of the work of Christ for forgiveness of sins. For example, the sincerity of godly Cornelius wasn't enough—he needed to hear the gospel (Acts 10).

Taking time to listen to what non-Christians say is a vital preliminary step. When we grasp "where people are" in their relationship to God, we can better help them reach a deeper understanding of the truth of God and His gospel.

5. In this age of easy access to restaurants and motels, is "in-home" hospitality really all that important? Why, or why not?

Our homes can be used in many ways to honor God and serve others. Hosting Bible fellowships is one—something that restaurants and motels are often not suited for. An offer of our homes as a place for visiting missionaries, etc., provides time for "holy interaction." In some communities, there are organizations that help battered women or abused children find temporary lodging. Working with such agencies can open doors for evangelism as we make our homes a haven for those in need.

Every year at Thanksgiving, a certain Christian family would prepare a big dinner. But before sitting down to eat, the father would go the local emergency room to see if there were any out-of-state visitors who needed a meal because they had had their trips interrupted due to sickness or injury. There always were. Such hospitality!

November 20
Lesson 12

Priscilla and Aquila Serve Together

DEVOTIONAL READING: Luke 10:1-11.

BACKGROUND SCRIPTURE: Acts 18:1–19:10.

PRINTED TEXT: Acts 18:1-4, 18-21, 24-28.

Acts 18:1-4, 18-21, 24-28

1 After these things Paul departed from Athens, and came to Corinth;

2 And found a certain Jew named Aquila, born in Pontus, lately come from Italy, with his wife Priscilla, (because that Claudius had commanded all Jews to depart from Rome,) and came unto them.

3 And because he was of the same craft, he abode with them, and wrought: (for by their occupation they were tentmakers.)

4 And he reasoned in the synagogue every sabbath, and persuaded the Jews and the Greeks.

. . . .

18 And Paul after this tarried there yet a good while, and then took his leave of the brethren, and sailed thence into Syria, and with him Priscilla and Aquila; having shorn his head in Cenchreae: for he had a vow.

19 And he came to Ephesus, and left them there: but he himself entered into the synagogue, and reasoned with the Jews.

20 When they desired him to tarry longer time with them, he consented not;

21 But bade them farewell, saying, I must by all means keep this feast that cometh in Jerusalem: but I will return again unto you, if God will. And he sailed from Ephesus.

. . . .

24 And a certain Jew named Apollos, born at Alexandria, an eloquent man, and mighty in the Scriptures, came to Ephesus.

25 This man was instructed in the way of the Lord; and being fervent in the spirit, he spake and taught diligently the things of the Lord, knowing only the baptism of John.

26 And he began to speak boldly in the synagogue: whom when Aquila and Priscilla had heard, they took him unto them, and expounded unto him the way of God more perfectly.

27 And when he was disposed to pass into Achaia, the brethren wrote, exhorting the disciples to receive him: who, when he was come, helped them much which had believed through grace:

28 For he mightily convinced the Jews, and that publicly, showing by the Scriptures that Jesus was Christ.

GOLDEN TEXT: Because he was of the same craft, he abode with them, and wrought: (for by their occupation they were tentmakers.)—Acts 18:3.

> *You Will Be My Witnesses*
> Unit 3: Unto the Uttermost Part of the Earth
> (Lessons 10-13)

Lesson Aims

After participating in this lesson, each student will be able to:

1. Tell how Paul, Priscilla, and Aquila demonstrated the benefits of teamwork in spreading the gospel.
2. Identify modern-day examples of Christian teamwork.
3. Plan a specific way to minister cooperatively for Christ.

Lesson Outline

INTRODUCTION
    A. Teamwork
    B. Lesson Background
I. MINISTRY WITH PAUL (Acts 18:1-4)
    A. Paul Arrives in Corinth (v. 1)
    B. Paul Receives Assistance (vv. 2-4)
II. MINISTRY IN EPHESUS (Acts 18:18-21)
    A. Departure for Ephesus (v. 18)
    B. Arrival in Ephesus (v. 19)
    C. Departure from Ephesus (vv. 20, 21)
       Unwelcome Guests
III. MINISTRY WITH APOLLOS (Acts 18:24-28)
    A. Preaching of Apollos (vv. 24, 25)
    B. Instruction of Apollos (vv. 26-28)
       Influential People
CONCLUSION
    A. Working Side by Side
    B. Prayer
    C. Thought to Remember

Introduction

A. Teamwork

Two men were riding a bicycle built for two, and they came to a big, steep hill. It took a great deal of struggle for the men to complete the stiff climb. When they got to the top, the man in front turned to the other and said, "That sure was a hard climb." The fellow in back replied, "Yes, and if I hadn't kept the brakes on all the way we certainly would have rolled down backward."

I wonder how many of us have the brakes on with God? Progress is always more difficult when half the team refuses to cooperate. The body of Christ depends on the cooperation of all its members. Only then can Christ's work be accomplished fully in the church.

Today's lesson brings Priscilla and Aquila to the forefront as a married couple whose ministry spanned several cities in the Roman world. Their example reminds modern believers of the cooperation required for effective ministry for Christ. [See question #1, page 118.]

B. Lesson Background

The ancient Jews who lived outside their homeland of Palestine came to be called the Diaspora. Such Jews could be found in cities such as Rome, Alexandria in Egypt, and Antioch of Syria. The term *Diaspora* came from the idea of scattering seed. Since the days of the Assyrian and Babylonian captivities (the eighth through sixth centuries before Christ), the Jews had been scattered widely outside of Palestine.

Priscilla and Aquila were Diaspora Jews who became Christians. Diaspora Jews were not always popular in Roman society. Romans looked with suspicion on Jewish religious practices, and they loathed the Jewish contention that there was but one God. From time to time, conflicts surfaced between Jewish and Roman elements within society, as happened during the reign of Claudius Caesar, who reigned A.D. 41–54. The Roman historian Suetonius describes how Claudius expelled the Jews from the city of Rome because of riots between Jews and Gentiles, which apparently were caused by disputes about someone called Chrestus. Most scholars take this name as a reference to Christ, and believe that Claudius wanted the Jews to leave because of their supposed role in the instigation of this trouble. The date for this decree was A.D. 49 or 50. The Roman leadership of the time really didn't see Christianity as a separate religion, but as an offshoot or variation of Judaism.

So Jewish residents such as Priscilla and Aquila were forced from their homes. Conditions in the Roman world were relatively favorable to travelers, so Jews driven from Rome did have options. The commercial centers of the Mediterranean world were connected by a network of roads, and travelers moved along these thoroughfares on a regular basis. Roman shipping lanes crisscrossed the Mediterranean Sea, so travelers could journey from Rome to any site in an eastward direction in a matter of a few weeks.

Today's lesson picks up the story of Aquila and Priscilla in Acts 18. They enter the narrative of Paul's travels because of his encounter with them in the city of Corinth.

I. Ministry with Paul
(Acts 18:1-4)
A. Paul Arrives in Corinth (v. 1)

1. After these things Paul departed from Athens, and came to Corinth.

These things refers to the events of Acts 17:16-34. Paul's departure *from Athens* comes after his address before the Areopagus on Mars' Hill. Paul is leading a missionary tour, which had begun in Antioch of Syria (Acts 15:35, 36). He had left Silas and Timothy behind in Berea while he moved on without them to Athens and Corinth (17:14, 15). Even so, there is some traveling back and forth by Silas and Timothy (see Acts 18:5; 1 Thessalonians 3:1). The year is most likely A.D. 50.

Corinth is an important Roman city. It is located on an isthmus some 40 miles west of Athens. Corinth has access to harbors on both sides of the city: Lechaeum on the west and Cenchreae on the east. Corinth thus commands a powerful position for commercial activity with its access to the Roman sea-lanes. The Romans had even developed a quick way to move ships across the isthmus on a track, thus saving the voyage around the dangerous southern coastline.

With its mixture of cultures and pagan religions, Corinth offers the same moral conditions that one would expect in larger commercial cities today. Paul wants to see the gospel take root in this pagan city. [See question #2, page 118.]

B. Paul Receives Assistance (vv. 2-4)

2, 3. And found a certain Jew named Aquila, born in Pontus, lately come from Italy, with his wife Priscilla, (because that Claudius had commanded all Jews to depart from Rome,) and came unto them. And because he was of the same craft, he abode with them, and wrought: (for by their occupation they were tentmakers.)

For the first time in the New Testament, *Aquila* and *Priscilla* make their appearance. They may have been Christians before coming to Corinth *from Rome*, though nothing specifically is said about this. The emperor *Claudius* made no distinction between Jews who are believers in Jesus and those who are not when issuing his edict.

Paul arrives in Corinth with no means for earning an income except for his trade. If he carries any funds from the church that commissioned him in Antioch, these do not appear evident in the account of Acts. The arrival of Silas and Timothy from Macedonia probably provides some support from these churches because after their appearance, Paul turns from tentmaking to full-time preaching (Acts 18:5).

Fortunately for Paul, Jewish families of the day are very careful to equip male children with a trade for life. That trade is tentmaking in the case of Paul. The phrase can include various kinds of leather-working, including the fashioning of tents, awnings, and coverings. Whatever prayers Paul offers for daily needs in Corinth are answered by the God who matches Paul with these fellow *tentmakers*. [See question #3, page 118.]

4. And he reasoned in the synagogue every sabbath, and persuaded the Jews and the Greeks.

How to Say It

ACHAIA. Uh-*kay*-uh.
ANTIOCH. *An*-tee-ock.
APOLLOS. Uh-*pahl*-us.
AQUILA. *Ack*-wih-luh.
AREOPAGUS. Air-ee-*op*-uh-gus.
ATHENS. *Ath*-unz.
BEREA. Buh-*ree*-uh.
CENCHREAE. *Sen*-kree-uh.
CLAUDIUS CAESAR. *Claw*-dee-us *See*-zur.
EPHESUS. *Ef*-uh-sus.
JUDAISM. *Joo*-duh-izz-um or *Joo*-day-izz-um.
LECHAEUM. Lek-uh-*ee*-um.
NAZARITE. *Naz*-uh-rite.
PISIDIA. Pih-*sid*-ee-uh.
PONTUS. *Pon*-tuss.
SUETONIUS. Soo-*toe*-nee-us.
SYNAGOGUE. *sin*-uh-gog.
SYRIA. *Sear*-ee-uh.
THESSALONICA. *Thess*-uh-lo-*nye*-kuh (strong accent on *nye*; th as in *thin*).

During the time that he spends tentmaking, Paul's pattern is to preach part-time by using *synagogue* meetings as his opportunity to reach the worshipers for Christ. Synagogues in the Diaspora include not just Jewish worshipers, but also Gentile worshipers called "God-fearers," who had not received circumcision.

Paul's entire effort in Corinth is off and running because of the help of Aquila and Priscilla. This couple provides the right amount of help to Paul for his preaching. It is possible that their leather-working shop is also the meeting place for the believers at Corinth.

II. Ministry in Ephesus
(Acts 18:18-21)

A. Departure for Ephesus (v. 18)

18. And Paul after this tarried there yet a good while, and then took his leave of the brethren, and sailed thence into Syria, and with him Priscilla and Aquila; having shorn his head in Cenchreae: for he had a vow.

Paul's ministry in Corinth lasts at least 18 months (see Acts 18:11). This verse comments on the end of that period, as *Paul* decides to move on. So he says good-bye to the Corinthian *brethren,* and sails back for *Syria.* That is the Roman province that includes Antioch, his ultimate destination (Acts 18:22). *Priscilla and Aquila* leave Corinth *with him* because Paul has plans for their continuing work for the Lord.

Before boarding the sailing vessel, Paul has his *head* shaved at *Cenchreae,* the eastern port city for Corinth. The *vow* is probably a kind of Nazarite vow (see Numbers 6:1-21), which in some cases can be taken for a period of 30 days. Paul's act may be either the beginning or the conclusion of the vow. If it's the beginning of the vow, Paul may be shaving his head in order to take his hair with him to the temple in Jerusalem. There he may intend to throw it into the fire of a burnt offering, thus bringing the vow to completion. Such an action on Paul's part illustrates his firm connection with his Jewish heritage, even after his conversion to Christ. Naming the name of Jesus does not prevent him from participating in Jewish ceremonies at the temple (see also Acts 21:17-26).

Priscilla and Aquila's willingness to uproot and accompany Paul for an uncertain future speaks to their devotion and faith. Did they volunteer or did Paul ask them to accompany him? There is no way to know, but one easily imagines the idea springing almost spontaneously as the three discuss Paul's future labors.

B. Arrival in Ephesus (v. 19)

19. And he came to Ephesus, and left them there: but he himself entered into the synagogue, and reasoned with the Jews.

At this point Paul's plans for traveling to and through *Ephesus* become clear. Stopping there on his way to Syria, his message to the *synagogue* worshipers would be similar to his presentation in synagogues at Antioch of Pisidia (Acts 13:13-41) and Thessalonica (Acts 17:1-4).

Paul's plans for Aquila and Priscilla also become clear as he leaves *them* in Ephesus for further ministry. Here again the cooperation of this couple as a team working for Christ is important. They evidently listen to Paul's encouragement about leaving Corinth and traveling to Ephesus, setting up their leather-working business there, and working for the cause of Christ. Whatever the sacrifice to them personally, Aquila and Priscilla are willing to bear it in order to present their witness for Christ. [See question #4, page 118.]

C. Departure from Ephesus (vv. 20, 21)

20, 21. When they desired him to tarry longer time with them, he consented not; but bade them farewell, saying, I must by all means keep this feast that cometh in Jerusalem: but I will return again unto you, if God will. And he sailed from Ephesus.

Paul has a schedule set in his mind. So when some in *Ephesus* want him to stay *longer,* he declines in favor of moving on. The phrase *I must by all means keep this feast that cometh in Jerusalem* does not appear in the earliest manuscripts of this verse. But a similar phrase is found in Acts 20:16. There Paul is nearing the end of his third missionary journey, and Ephesus is also part of the equation. Whatever reason Paul has for not staying on, he promises to *return* to Ephesus. This is a promise he keeps on that third missionary journey (Acts 19). Apparently it is more important for Priscilla and Aquila to remain in Ephesus than to accompany Paul to Syria.

UNWELCOME GUESTS

Newspaper advice columns often carry letters from readers whose relatives come to visit and overstay their welcome. But humans aren't the only ones who have unwelcome guests. Pristine Lake Davis, in California's northern Sierra Nevada, has had some unwanted visitors for a couple of decades. Someone had introduced illegally a foreign fish species, namely the northern pike.

Pike are a popular game fish elsewhere, but these vicious predators have been killing off native species in Lake Davis. The fear is that the pike will wipe out the native trout as well as salmon downstream. Wildlife officials have poisoned the lake and used dynamite, nets, traps, and electric shocks—all to no avail. The pike still thrive, proving that visitors can cause trouble regardless of their species!

The apostle Paul was not that kind of guest. He had stayed with Aquila and Priscilla during the many months he had ministered in Corinth. They moved with Paul to Ephesus, and they begged him to continue as their guest when he announced other plans. To have found such a bond, they must have shared with him an affinity of personality as well as involvement in the same trade. More important, they also shared a firm commitment to the ministry of the gospel. That is the strongest basis for a lasting friendship, as well as for being a welcome guest. —C. R. B.

III. Ministry with Apollos (Acts 18:24-28)

A. Preaching of Apollos (vv. 24, 25)

24. And a certain Jew named Apollos, born at Alexandria, an eloquent man, and mighty in the Scriptures, came to Ephesus.

Home Daily Bible Readings

Monday, Nov. 14—Jesus Sends Disciples Out in Pairs (Luke 10:1-11)

Tuesday, Nov. 15—Go and Find a Colt (Luke 19:28-34)

Wednesday, Nov. 16—Paul Preaches in Corinth (Acts 18:1-8)

Thursday, Nov. 17—Paul's Preaching Stirs Up Controversy (Acts 18:9-17)

Friday, Nov. 18—Paul, Priscilla, and Aquila Travel Together (Acts 18:18-23)

Saturday, Nov. 19—Priscilla and Aquila Help Apollos (Acts 18:24-28)

Sunday, Nov. 20—Paul Thanks Priscilla and Aquila (Romans 16:3-16)

This verse introduces us to *Apollos*. His background is Jewish, and he hails from *Alexandria* in Egypt, a city well known for its large Jewish community. The fact that he is *mighty in the Scriptures* tells us that he is a scholar. Being *eloquent* reveals skills in public speaking. His arrival in *Ephesus* comes between the time of Paul's departure for Syria and Paul's return several months later (compare Acts 19:1).

25. This man was instructed in the way of the Lord; and being fervent in the spirit, he spake and taught diligently the things of the Lord, knowing only the baptism of John.

Although a scholar, Apollos comes to Ephesus with some deficiencies. He apparently knows something about Jesus already. But when it comes to the subject of Christian baptism, he does not know more than *the baptism of John*. Thus his teaching about baptism lacks reference to those promises that come after Jesus' resurrection, such as forgiveness of sins and the gift of the Holy Spirit (see Acts 2:38; 22:16). John's baptism was designed to be temporary (Acts 19:1-5).

B. Instruction of Apollos (vv. 26-28)

26. And he began to speak boldly in the synagogue: whom when Aquila and Priscilla had heard, they took him unto them, and expounded unto him the way of God more perfectly.

Aquila and Priscilla hear the preaching of Apollos in Ephesus. Given all of the deficiencies they notice in his preaching, they could merely avoid him entirely. But instead, they take *him unto them* as they gently lead him to understand the facts about Jesus Christ. Nothing is said about the baptism of Apollos, but it is reasonable to assume that their teaching is followed by his baptism into Christ (compare again Acts 19:1-5).

Here again the example of this couple should encourage us to think of how cooperation can contribute to effective ministry. Both husband and wife are ready to be used by God in a private teaching ministry. [See question #5, page 118.]

INFLUENTIAL PEOPLE

Michael Hart's book *The 100: A Ranking of the Most Influential Persons in History* may surprise us. He ranked Muhammad No. 1, Isaac Newton No. 2, and Jesus No. 3. Anticipating our objections, Hart said he would have ranked Jesus first if all the people who today identify themselves as Christians actually followed Jesus' teachings more substantially. Hart believes that modern Muslims show more of the influence of Muhammad in their lives than Christians do of Christ in theirs. Hmmm!

After we have recovered from our shock, we may take solace in the fact that Hart's list is a secular evaluation. Muhammad created a geographic empire; Jesus did not.

Not one of us is likely to make it into anyone's book about the 100—or 1,000 or even 10,000—most influential people in history. But that is not nearly as important as the kind of influence we can have on the people close to us. Aquila and Priscilla are good examples of this truth. In mentoring Apollos, their influence reached many others through the ministry of that man.

In a way that really counts, Aquila and Priscilla were *influential* people! We can be, too, if our concern is more for Christ than for worldly recognition. Can you think of someone whom you might mentor in the faith? —C. R. B.

27. And when he was disposed to pass into Achaia, the brethren wrote, exhorting the disciples to receive him: who, when he was come, helped them much which had believed through grace.

Apollos moves on to *Achaia*, the province in which Corinth is prominent. Paul's ministry had finished there several months before, and now Apollos is ready to add his influence. The believers in Ephesus wrote letters to the Christians in Achaia to encourage them to accept Apollos as a preacher of the truth. Paul later comments on the work of Apollos by remarking that he (Paul) had planted the seed in Corinth, "Apollos watered; but God gave the increase" (1 Corinthians 3:6). It was the ministry of Priscilla and Aquila that made this "watering" possible.

28. For he mightily convinced the Jews, and that publicly, showing by the Scriptures that Jesus was Christ.

Apollos's preaching method of *showing by the Scriptures that Jesus was Christ* is consistent with the method of the apostles. Think about Peter's sermon on the Day of Pentecost (Acts 2:1-36), which drew from Psalm 16:8-11; 110:1; and Joel 2:28-32 to prove that Jesus is both Lord and Christ. Compare also Paul's sermon in the synagogue of Antioch of Pisidia (Acts 13:16-41).

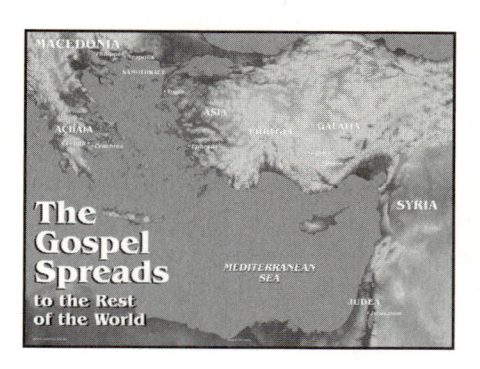

Visual for lesson 12

Use this map to help your students see the broader framework for Lessons 10 through 13.

There he presented a grand review of Old Testament history as a backdrop for the Messiah—Jesus Christ. The preaching of Apollos follows this method of establishing proof as he engages the Jews *publicly*.

Even so, the strength in the words of Apollos is not just his factual knowledge. He speaks with power. He himself is convinced utterly that Jesus is the Christ. When Jewish audiences hear him, they are presented with authoritative persuasion to reach the same conclusion. And behind this powerful preaching stands the solid, low-key ministry of Aquila and Priscilla!

Conclusion
A. Working Side by Side

In three different cities—Rome, Corinth, and Ephesus—Priscilla and Aquila worked in the ministry of Christ. Their work in Rome may have contributed to the order from Claudius Caesar to expel the Jews from the city. That's speculation, however. We know for certain that this couple went back to that great city as witnesses for Christ (Romans 16:3-5a).

The work of this couple in Corinth enabled the apostle Paul to survive in a difficult situation without income and without friends. Priscilla and Aquila turned their business into something of a support system for mission work, and their home into a place for believers to meet. Their work in Ephesus exemplified what it means to guide someone who needs more of the truth into a productive ministry for the Lord.

The New Testament presents Priscilla and Aquila working together. Whether referred to as Priscilla and Aquila (see Acts 18:18; Romans 16:3) or as Aquila and Priscilla (see Acts 18:2; 1 Corinthians 16:19) seems to make no difference. This couple consistently appears united in their service to Christ. They accomplish things together that could not have been accomplished apart. The fact that Priscilla's name can appear first has been noticed by scholars, who sometimes take it to mean that she had a prominence in the church separate from her husband. Yet the fact that their names can be interchanged may tell us that their cooperation was so complete that who received the credit meant nothing to them or anyone else, as long as the work was accomplished.

Whether thinking of husbands and wives or best friends who serve Christ side by side, the team of Priscilla and Aquila is a model for modern believers. Their unity in service is something we should imitate, especially when it comes to presenting Christ before a pagan society. Our efforts to influence the world for Christ will be hampered if our service is fractured and sporadic. When our faith operates consistently and cooperatively with other believers, the world will take note that we have been in the presence of Jesus.

B. Prayer

Father of all believers in Jesus, we ask You today to remind us that we belong to Your family. We ask that all rivalry, jealousy, and triumphalism against other Christians will disappear in favor of the unity and peace that comes to Your people wherever Jesus is truly honored as Lord. Through Christ who adds us to His church we pray, amen.

C. Thought to Remember

May the voices of Christians working together for Christ blend as one.

Learning by Doing

This page contains an alternate lesson plan emphasizing learning activities. Classes desiring such student involvement will find these suggestions helpful.

Learning Goals

After participating in this lesson, each student will be able to:

1. Tell how Paul, Priscilla, and Aquila demonstrated the benefits of teamwork in spreading the gospel.
2. Identify modern-day examples of Christian teamwork.
3. Plan a specific way to minister cooperatively for Christ.

Into the Lesson

Provide paper and pens for students, and ask them to make a list of all the places they have lived. After a few minutes, ask students to compare their lists. Give a small prize (such as an atlas from a dollar store) for the one who has lived in the most places.

Next, say, "We think of our modern society as a highly mobile one. But the Roman Empire had a transient population as well. Priscilla and Aquila are noted to have lived in Pontus, Rome, Corinth, and Ephesus—some places more than once. Of course, God does care where you live; but more importantly He cares about what you *do* where you live. Priscilla and Aquila did the right thing wherever they were."

Into the Word

Prepare index cards with the questions and answers that follow. Place either a question or an answer on each card. (Use only one answer or one question per index card. Do not put questions and answers on the same cards.) Randomly distribute the cards to the class; keep one card for yourself if you have an uneven number of students.

Q: Where was Paul before he came to Corinth? *A:* Athens.

Q: Why had Priscilla and Aquila left Rome? *A:* The emperor had ordered all Jews out of the city.

Q: Why did Paul initially associate with Priscilla and Aquila? *A:* All were tentmakers.

Q: What was the plan for evangelism in Corinth? *A:* To instruct in the synagogue.

Q: Where did Paul go after he left Corinth? *A:* To Ephesus.

Q: Why did Paul shave his head before sailing for Syria? *A:* He had taken a vow of some sort.

Q: What was the shortcoming in Apollos's religious education? *A:* He knew only of the baptism of John, not of baptism into Christ.

Q: Where did Paul leave Priscilla and Aquila as he traveled on to Syria? *A:* At Ephesus.

Q: What did Paul do in the synagogue at Ephesus? *A:* He reasoned with the Jews about Christ.

Q: Where was Apollos from? *A:* Alexandria in northern Africa.

Q: Where did Aquila and Priscilla hear Apollos's teaching? *A:* In the synagogue at Ephesus.

Q: How did Aquila and Priscilla deal with Apollos's incomplete doctrinal understanding? *A:* They took him aside privately and taught him the complete gospel.

Q: What was Apollos's plan when he left Ephesus? *A:* He wanted to visit the churches in Achaia.

Q: By what means did the Ephesian Christians commend Apollos to the believers in Achaia? *A:* They gave him a letter of recommendation.

Once the cards are distributed, say, "Circulate among yourselves until you find the question or answer that is a pair with your card." After pairs are made, ask students who are paired up to read their questions and answers. Then ask the group to identify the verse where the information is found.

Into Life

Provide your class with the names and addresses of missionary couples that your congregation supports. Ask for volunteers to write thank-you letters to those couples during the next week, commending them for their cooperative effort in spreading the gospel. If there is one missionary couple that your class is especially close to, consider collecting a special offering to send them as an "Aquila and Priscilla award" and as a thank-you.

If your congregation has a preacher whose wife faithfully serves the congregation with him, present the "Aquila and Priscilla award" to them. (The gift could be matching leather wallets in honor of Aquila and Priscilla's craft in leather.) Invite the preacher and his wife to the beginning of your class next Sunday and make the presentation with a reference to your study of the ministry team of Aquila and Priscilla.

Let's Talk It Over

These questions are designed to promote discussion of the lesson. The answers here are only discussion starters. Let your class talk it over from there.

1. *Synergy* is combined action. Combined, cooperative efforts produce greater results than separate, individual efforts. How can the church use the principle of synergy?

Churches can waste resources and effort by failing to work together. Even within a church people can promote "pet" ministries instead of seeing each ministry as part of a bigger picture. Recognizing that the various ministries of the church are not in competition with each other but rather working toward one common goal is necessary for synergy to take place.

Your church's leadership will foster combined, cooperative efforts by creating an atmosphere in which the differing gifts and talents of people are recognized and honored. Also, when church leadership can help people see a larger, overall vision or plan, there will be less friction between individual ministries.

2. Corinth was a major cultural and commercial center of its day. Should the church be more aggressive in reaching major cities instead of focusing so much on suburbs, exurbs, and rural settings? Why, or why not?

Commercial and cultural centers play key roles in determining the direction of cultural movements. Major cities such as Chicago, London, Los Angeles, Mexico City, New York City, and Toronto are such centers. The opportunity exists to change the direction of culture as the gospel is taken to such strategic places.

We will gain a commitment to reach such places when we remember that the church exists not only for evangelism, teaching, and worship, but also to be the conscience of the nation and community. Where Christian influence is absent, culture decays. The continuing press for legalization of homosexual marriage is an example. Some have suggested that if Paul were alive today, the first place he would go to establish a church would be New York City.

3. Today we use the term *tentmaker* to describe missionaries and others in ministry who are self-supporting in their work. When should this be a pattern for ministry today, if ever?

Some church planters earn their living at one job while laboring to launch a new church because of a lack of start-up funds for the work. They use a tentmaking strategy out of financial necessity. Some go into other lands and serve as English teachers while evangelizing the lost. Perhaps the government of the host country won't let them in unless they have a "legitimate" job.

The requirements of the moment thus can determine if a tentmaker strategy is appropriate. Remember that Paul chose to support himself on some occasions while recognizing his right to accept support at other times (1 Corinthians 9:4, 6).

4. What is the value in a husband-wife team ministry? What are the drawbacks?

A married couple can be very effective because the two can reach the needs of men and women in their separate spheres of influence and ministry. For example, the wife of the team may be much better at counseling other women than her husband might be.

A problem exists, however, when a church hires a new pulpit minister with the unstated assumption that it's a "two for the price of one" deal. This is a particular danger in smaller churches. Unreasonable expectations placed on the unpaid preacher's wife can sour a ministry (and a marriage) in a hurry!

5. What do we learn from the account of Aquila and Priscilla about how to approach those who have an incomplete or false knowledge of Scripture? Give an example of a time when you did not follow the pattern of Aquila and Priscilla; explain what happened.

Aquila and Priscilla took time to hear what Apollos had to say. Understanding *why* someone is following an incomplete or false teaching is vital. Has the person simply never been exposed to the truth, or has the person for some reason rejected the truth as it has been taught?

Another important principle we learn is that the gentle confrontation with Apollos was done in private. Confronting someone publicly on sensitive issues can be counterproductive, although Galatians 2:14 presents us with an exception.

Paul Says Good-Bye

November 27
Lesson 13

DEVOTIONAL READING: Acts 20:31-35.

BACKGROUND SCRIPTURE: Acts 20:17-38.

PRINTED TEXT: Acts 20:17-28, 36-38.

Acts 20:17-28, 36-38

17 And from Miletus he sent to Ephesus, and called the elders of the church.

18 And when they were come to him, he said unto them, Ye know, from the first day that I came into Asia, after what manner I have been with you at all seasons,

19 Serving the Lord with all humility of mind, and with many tears, and temptations, which befell me by the lying in wait of the Jews:

20 And how I kept back nothing that was profitable unto you, but have showed you, and have taught you publicly, and from house to house,

21 Testifying both to the Jews, and also to the Greeks, repentance toward God, and faith toward our Lord Jesus Christ.

22 And now, behold, I go bound in the spirit unto Jerusalem, not knowing the things that shall befall me there:

23 Save that the Holy Ghost witnesseth in every city, saying that bonds and afflictions abide me.

24 But none of these things move me, neither count I my life dear unto myself, so that I might finish my course with joy, and the ministry, which I have received of the Lord Jesus, to testify the gospel of the grace of God.

25 And now, behold, I know that ye all, among whom I have gone preaching the kingdom of God, shall see my face no more.

26 Wherefore I take you to record this day, that I am pure from the blood of all men.

27 For I have not shunned to declare unto you all the counsel of God.

28 Take heed therefore unto yourselves, and to all the flock, over the which the Holy Ghost hath made you overseers, to feed the church of God, which he hath purchased with his own blood.

. . . .

36 And when he had thus spoken, he kneeled down, and prayed with them all.

37 And they all wept sore, and fell on Paul's neck, and kissed him,

38 Sorrowing most of all for the words which he spake, that they should see his face no more. And they accompanied him unto the ship.

GOLDEN TEXT: Take heed therefore unto yourselves, and to all the flock, over the which the Holy Ghost hath made you overseers, to feed the church of God, which he hath purchased with his own blood.—Acts 20:28.

> *You Will Be My Witnesses*
> Unit 3: Unto the Uttermost Part of the Earth
> (Lessons 10-13)

Lesson Aims

After participating in this lesson, each student will be able to:

1. Recall the main points of Paul's final talk with the Ephesian elders.
2. Identify some of the "sad good-byes" that Christians experience today.
3. Write a letter of encouragement to a fellow Christian who lives in a foreign country.

Lesson Outline

INTRODUCTION
    A. Comfort for the Grieving
    B. Lesson Background
I. GOOD-BYE, WITH MEMORIES (Acts 20:17-21)
    A. Call for the Ephesian Elders (v. 17)
    B. Reflections on Ministry (vv. 18-21)
II. GOOD-BYE, WITH COMMITMENTS (Acts 20:22-24)
    A. Anticipation of Suffering (vv. 22, 23)
    B. Commitment to a Cause (v. 24)
    The Priorities of Life
III. GOOD-BYE, WITH CHALLENGES (Acts 20:25-28)
    A. Faithfulness in Preaching (vv. 25-27)
    B. Challenge to Leaders (v. 28)
    Famous Last Words
IV. GOOD-BYE, WITH PRAYER (Acts 20:36-38)
    A. Kneeling in Prayer (vv. 36, 37)
    B. Sadness of Parting (v. 38)
CONCLUSION
    A. Words That Inspire
    B. Prayer
    C. Thought to Remember

Introduction

A. Comfort for the Grieving

In his book *Helping the Hurting*, Philip Yancey tells a story about the famous composer Ludwig van Beethoven (1770–1827), a man who was not known for social grace. Because of his deafness later in life, Beethoven found conversation difficult and humiliating. When he learned of the death of a friend's son, Beethoven hurried to the house, overcome with grief. He had no words of comfort to offer. But he saw a piano in the room. For the next half hour he played the piano, pouring out his emotions in the most eloquent way he could. When he finished playing, he left. The friend later remarked that no one else's visit had meant so much.

We may contrast that remark with the words of Job to the friends who thought they were helping: "miserable comforters are ye all" (Job 16:2). Believers are sometimes faced with challenging times that include grief and sadness. Spiritual leaders must learn to use their words to help the sorrowing find comfort and perspective. Paul's words to the Ephesians accomplished this purpose.

B. Lesson Background

During his third missionary journey, Paul was headed for Jerusalem but planning to go to Rome as well (Acts 19:21). He had established new churches in territories such as southern Galatia, Asia, Macedonia, and Achaia. Many had been baptized into Christ, and churches had grown stronger in spite of the persecution they often faced. Paul's journeys were carried out with the help of several traveling companions. Frequently he depended on coworkers to provide leadership in his absence.

The book of Acts records much of this activity, but many of the details must be collected from the letters of Paul. Among the churches he established, the evidence tells us that at least some congregations formed a very close bond with the apostle. (See Philippians 4:10-20 and 1 Thessalonians 2:1-16.) Today's text will show us that Paul also developed a close relationship with the Ephesian elders.

I. Good-bye, with Memories
(Acts 20:17-21)

A. Call for the Ephesian Elders (v. 17)

17. And from Miletus he sent to Ephesus, and called the elders of the church.

Miletus (also in 2 Timothy 4:20) is a city of Asia located on the coast of the Aegean Sea. It is about 30 miles south of *Ephesus*, meaning that messengers will have to be *sent to* call for the Ephesian *elders*. The distance is about two days to walk, thus the round-trip requires four days or so. In spite of the inconvenience of the distance, Paul wants to see these elders again, and they are more than happy to meet him in Miletus.

Paul's Ephesian ministry is recorded in Acts 19. That ministry included the rebaptism of the disciples of John the Baptist, the defeat of the Jewish exorcists, and the riot energized by the silversmiths. Paul's ministry at Ephesus occupied a great deal of his time (see Acts 19:10). These elders had served with Paul in all kinds of circumstances, and he is grateful for his relationship with them.

Paul's reasons for summoning the elders rather than traveling to Ephesus to see them probably have to do with the delays that may occur should he return to there. People had rioted during his last visit there (see Acts 19:23-41)! Yet sensing the difficulties before him, Paul wants to make arrangements to meet with these special believers for this occasion.

B. Reflections on Ministry (vv. 18-21)

18, 19. And when they were come to him, he said unto them, Ye know, from the first day that I came into Asia, after what manner I have been with you at all seasons, serving the Lord with all humility of mind, and with many tears, and temptations, which befell me by the lying in wait of the Jews.

Paul's first words to the Ephesian elders *when they were come to him* are a reminder of shared experiences in ministry. Paul's reference to the *first day* he *came into Asia* takes us back to Acts 18:19-21. He had left Corinth with Priscilla and Aquila and had arrived in Ephesus to preach and teach briefly. He then left for Jerusalem and Antioch of Syria, returning later to spend many months in Ephesus (Acts 19:8-10; 20:31).

Paul's mention of *humility* and *tears* calls attention to his style of ministry. When he reminds the Thessalonians of his ministry with them, he points out that he had not used flattery or coveted praise, but had ministered among them as gently as a mother cares for her young (1 Thessalonians 2:4-9). This often included working to pay his own bills (see also 1 Corinthians 9:12-18). Similarly, he now reminds the Ephesian elders now that he has not ministered in a selfish way, looking for what advantage he could gain for himself. His ministry was marked by tears for their progress, giving the glory to God. His attitude in ministry is always that he and his coworkers are merely instruments through which God accomplishes His work (see 1 Corinthians 3:5-9).

The phrase *lying in wait of the Jews* reminds us that trouble from Jewish opponents seems to follow Paul wherever he goes. He was stoned at Lystra (Acts 14:19). At Thessalonica Jews rounded up some men of low repute to attack the house where Paul was staying (Acts 17:5). In Corinth the Jewish elements of the population initiated an action that placed Paul in front of Gallio, proconsul of Achaia (Acts 18:12). Even in Ephesus he met resistance from Jews, which moved him to begin a ministry in the lecture hall of Tyrannus (Acts 19:9, 10).

20, 21. And how I kept back nothing that was profitable unto you, but have showed you, and have taught you publicly, and from house to house, testifying both to the Jews, and also to the Greeks, repentance toward God, and faith toward our Lord Jesus Christ.

Paul speaks with confidence that he has not robbed the Ephesians of any part of the truth during his months of preaching. His efforts included both public preaching and teaching in private settings. His target is not only Jews, but also Gentiles (compare Acts 18:6). His ministry in Ephesus gave him an opportunity to preach to both Jews and Gentiles.

Paul sketches the content of his gospel as *repentance toward God, and faith toward our Lord Jesus Christ.* Though Paul's letters emphasize faith more frequently than repentance, both of these themes can be found (see, for example, Romans 1–3). Repentance emphasizes sorrow for sin as one turns away from evil; faith focuses on

---

Home Daily Bible Readings

Monday, Nov. 21—Naomi and Ruth Part with Orpah (Ruth 1:6-14)

Tuesday, Nov. 22—David and Jonathan Part (1 Samuel 20:32-42)

Wednesday, Nov. 23—Paul Stops in Greece and Macedonia (Acts 20:1-6)

Thursday, Nov. 24—Paul's Farewell Visit to Troas (Acts 20:7-12)

Friday, Nov. 25—Paul Speaks to the Ephesian Elders (Acts 20:17-24)

Saturday, Nov. 26—Paul Warns Elders to Be Alert (Acts 20:25-31)

Sunday, Nov. 27—Paul and the Elders Say Good-Bye (Acts 20:32-38)

> **How to Say It**
>
> ACHAIA. Uh-*kay*-uh.
> AEGEAN. A-*jee*-un.
> ASIA. *Ay*-zha.
> CAESAREA. Sess-uh-*ree*-uh.
> COLOSSIANS. Kuh-*losh*-unz.
> CORINTH. *Kor*-inth.
> CORINTHIANS. Ko-*rin*-thee-unz (*th* as in *thin*).
> EPHESIANS. Ee-*fee*-zhunz.
> EPHESUS. *Ef*-uh-sus.
> EZEKIEL. Ee-*zeek*-ee-ul or Ee-*zeek*-yul.
> GALATIA. Guh-*lay*-shuh.
> GALLIO. *Gal*-ee-o.
> LYSTRA. *Liss*-truh.
> MACEDONIA. Mass-eh-*doe*-nee-uh.
> MILETUS. My-*lee*-tus.
> SILAS. *Sigh*-luss.
> THESSALONIANS. *Thess*-uh-*lo*-nee-unz (strong accent on *lo*; *th* as in *thin*).
> THESSALONICA. *Thess*-uh-lo-*nye*-kuh (strong accent on *nye*; *th* as in *thin*).
> TYRANNUS. Ty-*ran*-nus.
> TYRE. Tire.

the commitment of the heart to Christ. [See question #1, page 127.]

This review of Paul's history with the Ephesians reminds those elders of their common bond. Their shared experiences give Paul a high degree of respect that make his words more powerful. When believers want to express comfort to people facing grief, the words will be more powerful if they come from someone whose life has been intertwined with those who are listening.

II. Good-bye, with Commitments (Acts 20:22-24)

A. Anticipation of Suffering (vv. 22, 23)

22, 23. And now, behold, I go bound in the spirit unto Jerusalem, not knowing the things that shall befall me there: save that the Holy Ghost witnesseth in every city, saying that bonds and afflictions abide me.

Paul feels an obligation *in the spirit* to go back to *Jerusalem*. It is a trip he must take! In his letter to the Romans (probably written during the time mentioned in Acts 20:1-3), he urges the believers to pray for this trip because he sensed danger ahead (Romans 15:31). [See question #2, page 127.] In the text before us, he makes clear that difficult challenges are coming on this journey to Jerusalem and that he has been warned of this by the Holy Spirit.

The cities that Paul has in mind here are not mentioned specifically. But later in the book of Acts, warnings will come from people in cities such as Tyre and Caesarea (Acts 21:3, 4, 8-11). Paul mentions the Holy Spirit because the warnings he receives are often directed at him by people who are moved by the Spirit to speak such messages.

B. Commitment to a Cause (v. 24)

24. But none of these things move me, neither count I my life dear unto myself, so that I might finish my course with joy, and the ministry, which I have received of the Lord Jesus, to testify the gospel of the grace of God.

The warnings, however, do not diminish Paul's determination to continue his ministry for Christ. His attitude about his *life* is that he has given himself to the *Lord* to be crucified with Christ (Galatians 2:20). Therefore whatever life he has belongs to Christ. His focus is on serving Christ, not on preserving his own life. Therefore, he will not be discouraged at the warnings regarding dangers to come.

Instead, Paul is determined to *finish* his *course with joy*. His choice of terms here refers to the course set out for the runners of a race. Paul uses athletic terminology elsewhere in his letters (see 1 Corinthians 9:24; 2 Timothy 4:7). [See question #3, page 127.]

This *ministry* of Paul is his because the Lord Jesus Christ has given it to him. Such language takes the listener back to Paul's experience on the road to Damascus (Acts 9:1-19). There Jesus revealed to Paul that he was chosen for the purpose of carrying the gospel to both Jews and Gentiles. Paul will refer to this moment as his commissioning from the Lord into this ministry (see Acts 26:12-18). So Paul expresses his sentiments to the Ephesian elders by reminding them of his commitments to the Lord and to his ministry. Just because he will not be present with them does not mean that he has forgotten his calling.

There are always times in life when parting from friends or coworkers will mean offering words of encouragement. Paul's use of his own example of dedication should inspire us to consider how our own dedication to Christ lifts others in times of sadness. Speaking about our love of Christ and His ministry to those facing sadness, loss, or grief can sometimes help friends take heart for the future.

THE PRIORITIES OF LIFE

The *Guinness Book of World Records* is an amazing collection of human endeavors. These endeavors can be serious, whimsical, significant, and ridiculous. If any human activity can be counted or measured, be assured that someone has done it and it is certified by Guinness. For example, Sammy and Billy Kishek spent several years (sometimes working 11 hours a day) and $15,000 creating a ball of rubber bands big enough to make it into the record book. At last count the ball was 5 feet high and weighed 2,700 pounds—and it was still growing!

The nearest known competitor of the Kishek brothers is no longer a threat. The competitor's 2,500-pound rubber band ball made the Guinness Book in 2002. In celebration the *Ripley's Believe It or Not* TV show dropped the ball from an airplane a mile above the Arizona desert to see how high it would bounce. It didn't; it just made a cloud of dust and a crater, exploding in the process.

With a great variety of things to which we might commit our lives, rubber band balls should be pretty low on our list. How much different Paul's priority was! Regardless of cost to freedom and life, he was prepared to fulfill the mission God had given him. As a result, his name is in God's book, which is much better than being in the Guinness book. Does our commitment measure up to his? What is our greatest priority in life?   —C. R. B.

III. Good-bye, with Challenges (Acts 20:25-28)

A. Faithfulness in Preaching (vv. 25-27)

25. And now, behold, I know that ye all, among whom I have gone preaching the kingdom of God, shall see my face no more.

The danger that lies ahead in Jerusalem is great indeed! The narrative moves forward in the next chapter with details about Paul's arrest there (Acts 21:33), followed by his hearings, leading to this imprisonment in Rome (Acts 28:16). This is indeed a touching moment as Paul confesses this conviction in clear language to his friends from Ephesus. With their love and respect for Paul, how can they not be affected emotionally by his words?

26, 27. Wherefore I take you to record this day, that I am pure from the blood of all men. For I have not shunned to declare unto you all the counsel of God.

Paul's language calls upon the Ephesians to "mark this down." He has fulfilled his duty to serve as a watchman on the city wall, as the prophet Ezekiel described his own job (Ezekiel 33:1-6). He had seen the danger and had warned the people of Ephesus with every ounce of strength he could generate. He had declared *all the counsel of God* so that every listener would know God's will.

Paul implies that he could have *shunned* this effort by speaking only what was safe or popular for him to speak. He calls upon the Ephesians to remember that he did not limit his words to the "safe" things. Rather, he had spoken the entirety of God's truth fearlessly. Thus he is innocent of *the blood of* any who will be destroyed when judgment day comes because they did not heed his gospel call.

B. Challenge to Leaders (v. 28)

28. Take heed therefore unto yourselves, and to all the flock, over the which the Holy Ghost hath made you overseers, to feed the church of God, which he hath purchased with his own blood.

So Paul leaves the Ephesian elders with a challenge to imitate his own ministry. First he challenges them to pay attention to themselves as elders. If they don't guard their own lives, who will? To Timothy, a leader at Ephesus, Paul will expand this discussion by saying, "Take heed unto thyself, and unto the doctrine; continue in them: for in doing this thou shalt both save thyself, and them that hear thee" (1 Timothy 4:16).

Visual for lesson 13

Refer to this photograph as you ask, "What are some ways that the people of the church are to be cared for?"

Paul also urges the elders to remember the importance of watching over *the flock*. This describes the teaching needed by the church to grow in faith. The apostle Peter echoes something of the same thing in 1 Peter 5:1-3. Paul's reference in the verse before us is especially to the threat of false teachers, as in his other writings such as Ephesians 5:6, 7 and Colossians 2:8.

As these elders present doctrine that nourishes the church, they should remember that they are not the owners of the church. Christ Jesus *purchased* the church *with His own blood* when He died on the cross. Paul's farewell to the Ephesian elders *(overseers)* is thus an appeal to continue to minister as if they were handling a precious possession bought with Christ's blood—which they are! Those who give their lives to shepherding the flock of God can influence fellow believers by accepting this challenge as their own.

Famous Last Words

People's last words give insight into their character. Consider these last words: P. T. Barnum asked, "How were the receipts today at Madison Square Garden?" Poet Dylan Thomas said, "I've had 18 straight whiskies, I think that's the record." As Joan Crawford's housekeeper prayed, the actress said, "Don't you dare ask God to help me."

Some people express their despair at what awaits them. The writer Thomas Hobbes said, "I am about to take my last voyage, a great leap in the dark." "Lord, help my poor soul" were Edgar Allan Poe's last words. The Emperor Vespasian, perhaps speaking sarcastically, said, "Woe is me. Methinks I'm turning into a god." Leonardo da Vinci's last words may surprise us: "I have offended God and mankind because my work did not reach the quality it should have."

Then there are the distinctly Christian farewells. Author Joseph Addison said, "See in what peace a Christian can die." Thomas à Becket, Archbishop of Canterbury who was martyred at the instigation of King Henry II, said, "I am ready to die for my Lord, that in my blood the Church may obtain liberty and peace."

Paul's words in our text were not his dying words, but they were the last words some of his colaborers would hear from him. They were a fond good-bye and a challenge to faithfulness. When the time comes for our farewells or last words, we can do no better. —C. R. B.

IV. Good-bye, with Prayer
(Acts 20:36-38)
A. Kneeling in Prayer (vv. 36, 37)

36, 37. And when he had thus spoken, he kneeled down, and prayed with them all. And they all wept sore, and fell on Paul's neck, and kissed him.

Kneeling in prayer is an expression of seriousness and humility (Ephesians 3:14), since standing in prayer is more often the posture used (Luke 18:9-14). Paul's friends are not only ready to pray with him, they also express their deep feelings in the form of tears. This is a farewell that touches everyone who loves and respects him. They show this by throwing their arms around him and kissing him on the cheeks.

Working for Christ can form bonds that are closer than family. These spiritual brothers of Paul are now parting with someone dear to them, and they cannot resist expressing their heartfelt love. Believers should never be ashamed of expressing their sadness and comfort in visible ways. [See question #4, page 127.]

B. Sadness of Parting (v. 38)

38. Sorrowing most of all for the words which he spake, that they should see his face no more. And they accompanied him unto the ship.

There is no avoiding the sadness of Paul's message. The emotional reaction to it is inspired by the news that this could be his final contact with them. Obviously there is concern for his coming hardships, the persecutions, and the suffering for his faith. But as they say good-bye at *the ship*, they understand that they are looking into the eyes of Paul for the final time.

So Paul's departure from Miletus is sad but not lonely. His Christian friends surround him with their love and support. At the same time, Paul does not leave these Christian friends before forcing them to ponder their future without his personal leadership. Even in his final moments with these friends, his focus is not on his own sufferings but on what he hopes that they will do in the ministry for Christ.

Conclusion
A. Words That Inspire

When times are difficult it is important that Christian leaders share words that keep the church focused on the things of God. Paul's

LESSON 13   125   NOVEMBER 27

words were spoken at a moment when believers saw gloomy times coming. But his words and example gave them courage. What opportunities will we have to speak words that bring comfort and courage? Can we use our words to lift the spirits of those whose faith may be threatened or overwhelmed? Our words can inspire faith and dedication in those who are weak and vulnerable. May the Lord help us to find ways to build up the church in times of distress. [See question #5, page 127.]

B. Prayer

Lord of all hope and comfort, help us this day to realize the power of our words when times are difficult. When people need to see in us a reason to trust You through hardships, may we have the strength to show them the way. In Christ, amen.

C. Thought to Remember

Words of faith and courage can make good-byes easier to bear.

Learning by Doing

This page contains an alternate lesson plan emphasizing learning activities. Classes desiring such student involvement will find these suggestions helpful.

Learning Goals

After participating in this lesson, each student will be able to:

1. Recall the main points of Paul's final talk with the Ephesian elders.
2. Identify some of the "sad good-byes" that Christians experience today.
3. Write a letter of encouragement to a fellow Christian who lives in a foreign country.

Into the Lesson

Put a variety of verbal farewells on classroom display from several different languages; for example, "Good-bye," "Vaya con Dios," "Adieu." If you have class members who know other languages, call them ahead of time and add their farewell expressions to your list.

As class begins, ask class members, "How do some of these expressions call for the blessing of God on the one being greeting?" (*Good-bye* represents the English "God be with you"; *vaya con Dios* is simple Spanish for "go with God"; *adieu* is French representing "to God.") After explanations, say, "Today's study is of a poignant good-bye that the Christians of Ephesus and Paul experienced. A desire for God's presence and blessing is always appropriate when Christians part."

Into the Word

Divide your class into three groups (six groups if you have more than 24 students). Give the first group(s) this assignment: "Luke records Paul's initial ministry in Ephesus in Acts 19. Skim that chapter and develop a summary of Paul and the Spirit's ministry in that city. You will be asked to review that history before the other groups give their reports."

Give the second group(s) this assignment: "Look at today's text in Acts 20:17-38. Paul is meeting, advising, and encouraging the elders of the Ephesian church. Make a list of attributes that are overt or implied in those elders. Identify verses where you see the characteristics. For example, they were overseers (v. 28); they were teachable (v. 20). When you give your report to the class, list the attributes, but ask the class to identify the relevant verses."

Give the third group(s) this assignment, "Look at today's text in Acts 20:17-38. Paul is meeting, advising, and encouraging the elders of the Ephesian church. Make a list of attributes that are overt or implied in the apostle Paul. He represents what all preaching ministers should be like. For example, he is demonstrative (v. 37); he is unprejudiced (v. 21). When you give your report to the class, list the attributes, but ask the class to identify relevant verses."

Give each group at least eight minutes to work. Then ask groups (in the order you passed out the assignments) to give reports. If you have two groups working on the same assignment, ask for one of the groups to begin the summary and the other one to finish it or else alternate between groups. (A similar activity is included in the student book.)

Your class can encourage the elders of your church with a "thinking of you"-type card. You may want to make such cards available; most Christian bookstores can provide boxed quantities. (One with a picture of Jesus as the good shepherd would be especially suitable, with today's Golden Text added and personalized with a note of thanks.) For example, begin with "Dear brother _____," then quote Acts 20:28, then add a personal note of thanks.

Into Life

Ask the class to develop a list of sad good-byes that each of us experience in life. If the group is slow to respond, give some examples: good-bye to a retiring minister; good-bye to a trusted family business that goes out of business; good-bye to a church family moving to a different community. After the list is made, ask the class to suggest an appropriate word to be given in each situation.

Provide a list of seven e-mail (or regular mail) addresses of Christians serving in foreign lands. Discuss with your class the appropriate words of encouragement that could be shared with each of the people on the list of addresses that you are providing.

Encourage students to send an e-mail per day to one of the seven names provided. Ask those who use regular mail to select one person to send an air letter and use the same encouraging words. (A similar activity is included in the student book.)

Let's Talk It Over

These questions are designed to promote discussion of the lesson. The answers here are only discussion starters. Let your class talk it over from there.

1. Paul's preaching included a call to repentance. Why is repentance necessary? How can your church do a better job of calling people to repent?

Repentance involves a change of lifestyle based upon a change of heart. It requires a noticeable difference in attitudes and actions. Repentance is necessary because it is part of making Jesus master of one's life. To refuse to repent is to make personal wishes and desires the focus of one's life.

The church, in an effort to grow, may sometimes shrink back on the teaching of repentance, not wanting to be seen as judgmental by challenging people's lifestyles (or deathstyles!). Repentance includes a recognition that there is something to repent *of,* namely *sin.* Churches that downplay the seriousness of sin will naturally minimize the importance of repentance as well.

2. Paul spent much of his ministry in bondage. Why would God allow such a great preacher of the Word to be restricted by captivity? What bondage are you experiencing that can be beneficial to God's kingdom in the long run?

God's ways are higher than ours, His thoughts much deeper than we can imagine. In a human way of looking at things, having Paul, the chief proponent of the faith, bound would be tantamount to stopping the forward movement of the cause. But God was still able to use Paul, though bound, to write powerful letters of encouragement and correction to the churches. Without those periods of bondage, we might not have those letters today!

Paul's faith in the midst of his trials and his ability to share the gospel before high-ranking officials further demonstrate the wisdom of God. God can use people, no matter the circumstances they find themselves in, to advance the work of His kingdom in ways we cannot see until after the fact.

3. Even in the face of more persecution, Paul kept pressing forward in his ministry. How is this focus a model for us today? How are our struggles in the faith similar to and different from those of Paul?

Revelation 2:10 encourages the Christian to be faithful even to the point of death. It is the Lord who will give the reward of a crown of life. Paul knew this, and he is a model for us in this regard. Faithfulness is necessary to receive the reward of Heaven.

Faithfulness is also needed to prove the effectiveness of the gospel we proclaim. To say that Jesus is Lord through all circumstances only to forsake Him when the going gets tough is to deny our words by our actions. We stand with Paul in this regard. Even so, few Christians who live in western democracies will be bound in chains as Paul was. Our bondage may take other forms.

4. In the church we often have to say good-bye to members who move away. What are some ways we can do this effectively?

As a show of encouragement, love, and support, those who are leaving need to receive a good send-off. This takes prayer and advance planning. A last-minute potluck supper probably won't be very effective. The idea is to say, "We value how you have served with us here, and we know you will be effective for Christ in the future." Send-offs can involve a time of prayer for those leaving and possibly a gift that brings to mind their service with your congregation for years to come.

5. Paul was aware of the pain that his words brought to the Ephesian elders. He therefore spoke words of encouragement as well. How can we be more ready to offer such words? At what times should we be ready to do this?

Maintaining open lines of communication within the church family is essential; e-mail can actually be a hindrance since it is rather impersonal. Monitoring the attendance and participation level of people can help point to times when encouragement may be needed. A sudden drop in church participation may be an indicator of a problem where encouragement is needed.

Of course, there is the need of being visible in times of extreme hardships and heartache, such as the death of a loved one or sickness. Often it is not necessary to speak. Your presence can be a great means of encouragement in and of itself.

Quarter Review

Use this page to form questions for the class to answer and discuss. Then provide the information as a handout to summarize the lessons of the past quarter.

Lesson 1: The Spirit Comes

Just as Jesus had promised, the apostles received power from on high on the day of Pentecost. The sights and sounds of the day attracted a crowd, so Peter and the Eleven delivered the Spirit-prompted gospel message.

Lesson 2: The Believers Share

"The poor you will always have with you," Jesus had said. The early church did not forget. The spirit of generosity present among the first Christians met the needs of all and testified greatly of Christ's love to a watching world.

Lesson 3: Peter and John Heal a Lame Man

The title only begins to tell the story. Peter and John did heal a lame man, but so much more then happened. The lame man praised god, a crowd gathered, and Peter preached the gospel once again.

Lesson 4: The Church Is Bold

Peter and John were haled before the Sanhedrin and threatened. When they were released, they quickly joined the other believers in prayer. More than a prayer of thanks for their release, it was a prayer for further boldness!

Lesson 5: Stephen Is Faithful to the End

Envy turned to rage and threats turned to violence in the case of Stephen. Having defended his faith so eloquently that his adversaries had nothing to say, he was left to face their angry hatred. Even so, they took only his life, not his witness.

Lesson 6: Philip Preaches in Samaria

Stephen was not the only one of "the seven" (Acts 6) who could defend the faith eloquently. Philip was another, and his efforts in Samaria brought a great revival. Even Simon, a sorcerer, was convinced.

Lesson 7: Philip Teaches an Ethiopian

Why Philip was called to leave an exciting ministry in the city of Samaria to preach to one man in the desert, only God knows. But Philip answered the call, and the gospel spread to Africa when the eunuch went on his way rejoicing.

Lesson 8: God Welcomes Gentiles

Cornelius is the first known Gentile to receive the gospel. But this lesson does not tell that story so much as it tells what it took to get Peter to be God's instrument in that historic event. May we not be so slow to open our hearts to others!

Lesson 9: Peter Escapes Prison

Things were getting desperate. James had been murdered, and it looked as if Peter were next. The church prayed, Peter slept, and God acted. But Peter found the prayer meeting harder to get into than the prison was to get out of!

Lesson 10: Paul Meets the Lord

For the second time in our studies a heavenly manifestation gets someone's attention, but a human messenger is required to deliver the good news. Human messengers are still the only way the gospel is spread. Are we doing our part?

Lesson 11: Lydia Demonstrates Faithfulness

Lydia was the first known European to receive the gospel. Immediately she began to demonstrate her gratitude for salvation. When we practice the gifts of the spirit, such as hospitality, we also demonstrate that kind of gratitude.

Lesson 12: Priscilla and Aquila Serve Together

We almost never hear of one without the other—Priscilla and Aquila. Nor do we ever hear of them idle! Do you have a partner? Are you as eager to serve as were they?

Lesson 13: Paul Says Good-Bye

It was a sad scene there on the beach as Paul bade what could have been his final farewell to his friends from Ephesus. But faithfulness to the Lord demanded it, even as it makes demands for hard choices from us.

Copyright © 2005. STANDARD PUBLISHING, Cincinnati, Ohio. Permission is granted to reproduce this page for ministry purposes only. Not for resale.

Winter Quarter, 2005-2006

God's Commitment— Our Response

Special Features

	Page
Quarterly Quiz	130
God's Plans for Humanity .... Lloyd Pelfrey	131
The World of Paul, Timothy, and Titus (Map Feature)	133
Mary's Song (Chart Feature)	134
Teaching for Transformed Lives (Teacher Tips) .... Eleanor Daniel	135
How to Say It	138
Quarter Review	256

Lessons

Unit 1: God's Redeeming Love

December	4	Justice for All	Isaiah 42:1-9	139
	11	Strength for the Weary	Isaiah 49:5, 6; 50:4-11	148
	18	Hope for the Suffering	Isaiah 53:1-3; Luke 1:46-55	157
	25	Good News for the World	Isaiah 61:1, 2; Luke 2:8-20	166

Unit 2: God's Gifts of Leadership

January	1	Rely on God's Strength	1 Timothy 1:12-20	175
	8	Pray for Everyone	1 Timothy 2:1-8	184
	15	Call Godly Leaders	1 Timothy 3:1-15	193
	22	Teach for Godliness	1 Timothy 4	202
	29	Practice Justice and Mercy	1 Timothy 5:1-8, 17-25	211

Unit 3: Faithful Followers, Faithful Leaders

February	5	Be True to Your Christian Heritage	2 Timothy 1:3-14	220
	12	Develop Christian Character	2 Timothy 2:14-26	229
	19	Follow a Good Mentor	2 Timothy 3:10–4:8	238
	26	Live and Teach the Truth	Titus 2	247

About These Lessons

Have you ever had the unsettling experience of committing yourself to planning an elaborate event, only to have people ignore your invitation? The God of the universe has committed himself to making big plans for us. But He expects a response! This quarter's lessons show us why and how.

Quarterly Quiz

This quiz can be used to preview the lessons, to review at the end of the quarter, or as a review after each lesson. The quiz may be copied and distributed to students. **The answers are on page 136.**

Lesson 1
1. The servant was to be a light for whom? (Gentiles, Satan, the temple?) *Isaiah 42:6*
2. The Lord declares new things. T/F *Isaiah 42:8, 9*

Lesson 2
1. The servant was to bring salvation to the end of the _____. *Isaiah 49:6*
2. Those who try to walk by their own light will lie down in what? (peace, bed, sorrow?) *Isaiah 50:11*

Lesson 3
1. The Lord's servant (Jesus) was _____ and _____ by men. *Isaiah 53:3*
2. Mary believed that the Lord's mercy extended from _____ to _____. *Luke 1:50*

Lesson 4
1. Isaiah predicted that the Lord's anointed would preach what kind of tidings to the meek? (good, bad, sobering?) *Isaiah 61:1*
2. What shone round about the shepherds? (sunlight, moonlight, glory of the Lord?) *Luke 2:9*

Lesson 5
1. Paul told Timothy to maintain a good conscience. T/F *1 Timothy 1:19*
2. Two who shipwrecked their faith were whom? (Silas and Barnabas, Hymeneus and Alexander, Nero and Caligula?) *1 Timothy 1:20*

Lesson 6
1. How many mediators are there between God and humanity? *1 Timothy 2:5*
2. Paul wanted everyone to lift up holy what? (hands, arms, elbows?) *1 Timothy 2:8*

Lesson 7
1. One method for evaluating someone's suitability to be an elder is to see how well he runs his own house. T/F *1 Timothy 3:4, 5*
2. What did Paul tell Timothy was "the pillar and ground of the truth"? (his own behavior, the church, the prophet Isaiah?) *1 Timothy 3:15*

Lesson 8
1. What was Timothy to do with profane and old wives' fables? (debate them, write a letter refuting them, refuse them?) *1 Timothy 4:7*
2. Timothy received his gift through the laying on of _____. *1 Timothy 4:14*
3. Paul did not think it was very important for Timothy to pay attention to doctrine. T/F *1 Timothy 4:16*

Lesson 9
1. Paul told Timothy to rebuke older men sharply so they would be sure and get the message. T/F *1 Timothy 5:1*
2. Anyone who doesn't provide for his own house is worse than what? (a Pharisee, a Sadducee, an infidel?) *1 Timothy 5:8*

Lesson 10
1. Paul's grandmother was named Lois and his mother was named Eunice. T/F *2 Timothy 1:5*
2. In bringing life and immortality, Christ abolished _____. *2 Timothy 1:10*

Lesson 11
1. The doctrinal error of Hymeneus and Philetus was that the resurrection would never occur. T/F *2 Timothy 2:17, 18*
2. With what kind of spirit is the Lord's servant to instruct those of the opposition? (confrontational, meek, casual?) *2 Timothy 2:25*

Lesson 12
1. Paul tells Timothy that all who live godly lives in Christ Jesus will suffer what? (persecution, inconvenience, heartburn?) *2 Timothy 3:12*
2. Among other things, Timothy was to reprove, rebuke, and exhort. T/F *2 Timothy 4:2*
3. Timothy was to do the work of what? (an apostle, a prophet, an evangelist?) *2 Timothy 4:5*

Lesson 13
1. Paul told Titus that the older women were to teach the young _____. *Titus 2:3, 4*
2. Titus was to rebuke with all authority. T/F *Titus 2:15*

God's Plans for Humanity

by Lloyd Pelfrey

A CHRISTIAN BUSINESSMAN in south-central Illinois was often associated with this statement: "If God is your partner, make your plans big." Almost a century ago, a similar sentiment was offered: "Make no little plans; they have no magic to stir men's blood and probably themselves will not be realized. Make big plans; aim high in hope and work."

The lessons for the next three months provide a study of God's plans for humanity. These are big plans! Our study of them will involve passages concerning God's prophecies about the Christ who was to come. We will also study God's expectations for those who respond favorably to His gracious designs.

The plans begin in the Old Testament. There we discover the basic theme is that *Someone is coming!* God will send His anointed one (Messiah) for the spiritual benefit of all. The first promises are found in the book of Genesis, and they continue on through the Minor Prophets. God's preparations for the promised one included individuals and nations. This divine determination for sending the Messiah was made before the foundation (or creation) of the world (1 Peter 1:20).

Unit 1: December
God's Redeeming Love

British statesman William Gladstone remarked in 1878 that "National injustice is the surest road to national downfall." The fall of great nations is normally accompanied by injustices among the leaders and their people. In **Lesson 1** we will see the prophet Isaiah predict that one aspect of the Messiah's work will be to bring judgment and justice. Nations and individuals can receive the promised blessings only as justice is applied throughout their lives.

Lesson 2 teaches us about strength. When it seems that no one cares, there is a temptation simply to quit. It is in such circumstances that God's people find strength in the redemptive work of the Messiah. The fact that the Lord has demonstrated His concern in the past provides a renewed determination for His people to encourage one another today. Together we can handle the tribulations, trials, and testings of life.

Lesson 3 starts us in Isaiah 53. That grand passage prophetically depicts the suffering of the Messiah for the sins of others. The lesson text also includes part of the Gospel of Luke. Attention there is given to the famous expression of Mary during the time that she visited Elisabeth (who was to be the mother of John the Baptist). In the midst of her unusual circumstances, Mary expressed confidence in God. Her expression of praise included reflections on her blessings and the mighty acts of God through the centuries.

Lesson 4 combines a prophecy in Isaiah about the ministry of Jesus with the passage in Luke that proclaims that the Savior is born. Angelic messengers brought the good news. The shepherds from the Bethlehem area then set the example as they made known to others the good things that they had seen and heard. How appropriate it is that our study takes place on the day when we traditionally celebrate the Savior's birth!

Unit 2: January
God's Gifts of Leadership

Leaders of any group or organization must be concerned about the next generation. If they're not, then their groups will die off! **Lesson 5** shows us Paul's concerns in this regard. We will see the apostle describe to Timothy his own experiences, and then encourage his son in the faith to follow his example in fighting the good fight. Sadly, not everyone remains true to the affirmations that they made about following Jesus, and Paul cites examples for Timothy to note. The first Sunday of a new year is a good time to consider how we will pass the mantle of church leadership to future generations.

Prayer is the emphasis in **Lesson 6**. Again we take our text from Paul's first letter to Timothy. There the apostle's exhortation is for Timothy—and indeed everyone—to pray. One major consideration is that such prayers are to be for governmental leaders. The spiritual qualities of presidents, prime ministers, and others in authority should always concern us. But the real purpose in such prayers is to allow the followers of God to be able to live in peace as they fulfill their obligations to God and humanity.

Lesson 7 focuses on leaders in the church. In this focus Paul sets forth the qualities that the church should expect elders and deacons to exhibit as they serve. Genuine leaders have genuine faith. Their lives may be noted as positive examples both in and out of the church. To have leaders with anything less than what the apostle describes is not only disappointing, but also harmful to the body of Christ.

Teaching is also a major part of the work of the church. Jesus emphasized this in Matthew 28:20 as a part of the Great Commission. **Lesson 8,** from 1 Timothy, gives us Paul's perspectives on teaching. He sounds warnings that there will be teachers who promote false doctrine. Such falsehood has its origins in evil spirits and demons who deceive. Teachers in the church must be examples in all aspects of their lives. The task of teaching is of the utmost importance, for eternal destinies are at stake.

Lesson 9. The last Sunday in January continues our study of church leadership. The tasks of leaders necessarily include maintaining proper relationships, and Paul offers needed cautions in this regard. A further thought concerns duties to see that the needs of the others (especially widows) are met. Warnings and advice about the lives of leaders and prospective leaders enrich this lesson.

Unit 3: February
Faithful Followers, Faithful Leaders

Every Christian is grateful for being a child of God. Many have a spiritual heritage that has helped to shape their lives. **Lesson 10** advances into 2 Timothy, where Paul reminds Timothy of two people whom he must remember: a godly mother and grandmother. They guided him spiritually in his formative years. Not every believer has such a benefit, but every Christian has someone who taught him or her in the faith.

The apostle goes on to warn Timothy about being ashamed; Paul reminds his younger colleague that he (Paul) was never ashamed of the gospel of Christ. Timothy must not be timid concerning his faith in Christ. Key tasks for Timothy will be to develop the virtues of love and personal discipline.

Contention causes tensions, and **Lesson 11** gives advice about quarrelsome words. The rhyme from school days that words do not hurt is simply not true. What a person says is important! Words may become a blessing to others or they may severely damage the church and its members.

The text is again from 2 Timothy, which includes a caution about handling the Word of God correctly. The abuse of what God's Word really says is a major factor in producing division. The lesson concludes with advice on responding to those who have been a part of the opposition. The goals are to treat them gently, lead them to repentance, and instill a knowledge of the truth.

Albert Schweitzer (1875–1965) wrote, "Example is not the main thing in influencing others. It is the only thing." **Lesson 12** emphasizes the importance of selecting a good mentor to be one's example of a godly life. This mentor-apprentice methodology always has been in God's plan for us. We see it stated forcefully in Deuteronomy 6:7, 8, one of the famous passages of the Bible. The concept is repeated in the final charges by the aged apostle to his son in the faith. There is also a vivid reminder that the crowns of righteousness are for all who eagerly await the return of the Savior.

Lesson 13, the final lesson of the quarter, is somewhat of a review. As such, it reinforces Paul's thoughts concerning attitudes and actions of Christians. The text is Paul's letter to Titus. There we see that every leader must live and teach the truth of the Word. There can be no disharmony between what is taught and what is done.

A Great Commitment, A Great Response

The quarter begins with God's initiative in promising that the Christ would come into the world. It concludes with words of instruction for leaders and other followers of the Christ, who has indeed come. His redemptive work by necessity demands that every one who hears the gospel must respond. The response is either to reject or accept the Son of God. That's the theme of these lessons: "God's Commitment—Our Response." As we grow in maturity and leadership skills, we continue to respond to Him.

The World of Paul, Timothy, and Titus

- Paul wrote 2 Timothy from Rome.
- Paul wrote 1 Timothy from Macedonia.
- Timothy was in Ephesus when he received both letters from Paul.
- Titus was on Crete when he received his letter from Paul.

ADRIATIC SEA
ITALY
Rome
Puteoli
Rhegium
SICILY
Syracuse
MALTA
MEDITERRANEAN SEA
MACEDONIA
Philippi
Thessalonica
Troas
Corinth
ASIA
Ephesus
CRETE

Mary's Song
(Luke 1)

WHAT MARY DOES: Magnifies the Lord (46); Rejoices in God (47)

WHAT GOD DOES

Regards Mary's low estate **(48)**

Does great things **(49)**

Is merciful **(50)**

Shows strength **(51)**

Scatters the proud **(51)**

Puts down the mighty **(52)**

Exalts those of low degree **(52)**

Fills the hungry **(53)**

Sends the rich away empty **(53)**

Helps His servant Israel **(54)**

Remembers to be merciful **(54)**

WHAT OTHERS DO: Call Mary blessed (48)

Teacher Tips

Teaching for Transformed Lives

Our Privilege

by Eleanor Daniel

TEACHING GOD'S WORD is a special privilege. But teaching God's Word to transform lives is more than a privilege—it is both work and a craft.

Effective teaching is always more than merely presenting a body of information, providing interpretation of the material, and suggesting a bit of an application. It also demands that the teacher "read" the learners and the needs, interests, and concerns they bring to the learning situation. It is this reality that always makes me muse longest as I prepare to teach.

Begin with a Central Truth

If you plan to teach the Word of God to transform lives, you must do the careful work of understanding the text and figuring out how it intersects with the lives of contemporary learners. It is by using your study of the text and your knowledge of your learners that you put together what I call the central truth for the lesson.

The central truth is a simple declarative sentence that provides the focus for the lesson and your preparation of it. It frequently combines Scripture content and student response. It is the thread that holds the lesson together. It is what you want the learners to remember even if they should forget all the details. It helps you decide how to approach the lesson, how many details to include, and what can wait until another teaching of the text.

The central truths for the lessons of this quarter are not hard to find. Here are some possibilities for Unit 1, entitled "God's Redeeming Love." **Lesson 1:** God's servant came to deliver hope, justice, and righteousness to all people, even, perhaps especially, the disenfranchised among us. **Lesson 2:** God's servant came to deliver salvation to all people, whatever their ethnic or personal background. **Lesson 3:** God's suffering servant meets our deepest need: personal salvation. **Lesson 4:** Our response to the Lord's servant should be one of joyful praise and proclamation.

Consider making a large display of Isaiah 61:1 to display for the duration of this unit. This also would be a worthwhile verse for students to commit to memory.

For the five lessons of Unit 2, entitled "God's Gifts of Leadership," consider the following possibilities as central truths. **Lesson 5:** The effective leader is the one who has been transformed by Christ. **Lesson 6:** Effective leaders are characterized by a distinctively Christlike lifestyle that is marked by prayer. **Lesson 7:** Effective Christian elders model a life of piety and service for Christ. **Lesson 8:** Effective Christian leaders give close attention to biblical teaching. **Lesson 9:** Effective Christian leaders and followers are marked by behavior that puts the needs of others first.

A helpful verse to display before the class (and for them to commit to memory) is 1 Timothy 1:16. You may find another verse that suits your class better.

For Unit 3, entitled "Faithful Followers, Faithful Leaders," consider the following as central truths. **Lesson 10:** Effective Christian leaders and followers are called to influence others. **Lesson 11:** Effective Christian leaders and followers seek God's approval. **Lesson 12:** Effective Christian leaders and followers faithfully perform their duties, despite the circumstances. **Lesson 13:** All Christians are responsible to see that the Word of God is taught to those of all ages. Second Timothy 4:2, among many other verses from this unit, would be good for display and memorization.

Next, Think About Presentation

When your course is set by a clear central truth, you are ready to think about how you will present the material. Bible lessons designed to transform lives have four building blocks that, when taken altogether, lead the student to the Word of God and from there to life.

Building Block #1: Approach. How will you gain the learners' attention? To begin by announcing the Scripture reference is not likely to engage adults. Instead, you could open with a good illustration and ask how it applies. Another approach is to have the learners interact with a concept relevant to the lesson. Still another option is to make a statement related to the lesson and ask students to agree or disagree.

Starting the lesson with a question is another tried-and-true method of gaining attention. You could take your central truth and modify it to be this question. Or you may wish to consider the following sample questions. **Lesson 1:** What do people hope for today? Why? **Lesson 2:** What is salvation? What do people want to be saved from? to? **Lesson 3:** What are some words related to salvation? **Lesson 4:** What do you do when you learn good news? **Lesson 5:** What qualities do leaders need most to be effective in the church? **Lesson 6:** Is it possible for a leader who does not demonstrate fully the qualities of Christ to lead effectively? Why, or why not? **Lesson 7:** If you were to craft a statement of what an elder in our church should be like, how would you illustrate this list for modern culture? **Lesson 8:** What does it mean to say that our church provides biblical teaching? **Lesson 9:** How is it possible for Christian leaders to put the needs of others first, yet attend to their own needs? **Lesson 10:** How have others influenced you? **Lesson 11:** As you were growing up, whose approval did you seek most of all? Why? How has that changed—or stayed the same—since childhood and adolescence? **Lesson 12:** What are some words that you associate with the concept of "duty"? **Lesson 13:** What do each of the age groups of preschool, elementary school, youth, and adults in our church need to learn? Who should teach them?

These are just possibilities—there are many more! You can develop your own approach or refer to the Into the Lesson part of the "Learning by Doing" section in each lesson for ideas. You can also develop this building block for the class as a whole or for small groups. Your decision here will depend on the nature of your class and the type of approach you decide on from week to week.

Remember that your goal is to engage your students from the very outset. This building block could be your most important, so don't bypass it! When you engage learners' attention at the very beginning, they are far more likely to remain involved as you move to the more complex material. When learners hear their own voices early in the session, they are much more likely to continue participating.

Building Block #2: Bible Study. The second building block is a study of the Scripture itself. What does it say? What questions does it answer? What questions does it raise? How should it be interpreted? Lesson Aims #1 (the *content* aim) and #2 (the *concept* aim) address these issues in each lesson.

You have many tools at your disposal. Each lesson suggests ways of engaging learners in the lesson. Try some of them. You may be surprised at how well they work. The discussion questions, for instance, are designed to elicit productive interaction. The ideas in the Into the Word part of the "Learning by Doing" section mean that you need not resort to lecture for every session—or even for many sessions, given the relevancy of the topics at hand.

If you are serious about wanting your learners to participate in discussion, encourage it from the beginning and throughout. People rarely participate in discussions that are tacked on as an afterthought following a lengthy lecture.

Building Block #3: Application. The proof of the lesson is in how learners are challenged to weave the teaching of the Bible text into their lives. Many will do it on their own. But don't assume that. Take some time to raise questions, suggest applications, and think through how Bible lessons learned can transform lives.

Lesson Aim #3 (the *conduct* aim) in each lesson points you in the right direction in this re-

---

Answers to Quarterly Quiz on page 130

Lesson 1—1. Gentiles. 2. true. **Lesson 2**—1. earth. 2. sorrow. **Lesson 3**—1. despised and rejected. 2. generation to generation. **Lesson 4**—1. good. 2. glory of the Lord. **Lesson 5**—1. true. 2. Hymeneus and Alexander. **Lesson 6**—1. one. 2. hands. **Lesson 7**—1. true. 2. the church. **Lesson 8**—1. refuse them. 2. hands. 3. false. **Lesson 9**—1. false. 2. an infidel. **Lesson 10**—1. false. 2. death. **Lesson 11**—1. false. 2. meek. **Lesson 12**—1. persecution. 2. true. 3. an evangelist. **Lesson 13**—1. women. 2. true.

gard. You can also find help in the Into Life part of the Learning by Doing sections, which offers one or two specific ideas each lesson. Try those ideas or think of your own. But whatever you do, don't skip the application!

Building Block #4: Conclusion. When you get to the end of the text and application, don't just stop. Take some time to summarize what you have discovered. Tell a story that elicits response. Challenge the learners. Pray with the class members to encourage them in their Christian journey.

The conclusion does not have to be long—in fact, it probably should not be. It need not be if you have followed the procedure suggested thus far. Your conclusion can be as short as verbalizing the Thought to Remember and asking the class to repeat it with you. The Conclusion section of the lesson may provide an illustration as a memorable summary or wrap-up.

After Class

Take a few minutes after you have finished teaching to reflect on how things went. Which activities did the learners respond to well? What needs to be modified? Which explanations did they "get"? Which ones should you have thought through more carefully? Self-reflection may be one of the best tools that you have for consistently improving your teaching.

One last word: Relax and enjoy your teaching experience. If you have prepared well, you will have far more successes than failures. And even a bad day isn't the end. Usually your class is forgiving. And it is amazing what we learn from a bad day now and then!

How to Say It

Use this list to help you pronounce the names and hard to pronounce words in the lessons of the winter quarter.

A

ABRAHAM. *Ay*-bruh-ham.
AHAZ. *Ay*-haz.
AMOS. *Ay*-mus.
ANTIOCH. *An*-tee-ock.
ASSYRIA. Uh-*sear*-ee-uh.

B

BABYLON. *Bab*-uh-lun.
BABYLONIANS. Bab-ih-*low*-nee-unz.
BARNABAS. *Bar*-nuh-bus.
BETHLEHEM. *Beth*-lih-hem.

C

CORINTHIANS. Ko-*rin*-thee-unz (*th* as in *thin*).
CORNELIUS. Cor-*neel*-yus.
CRETAN. *Cree*-tun.
CRETE. Creet.

D

DAMASCUS. Duh-*mass*-kus.
DEUTERONOMY. Due-ter-*ahn*-uh-me.

E

ECCLESIASTES. Ik-*leez*-ee-*as*-teez (strong accent on *as*).
EGYPT. *Ee*-jipt.
ELIJAH. Ee-*lye*-juh.
ELISHA. E-*lye*-shuh.
EPHESIAN. Ee-*fee*-zhun.
EPHESIANS. Ee-*fee*-zhunz.
EPHESUS. *Ef*-uh-sus.
EPIMENIDES. Ep-ih-*men*-ih-deez.
EUNICE. U-*nye*-see or *U*-nis.
EUTHANASIA. you-thuh-*nay*-zhuh.
EZRA. *Ez*-ruh.

G

GALATIANS. Guh-*lay*-shunz.
GAMALIEL. Guh-*may*-lih-ul or Guh-*may*-lee-al.
GENTILE. *Jen*-tile.
GENTILES. *Jen*-tiles.
GNOSTICS. *Nahss*-ticks.

H

HANNAH. *Han*-uh.
HEBREWS. *Hee*-brews.
HEZEKIAH. Hez-ih-*kye*-uh.
HOSEA. Ho-*zay*-uh.
HYMENEUS. Hi-meh-*nee*-us.

I

ICONIUM. Eye-*ko*-nee-um.
ISAIAH. Eye-*zay*-uh.
ISRAEL. *Iz*-ray-el.

J

JACOB. *Jay*-kub.
JEREMIAH. Jair-uh-*my*-uh.
JOSHUA. *Josh*-yew-uh.
JUDAH. *Joo*-duh.
JUDAS ISCARIOT. *Joo*-dus Iss-*care*-ee-ut.

L

LAMENTATIONS. Lam-en-*tay*-shunz.
LEVITICUS. Leh-*vit*-ih-kus.
LYSTRA. *Liss*-truh.

M

MACEDONIA. Mass-eh-*doe*-nee-uh.
MAGNIFICAT. Mag-*nif*-ih-cot.
MALACHI. *Mal*-uh-kye.
MESSIAH. Meh-*sigh*-uh.
MICAH. *My*-kuh.

N

NAZARETH. *Naz*-uh-reth.
NEBUCHADNEZZAR. *Neb*-yuh-kud-*nez*-er (strong accent on *nez*).
NICODEMUS. *Nick*-uh-*dee*-mus (strong accent on *dee*).

P

PENTECOST. *Pent*-ih-kost.
PHARISEES. *Fair*-ih-seez.
PHILETUS. Fuh-*lee*-tus.
PHILIPPIANS. Fih-*lip*-ee-unz.

R

RABBI. *rab*-eye.

S

SILAS. *Sigh*-luss.
SIMEON. *Sim*-ee-un.
SYNAGOGUE. *sin*-uh-gog.

T

TARSUS. *Tar*-sus.
THESSALONIANS. *Thess*-uh-*lo*-nee-unz (strong accent on *lo*; *th* as in *thin*).
TITUS. *Ty*-tus.

U

UZZIAH. Uh-*zye*-uh.

Z

ZACCHEUS. Zack-*key*-us.
ZAREPHATH. *Zair*-uh-fath.
ZECHARIAH. Zek-uh-*rye*-uh (strong accent on *rye*).
ZEUS. Zoose.

Justice for All

139

December 4
Lesson 1

Dec 4

DEVOTIONAL READING: Isaiah 41:8-13.

BACKGROUND SCRIPTURE: Isaiah 41, 42.

PRINTED TEXT: Isaiah 42:1-9.

Isaiah 42:1-9

1 Behold my servant, whom I uphold; mine elect, in whom my soul delighteth; I have put my Spirit upon him: he shall bring forth judgment to the Gentiles.

2 He shall not cry, nor lift up, nor cause his voice to be heard in the street.

3 A bruised reed shall he not break, and the smoking flax shall he not quench: he shall bring forth judgment unto truth.

4 He shall not fail nor be discouraged, till he have set judgment in the earth: and the isles shall wait for his law.

5 Thus saith God the LORD, he that created the heavens, and stretched them out; he that spread forth the earth, and that which cometh out of it; he that giveth breath unto the people upon it, and spirit to them that walk therein:

6 I the LORD have called thee in righteousness, and will hold thine hand, and will keep thee, and give thee for a covenant of the people, for a light of the Gentiles;

7 To open the blind eyes, to bring out the prisoners from the prison, and them that sit in darkness out of the prison house.

8 I am the LORD; that is my name: and my glory will I not give to another, neither my praise to graven images.

9 Behold, the former things are come to pass, and new things do I declare: before they spring forth I tell you of them.

GOLDEN TEXT: I the LORD have called thee in righteousness, and will hold thine hand, and will keep thee, and give thee for a covenant of the people, for a light of the Gentiles.—Isaiah 42:6.

DECEMBER 4

God's Commitment—Our Response
Unit 1: God's Redeeming Love
(Lessons 1-4)

Lesson Aims

After participating in this lesson, each student will be able to:

1. Describe how the servant demonstrates justice.
2. Explain how the figures of speech concerning the servant are fulfilled in the New Testament.
3. Suggest one specific way to promote God's justice in the coming week.

Lesson Outline

INTRODUCTION
    A. "Justice for All!"
    B. Lesson Background
I. DISCLOSING THE SERVANT (Isaiah 42:1)
    A. Selection of the Servant (v. 1a, b)
    B. Spirit for the Servant (v. 1c)
    C. Significance of the Servant (v. 1d)
II. DESCRIBING THE SERVANT (Isaiah 42:2-4)
    A. His Disposition (vv. 2, 3a)
    B. His Duties (vv. 3b, 4)
III. DECLARATIONS TO THE SERVANT (Isaiah 42:5-9)
    A. Power of God (v. 5)
    B. Protection of God (v. 6a)
    C. Purposes of God (vv. 6b, 7)
        Restored to Usefulness
    D. Preeminence of God (vv. 8, 9)
        Guaranteed Protection
CONCLUSION
    A. Justice and You
    B. Prayer
    C. Thought to Remember

Introduction

A. "Justice for All!"

To hear the word *justice* may bring to mind the aspects of deserved reward or punishment. The definitions may also have these facets: rightness, lawfulness, to exercise a proper power and authority to maintain what is right. When all the facets of justice are considered, it is plain why only God's plan can bring "justice for all." When differing levels of government are falling over themselves to outdo each other in abandoning absolutes, it becomes evident that what is really needed is godly justice. Only then can the singing about peace in the Christmas carols bring the desired results.

Occasionally, a news item appears that does not pass the "sniff test" for justice. The story may be of a robber who was injured by the defensive actions of the intended victim. The robber then sues the victim and receives much more than the robbery would have gained for him. A recent article has this comment: "You may . . . have to compensate those who would have harmed you on your property!"

John Jay, an early justice of the U.S. Supreme Court, wrote, "Justice is indiscriminately due to all, without regard to numbers, wealth, or rank." Some of the high-visibility court trials in recent years have demonstrated that those with wealth can afford very capable attorneys who are more likely to win in the justice system. Wealth, however, is not the only factor. In the past it often seemed that the person's race, country of origin, etc., produced miscarriages of justice.

One of the symbols of justice is "The Blind Lady." You've seen her with her eyes covered as she holds a sword in one hand and the scales of justice in the other. Combining the ideas of the blindfold and the scales suggests that the true courts of justice are blind to prejudice. But what about the sword? As one thoughtful observer put it, "Justice that does not bear a sword beside its scales soon falls into ridicule" (perhaps by Charles de Gaulle, 1890–1970).

Before we move through today's lesson, we should note that the word translated *judgment* in the *King James Version* usually is the same as *justice* in modern English.

B. Lesson Background

Each of the four lessons for December has selections from the book of Isaiah, and the final two lessons of the month will also have passages from the Gospel of Luke. The book of Isaiah is usually dated over the period of 740–700 B.C. Isaiah lived and wrote during the reigns of four kings of Judah (see Isaiah 1:1). Isaiah's task was formidable, for King Ahaz was one of the worst kings of ancient Judah. The idolatry that he introduced marked the beginning of the end for that nation (2 Chronicles 28:1-4). Godly

Hezekiah succeeded Ahaz, but his personal righteousness could not tip the scales of justice away from the sentence that the people deserved for their idolatry.

Although Assyria was the dominant power in his day, Isaiah prophesied that the nation would eventually fall to the Babylonians (Isaiah 39:5-7). Nebuchadnezzar and his Babylonian army ultimately destroyed Jerusalem and the temple in 586 B.C. As Isaiah begins chapter 40, the entire nature of the book changes. The prophet writes to provide comfort for people who will be in exile, and he instructs them to leave Babylon with joy when the opportunity comes (Isaiah 48:20).

But Isaiah also prophesies even greater deliverance. In so doing, he uses four poems about a special servant of the Lord who would come. (See Lesson 7 from the fall quarter.) These poems give new dimensions to the one who already had been the subject of earlier prophecies. (See especially Isaiah 7:14; 9:1-7; and all of chapter 11 for those prophecies.) Sections of each poem are noted in the New Testament as being fulfilled in Jesus.

I. Disclosing the Servant (Isaiah 42:1)

A. Selection of the Servant (v. 1a, b)

1a, b. Behold my servant, whom I uphold; mine elect, in whom my soul delighteth.

Matthew 12:18-21 cites the first four verses of Isaiah 42. This is the longest quotation in the Gospel of Matthew from the Old Testament. We may take note of the larger context by observing that several chapters in this part of Isaiah challenge the idols to do what God can do. The verses before Isaiah 42:1 present vivid contrasts to what God sets forth in today's text. The word *behold* occurs in 41:24, 29 and seems to be addressed to the images that are "wind and confusion" (41:29). God now introduces His *servant*, and the difference is dramatic!

Some have thought that the use of the word *servant* is intended to show the humility of the one sent. Jesus certainly was meek (see Matthew 11:29), but this is not the text for it. In royal circles it is a great honor to be the servant of a king. [See question #1, page 147.]

The fact that this servant is fully endorsed by the Lord is expressed in three ways. First, God states that He will *uphold* Him. The thought is that the servant will be sustained by God. Enemies will not prevail against the servant. Second, this servant has been specially appointed by God. Finally, He is the one *in whom* God finds a special joy. This is but a preview of the statements made by God at the baptism and the transfiguration of Jesus (Matthew 3:17; 17:5).

B. Spirit for the Servant (v. 1c)

1c. I have put my Spirit upon him.

The presence of the *Spirit* is also mentioned in Isaiah 11:2 and 61:1. The latter passage will be cited centuries later by Jesus at the synagogue in Nazareth. He will note that the passage is fulfilled that day (Luke 4:17-21).

C. Significance of the Servant (v. 1d)

1d. He shall bring forth judgment to the Gentiles.

Achieving justice or *judgment* always has been difficult. One of the Ten Commandments warns about giving a false testimony (Exodus 20:16). This judicial feature is a part of God's judgment for all humanity; it is not restricted to Old Testament Israel. These messages are found throughout the prophetic writings. They affirm that even though other nations will be severely judged, God also promises that they would have the opportunity to know the one God.

II. Describing the Servant (Isaiah 42:2-4)

A. His Disposition (vv. 2, 3a)

2. He shall not cry, nor lift up, nor cause his voice to be heard in the street.

The word *not* is very vivid in the original Hebrew; it is emphasized by being the first word in the sentence. This is the first of seven uses of this word into the first part of verse four. (The *King James Version* translates this word as both *not* and *nor* for a bit of variety.)

VISUALS FOR THESE LESSONS

The visual pictured in each lesson (e.g., page 142) is a small reproduction of a large, full-color poster included in the Adult Resources packet for the Winter Quarter. The packet is available from your supplier. Order No. 292.

The use of the word *not* may seem to give a negative implication, but this is not the case. All seven phrases emphasize the peaceful approach that characterizes Jesus' ministry to those who receive His teaching. Jesus could, however, use a whip (John 2:15), overturn tables, and prohibit anyone from using the temple for a shortcut (Mark 11:16).

This servant is not going to raise his *voice* in a boisterous way so as to drown out others by sheer volume. Physically, however, His voice will have tremendous power by the way He will be able to preach to thousands. His quiet manner is enhanced by the power of the message. The Son of God will not need to publicize himself with excessive noise. He will not force His way on anyone. [See question #2, page 147.]

3a. A bruised reed shall he not break, and the smoking flax shall he not quench.

A *bruised reed* is one that has been bent or broken over. It is normally considered to be useless, and it is therefore despised. In this case it represents those who may be considered as outcasts, but Jesus welcomes them also. It may also represent one who is hurting, struggling with sin or sorrow. The church is a place where all are to be welcomed and given genuine love, either tender or tough as the situation warrants.

The smoking flax is a wick that is not really producing light as it should. It is almost spent, simply useless, and ready to be discarded—but it can be restored! The flax or wick can be trimmed and the oil in the lamp replenished. Then the flame is renewed to its intended brightness. So lives that have been almost spent can be restored if they choose to be; but first the message must be communicated to them.

B. His Duties (vv. 3b, 4)

3b. He shall bring forth judgment unto truth.

This is the second time in the passage that the word *judgment* or justice is used. In verse one it was announced that God's judgments are for all nations. This time the emphasis is on the truthfulness of the justice of God. [See question #3, page 147.]

Unto truth carries the idea of administering justice faithfully or with fidelity. In an age when truth and fidelity are diminished or considered to be relative, it is interesting to compare how many times the word *truth* occurs in the New Testament. Jesus says that He is the truth (John 14:6). If an individual holds to His teaching, then he or

Use this visual as a discussion starter on the topics of justice, strength, hope, and good news.

Visual for lesson 1

she will know the truth and be set free (John 8:31, 32). God's Word is declared to be the "word of truth" (Ephesians 1:13; 2 Timothy 2:15; James 1:18). This truth must be spoken in love (Ephesians 4:15). The balance between love and truth must be a foundation of personal relationships, especially in those situations when the truth of the Word is presented to those who are lost.

4. He shall not fail nor be discouraged, till he have set judgment in the earth: and the isles shall wait for his law.

The final two uses of the word *not* and *nor* occur in this verse. The words that they modify, namely *fail* and *discouraged*, are fascinating, for they are words from the previous verse. There they were translated as "smoking" (smoldering) and "bruised." In other words, the servant will burn brightly and will not be broken. He will understand when others experience these things.

The purpose of His coming is again set forth: to establish *judgment* (justice) so that throughout the world the people who have placed their confidence in Him will not be disappointed. God's plans will come to fruition! This is the type of Savior that everyone should desire. [See question #4, page 147.]

III. Declarations to the Servant (Isaiah 42:5-9)

A. Power of God (v. 5)

5. Thus saith God the L*ord***, he that created the heavens, and stretched them out; he that spread forth the earth, and that which cometh out of it; he that giveth breath unto the people upon it, and spirit to them that walk therein.**

The final five verses of this servant poem or song express assurances to the servant. They also provide insights into the actual ministry that Jesus will have centuries later while on earth.

In an Old Testament context, we recall that each nation tended to have its own god or gods, and sometimes a god's sphere of influence was limited to a single city. Not so with the God of Israel! He is the one who *created the heavens* and *spread forth the earth*. That concept was used by Jonah to identify his God to pagan sailors (Jonah 1:9). During and after the exile in Babylon, it becomes a custom to refer to the God of Israel as the "God of heaven" (Ezra 1:2; 7:12; Daniel 2:37, 44).

In this section of Isaiah (chapters 40–48), one of the main points is to contrast the one true God with the idols—idols that had to be made (44:17), had to be carried and set up (45:20), and that cannot answer (46:7). The God of Israel, by contrast, is the one who created the stars and calls them by name (40:26). It is the power of this God that is behind the promise of sending a servant who will bring justice to all.

The latter part of the verse gives another great truth. It states that *God the Lord* is the one who provides *breath* and *spirit* of life. The life principle does not exist in the earth itself, nor is it a result of a lightning strike. Life is the gift of God.

B. Protection of God (v. 6a)

6a. I the LORD have called thee in righteousness, and will hold thine hand, and will keep thee.

The coming of the servant will be no accident, for *the Lord* is the one calling Him as a part of His redemptive purposes. He will come *in righteousness,* thus reflecting all the standards of ethics, morals, and conduct that a holy God has by His very nature.

The servant has the assurance that He will be protected so as to fulfill His mission. To *hold* the *hand* expresses a constant affirmation of security and safety. To *keep* could also be given as to "guard." The Savior who comes into the world will be kept from the wrath of Herod and from early attempts to end His life. Finally, however, He has to die for the sins of humanity. At that moment, the Lord will give expression to the thought that He has been forsaken (Matthew 27:46), but this also is part of God's plan.

C. Purposes of God (vv. 6b, 7)

6b. And give thee for a covenant of the people, for a light of the Gentiles.

Two aspects of the servant's mission are stated, and most students consider that there are two distinct recipients. The word *people* is a prophetic term for those who belong to God, and in this case it refers to the people of Israel (compare Hosea 2:1, 23). The other entity to receive a blessing is *the Gentiles*.

Two terms are used to depict the purposes of the servant. They are *covenant* and *light*. Just as Jesus is light, so in this passage He is portrayed as a covenant. He is the very foundation and essence of the New Covenant.

The ancient Hebrew mind is fully aware of the implications of covenants. The word is first used in the covenant God made with Noah after the flood, and then to the patriarchs, the nation of Israel, and with David. In such covenants God makes promises that He will keep, but conditional factors often play an important part. Humans can lose the benefits unless they keep their part. It is necessary both to accept and then to keep a covenant that God offers.

We may also note that this verse seems to be behind the statement of Simeon at the dedication of Jesus. Simeon rejoiced that his eyes had seen the salvation that God had prepared: a light for the Gentiles and the glory for the people of Israel (Luke 2:30-32).

7. To open the blind eyes, to bring out the prisoners from the prison, and them that sit in darkness out of the prison house.

Jesus will cause *blind eyes* to see during His time on earth. But here figurative language means that the servant will eliminate spiritual

---

Home Daily Bible Readings

Monday, Nov. 28—An Eastern Victor Is Roused (Isaiah 41:1-7)

Tuesday, Nov. 29—God Will Strengthen Israel (Isaiah 41:8-13)

Wednesday, Nov. 30—God Will Care for the People (Isaiah 41:14-20)

Thursday, Dec. 1—God Is Greater Than Babylon's Deities (Isaiah 41:21-29)

Friday, Dec. 2—My Servant Will Bring Forth Justice (Isaiah 42:1-9)

Saturday, Dec. 3—Sing Praise to God (Isaiah 42:10-17)

Sunday, Dec. 4—Blind and Deaf to God's Instruction (Isaiah 42:18-25)

blindness and *darkness*, bringing freedom from the *prison* of sin. [See question #5, page 147.]

RESTORED TO USEFULNESS

In the field of mortuary science, there exists the practice known as restorative arts. The goal of this work is to restore a dead body to an appearance closely resembling the person while living. To perform restorative arts successfully involves learning principles of color theory in pigments, principles of cosmetology, as well as a consideration of normal complexion types and deviations from those. Yet long before there was any such thing as restorative arts, there was God, the greatest restorer of all.

Think about it: God takes what is dead—what appears to be of no value—and restores it by the power of His Son, Jesus. God's restoration process comes as He works on people's hearts through His Word and the Holy Spirit. Seemingly useless people with nothing to offer are restored by the gospel; those who are dead in their sins are restored by the sanctifying power of God's Spirit to new life and purpose.

God is such a powerful restorer! The church as a whole and Christians as individuals seek to be His agents of restoration. Instead of labeling others as beyond help and hope, it is our task to be ministers of reconciliation and restoration. Through the power of the Holy Spirit, that's exactly what God expects of us. —A. E. A.

D. Preeminence of God (vv. 8, 9)

8. I am the LORD: that is my name: and my glory will I not give to another, neither my praise to graven images.

The personal *name* of *the Lord* is behind all that is being promised. That name had a special significance at the time that Moses was called (Exodus 3:13, 14). Exodus 34:14 says that God is a jealous God. This is jealousy in the right sense: there are no real rivals to the one God. *Graven images* (idols) are worthless.

9. Behold, the former things are come to pass, and new things do I declare: before they spring forth I tell you of them.

The former things, those that had been prophesied in the past, are fulfilled as predicted in the course of time. The Lord proclaims new blessings long *before they* are accomplished. It is indeed a blessing today for us to know that these really were predictive prophecies. The discovery of the Dead Sea Scrolls with copies of the book of Isaiah proves that God truly had spoken these things centuries ahead of time. They came to pass just as He said. Fulfilled prophecy is a guarantee of truth; it is a vital part of the Christian's guarantee of eternal life.

GUARANTEED PROTECTION

People spend a lot of money on security and safety. Alarm systems to prevent theft of cars and laptop computers are considered necessities by many. There are systems designed for detecting smoke or carbon monoxide levels in our homes. Bars on the windows and multiple dead bolts on the doors are common in high crime areas.

Celebrities, for their part, have personal bodyguards. So do political figures. This is especially true of heads of state, who are constantly under the watchful eye of trained protectors. For years there has been screening of bags and people at airports. In a post–September 11 world, this security has been heightened. We all want to feel secure, don't we? Yet we know all too well that earthly security is never perfect.

The only perfect security comes from God. His promise of "new things" is, among others, a promise of eternal security. "Behold, I make all things new" (Revelation 21:5). This "newness" is for those who are His children of righteousness. The newness includes the fact that "there shall be no more death . . . for the former things are passed away" (Revelation 21:4). This protection is available to all who call upon the name of Jesus and submit themselves to what His

---

How to Say It

AHAZ. *Ay*-haz.
ASSYRIA. Uh-*sear*-ee-uh.
BABYLONIANS. Bab-ih-*low*-nee-unz.
EPHESIANS. Ee-*fee*-zhunz.
EZRA. *Ez*-ruh.
GENTILES. *Jen*-tiles.
HEZEKIAH. Hez-ih-*kye*-uh.
HOSEA. Ho-*zay*-uh.
ISAIAH. Eye-*zay*-uh.
JUDAH. *Joo*-duh.
NAZARETH. *Naz*-uh-reth.
NEBUCHADNEZZAR. *Neb*-yuh-kud-*nez*-er (strong accent on *nez*).
SYNAGOGUE. *sin*-uh-gog.

Word has to say. Jesus is with His people as protector, now and forevermore. —A. E. A.

Conclusion

A. Justice and You

Jesus came to the earth to bring justice. Some of its applications may include the influences that Christians have had in their homes, at work, and in their communities. It also includes the larger scene as described in Matthew 25:31-46 when the nations will be judged. But the criteria that are mentioned there are challenging: they are acts of benevolence to those brothers in need! When we do such things, we demonstrate our faith in Christ by what we do (James 2:14-26). It is the responsibility of each Christian to resolve to do his or her part in bringing "justice for all."

B. Prayer

Almighty God, just as You have demonstrated Your compassion to us, we resolve today to make a difference in the lives of others by acts of justice and benevolence in the name of the servant whom You sent. In Jesus' name, amen.

C. Thought to Remember

Each person decides if he or she will receive God's justice or God's mercy—mercy given only to those who accept the servant of the Lord as personal Savior.

Learning by Doing

This section contains an alternative lesson plan emphasizing learning activities. Classes desiring such student involvement will find these suggestions helpful.

Learning Goals

After this lesson, each student will be able to:
1. Describe how the servant demonstrates justice.
2. Explain how the figures of speech concerning the servant are fulfilled in the New Testament.
3. Suggest one specific way to promote God's justice in the coming week.

Into the Lesson

Wear a black robe (symbolizing a judge) to class. Carry a gavel and a large book. Strike the gavel onto the table and declare, "Hear ye! Hear ye! Justice for all."

Display the following fill-in-the-blanks activity to highlight the lesson titles and themes for the first four lessons of this series: ___ for ___; ___ for the ___; ___ for the ___; ___ ___ for the ___. Display also this list of words: *all, good, hope, justice, news, strength, suffering, weary, world*. Say, "Fit the words into the blanks without looking at the lesson materials. What I said when I struck the gavel is a clue to one of the phrases."

Into the Word

After introducing the lesson with the opening activity, distribute to each student an index card with one of these letters: *S, E, R, V, A, N, T*. Duplicate each letter, as necessary, to have enough cards for your typical class attendance. Give these directions: "For the letter you have been given, identify a descriptive word (or words) that characterize the servant in today's text in Isaiah 42:1-9. Also note a verse or verses from today's text where each descriptive word is noted or implied." Give this example: "For the letter *S* one may note 'Spirit-filled,' based on verse 1."

Here are a few possibilities that you may suggest: S—successful (v. 4); E—excellent (v. 1); R—righteous (v. 6); V—valued (v. 1); A—anticipated (v. 4); N—nurturing (v. 3); T—true (v. 6).

Say, "When God speaks to the servant, He reveals the special relationship they share." Divide the class into three sections. Ask the first section, "What do you see characterizing the servant and the Father's special relationship?" Expect such responses as "loving support," as seen in verses 1 and 6. Ask the second section, "What elements of that relationship does the individual Christian share with the Father?" Expect such responses as the loving support we also receive, as seen in 1 John 3:1. Ask the third section, "What attributes of the servant must one adopt to enable such a relationship with the

Father?" Expect such responses as "submission to His will," as seen in Romans 12:2.

Next, divide the class quickly into seven groups of people seated next to each other. Say, "Several of the images in our text bring to mind specific examples of what Jesus-the-servant and His disciples did, as recorded in the Gospels and in Acts." Then give each group one of the following phrases/verse numbers from Isaiah 42: (1) v. 2; (2) v. 3a; (3) "a light of the Gentiles," v. 6; (4) "to open the blind eyes," v. 7a; (5) "I am the Lord; that is my name", v. 8; (6) "new things do I declare," v. 9; (7) v. 4b, regarding the islands placing hope in Him.

Say, "Quickly select a good New Testament example of the fulfillment of your assigned verse." Allow for a variety of responses, but these are possibilities: (1) the whole tenor of Jesus' ministry; (2) one of Jesus' rescues of someone nearly lost to Satan's power, such as the Gadarene demoniac; (3) the Greeks coming to Jesus, as recorded in John 12:20, 21; (4) the healing of the blind man of John 9; (5) Jesus' designation of himself as "I am" in John 8:58; (6) the people's conclusion at the end of the Sermon on the Mount in Matthew 7:28, 29; (7) Paul and Barnabas's work on the island of Cyprus as recorded in Acts 13:4-12.

Into Life

Say, "Today's lesson shows us that God has a special concern for justice. At the final judgment, He will establish complete justice to eliminate injustice for eternity." Then give to each student a three-inch slip of paper, which you have prepared in advance, printed with the word **INJUSTICE**. Say, "When you see or read of an occasion of injustice this week at work, home, or in the news, decide what you can do—even in a small way—to see that injustice corrected. After you take the action, tear off the letters *IN* from *INJUSTICE* from your slip of paper. Then pray that God will see justice done in all circumstances."

Let's Talk It Over

These questions are designed to promote discussion of the lesson. The answers here are only discussion starters. Let your class talk it over from there.

1. Culture can influence our understanding of the Bible. In Isaiah 42:1 we may cringe at references naming the coming Messiah as a *servant*. How do we view servanthood today vs. how that idea may have been understood in Isaiah's day? Why is this distinction important?

The American Civil War and the worldwide slave trade of the nineteenth century heightened sensitivity to the idea of "ownership" of another human being. Servants, in the sense of being slaves, have been dehumanized and abased. In modern Western democracies, on the other hand, the term *servant* is often thought of as something like a butler or a maid. Such servants often are hired hands for specific tasks.

Servants in the ancient world, however, often had much influence even though they lacked full freedom. They could become the teachers of their master's children and managers of their wealth (compare Genesis 39:2-6). Jesus fulfilled the will of the Father in the spirit of a fully devoted, fully capable servant—when we think of servant in the ancient sense. Philippians 2:8 identifies Jesus as one who willingly humbled himself to become such a servant.

2. The secular world sometimes identifies Christians by all the things we will "not" do. Do you think this is fair? Why, or why not?

Being judged by what we will "not" do can come from either scorn at "what we're missing" or from admiration at our self-control. Much depends on the eye of the beholder!

In Isaiah 42 we see the description of a servant who has great control. He was not interested in being the loudest. Instead, He quietly persisted at His task. We do not see Him seeking out the high and mighty to help boost His popularity. Instead, He spoke to those who had "ears to hear." He intentionally sought out society's outcasts. This type of character is a model for those looking to lead others to salvation (compare Ecclesiastes 9:17).

3. Drawing on Isaiah 42:3 and other passages, what differences do you see between the judgment found in human courts and that which will occur in the final judgment? How can we explain this difference to unbelievers? Why is it important to do so?

Many contrasts can be presented. Human judges are imperfect as are the juries that issue the verdicts. Human laws do not cover all issues. Our laws are constantly changing, depending on who is in office. Investigators make mistakes. The quality of a person's defense often depends on how much money he or she has available to spend on lawyers. The list can go on!

God's courtroom, of course, suffers from none of these restrictions. Truth is primary in His judgment, and He knows the truth about us perfectly. Without Christ this is bad news indeed! But those who have Christ as Savior have had the penalty for their sins paid at Calvary. This is what God requires for us to "go free" at His final judgment. What truth could be more important?

4. In what ways is the servant setting "judgment in the earth" yet today? What are some things we can do to help bring this about?

We may begin by noticing the persistence of the servant in this regard as seen in Isaiah 42:4. For Him, failure is not possible!

Administering judgment and justice includes upholding God's standards of right and wrong. In a general sense, our part is to live out the truth of God's Word in that regard. Bringing about God's judgment and justice in specific instances requires prayerful reflection in asking God to open doors. To neglect the battle for justice would mean a failure to uphold the holiness of God.

5. Few seem open to hearing the idea that they live in spiritual darkness! How does Christ's compassion toward those who rejected Him serve as a model for us in this regard?

To respond to enemies as Jesus did may seem superhuman to us. We are not the creators of the universe and are acutely aware of our limitations. We hope to be righteous, but someone is sure to catch us in a weak moment.

But God promises to give us extraordinary help to accomplish that which we could not do on our own. First Peter 1:3-9 explains how the resurrection of Jesus can make us overcomers.

December 11
Lesson 2

Strength for the Weary

DEVOTIONAL READING: Isaiah 49:7-13.

BACKGROUND SCRIPTURE: Isaiah 49, 50.

PRINTED TEXT: Isaiah 49:5, 6; 50:4-11.

Isaiah 49:5, 6

5 And now, saith the Lord that formed me from the womb to be his servant, to bring Jacob again to him, Though Israel be not gathered, yet shall I be glorious in the eyes of the Lord, and my God shall be my strength.

6 And he said, It is a light thing that thou shouldest be my servant to raise up the tribes of Jacob, and to restore the preserved of Israel: I will also give thee for a light to the Gentiles, that thou mayest be my salvation unto the end of the earth.

Isaiah 50:4-11

4 The Lord God hath given me the tongue of the learned, that I should know how to speak a word in season to him that is weary: he wakeneth morning by morning, he wakeneth mine ear to hear as the learned.

5 The Lord God hath opened mine ear, and I was not rebellious, neither turned away back.

6 I gave my back to the smiters, and my cheeks to them that plucked off the hair: I hid not my face from shame and spitting.

7 For the Lord God will help me; therefore shall I not be confounded: therefore have I set my face like a flint, and I know that I shall not be ashamed.

8 He is near that justifieth me; who will contend with me? let us stand together: who is mine adversary? let him come near to me.

9 Behold, the Lord God will help me; who is he that shall condemn me? lo, they all shall wax old as a garment; the moth shall eat them up.

10 Who is among you that feareth the Lord, that obeyeth the voice of his servant, that walketh in darkness, and hath no light? let him trust in the name of the Lord, and stay upon his God.

11 Behold, all ye that kindle a fire, that compass yourselves about with sparks: walk in the light of your fire, and in the sparks that ye have kindled. This shall ye have of mine hand; ye shall lie down in sorrow.

GOLDEN TEXT: For the Lord GOD will help me; therefore shall I not be confounded: therefore have I set my face like a flint, and I know that I shall not be ashamed.—Isaiah 50:7.

LESSON 2   DECEMBER 11

> *God's Commitment—Our Response*
> Unit 1: God's Redeeming Love
> (Lessons 1-4)

Lesson Aims

After participating in this lesson, each student will be able to:

1. Recite at least two purposes that Isaiah prophesied for the Messiah to fulfill.
2. Tell how Jesus fulfilled those prophecies.
3. Prepare an explanation of how the shame Christ underwent saves us.

Lesson Outline

INTRODUCTION
    A. Cheery or Weary?
    B. Lesson Background
 I. COMMISSION OF THE SERVANT (Isaiah 49:5, 6)
    A. Stated by the Servant (v. 5)
    B. Stated by the Lord (v. 6)
       Light Attracts
 II. COMFORT BY THE SERVANT (Isaiah 50:4, 5)
    A. Tongue to Tell (v. 4a)
    B. Ear to Listen (vv. 4b, 5)
III. COMPOSURE OF THE SERVANT (Isaiah 50:6-9)
    A. In Suffering (v. 6)
    B. In Standing Firm (vv. 7-9)
IV. COUNSEL ON BEHALF OF THE SERVANT (Isaiah 50:10, 11)
    A. To Those Who Accept Him (v. 10)
       Trust for the Journey
    B. To Those Who Reject Him (v. 11)
CONCLUSION
    A. The Verdict
    B. Prayer
    C. Thought to Remember

Introduction

A. Cheery or Weary?

Christmas is two weeks away. For many it seems that much of the cheeriness is gone, for they are exhausted with the preparations for the events that accompany this special holiday.

A church paper gave the lament of one young preacher about a planned outing for his wife and himself. They intended to purchase all the necessary Christmas gifts within a set period of time and within a certain cost limit. The results were that the shopping expedition took five times longer than anticipated and cost twice as much as their agreement. At the end of the trip they were weary, not cheery.

The title of today's study is "Strength for the Weary," but is this the weariness described above? We would have to be *very careful* to think through the question before answering. The Messiah did indeed come to comfort His people and to provide comfort for the poor in heart. Isaiah 40:31 affirms that those who wait or hope in the Lord will renew their strength, and that they can run or walk without being weary or faint. In context, that passage may refer to the people to be exiled in Babylon. When they receive word that they can return to their homeland, the excitement would invigorate them. Good news is definitely a factor in providing "strength for the weary." And the message of Christmas is definitely *good news!*

Returning to our story about the weary preacher and his wife, we should note that physical weariness can lead to spiritual defeat. Comfort for both physical and spiritual weariness can come from prayer, by the examples of how other Christians handle stresses, or through the genuine love and compassion of those who minister personally in the name of Christ. Comfort and strength are also available through today's lesson as we reflect anew on God's plan to save us.

B. Lesson Background

The background for this lesson is approximately the same as for the previous study. We already noted the fact that there are four servant poems or servant songs in the book of Isaiah

---

How to Say It

AMOS. *Ay*-mus.
BABYLON. *Bab*-uh-lun.
DEUTERONOMY. Due-ter-*ahn*-uh-me.
GENTILES. *Jen*-tiles.
ISAIAH. Eye-*zay*-uh.
ISRAEL. *Iz*-ray-el.
JACOB. *Jay*-kub.
JEREMIAH. Jair-uh-*my*-uh.
JOSHUA. *Josh*-yew-uh.
MESSIAH. Meh-*sigh*-uh.
PHILIPPIANS. Fih-*lip*-ee-unz.

(42:1-9; 49:1-13; 50:4-11; 52:13–53:12; see also page 60 of Lesson 7 for the fall). The previous lesson, from Isaiah 42, was the first of such poems.

Today's lesson involves selected verses from the next two poems or songs. In the fullness of time, the Son of God would come to earth. The ultimate purpose was to provide a way for men and women to experience freedom from the weight of sin. Thus does Jesus give strength for the weary for eternity.

I. Commission of the Servant (Isaiah 49:5, 6)

A. Stated by the Servant (v. 5)

5. And now, saith the LORD that formed me from the womb to be his servant, to bring Jacob again to him, Though Israel be not gathered, yet shall I be glorious in the eyes of the LORD, and my God shall be my strength.

The speaker in this verse is the *servant*, and several features of His special commission are given. First, there is an awareness that *the Lord* has a divine plan. Second, it is stated figuratively that this plan always has been in the mind of God. To say that it is *from the womb* is a way of making this affirmation in a common figure of speech (see also Isaiah 49:1).

The commission is that He is to return *Jacob* to the Lord again. *Jacob* is another term for Israel (see Deuteronomy 33:10). Jacob later came to be used to refer to Judah, the southern part of divided Israel (Jeremiah 5:20; Lamentations 2:2).

While the exiles in captivity may read this and interpret it as a return from Babylon, its ultimate meaning is much greater. The emphasis here (and in the next verse) indicates a spiritual return by the people of Israel. It is sin that will cause the Babylonian captivity, and God's primary concern is spiritual reform.

The identification of the *servant* has been much debated, with at least five options suggested. The apostle Paul applies the final part of the next verse to his work in going to the Gentiles (Acts 13:47) and makes it a messianic command. This is in accord with the traditional view that the word *servant* applies to the Messiah. This concept means that the reference to the *servant* as *Israel* in verse three of this poem could be providing yet another name for the Messiah. Similar to Jacob of old (Genesis 32:22-32), Jesus wrestled to a victory in His service for God (Luke 22:44).

The careful student who compares translations will notice that there is a problem in the middle part of the verse at hand. The *King James Version* says that *Israel* was *not gathered*. Other translations have that phrase as parallel to the previous one and therefore give the opposite meaning—that Israel *was* gathered. The ancient manuscripts and translations also differ on this passage. The difficulty is that the Hebrew word for *not* sounds exactly like the word that means *to him*. Copying in ancient times was sometimes done by listening to a reader, and this could have caused the seeming discrepancy. The wonderful thing is that either way there is a positive interpretation: Either the second phrase is intended to emphasize the commission *to bring Jacob again to him* by repeating it in slightly different words (which is good Hebrew poetry), or (as the *KJV*) we have fulfilled prophecy in that Jesus came to His own people and many of them did not receive Him when they refused to be gathered (John 1:11).

The servant's determined faithfulness guarantees that His mission will be accomplished. He will therefore be exalted *in the eyes of the Lord*.

We may also note that the title for this lesson has an application here. In prophetic fashion the servant states that *God* is the source of His *strength*. Psalm 46:1 contains a similar statement, that God is "our refuge and strength."

B. Stated by the Lord (v. 6)

6. And he said, It is a light thing that thou shouldest be my servant to raise up the tribes of Jacob, and to restore the preserved of Israel: I will also give thee for a light to the Gentiles,

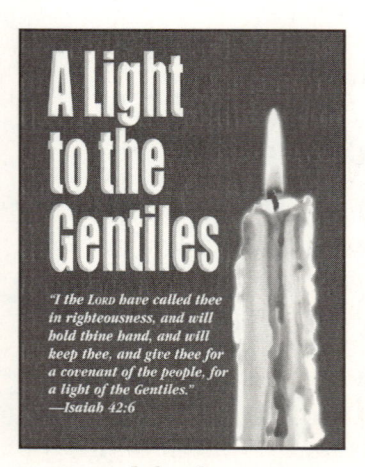

Start a discussion with this visual as you ask "How are we part of Jesus' ministry of light?"

Visual for lesson 2

that thou mayest be my salvation unto the end of the earth.

Parents today often encourage their children to advance to a higher level of achievement. Here, the Lord, God the Father, uses that concept in language that we can understand. The servant's mission is enlarged beyond the people *of Israel*. It also must include *the Gentiles*. It is this prophecy that shows that much more than a physical return from Babylonian captivity is in view. It is this verse that Paul cites to justify his going to the Gentiles (Acts 13:47).

God had told the people of Israel through a prophet that they, of all the families of the earth, were the only ones chosen by Him (Amos 3:2); yet God's ultimate plan includes all peoples. The text before us is intended to give instruction not only to encourage the servant but also to tell Israel to be ready to implement the promise of *salvation* to the extremities *of the earth*. This is to happen at the appointed time in God's plan of redemption. The concept of the Messiah as developed by the ancient rabbis did not include the thought that He would be a *light to* [for] *the Gentiles*. Their faulty concept produced much tension in the early church, as we see in Acts 11:1-3. [See question #1, page 156.]

LIGHT ATTRACTS

We are all familiar with the ability of light to attract. Sometimes this is a positive thing, sometimes negative. Insects attracted to a light can be pests as they enter our homes. But an airport searchlight that brings an airplane to a safe arrival is a very positive attraction. In many communities there are very large displays of Christmas lights at this season of the year. This too can be either positive or negative.

In a positive sense, such lights at Christmas can witness to the one who is the "light of the world": Jesus, who came as a baby born in Bethlehem. In a negative sense, such lighting displays can merely be witness to the extravagance of the one putting them up. You've probably noticed that the displays seem to get more elaborate every year. No longer does decorating a single evergreen in the front yard suffice. It's as if every tree demands its own ropes of light, wrapping trunks as well as branches. The same trends that lead to conspicuous consumption in other areas also make Christmas lights more abundant.

As we put up Christmas lights in our homes and churches this year, may those lights point to the source of true light and not to our own cleverness or extravagance. Our Christmas lights will attract in either a positive or a negative way. The choice is ours. —A. E. A.

II. Comfort by the Servant (Isaiah 50:4, 5)
A. Tongue to Tell (v. 4a)

4a. The Lord GOD hath given me the tongue of the learned, that I should know how to speak a word in season to him that is weary.

The printed text moves to the third servant poem in the book of Isaiah. The subject changes from the larger mission of the servant to personal aspects of His task. Overall, it examines His personal responsibilities in speaking, listening, suffering, and showing determination. Many of the prophets of ancient Israel are threatened, abused, imprisoned, and put to death because they faithfully proclaim the message they received (Acts 7:52). Jesus' experiences will be very similar hundreds of years after Isaiah writes. Jesus may come as the precious babe in the manger, but eventually He will be fully aware of the temptations, trials, and rejections that exist on this planet.

Moses predicted that someday there would be a prophet like himself (Deuteronomy 18:15). Various comparisons may be made between Moses and Jesus, but there is one contrast especially interesting here: Moses claimed that he lacked eloquence and could not speak (Exodus 4:10); the servant, on the other hand, declares that the *Lord* has *given* Him a *tongue* that is capable and ready to speak. He will be taught, evidently, by God and man (Luke 2:40, 52). He will know what needs to be said, and He will say it.

The ministry of Jesus will produce weariness for Him. It will be tiring to speak to thousands, to know that people are seeking to be with Him for the wrong reasons, and to tolerate the quarrels of the disciples. At such times the Word of God from what we call the Old Testament will bring strength to Him. He is the one who brings us strength *in season* through His Word today. [See question #2, page 156.]

B. Ear to Listen (vv. 4b, 5)

4b. He wakeneth morning by morning, he wakeneth mine ear to hear as the learned.

This commentary is being written in the evening, and the alarm must be set to one of those early hours—my designated slot for a prayer vigil in the *morning*. Jesus did not need an alarm clock; God the Father could awaken Him each morning and begin the day's interactions. The figure of speech is fascinating: the *ear* also is awakened so as to be alert to this special instruction from on high.

5. The Lord GOD hath opened mine ear, and I was not rebellious, neither turned away back.

It fills the mind with wonder to speculate on what God the Father and God the Son shared whenever Jesus prayed. The Son imposed limitations on himself when He gave up the glories of Heaven temporarily (Philippians 2:7). Minimal records are given of these prayers (Mark 14:36), but they must have been times of intense mental interchange between the heavenly Father and the Son.

The response of the servant when God opens his *ear* is a great example. He does not resist; He is *not rebellious*. The servant Son listens, obeys, and does not turn *back* from His appointed mission. He is fully aware that the things before Him will lead to rejection, physical torture, public shame, and humiliation. But He continues to have an ear that is open to His Father. [See question #3, page 156.]

III. Composure of the Servant (Isaiah 50:6-9)

A. In Suffering (v. 6)

6. I gave my back to the smiters, and my cheeks to them that plucked off the hair: I hid not my face from shame and spitting.

A local church had a candlelight service on Christmas Eve. The theme was "From the Manger to the Cross." The emphasis that December night is the same as that of this verse. The gradual intensification of the servant's mission tells of things that take place before He reaches the cross. This poem is the servant's own predictive statement of what He will endure over 700 years after Isaiah writes these words.

The New Testament writers record that God's servant underwent the torture of being scourged or flogged (Matthew 27:26; Mark 15:15; John 19:1). The Gospels also record the mockery and *spitting* that the servant comes to endure (Matthew 27:27-31; Mark 15:16-20).

The divine prophecy states that Jesus *hid not* His *face* from these things. Matthew records Jesus as saying that He could call 12 legions of angels, but He was determined that the Scriptures be fulfilled (Matthew 26:53, 54). [See question #4, page 156.]

B. In Standing Firm (vv. 7-9)

7. For the Lord GOD will help me; therefore shall I not be confounded: therefore have I set my face like a flint, and I know that I shall not be ashamed.

The servant expresses an emphatic confidence that *the Lord* will sustain Him. In this He sets the example that has been followed through the centuries. Psalm 46:1, a favorite passage of many, agrees: "God is our refuge and strength, a very present help in trouble." Every Christian who is struggling with weariness—physical, emotional, or spiritual—must occasionally be reminded of this fact. The problem may persist, but strength for coping comes.

The conviction of the servant shows real determination with the phrase *set my face like a flint*. One of the famous sermons of history is entitled "The Christ of the Flint Face." It is connected with a statement in Luke 9:51 where Jesus sets "his face to go to Jerusalem." There He eventually is to face an agonizing death. (Compare Paul's own statement in Acts 20:22.)

The result is that the servant is confident that the disgrace of failure will not be in His experiences. His actions always will be pleasing to the Lord. While reproach may be cast upon Him, He will never suffer the humiliation of failure.

8. He is near that justifieth me; who will contend with me? let us stand together: who is mine adversary? let him come near to me.

The language changes to a court scene, and the servant expresses several things. First, He is aware of the nearness of God. Second, it is His vindication that is the only thing that matters. Third, the servant dares anyone to bring an accusation against Him. The servant may suffer, but He has confidence in the ultimate court of justice.

9. Behold, the Lord GOD will help me; who is he that shall condemn me? lo, they all shall wax old as a garment; the moth shall eat them up.

The servant again declares that it is *the Lord* who is the source for His strength. And again He challenges anyone to *condemn* Him or prove Him guilty in any way.

The final words of the servant give the end of those who would presume to sentence Him. The figure of *a garment* is used to show the outcomes. Clothing is a valuable commodity in primitive cultures (see Joshua 7:21). But clothing usually suffers destruction from use *(wax old)* or from insects such as *the moth*. So will the enemies of the servant be destroyed.

IV. Counsel on Behalf of the Servant (Isaiah 50:10, 11)

A. To Those Who Accept Him (v. 10)

10. Who is among you that feareth the Lord, that obeyeth the voice of his servant, that walketh in darkness, and hath no light? let him trust in the name of the Lord, and stay upon his God.

The words of the *servant* come to an end. But the poem continues with an exhortation and a warning on behalf of the servant who will someday come to earth.

One question about this verse and the next is the identity of the speaker. Is it Isaiah, or is it the Lord? In the final analysis it is God.

The exhortation here is addressed to anyone who reveres *the Lord* and who is obedient to *his servant*. This serves as a reminder that it is the fear of the Lord that is foundational to true wisdom (Proverbs 9:10).

Involved in such obedience is a recognition that the person has previously walked in darkness and has had *no light* for the journey of life. Now the plea is to *trust* in *the Lord* and be determined to have continual faithfulness. [See question #5, page 156.]

Trust for the Journey

As we start out on a trip, there are many things in which we place our trust. We trust in our automobile to give us good service. We trust the traffic enforcement officers to maintain the laws of the highway so the journey will be safe. We trust that the gas stations will be open for the purpose of refueling and restaurants will be open for food. The map we read we trust to be accurate. We are confident that the road signs point the right direction.

Our walk with God also demands trust. On this spiritual journey, we depend upon God's protection that He will build a hedge of safety around us. We depend upon spiritual nourishment from the encouragement of others and a refueling and renewing by the Holy Spirit. The Word of God is our road map, and we can be sure that following this will never lead us down a wrong road.

Before we start out on a journey, it's best that we plan ahead. The same is true for our spiritual journey. Time spent with God in prayer and Bible reading at the beginning of the day puts us on the right road. Times of encouragement as we interact with fellow Christians provide nourishment and fuel for the journey. God has promised that He will never abandon those who belong to Him. It is He, and only He, who can be trusted to provide guidance, protection, and strength for our journey toward eternity. —A. E. A.

B. To Those Who Reject Him (v. 11)

11. Behold, all ye that kindle a fire, that compass yourselves about with sparks: walk in the light of your fire, and in the sparks that ye have kindled. This shall ye have of mine hand; ye shall lie down in sorrow.

A warning is given to the many who are self-sufficient in trying to provide their own light for life. It is easy to accept the world's lie that we can take care of ourselves, protect ourselves, and handle life if we have health, wealth, and good luck. Many choose to *walk in the light* that they *kindle* for themselves.

God makes a promise that from His *hand* such people will be compelled to *lie down* in anguish. Make sure you're not one of those!

Conclusion

A. The Verdict

The verdict is clear: there is strength for the weary! We tap in to the ultimate source of that strength by fearing the Lord and obeying His

---

Home Daily Bible Readings

Monday, Dec. 5—Comfort, O Comfort My People (Isaiah 40:1-5)
Tuesday, Dec. 6—God Strengthens the Powerless (Isaiah 40:27-31)
Wednesday, Dec. 7—My God Has Become My Strength (Isaiah 49:1-7)
Thursday, Dec. 8—The Lord Has Comforted His People (Isaiah 49:8-13)
Friday, Dec. 9—I Will Not Forget You (Isaiah 49:14-18)
Saturday, Dec. 10—I Am the Lord, Your Savior (Isaiah 49:22-26)
Sunday, Dec. 11—The Lord God Helps Me (Isaiah 50:4-11)

voice (v. 10, above). The factor of obedience must not be overlooked. Many people desire physical blessings in abundance from God, but there are few attempts to live faithfully in obedience to God's commands. Should God be expected to strengthen the weary who live in flagrant disobedience to Him?

The Sermon on the Mount ends with the familiar account of the two builders (see Matthew 7:24-27). One built on the rock, and the other built on sand. Jesus said that building on the rock means hearing His words and obeying them. To obey God brings with it a certain assurance and joy that give strength to live for God every day.

B. Prayer

Our God in Heaven, in Jesus' name give us strength for today, just for this day. As we seek our physical and spiritual strength daily, remind us that our task is to live for You one day at a time. In Jesus' name, amen!

C. Thought to Remember

"God is able to make all grace abound toward you" (2 Corinthians 9:8).

Learning by Doing

This section contains an alternative lesson plan emphasizing learning activities. Classes desiring such student involvement will find these suggestions helpful.

Learning Goals

After participating in this lesson, each student will be able to:

1. Recite at least two purposes that Isaiah prophesied for the Messiah to fulfill.
2. Tell how Jesus fulfilled those prophecies.
3. Prepare an explanation of how the shame Christ underwent saves us.

Into the Lesson

Display the following as class begins: "What makes one WEARY?" Ask students to suggest answers using the letters of the word. For example, for *W*, *work* is a possibility. If students seem to be stuck at points, some additional examples include *worry, exercise, emotions, argument, anxiety, running, yearning, yelling*. At the end of the activity, point out the lesson title, "Strength for the Weary" and draw attention to today's text.

Into the Word

The lesson outline uses *commission, comfort, composure, counsel*. There are 33 letters in those words. Divide the words so that you have the number typically in your class. For example, if you usually have 15 students, divide the words into these 15 sets: CO, MM, IS, SI, ON, CO, MFO, RT, CO, MP, OS, URE, CO, UN, SEL. Put each combination on a separate card. Mix the cards and give one to each student.

Say, "To discover an emphasis in today's lesson, find others whose letters, when combined, make a key word related to the text." Encourage students to stand and "mill around" for this activity. If they need help, say that each word begins with *CO*. After students gather into their four groups (because there are four words), assign each a sitting area for the discussion to follow.

Put the four-part lesson outline on display. Give one of the following discussion stimulus assignments to each of the appropriate groups.

Commission—As the servant speaks in Isaiah 49:5, what insight does He show into God's eternal plan? What confidence does He express in God? What do we understand God's eternal plan to be? As the Lord speaks in Isaiah 49:6, how does He state His eternal purpose? What would be surprising in God's declaration to Isaiah's first hearers? What special relationship do we as Christians have to the servant's purpose? How do we fulfill the servant's purpose?

Comfort—Look at Isaiah 50:4, 5. What essential difference do you see between Moses as God's servant and the servant of Isaiah? What examples from the Gospels come to mind of Jesus saying the right thing at the right time? How and what did the Father speak to the Son in His earthly state? What is the servant's response to the Father's instructions? How far are we from affirming the servant's vow of Isaiah 50:5 for ourselves?

Composure—Read Isaiah 50:6-9. What similarities do you see between the servant's description of the way He reacts to persecution and the way Christ reacted after His arrest? What is commendable about the nonresistance of the servant to His enemies? How does one develop a similar composure in the face of such attacks?

Counsel—Read Isaiah 50:10, 11. What are the two secrets to a godly life? In what sense does a person without God walk in darkness? How does self-sufficiency cause a multitude of sins? In what way does a person have no more than sparks when trying to light his or her own path?

Allow time for groups to present at least some of their conclusions.

Into Life

Next, divide your class into six groups where they are already seated. Say, "Verse 10 of Isaiah 50 has a grand question and God's grand answer for the weary." Assign each group one of these segments of the verse: "Who is among you that feareth the Lord"; "that obeyeth the voice of his servant"; "that walketh in darkness"; "and hath no light?"; "let him trust in the name of the Lord,"; "and stay upon his God." Say the part of the verse relevant to each group, and let them repeat it. Then ask the groups to say the parts in sequence three times as quickly as they can.

Finally, ask, "What words to the weary will you use personally this week?" Suggest that verse 10 holds the answers: fearing, obeying, trusting, and staying. Distribute small pieces of paper. Say, "Write down the verse and carry it with you this next week as 'defense against world-weariness.'" You can also suggest that some may wish to put their notes where they will see it each day rather than carry it.

Let's Talk It Over

These questions are designed to promote discussion of the lesson. The answers here are only discussion starters. Let your class talk it over from there.

1. Many first-century Jews seemed to have overlooked the ancient promise that the coming servant would be a light to the Gentiles. How have we been guilty in allowing our own expectations and experiences to color our understanding of Scripture? How do we guard against this?

The Jews of the first century were under Roman occupation. Jewish hatred of this arrangement undoubtedly served to block any idea that those Gentiles somehow could gain God's favor. Our own expectations and experiences also slant our view about what we think God should or should not do. This seems especially so when we suffer personal injustice or see people lose their lives on a massive scale.

We guard ourselves from wrong interpretations through constant awareness of the danger of imposing our ideas on the Scripture. When we focus on finding the inspired author's original intent, we rarely will go wrong.

2. Weary people often feel alone as they carry their heavy loads. Certainly Moses had these feelings (see Numbers 11:14, 15). Drawing upon Isaiah 50:4, 5, how will you use these verses to allow God to relieve your own weariness?

These verses speak of Jesus' suffering. When we read them, we realize that God would not go to all the trouble of sending Jesus to die for our sins only to abandon us to our own despair. That wouldn't make sense! Immanuel—"God with us"—is still the message of Christmas.

Isaiah 50:5 also speaks of how the servant (Jesus) had an open ear. For ways that that fact can help us personally, see the next question.

3. If the Messiah needed an open ear, how much more do we need the same thing! What are some ways to keep our ears open to God's leading? How would we guard against mistaking our own desires for God's voice?

Jesus had an open ear in order to know how to serve the Father more effectively. We see this very clearly in the Garden of Gethsemane as Jesus refuses to listen to His own desires (Luke 22:42). For our part, we serve God best when our eyes and ears are attuned to God's written Word. It is the Word, first and foremost, that teaches us God's desires.

We should not forget that an important part of our service involves keeping our eyes and ears open to the needs around us. Matthew 25:35, 36 makes this clear. God may lead us in this regard by opening and closing various doors of opportunity. Sometimes it takes great spiritual sensitivity and prayer to recognize these opportunities when they present themselves.

4. Self-help tools often do not prepare leaders for attacks they are likely to encounter. Isaiah 50:6-9 gives us an unusual perspective on how the perfect leader was called upon to suffer. How can suffering actually help to define a person's ability to lead?

How a person deals with rebuke or pressure speaks volumes about strength of character or personal commitment. Someone who falls apart under light stress is unlikely to be an effective leader when the pressure is really on.

Of all the leaders who ever walked the earth, it is Jesus who best exemplifies how to keep focus under harassment and persecution. Jesus had become a threat to the prevailing power structures (John 11:48). His suffering and rejection caused him to take a good, hard look at His mission (Luke 22:37). Our suffering also will challenge us to examine our commitments. God may be preparing us for greater leadership roles through our sufferings (compare Acts 9:16).

5. The text recognizes that certain resources are available to those who yield to the Lord. How do you draw upon these resources on a day-to-day basis? What were some times that you tried to manage by your own strength?

An old hymn says, "You'll never walk alone." The same promise is presented in the poem "Footprints." It reminds us that there are times we will make it only if God is carrying us. It's a beautiful thought, but it is conditional. To know that the Father, the Son, and the Holy Spirit are going to be there as our resource, we must first agree to give up some of our own self-sufficiency. Many fail to yield and therefore fail to know God's power.

Hope for the Suffering

December 18
Lesson 3

DEVOTIONAL READING: Romans 12:9-16.

BACKGROUND SCRIPTURE: Isaiah 53; Luke 1.

PRINTED TEXT: Isaiah 53:1-3; Luke 1:46-55.

Isaiah 53:1-3

1 Who hath believed our report? and to whom is the arm of the Lord revealed?

2 For he shall grow up before him as a tender plant, and as a root out of a dry ground: he hath no form nor comeliness; and when we shall see him, there is no beauty that we should desire him.

3 He is despised and rejected of men; a man of sorrows, and acquainted with grief: and we hid as it were our faces from him; he was despised, and we esteemed him not.

Luke 1:46-55

46 And Mary said, My soul doth magnify the Lord,

47 And my spirit hath rejoiced in God my Saviour.

48 For he hath regarded the low estate of his handmaiden: for, behold, from henceforth all generations shall call me blessed.

49 For he that is mighty hath done to me great things; and holy is his name.

50 And his mercy is on them that fear him from generation to generation.

51 He hath showed strength with his arm; he hath scattered the proud in the imagination of their hearts.

52 He hath put down the mighty from their seats, and exalted them of low degree.

53 He hath filled the hungry with good things; and the rich he hath sent empty away.

54 He hath holpen his servant Israel, in remembrance of his mercy;

55 As he spake to our fathers, to Abraham, and to his seed for ever.

GOLDEN TEXT: His mercy is on them that fear him from generation to generation.—Luke 1:50.

> *God's Commitment—Our Response*
> Unit 1: God's Redeeming Love
> (Lessons 1-4)

Lesson Aims

After participating in this lesson, each student will be able to:

1. Compare and contrast the predictions of Isaiah 53:1-3 with Mary's song.
2. Explain why the suffering-servant concept is important to understanding the significance and joy of Christ's birth.
3. Express Mary's joy in a personal way.

Lesson Outline

INTRODUCTION
    A. Hope Defined
    B. Hope at Christmas
    C. Lesson Background
 I. DESPISING THE SERVANT (Isaiah 53:1-3)
    A. Declarations About the Servant (v. 1)
    B. Descriptions of the Servant (v. 2)
    C. Disdaining the Servant (v. 3)
      Rising Above Rejection
II. DELIBERATIONS BY MARY (Luke 1:46-55)
    A. Rejoicing in the Lord (vv. 46, 47)
    B. Recognition by the Lord (v. 48a)
    C. Recognition by Others (v. 48b)
    D. Regarding the Lord (v. 49)
    E. Relating to the Lord (v. 50)
    F. Repercussions from the Lord (vv. 51-53)
      A Healthy Diet
    G. Remedy from the Lord (vv. 54, 55)
CONCLUSION
    A. Hope for the Needy
    B. Prayer
    C. Thought to Remember

Introduction

A. Hope Defined

Hope sometimes has been defined as "confident expectation" or a "union of desire and expectation." By its very nature, the concept of hope is restricted to those who are alive (Ecclesiastes 9:4).

The Christian has the great joy of having a living hope that has been guaranteed by the resurrection of Jesus Christ. That hope looks forward to an incorruptible inheritance that is reserved in Heaven (1 Peter 1:3, 4). That hope sustains the believer, regardless of the trials that may come in this life. That hope serves as an anchor of the soul to everyone who finds refuge in the sure promises of God (Hebrews 6:18, 19).

Hope is a part of that famous trilogy of faith, hope, and charity (love). Each serves an important role in defining the Christian experience.

B. Hope at Christmas

The celebration of the Savior's birth has the concept of hope associated with it in many ways. For children it is usually what they expect to receive as gifts. Sometimes those hopes are fulfilled, but often those hopes are unrealistic.

Christmas also is associated with a certain nostalgia that family members should attempt to be together. People often hope (sometimes unrealistically) that travel plans, weather, and schedules will permit such reunions.

Many families indeed will be together for Christmas in a few days. But one or more family members may be absent because of death in the past year. The lesson for the day is entitled "Hope for the Suffering," and some will be hurting because of the deaths of those loved ones. In Christ, however, they are able also to express the confident hope of being able to be reunited with Christian loved ones. The Christ whose arrival we celebrate at Christmas is the one who brings this hope.

C. Lesson Background

Passages from Isaiah and Luke are the texts for this lesson. The first three verses of Isaiah 53 are a part of the fourth servant poem or servant song. (See the discussion of these four in our previous two lessons.) The poem at issue today begins at Isaiah 52:13 and it continues to the end of Isaiah 53. Polycarp, a Christian writer of the second century, refers to Isaiah 53 as "the golden passional of the Old Testament." This is the passage that has given rise to the phrase *suffering servant*. A prophetic view of the substitutionary death of the Messiah is clearly shown in the poem.

Isaiah 53 is quoted at least six times in the New Testament. (See Matthew 8:17; Luke 22:37; John 12:38; Acts 8:32, 33; Romans 10:16; and 1 Peter 2:22.) There are 30 or so other references to it that are not direct quotations. What an important passage this is!

The Gospel of Luke, for its part, gives careful attention to the birth of Jesus, which occurs some 700 years after Isaiah writes. The occasion of the passage from Luke for today's lesson is Mary's visit to Elisabeth, a relative. Elisabeth was with child herself, and that child would come to be known as John the Baptist. Mary's response to Elisabeth's blessing is sometimes called The Magnificat, following the Latin translation.

I. Despising the Servant (Isaiah 53:1-3)

As indicated above, this servant poem actually began at Isaiah 52:13. The word *servant* appears in Isaiah 52:13 and 53:11. This is the longest of the four servant songs or servant poems.

A. Declarations About the Servant (v. 1)

1. Who hath believed our report? and to whom is the arm of the LORD revealed?

Isaiah is the speaker, and the word *our* may refer to the collective statements of all that the prophets had made about the Messiah's coming. It even could include the actual statements to be made by the Messiah himself during His ministry. The two questions are rhetorical. In this context they become affirmations that God's servant does not enjoy positive responses by His people (see John 1:11).

God's communication to His people is said to be done in two ways. The first is by what is said *(report)*. The second is what is done by *the arm of the Lord*. That is a figure of speech to refer to the mighty acts of God. It therefore includes the miracles that Jesus will perform. This is the interpretation that John 12:37, 38 gives to this verse. Romans 10:14-17 establishes that faith comes by hearing the message. Yet Romans 10:16, which quotes Isaiah 53:1, tells us of those who reject the message. Some people hear and know, but their lives show that they do not believe in the Messiah who was born in Bethlehem.

B. Descriptions of the Servant (v. 2)

2. For he shall grow up before him as a tender plant, and as a root out of a dry ground: he hath no form nor comeliness; and when we shall see him, there is no beauty that we should desire him.

The phrasing *for he shall grow up before him* clearly shows a distinction between God the Son and God the Father as the servant grows up before (in the sight of) the Lord. The statement *shall grow up* is predictive prophecy that requires some 700 years to come to completion. Yet on God's timeline it is indeed completed!

Two words from agriculture are used to describe the servant. They are *plant* and *root*. Both words reflect qualities in the Messiah that do not make Him attractive to those who will prefer a militaristic Messiah who would make Israel to be supreme among the powers of the world.

Another figure of speech is that this growth will be from *dry ground*. Thus it would appear to be weak and of no value. To the casual observer, it is not something to be desired. [See question #1, page 165.]

Jesus' kingdom is not of this world, and the preconceived notions of many will not match what Jesus will have to say. There are prophecies that the Messiah will be a branch and out of the roots of Jesse, the father of David (Isaiah 4:2; 11:1). But many ancient Jews hope that the branch will turn into a mighty cedar.

Many also prefer that their leaders be handsome or attractive physically, don't they? David, Jesus' ancestor, had this quality (see 1 Samuel 16:18). When Jesus arrives following this prophecy, it will seem that He does not have the kind of physical attributes that compels instant endorsement from those who see Him.

C. Disdaining the Servant (v. 3)

3. He is despised and rejected of men; a man of sorrows, and acquainted with grief: and we hid as it were our faces from him; he was despised, and we esteemed him not.

The words *despised* and *rejected* are forceful ways of showing an intensity in the disfavor that Jesus is to receive during His earthly ministry. Jesus will not be just disregarded or ignored. Rather, He will be rejected and renounced deliberately. It has been said that unreturned love is one of the cruelest experiences that a person can have. When applied to the way that many have shown a total disregard for the love of God, it takes on gigantic proportions and implications. This has eternal consequences. [See question #2, page 165.]

RISING ABOVE REJECTION

In the summer of 1807, Robert Fulton's crude little steamboat was prepared to move up the

Hudson River on its maiden voyage. Critics called the boat *Fulton's Folly*. But we know now that this was no folly, it was no fluke. Fulton rose above his critics. As a result his boat became the predecessor to today's large ocean liners.

It is easy to cast doubt, isn't it? Parents are guilty at times of stifling creativity in their children. The road of life is littered with people who have been told that they would never amount to anything—and believed it. But there are always the overcomers, those who refuse to listen to the naysayers. Such people go on to greatness.

The ultimate example of this is Jesus, although His greatness is like no other. He was loathed by many. And His way is still rejected today by the masses. But Scripture reminds us that "the stone which the builders disallowed, the same is made the head of the corner" (1 Peter 2:7).

Just as God has raised Jesus to the place that is above all, so He continues to exalt His will and His way in the world. The example of Jesus, the supreme overcomer, encourages us to serve our Lord and seek to promote His will in a critical, hostile world. Jesus himself will help us. What appears folly to the world will in the end be the triumph of the plan of God. —A. E. A.

II. Deliberations by Mary (Luke 1:46-55)

In keeping with the season, Isaiah 53 leads us to think on the coming of the infant Jesus. We approach Him in this lesson through His mother Mary. She is at the house of Elisabeth as we pick up the story. Mary's statement in reply to Elisabeth has the qualities of one of the psalms of the Old Testament. It also offers several similarities to the exaltation expressed by Hannah after she had dedicated her son Samuel to the Lord (1 Samuel 2:1-10).

A. Rejoicing in the Lord (vv. 46, 47)

46, 47. And Mary said, My soul doth magnify the Lord, and my spirit hath rejoiced in God my Saviour.

Just before Mary's expression of praise, Elisabeth blessed her through the inspiration of the Holy Spirit. Mary's own personal piety undoubtedly assists her in drawing upon phrases and other songs from the Old Testament, especially the song by Hannah. Her spontaneous com-

---

How to Say It

BETHLEHEM. *Beth*-lih-hem.
DEUTERONOMY. Due-ter-*ahn*-uh-me.
ECCLESIASTES. Ik-*leez*-ee-*as*-teez (strong accent on *as*).
ELIJAH. Ee-*lye*-juh.
ELISHA. E-*lye*-shuh.
HANNAH. *Han*-uh.
HEBREWS. *Hee*-brews.
ISAIAH. Eye-*zay*-uh.
LEVITICUS. Leh-*vit*-ih-kus.
MAGNIFICAT. Mag-*nif*-ih-cot.
MESSIAH. Meh-*sigh*-uh.
MICAH. *My*-kuh.
ZAREPHATH. *Zair*-uh-fath.

---

ments in reply to Elisabeth give evidence of a genuine and sincere faith.

Mary states two emotions from the depths of her *soul*, and they seem to be expansions of previously held concepts. First is her exaltation of *the Lord;* second is the joy that she is experiencing in *God,* her *Saviour.*

B. Recognition by the Lord (v. 48a)

48a. For he hath regarded the low estate of his handmaiden.

One aspect of Jesus' life that goes unesteemed is *his* modest origin (to earthly eyes) in the family of Mary and Joseph. This is confirmed by the offering of two doves or pigeons when the family goes to Jerusalem to observe the purification rites (Luke 2:21-24). The usual sacrifices are a lamb plus a pigeon or a dove. But two birds are permitted if a family is too poor to afford a lamb (Leviticus 12:6-8). This is part of being of *low estate.*

Mary often is portrayed as being rather young, but the concepts in the statements she makes reflect a maturity beyond her age. She is fully aware of her origins and of the blessing of being selected by God to be the mother of the Savior.

C. Recognition by Others (v. 48b)

48b. For, behold, from henceforth all generations shall call me blessed.

Two beatitudes about Mary have been stated already by Elisabeth, one in verse 42 and the other in verse 45. [See question #3, page 165.] Mary's words show that she understands her distinctive part in bringing the Messiah into the world. It is thus appropriate to honor Mary for the responsible task that she has. Some have elevated her to a status beyond what the Bible suggests, however. Others, in a reaction to this extreme, almost ignore her importance in the plan of God.

D. Regarding the Lord (v. 49)

49. For he that is mighty hath done to me great things; and holy is his name.

Mary is filled with reverence for the *mighty* God. He is the one choosing her for the *great things* being done. She is also fully aware of the importance of God's holiness. The Lord confronted the nation of Israel about being holy (Leviticus 11:44, 45; see also 1 Peter 1:15, 16).

When Mary says *holy is his name*, she may have in mind Isaiah 57:15. That passage refers to God and says that His "name is Holy." Mary knows something about God!

E. Relating to the Lord (v. 50)

50. And his mercy is on them that fear him from generation to generation.

The Ten Commandments prohibit making any graven image. The seriousness of this is seen in the promise of judgment to the third and fourth generations for those who bow down to such idols (Exodus 20:4, 5). Yet *mercy* is promised for thousands—for generations who love and keep God's commandments (Exodus 20:6). Many things are happening in Mary's life. These include her message from Gabriel, the dream to Joseph, and Elisabeth's situation. These things cause her to realize that God is still keeping His promises *from generation to generation,* even after so many centuries. [See question #4, page 165.]

In Mary's statement a condition for receiving mercy is *fear* of the Lord, whereas in the Ten Commandments it is obedience. These are not in conflict. Micah 6:8 enriches both ideas of fear and obedience when it tells us of the Lord's desire for His people "to do justly, and to love mercy, and to walk humbly with thy God."

F. Repercussions from the Lord (vv. 51-53)

51. He hath showed strength with his arm; he hath scattered the proud in the imagination of their hearts.

The *arm* as a source of power is a frequent figure of speech for the ancient Hebrews (examples: Exodus 6:6; Deuteronomy 5:15). Except for the labor performed by livestock, the human arm is the most visible means of power in ancient domestic and military achievements.

The deliverance of Israel from Egypt was one of the great events in the history of that nation. God used His mighty arm to bring about the plagues, the crossing of the sea, and the provision of water and food to sustain the nation for its 40 years of wandering in the wilderness. A nation that was suffering under slavery was able to experience hope in its distress.

Sadly, there were episodes of rebellion. But hope eventually won the battles: Israel crossed the Jordan under Joshua's leadership; the walled city of Jericho collapsed according to God's divine plan; the nations of the land of Canaan were conquered; and the people of Israel took over cities that they had not built. In each instance of victory, the Lord was scattering the *proud* who were opposing the people of God.

52. He hath put down the mighty from their seats, and exalted them of low degree.

Mary's mental catalog of great victories over Israel's enemies is similar to portions of Hebrews 11, the Faith Chapter. Some of the incidents of the book of Judges may also be in her mind. In those instances, the people of Israel had been suffering, and God provided judges who gave them new hope. After the period of the judges, David delivered his people from oppression when he defeated Goliath, the giant warrior of the Philistines. God had truly brought low the powerful and elevated the people who had been subdued.

The language employed here seems to be more than just a poetic expression. It is based on Mary's comprehension of the greatness of God.

53. He hath filled the hungry with good things; and the rich he hath sent empty away.

Visual for lesson 3

Point to this visual as you ask "How is the hope that Jesus brings different from the hope that many people actually have?"

The emphasis changes from the events of war to meeting the basic need of hunger. The expressions of praise here are more likely to be poetic and general rather than referring to actual events.

There are specific occasions in the Old Testament, however, that involve miraculous multiplications of food for *the hungry*. One example involves the widow of Zarephath, who fed Elijah the prophet for quite some time (1 Kings 17:14-16). Another example is the feeding of 100 men with 20 loaves of barley bread in the time of Elisha (2 Kings 4:42-44). We should not overlook the possibility that spiritual hunger may be an issue (or even *the* issue) for Mary (compare Psalm 107:9). [See question #5, page 165.]

A Healthy Diet

Go to the Web site www.bread.org. Then click on the "hunger basics" link. There you will see startling statistics. Hunger and malnutrition are problems that need to be addressed in our world today.

Even so, there is a more serious type of hunger all around us: it is spiritual hunger and malnutrition. In one sense, hunger can be a good thing because it pushes us to seek nutrition. In the Sermon on the Mount, Jesus said, "Blessed are they which do hunger and thirst after righteousness: for they shall be filled" (Matthew 5:6). Beyond the miraculous provisions of food God made for people in various times and places in the Bible, spiritual food also is provided at the Lord's banquet table. In John 6:27 Jesus cautions His followers with these words: "Labor not for the meat which perisheth, but for that meat which endureth unto everlasting life, which the Son of man shall give unto you."

Sadly, opportunities for a solid spiritual diet are often neglected by God's people. Instead of finding the food that Jesus serves, many Christians gorge themselves on spiritual junk food. Some devotional books and Christian fiction are little more than pop culture with a spiritual spin. A world that is spiritually hungry is often treated to a version of the Word of God that bears little resemblance to the nutritional "meat" of the original.

Does your church continually monitor its programs to be sure a steady and healthy spiritual diet is offered? Do you as an individual take care to be sure that your spiritual diet is one that provides the essential ingredients for healthy, godly living? —A. E. A.

G. Remedy from the Lord (vv. 54, 55)

54. He hath holpen his servant Israel, in remembrance of his mercy.

It is very obvious to Mary that the nation of *Israel* is truly blessed. Some conjecture that Mary's recollections include some of the great promises of a coming one who would be the Savior. In the book of Isaiah the word *servant* does apply several times to the nation of Israel, but the ultimate purpose of that nation was to be the channel through which the Messiah would come into the world. It was essential that there be a righteous remnant, including godly people such as Mary, so that at the appointed time there would be a birth of the Son of God in Bethlehem. All of these things would work together to show both the longsuffering and the grace of God.

55. As he spake to our fathers, to Abraham, and to his seed for ever.

The final words of Mary's song show that the promises made to *Abraham* are a part of her understanding of God's redemptive plan. God has been faithful. He has kept His word from generation to generation, and now the grand climax is ready to begin its fulfillment through the Son she will deliver.

It has often been said that Mary herself may have suffered because of the comments others probably made about her out-of-wedlock pregnancy. That is speculation, but one thing that is sure is that Mary has a tremendous faith that

---

Home Daily Bible Readings

Monday, Dec. 12—Despised, Rejected, a Man of Sorrows (Isaiah 52:13–53:3)

Tuesday, Dec. 13—He Bore the Iniquities of Many (Isaiah 53:4-12)

Wednesday, Dec. 14—John the Baptist's Birth Foretold (Luke 1:5-17)

Thursday, Dec. 15—The Birth of Jesus Foretold (Luke 1:26-38)

Friday, Dec. 16—Mary Visits Elisabeth (Luke 1:39-45)

Saturday, Dec. 17—Mary's Song of Praise (Luke 1:46-55)

Sunday, Dec. 18—Hope Comes Through Tribulations (Romans 5:1-11)

enables her to express her hope. She experiences this hope even in the midst of any such suffering that her situation may produce.

Conclusion

A. Hope for the Needy

Some have a different hope at Christmas: they simply hope to be able to have a meal for the day. Some groups sponsor such meals for the needy in their communities. Churches often have benevolent programs that include delivering baskets of food to the underprivileged. Yes, there are some who take advantage of such kind acts, but there are others who express their sincere appreciation for these labors of love in the name of Christ. Such experiences in helping others to have their physical hopes fulfilled make the efforts worthwhile.

God has done so much for us. What will you do to provide hope for those who suffer physically and spiritually at this time of year?

B. Prayer

Our Father in Heaven, we read daily of suffering in the world, and that Christians are often the targets for persecution. We pray for them and for us that we may be steadfast because of the hope that we have in Christ, the hope of the world. In Jesus' name, amen.

C. Thought to Remember

"The God of hope fill you with all joy and peace in believing" (Romans 15:13).

Learning by Doing

This section contains an alternative lesson plan emphasizing learning activities. Classes desiring such student involvement will find these suggestions helpful.

Learning Goals

After participating in this lesson, each student will be able to:

1. Compare and contrast the predictions of Isaiah 53:1-3 with Mary's song.
2. Explain why the suffering-servant concept is important to understanding the significance and joy of Christ's birth.
3. Express Mary's joy in a personal way.

Into the Lesson

Say, "Suffering contorts and disfigures. Look at these 'contorted' words and identify things that accompany suffering." Have each of the following scrambled words on a separate card or sheet: *ainp* (pain), *aegnr* (anger), *efgir* (grief), *aceeiimnpt* (impatience), *adensss* (sadness), *deeinoprss* (depression), *acdeegimnorstu* (discouragement). Show one word at a time, starting with the shorter ones. As words are unscrambled, write them for group display. Once all seven words are identified, ask, "What are other things that accompany suffering?"

As an alternate introduction, use the following activity that is included in the student books. Display this fill-in statement, "Christmas _____ hope," and ask the class for verbs they believe accurately complete the thought. If a suggested answer seems unclear, ask for an explanation. (Sample responses are *is, satisfies, gives, delivers, promises, completes, fulfills.*)

Into the Word

Invite someone with music skills to bring a keyboard to class and play a few measures of some hymns and choruses. Give the musician your list of songs (see below) a week ahead of time for preparation.

First, ask the class to identify the song being played. Then ask students to identify Bible verses from today's text (in Isaiah 53 and Luke 1) that relate to that particular song. Suggested Bible verses are given in parentheses by each song, but accept student's suggestions for other Bible verses they may see relating to a particular song. Songs: "Hallelujah, What a Savior!" *(Isaiah 53:3)*; "Magnify, O Magnify" *(Luke 1:46)*; "What a Mighty God We Serve" *(Luke 1:49)*; "Come, Desire of Nations, Come" *(Isaiah 53:2)*; "O Sacred Head Now Wounded" *(Isaiah 53:3)*; "Holy, Holy, Holy" *(Luke 1:49)*; "Leaning on the Everlasting Arms" *(Luke 1:51)*; "Bread of Heaven, on Thee

We Feed" *(Luke 1:53);* "God of Our Fathers" *(Luke 1:55);* "Man of Sorrows" *(Isaiah 53:3).* Add other hymns and choruses that your class knows. As Bible verses are identified, you will have opportunity for explanations about the text that you wish to add.

Also, recruit two women to present the following dialogue between Hannah (see 1 Samuel 2:1-10) and Mary. Introduce the activity to your class by saying, "Hannah and Mary had similar experiences with God. They sang similar songs of praise. Imagine what it would be like if they stood face to face." Have your actresses ready to stand at those words and begin the dialogue.

Hannah (H): Mary, you are indeed blessed of God, even more so than I was.

Mary (M): O Hannah, God has heard the prayers of His people. He answered with a Savior.

H: From my place of disgrace and shame, He has exalted me in the eyes of all.

M: Yes, praise His name. From my humble home of poverty, He has made me rich indeed.

H: God's people for all time will call our names in joy. Hannah . . . Mary . . . chosen!

M: With His strong hand He has touched me in holiness and power. He does great things.

H: In the midst of my pain, He showed His mercy. His loving kindness endures forever.

M: He has brought down the pride of queens and noble women, but He has lifted me up.

H: His promise of seed to Abraham continues in my son Samuel and in your son, the Messiah.

M: Blessed be our God, dear Hannah; He keeps His word in love. You and I have seen it.

Next, have half the class turn to 1 Samuel 2:1-10. Have students compare and contrast the dialogue with both Hannah and Mary's songs.

Into Life

The lesson writer uses part of Romans 15:13 as the Thought to Remember. Print that half-verse and reference on address labels. (If your home computer cannot do this, check with your church's office about the possibility.) Give each class member two or more copies to add to a card or letter to be sent during this holy season.

Let's Talk It Over

These questions are designed to promote discussion of the lesson. The answers here are only discussion starters. Let your class talk it over from there.

1. In Isaiah 53:2 we read of "a tender plant." What environmental factors that cause a plant to grow can be used to illustrate the growth of young Jesus "in wisdom and stature, and in favor with God and man"? How do we tap into the same factors for our own growth?

Young plants will grow if they are given the right environment of light, nutrients, soil, and water. You may find your class being very creative in connecting these four with various aspects of Jesus' home life and His early spiritual training. He was no doubt heavily affected by the teachings of His parents and the synagogue leaders. Stress that without growth there is stagnation (see 1 Corinthians 3:1, 2; Hebrews 5:11–6:3).

2. Isaiah 53:1-3 describes attributes that appear to make Jesus an unlikely candidate as God's ultimate servant. Why do you think these characteristics were part of God's deliberate plan for the Messiah?

To our way of thinking, leaders are supposed to have a certain commanding presence (compare 1 Samuel 9:2; 16:7, 12). They are to be positive thinkers whose emotions can be masked. They appear to be winners in every way.

But Jesus was different. On the cross, He appeared to be the ultimate loser. Yet His followers did not identify with Him because of earthly prestige. Rather, it was because they understood (eventually) who the resurrected Jesus really was and what He could do in the context of eternity.

The Son still draws to himself those who have eyes and ears attuned to eternity. God requires such eyes to look beyond worldly definitions of success to see ultimate truth about His Son.

3. Elisabeth provided a safe haven for Mary that included a listening ear. As we approach the end of the year, we can reflect on the ways in which we have served and can serve others. How can we do better in this regard?

Matthew 25:40 sets the stage for the discussion: "Inasmuch as ye have done it unto one of the least of these my brethren, ye have done it unto me." There are many, many ways to apply this principle, so expect a wide-ranging discussion.

If the discussion begins to focus too heavily on meeting physical and emotional needs, remind your students that spiritual matters are the most important. This reminder can lead to a discussion of the importance of prayer lists, etc.

4. Luke 1:50 states that God's mercy is extended "from generation to generation." Certainly the words *forever* or *eternally* could have been used. Why do you think the reference to generations is a stronger statement?

God uses people to spread His message—that's His plan as one generation gives way to the next. The responsibility of parents in sharing the gospel message with their children cannot be overstated. A minister was turned away from talking with a sixth-grade boy because the parents didn't want Christianity "forced" on their son. When the child's life came to a tragic end several years later, there was little comfort that could be given to the parents regarding their son's lack of response to the gospel. Those of one generation had failed someone of the next!

Whether it is through the family unit or through acquaintance, we are accountable for sharing the good news with the next generation. The lesson from Old Testament Israel is that they were always just one generation away from rejecting God.

5. Some think that God stepped back after creation to take a passive role. Luke 1:51-53 presents a different view! How does God still shape history? Discuss times in your life when you believe God intervened directly.

In the ancient past, God occasionally worked by means of unmistakable miracles. Under the New Covenant, all of God's subsequent works in history (miraculous or not) occur in light of the fact that He already has sent His Son.

Recognizing situations in which God intervenes directly in our lives is tricky! This can be very subjective, especially in cases when someone thinks that "God is telling me to do such and such." Often God seems to work through opening and closing doors of opportunity. God's plans in this regard might not be recognized as His intervention until much later.

December 25
Lesson 4

Good News for the World

DEVOTIONAL READING: Isaiah 52:7-12.

BACKGROUND SCRIPTURE: Isaiah 61:1-3; Luke 2:8-20.

PRINTED TEXT: Isaiah 61:1, 2; Luke 2:8-20.

Isaiah 61:1, 2

1 The Spirit of the Lord God is upon me; because the Lord hath anointed me to preach good tidings unto the meek; he hath sent me to bind up the brokenhearted, to proclaim liberty to the captives, and the opening of the prison to them that are bound;

2 To proclaim the acceptable year of the Lord, and the day of vengeance of our God; to comfort all that mourn.

Luke 2:8-20

8 And there were in the same country shepherds abiding in the field, keeping watch over their flock by night.

9 And, lo, the angel of the Lord came upon them, and the glory of the Lord shone round about them; and they were sore afraid.

10 And the angel said unto them, Fear not: for, behold, I bring you good tidings of great joy, which shall be to all people.

11 For unto you is born this day in the city of David a Saviour, which is Christ the Lord.

12 And this shall be a sign unto you; Ye shall find the babe wrapped in swaddling clothes, lying in a manger.

13 And suddenly there was with the angel a multitude of the heavenly host praising God, and saying,

14 Glory to God in the highest, and on earth peace, good will toward men.

15 And it came to pass, as the angels were gone away from them into heaven, the shepherds said one to another, Let us now go even unto Bethlehem, and see this thing which is come to pass, which the Lord hath made known unto us.

16 And they came with haste, and found Mary and Joseph, and the babe lying in a manger.

17 And when they had seen it, they made known abroad the saying which was told them concerning this child.

18 And all they that heard it wondered at those things which were told them by the shepherds.

19 But Mary kept all these things, and pondered them in her heart.

20 And the shepherds returned, glorifying and praising God for all the things that they had heard and seen, as it was told unto them.

GOLDEN TEXT: Unto you is born this day in the city of David a Saviour, which is Christ the Lord.—Luke 2:11.

LESSON 4 · 167 · DECEMBER 25

> *God's Commitment—Our Response*
> Unit 1: God's Redeeming Love
> (Lessons 1-4)

Lesson Aims

After participating in this lesson, each student will be able to:

1. Retell the events in the lives of the shepherds on the night Jesus was born.
2. Explain how Isaiah 61:1, 2 applies to the lives of the shepherds.
3. Glorify and praise God for Jesus as the shepherds did.

Lesson Outline

INTRODUCTION
    A. Jesus Is Coming—Again!
    B. Lesson Background
 I. ANOINTED ONE SPEAKS (Isaiah 61:1, 2)
    A. His Claims (v. 1a)
    B. His Commission (vv. 1b, 2)
    Breaking Free
 II. ANNOUNCEMENTS TO THE SHEPHERDS (Luke 2:8-14)
    A. Savior for All (vv. 8-11)
    B. Sign of a Baby (v. 12)
    C. Heavenly Host (vv. 13, 14)
 III. JOURNEY TO BETHLEHEM (Luke 2:15-20)
    A. Decision (v. 15)
    B. Discovery (v. 16)
    C. Declarations (v. 17)
    Can You Believe It?
    D. Different Responses (vv. 18-20)
CONCLUSION
    A. Making a Difference!
    B. Prayer
    C. Thought to Remember

Introduction

A. Jesus Is Coming—Again!

What would life be like if Christ had not come? Sermons, books, and poems have presented their speculation on the subject. During the last 2,000 years, the influence of Christ cannot be discounted. His followers have had a profound impact in the areas of benevolence, education, the fine arts, and the histories of civilizations and nations. We shudder to think of a world without Christ and the forgiveness of sin he brought.

But Jesus was indeed born into the world. And that fact causes us to remember that He is coming again! Jesus came the first time as the suffering servant, giving His life as an atonement for sin. He also warned that His return will be a time of judgment and condemnation for those who have lived in rebellion to Him and His Word.

As this is being written, a prophecy seminar is being advertised as giving all there is to know about when Jesus will return. Jesus himself said that He did not know the day or the hour (Mark 13:32). The urgency is not to set a date, but to set one's life in order and be ready for the return of the Lord at any time.

The prophecies of Jesus' first coming covered a time period of centuries. A final exhortation of the apostle Peter was, "The Lord is not slack concerning his promise, as some men count slackness; but is long-suffering to us-ward, not willing that any should perish, but that all should come to repentance" (2 Peter 3:9). Jesus said that He will return—and He will!

B. Lesson Background

The theme for the month of December has been "God's Redeeming Love." The Scriptures selected have included Old Testament passages that set forth God's plan to demonstrate His love for the world by sending a special servant. Each lesson has included passages from the book of Isaiah, and the final two Sundays of December also use portions from the book of Luke.

Home Daily Bible Readings

Monday, Dec. 19—God's Justice and Deliverance Never End (Isaiah 51:1-6)
Tuesday, Dec. 20—God's Messenger Brings Good Tidings (Isaiah 52:7-12)
Wednesday, Dec. 21—God Will Be Your Glory (Isaiah 60:15-22)
Thursday, Dec. 22—Good Tidings for the Oppressed (Isaiah 61:1-7)
Friday, Dec. 23—God Gives Salvation and Righteousness (Isaiah 61:8–62:3)
Saturday, Dec. 24—Mary Has a Baby (Luke 2:1-7)
Sunday, Dec. 25—The Angels Bring Good Tidings (Luke 2:8-21)

Isaiah sometimes has been designated as "the gospel prophet" or "the fifth evangelist" (adding Isaiah to Matthew, Mark, Luke, and John). Much of Jesus' life is given in predictive prophecy by Isaiah, from Jesus' being born of a virgin to His ministry and death. The first few verses of Isaiah 61, the passage for today, will confirm the mission of Jesus.

The event from Luke in today's text is that which takes place immediately after Jesus' birth. It is the announcement to shepherds that the Savior, the Christ, is in nearby Bethlehem as a baby in a manger. This part of God's plan for the ages had come to pass, just as it had been predicted through Isaiah and other prophets for centuries.

I. Anointed One Speaks
(Isaiah 61:1, 2)
A. His Claims (v. 1a)

1a. The Spirit of the Lord GOD is upon me; because the LORD hath anointed me to preach good tidings unto the meek.

All of the previous selections from Isaiah this month have been from what are called the servant poems or servant songs. The word *servant* is not found in Isaiah 61, but that chapter is sometimes included as one of the poems because of its content and form.

Three interesting facts pertain to this verse and those that follow. First, this verse is quoted almost word for word by Jesus while in His hometown of Nazareth. That occasion is at the beginning of His ministry (Luke 4:16-19). When Jesus reads the opening verses of Isaiah 61, He will say that this Scripture is fulfilled that very day!

After an initial gracious reception, Jesus' words will anger the assembled people. They will usher Jesus out of the city to throw Him down a precipice. But Jesus, manifesting a portion of His divinity, will walk back through the hostile crowd without suffering any harm (Luke 4:28-30). [See question #1, page 174.]

Second, the opening words of the verse at hand are fascinating in that all three personalities of the Godhead are mentioned: *the Spirit, the Lord,* and the *anointed* one speaking (the Christ or Messiah). The word *anointed* gives a different perspective to the role of the servant who had been introduced earlier. Anointing is a setting aside to a special office. In the Old Testament it is often reserved for prophets (example: Elisha's anointing by Elijah in 1 Kings 19:16b); kings (example: David's anointing by Samuel in 1 Samuel 16:1, 12, 13; 2 Samuel 2:7); and priests (examples: Exodus 28:41; 29:7; Leviticus 8:12, 30). A study of the person and work of Jesus in the New Testament shows that He fulfills all three functions: prophet, priest, and king.

Third, the foremost duty for the anointed one is *to preach*. The message of this preacher is the *good tidings* of the gospel. The specified audience consists of those who are not arrogant in their attitudes; they are those who are *the meek* (compare Matthew 5:3-5). Such people understand the burden of sin, and they are receptive. (Some have attempted to say that the speaker in this passage is Isaiah. But Jesus applies it to himself in Luke 4:18.)

B. His Commission (vv. 1b, 2)

1b. He hath sent me to bind up the brokenhearted, to proclaim liberty to the captives, and the opening of the prison to them that are bound.

To bind up the brokenhearted is a figure of speech, as if a bandage is to be applied to the heart that is broken because of sin. Several things can cause a broken heart, but the spiritual is foremost here.

The commission of the Savior includes proclamations for those who are in confinement. This does not mean that becoming a Christian removes the shackles of physical confinement, whatever that consists of. Rather, there is a spiritual liberation that enables a person to experience a freedom that does not depend on physical circumstances.

BREAKING FREE

Johnny had dropped out of church. He was disenchanted with the people of God, so he disassociated himself from them. He considered a relationship with the church to be unnecessary.

Then one day a fire destroyed his home and all family possessions. Churches and individual Christians responded with an outpouring of financial gifts, clothing, toys for the children, and prayers. Johnny was touched by the love of God's people. He and his family renewed their walk with God through a local church. Shortly after this, the best friend of Johnny's 7-year-old son was killed in a car accident. Johnny, motivated by the outpouring of love he had received, helped this family in their time of need.

Jesus came to bind up the broken, to liberate those captured by sin. He provided this relief while on earth in a physical body. He continues to provide this same help today through His spiritual body, the church. To be the people of Christ is to take on the work of Christ. Churches are often good at demonstrating this gift of love in the Christmas season. But it is a gift that needs to be a daily part of the church of Christ. The gift of love exhibited by the people of God is a gift that keeps on giving. Just ask Johnny. —A. E. A.

2. To proclaim the acceptable year of the LORD, and the day of vengeance of our God; to comfort all that mourn.

Several things are of special interest in this verse. One is the contrast in the designated periods of time: *year* vs. *day*. These terms are figures of speech in the ancient culture, and they are meant to express periods without concern for a precise number of hours or minutes.

The first phrase of the verse reminds us of the concepts associated with the Year of Jubilee, which was to occur every fifty years (Leviticus 25:8-17). In that year debts were to be canceled, servants were freed, and land went back to the original families. (So far no one is complaining that a phrase, found in Leviticus 25:10 and associated with the Year of Jubilee, is on the Liberty Bell in Philadelphia!)

We also note that justice in God's sight demands the *vengeance of our God*. There are many precious promises in the message of "good news," but there are also powerful warnings to those who do not listen to this preacher. Interestingly, when Jesus quotes Isaiah 61:1, 2 in Luke 4:18, 19, He stops with the phrase "to preach the acceptable year of the Lord." It's as if Jesus is saying that His ministry ushers in the positive message of hope right then and there, while the dire reality of judgment will be delayed somewhat. [See question #2, page 174.]

The final phrase of the verse at hand moves back to the message of *comfort*. What a great word at Christmas! The phrase is similar to one of Jesus' statements in the Sermon on the Mount in Matthew 5:4.

II. Announcements to the Shepherds (Luke 2:8-14)

A. Savior for All (vv. 8-11)

8, 9. And there were in the same country shepherds abiding in the field, keeping watch over their flock by night. And, lo, the angel of the Lord came upon them, and the glory of the Lord shone round about them; and they were sore afraid.

The message of Jesus' birth is not given to an emperor in Rome or to a high priest in Jerusalem. Rather, it is to humble *shepherds* that the heavenly *angel* appears.

The shepherds will remember this night for the rest of their lives, telling about it over and over. Perhaps these shepherds, like Simeon in Luke 2:25, are looking for the consolation of Israel. Perhaps some, like Joseph and Mary, are also descendants of David. Perhaps they know the prophecy about Bethlehem in Micah 5:2, and therefore speak of such spiritual matters during the long hours of the night watches.

One of our favorite Christmas songs says that it was a "silent night," but we do not know that to be a fact. The shepherds are guarding their flocks from predatory animals, and they are alert to the sounds of the night. The sudden appearance of an *angel of the Lord* is startling in the darkness, and the added factor of *the glory of the Lord* combines to produce fright. That is the usual reaction whenever a person receives a heavenly visitor (examples: Luke 1:12; Acts 10:4).

10. And the angel said unto them, Fear not: for, behold, I bring you good tidings of great joy, which shall be to all people.

The words of *the angel* provide assurance to the frightened shepherds. The impact of the

---

How to Say It

BETHLEHEM. *Beth*-lih-hem.
EGYPT. *Ee*-jipt.
ELIJAH. Ee-*lye*-juh.
ISAIAH. Eye-*zay*-uh.
LEVITICUS. Leh-*vit*-ih-kus.
MESSIAH. Meh-*sigh*-uh.
MICAH. *My*-kuh.
NAZARETH. *Naz*-uh-reth.
SIMEON. *Sim*-ee-un.
ZECHARIAH. *Zek*-uh-*rye*-uh (strong accent on *rye*).

angel's words builds to a positive climax that gives even more confidence.

Some students restrict the word *people* in this context to mean only the Jews. The reason for this is that other accounts mention salvation of "his people" (Matthew 1:21) as Jesus reigns over "the house of Jacob" (Luke 1:33). It is true that the church was primarily Jewish in background for the first few years of its existence. The prophecies of Isaiah, Amos, and others, however, support the view that the pronouncements include Gentiles—that they mean the same as the title for this lesson: "good news for the world." God intends salvation to be for Jew and non-Jew alike (Acts 10:34, 35; 11:18).

11. For unto you is born this day in the city of David a Saviour, which is Christ the Lord.

The *Saviour* does not come as a mature warrior. Instead, He arrives as a newborn baby. The terms continue to build in their significance, words such as *David, Saviour, Christ,* and *Lord.* The shepherds undoubtedly have confirming thoughts with each word. We may safely conjecture that the shepherds are aware of the ancient connection between David and the *city* of Bethlehem.

B. Sign of a Baby (v. 12)

12. And this shall be a sign unto you; Ye shall find the babe wrapped in swaddling clothes, lying in a manger.

The extraordinary happenings would seem unbelievable, even to those experiencing them. When it's all over, they may just think it was a hallucination. But to be given *a sign* will promote acceptance and belief. It's real! The sign is that of a *babe . . . lying in a manger.*

The birthing place for the Savior is not a sterilized room in a hospital, but a place that includes a feed box for animals. The traditional pictures show animals nearby, and that may be a valid assumption. [See question #3, page 174.]

C. Heavenly Host (vv. 13, 14)

13, 14. And suddenly there was with the angel a multitude of the heavenly host praising God, and saying, Glory to God in the highest, and on earth peace, good will toward men.

The appearance and announcement of one *angel* is dramatically emphasized with the sudden manifestation of a *heavenly host.* This angelic army has the joy and privilege of being a part of this special event.

Visual for lesson 4

Red and gold are important colors in this visual. Ask how each can remind us of Christ at Christmas.

A careful reading of the text indicates that the angels come *praising God and saying* something. There is no reference to singing as such. Yet over the years, composers have set the angelic words to music, with marvelous effect.

The messages of the angels are bidirectional: *to God* and *toward men.* This birth will be more reason than ever before to give *glory* to God.

The second part of the statement refers to the genuine *peace* that can now be *on earth.* Rome had brought a military peace that would later permit the early Christians to spread the gospel. The peace mentioned here, however, is a peace between God and people. One of the greatest peace pronouncements of the New Testament is Romans 5:1: "Therefore being justified by faith, we have peace with God through our Lord Jesus Christ."

It is also fitting to note that Jesus said that He brought not only peace but also a sword (Matthew 10:34). Even today the very mention of the name *Jesus* in various parts of the world can produce tension and hostility that may turn violent.

III. Journey to Bethlehem (Luke 2:15-20)

A. Decision (v. 15)

15. And it came to pass, as the angels were gone away from them into Heaven, the shepherds said one to another, Let us now go even unto Bethlehem, and see this thing which is come to pass, which the Lord hath made known unto us.

The angels deliver their praises and their message to humanity and then depart *into heaven.* This raises some intriguing questions.

LESSON 4 171 DECEMBER 25

Do they simply disappear? Is there a visible departure until eventually they no longer can be seen? We are left to conjecture. What is not in doubt, however, is the shepherds' response. Stunned, they collect their thoughts and take the only reasonable actions that their experiences lead them to do.

First, *the shepherds* speak *one to another*. It is almost as if they need to have further confirmation among themselves that they had really seen and heard the heavenly messengers. Except for their own voices, only the sounds of night now are heard. But their conclusion is that they must leave in order to confirm what the angel had announced. They want to *see this thing* that has occurred in their own little town of *Bethlehem*.

B. Discovery (v. 16)

16. And they came with haste, and found Mary and Joseph, and the babe lying in a manger.

It is just as the angel had said: shepherds find the infant Jesus *lying in a manger*, with *Mary and Joseph* in attendance. Without doubt, this is a privileged group that meets together this night.

As the shepherds come with all good speed to Bethlehem, does the excitement cause them to leave the flocks unguarded? Does someone volunteer to stay behind? Do they bring their flocks along? How long do they stay? The story may be familiar, but there is still much that arouses our curiosity!

C. Declarations (v. 17)

17. And when they had seen it, they made known abroad the saying which was told them concerning this child.

An evangelist is someone who tells good news. These shepherds thus become the very first evangelists to testify about Jesus Christ, who has come in the flesh. What an amazing way that God works!

CAN YOU BELIEVE IT?

A man who worked on the streets near the World Trade Center in New York City was thought to be dead following the September 11, 2001 attacks. But almost a year later, his family received word that he was alive. The family of George V. Sims, 46, said they learned of his whereabouts in August 2002 when a hospital called and said that they believed Sims was a patient there.

How would you have responded to such good news? Stunned silence? Disbelief? Jump for joy? Maybe your response would be to grab the nearest person for a big hug. Many times good news is something we just have to share with others. One thing is certain though: when we hear really good news, something happens.

The response of the shepherds to the news of the birth of Jesus presented by the angels was one of desire. They wanted to check this out for themselves. And when they went to Bethlehem and saw that the good news was really true, they rejoiced and spread the message.

On this Christmas Day we reaffirm our belief that the coming of Jesus into the world actually happened. A proper response to this is rejoicing and sharing this good news with others.

—A. E. A.

D. Different Responses (vv. 18-20)

18. And all they that heard it wondered at those things which were told them by the shepherds.

The people who hear the accounts of *the shepherds* can do only what is stated here. The angels do not appear to these people to provide additional confirmation. Thus they can only wonder and think about what they are told. The rest of the story is still to unfold in the years ahead. That will provide their confirmation! [See question #4, page 174.]

19. But Mary kept all these things, and pondered them in her heart.

Mary's list of *things* associated with the birth of Jesus continues to grow. In the near future she will experience the visit by the wise men (Matthew 2:11), and then there will be the unexpected sojourn to Egypt (Matthew 2:13-15). Will she hear of the slaughter of the male infants in the vicinity of Bethlehem (Matthew 2:16)?

And then there are her thoughts when she finally finds her lost son in the temple, reasoning with scholars about the Law (Luke 2:41-51). What will she think as she sees Him dying on a cross (John 19:25-27)? Mary will have much to ponder throughout her life.

20. And the shepherds returned, glorifying and praising God for all the things that they had heard and seen, as it was told unto them.

We turn our attention once again to the *shepherds*. They must wonder why they are chosen to be a part of this special event. But then they do the right thing: they glorify and praise *God for all the things* they had been privileged to hear and see. [See question #5, page 174.]

Conclusion

A. Making a Difference!

The prophecies and the birth of Jesus combine to make an unusual story. The prophecies that had accumulated through the centuries were fulfilled when Jesus became God incarnate—God in the flesh. As a new year dawns, will these things be just another telling of a familiar account, or will they make a difference in the lives of each one who has considered them again? As a new year dawns, will we resolve to make differences for Christ in the lives of others—differences that can determine where they spend eternity?

The events associated with Jesus' birth were not ordinary! They are a part of the message of Christ, and they are to be preached and taught by His followers to those who have never heard. It bears repeating: The purpose is to make a difference in the eternal destinies of those who hear.

B. Prayer

Almighty God, on a day when meals are served in ways that show abundant blessings, may we remember to give thanks for daily bread and for the coming of Jesus, the bread of life. In Jesus' name, amen.

C. Thought to Remember

To celebrate Christmas without remembering Jesus is unthinkable!

Learning by Doing

This section contains an alternative lesson plan emphasizing learning activities. Classes desiring such student involvement will find these suggestions helpful.

Learning Goals

After participating in this lesson, each student will be able to:
1. Retell the events in the lives of the shepherds on the night Jesus was born.
2. Explain how Isaiah 61:1, 2 applies to the lives of the shepherds.
3. Glorify and praise God for Jesus as the shepherds did.

Into the Lesson

As class begins, have one of your better oral readers stand and read Luke 4:14-21. At the end of the reading say, "The text Jesus quoted from Isaiah would have sounded familiar to Jews of the first century. The rabbis had long taught that it was messianic. When Isaiah wrote it, it certainly brought hope to his first readers. It was good news then. It is good news now."

Then ask, "But what if Christ had not been born?" Write on the board "If Christ had not been born, then _____." Ask class members to think of different ways to complete this sentence. For example, "If Christ had not been born, then the church would not exist." Let students offer completions for two or three minutes. Then lead into the lesson by saying, "That is all very bad news indeed. But we have, as the lesson title affirms, 'Good News for the World.'"

Into the Word

Prepare copies of the following to be read antiphonally. It is today's text from Isaiah 61:1, 2 with a response added to each truth. Either read the leader's part yourself or have another do so. L=leader; G=group.

L: **The Spirit of the Lord is upon me.**
G: God's Spirit has come to dwell in us.
L: **Because the Lord hath anointed me to preach good tidings unto the meek.**
G: God wants the good news told to all.
L: **He hath sent me to bind up the brokenhearted.**
G: God cares when our hearts are broken.
L: **To proclaim liberty to the captives.**
G: There is an escape from the bondage of sin.
L: **And the opening of the prison to them that are bound.**
G: God offers freedom in Christ for the asking.
L: **To proclaim the acceptable year of the Lord.**

G: Now is the acceptable time.
L: **And the day of vengeance of our God.**
G: God will see justice done.
L: **To comfort all that mourn.**
G: God has given His Holy Spirit to be our comforter.

Next, ask learners to look at the text in Luke 2:8-20 and describe what the front of a Christmas card could look like that featured each verse (or a segment thereof). Suggest that students come up with some cards not typically found. For example, for "and they were sore afraid" (the last clause in verse 9) the card may show a close-up of shepherd faces with looks of terror. As a second example, "which shall be to all people" (the last phrase of verse 10) may be depicted as a collage of photos of twenty-first-century ethnic groups. (A similar activity is included the student book.)

Into Life

Prepare and distribute copies of a document containing the heading, "Resolutions!" with the following five statements printed beneath.

1. Mary actively meditated on the grand truths of the incarnation as well as her part in it. **Resolved:** I will incorporate into my meditative life _____.

2. The shepherds set the example of telling everyone they saw about the Messiah's birth. **Resolved:** I will tell _____.

3. Isaiah's description of the Messiah (Isaiah 61:1, 2) includes a variety of graces to those who are hurting. **Resolved:** I will show grace by _____.

4. The angels fulfilled their ministry of praise to God at Jesus' birth. **Resolved:** I will enlarge my ministry of praise by _____.

5. God loves me so much that He has given His Son. **Resolved:** I will love Him so much I will _____.

Say to your class, "Take this resolution sheet home with you. This coming week is the traditional time when many people write resolutions for life changes. Use these stimulus statements to give consideration to some new commitments for the year ahead."

Let's Talk It Over

These questions are designed to promote discussion of the lesson. The answers here are only discussion starters. Let your class talk it over from there.

1. People initially thought well of Jesus when He quoted Isaiah 61:1, 2 (see Luke 4:20-22). But the mood turned ugly when He drew a comparison with the time of Elijah (Luke 4:24-29). What was the flaw in their attitudes that made them resistant to the good news Jesus was sharing? How are we susceptible to this flaw today?

What Jesus had to say in Luke 4:24-27 is similar to Stephen's speech in Acts 7. Both Jesus and Stephen accuse people of rejecting the prophets (compare Acts 7:52 with Luke 4:24). Such people are, as a result, outside the will of God (compare Acts 7:51 with Luke 4:25-27). This is what incited murderous rage in both cases (compare Acts 7:54 with Luke 4:28, 29).

Arrogance is part of a trap that thinks "How could I *not* be one of God's favorite people?" Those who have that attitude cannot hear God's voice. They are not humble. Yet Jesus' message is for the humble and meek (Matthew 5:3-10).

2. The phrase "and the day of vengeance of our God" in Isaiah 61:1, 2 may seem to be out of place in not being part of the "good news." What relationship do you see between that phrase and the other prophecies of that passage?

Several religious groups reject the concept of judgment and Hell. When that happens, the compassionate and redemptive side of Jesus becomes the sole focus.

The love of Jesus should indeed captivate us! But we must not allow ourselves to forget that our God also is just, holy, and righteous. He cannot allow sin to continue. A day will come when He purges any and all challenges to His people and to His own holiness. This is an important part of the "comfort" spoken of in our lesson text.

3. We sometimes hear people say things like, "God told me that . . . " or "God has shown me that . . . " How can we determine if a claimed revelation or sign is really a message from God? Why is it important to do so?

When Aaron threw down his staff, it became a snake as a sign of God's power. Pharaoh's magicians seemingly replicated that sign—until their props were swallowed! (See Exodus 7:8-13.) This may be an early indicator that we must be somewhat cautious about signs being the sole evidence for God's intervention.

Zechariah 13:1-6 and Hebrews 1:1, 2 seem to say that there are no more prophets after Christ. This should make us cautious about additional "revelations" over and above what the New Testament says. Second Thessalonians 2:9 warns that Satan also will use signs to deceive us. A key difference between the signs of Satan and the words of the angels is their ability to be verified. Modern-day signs that come only to an individual and cannot be traced to a gospel promise should make us very cautious.

4. In Luke 2:18 we read of wonder (or amazement) as a reaction to the good news told by the shepherds. What does this response teach us?

A good salesman can usually land at least one out of every eight sales. A baseball player who gets a hit four out of ten times at bat is an extremely good hitter. Christian evangelists sometimes become discouraged, however, if the response does not come the first time the good news is presented or if more people reject than accept the message. We may feel this way because we know the consequence if the message is permanently rejected.

Most people, however, will need time. Personal history, lack of education, or suspicion can delay responses. There may be value in having a person work through an informed decision rather than reacting on emotion. This calls for patience and persistence in witnessing.

5. What a spectacular evening the shepherds had! We may wonder how long the feeling lasted. Did you ever have trouble renewing a sense of dedication for Christ once a spiritual mountaintop experience had passed? Explain.

The Christmas season gives us a special, focused time to refresh our Christian hope. But limiting this refreshing to a few events per year that give us a spiritual high can leave us down in the valley the rest of the time. A key to staying out of the valley is to be involved in the lives of other Christians. Worshiping, praying, and studying the Scriptures with fellow believers adds an important dimension.

Rely on God's Strength

January 1
Lesson 5

DEVOTIONAL READING: Romans 16:17-27.

BACKGROUND SCRIPTURE: 1 Timothy 1.

PRINTED TEXT: 1 Timothy 1:12-20.

1 Timothy 1:12-20

12 And I thank Christ Jesus our Lord, who hath enabled me, for that he counted me faithful, putting me into the ministry;

13 Who was before a blasphemer, and a persecutor, and injurious: but I obtained mercy, because I did it ignorantly in unbelief.

14 And the grace of our Lord was exceeding abundant with faith and love which is in Christ Jesus.

15 This is a faithful saying, and worthy of all acceptation, that Christ Jesus came into the world to save sinners; of whom I am chief.

16 Howbeit for this cause I obtained mercy, that in me first Jesus Christ might show forth all long-suffering, for a pattern to them which should hereafter believe on him to life everlasting.

17 Now unto the King eternal, immortal, invisible, the only wise God, be honor and glory for ever and ever. Amen.

18 This charge I commit unto thee, son Timothy, according to the prophecies which went before on thee, that thou by them mightest war a good warfare;

19 Holding faith, and a good conscience; which some having put away, concerning faith have made shipwreck:

20 Of whom is Hymeneus and Alexander; whom I have delivered unto Satan, that they may learn not to blaspheme.

GOLDEN TEXT: I thank Christ Jesus our Lord, who hath enabled me,
for that he counted me faithful, putting me into the ministry.
—1 Timothy 1:12.

> *God's Commitment—Our Response*
> Unit 2: God's Gifts of Leadership
> (Lessons 5-9)

Lesson Aims

After participating in this lesson, each student will be able to:

1. Compare and contrast Paul's life before and after his transformation in Christ.
2. Tell how the power of the gospel can effect similar transformations today.
3. Write a letter to a young person in the church, encouraging progress in his or her faith.

Lesson Outline

INTRODUCTION
    A. Church Leadership and Church Purity
    B. Lesson Background
I. PAUL RECEIVED MERCY (1 Timothy 1:12-14)
    A. Humble Gratitude (vv. 12, 13)
        Counted Faithful
    B. Amazing Grace (v. 14)
II. CHRIST CAME TO SAVE (1 Timothy 1:15-17)
    A. Christ's Mission (v. 15)
    B. Paul's Need (v. 16)
    C. Paul's Doxology (v. 17)
III. TIMOTHY HAS A CHARGE (1 Timothy 1:18-20)
    A. Faith and Instruction (vv. 18, 19a)
    B. Apostasy and Discipline (vv. 19b, 20)
        Shipwrecked Faith
CONCLUSION
    A. Gratitude and Service
    B. Prayer
    C. Thought to Remember

Introduction

A. Church Leadership and Church Purity

There is an old story of a young man who entered a bank and asked to see the president. He stated that for a modest fee he would show him how to recognize all counterfeits. The president, upon hearing the proposition, saw the possibility of saving himself and the bank thousands of dollars. So he had the young man ushered in.

Expecting the young man to open his briefcase and spread out before him many counterfeits, the bank president was surprised when he simply removed a dollar bill from his billfold. The young man said, "Sir, if I can teach you to recognize all the marks of the genuine, then you will automatically recognize all that is counterfeit." Even in a modern era when currency contains watermarks, multicolored ink, and security threads, this is good advice!

An important part of today's lesson is the charge of "holding faith" (1 Timothy 1:19). Not everyone does this, as the rest of that verse and 1:6 make clear. "Holding faith" comes about through study. The psalmist said, "Thy word is a lamp unto my feet, and a light unto my path" (Psalm 119:105). When leadership accepts the charge to study the Word of God, their familiarity with it will enable them to protect the church from false doctrine. What a New Year's resolution this can be for 2006!

B. Lesson Background

In the previous four lessons, we have studied God's marvelous plan for meeting humanity's desperate need. God met that need by sending His Son. The radical change Jesus makes in a person's life prepares him or her for service. Jesus becomes the great change agent. His presence in a person's life decisively alters one's eternal destiny. And the more a person walks by faith, the more the Lord is able to use him or her. This was the apostle Paul's experience. Paul wrote letters to his son in the faith, Timothy, to encourage him to walk the same path.

Some suggest that Timothy was converted during Paul's first missionary trip to Asia Minor (modern Turkey). This trip included a visit to Timothy's hometown of Lystra (see Acts 14:8-20). The examples of Paul's life and preaching undoubtedly made an indelible impression on Timothy. These examples, coupled with the godly role models of Timothy's mother and grandmother (2 Timothy 1:5; 3:15), most likely are what led to his conversion to Christ. Timothy then became a coworker in Paul's evangelistic enterprise.

When Paul revisited the churches he had established, he recruited Timothy as a traveling companion. As Acts 16:1-4 tells us, Timothy's father was Greek but his mother was a Jewish believer. Paul circumcised Timothy because of his Greek background so that his influence among Jews would not be diminished.

The letter of 1 Timothy was written sometime after Paul's first imprisonment. The date was likely between A.D. 62 and 65, and Paul was probably somewhere in Macedonia as he composed. The letter was written to reinforce certain instructions that Paul had given to Timothy after leaving him in Ephesus.

I. Paul Received Mercy (1 Timothy 1:12-14)

In the section preceding today's text, Paul reminded Timothy to repudiate false teachers and their erroneous doctrines. Paul began by citing the hostile culture into which he and Timothy had been called to minister. It was a culture that included reliance on "fables" and "endless genealogies" (1:4).

A. Humble Gratitude (vv. 12, 13)

12. And I thank Christ Jesus our Lord, who hath enabled me, for that he counted me faithful, putting me into the ministry.

Humility acknowledges that effective *ministry* is not accomplished by one's own efforts. Rather, effective ministry is through God's enablement (Acts 26:22; Philippians 4:13). A leadership role does not leave place for one to boast, but gives the glory to God.

Paul had been specially called (Acts 9:15; 22:14-21; 26:16-20). [See question #1, page 183.] Christ knew the character of Paul and knew he could be counted on. Paul, in turn, acknowledges the source of power in his ministry. Notice the terms Paul uses concerning the one who empowers him. The very nature of the one who put Paul into ministry signifies His enabling power: *Christ*, God's anointed one, is *Jesus our Lord*, which denotes His sovereignty. Paul is humbled by the fact that the Lord has seen fit to use him. This is the spirit of anyone involved in a church leadership role.

God has a work that each of us can do. If we don't do it, then it may not be done. It is awe inspiring to realize that God sees fit to use us in His work. It should humble us to think that we are privileged to labor in areas that have eternal consequences. Anything we do in His name is as unto the Lord (Matthew 25:34-40).

COUNTED FAITHFUL

Joshua Chamberlain was a college professor in Maine in 1862 when he volunteered his services to the governor for the American Civil War. Subsequently, he was appointed to be a senior officer in a regiment designated the Twentieth Maine. Wounded at the Battle of Fredericksburg, he commanded that regiment at Gettysburg when it had its appointment with destiny.

The Twentieth Maine was placed on a piece of ground known as Little Round Top at the extreme left flank of the Union Army. Chamberlain had to hold that position at all costs. If the Confederates turned his flank, they could roll up the entire Union Army. When his men were attacked by a much higher number of Confederates, they fought back until their ammunition was gone.

Then in an audacious move, Chamberlain led his troops in a bayonet attack that pushed the stalled Confederates off the hill and saved the left flank. Wounded again, he would later receive the Congressional Medal of Honor for his actions on Little Round Top. He received four more wounds in the war, was promoted to major general, and was given the honor of commanding the troops that received the surrender of Robert E. Lee's army at Appomattox.

Chamberlain had a weighty responsibility at Gettysburg. But he was faithful to his assigned duties, then and afterward. His wounds did not deter him from further service. Paul also was one who was "wounded in action" many times (see 2 Corinthians 6:3-10). But he stood firm. He could still be thankful that the Lord considered him faithful. He encourages Timothy—and us—to stand firm as well. —J. B. N.

13. Who was before a blasphemer, and a persecutor, and injurious: but I obtained mercy, because I did it ignorantly in unbelief.

Paul now cites the reason for his gratitude and sense of unworthiness: he once had been a violent opponent of Christianity. Jesus, appearing on the Damascus road, confirmed what Paul now affirms for himself: "Saul, Saul, why persecutest thou me?" (Acts 9:4). Saul (before being renamed Paul) had sanctioned the death of Stephen (Acts 7:58–8:1). Further, Saul had intended to take into custody any Christians to be found in Damascus (Acts 9:1, 2). [See question #2, page 183.]

Paul earlier affirmed that he had acted "in all good conscience" (Acts 23:1). From this we may conclude that conscience is not always a reliable guide. Conscience can operate only on the information it receives. Paul sincerely thought he was serving God while persecuting Christians. Paul thought he was preserving the Law of Moses. But he was sincerely wrong. Sinning in ignorance is still sin. As a judge will tell you, "Ignorance of the law is no excuse." Paul obtained mercy because he repented of his error.

This is also illustrated in the 3,000 who were saved on the Day of Pentecost. According to Peter's charge in his sermon, those present had been party to Jesus' crucifixion (Acts 2:36). When confronted by Peter's sermon, the people became convinced that this Jesus, whom they had crucified, was Lord and Christ. Similar to what Saul said on the Damascus road (Acts 22:10), they had cried out, "What shall we do?" (Acts 2:37). And like Saul (Acts 22:16), they submitted to the gracious conditions of pardon and were saved (Acts 2:38, 41).

What a lesson for all of us! Psalm 103:12 says, "As far as the east is from the west, so far hath he removed our transgressions from us." The life and witness of Saul (Paul) illustrates the dramatic change that can take place through the power of God. [See question #3, page 183.]

B. Amazing Grace (v. 14)

14. And the grace of our Lord was exceeding abundant with faith and love which is in Christ Jesus.

Given all that has happened to him, it is no wonder that Paul writes so much about *the grace of our Lord*. Arrogance and pride because of accomplishments have no place in God's service. That was the downfall of the Pharisees who loved to boast (Luke 18:11, 12). We owe to the riches of God's grace all that we are and hope to be.

II. Christ Came to Save (1 Timothy 1:15-17)

The greatest love story of all time is now retold. It affirms what Jesus told Nicodemus (John 3:16) and Zaccheus (Luke 19:10).

A. Christ's Mission (v. 15)

15. This is a faithful saying, and worthy of all acceptation, that Christ Jesus came into the world to save sinners; of whom I am chief.

A faithful saying means that what Paul is about to relay is true and can be believed by everyone. That goes for us too!

Paul is overwhelmed by the realization that God's love embraces someone such as himself—whom he considers to be the worst of *sinners*. Think about it: God incarnate came into the world for the express purpose of saving people as evil as Saul had been! We all need to believe this. A hopeless world needs to be told this good news over and over. We are the only vehicles through whom it will hear this message.

Earlier, Paul exclaimed "Woe is unto me, if I preach not the gospel!" (1 Corinthians 9:16). Our challenge is to see non-Christians as those needing salvation rather than as our enemies. We need to let them know that Jesus is the answer to the sinner's problem (John 3:17).

B. Paul's Need (v. 16)

16. Howbeit for this cause I obtained mercy, that in me first Jesus Christ might show forth all long-suffering, for a pattern to them which should hereafter believe on him to life everlasting.

The conversion of a man like Paul should be an encouragement. "Wherefore he is able also to save them to the uttermost that come unto God by him" (Hebrews 7:25). No person is hopeless.

If you think about it, Paul had been a most unlikely prospect. His conversion reminds us of the old cliché that the darkest hour is just before dawn. When a person is fighting the hardest may be when he or she is closest to surrendering to Christ, as in Paul's case. Jesus had chided Saul, "it is hard for thee to kick against the pricks" (Acts 26:14). How many times during revivals have I left someone's home thinking it was a hopeless case, only to see that individual

---

Home Daily Bible Readings

Monday, Dec. 26—Strengthen Me, O God (Psalm 119:25-32)

Tuesday, Dec. 27—God Is Able to Strengthen You (Romans 16:17-27)

Wednesday, Dec. 28—We Sent Timothy to Strengthen You (1 Thessalonians 3:1-5)

Thursday, Dec. 29—May God Strengthen Your Hearts (1 Thessalonians 3:6-13)

Friday, Dec. 30—Paul, Silas, and Timothy Strengthen Churches (Acts 16:1-5)

Saturday, Dec. 31—Paul Writes to Timothy (1 Timothy 1:1-11)

Sunday, Jan. 1—Strengthened by Christ (1 Timothy 1:12-20)

respond to the gospel on that very night. So don't give up easily! Don't underestimate the work of the Holy Spirit and the power of the gospel.

Christians may be reluctant to share their faith because of the fear of failure in dealing with people like Paul. Remember, God has not called us to be successful, but to be obedient. We are simply seed sowers. It is God who does the harvesting. Only He can convert (see 1 Corinthians 3:6, 7). So don't be afraid of failure. When you share your faith in love, inevitably there will be a harvest.

Paul was saved by grace, not only for his own sake but for the sake of others. He is an example of God's love, grace, power, and long-suffering (2 Peter 3:15). Where would we be were it not for God's great patience? God doesn't give up on us easily. Nor should we give up easily when working to win people to Christ. What Paul is saying is, "If Christ can save a sinner such as me, He can save anyone. My example gives hope to all."

C. Paul's Doxology (v. 17)

17. Now unto the King eternal, immortal, invisible, the only wise God, be honor and glory for ever and ever. Amen.

Such an expression of praise is inevitable from one who realizes that he or she is a sinner saved by grace. It is uttered in admiration and awe.

The God whom Paul describes is the only God there is! He was willing to become incarnate in His Son. Although *invisible,* we catch a glimpse of God through Jesus: "he that hath seen me hath seen the Father" (John 14:9). There is nothing hidden from God (Matthew 10:26). This one alone is the God able to fulfill His promise to aged Abraham for a son (Romans 4:18, 19), to deliver three Israelites from the fiery furnace (Daniel 3), to raise Jesus from the dead (Galatians 1:1), and to save to the uttermost all "that come unto God by him" (again, Hebrews 7:25).

Pagan deities—who are really no deities at all—have none of the attributes ascribed to God. Since these so-called gods find their origin in the minds of finite people, there is found in them only the attributes commonly found in humanity. But we serve the living God. He is transcendent, above all things. Yes, God is able. God alone is praiseworthy. He alone can do for us what we cannot do for ourselves.

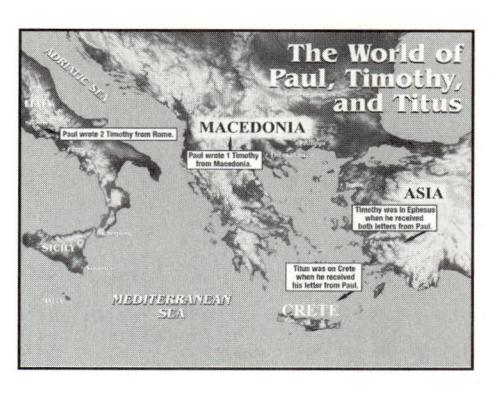

Visual for lesson 5

Keep this map posted for the final nine lessons of the quarter to help your students maintain a geographical perspective.

God's name is thrown around very casually in postmodern culture. Even many Christians use it thoughtlessly in expressions of surprise or dismay. Have we lost our sense of reverence? (See Exodus 20:7.) He is our creator, our redeemer; we are the objects of His grace. He and He alone deserves the worship of our lips and hearts (Psalms 95:3-6; 96:1-9).

III. Timothy Has a Charge (1 Timothy 1:18-20)

Paul's first charge to Timothy at the beginning of the letter reveals the purpose for writing (1:3-10). Now the charge is expanded, taking on an increased urgency.

A. Faith and Instruction (vv. 18, 19a)

18. This charge I commit unto thee, son Timothy, according to the prophecies which went before on thee, that thou by them mightest war a good warfare.

Paul encourages *Timothy* to proceed in the task entrusted to him. That encouragement comes from the fact that there have been *prophecies* made concerning him and his call to ministry and service in the kingdom.

The charge includes Timothy's participation in *a good warfare.* It is not a warfare against flesh and blood (see Ephesians 6:12). It is a good warfare because it is against sin and Satan and because Timothy is in the Lord's army. So he is to stand up against false teachers and not be intimidated by their arrogance and rebellious spirit.

We twenty-first-century Christians are engaged in this same kind of spiritual warfare. We dare not be pacifists in this regard. [See question #4, page 183.]

19a. Holding faith, and a good conscience.

Paul depends on Timothy not to abandon either his *faith* or his *good conscience*. There is no hint that Paul thinks it is OK for Timothy to tolerate, in the name of "diversity," the attitudes of those who do. The next verse shows why.

B. Apostasy and Discipline (vv. 19b, 20)

19b. Which some having put away concerning faith have made shipwreck.

When *some* forsook *faith,* their consciences were left without any guidelines. As a result, their faith was wrecked like a ship that runs up on rocks because it has no rudder. We do well to heed Paul's admonition to Timothy: We must hold on to the Christian faith, because in so doing we will have an enlightened conscience. Then we won't blaspheme or contradict God and end up in apostasy (Hebrews 11:6). That is the danger these false teachers are in. [See question #5, page 183.]

20. Of whom is Hymeneus and Alexander; whom I have delivered unto Satan, that they may learn not to blaspheme.

Two men by the names of *Hymeneus and Alexander* are examples of those who have defected from faith. Their consciences are seared (1 Timothy 4:2). They have sold out to *Satan.* Perhaps Paul had tried to teach these two men personally, so the sting of their apostasy hits him hard.

We learn of the necessity of church discipline in this verse. The New Testament sets forth three instances that call for church discipline: doctrinal defection (see Romans 16:17, 18; 1 Timothy 6:3, 4; and Titus 1:10-16); moral defection (see 1 Corinthians 5); and divisiveness (again, Romans 16:17, 28; plus Titus 3:10). This is consistent with Jesus' teaching in Matthew 18:15-17. A bad apple tolerated can destroy a whole bushel. This is true in the church.

These two propagators of false teaching needed to be dealt with. How many times has a church's witness in a community been nullified because it tolerated sin? Even so, the motivation for biblical discipline is to restore the errant person (2 Corinthians 2:5-11). It also is only a last resort (notice the sequence in Matthew 18:15-17). A diseased member of the body is removed only if the welfare of the body is in jeopardy.

When done properly, many times the object of discipline is brought to repentance and restored.

How to Say It

ABRAHAM. *Ay*-bruh-ham.
DAMASCUS. Duh-*mass*-kus.
EPHESUS. *Ef*-uh-sus.
HEBREWS. *Hee*-brews.
HYMENEUS. Hi-meh-*nee*-us.
LYSTRA. *Liss*-truh.
MACEDONIA. Mass-eh-*doe*-nee-uh.
NICODEMUS. *Nick*-uh-*dee*-mus (strong accent on *dee*).
PENTECOST. *Pent*-ih-kost.
ZACCHEUS. Zack-*key*-us.

Restoration may be in view here as Paul expresses his desire that Hymeneus and Alexander *learn not to blaspheme.*

SHIPWRECKED FAITH

Many factors can be involved in a shipwreck. At 11:10 P.M. on July 25, 1956, in a heavy fog off Nantucket Island, the reinforced icebreaking bow of the Swedish-American liner *Stockholm* sliced into the starboard side of the Italian luxury liner *Andrea Doria.* Other ships quickly responded to the SOS, and within seven hours all survivors of the 1,662 passengers and crew were safely removed from the doomed ship. But 52 lives were lost. At 10:09 A.M., only 11 hours after impact, the *Andrea Doria* sank.

Later investigation indicated that the *Andrea Doria's* radar was not used properly. And at the last moment, the ship turned left into the *Stockholm's* path, rather than turning to the right, which was standard procedure for a head-on crossing at sea. Carelessness caused the loss of a $30 million ship, as well as the 52 lives.

Paul already had survived a shipwreck on the coast of Malta (Acts 27, 28). And he knew that bad judgment could bring on such a disaster. But even more tragically, he knew what could happen with spiritual carelessness. He mentions two men who had made spiritual shipwreck of their lives because they had not paid attention to faith and conscience. Neglect of either can lead to stormy times, malfunctioning relationships, too-late warnings, and an ignorance-is-bliss attitude that leads straight to disaster, spiritual and otherwise. Take heed: the ruins of shipwrecked lives litter the fields of history just

LESSON 5 · JANUARY 1

as much as the ruins of ships litter the ocean's floors. —J. B. N.

Conclusion

A. Gratitude and Service

Today's lesson should make each of us grateful for the grace of God that forgave us our sins. Our challenge is to translate that gratitude into a life of useful service. Paul's example and our own experience should teach us that we can trust God for He "is able to do exceeding abundantly above all that we ask" (Ephesians 3:20).

Sadly, many would be willing to serve in leadership roles if such roles entailed no responsibility. But then that would not be leadership! The implementation of God's plan depends on leaders remembering that God never asks us to do anything that He will not enable us to do. Paul recognized his personal inability to carry out the task God had set before him. But he also recognized, as should we, that God uses the weak things of the world to demonstrate His power so that we have no basis to glory. As a result, it is God who is glorified (1 Corinthians 1:26-31).

B. Prayer

Forgive us, Father, for those times when we have relied on our own feeble resources rather than depending on You. On this first day of a new year, help us as we endeavor to walk by faith, trusting You to give us victory in every circumstance. We ask it in Jesus' name, amen.

C. Thought to Remember

"The Lord is the strength of my life; of whom shall I be afraid?" (Psalm 27:1).

Learning by Doing

This section contains an alternative lesson plan emphasizing learning activities. Classes desiring such student involvement will find these suggestions helpful.

Learning Goals

After participating in this lesson, each student will be able to:

1. Compare and contrast Paul's life before and after his transformation in Christ.
2. Tell how the power of the gospel can effect similar transformations today.
3. Write a letter to a young person in the church, encouraging progress in his or her faith.

Into the Lesson

Personal testimonial: Recruit a young Christian, whose conversion to Christ brought a dramatic turnabout in his or her life, to give a short, life-change testimonial. The main focus should be on how his or her life has changed since accepting Christ, rather than on the specific conversion experience itself. (Caution your recruit about making too graphic a description of an earlier sinful lifestyle.)

Into the Word

Photocopy the following word-find puzzle (it is included in the student books). Make a transition from the testimonial to this activity by saying, "Christ has been changing people for 2,000 years. Paul, when he was Saul, approved of the murder of Christians. But Christ changed him. This word-find puzzle draws attention to the characteristics of Christian leadership that the Christ-changed Paul could commend to Timothy in today's text of 1 Timothy 1:12-20."

```
H L R O I R R A W E
A U D R E R D L T E
C A M D E E E N R F
H L E B L N E E E A
A A X B L D N V D I
N E A R N E L I E T
G N M E D L N G S H
E A P E R L L R E F
D E L A E A D O E U
D R E R L C E F A L
```

The following words can be found in the puzzle, with the Bible verse references in parentheses: *called* (12), *changed* (13), *dependent, enabled* (12), *example* (16), *faithful* (12), *forgiven* (16), *humble* (15), *sinner* (15), *warrior* (18). Be sure to include all 10 words at the bottom of the puzzle as hints (but don't include the verse references). Also say "We're not looking for the exact words from the Bible text. Instead, we're looking for words that tell us of the concepts that we find in our text."

When all 10 words have been identified, ask students to identify which Bible verses from today's text match each of the characteristics found in the puzzle. Finally, challenge students to create one remaining word using only the letters that served as filler spaces. (The word is *leader*.)

As an alternative or additional activity, put these three words on the board: *blasphemer, persecutor, injurious*. Tell the class, "Paul's change in Christ was sudden and complete." Have a student read Acts 9:1-6, 17-22.

Then say, "Select a letter in one of these three words, and I'll change it to a letter of another word that characterizes Paul's new lifestyle in the Spirit." As learners select letters, replace them as follows: **Word 1:** *b* to *e*; *l* to *v*; *a* to *a*; *s* to *n*; *p* to *g*; *h* to *e*; *e* to *l*; *m* to *i*; *e* to *s*; *r* to *t*—from *blasphemer* to *evangelist*; **Word 2:** *p* to *e*; *e* to *n*; *r* to *c*; *s* to *o*; *e* to *u*; *c* to *r*; *u* to *a*; *t* to *g*; *e* to *e*; *r* to *r*—from *persecutor* to *encourager*; **Word 3:** *i* to *n*; *n* to *o*; *j* to *u*; *u* to *r*; *r* to *i*; *i* to *s*; *o* to *h*; *u* to *e*; *s* to *r*—from *injurious* to *nourisher*.

As each new word is deciphered, complete the conversion of the letters. When all three are identified, say, "Paul went from saying bad things to saying the best things; he went from treating enemies harshly to loving brothers kindly; he went from attacking others' well-being to building up others' health and strength. Those are changes each of us needs to make in Christ."

Into Life

Obtain a list of teenagers who participate in your church's youth ministry. Write each teen's name and address on a slip of paper and put the slips into a bag.

Say, "In this bag I have the names and addresses of several of our church's teenagers. We need volunteers to write short encouragement notes to them during this next week. Our study has been that of an 'encouragement letter' Paul sent to the younger Timothy. That biblical letter of 1 Timothy may offer ideas for your own note." Set the bag near the classroom's exit and recommend that each student take a name as they leave.

Let's Talk It Over

These questions are designed to promote discussion of the lesson. The answers here are only discussion starters. Let your class talk it over from there.

1. Paul's calling into ministry was spectacular, to say the least! How are Christians called to Christian leadership today? How can we tell the difference between a true call and a false call?

Although God can still work in any manner He chooses, He seems to call people to Christian leadership roles today in ways that are less spectacular than in the first century A.D. We can be drawn to God's service by the influence of parents, by the encouragement of friends, etc. Strong calls are often perceived when needs and opportunities present themselves, especially when combined with the impact of the Bible working on our hearts. Any perceived call that violates Scripture cannot be from God.

2. Why do you think that God chooses to use human agents to accomplish His purposes when we are so prone to be weak and wrong?

God obviously possesses the power and wisdom to do all of His work alone or through angels. Yet, He consistently enlists humans! He works in and through people who submit to His will. He also works through people who reject His will (one example is Pharaoh).

Our obedience demonstrates whose side we're on (see James 2:18). It is for our good and for our spiritual development that we are saved "unto good works" (Ephesians 2:10) and commissioned to make disciples (Matthew 28:19, 20). Think of how strange it would be if angels were the only ones spreading the gospel, meeting needs of the poor, etc., while we did nothing!

3. How can we describe God's love and grace in terms that unbelievers will understand?

The apostle Paul had experienced such a transformation of conviction and commitment that he delighted in giving his personal testimony to anyone who would listen. Most of us long to be effective in evangelism. Paul's example can be instructive.

To Timothy and other believers, Paul used vocabulary and arguments familiar to God-fearing people. But his witness to pagan soldiers, Greek philosophers, and hostile Hebrews involved language suited to their frames of reference (examples: Acts 17:16-34; 22:1-21). We too have opportunities and obligations to share the gospel with a wide variety of individuals and groups. Religious terminology can be modified for the situation without compromising the truth.

One good tactic is to tell our own life story—our personal experience of God's grace and Christ's love, the account of our connection with divine forgiveness and spiritual peace. We also can follow Christ's example by creating parables to illustrate the good news with word pictures. Author Max Lucado is particularly good at this.

4. How would you respond to someone who said, "Christian discipleship involves primarily a life of peace"?

War and Peace is not only a book title; it is also a phrase that describes our Christian walk. Jesus, the prince of peace (Isaiah 9:6), once said He had come to bring "a sword" (Matthew 10:34). The peace we have with God (Romans 5:1) means spiritual battles against whatever would pull us away from Him (Luke 14:26). We must be committed to peace, yet prepared to wage war against "the wiles of the devil" and "spiritual wickedness in high places" (Ephesians 6:11, 12). Spiritual warfare includes confronting false teaching (1 Timothy 4:1-3). We wear spiritual armor and use the "sword of the Spirit" (Ephesians 6:17) even as we're called to present "the truth in love" (Ephesians 4:15).

5. How can the postmodern emphasis on tolerance shipwreck faith and disarm the church? What do we do to avoid this?

A postmodern culture's devotion to tolerance leads people to close their ears to blasphemy and close their eyes to sinful behavior. Centuries ago, God told at least three churches that this kind of tolerance was very displeasing to Him (see 1 Corinthians 5:1-5; Revelation 2:14-16, 20-23).

Tolerance of false teaching or immorality will poison Christians, disable the church, and disgrace our holy God. Tolerance in this sense is a disservice to the unrepentant as well. In John 4 we see Jesus accepting the woman at the well, but also unveiling her sinful lifestyle and false religious belief. That distinction is still important.

Pray for Everyone

January 8
Lesson 6

DEVOTIONAL READING: Colossians 4:2-6.

BACKGROUND SCRIPTURE: 1 Timothy 2.

PRINTED TEXT: 1 Timothy 2:1-8.

1 Timothy 2:1-8

1 I exhort therefore, that, first of all, supplications, prayers, intercessions, and giving of thanks, be made for all men;

2 For kings, and for all that are in authority; that we may lead a quiet and peaceable life in all godliness and honesty.

3 For this is good and acceptable in the sight of God our Saviour;

4 Who will have all men to be saved, and to come unto the knowledge of the truth.

5 For there is one God, and one mediator between God and men, the man Christ Jesus;

6 Who gave himself a ransom for all, to be testified in due time.

7 Whereunto I am ordained a preacher, and an apostle, (I speak the truth in Christ, and lie not,) a teacher of the Gentiles in faith and verity.

8 I will therefore that men pray every where, lifting up holy hands, without wrath and doubting.

GOLDEN TEXT: I exhort therefore, that, first of all, supplications, prayers, intercessions, and giving of thanks, be made for all men.
—1 Timothy 2:1.

> *God's Commitment—Our Response*
> Unit 2: God's Gifts of Leadership
> (Lessons 5-9)

Lesson Aims

After participating in this lesson, each student will be able to:

1. List some methods and reasons Paul says believers should pray.
2. Identify some specific people for whom we should pray, based on Paul's general description.
3. Adjust his or her prayer life to match the pattern Paul sets forth.

Lesson Outline

INTRODUCTION
    A. What Makes the Difference?
    B. Lesson Background
I. OUR PRAYERS (1 Timothy 2:1-3)
    A. Types of Prayers (v. 1)
    B. Special Objects of Prayer (v. 2a)
    C. Results of Prayer (vv. 2b, 3)
II. GOD'S PLANS (1 Timothy 2:4-8)
    A. Salvation, Knowledge, Truth (v. 4)
    B. God, Man, Christ (v. 5)
       One Mediator
    C. Ransom, Testimony, Time (v. 6)
    D. Preacher, Apostle, Teacher (v. 7)
    E. Holiness, Prayer, Attitude (v. 8)
       Holy Hands
CONCLUSION
    A. Power!
    B. Prayer
    C. Thought to Remember

Introduction

A. What Makes the Difference?

For years our church has had a prayer chain. This is an organized network of people who believe in the power of prayer. They have volunteered to spend time praying for others who may be in a crisis situation or who have emotional, financial, physical, relational, or spiritual problems. Our prayer chain is also the vehicle to communicate praises for answered prayers.

What a blessing this has been! The blessings are not only for the participants and the objects of prayer, but for the entire church. Our prayer chain has gained such a reputation that people outside of our church frequently will request to be put on our prayer chain. The inspiring testimonies many give with regard to answered prayers serve as towers of strength, encouragement, and rejoicing among fellow Christians.

Our prayer chain helps take the focus off self and place it on others. This in itself has curative value. Even the medical profession increasingly acknowledges the beneficial influence that prayer has on people.

If your church does not have a prayer chain or prayer ministry of some type, I would recommend it highly. Such a ministry recognizes the priority of prayer in the life of the church. It heightens church members' awareness of concerns that need attention. It focuses on God, who is able to meet those needs. It alters attitudes from being critical or judgmental to that of sympathetic concern.

Remember: "Pray one for another, that ye may be healed. The effectual fervent prayer of a righteous man availeth much" (James 5:16). Paul knew this too. That's why he stresses prayer in this letter to Timothy, who is ministering to a troubled church.

B. Lesson Background

Paul had left his "son in the faith" Timothy in Ephesus sometime during the interim between his own imprisonments in Rome. It was a daunting task that he had assigned this young preacher. The great Ephesian church had some doctrinal problems that needed to be addressed. Timothy also had to cope with some strong personalities who were espousing false teaching. This situation is what brought forth Paul's letter of instruction and encouragement.

In last week's lesson, Paul reminded Timothy of his charge. Paul accompanied this reminder with further instruction. Paul also encouraged Timothy by citing himself as an example of the sufficiency of God's grace and His enabling power. With this as background, we make a transition into today's text.

I. Our Prayers (1 Timothy 2:1-3)

Remember that in the original manuscript, written in Greek, there were no chapter headings or breaks. Those were not put in until hundreds of years later. So Paul shows a movement in thought by connecting his preceding and following thoughts with a transitional form. His thought now stresses the role of prayer and its priority.

A. Types of Prayers (v. 1)

1. I exhort therefore, that, first of all, supplications, prayers, intercessions, and giving of thanks, be made for all men.

The transitional word *therefore* connects what Paul is about to say with his foregoing statements. On the basis of the charge, encouragement, and instruction he has given to Timothy already (see last week's lesson), Paul now proceeds to cite the place and types of *prayers* in the church.

In addition to the general idea of *prayers,* Paul mentions *supplications, . . . intercessions, and giving of thanks* as specific ways of coming before God's throne. Supplications are requests. They may address our deep personal needs—strength for resisting temptation, the asking of forgiveness.

Intercessions are petitions that we offer up to God on behalf of others. Christ was a model of intercessory prayer (John 17:6-26) even as He prepared to make the ultimate intercession in His death (see Romans 8:34). The Holy Spirit also has a vital ministry of intercession for us before our heavenly Father (Romans 8:26). In 2 Thessalonians 3:1, Paul is specific in his request that others make intercession for him. Just because he is an apostle doesn't mean that he doesn't need prayer support too! Modern Christians are to offer intercessory prayer on a regular basis.

Thanksgivings are the outpouring of our hearts for God's beneficence, for the blessings He bestows upon us in so many ways. We thank God for the provision He makes for all our needs, both physical and spiritual. We do well to remember that "every good gift and every perfect gift is from above, and cometh down from the Father of lights, with whom is no variableness, neither shadow of turning" (James 1:17).

Notice that Paul does not prescribe a certain form or ritual to these prayers. There is no instruction for liturgical form. Rather, Paul cites the types of communication with God that have different meanings and applications.

Christians not only major in prayer for themselves but also in prayers *for all men.* What Paul

Point to these prayer categories as you ask "Who do you know that most needs your prayers?"

Visual for lesson 6

has in mind by that word *all* is the subject of the next verse.

B. Special Objects of Prayer (v. 2a)

2a. For kings, and for all that are in authority.

Concerning the *all men* in verse 1, Paul now makes clear that he is thinking of civil leaders. We are more prone to criticize them than to pray for them, aren't we? Government officials in Paul's day are pagans, of course. Such leaders include the infamous Nero, who eventually would have Paul beheaded. In another letter, Paul says "Bless them which persecute you: bless, and curse not" (Romans 12:14). Prayer, with the strength that comes from the Lord, is the only way we can do this.

Before we pray it will help to remember that civil government is ordained of God (Romans 13:1). For this reason we pray for those who are entrusted with the oversight of civil life. People in authority need our prayers because they are confronted daily with difficult decisions that affect the peace and safety of society as a whole. They have to deal with pressures exerted by all types of special interest groups whose offer of monetary support is very tempting.

A study of history makes clear that God rules in the affairs of humanity. *Kings* and kingdoms come and go, but God is still sovereign in His universe. Prayer can lead to a change in the attitudes and decisions of authorities.

God may answer your prayers for governing authorities by using you as an influence through your respectful e-mails, letters, and phone calls to those in government. As you voice your concerns, remember also to express gratitude for their support of what is right and good. Tell them that you are praying for them. This is a much-neglected ministry on the part of Christians. [See question #1, page 192.]

C. Results of Prayer (vv. 2b, 3)

2b, 3. That we may lead a quiet and peaceable life in all godliness and honesty. For this is good and acceptable in the sight of God our Saviour.

Paul cites something that every Christian should long for: *a quiet and peaceable life in all godliness and honesty.* Paul does not say to pray for government leaders so that we will have all of our physical needs supplied by a "nanny" state. Rather, our prayers are for an environment in which we can function best as godly and honest people. In other words we pray for the government to protect our safety as opposed to giving us what we think are our "entitlements." This matches Paul's thoughts in Romans 13:1-5 (see also 1 Peter 2:13-17).

When we pray like that and the result is a quiet and peaceful life, our gratitude is to be expressed in godly and honest living. But a quiet and peaceful life will not be our lot if we do not live godly and honest lives. The trait of godliness is found in our right relationship with God as seen in personal holiness. Honesty is the trait that is expressed in all our dealings with others. The two are inseparable. One cannot truly exist without the other (compare 1 Peter 3:8-12). This is a vital part of discovering what is *good and acceptable in the sight of God our Saviour.* [See question #2, page 192.]

II. God's Plans (1 Timothy 2:4-6)

When we Christians try to see the world through the eyes of God, it alters our prayer lives in profound ways. True, our world is sinful and rebellious. But that fact does not diminish God's love for all people. This is a love so great that He sent His one and only Son to save them (John 3:16; Romans 5:8). It is a love we must share!

A. Salvation, Knowledge, Truth (v. 4)

4. Who will have all men to be saved, and to come unto the knowledge of the truth.

Here Paul asserts God's will for *all* humanity. Some may ask, "If it is God's will that everyone be saved, then why doesn't He save everyone?" The answer is that God created us to be free moral agents, with free will, with the ability to make opposite choices. When a person reads or hears the Word of truth, it causes his or her life to arrive at a fork in the road. Standing at the crossroads of accepting or rejecting Christ, that individual makes a freewill choice. It is a decision that will determine his or her eternal destiny (Matthew 7:13, 14).

God created all people in His own image. He wants us to enjoy eternal fellowship with Him. Our choice to disobey God alienates us from Him. But God's love for His creation has made provision for the problem of sin so that anyone can be saved (Romans 10:13; 2 Peter 3:9).

We should not think that Paul is teaching a doctrine of universalism—that everyone will indeed be saved. Being saved requires that we comply with the gracious conditions of pardon that God has revealed to us. Having *the knowledge of the truth* is part of this. Jesus is the embodiment of truth (John 14:6). He said, "And ye shall know the truth, and the truth shall make you free. . . . If the Son therefore shall make you free, ye shall be free indeed" (John 8:32, 36). We study the Word of God because there we learn not only of truths but also of the one who was and is truth (2 Timothy 2:15; 3:14-17).

The fact that God wants *all men to be saved* has obvious evangelistic implications. Our role as Christians is to implement God's desire for the salvation of all. Jesus' Great Commission is the marching order of the church (Matthew 28:19, 20). Paul is very conscious of this (Romans 10:14-17). [See question #3, page 192.]

B. God, Man, Christ (v. 5)

5. For there is one God, and one mediator between God and men, the man Christ Jesus.

Contrary to the pagan world all around him, Paul affirms that *there is one God.* The Bible affirms that fact time and again in both Old and New Testaments (examples: Malachi 2:10; 1 Corinthians 8:6). The pagan world, by contrast, has many "gods." That world worships created things rather than the creator (Romans 1:23, 25). The one true God is the God who has revealed himself; it is He alone who is to be worshiped and served (Exodus 20:3-5).

In His infinite love and mercy, the one true God has provided the means by which all can be reconciled to Him. And that is through the *one mediator . . . the man Christ Jesus.* The fact that Jesus is the one mediator is a truth that a person must accept to be saved (see Acts 4:12).

This eliminates a popular notion that there are many roads to God. It also disavows the idea that others can mediate. For example, we cannot (and need not) invoke "the saints" or the virgin Mary to intercede for us. No human can take the place of Jesus. It is because of what He has done for us on the cross that enables Him to be our only mediator, intercessor, advocate (1 John 1:7–2:2). [See question #4, page 192.]

ONE MEDIATOR

On numerous occasions I have been asked to pray at various functions other than church services. Sometimes these are meetings of service clubs (Lions, Kiwanis, Rotarians, etc.), or community memorial services, or giving the blessing for the meal at some civic occasion. Many times I have been asked politely to refrain from closing "in Jesus' name." Many of their members were Jews, my host would explain. Some were Muslims, or some had no religious inclination at all. To end my prayer in the traditional way would therefore be offensive to them.

In every instance, I have refused. That was probably not the time or place to go into a theology lesson, but I have tried to point out, briefly and just as politely as they asked, that the only way I can approach God is through Jesus. If I can't pray in Jesus' name, then I can't pray to God at all. "Oh," they would say, somewhat puzzled. And the conversation usually ended there, on a very awkward note.

In these days of political correctness, non-Christian people are often bewildered by the Christian's insistence that Jesus is the only way to God and eternal life. This stance seems so bigoted to flexible and "tolerant" societies. In John 14:6, Jesus said, "No man cometh unto the Father, but by me." Paul rightly states there is only one mediator. It may be politically incorrect, but it is certainly theologically correct. —J. B. N.

C. Ransom, Testimony, Time (v. 6)

6. Who gave himself a ransom for all, to be testified in due time.

The reason that Jesus is the one mediator between God and humanity is that He alone is the one who paid the *ransom* for our deliverance from God's wrath. The price that Jesus paid was His blood that He shed when He died on the cross for sin (Romans 3:21-27; 1 Peter 1:18, 19). In His death Jesus canceled the effects of Adam's sin that have been passed on to all (Romans 5:12-21). He also paid the penalty for our own, personal sins.

Being our mediator required that Jesus give himself to be a ransom (Mark 10:45; Hebrews 9:15). Jesus' death is the basis that made His mediation possible. He was the only one worthy (God-man) to perform such a deed. That's the reason no "saint" can qualify as a mediator.

That which was *testified in due time* was Jesus' redemptive work on the cross. That's the reason Paul said, "We preach Christ crucified" (1 Corinthians 1:23). And now this testimony is to be preached everywhere.

D. Preacher, Apostle, Teacher (v. 7)

7. Whereunto I am ordained a preacher, and an apostle, (I speak the truth in Christ, and lie not,) a teacher of the Gentiles in faith and verity.

Here Paul expands a bit on his opening assertion in 1 Timothy 1:1. Paul's actions are consistent with the commission the Lord had given him (Acts 9:15; 22:15; 26:16-18). So Paul affirms again his apostleship, his special call of the Lord, as one sent to *Gentiles* (see also Acts 13:46-48; 18:6; Romans 11:13; Galatians 1:16). As such, he was to preach good news to non-Jews, even as Peter was to preach primarily to the Jews.

Paul's integrity and credibility in this regard are obviously quite important to him. This isn't the first time that he has felt obligated to defend that integrity and authority (see 1 Corinthians 9). A vital part of this integrity is preaching *in faith and verity* (truth). He trusts the Holy Spirit

---

Home Daily Bible Readings

Monday, Jan. 2—Paul Prays for the Philippians (Philippians 1:3-11)

Tuesday, Jan. 3—Pray Without Ceasing (1 Thessalonians 5:16-22)

Wednesday, Jan. 4—God Hears Our Prayers (1 Peter 3:8-12a)

Thursday, Jan. 5—A Parable About Praying (Luke 18:1-8)

Friday, Jan. 6—Pray for Your Enemies (Matthew 5:43-48)

Saturday, Jan. 7—Pray for Everyone (1 Timothy 2:1-7)

Sunday, Jan. 8—Prayer Is Powerful and Effective (James 5:13-18)

of God to do His work through the Word of truth that he (Paul) faithfully preaches and teaches (Romans 1:15; 15:20; 1 Corinthians 1:17; Ephesians 3:8).

Our challenge is to share our faith with the same confidence. And we can if we teach the Word of God in love and leave the results to Him. He just asks us to be faithful and go.

E. Holiness, Prayer, Attitude (v. 8)

8. I will therefore that men pray every where, lifting up holy hands, without wrath and doubting.

We know, of course, that God gives us wide latitude concerning time and place of prayer. We can pray in solitude at home (Matthew 6:6), with others at mealtime (Acts 27:35), and in public settings (Acts 20:36). That is part of what it means to "pray without ceasing" (1 Thessalonians 5:17). But what about our posture during those times with God? In the verse before us, is Paul telling us that raised *hands* is a requirement for prayer?

In the Scriptures we find that some kneel to pray (Luke 22:41; Acts 20:36; 21:5), some stand (Luke 18:13), and some prostrate themselves (Deuteronomy 9:18; Mark 14:35). There also are occasions when people raise their hands as they address God (Exodus 9:29; 1 Kings 8:22, 54; Psalm 141:2; Lamentations 3:41). The thing that is stressed is that they be *holy* hands. To use one's hands in an unholy way one minute only to lift those same hands in prayer the next minute would be an abomination to the holy God. [See question #5, page 192.]

Hands lifted up in prayer should be expressions of sincere faith and pure motives, not for show or as a prescribed form. To offer prayers *without wrath and doubting* is an important part of this. Our motives and mind-set are important while praying. The Lord's own prayer can teach us even more in this regard (Matthew 6:9-15).

HOLY HANDS

In Lincoln, Illinois, there is a replica of the original Postville Courthouse where Abraham Lincoln once practiced law as a circuit-riding lawyer. Just a block away is Postville Park. One day Lincoln had taken the case of a farmer who was suing a man who had bought a pig but had never paid for it. The other man protested that he had paid for it and refused to pay again. As

> ### How to Say It
> CORINTHIANS. Ko-*rin*-thee-unz (*th* as in *thin*).
> DEUTERONOMY. Due-ter-*ahn*-uh-me.
> EPHESIANS. Ee-*fee*-zhunz.
> EPHESUS. *Ef*-uh-sus.
> GENTILES. *Jen*-tiles.
> LAMENTATIONS. Lam-en-*tay*-shunz.
> MALACHI. *Mal*-uh-kye.
> THESSALONIANS. *Thess*-uh-*lo*-nee-unz (strong accent on *lo*; *th* as in *thin*).

the case developed during the court proceedings, Lincoln came to the conclusion that his client indeed had been paid and was trying to collect twice.

During the noon recess, Lincoln went down to Postville Park to pitch horseshoes. When it was time for court to reconvene, Lincoln did not show up. The judge sent a clerk down to call Lincoln back to the courtroom. Lincoln sent the answer: "I can't. My hands are dirty." The judge, who had come to the same conclusion as Lincoln during the testimony, knew exactly what Lincoln meant. He dismissed the case.

By presenting the case of a man who was trying to extort extra money from a purchaser, Lincoln knew he had dirtied his own hands. Thus he refused to proceed with the case. How different it would be for most modern lawyers! They would say that they are only presenting the case for a client; it is not their place to determine the morality involved. Paul calls us to a different and higher standard. We are to lift up holy hands—not hands that have been soiled by defending immorality.   —J. B. N.

Conclusion

A. Power!

Even as Paul charged Timothy, it is incumbent upon church leaders to teach the necessity and the powerful role of prayer in the lives of Christians. Church leaders do this, in part, by setting examples in their own worship lives.

Isn't it easy to fall into a rut and pray the same trite prayers, using the same phrases, year after year? We do well to give thought to praying for *specific* people and *specific* needs. Prayer at specific occasions ought to reflect those occasions. Invocations, for example, ought to be what the word implies—asking God's presence and blessing as we lift up pleasing worship to Him. Communion prayers should focus on the event it commemorates and not wander over every other subject.

The same kind of focus should be true of prayers during the time of offering. Such prayers acknowledge God as the giver of every good gift, express gratitude, and dedicate our gifts. We offer such prayers with an acknowledgment of our stewardship.

Prayer is God's powerhouse in the life of a Christian and the church. As we learn to pray, we will pray not only for our own needs, but also for the needs of others, for our civil and church leadership, and especially for the salvation of those still outside of Christ.

B. Prayer

Father, help us to pray more intentionally, keeping in mind the things You have taught us in our lesson today. Help us to be more sensitive to the needs of others, both physical and spiritual. We trust You to create circumstances that will help bring about the answers to our prayers that are according to Your will and for Your glory. In Jesus' name we pray, amen.

C. Thought to Remember

Prayer comes first.

Learning by Doing

This section contains an alternative lesson plan emphasizing learning activities. Classes desiring such student involvement will find these suggestions helpful.

Learning Goals

After participating in this lesson, each student will be able to:

1. List some methods and reasons Paul says believers should pray.
2. Identify some specific people for whom we should pray, based on Paul's general description.
3. Adjust his or her prayer life to match the pattern Paul sets forth.

Into the Lesson

Have this question on display as students arrive: "Why Pray?" As class begins, solicit students' responses. Expect such answers as the following: "because we are commanded to pray," "because Jesus set us an example," "because some matters are simply beyond our abilities," and "we need help." Ask students to cite relevant Scriptures. (Suggest they use Bible concordances, if necessary.)

Into the Word

Give each learner eight strips of paper, 5-1/2 inches long and 1-1/2 inches wide (cut from sheets of 8-1/2 by 11 inches). Ask students to write on each of their slips of paper a prayer request derived from Bible verses in today's text of 1 Timothy 2:1-8. Share these examples: "Give thanks for public workers who serve you, such as garbage collectors" (v. 4) and "Pray for those in difficult cultures who are trying to help people come to the knowledge of God's truth" (v. 4).

After allowing time for students to work, collect the completed slips, saying, "It is OK if you have fewer than eight." To make sure you have prayer thoughts related to all eight verses, you may want to add the following slips for any verses your students did not complete: "Pray for individuals whom you never have prayed for" (v. 1); "Pray that God's Spirit will enable a peaceful, quiet life for you" (v. 2); "Pray that you will please God with your prayers" (v. 3); "Pray for the convicting work of the Spirit in the life of someone whom you—and God—want to be saved" (v. 4); "Thank God that in His wisdom He provided a mediator for us in Jesus Christ" (v. 5); "Praise God that the Lord Jesus offered himself for our sins" (v. 6); "Thank God for the apostle Paul and for his ministry to us in the Word" (v. 7); "Pray for the personal holiness that makes your prayers effective before God" (v. 8).

Once the slips are collected, mix them up and then pull out one at a time. Read each one aloud and ask the class, "To which of the eight verses does this prayer request relate?" Some may be identified in ways other than the writer intended, but that will increase the group's examination of the text and possibly create more discussion.

Return to the question you displayed at the beginning, and ask the class, "What answers to our original question do you see Paul giving in these admonitions to Timothy?" Let the class respond freely, but if the following ideas are not suggested, do so yourself: "Paul says to pray because there is one God and one mediator between us and Him" (v. 5); "Paul says to pray because all people need our intercession" (v. 1); "Paul says to pray that all will know the truth of the gospel" (vv. 4, 7).

Into Life

Before class, make up some slips of paper that contain the identity of people with whom we often interact but for whom we are unlikely to pray. Some ideas include the checkout clerk at the grocery store, the cashier at a gas station, the garbage collector, the mayor, the receptionist at the doctor's office, construction workers, a neighbor whose property joins my own, the letter carrier, the hair stylist, the principal and teachers of a nearby school, police officers, airline pilots, etc. Have each student draw a slip of paper from a bag or box.

Ask the class members to post and use the slips they drew as a prayer stimulus for the coming week. Suggest that the prayers will be more focused if they know some specifics to add to their prayer. These specifics include the name of a person holding the occupation on the paper and the exact need that that person has. Challenge them to offer prayers of thanks for this person and to petition God for his or her spiritual well-being.

Bring the class to a close by asking your students to join you in unison in repeating as a prayer this petition offered by one of Jesus' disciple: "Lord, teach us to pray" (Luke 11:1).

Let's Talk It Over

These questions are designed to promote discussion of the lesson. The answers here are only discussion starters. Let your class talk it over from there.

1. Is it possible to make a prayer list too long? Why, or why not?

Christians like to make prayer lists—in Sunday school, at in-home small group meetings, in congregational newsletters, on their church's Web site, etc. Criticizing the practice is risky; who wants to be known as someone against praying? There is a dilemma, however, when maintaining prayer lists begins to take away substantial time from actually praying.

Perhaps some guidelines will help us keep prayer lists manageable. For example, we can limit public intercessions to family members or to the "household of faith" (Galatians 6:10). Prayers for all others can be made in private. Even on a private level, however, overly long lists can be unfeasible due to time constraints. Each individual must decide how many specific intercessions to make. Some prayer warriors will have more time than others to devote to praying for particular people and causes.

2. Do godliness and honesty produce a quiet and peaceable life, or is it the other way around? Explain.

Undoubtedly, these two sets of virtues facilitate one another. So the answer to our question, whichever way we state it, is "yes." This is what is called a reciprocal dynamic: just as chickens produce eggs, chickens are also produced by eggs. Those who live godly and honest lives should find those lives to be more peaceable as a result. (If nothing else, this will be an inner peace with God.) Quiet and peaceable lives should, in turn, have greater opportunities to become more and more godly.

3. How can we become more intentional about praying for the unsaved?

There are many ways to answer this. Some small groups make a "Ten Most Wanted" list of non-Christians, then concentrate fervent and persistent prayer on those lost souls. Other congregations organize prayer walks where certain streets are assigned to individuals, pairs, or teams. As they walk past houses, they pray for the residents inside, even though they are strangers.

Praying for unsaved family members should be a priority. Such a practice can result in a special sensitivity to opportunities for words of witness. Since "faith cometh by hearing" (Romans 10:17), prayer for the unsaved starts with asking that we may have words of witness at the proper time.

4. How would you respond to someone who asks, "Aren't all religious people headed for Heaven?"

The postmodern world thinks of Christians as exclusive and intolerant. What offends our accusers is our insistence that Jesus Christ alone points the way to God and eternal life. "There is none other name under heaven given among men, whereby we must be saved" (Acts 4:12).

Rather than starting with Acts 4:12 as our answer, perhaps we will make more progress by responding with a question of our own: "Why do you think that all religious people are headed for Heaven?" This will help us uncover hidden presuppositions. For example, the person may respond that he or she thinks that all religious people are sincere and that "sincerity" is the key to gaining eternal life. Upon hearing that, we could mention examples of cult leaders whose religious sincerity clearly had an evil or unholy bent. With the sincerity foundation shaken, the other person may be ready to consider Acts 4:12.

5. What posture do you prefer for praying? Why?

Charlie Shedd, author of *How to Develop a Praying Church,* says his best prayer was prayed while he was stuck upside-down in a well! Attitude, of course, is more important than position. Some prefer kneeling because it demonstrates reverence. Standing, sometimes with uplifted hands, expresses praise and adoration. Those in Bible times who prostrated themselves before the Lord did so to indicate their humility and repentance. In one case, however, the Lord showed His displeasure with Joshua's praying in this posture when He said, "Get thee up; wherefore liest thou thus upon thy face?" (Joshua 7:10). None of these postures, however, is a viable substitute for godly sincerity, trust, and love.

Call Godly Leaders

January 15
Lesson 7

DEVOTIONAL READING: Mark 9:33-37.

BACKGROUND SCRIPTURE: 1 Timothy 3.

PRINTED TEXT: 1 Timothy 3:1-15.

1 Timothy 3:1-15

1 This is a true saying, If a man desire the office of a bishop, he desireth a good work.

2 A bishop then must be blameless, the husband of one wife, vigilant, sober, of good behavior, given to hospitality, apt to teach;

3 Not given to wine, no striker, not greedy of filthy lucre; but patient, not a brawler, not covetous;

4 One that ruleth well his own house, having his children in subjection with all gravity;

5 (For if a man know not how to rule his own house, how shall he take care of the church of God?)

6 Not a novice, lest being lifted up with pride he fall into the condemnation of the devil.

7 Moreover he must have a good report of them which are without; lest he fall into reproach and the snare of the devil.

8 Likewise must the deacons be grave, not double-tongued, not given to much wine, not greedy of filthy lucre;

9 Holding the mystery of the faith in a pure conscience.

10 And let these also first be proved; then let them use the office of a deacon, being found blameless.

11 Even so must their wives be grave, not slanderers, sober, faithful in all things.

12 Let the deacons be the husbands of one wife, ruling their children and their own houses well.

13 For they that have used the office of a deacon well purchase to themselves a good degree, and great boldness in the faith which is in Christ Jesus.

14 These things write I unto thee, hoping to come unto thee shortly:

15 But if I tarry long, that thou mayest know how thou oughtest to behave thyself in the house of God, which is the church of the living God, the pillar and ground of the truth.

GOLDEN TEXT: Holding the mystery of the faith in a pure conscience.
—1 Timothy 3:9.

> *God's Commitment—Our Response*
> Unit 2: God's Gifts of Leadership
> (Lessons 5-9)

Lesson Aims

After participating in this lesson, each student will be able to:

1. Compare and contrast the "must be" characteristics of elders (bishops) with that of deacons.
2. Cite some contemporary situations that especially call for, or especially challenge, the qualities Paul describes as essential to leadership.
3. Write a proposal for his or her church on how to cultivate leaders.

Lesson Outline

INTRODUCTION
    A. The Stories We Know So Well
    B. Lesson Background
 I. WHO CAN BE AN ELDER? (1 Timothy 3:1-7)
    A. Willingness to Serve (v. 1)
    B. Eligibility to Serve (vv. 2-7)
      A Model of Hospitality
 II. WHO CAN BE A DEACON? (1 Timothy 3:8-13)
    A. Eligibility to Serve, Part 1 (vv. 8-10)
      Forked Tongue?
    B. Character of Wives (v. 11)
    C. Eligibility to Serve, Part 2 (v. 12)
    D. Result of Faithful Service (v. 13)
III. WHY THESE INSTRUCTIONS? (1 Timothy 3: 14, 15)
CONCLUSION
    A. Church Leadership Today
    B. Prayer
    C. Thought to Remember

Introduction

A. The Stories We Know So Well

"Let me tell you a story about a church elder I once knew." After hearing that statement, is there any one of us who *doesn't* have a sad story that involved a church leader who besmirched the integrity of his office? On the one hand, such stories can serve as valuable case studies to help future leaders not make the same mistakes. But on the other hand, such stories can cause us to have a jaded outlook toward all church leaders.

Having a kingdom perspective makes the difference in one's attitude toward positions of leadership and toward the people in those positions. If one perceives power, control, and "calling the shots" to be the main issues of church leadership positions, then skepticism and cynicism will result. Such attitudes inhibit a willing and joyful support of church leadership.

Negative attitudes can be turned around by those who serve in leadership positions. The turnaround occurs when service comes from a love of Christ, of the church, and an opportunity for service. When that happens, the members of the church respond with a like attitude. Self or kingdom: that choice is what makes the difference in the spirit and life of a church.

B. Lesson Background

The apostle Paul was concerned about the care of the churches. The first-century churches needed wise oversight because of a diversity of ethnic, cultural, and economic backgrounds. The needs were complex (compare Acts 6:1; 1 Corinthians 11:20-22; James 2:2-4). What was required was church leadership that would give proper direction, make wise decisions, and be a role model that inspired confidence and compliance on the part of its members.

So Paul set forth characteristics that were to be found in the lives of those who assume leadership responsibility in the church. Generally speaking, these characteristics should be found in every Christian's life. Those who have become mature in the ways that Paul speaks about are the ones to be considered as leaders. As such, they become examples for the entire body of believers (1 Timothy 4:12; Titus 2:7, 8).

The term *qualifications* is most frequently associated with the listing that Paul provides in today's text. (See, for example, the title of the visual on page 196 and headings in the daily Bible readings on page 198.) This terminology can lend itself to a legalistic approach to the selection process if it means a harsh, severe demand for perfection. Perhaps a better term would be *qualities.* This does not imply a casual or indifferent approach to Paul's instructions. Nor does it compromise the traits desired for biblical leadership. Rather, the term *qualities* speaks of a type of a man whose life is exemplary and commands respect; he is one who has demonstrated ability and a Christian spirit.

I. Who Can Be an Elder? (1 Timothy 3:1-7)

So who can be called to church leadership? Does a man's past prohibit his serving? In a letter to the Corinthian Christians, Paul gives a litany of sins and indicates that these had been the lifestyle of some of them prior to their conversion (1 Corinthians 6:9-11). If a man's past constitutes a prohibition, who could serve?

The principle we shall see Paul establish is that a man must prove himself. His commitment over time warrants his consideration for leadership. He must have a track record. The guidelines within which a man proves himself are set forth in Paul's instructions to Timothy.

A. Willingness to Serve (v. 1)

1. This is a true saying, If a man desire the office of a bishop, he desireth a good work.

The New Testament uses three distinct Greek words to denote *the office* that Paul is talking about. These three words come across in English as *bishop* (or overseer), *pastor* (or shepherd), and *elder*. These three are used interchangeably in the New Testament. It is a mistake to make them mean different things (compare Acts 20:17, 28; Titus 1:5, 7; 1 Peter 5:1, 2).

In discussing this office, Paul deals first with motivation or *desire*. A man who has to be coerced into serving will not serve well. Grudging service blesses no one. [See question #1, page 201.] Men need to realize that the office of elder is the highest that God has ordained in the local church. It is a single honor and privilege to serve God and the church in this capacity.

However, a man is not to be motivated to serve by the honor of the office, to satisfy ego, or to occupy a position of authority. The emphasis here is not on *office* but on *work*. A love of Christ and the church, gratitude for His amazing grace, and a desire to see the work of the kingdom prosper are what lead a man to commit himself willingly to this position of leadership. How sad to see those who desire the office but not the work! [See question #2, page 201.]

B. Eligibility to Serve (vv. 2-7)

2a. A bishop then must be blameless.

To *be blameless* need not imply perfection. If it did, no one could be an elder! A better interpretation is that a man should have no moral flaw that would be an occasion to bring him into disrepute and thus nullify his witness.

2b. The husband of one wife.

This particular issue has resulted in much controversy—perhaps more so than any other issue in Paul's list! Does *husband of one wife* exclude a man (1) who was divorced before he became a Christian? (2) who divorced his wife after he became a Christian? (3) whose wife died and he remarried? or (4) whose wife died and he does not remarry? Discussion of all these would require more space than is allowed here. Certainly the issue must include demonstrated faithfulness of a man to his wife over time.

2c. Vigilant, sober, of good behavior.

These three go together. One must be careful about lifestyle (Ephesians 5:15-18; 1 Peter 5:8). This is true not only for the sake of the elder himself but also for the sake of those over whom he is exercising oversight. He must use good judgment in all his actions.

2d. Given to hospitality, apt to teach.

Being *given to hospitality* and being *apt to teach* can go hand in glove. Informally sharing spiritual nourishment around the dinner table is one of the most effective ways of building bridges. This kind of hospitality can open doors by which people are led to Christ and can grow in Him.

Being *apt to teach* also means that a mature elder knows what he believes and why. He is a man of conviction who has a desire to share his faith. He can recognize false doctrine (1 Timothy 4:16; Titus 1:9; 2:1). A church that has

---

How to Say It

CORINTHIANS. Ko-*rin*-thee-unz (*th* as in *thin*).
EPHESIANS. Ee-*fee*-zhunz.
EPHESUS. *Ef*-uh-sus.
HEZEKIAH. Hez-ih-*kye*-uh.
JERUSALEM. Juh-*roo*-suh-lem.
JUDAS ISCARIOT. *Joo*-dus Iss-*care*-ee-ut.
UZZIAH. Uh-*zye*-uh.

shepherds (elders) who cannot recognize false viewpoints that are masquerading as "diversity of expression" is a church that is headed for trouble.

A Model of Hospitality

Alexander Campbell came to the United States from Ireland (via Scotland) in 1809 with little more than the clothes on his back. Yet by hard work and the fortunate occurrence of acquiring his wife's family farm, he ended his life in 1866 a considerably wealthy man. He realized that God had granted him comfortable resources, and he did not withhold those resources from others. He was a man given to hospitality.

Although his own family was large (14 children), the dining table was often set for 30—and sometimes 60. Selina Campbell, Alexander's second wife, reported that no needy person was ever turned from the door. Travelers, both foreign and American, were welcome. Even strangers caught by nightfall were taken in. Guests came to spend a week, a month, and some even a year, but all were made to feel at home. Campbell eventually added a wing to his house, which the local inhabitants began to call *Strangers Hall* because of the number of people who stayed for a while.

Hospitality can take many forms and may be governed by the limits of financial ability. But all Christian leaders are expected to demonstrate this virtue.
—J. B. N.

3. Not given to wine, no striker, not greedy of filthy lucre; but patient, not a brawler, not covetous.

These characteristics speak much about social conduct and relationships. They describe a self-controlled man. These characteristics can influence one another. For instance, an alcoholic (someone *given to wine*) is often *a brawler* as a result of intoxication (compare Proverbs 20:1).

4, 5. One that ruleth well his own house, having his children in subjection with all gravity; (for if a man know not how to rule his own house, how shall he take care of the church of God?)

How one conducts his own household can indicate fitness to serve as elder. How does he treat family members? Do they honor and respect him? A man who cannot make responsible decisions at home probably will not be able to *take care of the church of God.*

6. Not a novice, lest being lifted up with pride he fall into the condemnation of the devil.

Spiritual immaturity mixed with *pride* is a disastrous combination for anyone but especially for a church leader (compare Proverbs 16:18). Pride was the downfall of Satan, *the devil*, and it led to his punishment or *condemnation*. Pride could place *a novice* Christian in great danger as an elder if a sense of authority goes to his head (compare the cases of Kings Uzziah and Hezekiah in 2 Chronicles 26:16; 32:25, 26).

There are other dangers. For instance, a novice Christian who becomes an elder can be too vulnerable to criticism. He also would lack the mature spiritual discernment to handle difficulties regarding doctrine or personal relationships. If this happens, a man can become discouraged, disillusioned, and ruined for future leadership opportunities (compare 1 Timothy 5:22).

7. Moreover he must have a good report of them which are without; lest he fall into reproach and the snare of the devil.

A man's reputation outside the church *(them which are without)* is important. Does he exhibit integrity to non-Christians? Is he considered moral, ethical, and honest by unbelievers? If his lifestyle becomes the occasion of ridicule, it may lead non-Christians to become skeptical and cynical. [See question #3, page 201.]

The devil is an expert at setting traps. Hypocrisy is one of the devil's most deadly snares. When a leader falls into this trap, his credibility

Visual for lesson 7

Point to the word qualifications *as you open a discussion on the difference between that word and the word* qualities.

and witness are destroyed. A man needs to walk circumspectly lest he stumble into this danger.

II. Who Can Be a Deacon? (1 Timothy 3:8-13)

Deacon is actually a Greek word. Translated it means "one who serves," "servant," and sometimes "minister" (2 Corinthians 3:6). Every Christian serves or ministers, but not in the technical sense of deacon as used in today's lesson. A Christian who serves the church in a general sense is not a deacon any more than an older man is automatically an elder.

Bible students generally assume that the seven men selected in Acts 6:1-6 to serve the church were the first deacons, even though that term is not actually used there. The role of deacon exists to meet certain needs. It was not created because the apostles thought they were too good to wait on tables (Acts 6:2), but because it was taking them away from their primary function as ordained by the Lord: prayer and teaching of the Word (Acts 6:4).

To show that this service was not considered menial, note the caliber of men Peter had the church in Jerusalem select: "men of honest report, full of the Holy Ghost and wisdom" (Acts 6:3). Paul sets before Timothy a similar high standard for those who would serve as deacons in Ephesus. High standards of moral character, practical qualities, and doctrinal soundness are expected for deacons as well as for elders.

A. Eligibility to Serve, Part 1 (vv. 8-10)

8. Likewise must the deacons be grave, not double-tongued, not given to much wine, not greedy of filthy lucre.

Deacons have a great trust. The service they render is very public. Moral character is a prerequisite. Their service is as much a serious matter as is the service by elders. [See question #4, page 201.]

In moving among people as they serve, deacons can fall into the trap of saying different things to different people to keep everyone happy. Hence the warning against being *double-tongued*. Deacons, as all Christians, need to be truthful consistently. This honors God.

The potential danger in the use of alcoholic beverages is revealed both in Scriptures (Proverbs 21:17; 23:20, 21, 29-32) and in modern society. One who is trying to exemplify the Christian life may need to abstain completely in certain cultural settings. This will help avoid the appearance of evil. It will help avoid becoming a stumbling block to others. This is the same standard that elders must meet (see v. 3, above).

The warning about being *greedy of filthy lucre* speaks to a deacon's attitude toward money. This warning is especially important since many deacons have oversight of the church's material resources. Judas Iscariot's fascination with money led him to be a thief and a betrayer (Matthew 26:15; John 12:6).

FORKED TONGUE?

On the American frontier, a common saying among the Indians was "White man speaks with forked tongue." This was because so many times the Indians were told one thing, and then later they were told something entirely different. Sometimes this had to do with treaties when Indians ceded land to the U.S. government. Often Indians were told, "If you cede this land, we will guarantee that no settlers will cross over and interfere with your land west of this line."

Trusting the government, the Indians accepted the treaty only to discover later that the government was either unable or unwilling to stop westward settlement. Sometimes the government did indeed deal in subterfuge, realizing that the treaty was only a stopgap in the constant westward migration of settlers. Sometimes the government acted in good faith, fully intending to keep the settlers out, only to have things get out of control. One way or another, the Indians learned they could not trust the government promises.

Paul insists that the leaders in the church must not be known to speak with "forked tongue." As Jesus said, "Let your communication be, Yea, yea; Nay, nay" (Matthew 5:37; compare James 5:12). Anything else invites a mockery of truth and the integrity of the church. —J. B. N.

9. Holding the mystery of the faith in a pure conscience.

Mystery of the faith refers to what had been concealed, meaning God's eternal purposes as prophesied in the Old Testament. This mystery has now been revealed through apostles (see Romans 16:25, 26; Ephesians 1:9; 3:2-5, 9). Deacons are to live lives consistent with the Word.

Many such conscientious men eventually are considered for the ministry of the eldership. Even so, some men may remain deacons for the remainder of their earthly service. The office of elder and the office of deacon each have a purpose. Both are important.

10. And let these also first be proved; then let them use the office of a deacon, being found blameless.

A man is *proved* for *the office of a deacon* over time. People should see in a potential leader faith and involvement in the life of the church. Only then will a church give a man prayerful consideration for this responsible position. It is a big mistake to place a man in this office in the hope that this will "get him involved."

B. Character of Wives (v. 11)

11. Even so must their wives be grave, not slanderers, sober, faithful in all things.

The character of a man's wife can commend him or disqualify him for this type of service. It is a real blessing to a church to have leaders whose spouses are supportive. A deacon whose wife has serious shortcomings in the areas mentioned in this verse may indicate a chaotic home life. [See question #5, page 201.]

C. Eligibility to Serve, Part 2 (v. 12)

12. Let the deacons be the husbands of one wife, ruling their children and their own houses well.

In regard to what Paul says here, we refer back to what was said of the elders in verses 2, 4, and 5, above. Respected leaders model what God desires for the home.

D. Result of Faithful Service (v. 13)

13. For they that have used the office of a deacon well purchase to themselves a good degree, and great boldness in the faith which is in Christ Jesus.

A man who shows his passion for the Lord's work soon gets the attention of a congregation. When that happens, he comes under consideration for greater responsibility. With increased experience, deacons become stronger and more confident in their faith. They grow both in the grace as well as the knowledge of *Christ Jesus.*

Would that there could be raised up a host of deacons like this in our churches! What a blessing that would be. No wonder Paul speaks so well of those who serve faithfully. And someday there will be the divine benediction "well done, thou good and faithful servant" (Matthew 25:21). This is more than adequate compensation for the time and energy expended in serving the Lord and His church faithfully.

III. Why These Instructions? (1 Timothy 3:14, 15)

Paul has just told us "what's so." Now he answers the question "so what?"

14. These things write I unto thee, hoping to come unto thee shortly.

You can sense Paul's yearning to be with Timothy! Paul's presence would provide tremendous moral support. Face-to-face teaching would offer an opportunity to give further instruction.

15. But if I tarry long, that thou mayest know how thou oughtest to behave thyself in the house of God, which is the church of the living God, the pillar and ground of the truth.

There are no double standards of conduct in the kingdom of God. But it is incumbent upon leaders to set an example of Christian behavior. Paul is not talking about how Timothy is to *behave* inside a church building. Rather, *the house of God* refers to the body of Christ. It refers to Christians, to that great assembly of the called ones wherever they may be.

And note the emphasis that Paul places on God as *living.* He is not as the lifeless gods and idols of the pagan world. Only the living God can be the source of all *truth.* Apart from God, truth is suppressed (Romans 1:18). When that happens, hu-

---

Home Daily Bible Readings

Monday, Jan. 9—Moses Appoints Israel's Tribal Judges (Deuteronomy 1:9-18)
Tuesday, Jan. 10—Paul Is Welcomed as a Leader (Galatians 2:1-10)
Wednesday, Jan. 11—Respect Those Who Labor Among You (1 Thessalonians 5:6-15)
Thursday, Jan. 12—Qualities of a Leader (Titus 1:5-9)
Friday, Jan. 13—The Greatest Is Servant of All (Mark 9:33-37)
Saturday, Jan. 14—Qualifications of Overseers (1 Timothy 3:1-7)
Sunday, Jan. 15—Qualifications of Helpers (1 Timothy 3:8-13)

mans become a law unto themselves. We are in a culture of increasing relativism and pluralism, where absolutes are denied (compare Judges 21:25). The church has a divinely given mandate to proclaim and defend truth. The church is both pillar (supporter) and preserver of God's truth as revealed in Christ (John 14:6) and in His Word (John 17:17).

Conclusion

A. Church Leadership Today

A biblical eldership does not have to rule by mandate. Better is to lead by example in Bible study, prayer, generosity, and godliness. This type of leadership inspires trust and a willingness to follow. The biblical concept of leadership is not that of a business corporation where orders are given. Church leaders are out in front leading the flock, not driving it. On a tour of the Holy Land, we observed this to be true of the Bedouin shepherds. At the start of the day they would lead their flocks to pasture. That's the way the psalmist, the shepherd David, described it. "He leadeth me beside the still waters. . . . he leadeth me in the paths of righteousness" (Psalm 23:2, 3).

Such leadership is all the more urgent given the doctrinal and moral laxity of our age. Young Timothy labored in a very secular culture, and so do we. At no time in history is today's passage any more relevant than now. A prayerful commitment to a restoration of the biblical practice of church government is a priority. God always honors a people committed to doing His will.

B. Prayer

Gracious Father, thank You for caring for Your church that was purchased by the blood of Jesus Christ, Your Son. We praise You for Your wisdom in Your plan for governing it. Forgive us when we have failed to follow Your instructions. Help us in our resolve to do Your will that You may be glorified in the church. We ask it in Jesus name, amen.

C. Thought to Remember

Embrace God's plan for church leadership.

Learning by Doing

This section contains an alternative lesson plan emphasizing learning activities. Classes desiring such student involvement will find these suggestions helpful.

Learning Goals

After this lesson, each student will be able to:

1. Compare and contrast the "must be" characteristics of elders (bishops) with those of deacons.

2. Cite some contemporary situations that especially call for, or especially challenge, the qualities Paul describes as essential to leadership.

3. Write a proposal for his or her church on how to cultivate leaders.

Into the Lesson

Say to the class, "I'm going to read 10 statements about church leadership. Decide whether you agree or disagree—no qualifiers. Do not answer aloud." Then read to the class the following:

   1. Most church leaders are honorable and godly.

   2. Church leaders are to be elected by congregational vote.

   3. Church leaders are to be followed.

   4. All church leaders need a thorough knowledge of the Scriptures.

   5. There are various church leadership ministries according to the New Testament.

   6. All ages of adults can be selected as church leaders.

   7. Others suffer when church leaders make mistakes.

   8. In His ministry, Jesus set the example for all spiritual leaders.

   9. Church leaders should serve a preset, limited term and then be replaced.

   10. Only God knows the heart well enough to appoint people to leadership.

Return to the statements one at a time and let learners express their views. Don't prolong the discussion. At the end say, "We may have differing views on church leaders in general, but we must agree on the attributes for church leaders that the Spirit reveals. Let's look at 1 Timothy 3:1-15."

Into the Word

Use this "Another Word" activity to explore today's Bible text. Ask class members each to number a sheet of paper from 1 to 25. Tell them to write another word for each of the following words you will say aloud. Also tell students to skip any words about which they are unsure.

Words: 1. desire (verb); 2. bishop; 3. work (noun); 4. blameless; 5. one; 6. vigilant; 7. sober; 8. hospitality; 9. apt; 10. striker; 11. greedy; 12. lucre; 13. brawler; 14. covetous; 15. novice; 16. condemnation; 17. reproach; 18. snare; 19. mystery; 20. pure; 21. deacon; 22. grave (adjective); 23. slanderers; 24. purchase (verb); 25. pillar.

Now read 1 Timothy 3:1-15 aloud, pausing after each verse to ask for the "another word" students have on their lists. If an answer seems unclear, ask for an explanation. Be alert to substitutions that alter the meaning of the Spirit's intent.

If your class uses the student books, you may like to fill in the chart as a class under the "Who Needs It?" activity.

Into Life

Verse 9 gives a core characteristic of those who would be leaders in God's church: "holding the mystery of the faith in a pure conscience." Put the 10 words of the Bible verse on 10 half sheets of paper (8-1/2 by 5-1/2 inches). On an 11th half sheet of paper, put the reference "1 Timothy 3:9."

Shuffle those sheets of paper and put them on the wall or bulletin board in three rows of three and one row of two. Put them far enough apart to be able to cover each of the 11 half sheets with a full sheet of 8-1/2 by 11 inch opaque paper. Tape those full sheets of paper over the half sheets as liftable flaps. Number the flaps 1 through 11.

Very quickly lift each of the flaps, in numerical order, to let your class see the words underneath. Students are to take turns trying to say the Bible verse by calling out the correct flap numbers in the proper order for each of the hidden words of the verse.

Let a person continue as long as he or she is correct. After an error, let another student start at the beginning. (From time to time, as needed, you may want to lift the flaps one at a time for another look.) Continue until someone gets all the words in proper order. Use that moment to emphasize the high standards we must hold for our spiritual leaders.

Finish by asking "Does our church have a 'successor strategy' in place to develop new leaders?" Ask for volunteers to write a proposal (as homework) for cultivating leaders in your church.

Let's Talk It Over

These questions are designed to promote discussion of the lesson. The answers here are only discussion starters. Let your class talk it over from there.

1. How do we go about finding men who truly are willing to *serve* as elders, rather than those who are merely interested in title and position?

One good plan is for incumbent elders to nominate candidates for the eldership. Such elders may have confidential knowledge that serves to exclude certain men from nomination. Discerning elders will be well acquainted with each nominee. They will make certain that qualities (or qualifications) of each match the list in today's lesson text. In larger churches no one is expected to know every man in the congregation well enough to evaluate his suitability for nomination as elder. This elder-nomination plan is especially expedient in those cases. The congregation then casts votes to approve the nominations.

2. Can or should a church's pulpit minister also be an elder? Why, or why not?

Churches have approached this question in at least three ways. Some churches say "Yes—our preacher is automatically considered to be part of the eldership because a pulpit minister is really just a specialized type of elder." Other churches say "No—for the preacher to be an elder would be a conflict of interest." Still other churches say "It's possible—but the preacher has to be voted on by the congregation for the office of elder just as any elder would be." In this third case, the periodic congregational vote on the preacher to be an elder serves, in effect, as a vote of confidence (or no confidence) on his ministry as a whole.

The New Testament itself doesn't answer this question. Even the idea of voting, as Western democracies value that concept, is not developed by the New Testament writers. Churches thus should approach this issue with a great deal of thought and prayer, seeking God's will.

3. How much weight should be given to reputation (whether deserved or undeserved) when discerning a man's suitability for church leadership? Are "minor" things like speeding tickets important in this regard? Why, or why not?

Such judgments can be difficult. Some men may be burdened with reputations they don't deserve. The general public sometimes jumps to conclusions about people from hearsay. They may base their prejudice against a man on behavior and events of his pre-Christian life, not allowing for the transforming power of Christ.

On the other hand, elders and deacons are especially accountable to "abstain from all appearance of evil" (1 Thessalonians 5:22). Christian liberty may allow more lifestyle freedom than is really expedient at times, especially for church leaders (1 Corinthians 8). Selecting leaders for the church requires much care and prayer in this regard.

4. In recent years some congregations have opted for "ministry teams" in place of deacons. Is this a good idea? Why, or why not?

Often the works of service performed by ministry teams and deacons are the same. An advantage of ministry teams is that more volunteers frequently are involved. Many members are assimilated effectively by this plan, and the system seems to "work" in most cases.

However, the loss of deacons as a biblical office of the church can result in a lowering of standards for church leaders. It can be easy to rationalize that since ministry team members "aren't really deacons," then the high standards of godly deacons as seen in today's text don't really apply. Yet, God established the office of deacon for a reason! Ultimately, we will not achieve God's results if we ignore God's processes.

5. How do the wives of church leaders affect the work of their husbands, for good or for ill? How can a leader affect his wife's attitude?

If the wives of leaders are judgmental, gossips, immodest, materialistic, or hypocritical, their husbands' leadership (no matter how consecrated) will not long survive. The elders, deacons, and preachers who are truly blessed are those whose wives are faithful to God in all respects (compare Proverbs 31:10-31).

One way an elder or deacon can influence his wife's attitude is by keeping a certain balance in life. A man who is absorbed with church committee meetings, etc., can foster resentment in his wife, who feels as though she and the children have to compete for his time.

January 22
Lesson 8

Teach for Godliness

DEVOTIONAL READING: 1 Timothy 6:2b-10.

BACKGROUND SCRIPTURE: 1 Timothy 4.

PRINTED TEXT: 1 Timothy 4.

1 Timothy 4:1-16

1 Now the Spirit speaketh expressly, that in the latter times some shall depart from the faith, giving heed to seducing spirits, and doctrines of devils;

2 Speaking lies in hypocrisy; having their conscience seared with a hot iron;

3 Forbidding to marry, and commanding to abstain from meats, which God hath created to be received with thanksgiving of them which believe and know the truth.

4 For every creature of God is good, and nothing to be refused, if it be received with thanksgiving:

5 For it is sanctified by the word of God and prayer.

6 If thou put the brethren in remembrance of these things, thou shalt be a good minister of Jesus Christ, nourished up in the words of faith and of good doctrine, whereunto thou hast attained.

7 But refuse profane and old wives' fables, and exercise thyself rather unto godliness.

8 For bodily exercise profiteth little: but godliness is profitable unto all things, having promise of the life that now is, and of that which is to come.

9 This is a faithful saying, and worthy of all acceptation.

10 For therefore we both labor and suffer reproach, because we trust in the living God, who is the Saviour of all men, specially of those that believe.

11 These things command and teach.

12 Let no man despise thy youth; but be thou an example of the believers, in word, in conversation, in charity, in spirit, in faith, in purity.

13 Till I come, give attendance to reading, to exhortation, to doctrine.

14 Neglect not the gift that is in thee, which was given thee by prophecy, with the laying on of the hands of the presbytery.

15 Meditate upon these things; give thyself wholly to them; that thy profiting may appear to all.

16 Take heed unto thyself, and unto the doctrine; continue in them: for in doing this thou shalt both save thyself, and them that hear thee.

GOLDEN TEXT: Take heed unto thyself, and unto the doctrine; continue in them: for in doing this thou shalt both save thyself, and them that hear thee.
—1 Timothy 4:16.

> *God's Commitment—Our Response*
> Unit 2: God's Gifts of Leadership
> (Lessons 5-9)

Lesson Aims

After participating in this lesson, each student will be able to:

1. Summarize Paul's warning about false teaching and the need for Timothy to pursue godliness.
2. Suggest some specific blessings that come to the one who pursues godliness.
3. Tell of one way that he or she will set an example of godliness in the coming week.

Lesson Outline

INTRODUCTION
    A. What Deceivers Do
    B. Lesson Background
 I. WARNING ABOUT FALSE TEACHERS (1 Timothy 4:1-5)
    A. Apostasy Predicted (vv. 1-3)
       A Seared Conscience Renewed
    B. Thanksgiving Practiced (vv. 4, 5)
       God's Goodness
 II. DUTIES OF A FAITHFUL MINISTER (1 Timothy 4:6-11)
    A. Things to Communicate (v. 6)
    B. Things to Avoid (v. 7)
    C. Things of Value (vv. 8-10)
    D. Things to Do (v. 11)
III. COUNSEL ON PERSONAL CONDUCT (1 Timothy 4:12-16)
    A. Youth, Example, Devotion (vv. 12, 13)
    B. Gift, Prophecy, Elders (v. 14)
    C. Diligence, Progress, Salvation (vv. 15, 16)
CONCLUSION
    A. Help Wanted: More People Like Timothy!
    B. Prayer
    C. Thought to Remember

Introduction

A. What Deceivers Do

Semantics. These are the word games that deceivers employ in leading people astray. They use good words with which everyone is familiar but give them different meanings.

In a sermon one Sunday, I cited a preacher who denied the deity of Christ and the inspiration of Scripture. Afterward a lady confronted me and vehemently denied that this was true of the man who had been her preacher for many years. The next week she confronted me again and said she had talked to her former preacher. Upon her inquiry, he responded that he believed Jesus was the Son of God and that the Bible was inspired.

I then suggested that she had asked the wrong questions. She should ask him if he believed Jesus was the Holy Spirit–conceived, virgin-born Son of God. I also suggested that she ask him if he believed the Bible to be the Holy Spirit–inspired, infallible, authoritative Word of God. The following week she approached me crestfallen. He had scoffed at her questions and said he only believed Jesus was "a" son of God, only to a greater degree than we are all sons of God. He also believed that the Bible was inspired only in the sense that the poet Tennyson was inspired when he wrote. False teachers are still with us!

B. Lesson Background

Last week we saw the apostle Paul give instruction to Timothy with regard to leadership in the local church. Paul specifically wrote with regard to the selection of elders and deacons. He cited the qualities that should be found in men upon whom would be laid the responsibility of overseeing the affairs of the church and ministering to the material needs of its members.

Now Paul turns his attention to Timothy's responsibilities as an evangelist (see this description in 2 Timothy 4:5). These would relate to Timothy's duties in teaching and preaching as well as in his personal life. This retraces the charge Paul had given him earlier in this letter (see 1 Timothy 1:3, 18).

I. Warning About False Teachers (1 Timothy 4:1-5)

A. Apostasy Predicted (vv. 1-3)

1. Now the Spirit speaketh expressly, that in the latter times some shall depart from the faith, giving heed to seducing spirits, and doctrines of devils.

False teaching infiltrated the church even as early as the first century. Timothy has to come to grips with this issue for his own sake as well as for the sake of the church at Ephesus. To *depart from the faith, giving heed to seducing spirits, and doctrines of devils* is summed up in our single word *apostasy*.

This prediction of apostasy comes about by direct revelation to the apostle Paul by the Holy *Spirit*. The *latter times* refers to the Christian era—the church age, from Pentecost to the Lord's return (compare Acts 2:17; 2 Timothy 3:1; 4:3; Hebrews 1:1, 2) rather than only to the time of the second coming of Christ. The spread of false doctrine should come as no surprise to us. Paul notes its demonic origin.

It is a terrible thing to *depart from the faith* after once having accepted Jesus as Lord and Savior. Scripture offers several warnings in this regard (Galatians 5:4; Hebrews 6:4-6; 10:26-31; 2 Peter 2:20-22). Those who depart from the faith in Paul's day are those who allow their ambition and pride to control them (compare 2 Timothy 3:1-9). This makes them vulnerable to the seductive influence of demons. Such false teachers secure a following within the church through their pretensions (Titus 1:11). Church history reveals a dismal record of departures from biblical doctrine and apostolic practice.

2. Speaking lies in hypocrisy; having their conscience seared with a hot iron.

The Holy Spirit is the Spirit of truth. Truth is eternal. God is the source of all truth. False teachers tell *lies* because, as Jesus affirmed, they are of their father the devil (John 8:44).

False teachers are deceivers. In their *hypocrisy* they pose as one thing but are really something else entirely. They are masters at producing counterfeit religion. It has the appearance of the real thing but is flawed. Unfortunately, many people have a hard time recognizing truth and are easily fooled.

Those who go against the truth have to sear *their conscience* (compare Titus 1:15). Their hearts become scarred, tough, and hardened—dead. Truth no longer fazes them. Perhaps they lose the ability to distinguish truth from falsehood. Such folks often go instead with "whatever works" and see truth as relative (compare Judges 21:25). How sad—and dangerous—when one becomes an apostate.

A Seared Conscience Renewed

John Newton (1725–1807) grew up fully aware of the teachings of Christianity, but they had made little impression upon him. He entered into naval service as a young man and became involved in the slave trade. He saw the suffering of black slaves as they were separated from family and homeland. He saw them held in pens awaiting shipment to America, and he himself transported several shiploads to the New World. He saw young black women helplessly used to satisfy sailors' lust. He saw all this, but his conscience was seared, and it gave him no remorse at the time.

Later Newton experienced conversion, became an Anglican minister, supported the evangelical revival in the church, and labored to stop the evils of slavery in the British Empire. He is perhaps best known today as the author of the hymn "Amazing Grace." The line that says "that saved a wretch like me"—Newton knew what that meant.

When Newton's conscience was seared, he was totally insensitive to the evils and horror of slavery in which he participated. It took a conversion experience to remove the hard crust of his conscience and open him up to Christian virtue. Christ is working this way in lives right now!
—J. B. N.

3. Forbidding to marry, and commanding to abstain from meats, which God hath created to be received with thanksgiving of them which believe and know the truth.

Paul likely is striking at the Gnostics. This movement teaches that the flesh and the material world are evil by their very nature. Thus the joining of husband and wife in marriage would be evil as well. The Gnostics carry their philosophy to the point where they even deny that Jesus had come in the flesh. The apostle John

---

How to Say It

CORINTHIANS. Ko-*rin*-thee-unz (*th* as in *thin*).
CORNELIUS. Cor-*neel*-yus.
EPHESIANS. Ee-*fee*-zhunz.
EPHESUS. *Ef*-uh-sus.
GALATIANS. Guh-*lay*-shunz.
GENTILE. *Jen*-tile.
GNOSTICS. *Nahss*-ticks.
HEBREWS. *Hee*-brews.
LYSTRA. *Liss*-truh.
TITUS. *Ty*-tus.

deals with this issue extensively in his letters (compare 2 John 7).

Yet there is nothing wrong with marriage and food. These are not evil in and of themselves (see Mark 7:17-19; Hebrews 13:4). There is nothing so refreshingly liberating as truth!

B. Thanksgiving Practiced (vv. 4, 5)

4. For every creature of God is good, and nothing to be refused, if it be received with thanksgiving.

Paul repudiates outright what the false teachers promote. Those who know God's Word acknowledge that everything God created is good (Genesis 1:31). To abuse the things God gives us is wrong. But a proper regard and *thanksgiving* for all that God has created honors Him. [See question #1, page 210.] God used this truth in an illustration to the apostle Peter in preparation for his visit to Cornelius, a Gentile (Acts 10:15).

GOD'S GOODNESS

James Alfred Wight (1916–1995), better known under his pen name of James Herriot, was a country veterinarian in Yorkshire, England. In 1966 he began to write a series of books about his experiences with animals. His books became best-sellers. In winsome stories, he talks about dogs, cats, horses, sheep, and other livestock that he encountered in 50 years as a vet. He evokes a nostalgic love of animals and a slower country living that has given his books an appealing quality. In all, he wrote 15 books, which have sold 50 million copies in 20 countries.

Probably, his four best-known books are titles borrowed from the refrain of a hymn written by Cecil Frances Alexander, wife of an Anglican bishop in the nineteenth century. She wrote over 400 hymns, but "All Things Bright and Beautiful" is probably her best known.

> All things bright and beautiful,
>   All creatures great and small,
> All things wise and wonderful:
>   The Lord God made them all.

These words, together with the appeal of Herriot's stories, sum up what Paul is referring to. Genesis tells us that when God created, He saw that it was good. Paul reminds us that the creation is still good, and the bounty God has provided is to be enjoyed with thanksgiving. —J. B. N.

5. For it is sanctified by the word of God and prayer.

To be *sanctified* means to be set apart, usually for a holy purpose as ordained by God. And what was the purpose for which God created all things? The answer is recorded as early as Genesis 9:3: they are for humanity's use. That is why offering grace before eating is appropriate.

II. Duties of a Faithful Minister (1 Timothy 4:6-11)

A. Things to Communicate (v. 6)

6. If thou put the brethren in remembrance of these things, thou shalt be a good minister of Jesus Christ, nourished up in the words of faith and of good doctrine, whereunto thou hast attained.

The mark of *a good minister of Jesus Christ* is keeping the people informed about what is going on around them—about the things that jeopardize their faith. If a person is not *nourished* in *faith* and sound *doctrine*, he or she will not be equipped to recognize false doctrine when it comes. [See question #2, page 210.]

Timothy had been spiritually equipped earlier by a godly grandmother and mother (2 Timothy 1:5; 3:14, 15). Now the apostle Paul continues that practice. This type of teaching in Christian homes and churches is an imperative. It is the best antidote for the high doctrinal and spiritual mortality rate that we are experiencing in our churches, especially among our young people.

B. Things to Avoid (v. 7)

7. But refuse profane and old wives' fables, and exercise thyself rather unto godliness.

Home Daily Bible Readings

Monday, Jan. 16—Moses Teaches Israel to Obey (Deuteronomy 4:1-8)

Tuesday, Jan. 17—Give Ear to My Teaching (Psalm 78:1-8)

Wednesday, Jan. 18—Rules for the New Life (Ephesians 4:25–5:2)

Thursday, Jan. 19—The Teacher's Gift Is Teaching (Romans 12:3-8)

Friday, Jan. 20—A Warning Against False Teaching (1 Timothy 4:1-5)

Saturday, Jan. 21—Exercise Yourself in Godliness (1 Timothy 4:6-10)

Sunday, Jan. 22—Put All These Things into Practice (1 Timothy 4:11-16)

Paul is blunt: Timothy doesn't have the time to listen to nonsense. It is easy to get caught up in theological fads, hand-me-down traditions, and various *fables* (compare Titus 1:14). Some people exploit every crisis by forcing interpretations on Scripture to fit the occasion. These interpretations often have their origin in legends and myths. Paul says to ignore them, whatever they are, and to expend energy on cultivating *godliness* instead.

The term *exercise* indicates that godliness takes effort. It doesn't just happen. It requires the discipline to study the Word in order to determine God's will and live it out (Psalm 119:11, 105; 2 Timothy 3:15, 16).

C. Things of Value (vv. 8-10)

8. For bodily exercise profiteth little: but godliness is profitable unto all things, having promise of the life that now is, and of that which is to come.

Physical fitness is a booming industry today. The malls are favorite walking places. Hiking trails are popular. When one feels good physically, he or she functions better. Paul is not belittling physical fitness. Paraphrased, what he is saying is, "What good is it to gain a benefit from a physical fitness program if at the same time we are out of shape morally and spiritually for the life that *is to come*?"

9. This is a faithful saying, and worthy of all acceptation.

There is a bit of doubt as to whether *this . . . faithful saying* refers to what Paul has just said in verse 8 or what comes next in verse 10. In either case we can be sure that everything Paul writes is under the inspiration of the Holy Spirit.

10. For therefore we both labor and suffer reproach, because we trust in the living God, who is the Saviour of all men, specially of those that believe.

Paul affirms why he is willing to *labor* so hard. To appreciate his struggles, read in 2 Corinthians 11:23-28 what Paul suffered for the cause of Christ. And what was Paul's view of all this? His sufferings "are not worthy to be compared with the glory which shall be revealed in us" (Romans 8:18). Yes, God calls people to labor diligently, no matter the cost. This labor can result in suffering. The apostle Peter says that if we suffer as Christians, we are not to be ashamed but to glorify God in this (1 Peter 4:16).

This visual may cause your learners to ask themselves "What am I really doing with my Bible?

Visual for Lessons 8, 12

God *is the Saviour of all men* in the sense that He offers salvation to everyone. Jesus died for all and thereby draws everyone to Him (John 12:32). But Jesus' drawing can be resisted, as the pages of Scripture and experience tell us. Thus Paul is not teaching universal salvation. He simply means that anyone and everyone can be saved. But there are conditions to meet (Acts 2:38; Romans 10:13; James 2:24; etc.).

D. Things to Do (v. 11)

11. These things command and teach.

The phrase *these things* refers to what Paul said in verses 6-10. Paul's charge to Timothy is very clear! As a result, those in the church at Ephesus are to be impressed with the necessity of Timothy's message regarding false teachers and godly living. The duty of every Christian leader is to impress upon all whom they teach the imperative nature of this kind of life. The result should be that the world may see the glory of God reflected in us (Matthew 5:14-16).

III. Counsel on Personal Conduct (1 Timothy 4:12-16)

A. Youth, Example, Devotion (vv. 12, 13)

12. Let no man despise thy youth; but be thou an example of the believers, in word, in conversation, in charity, in spirit, in faith, in purity.

The Christian life is proactive. It is not enough to refrain from doing evil. No, the Christian must do good as well. So Paul encourages Timothy to continue living an exemplary life as the best way to silence any critics (compare Titus 2:8).

Although Timothy is to "command and teach" (v. 11), this may cause a problem because of his *youth.* There even may be godly people in Ephesus who believe that youth disqualifies one to be a leader. [See question #3, page 210.] The way to overcome this is for Timothy to live a life that will lead people to respect him. The reality is that the preacher lives a "goldfish bowl existence." He needs to be sensitive to the fact that people are watching. The very nature of his calling makes him a role model.

Paul expands on the importance of being a role model when he says, "Be ye followers of me, even as I also am of Christ" (1 Corinthians 11:1). One teaches by life as well as by doctrine. In the antique language of the *King James Version,* the phrase *in conversation* refers to "manner of life." One's lifestyle is to be above reproach.

13. Till I come, give attendance to reading, to exhortation, to doctrine.

Paul's intends to join Timothy at an unspecified date. Until then he provides Timothy certain instructions. We can see that when Timothy focuses on *reading,* he will be better equipped for *exhortation* and instruction in *doctrine.* As such, he will be fulfilling Jesus' last directive as recorded in Matthew's gospel: "Teaching them to observe all things whatsoever I have commanded you" (Matthew 28:20). This is a good agenda for every preacher and Christian leader. [See question #4, page 210.] We must never stop learning! The Word of God is inexhaustible.

Sadly, however, there is very little attention given *to doctrine* in many pulpits today. In place of doctrine are feel-good sermons in many cases. There is an important place in sermons for meeting felt needs. But sound doctrine must serve as the basis. Feel-good sermons without that sound doctrinal basis may appeal to the emotions, but will not strengthen one against assaults on his or her faith (compare Ephesians 4:11-15).

This is not an either-or issue. God's Word appeals to both the intellect and the emotions (Acts 2:37; Hebrews 4:12). But these two must come in that order. That is the way the conscience is educated. Truth leads to right feelings and conduct. Emotions without intellect lead to "a zeal of God, but not according to knowledge" (Romans 10:2).

B. Gift, Prophecy, Elders (v. 14)

14. Neglect not the gift that is in thee, which was given thee by prophecy, with the laying on of the hands of the presbytery.

These instructions given to Timothy are not to be construed as rebukes. Rather, they are encouragements to "hang in there," to keep doing what he is already doing. There is the old saying: "If you don't use it, you will lose it."

To be able to "do the work of an evangelist" (2 Timothy 4:5) may be *the gift* alluded to (see also Ephesians 4:11). If so, this was bestowed by God through *the laying on of the hands of the* body of elders *(presbytery).*

This action may have occurred when Paul recruited Timothy on the second missionary tour at the time when Paul stopped to confirm the church at Lystra (Acts 16:1-3). That was a church that Paul had established on his first journey (Acts 14:8-20). All of this had been revealed through Paul concerning the way Timothy was going to be used (1 Timothy 1:18).

C. Diligence, Progress, Salvation (vv. 15, 16)

15. Meditate upon these things; give thyself wholly to them; that thy profiting may appear to all.

The matters of which Paul speaks are not frivolous. Timothy is to reflect not only upon the blessings and privileges that accrue to leadership but also on the corresponding responsibilities of the stewardship that have been given him. Such personal reflection takes time! If Timothy gets to be "too busy" doing his various daily tasks, he won't be able to *meditate upon these things.* This should be a facet of Timothy's leadership role. It is a facet that should not be overlooked by leaders in the church today. [See question #5, page 210.]

One happy result will be that Timothy will be more able to give himself *wholly* to his God-given role. When that happens, everyone will take note of his commitment to ministry. What a witness!

16. Take heed unto thyself, and unto the doctrine; continue in them: for in doing this thou shalt both save thyself, and them that hear thee.

Paul sums up his instructions by telling Timothy to pay close attention to his own heart, beliefs, and conduct. A little indiscretion can jeopardize Timothy's influence and role as a leader. It is heartbreaking to see those who are disillusioned by the moral downfall of a leader they had trusted.

Timothy is to be careful also in what he teaches. How sad to see people espousing false *doctrine* because they themselves were taught wrongly. A life of faithfulness in ministry adds to the assurance of Timothy's own salvation. The crown of life is his (Revelation 2:10). A life of faithfulness also influences the eternal destinies of all those he is responsible for leading.

Conclusion

A. Help Wanted: More People Like Timothy!

A host of leaders like Timothy would shake the church! They would be willing to let God use them in building up His kingdom on earth. They would be leaders who are well trained in the Scriptures, are willing to take a stand for truth, and will back it up with a godly life. What is our church doing to train and mentor its Timothys to come?

B. Prayer

Father, may our homes and churches be so wholly committed to You in word, spirit, and deed that our children will be inspired to lives of faithful service. May You find among them those who will be Your Timothys in the church of tomorrow. We pray this in Jesus' name, amen.

C. Thought to Remember

"The things that thou hast heard of me among many witnesses, the same commit thou to faithful men, who shall be able to teach others also" (2 Timothy 2:2).

Learning by Doing

This section contains an alternative lesson plan emphasizing learning activities. Classes desiring such student involvement will find these suggestions helpful.

Lesson Aims

After this lesson, each student will be able to:

1. Summarize Paul's warning about false teaching and the need for Timothy to pursue godliness.
2. Suggest some specific blessings that come to one who pursues godliness.
3. Tell of one way that he or she will set an example of godliness in the coming week.

Into the Lesson

Bring to class a clear example of false doctrine from a religious group that considers its members to be following Christ. Your example could be in the form of a video clip, a newspaper clipping, magazine article, etc.

Discuss this problem, but don't get bogged down in details. Use this to stress that false doctrine is still with us. To prepare for the Into the Word segment, say, "Recognizing false doctrine is just one issue among many for the church. I have several more issues for us to consider today."

Into the Word

Prepare in advance the following statements on 10 slips of paper, one statement per copy.

1. There is nothing more practical than sound doctrine.

2. Hardening of the arteries is not nearly as serious as hardening of the conscience.

3. All false doctrine originates in the mind of the devil.

4. A young person's folly is more forgivable than that of an older person.

5. Physical fitness is at the base of godly stewardship.

6. A minister's most important attribute is his gracious and friendly personality.

7. An effective evangelist/minister must be a reader.

8. Meditation speaks of Eastern mysticism and has no place in the Christian lifestyle.

9. A cauterized conscience has no value in terms of morality.

10. Recognizing that "the Spirit speaketh expressly" is the basis for sound doctrine.

Have the class divide into groups of two or three. Give each group one of the statements. Say, "Read 1 Timothy 4 and then identify a verse or verses related to your statement. Discuss as a group whether you agree or disagree with your assigned statement. Did the Bible verses you identified change your initial opinion about the statement you received?" After a few minutes, have groups present their conclusions.

For an added activity, confer with several class members in advance and ask each to deliver in class a short defense for one of the following false doctrines:

1. "Truly spiritual Christians do not marry."
2. "Sometimes a lie is the kindest thing one can say to a friend."
3. "Every Christian should be a vegetarian."
4. "God is the Savior of all, as Paul declares, so missionary evangelism is unnecessary."
5. "One's lifestyle has nothing to do with his or her eternal destiny, for salvation is purely by God's grace."

Allow time for responses.

Into Life

Prepare a priority paper for each student using the heading, "More or Less" at the top. List the following seven priorities:

___Give more thanks to God for food and other daily provisions.
___Spend less time in idle talk about insignificant matters.
___Spend more time reading the Scriptures than I currently do.
___Read, watch, and listen to less false doctrine in the religious media.
___Share more of my understanding of God's truth with others.
___Use less of my time in sports and other physical pursuits.
___Deepen my trust in the living God and my Savior.

Distribute papers and say, "Number the items on this list from one to seven in the order that you think each item should be a priority for yourself as a Christian." Ask for volunteers to share the reasons for one or two of their answers.

Let's Talk It Over

These questions are designed to promote discussion of the lesson. The answers here are only discussion starters. Let your class talk it over from there.

1. How does mealtime prayer sanctify God's provisions and honor His name? How can we improve those prayers?

Grace before meals acknowledges that God supplies every need. More than that, it recognizes that God owns everything on the table—no matter who grows it, who sells it, who buys it, or who prepares and serves it.

This affirmation creates a spirit of thanksgiving, humility, and dependence upon divine providence. If the blessing of our food is sincere (meaning more than a mere ritual), the result is greater faith, trust, and reverence before God. Such prayers exalt His holy name by serving as a godly example to everyone who participates or observes.

2. It looks like Paul is giving Timothy what we would call a job description. How should job descriptions for ministers today be similar to or different from what Paul gave Timothy? Defend your answer.

Today's text and other passages already provide some general expectations: preach/teach sound doctrine; pursue personal holiness by practicing the spiritual disciplines; protect the flock and defend the faith; labor with diligence; be prepared and willing to suffer persecution; and challenge the congregation to evangelism.

Notice that there is nothing in the list about performing weddings and funerals, attending church conventions and seminars, earning advanced degrees, or writing church newsletters. Yet these are additional expectations that we put on our ministers (or they put on themselves). The wise board of elders will insist that a minister establish priorities.

3. Is there a problem of age discrimination in selecting church leaders today? If so, is such discrimination different from the problem of Timothy's youthfulness in Paul's day? Explain.

Timothy's issue was the possibility of having his counsel and witness ignored by older church members primarily because of an age difference. Haven't we all seen that at times?

Since Timothy's day, however, age discrimination has gone to the other end of the spectrum: congregations have been known to pass by mature, seasoned ministers in favor of younger men with far less experience. Perhaps this practice is in deference to a youth-oriented culture.

Those responsible for church staffing (pulpit committees, etc.) can make a good start by recognizing that this problem does exist at times. That recognition will help them evaluate candidates' qualifications without showing favoritism for certain age ranges. Fairness will result in balancing outlook and tempering expectations. On the one hand, not many 60-year-olds have the physical energy and stamina of a 30-year-old. But on the other hand, not many 30-year-olds have 40 years of experience in the ministry!

4. The challenges regarding reading, exhortation, and doctrine in 1 Timothy 4:13 and "teaching them to observe all things" in Matthew 28:20 are vital! How can a preacher make these a priority?

An interesting development in recent decades is that many church buildings provide an "office" rather than a "study" for the minister. That slight change of designation may reflect an expectation for the minister to be "out in the community" rather than at a desk preparing to teach and preach.

How many hours per week does your minister have available to prepare sermons and lessons? Ask and find out—the answer may be surprising!

5. Does your minister's contract or job description make provision for time to think and reflect? How much or how little is this emphasized?

Church leaders profit from the disciplines of prayer and meditation, but time must be set aside for these. Retreats, vacations, and sabbaticals have different purposes, but they all allow the minister to "do something different" for a while and thus grow (or recharge) spiritually.

Vocational ministers must be intentional about providing for themselves special people, places, books, quiet times, etc., to aid the process of spiritual growth and maintain spiritual health. A wise eldership will help a minister to avoid allowing "the tyranny of the urgent" to squeeze out the need for time to think and reflect.

Practice Justice and Mercy

January 29
Lesson 9

DEVOTIONAL READING: Matthew 23:23-28.

BACKGROUND SCRIPTURE: 1 Timothy 5.

PRINTED TEXT: 1 Timothy 5:1-8, 17-25.

1 Timothy 5:1-8, 17-25

1 Rebuke not an elder, but entreat him as a father; and the younger men as brethren;

2 The elder women as mothers; the younger as sisters, with all purity.

3 Honor widows that are widows indeed.

4 But if any widow have children or nephews, let them learn first to show piety at home, and to requite their parents: for that is good and acceptable before God.

5 Now she that is a widow indeed, and desolate, trusteth in God, and continueth in supplications and prayers night and day.

6 But she that liveth in pleasure is dead while she liveth.

7 And these things give in charge, that they may be blameless.

8. But if any provide not for his own, and specially for those of his own house, he hath denied the faith, and is worse than an infidel.

17 Let the elders that rule well be counted worthy of double honor, especially they who labor in the word and doctrine.

18 For the Scripture saith, Thou shalt not muzzle the ox that treadeth out the corn. And, The laborer is worthy of his reward.

19 Against an elder receive not an accusation, but before two or three witnesses.

20 Them that sin rebuke before all, that others also may fear.

21 I charge thee before God, and the Lord Jesus Christ, and the elect angels, that thou observe these things without preferring one before another, doing nothing by partiality.

22 Lay hands suddenly on no man, neither be partaker of other men's sins: keep thyself pure.

23 Drink no longer water, but use a little wine for thy stomach's sake and thine often infirmities.

24 Some men's sins are open beforehand, going before to judgment; and some men they follow after.

25 Likewise also the good works of some are manifest beforehand; and they that are otherwise cannot be hid.

GOLDEN TEXT: Rebuke not an elder, but entreat him as a father; and the younger men as brethren; the elder women as mothers; the younger as sisters, with all purity.—1 Timothy 5:1, 2.

> *God's Commitment—Our Response*
> Unit 2: God's Gifts of Leadership
> (Lessons 5-9)

Lesson Aims

After participating in this lesson, each student will be able to:

1. Describe some ways that Christians are to treat one another.
2. Give an example of how his or her church has honored its older (and perhaps needier) members and how it has recognized its leaders.
3. State one way he or she will honor an elderly Christian or dedicated leader this week.

Lesson Outline

INTRODUCTION
  A. Too Busy?
  B. Lesson Background
I. BEHAVIOR TOWARD OTHERS (1 Timothy 5:1, 2)
  A. Toward Men (v. 1)
  B. Toward Women (v. 2)
II. CARE OF WIDOWS (1 Timothy 5:3-8)
  A. Categories (vv. 3, 4)
    Piety at Home
  B. Lifestyles (vv. 5-7)
  C. Obligation (vv. 8)
III. HONOR FOR ELDERS (1 Timothy 5:17-20)
  A. Worthy of Support (vv. 17, 18)
    Double Honor
  B. Accusations Against Elders (vv. 19, 20)
IV. NOTES TO TIMOTHY (1 Timothy 5:21-25)
  A. Partiality Forbidden (v. 21)
  B. Laying on of Hands Restricted (v. 22a)
  C. Purity Mandated (v. 22b)
  D. Advice Offered (v. 23)
  E. Actions Recognized (vv. 24, 25)
CONCLUSION
  A. Delay of Game
  B. Prayer
  C. Thought to Remember

Introduction

A. Too Busy?

Some of us can recall depressing images of the old county homes where the aged and orphans were left—forgotten, lonely, and despondent. And even with our modern, upscale, and highly regulated senior citizen facilities, the sense of loneliness often is no less. After being placed in a comfortable setting, many of the elderly are abandoned and forgotten by family and friends.

Many fine benevolent facilities try to compensate for this state of affairs by providing a broad program of activities and services. This helps alleviate the tendency of residents to lapse into self-pity and depression. Even with emotional well-being, however, advancing years are accompanied by breakdowns in health. That's the very nature of our humanity (see Psalm 90:10). The problems of the aging process are heightened with the loss of close friends and the neglect of family members. Here is where the family and the church must come into the picture.

Today's lesson is timely for those who live in a materialistic, self-centered culture. Paul gives a sobering reminder of those godly traits that should be inherent in family relationships, especially among believers.

B. Lesson Background

Last week we studied Paul's counsel to Timothy with regard to false teachers, their doctrines, and the necessity of exposing them. The lesson concluded with admonitions to Timothy concerning those things to which he needed to give continual attention in his personal life. Paul now makes a transition and calls attention to meeting needs among certain members of the church.

God's solutions to meeting needs are not always the same as human solutions. For example, the courts have made it legal to eliminate unwanted preborn children by way of abortion. In certain places and circumstances, the aged can be removed through a murderous process referred to as euthanasia. Some would eliminate all who, in their eyes, no longer contribute to society. But God created us in His own image and likeness (Genesis 1:26, 27). Every person is to be regarded with dignity and respect at all stages and situations of life.

I. Behavior Toward Others
(1 Timothy 5:1, 2)
A. Toward Men (v. 1)

1. Rebuke not an elder, but entreat him as a father; and the younger men as brethren.

With both older and *younger men*, the attitude of one who rebukes or reproves has everything to do with how the admonition is received. If one is harsh, vindictive, or impugns motives, then defensiveness and resentment may be the result.

Offering correction to those in error is not easy. In the first case, Paul probably is referring to an aged man as opposed to someone who holds the office of elder since there is an older/younger contrast in both verses 1 and 2.

Youth are prone to be impatient with older men, who tend to be more deliberate in their actions. Of course, one does not tolerate indolence or incompetence. But the corrective approach should be that of encouraging industry and ability. The purpose is to build up, not to tear down. So the approach to those who are older is to be done with respect and dignity that their years deserve. This is the import of the word *entreat* in contrast to the word *rebuke*.

Treatment of younger men as *brethren* or equals is self-explanatory. Reproving those that need reproving calls for meekness rather than arrogance, humility rather than haughtiness.

B. Toward Women (v. 2)

2. The elder women as mothers; the younger as sisters, with all purity.

Paul continues to outline the type of treatment Timothy is to accord to those in his congregation. He is not to overlook faults or flaws that truly are detrimental. But he should not be motivated in correction by a mean spirit or by an attitude of superpiety. That is the spirit that leads to noticing a speck in someone else's eye while having a beam hanging out of one's own (Matthew 7:1-5). Yes, judgments are required, but they are not to be hypocritical judgments (Matthew 7:15-20). This is part of treating one another with respect. This attitude allows Timothy to treat older *women as mothers*.

The Bible has much to say about *purity*, both of the sexual and non-sexual kinds. When men think of the *younger* women of the church *as sisters*, purity will be easier to maintain. A man should not be guilty of any indiscretions. His conversations should not carry innuendos or double meanings.

II. Care of Widows
(1 Timothy 5:3-8)
A. Categories (vv. 3, 4)

3. Honor widows that are widows indeed.

In the culture of Paul's time, a woman without a husband or family is in dire straits. It can be a heartless environment for those who have no means of support. Government-funded social insurance plans, heath care, and retirement centers do not exist. Paul's first instruction regarding the church's responsibility in this matter is that those who *are widows indeed* are to receive *honor.*

The type of widows that Paul has in mind are those who are destitute and have no family members to take care of them. The early church in Jerusalem set a good example of benevolence when it came to the care of widows (Acts 6:1-7). Attention to such widows is certainly "pure religion and undefiled before God" (James 1:27).

4. But if any widow have children or nephews, let them learn first to show piety at home, and to requite their parents: for that is good and acceptable before God.

The church as a whole is not responsible to provide for those widows who have family members who can support them (also 1 Timothy 5:16). The care given by children should be a normal expression of gratitude for the years their parents invested in them. It is also a duty imposed by the fifth of the Ten Commandments (Exodus 20:12). Jesus reiterated this in Matthew 19:19 and Mark 7:10-12. [See question #1, page 219.]

Modern long-term care of the elderly is very expensive, however, and help from various agencies may be needed. Even so, we dare not dishonor elderly parents with a "let the government handle it" mentality. Fulfillment of this duty pleases and honors God. It is a vital part of showing *piety at home.*

PIETY AT HOME

Martin Luther (1483–1546) was the major leader of the Protestant Reformation. It was a time of significant change in the European church as well as European society. One of the challenges

---

How to Say It

CORINTHIANS. Ko-*rin*-thee-unz (*th* as in *thin*).
DEUTERONOMY. Due-ter-*ahn*-uh-me.
EPHESUS. *Ef*-uh-sus.
EUTHANASIA. you-thuh-*nay*-zhuh.
HEBREWS. *Hee*-brews.
LEVITICUS. Leh-*vit*-ih-kus.
MICAH. *My*-kuh.

Luther faced was to reestablish the sanctity of marriage and family life for church leaders. When he married a former nun, Katherine von Bora, in 1525, it changed his life. It also changed Lutheran ministry for centuries to come.

This couple had six children and reared four orphaned children from his relatives as well. Luther saw the home as the school for character. Children were to learn to obey parents and also learn to fear God. Children learned daily Bible lessons, and in turn Luther learned of God's goodness by enjoying the presence of wife and family. The family shared the workload, with Luther doing the preaching, teaching, and writing, and Katie overseeing the home chores, the gardening, and the livestock. Under Luther's guidance, the home became the school for piety, manners, responsibility, and morality. Piety is responsible behavior as well as attitudes of devotion.

Paul's comment is that children should learn at home that part of their piety is supporting their parents in time of need. When that happens, more church resources become available to support those aged members who have no other means of support. —J. B. N.

B. Lifestyles (vv. 5-7)

5. Now she that is a widow indeed, and desolate, trusteth in God, and continueth in supplications and prayers night and day.

Paul describes a type of *widow* who is worthy of the church's help. Though without a visible means of support, she trusts God. She believes her prayers for her own needs *(supplications)* as well as her *prayers* on behalf of others will be honored. She is keenly aware of God's presence (compare Luke 2:36, 37). Through His church, God provides for members of His family who are in genuine need.

6. But she that liveth in pleasure is dead while she liveth.

In pagan Ephesus (the city where Timothy serves), there are strong temptations for a widow to resort to unholy means of livelihood. If she succumbs, she will become spiritually dead. The pleasures of sin are for a season (Hebrews 11:25). A widow who makes such a choice is not to be supported. Younger widows are not to be supported either (1 Timothy 5:9-15).

7. And these things give in charge, that they may be blameless.

Christians are to recognize the need for justice that is tempered by mercy. The world watches the church critically. How we treat and care for one another is a commentary on the genuineness of our profession.

C. Obligation (v. 8)

8. But if any provide not for his own, and specially for those of his own house, he hath denied the faith, and is worse than an infidel.

Jesus affirmed the obligation to support one's parents, as we saw earlier. Therefore, to refuse one's duty is to deny *the faith*. Any conduct that is inconsistent with these instructions is equivalent to a repudiation of Christianity. And because such people sin against what they know, they are worse than a nonbeliever *(an infidel)*.

The modern availability of pensions, insurance, social security, welfare, and retirement centers (mentioned with v. 3 earlier) causes us some challenges in applying this passage. These systems of support allow many seniors to maintain independent living. As much as possible, this should be honored.

The time may come, however, when hard decisions have to be made. When possible, elderly or indigent relatives can be taken into a family member's home. But there are circumstances where this is not possible or advisable. Assisted living and nursing care sometimes can be administered only through proper facilities. Placing loved ones in a care center or seeing their needs supplemented by government agencies

---

Home Daily Bible Readings

Monday, Jan. 23—God Loves Righteousness and Justice (Psalm 33:1-5)

Tuesday, Jan. 24—Show Justice, Integrity, Righteousness, and Mercy (Proverbs 28:4-13)

Wednesday, Jan. 25—Jesus Demands Justice, Mercy, and Faith (Matthew 23:23-28)

Thursday, Jan. 26—Mercy Triumphs over Judgment (James 2:8-13)

Friday, Jan. 27—Show Mercy to All Believers (1 Timothy 5:1-8)

Saturday, Jan. 28—Show Justice to the Widows (1 Timothy 5:9-16)

Sunday, Jan. 29—Show Justice to the Elders (1 Timothy 5:17-25)

does not relieve family members of responsibility of demonstrating financial and emotional support. [See question #2, page 219.] Churches demonstrate their appreciation for the lives of faithful servants by including Christian retirement homes in their budgets.

III. Honor for Elders
(1 Timothy 5:17-20)
A. Worthy of Support (vv. 17, 18)

17. Let the elders that rule well be counted worthy of double honor, especially they who labor in the word and doctrine.

Paul now specifies the regard in which *elders that rule well* are to be held. We know, of course, that elders serve as they are able and as time permits. A few elders are able to *labor* extensively *in the word and doctrine*, and they do a great job. Praise God for both part-time and full-time elders!

Some elders may no longer be in the workplace. They may have retired from occupations or livelihoods in order to serve full time in visitation, teaching, and preaching. Thoughtful churches can offer to subsidize the retirement income of such elders. Paul justifies such compensation by citing two biblical illustrations, as we see next.

18. For the Scripture saith, Thou shalt not muzzle the ox that treadeth out the corn. And, The laborer is worthy of his reward.

The first quote is from Deuteronomy 25:4. Paul also cites this same passage in 1 Corinthians 9:9 to justify his own right to receive support. Oxen are allowed to feed while they work. Thus they participate in the fruit of their labor.

The second citation is from Jesus. It concerns support for His disciples as they labor (Luke 10:7). Elders who rule well should be honored in this way. [See question #3, page 219.]

Double Honor

Numerous individuals have been honored throughout history, and we celebrate their achievements. But most have been honored for only one specific area of expertise. Perhaps this area has been in athletics, politics, business success, or military leadership. Even more impressive, however, are the individuals who have achieved success in two or more fields. They are worthy of double honor.

Eddie Rickenbacker was a race car driver who became a famous ace pilot in World War I and then the president of Eastern Air Lines. Benjamin Franklin was an inventor, a businessman, and a successful diplomat. Michelangelo was outstanding as both a painter and a sculptor. George Washington Carver was an outstanding college professor whose work also resulted in hundreds of uses for the peanut. John Glenn was an astronaut who served four terms in the U.S. Senate. George Washington was an outstanding military leader who became the greatest of American presidents. The list could go on and on.

Paul's comment, however, applies particularly to elders. Serving well as an elder is a significant achievement in itself and is certainly worthy of honor. But those who also serve in a more focused ministry "in the word and doctrine" are worthy of double honor. Does your church follow this pattern? —J. B. N.

B. Accusations Against Elders (vv. 19, 20)

19. Against an elder receive not an accusation, but before two or three witnesses.

Men who have the responsibility of oversight frequently become targets of criticism. A man's reputation can be destroyed so easily. So any accusation must be proven to be true by *two or three* credible *witnesses*. This helps avoid a miscarriage of justice (Deuteronomy 19:15; Matthew 18:16). [See question #4, page 219.]

20. Them that sin rebuke before all, that others also may fear.

If the charges are proven to be true, action must be taken. The church's credibility is at stake. Since an elder is elected by the congregation (in most cases), it has a right to hear the charges, the proof, and to take appropriate action. In modern terminology, due process is to be followed.

Any church discipline procedure, whether or not the accused is an elder, presupposes that every effort has been made first to bring the person to repentance (Matthew 18:15; 2 Corinthians 2:5-8). When a part of our body is diseased, we don't amputate immediately. First we do a diagnosis. We do everything within our power to restore or salvage it. But if it defies healing, and if its continuing existence threatens the survival of the body, then we amputate as a last resort. The scriptural procedure is outlined by Jesus in Matthew 18:15-17 and by Paul in 1 Corinthians 5. If the *sin* is public, the *rebuke* must be public *(before all)* for the church to maintain credibility. The example is a warning to others.

IV. Notes to Timothy (1 Timothy 5:21-25)
A. Partiality Forbidden (v. 21)

21. I charge thee before God, and the Lord Jesus Christ, and the elect angels, that thou observe these things without preferring one before another, doing nothing by partiality.

Administering justice is a serious matter. Of necessity it must be done impartially. *God, and the Lord Jesus Christ, and the elect angels* watch our actions. We will be held accountable. God does not like dishonest scales (see Leviticus 19:36; Proverbs 11:1; Micah 6:11). This especially applies to the scales of justice (compare Deuteronomy 1:17; 16:19; Proverbs 24:23).

Favoritism can destroy a church family the same as it can our earthly families (examples: Genesis 25:28; 37:3, 4). A leadership's judgments and actions are not to be based upon friendships, personality, position, or wealth, but on the basis of what is right and wrong.

B. Laying on of Hands Restricted (v. 22a)

22a. Lay hands suddenly on no man.

The laying on of *hands* is an issue of setting someone apart for an office or certain duties of the church (compare Acts 6:6; 13:3). This is not to be done hastily or *suddenly,* as ordination is based on a person's demonstrated spiritual growth (compare 1 Timothy 3:6; also see p. 196).

C. Purity Mandated (v. 22b)

22b. Neither be partaker of other men's sins: keep thyself pure.

Timothy also is told not to participate in anyone's unworthy conduct. A leader is to be *pure* or circumspect in all behavior.

D. Advice Offered (v. 23)

23. Drink no longer water, but use a little wine for thy stomach's sake and thine often infirmities.

We can only speculate about this parenthetical statement regarding Timothy's health. It may be connected to the admonition *keep thyself pure* in verse 22. Paul was concerned that Timothy keep himself physically fit so he could serve effectively.

This passage has been used as a proof text to justify moderate consumption of alcoholic beverages. However, insistence on exercising our "rights" in this area may disregard the important principle of foregoing "rights" for the sake of another person who may be watching our example. For in-depth study of this vital principle, read Romans 14 and 1 Corinthians 8, 9.

The most that can be assumed here is that Paul's recommendation is for medicinal purposes only *(thy stomach's sake).* There is also the question as to whether the *little wine* Paul recommends could intoxicate. Today we have other medications for gastrointestinal problems. [See question #5, page 219.]

Post this visual as you ask "Whom do you hesitate to shake hands with out of favoritism? Why?"

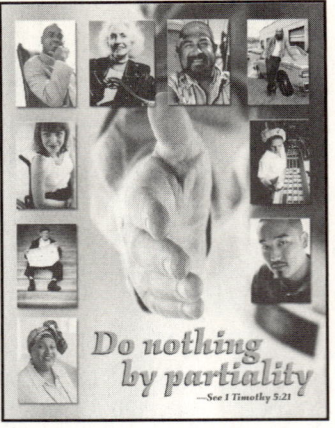

Visual for lesson 9

E. Actions Recognized (vv. 24, 25)

24. Some men's sins are open beforehand, going before to judgment; and some men they follow after.

The *sins* of *some* are very obvious, aren't they? A flagrantly sinful lifestyle obviously disqualifies a person for consideration to be a church leader.

In others, the sins are not so obvious. They may even be cleverly concealed. A modern example would be surfing the Internet in private to lust after pornographic images. Yet the Scripture says, "Be sure your sin will find you out" (Numbers 32:23). When Timothy refrains from laying on hands too soon to ordain elders (1 Timothy 5:22), he is allowing time for secret sins to surface.

25. Likewise also the good works of some are manifest beforehand; and they that are otherwise cannot be hid.

The same principle is true for *the good works of some.* Good works commend a person. Christian attitudes and conduct stand out. Even good deeds done in secret commend the person doing them; God will make sure of that (Matthew 6:3, 4). People respect integrity and credibility.

Conclusion
A. Delay of Game

In sports, a person or team can be penalized for "delay of game." By contrast, Paul's instruction is to allow enough time to pass to observe attitude, character, lifestyle, and commitment to the Lord's work before setting a person apart for the responsibility of leadership. "Wherefore by their fruits ye shall know them" (Matthew 7:20; compare Galatians 5:22, 23).

A church ignores God's instruction in the selection of leadership at its peril. No church will rise higher than its leadership. A congregation with godly leadership has a God-given gift; it should respect, encourage, support, and follow that leading.

B. Prayer

Father, we thank You for godly men who are willing to answer the high calling of eldership in Your church. Bless them and grant them the wisdom and insight that will enable them to administer the affairs of the church with justice and mercy. In Jesus' name we ask it, amen.

C. Thought to Remember

"Therefore all things whatsoever ye would that men should do to you, do ye even so to them: for this is the law and the prophets" (Matthew 7:12).

Learning by Doing

This section contains an alternative lesson plan emphasizing learning activities. Classes desiring such student involvement will find these suggestions helpful.

Learning Goals

After participating in this lesson, each student will be able to:

1. Describe some ways that Christians are to treat one another.
2. Give an example of how his or her church has honored its older (and perhaps needier) members and how it has recognized its leaders.
3. State one way he or she will honor an elderly Christian or dedicated leader this week.

Into the Lesson

Purchase candies wrapped with Christian sayings or Bible verses. Distribute one piece to each class member as he or she arrives. Instruct students not to eat their candies.

Once everyone is seated, say, "I want you to give your candy to another class member." After they have done so, say, "How Christians treat other Christians is the theme of today's study. Of course, our text is about more than just giving treats to one another. It is about how Christians treat one another in every aspect of life. Let's look at our text in 1 Timothy 5:1-8, 17-25."

Into the Word

Recruit two class members to represent the concepts of justice and mercy as they present the two monologues below. Prepare a label for each volunteer to wear. One label should have the word *JUSTICE* and the other *MERCY*. Give your recruits their monologues early enough that each can read through it before presenting it.

JUSTICE: "I am an elusive ideal. Though many peoples and nations avow allegiance to me, I am all too seldom seen. Many sins attack me: envy, greed, prejudice, lying, and self-centeredness. I am often pictured as a blindfolded lady, carrying scales of balance above my head.

"Fair and equal treatment is my intent. But when flawed humans step into my presence, they seek to warp the balance in my weights. The laws of God established me; the laws of humanity either protect me or annul me. Ultimately, only God has the knowledge of humanity's affairs and an individual's heart clearly enough to make certain that I am properly administered. And He will. I am *Justice*. I am an elusive ideal."

MERCY: "I am a most desired and a desirable presence. The sins of which my associate, Justice, speaks make me absolutely essential. Justice may make things fair, but I make life bearable and delightful.

"Those who sense my presence are those who sense the weaknesses of us all. Those who understand me know that I am from the heart of a loving God. Those who deny me deny that God exists or deny that He is anything but an indifferent, or even fiendish, creator. Ultimately, only those who love as God loves can show me in their words and behaviors. I am *Mercy*. I am a most desired and most desirable presence."

After the monologues, relate the ideas to the admonitions that Paul makes in 1 Timothy 5:1-8, 17-25. Have the text read aloud and use the following questions in your discussion.

1. How do verses 1 and 2 tell us to treat people? *Note that neither age nor gender should negate justice.*

2. How do Paul's words regarding widows in verses 3-6 maintain a concept of justice? *Note that personal responsibility is a component of justice.*

3. How does providing for one's own family (verse 8) relate to justice? *Note that justice involves moral decisions as well as legal ones.*

4. In verses 17 and 18, how is justice shown?

5. In verse 20, what role does justice play in church discipline?

6. How do the sins mentioned in the justice monologue interfere with justice in relationships? How do the principles of justice and mercy relate to verses 22 and 24?

Add other questions that you see as important for discussing the text and the dual concepts of justice and mercy.

Into Life

Distribute small slips of paper. Ask students to write the name of a widow they believe deserves congregational support. On the other side ask the students to write the name of an elder they believe merits a financial gift for special services to the local body of Christ. Say that you will tally the recommendations and address a letter to the church leadership noting the class's recommendations. Collect and make the recommendations as confidentially as the setting allows.

Let's Talk It Over

These questions are designed to promote discussion of the lesson. The answers here are only discussion starters. Let your class talk it over from there.

1. How can the church be selective with benevolence without creating offense?

The earliest church apparently had an assistance policy that excluded those whose families could help. Such a system reflects a commitment to thoughtful, faithful stewardship. There may have been complaints. But if the policy was applied consistently, no objection could be justified.

When widows, widowers, or aged couples exhaust their personal resources, then children and other family members should step up to provide for their needy relatives. That principle must be taught to believers to promote understanding and willing compliance within the household of faith. A written "benevolence policy" can help churches avoid complaints of being arbitrary, inconsistent, or uncaring as they selectively help.

2. Considering the availability of government assistance and megachurch resources today, how does a Christian know when it's time to ask for help in caring for an elderly parent?

Motive is important. One is not to ask for help merely to avoid expending personal financial assets or the assets of the parents. One who asks for help because he or she views the parent as an inconvenience or nuisance needs to pray for a different attitude!

On the other hand, some well-meaning Christians take 1 Timothy 5:8 to such an extreme that they do not ask for outside assistance under any circumstances. But requesting assistance is not sinful if a person has tried to apply 1 Timothy 5:8 to the best of his or her ability. Christians and their congregations should support faith-based benevolent institutions with generous contributions that will keep subsidy accounts solvent.

3. Greater numbers of paid staff and paid elders in a church mean less money available for missions, building programs, benevolence, etc. Or does it? What's the balance here?

With the growth of a church usually comes the hiring of additional staff members. These paid leaders often oversee various specialized ministries. Although the church is a volunteer organization, it will need more leaders to organize, train, and encourage the volunteers as it grows. Some suggest a general rule of one paid staff person for every 100 attendees. But there are churches with twice that, or more.

An option for some churches could be to retain greater numbers of part-time or bivocational leaders and fewer full-time staff members. The touchstone for such decisions should be the Great Commission in Matthew 28:19, 20. "What staffing arrangement will most help us to fulfill that command?" is a question that should be asked.

4. How should you respond to someone who criticizes a church elder? What are the different reactions you can expect to your response? What do those reactions say about the critic?

Criticisms of church leaders that are not handled according to biblical guidelines can become divisive gossip. Gently suggest that the person voicing the complaint consult the scriptural pattern for resolving conflict in Matthew 18:15-20.

How the person reacts to your suggestion can reveal true motives. Sometimes a critic merely is trying to line up support for a predetermined plan to change the church's leadership in some way. A person with a sincere concern will show interest in your suggestion. You can offer to study that passage together. A person with less noble motives, however, may just walk away with a shrug. Pray for such a person!

5. Must Christians be teetotalers, abstaining from alcoholic beverages? Why, or why not?

The Bible condemns drunkenness (Ephesians 5:18), but not drinking in moderation. But many Christians feel that the requirement to "abstain from all appearance of evil" (1 Thessalonians 5:22) means to forego alcohol since its use is associated with many evils (compare 1 Peter 4:3).

Paul writes that, "All things are lawful unto me, but all things are not expedient" (1 Corinthians 6:12). Since consumption of alcohol can place a stumblingblock in the paths of others who see our example, many Christians conclude that use of alcoholic beverages is not expedient for them. (The issue of eating meat sacrificed to idols in 1 Corinthians 8 offers parallels.)

February 5
Lesson 10

Be True to Your Christian Heritage

DEVOTIONAL READING: 2 Thessalonians 2:13-17.

BACKGROUND SCRIPTURE: 2 Timothy 1.

PRINTED TEXT: 2 Timothy 1:3-14.

2 Timothy 1:3-14

3 I thank God, whom I serve from my forefathers with pure conscience, that without ceasing I have remembrance of thee in my prayers night and day;

4 Greatly desiring to see thee, being mindful of thy tears, that I may be filled with joy;

5 When I call to remembrance the unfeigned faith that is in thee, which dwelt first in thy grandmother Lois, and thy mother Eunice; and I am persuaded that in thee also.

6 Wherefore I put thee in remembrance, that thou stir up the gift of God, which is in thee by the putting on of my hands.

7 For God hath not given us the spirit of fear; but of power, and of love, and of a sound mind.

8 Be not thou therefore ashamed of the testimony of our Lord, nor of me his prisoner: but be thou partaker of the afflictions of the gospel according to the power of God;

9 Who hath saved us, and called us with a holy calling, not according to our works, but according to his own purpose and grace, which was given us in Christ Jesus before the world began;

10 But is now made manifest by the appearing of our Saviour Jesus Christ, who hath abolished death, and hath brought life and immortality to light through the gospel:

11 Whereunto I am appointed a preacher, and an apostle, and a teacher of the Gentiles.

12 For the which cause I also suffer these things: nevertheless I am not ashamed; for I know whom I have believed, and am persuaded that he is able to keep that which I have committed unto him against that day.

13 Hold fast the form of sound words, which thou hast heard of me, in faith and love which is in Christ Jesus.

14 That good thing which was committed unto thee keep by the Holy Ghost which dwelleth in us.

GOLDEN TEXT: I call to remembrance the unfeigned faith that is in thee, which dwelt first in thy grandmother Lois, and thy mother Eunice; and I am persuaded that in thee also.—2 Timothy 1:5.

> God's Commitment—Our Response
> Unit 3: Faithful Followers, Faithful Leaders
> (Lessons 10-13)

Lesson Aims

After participating in this lesson, each student will be able to:

1. Identify some ways that Paul, Lois, and Eunice influenced Timothy's faith.
2. Explain how Paul's mentoring of Timothy can be a pattern for his or her church today.
3. Develop a plan for the week ahead to guard sound doctrine in his or her life.

Lesson Outline

INTRODUCTION
    A. The Teacher Who Made a Difference
    B. Lesson Background
 I. JOY OF A TEACHER (2 Timothy 1:3, 4)
    A. Proud to Pray for You (v. 3)
    B. Thrilled to See You (v. 4)
 II. FAITH OF GENERATIONS (2 Timothy 1:5-12)
    A. Foremothers of Faith (v. 5)
      Making a Difference
    B. Gift of God (vv. 6, 7)
    C. Power of God (vv. 8-10)
    D. Ministry Without Shame (vv. 11, 12)
III. PATTERN TO FOLLOW (2 Timothy 1:13, 14)
    A. Standard Bearer (v. 13)
      No Improvement Needed
    B. Treasure Guardian (v. 14)
CONCLUSION
    A. Training Our Successors
    B. Overcoming Family Unfaithfulness
    C. Prayer
    D. Thought to Remember

Introduction

A. The Teacher Who Made a Difference

Do you remember a teacher who had a huge, positive impact on your life? Recently I ran across the name of my junior high school principal. I don't remember much that I learned in junior high or even many of my teachers, but I remembered this man instantly. I remember sitting in his office, having been sent there as a consequence of some stupid action. I remember that he dealt with me firmly but patiently. He talked frankly about my future goals. He took a special interest in me, a scrawny 13-year-old, and he challenged me to be a better person, to dream big, to work hard. What he was doing was investing a bit of himself in me. He was more teacher than principal in these encounters.

This man was not satisfied with being the principal of a small-town junior high school. He eventually became the superintendent of the school district and then the State Superintendent for Public Instruction. After a successful tenure in this office, he "retired" and was elected to be a state senator, an office he still holds.

I took the time to write him a note and tell him that his pupil had turned out OK. I thanked him for his patience and interest in me so many years ago. As we grow older, are we able to identify those whom *we* have influenced in positive ways?

B. Lesson Background

As far as we know, the apostle Paul had no children and was never married. We do know that Paul had a sister and nephew, so he did play the role of uncle (Acts 23:16). We also know little about Paul's relationship to his father. We know that his father provided him with an excellent education, with a trade (tent-making), and with Roman citizenship.

Paul noted that he had grown up in Jerusalem under the tutelage of a great rabbi, Gamaliel (Acts 22:3). It is likely that Gamaliel had served as a substitute father for young Paul, if indeed Paul's formative years were spent in the temple city far from his family's home in Tarsus. Thus Paul well knew that the teacher-student bond could be more than a professional relationship. Teachers produce disciple-children. Teachers bear both joy and responsibility for the careers of these "offspring."

While Paul saw himself as the "father" of his converts (compare 1 Corinthians 4:15), he considered Timothy to be his "son" is a unique way. He had taken a personal, paternal responsibility for Timothy's circumcision, because Timothy's natural father was not a Jew. Paul's role of substitute father seemed so appropriate that Paul convinced Timothy's mother to let the boy travel with him, even though Timothy probably was no more than a teenager (Acts 16:1-3).

In this week's lesson we see Paul reflecting on this relationship from the vantage point of many years of fruitful association with Timothy. The book of 2 Timothy was written while Paul was in prison in Rome (2 Timothy 1:8, 16, 17), probably awaiting his execution (2 Timothy 4:6). Soon there would be no teacher to guide the student. Yet Paul was confident that Timothy was ready to assume full responsibility; Timothy was his prized pupil, his son in the faith, his joy and hope for the future.

I. Joy of a Teacher
(2 Timothy 1:3, 4)
A. Proud to Pray for You (v. 3)

3. I thank God, whom I serve from my forefathers with pure conscience, that without ceasing I have remembrance of thee in my prayers night and day.

Paul begins by reminding Timothy of his own rich heritage of faith. Paul's service to God is derived from his spiritual ancestors or *forefathers*.

We learn two important things from Paul by analyzing this expression. First, he sees no conflict between his service to God as a preacher of the gospel and the service to God given by ancestral Jews before Christ came. In other words, there is no necessary conflict between past service to God under the Old Testament and current service to God under the New Testament. In both cases true service to God is motivated by faith and love.

Second, we learn the importance of faith that is passed on from one generation to the next. Paul did not discover service to God by chance or accident. He was taught it and saw it modeled by his teachers. [See question #1, page 228.]

B. Thrilled to See You (v. 4)

4. Greatly desiring to see thee, being mindful of thy tears, that I may be filled with joy.

Isn't it amazing that in our world of instant communication, cell phones, and e-mail, we still long to see our loved ones in person? There is no substitute for face-to-face smiling, laughing, and hugging of ones whom we cherish! We will endure long plane flights or hours of driving just to spend a few days with friends or relatives.

Paul is no different. The trip from Rome to Ephesus would be a short plane hop today, but it is a journey of many weeks in the first century. Furthermore, the only hope Paul has for seeing Timothy is if the young man comes to Rome. Paul is in prison and travel is impossible for him. Paul desperately wants Timothy to come to Rome so he can see him one last time (2 Timothy 4:9).

Today, we who are able to get out and about should not forget the joy that a visit to a housebound friend can bring. A note or card is fine as far as it goes, but dropping in may bring great joy to a lonely person.

Visual for lesson 10

Start a discussion by repeating the question on this visual. Follow by asking "How?"

II. Faith of Generations
(2 Timothy 1:5-12)
A. Foremothers of Faith (v. 5)

5. When I call to remembrance the unfeigned faith that is in thee, which dwelt first in thy grandmother Lois, and thy mother Eunice; and I am persuaded that in thee also.

Acts 16:1 tells us that Timothy's *mother* was a Jewish woman who had become a Christian believer. They lived in Lystra, a city evangelized by Paul and Barnabas on the first missionary journey (see Acts 14:6-21). When Paul returned (now with Silas, perhaps three or four years later), he was impressed with Timothy. Luke, the author of Acts, describes Timothy as a disciple (Acts 16:1).

The verse before us fills in more details about Timothy's mother and *grandmother*. Acts 16:3 tells us that Timothy's father was not a Jew. How had *Lois* allowed daughter *Eunice* to marry a pagan Gentile? We do not know. We do know that the worship of the Greek gods was strong in Timothy's hometown of Lystra, as it supported a temple and a priest for Zeus (Acts 14:13).

Timothy, then, did not grow up with the benefit of a father to care for his proper religious development. These two godly women were the ones who had insisted that he know the Jewish Scriptures, our Old Testament (2 Timothy 3:15). They were concerned about more than his physical food and clothing!

Many preachers and missionaries today readily confess that the influence of a mother or grandmother was a key to their faith and commitment to ministry. These are the mothers who made sure their sons went to Sunday school, learned how to pray, memorized Bible verses, and lived by faith daily. Too often these women received little or no support from their husbands in this regard. Where would the church be without these grand foremothers in the faith! [See question #2, page 228.]

MAKING A DIFFERENCE

The names of John and Charles Wesley are familiar to many Christians. Charles was a prolific writer of hymns, including such standards as "Christ the Lord Is Risen Today," "Hark! the Herald Angels Sing," and "Love Divine, All Loves Excelling." John was a great eighteenth-century gospel preacher whose influence is felt yet today. Their father, though a minister of the gospel, was not the dominant influence in their lives. Instead, it was their mother, Susanna, who molded their character.

Susanna bore 19 children in the span of 19 years. Nine died in infancy. In spite of difficult circumstances, she was committed to caring for her family. She started a school for her children, though resources were limited. She said her purpose was "the saving of their souls," so academics never took priority over instruction in God's Word. Because Susanna wanted to develop a personal relationship with each child, she scheduled a private appointment with each of them once a week for encouragement. These bonds of faith and love helped them survive continual hardships.

Many celebrities from the popular culture are having a profound influence upon the children of today. When a mother abandons her role as modeled by Susanna Wesley, Eunice, and Lois, these wrong influences can win the day. What can your church do to encourage Christian mothers in their role of spiritual formation of children? —A. E. A.

B. Gift of God (vv. 6, 7)

6, 7. Wherefore I put thee in remembrance, that thou stir up the gift of God, which is in thee by the putting on of my hands. For God hath not given us the spirit of fear; but of power, and of love, and of a sound mind.

What is this *gift of God* that Paul gave Timothy by laying his *hands* on him? We should confess that we do not completely understand the nature of the specific gift or the significance of the laying on of hands. However, we do understand some of it.

Laying on of hands refers to the physical touching that accompanies a ceremony of commissioning a person for a task of ministry on behalf of the church (compare Acts 6:6; 13:3; Hebrews 6:2). This ceremony signifies the granting of authority necessary for accomplishing the task.

Today, this is usually part of an ordination service in which the elders of a congregation formally charge a person for ministry. There is nothing magical about this ceremony. The elders have no supernatural power that zaps from their hands to the person's shoulders. Supernatural power comes only from God and is not controlled by human beings.

We know also that this gift to Timothy is a type of empowerment (compare 1 Timothy 4:14). Timothy does not have a gift that causes him to *fear*. We do not need cowards in ministry! The authority given to Timothy is characterized by *power*, *love*, and *a sound mind*. Sloth and neglect will make us weak, selfish, undisciplined, and ineffective in ministry. Like Timothy, all disciples occasionally need to be called to accountability, to *stir up* our commitment. The power of the Holy Spirit is always available to us. We are the ones who quench this fire (1 Thessalonians 5:19). [See question #3, page 228.]

C. Power of God (vv. 8-10)

8-10. Be not thou therefore ashamed of the testimony of our Lord, nor of me his prisoner: but be thou partaker of the afflictions of the gospel according to the power of God; who hath saved us, and called us with a holy calling, not according to our works, but according to his own purpose and grace, which was given us in Christ Jesus before the world began; but is now made manifest by the appearing of our Saviour Jesus Christ, who hath abolished death, and hath brought life and immortality to light through the gospel.

Rather than operate from a position of fear or cowardice, Paul admonishes Timothy to not be *ashamed*. Jesus had prophesied that some disci-

> **How to Say It**
>
> BARNABAS. *Bar*-nuh-bus.
> EPHESUS. *Ef*-uh-sus.
> EUNICE. U-*nye*-see or *U*-nis.
> GAMALIEL. Guh-*may*-lih-ul or Guh-*may*-lee-al.
> GENTILES. *Jen*-tiles.
> JERUSALEM. Juh-*roo*-suh-lem.
> LYSTRA. *Liss*-truh.
> PHARISEES. *Fair*-ih-seez.
> RABBI. *rab*-eye.
> SILAS. *Sigh*-luss.
> TARSUS. *Tar*-sus.
> ZEUS. Zoose.

ples would be ashamed of Him (Mark 8:38). This is a lack of courage to take a bold stand for their *Saviour*. To be ashamed of the gospel, then, is to deny one's faith in Christ and His power to save (see Romans 1:16).

Paul mentions two areas that Timothy must address fearlessly: his *testimony of our Lord* and the fact that Paul, his mentor and spiritual father, is a jailbird. While Timothy's life probably was not threatened because of his preaching, Paul's was. Paul could have denied Jesus, begged for the intervention of the non-Christian Jewish leaders of Rome, and had his life spared. But he didn't. The time for faithful preaching is not determined by political climate or personal safety.

Paul goes on to give several essential elements to this fearlessly proclaimed message. First, the entire plan of salvation has been designed intentionally by God. We are not part of some make-it-up-as-you-go endeavor on God's part. God knows what He is doing.

Second, God has called us to be a part of this plan. This is a holy and noble calling, the summons to God's mighty service. God does not need us to accomplish His purposes, but God will use us powerfully if we commit to His service.

Third, the power of God's plan has been demonstrated in the life and resurrection of Jesus. His resurrection *abolished death* and shows us the way to salvation. This is precisely what Jesus saves us from: the terror and hopelessness of inevitable death (1 Corinthians 15:55).

D. Ministry Without Shame (vv. 11, 12)

11, 12. Whereunto I am appointed a preacher, and an apostle, and a teacher of the Gentiles. For the which cause I also suffer these things: nevertheless I am not ashamed; for I know whom I have believed, and am persuaded that he is able to keep that which I have committed unto him against that day.

Paul continues his theme of freedom from shame, from cowardice. He is beyond embarrassment and timidity.

A church in my area has the motto, "The Fellowship of the Unashamed." This does not mean there are no shameful things in their lives. It means they are committed to never being ashamed of being Christians. Christians in Western democracies do not live under the threat of death (unlike some countries). But many such Christians live with constant ridicule, belittlement, and pressure to compromise faith. It feels like it would be easier to keep our faith very private and personal.

Paul knows, however, that a hidden faith is an ashamed faith. This is why a good Jew like Paul —a Pharisee, a Hebrew of the Hebrews (Philippians 3:5), a former student of Rabbi Gamaliel— could accept shamelessly his call to be an evangelizer, *apostle*, and *teacher of the Gentiles*. [See question #4, page 228.]

To keep that which I have committed is literally "to safeguard my deposit." This is Paul's investment of biblical training in Timothy. Paul is confident that this "deposit" will be a credit on his account on *that day*, the day of reckoning or judgment. He is confident not only in Jesus but also in Timothy.

III. Pattern to Follow (2 Timothy 1:13, 14)

A. Standard Bearer (v. 13)

13. Hold fast the form of sound words, which thou hast heard of me, in faith and love which is in Christ Jesus.

Timothy's job is not to tinker with Paul's gospel message. Rather, Timothy's job is to pass along that message faithfully. He will be able to do this only if he holds *fast* to that message himself. That's our job too!

NO IMPROVEMENT NEEDED

Tim Taylor, the character in the long-running TV series *Home Improvement*, was always trying to tweak things to make them better. Whether it be putting a lawn-mower engine on a garbage disposal or turbo charging the engine of a garden tractor, his goal was to improve everything. Tim's recurring theme was to give "more power" to whatever he was working on. But more power usually resulted in hilarious problems!

The world is filled with people who want to practice "Scripture Improvement," but there's nothing funny about this. Many of these folks are well-meaning, sincere Christians. Others want to use Christianity to further a certain agenda. In either case, to change Scripture to make it say what it does not say is to pave a road to ruin, not relevancy. One thinks, for example, of attempts to reinterpret the Bible in order to give homosexuality a stamp of approval. When truth is undermined, collapse is not far away (Daniel 8:12).

Paul's words of warning to Timothy about maintaining soundness of doctrine ring as true today as they did in the first century. It is the task of Christians to hold on to this truth and spread this truth. It is only the truth of Jesus Christ that provides us anything solid upon which to stand for eternal life. —A. E. A.

B. Treasure Guardian (v. 14)

14. That good thing which was committed unto thee keep by the Holy Ghost which dwelleth in us.

Should we use or hoard? Several years ago, I ran across a beautiful plush lamb that had been given to me as a baby. It was so fine that my wonderful, conscientious mother had hidden it to save it from baby drool and dirt. But bugs had gotten into the box and destroyed the once beautiful lamb. Her noble intention to safeguard something of beauty had resulted in losing the item without its ever being used.

When it comes to the grand doctrines of the gospel, should they be safeguarded or used? Can we trust new Christians with our truths? Won't they be distorted, misused, and lost?

The answer is that we must do both. On the one hand, we always must contend for the faith (Jude 3) and measure what we teach by the apostles' teaching as found in the New Testament. This body of teaching was committed to Timothy by Paul. It has now been entrusted to us.

On the other hand, we must encourage new converts to begin learning and using Christian doctrine immediately. As Alexander Campbell (1788–1866) said, "Doctrine is what you live." It is in the use of the Bible that it lives and breathes. [See question #5, page 228.]

Conclusion

A. Training Our Successors

Veterans' organizations that are built around World War II service members have fallen on very hard times in America. Their few remaining members are old and ill. Their ranks are dwindling rapidly as more than 1,000 veterans of that era die every day. They all will be gone in a few years. The church too is always one generation removed from extinction. Without constant replenishment of its members, it will die.

Research by the Barna Group tells us that the average person's moral foundation is in place by age 9. Most people have come to lifelong faith conclusions by age 13, and most adult leaders in churches were heavily involved in training and ministry when children. Yet many church programs today are designed to serve adults. Aging "Baby Boomers" (those born between 1946 and 1964) clamor for worship according to their tastes. The "Gen Xers" (who are in their thirties) want churches that are responsive to their needs.

We cannot ignore these voices, but the leaders of tomorrow's church are found among our preteens of today. Are we investing funds, time, and our very best people in training children? That "deposit on account" today will have a rich yield of Timothys and Timothyettes for the future.

B. Overcoming Family Unfaithfulness

Where would Timothy have been without Paul as a mentor? He probably would not have

---

Home Daily Bible Readings

Monday, Jan. 30—God Gives the Heritage (Psalm 111)
Tuesday, Jan. 31—We Can Lose Our Heritage (Jeremiah 17:1-8)
Wednesday, Feb. 1—Stand Fast, Hold Traditions (2 Thessalonians 2:13-17)
Thursday, Feb. 2—Timothy's Mother Was a Believer (Acts 16:1-5)
Friday, Feb. 3—Lois and Eunice Passed On Faith (2 Timothy 1:1-5)
Saturday, Feb. 4—Be Not Ashamed of Your Testimony (2 Timothy 1:6-10)
Sunday, Feb. 5—Hold Fast the Good Treasure Given You (2 Timothy 1:11-18)

any books with his name in the New Testament, but I suspect he would have turned out all right. I think he would have become a strong leader in the little church in Lystra, perhaps its preacher. Why? Because of the faith of his mother and his grandmother. When Paul came to town, it was their training that allowed Timothy to leave on his first missionary trip to Macedonia!

Modern families are often incomplete in some way. But inadequate families can be wholly adequate for raising godly adults if training in the Scriptures is prized and modeled. Sometimes this task falls upon the mother because there is no one else. In some cases this responsibility falls upon grandparents because the parents are absent. If you are in this situation, don't despair. God will strengthen, support, and honor you.

C. Prayer

God of truth, as You used Paul to pass on the heritage of Christian faith to Timothy, use us to train and encourage the Timothys and Timothyettes You send our way. May we never hoard the gospel, but share it freely. We pray in the name of our Savior, Jesus Christ, amen.

D. Thought to Remember

You never know which of the teens of today will grow up to be the preachers of tomorrow, so invest your life in as many as you can.

Learning by Doing

This section contains an alternative lesson plan emphasizing learning activities. Classes desiring such student involvement will find these suggestions helpful.

Learning Goals

After participating in this lesson, each student will be able to:

1. Identify some ways that Paul, Lois, and Eunice influenced Timothy's faith.
2. Explain how Paul's mentoring of Timothy can be a pattern for his or her church today.
3. Develop a plan for the week ahead to guard sound doctrine in his or her life.

Into the Lesson

If your class does not use the student book, prepare a handout as follows. At the top of the page, write the heading "My Faith Family Tree." Under it draw a large tree with several branches. Do not include leaves. Also prepare a handout described in the Into Life portion of the lesson, below.

Open the lesson by asking class members to write the names of people who have been significant in the development of their faith and their service to Jesus. They may write these names on branches or at the ends of the branches.

Next, encourage class members to select and circle one name they would like to share with the class (or a small group). They should tell how that person influenced or encouraged his or her faith or service to Christ.

Make the transition to Bible study by telling the class, "There is a young man in the Bible who would include the names Lois, Eunice, and Paul on his faith family tree. Who is he?" *(Timothy).* Say, "From Timothy's experience we will learn principles for passing our faith along to others."

Into the Word

Say, "God has blessed us with two wonderful institutions that are charged with passing along the faith: the family and the church. Either one may do the job. However, there is a special strength in being blessed with both institutions working toward that goal."

Divide the class into three or four groups of two to five people each. Additional groups may be added, duplicating the activities mentioned here. Give each group some poster board, markers, and printed instructions as follows:

Group #1: "Your charge is to read today's printed text and list every word or phrase that teaches something about passing along the faith. Make notes beside these words or phrases about lessons learned."

Group #2: "Read the text to discover a few clues about how families may accomplish the task of passing on the faith. List these on the poster board. From your experiences and knowledge, list additional tips or principles in bringing up children to know and serve the Lord."

Group #3: [If there are grandparents present in the class, you may wish to create a special group with this challenge.] "Read the text and discover clues about how grandparents may be important in passing along the faith to grandchildren. List these. From your experiences and observations, list additional ideas or tips in helping grandchildren discover the Lord."

Group #4: "Make two columns on your poster board with the headings 'Encouraging Children/Youth' and 'Encouraging Young Adults.' Read the text and write clues about how the church may encourage its younger people, whom we may call Timothys and Timothyettes. Drawing on your experiences and observations, add additional ideas about how the church may accomplish this goal."

Allow no more than 12 minutes for discussion. Then ask the groups to report their discoveries and suggestions. Write their ideas to the board as appropriate.

Into Life

Thank the class for the abundance of ideas shared today. Explain that you would like to give an opportunity for each person to encourage faith or leadership in one young person or young adult. Distribute a piece of stationery you have designed with the following headings at appropriate intervals on the page.

Dear _____,
  I wanted to send you this note because . . .
  I especially have noticed and appreciate this particular quality in you: . . .
  I would encourage you to . . .
          Yours in Christ, _____.

Ask class members to use this format or one of their own making. (This activity is also in the student book.)

Let's Talk It Over

These questions are designed to promote discussion of the lesson. The answers here are only discussion starters. Let your class talk it over from there.

1. The best Christian teachers and mentors excel in prayer, teaching ability, knowledge of the Scripture, "practicing what they preach," and simply being available. Is any attribute more important than any other? Explain.

Each attribute is important, although not every Christian teacher will be equally skilled or gifted in all the areas. Further, the age level or spiritual maturity of the one being taught or mentored can determine which attribute is most valuable at the time. For example, a mentor does not need to have a Ph.D. in knowledge of the Scripture in order to teach simple Bible truths to a 5-year-old!

We should note that every teacher can tap a great resource of strength and wisdom from the discipline of prayer. This is foundational. Jesus' prayers included specific intercession for His students (see John 17). Paul persistently prayed for those he mentored. Paul knew his gifts were from God, and he depended on the indwelling Spirit to make his teaching skills effective.

2. How can we honor our teachers and mentors? Or should we focus strictly on honoring God? Explain.

Giving eulogies at funerals is fine, but a better way to pay tribute to parents, teachers, and other mentors (living or dead) is for us to "practice what they preached." Living out Christian values that are passed on to us is the finest praise and respect we can show for these significant persons. We can use cards, e-mails, and telephone calls to express our appreciation for our teachers. But putting into action the lessons they taught us will prove to be their most satisfying reward.

We also honor our mentors when we pass on to our physical and spiritual descendants the Christian truths that we have learned. As we do we may discover that God is the one who actually is receiving the most honor!

3. How can we stir up our God-given gifts for Christian service?

Developing to full potential requires persistent effort. "Use it or lose it" applies here. Your spiritual gifts, skills, and abilities—music, speech, drama, witnessing, personal evangelism, discipling, etc.— will be stirred up by consistent use and sharpening. This sharpening includes rehearsing, performing, working, helping, learning, and serving.

But *motivation* for developing our gifts is an important starting point. Unless we allow the Spirit to motivate us, there will be no improvement. Do you ever stop and ponder how many people die every day only to enter a Christless eternity? We may well find the Spirit motivating us when we think from such a perspective.

4. What is the difference between fear and reserve? How do we take into account this difference among our fellow Christians?

Paul wanted Timothy to be bold in his ministry. In this light, Paul wrote, "God hath not given us the spirit of fear; but of power, and of love, and of a sound mind" (2 Timothy 1:7). "No Fear!" should be a Christian motto.

Even so, reserve and quietness are natural characteristics of some introverted personalities. That doesn't mean that the introverts are fearful. The reason one of your fellow Christians never speaks up in class may be that he or she is involved in deep thought. Such folks may not have on-the-spot verbal witnessing as a strength. Instead, they may be better at giving prepared talks or at writing. Boldness has more than one outlet!

5. What are some ways that you have found to "keep the faith"? How have you been able to "give it away" at the same time?

Answers here will be highly individual, so expect a wide-ranging discussion. If the discussion centers too much on vaguely "living out the faith," encourage students to be more specific. Are your students depending on their Christian lifestyles to be their only witness for Christ? What about "faith cometh by hearing, and hearing by the word of God" (Romans 10:17)?

Many have found that the only way to keep the truths of Christianity vibrant in their lives is to give those truths away. We also take care, however, to refresh and restore our faith on a regular basis. There are many ways to do this, but study of the Bible and pondering how it relates to culture is important. Don't become stagnant!

Develop Christian Character

February 12
Lesson 11

DEVOTIONAL READING: **Colossians 3:5-11.**

BACKGROUND SCRIPTURE: **2 Timothy 2.**

PRINTED TEXT: **2 Timothy 2:14-26.**

2 Timothy 2:14-26

14 Of these things put them in remembrance, charging them before the Lord that they strive not about words to no profit, but to the subverting of the hearers.

15 Study to show thyself approved unto God, a workman that needeth not to be ashamed, rightly dividing the word of truth.

16 But shun profane and vain babblings: for they will increase unto more ungodliness.

17 And their word will eat as doth a canker: of whom is Hymeneus and Philetus;

18 Who concerning the truth have erred, saying that the resurrection is past already; and overthrow the faith of some.

19 Nevertheless the foundation of God standeth sure, having this seal, The Lord knoweth them that are his. And, Let every one that nameth the name of Christ depart from iniquity.

20 But in a great house there are not only vessels of gold and of silver, but also of wood and of earth; and some to honor, and some to dishonor.

21 If a man therefore purge himself from these, he shall be a vessel unto honor, sanctified, and meet for the master's use, and prepared unto every good work.

22 Flee also youthful lusts: but follow righteousness, faith, charity, peace, with them that call on the Lord out of a pure heart.

23 But foolish and unlearned questions avoid, knowing that they do gender strifes.

24 And the servant of the Lord must not strive; but be gentle unto all men, apt to teach, patient;

25 In meekness instructing those that oppose themselves; if God peradventure will give them repentance to the acknowledging of the truth;

26 And that they may recover themselves out of the snare of the devil, who are taken captive by him at his will.

GOLDEN TEXT: Flee also youthful lusts: but follow righteousness, faith, charity, peace, with them that call on the Lord out of a pure heart.—2 Timothy 2:22.

> *God's Commitment—Our Response*
> Unit 3: Faithful Followers, Faithful Leaders
> (Lessons 10-13)

Lesson Aims

After participating in this lesson, each student will be able to:

1. Summarize Paul's advice to Timothy about the development of Christian character.
2. Identify an example of ungodly behavior that is just as prevalent today as it was in the first century.
3. Identify one ungodly behavior in his or her life to modify or eliminate.

Lesson Outline

INTRODUCTION
    A. The Surveillance Society
    B. Lesson Background
 I. WORD WRANGLING (2 Timothy 2:14-18)
    A. Ruining Listeners (v. 14)
    B. Ratified Explainer (v. 15)
    C. Rotten Talk (vv. 16-18)
      The Power of Words
 II. FIRM FOUNDATION (2 Timothy 2:19-21)
    A. God's Inscriptions (v. 19)
    B. Our Preparation (vv. 20, 21)
      Clean and Ready
 III. SATAN'S SNARE (2 Timothy 2:22-26)
    A. Fleeing and Pursuing (v. 22)
    B. Arguments and Instruction (vv. 23-25a)
    C. Truth and Escape (vv. 25b, 26)
CONCLUSION
    A. Godly Living for the Long Haul
    B. Controversies in the Church
    C. Prayer
    D. Thought to Remember

Introduction

A. The Surveillance Society

Privacy. It has been cherished by most people, even touted as a constitutional right in America and other countries. Yet technological advances and the pressure to thwart terrorists and criminals have eroded personal privacy enormously. We use the Internet, scarcely aware that every move we make is being tracked, often for commercial purposes. We send personal e-mails, usually forgetting that they all are preserved on a network server somewhere. We drive around town, oblivious to the intersection cameras that are capable of reading our license plates and tracking our movements.

We use our credit cards, disregarding the fact that this use provides a permanent record of our purchases. We talk on cell phones, failing to remember that these are open lines on the public airways, and anyone with the right equipment can listen. We make withdrawals at cash machines, unmindful that cameras are taping us during the transaction. We deposit our trash after eating at the fast food restaurant, unaware that the napkin bearing a trace of our saliva could be used to pinpoint us via DNA testing.

Our smallest actions seem to be noticed and recorded. Even so, we certainly are not to the extreme of George Orwell's book *1984*, which depicted government cameras in citizens' houses to track them 24 hours per day. On the other hand, the Bible consistently presents God as one who *is* aware of everything we think, say, and do. Nothing is hidden from Him. As the psalmist wrote, "Thou understandest my thought afar off. . . . and art acquainted with all my ways" (Psalm 139:2, 3).

So often we behave contrary to this reality, don't we? We do things that we know displease God and somehow believe that He doesn't notice or care. Today's lesson teaches us that there is no room for hidden evil in the life of a Christian disciple. While God is gracious to forgive our sins, He also expects our best efforts in the pursuit of godliness. God is not the only observer of our behavior. Particularly if we are teachers, our actions will teach as much as our words.

B. Lesson Background

This week we get a disturbing look at the troubles of the Ephesian church where Timothy ministered. It is disturbing because it seems too much like churches we have known. Teachers were leading believers astray with ridiculous, speculative doctrines. Most disturbing of these, for Paul, was a denial of future resurrection. Paul identifies the main perpetrators of this error by name: Hymeneus and Philetus. Hymeneus is known to us from 1 Timothy 1:19, 20, where he is described as having shipwrecked his faith, requiring that he be "delivered unto Satan" (that is, cut off from the church and its fellowship).

The church at Ephesus had its choice of many flavors of false doctrine (as do Christians today). First Timothy 1:3-7 does give us some of the elements of the particular false teaching at Ephesus. Paul indicated that it contained a Greek, pagan element because of its concern for mythology (v. 4). It also had Jewish elements because of its concern for genealogies and the Law (vv. 4, 7). The part that is repeated in today's Scripture, however, was its characteristic of speculation that led to endless, meaningless discussion (compare 1 Timothy 1:4, 6).

I. Word Wrangling
(2 Timothy 2:14-18)

A. Ruining Listeners (v. 14)

14. Of these things put them in remembrance, charging them before the Lord that they strive not about words to no profit, but to the subverting of the hearers.

The power of public speech is startling. In A.D. 1095, Pope Urban II gave a single, fiery speech that mobilized the gentry of Europe for the first crusade and radically changed the course of history. During World War II, the speeches of Adolf Hitler enflamed the patriotic passions of the German people for war, while the addresses of Winston Churchill gave the British people hope in their darkest days.

Paul well knows the power of speech. It can mobilize the masses for great good. It may also result in *the subverting of the hearers*. There is nothing more disillusioning to new converts than to see their leaders embroiled in public bickering. If Christianity is about love and forgiveness, about fellowship and charity, why do mature Christians *strive . . . about words to no profit?* Paul is not talking about shying away from confronting false doctrine. He is talking about the damage that quarreling causes. Paul also had to warn the Corinthians about quarreling (1 Corinthians 1:11; 3:3; 2 Corinthians 12:20).

B. Ratified Explainer (v. 15)

15. Study to show thyself approved unto God, a workman that needeth not to be ashamed, rightly dividing the word of truth.

Timothy needs to show himself *approved unto God* above all else. God is the intended audience. Timothy is not to seek Paul's approval, but God's. Paul gives Timothy three ways to reach the status of a Christian who has God's approval. First, Timothy is to *study*. The idea is that of diligent, persistent learning.

I have a motto that I have long used with my college students: "Whining is no substitute for hard work." Books are not understood unless carefully read. Classroom lectures are not comprehended unless the student listens and takes good notes. Written assignments are not profitable unless the student takes time to think and write clearly. Timothy will be studying mainly on his own, but it will still take hard work.

Second, Paul recommends that Timothy strive to be a *workman* who has nothing to fear from having his work scrutinized. This does not mean that Timothy is to reach a level where he knows everything and does everything right. Rather, it means he should be working to the extent that his effort is above criticism, and his performance is constantly improving. He is never to fake it.

Third, Paul defines for Timothy the primary object of his studies: he is to *rightly* divide *the word of truth*. This refers to the interpretation of Scripture. [See question #1, page 237.]

Another saying that I drill into my students is this: "Biblical interpretation is hard work." Truly grasping the meaning of Scripture involves wrestling with the text: reading, rereading, pondering, meditating, praying. Too many Christians have an unnecessarily shallow knowledge of the Bible simply because they have not invested themselves in learning its truths. They expect to be spoon-fed by the preacher every week. Paul calls us to work hard and enrich ourselves through ever expanding knowledge of God's word.

C. Rotten Talk (vv. 16-18)

16-18. But shun profane and vain babblings: for they will increase unto more ungodliness. And their word will eat as doth a canker: of

---

How to Say It

CORINTHIANS. Ko-*rin*-thee-unz (*th* as in *thin*).
EPHESIAN. Ee-*fee*-zhun.
EPHESUS. *Ef*-uh-sus.
HYMENEUS. Hi-meh-*nee*-us.
PHILETUS. Fuh-*lee*-tus.

whom is Hymeneus and Philetus; who concerning the truth have erred, saying that the resurrection is past already; and overthrow the faith of some.**

Perhaps Paul knows that Timothy's keen mind is drawn to debate theological issues. In the realm of debate, truth is not always the prize. Winning is! [See question #2, page 237.] Paul uses some very descriptive words at this point. *Profane and vain babblings* can be thought of as "irreverent and empty chattering." If we were forced to read a transcript of every word we uttered at the end of the day, what percentage would be classified "profane" and what percentage would be "pointless babble"?

Paul warns Timothy that this careless, worthless talk is a bad influence on others. He calls it *a canker*. It is like rotten flesh that endangers the entire body. The only solution for gangrene is to cut it off. Irreverent and empty babbling, especially concerning doctrinal matters, can lead to spiritual decay and rottenness.

Paul then gives Timothy an example to show just how serious this issue is. He names two false teachers in Ephesus, *Hymeneus and Philetus*, and identifies their main doctrinal error: *the resurrection* is already past. This doctrine is so important that Paul elsewhere spends a great deal of time discussing it (see 1 Corinthians 15).

THE POWER OF WORDS

A *malaprop* is an absurd misuse of words. Baseball legend Casey Stengel used this malaprop: "I want you all to line up in alphabetical order according to your size." Movie mogul Sam Goldwyn is quoted as saying, "A verbal contract isn't worth the paper it's written on" and "Don't pay any attention to the critics—don't even ignore them."

At one extreme, misuse of words can be downright humorous! But at the other extreme, misused words can wound and destroy. The old adage "Sticks and stones may break my bones, but words can never hurt me" is simply not true. Abusive words destroy families, subvert friendships, and ruin business partnerships.

When it comes to communicating the Word of God, our challenge is to take utmost care in using proper words in the proper contexts. To fail in this can have negative eternal consequences for those who hear. Also it can have bearing upon the one speaking the words. James 3:1 offers the caution that teachers "shall receive the greater condemnation" because of what they may wrongly teach. Choosing the best words and the right words is vital in Christian communication. How are you doing in this regard?   —A. E. A.

II. Firm Foundation
(2 Timothy 2:19-21)
A. God's Inscriptions (v. 19)

19. Nevertheless the foundation of God standeth sure, having this seal, The Lord knoweth them that are his. And, Let every one that nameth the name of Christ depart from iniquity.

Paul gives a word picture for *the foundation* of our pursuit of biblical truth. The picture is that of a huge substructure upon which a building is erected. Paul pictures this immovable foundation as being sealed with two inscriptions. The *seal* would be understood as God's mark of ownership. The inscriptions or messages are public statements of the purpose of the building.

The first inscription is *The Lord knoweth them that are his.* This indicates that we cannot fool God with religious activities. Some seek truth because they want to know God better, and God knows who these individuals are.

The second inscription, which reads *Let every one that nameth the name of Christ depart from iniquity,* is for us. If teachers of doctrine are to be taken seriously, they must live lives of righteousness and integrity. There is no place for one who professes Christ with lips or in writings, but denies Christ daily in action. We have every right to judge teachers by their lifestyle and activities (Matthew 7:15-20). This is why public moral failure among Christian leaders is so devastating. Even the truths that these fallen leaders proclaim become suspect when they stumble.

B. Our Preparation (vv. 20, 21)

20, 21. But in a great house there are not only vessels of gold and of silver, but also of wood and of earth; and some to honor, and some to dishonor. If a man therefore purge himself from these, he shall be a vessel unto honor, sanctified, and meet for the master's use, and prepared unto every good work.

We are very familiar with the ideas of "everyday dishes" and "good china." Some families even have a special set of holiday dishes that is unpacked but once a year. Paul points out that

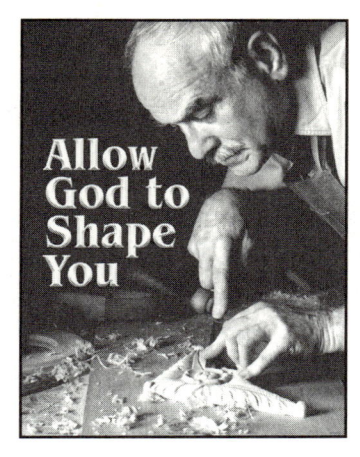

Ask "What part of your life is in most need of chiseling away?" as you point to this visual.

Visual for lesson 11

we use *some* dishes *to honor and some to dishonor*. There is an interesting play on words here in the Greek, for the word meaning "honor" is part of Timothy's name (which means "one who honors God"). Honor is Timothy's first name, not *dishonor!*

Paul's point is that in order for dishes to be used, whether for special occasions or every day, they must be clean. We may use flimsy paper plates for a cookout, but we don't mind as long as they're clean. We wash the Christmas plates after unpacking them because no one wants to eat from dusty, dirty dishes. Likewise, those teachers who will be most useful to God must care for more than perfecting their lectures and sermons. They must strive for godliness.

CLEAN AND READY

Contrary to what some may think, the phrase *cleanliness is next to godliness* is not in the Bible! Even so, we still place a high premium on cleanliness. We would not dream of allowing a doctor who had not properly scrubbed to operate on us. We expect that those who wait on us in restaurants will maintain proper personal hygiene. Moms send their children back to the sink before a meal if their hands are not properly washed.

Jesus stressed the importance of internal cleanliness when He pronounced a series of *woes* in Matthew 23. The objects of His criticism were people more interested in looks than life, more concerned about legalistic rules than living righteously. He tells them: "Woe unto you, scribes and Pharisees, hypocrites! for ye make clean the outside of the cup and of the platter, but within they are full of extortion and excess. Thou blind Pharisee, cleanse first that which is within the cup and platter, that the outside of them may be clean also" (Matthew 23:25, 26).

This kind of cleanliness is vital for those who would be effective servants of God. Outward behavior starts with inward attitude. Our lives need to reflect the holiness of God in both areas. The psalmist reminds us of this need for purity before God: "Who shall ascend into the hill of the Lord? Or who shall stand in his holy place? He that hath clean hands, and a pure heart; who hath not lifted up his soul unto vanity, nor sworn deceitfully" (Psalm 24:3, 4). —A. E. A.

III. Satan's Snare (2 Timothy 2:22-26)

A. Fleeing and Pursuing (v. 22)

22. Flee also youthful lusts: but follow righteousness, faith, charity, peace, with them that call on the Lord out of a pure heart.

We are made spiritually righteous and holy by the blood of Jesus (1 John 1:7). It is a gracious, supernatural act of God. But a righteous, holy lifestyle is not automatic. The Christian lifestyle must be pursued. We must study Scripture to know how God expects us to live. Then we must go for it!

Paul gives a quartet of virtues that we are to run after: *righteousness* (doing the right thing), *faith* (daily trusting God to provide for us), *charity* (love for others), and *peace* (respecting others and not fighting with them). Furthermore, Paul advises that this pursuit is much easier if we have some running companions: those who also follow God *out of a pure heart*. [See question #3, page 237.]

B. Arguments and Instruction (vv. 23-25a)

23-25a. But foolish and unlearned questions avoid, knowing that they do gender strifes. And the servant of the Lord must not strive; but be gentle unto all men, apt to teach, patient; in meekness instructing those that oppose themselves.

Why are some churches always in turmoil? And why are some Christians so downright quarrelsome? These are not new questions. The quarrels in Ephesus seem to have gotten so out of control that Paul heard about them in Rome. Timothy may be overwhelmed by these. [See question #4, page 237.]

Paul's advice to Timothy is that in the final analysis he can control only his own behavior.

He cannot change the behavior of every church member and immediately stop the fighting. Timothy's own behavior, however, will speak for itself if he follows five simple guidelines. First, quit arguing. Don't even worry about defending yourself. When things escalate into a quarrel, quit arguing. Second, *be gentle* to all. Respect all people, even those with whom you disagree.

Third, be ready *to teach* anyone who will listen. Don't let doctrinal quarreling dictate what you teach. Always be ready to teach the core doctrines of the faith. Fourth, have some patience. Sometimes, have a lot of patience! Quick anger and harsh words never defuse an explosive situation. Fifth, demonstrate *meekness* in all of this. Defend truth because it is the truth, not because it is your preference. Show some humility and you are more likely to gain a hearing.

C. Truth and Escape (vv. 25b, 26)

25b, 26. If God peradventure will give them repentance to the acknowledging of the truth; and that they may recover themselves out of the snare of the devil, who are taken captive by him at his will.

If we behave as Paul instructs Timothy, we may achieve our goal. This goal is the salvation of the wayward Christians. Seeking to crush and demolish their false teaching may destroy their faith altogether if we're not careful. God is concerned for their souls and for their salvation, and we must be as well.

Paul notes the spiritual realities that are at work here. False doctrines arise from more than idle human speculation. Quarrels and disputes come from more than human pride and egotism. They come ultimately from Satan, the hater of *the truth* and the father of lies (see John 8:44). His falsehoods are not excluded from our churches today.

The one thing that Satan cannot stand is the truth. The foundational truths of the gospel are that God loves us, He sent His Son to die for our sins, and He promises reconciliation and eternal life to those who trust and follow Him. These truths of the gospel serve as our lifeline from the sea of sin and death. The truth of Jesus sets us free (John 8:32).

Conclusion

A. Godly Living for the Long Haul

Church leadership demands a consistent Christian lifestyle. Teachers must do more than teach the truth. They must also live the truth. This is a lifelong commitment. They must be committed to teaching the truth about God and living lives according to God's will.

Take time to examine your own life. Are you daily striving to do the right things, to respect all people, to teach patiently those who will listen, to act humbly without arrogance? Or do you have other lifestyle issues that you are hiding from the church? Ask God to forgive you and to help you overcome these burdens. Remember, you won't shock God when you own up to these sins. He already knows.

God also will give you spiritual resources to assist your quest for holiness. You do not have to run this race alone. He will give you godly companions. Most of all, He will guide and protect you with His Holy Spirit. The hymn writer Cyrus Nusbaum (1861–1937) put it this way: "Would you live for Jesus, and be always pure and good? . . . Let Him have His way with thee. His power can make you what you ought to be."

B. Controversies in the Church

The list of controversies that has caused church quarrels is endless: One cup for Communion or separate cups? Immerse once for baptism or three times? Sing praise choruses or hymns? Red carpet or blue? One church I served actually had a major tiff over whether they should buy a Kirby® vacuum cleaner or a Hoover®!

But every church quarrel has casualties. Young people in particular are often spiritually

---

Home Daily Bible Readings

Monday, Feb. 6—God's Promise Is Realized Through Faith (Romans 4:13-25)
Tuesday, Feb. 7—So You May Grow in the Word (1 Peter 2:1-10)
Wednesday, Feb. 8—Grow in the Knowledge of God (Colossians 1:3-10)
Thursday, Feb. 9—A Good Soldier of Jesus Christ (2 Timothy 2:1-7)
Friday, Feb. 10—Remember Jesus Christ (2 Timothy 2:8-13)
Saturday, Feb. 11—Be a Worker Approved by God (2 Timothy 2:14-19)
Sunday, Feb. 12—Pursue Righteousness, Faith, Charity, and Peace (2 Timothy 2:20-26)

scarred when church leaders quarrel. Fighting churches are not growing churches. They are not involved in evangelism. How could they be? They are too busy bickering. [See question #5, page 237.]

We must remember that fighting in the church is a manifestation of Satan's power, not God's grace. We must strive to live in peace (Romans 12:18) and to follow truth (3 John 3, 4). Sometimes people have to be disfellowshiped because of divisiveness (Titus 3:10). More often we must have patience with those with whom we disagree. Part of our patience is based on the realization that we are all fallible. As such, we are open to correction from God's Word. Even in our own lives, let us pray that "truth will rise above falsehood as oil above water" (Miguel de Cervantes, 1547–1616).

C. Prayer

God of truth, may You guide us in our pursuit of truth and righteousness. May we avoid quarreling and quarrelsome people. If we have been guilty of quarreling, forgive us and give us a new heart for truth. We pray in the name of Jesus, who has freed us by the truth, amen.

D. Thought to Remember

Christian teachers communicate the truth by words and by actions.

Learning by Doing

This section contains an alternative lesson plan emphasizing learning activities. Classes desiring such student involvement will find these suggestions helpful.

Learning Goals

After this lesson, each student will be able to:
1. Summarize Paul's advice to Timothy about the development of Christian character.
2. Identify an example of ungodly behavior that is as prevalent today as it was in the first century.
3. Identify one ungodly behavior in his or her life to modify or eliminate.

Into the Lesson

Brainstorming! Say, "God expects certain spiritual and behavioral qualities in people who serve in Christian leadership roles. Help me create a list of desired characteristics of a Christian leader." Ask a "scribe" to jot these qualities or characteristics on the board as they are given.

Make the transition to Bible study by saying, "Our list, of course, is not complete. Paul also offers a list of characteristics and behavior traits of Christian leaders. Based on what Paul says elsewhere, we know that the list in 2 Timothy 2:14-26 is not a complete list. But it is a list that was appropriate for his audience."

Into the Word

Prepare a very brief lecture from the Lesson Background and the commentary on verse 14 of today's printed text. This will help the class understand a key reason why Paul wrote the letter we call 2 Timothy. As you lecture, have six letter-size pieces of card stock with the following (one word or phrase on each): *Ephesian Church; Wrong Teachings; Resurrection; Greek Mythology; Jewish Elements;* and *Endless Discussions.* Affix the one- or two-word phrases to the wall as you speak.

After introducing today's text this way, proceed to Activity #1. Use Activity #2 and/or Activity #3 as time permits. Decide in advance which activity or activities will be for the class as a whole and which you will do in small-group discussions.

Activity #1. Prepare a poster board with a heading "Approved by God." Under the heading make two columns with the headings "To Do" and "To Avoid." Explain that there are traits and practices that God expects of His leaders. Read through the text and ask the class to help you make a list of the things a Christian leader is to do or to avoid. Write the answers on the poster board in the appropriate column. As each is mentioned, you can ask what would be the result of failure concerning the particular trait under discussion.

Activity #2. Tell the class or the small groups that verses 17 and 20 contain some word pictures Ask the class as a whole (or give the small groups written copies) these two questions:

a. *Verse 17 says "And their word will eat as doth a canker." What was the problem? What lesson do we learn from this word picture?*

b. *In verse 20, what do you discover from the colorful language about vessels of gold and silver, wood and earth? What does this word picture teach Christian leaders?*

Allow time for discussion.

Activity #3. Before class prepare a poster board titled "Handling Troublesome Churches and People." Underneath, put the following phrases (but not the words in parentheses):

    a. Avoid foolish and unlearned _____ *(questions)*
    b. Do not _____ *(strive or argue)*
    c. Be _____ *(gentle or kind)*
    d. Apt or ready to _____ *(teach)*
    e. Be _____ *(patient)* and "Instruct in _____" *(meekness)*

Make a transition to this activity by asking "Have you noticed that some churches always seem to be in turmoil and that some Christians are so quarrelsome? How should Christian leaders handle those problems?" Ask for help in completing the phrases using verses 23-25a in the printed text. Comment on how these principles help diffuse problems.

Into Life

Distribute one index card to each student. Say, "Write 'Approved Status' at the top of your card, then look at the 'to do' and 'to avoid' poster lists we compiled earlier. From those lists, identify one characteristic, trait, or practice that you would like to eliminate, modify, or develop during the coming weeks. Write it on the card."

Encourage students to carry their cards with them or to put them in a conspicuous place at home to serve as reminders. Close with prayer.

Let's Talk It Over

These questions are designed to promote discussion of the lesson. The answers here are only discussion starters. Let your class talk it over from there.

1. When learning and applying Christian truth, how can we distinguish matters of doctrine from matters of expediency? Why is it important to do so?

Most issues are easy to categorize. For example, repentance, works, faith, baptism, resurrection, and judgment are just a few of the issues clearly revealed in Scripture as *doctrinal* (Hebrews 6:1, 2). God pays close attention to doctrines that are taught (Revelation 2:14, 15, 20).

Most matters of *expediency* also are easy to spot. Examples include times for worship services, the order of the worship service, and the style of the pulpit furniture. Differences of opinions can be expressed here as long as they don't become divisive. Since no biblical mandate exists, congregational preferences can prevail.

Asking "What does the Bible say about this issue?" will help resolve many discussions. It will also help us sort through so-called "gray" areas, where one person sees a doctrinal issue while another sees a matter of expediency. Passages such as Romans 14 and 1 Corinthians 8 show us how to work prayerfully through such matters.

2. Can all doctrines and issues be debated with love, or should we simply avoid certain controversial subjects? Explain.

As in childrearing, the best advice is often this: choose your battles! In many controversies, the best tactic is to choose not to battle. Christian values are not enhanced by quarreling. If a discussion begins to shed more "heat" than "light," it may be best simply to excuse yourself politely.

Some disagreements are unavoidable. In those cases, "speaking the truth in love" (Ephesians 4:15) is a priority. Respect for one who holds differing convictions is always appropriate: Remember, he or she is created in the image of God just as you are. Stick to the facts and inferences of the issue; don't attack character flaws or motives.

3. Paul talks about *youthful lusts*. As we grow older, can we expect to be less tempted to sin? Defend your answer.

Younger people generally have less instruction to guide them. They certainly have fewer life experiences than senior adults. These two factors may make younger people more susceptible to Satan's schemes.

Even so, the temptations of senior adults are not necessarily less intense than those of teens. One may hope that truly mature persons would react more wisely to temptations than they did in their youth. Years of experience in resisting evil should teach prudence and discretion. (Solomon is a notable exception; see 1 Kings 11:4.) No matter what our age, we all can be thankful that we never will be tempted beyond our capacity to resist (1 Corinthians 10:13).

4. How can we, in meekness and humility, let potential quarrelers know that their questions are foolish?

Common sense and Christian sensitivity tell us to avoid using the word *foolish*—even when that seems to be the best description (see also Matthew 5:22). A different choice of words, tone of voice, and even body language can convey a less adversarial attitude.

Certain classic phrases may help as long as they are not taken to be dismissive. "Some questions won't be answered for certain until we are in Heaven—and then we probably won't even care." "God has revealed all we need to know about that, and I'm willing to leave the details up to Him." "This question has been asked through the ages, and none of our answers seem satisfactory, so further discussion may be futile."

5. When have you seen incidents in which church strife could have been defused by eliminating pride and selfishness? Explain.

Use this question carefully if your own church has suffered this problem recently. Stress that dissension wounds the spirit of the church; broken relationships are not easily or quickly healed. How God must weep when His people behave in divisive ways! We know that God hates dissension and divisiveness among His people (Proverbs 6:19; Romans 16:17, 18). Humility at the outset will go a long way toward avoiding such problems (Matthew 5:5; Philippians 2:3; 1 Peter 5:5).

February 19
Lesson 12

Follow a Good Mentor

DEVOTIONAL READING: Psalm 119:9-16.

BACKGROUND SCRIPTURE: 2 Timothy 3, 4.

PRINTED TEXT: 2 Timothy 3:10—4:8.

2 Timothy 3:10-17

10 But thou hast fully known my doctrine, manner of life, purpose, faith, long-suffering, charity, patience,

11 Persecutions, afflictions, which came unto me at Antioch, at Iconium, at Lystra; what persecutions I endured: but out of them all the Lord delivered me.

12 Yea, and all that will live godly in Christ Jesus shall suffer persecution.

13 But evil men and seducers shall wax worse and worse, deceiving, and being deceived.

14 But continue thou in the things which thou hast learned and hast been assured of, knowing of whom thou hast learned them;

15 And that from a child thou hast known the holy Scriptures, which are able to make thee wise unto salvation through faith which is in Christ Jesus.

16 All Scripture is given by inspiration of God, and is profitable for doctrine, for reproof, for correction, for instruction in righteousness:

17 That the man of God may be perfect, thoroughly furnished unto all good works.

2 Timothy 4:1-8

1 I charge thee therefore before God, and the Lord Jesus Christ, who shall judge the quick and the dead at his appearing and his kingdom;

2 Preach the word; be instant in season, out of season; reprove, rebuke, exhort with all long-suffering and doctrine.

3 For the time will come when they will not endure sound doctrine; but after their own lusts shall they heap to themselves teachers, having itching ears;

4 And they shall turn away their ears from the truth, and shall be turned unto fables.

5 But watch thou in all things, endure afflictions, do the work of an evangelist, make full proof of thy ministry.

6 For I am now ready to be offered, and the time of my departure is at hand.

7 I have fought a good fight, I have finished my course, I have kept the faith:

8 Henceforth there is laid up for me a crown of righteousness, which the Lord, the righteous judge, shall give me at that day: and not to me only, but unto all them also that love his appearing.

GOLDEN TEXT: Continue thou in the things which thou hast learned and hast been assured of, knowing of whom thou hast learned them.—2 Timothy 3:14.

LESSON 12 — FEBRUARY 19

> *God's Commitment—Our Response*
> Unit 3: Faithful Followers, Faithful Leaders
> (Lessons 10-13)

Lesson Aims

After participating in this lesson, each student will be able to:

1. List some examples that Paul set as Timothy's mentor.
2. Explain how godly mentoring works and why it's important.
3. Take specific steps to have a mentor or be a mentor to someone.

Lesson Outline

INTRODUCTION
    A. The Perils of Ministry
    B. Lesson Background
I. PAUL'S GRIT IN MINISTRY (2 Timothy 3:10-13)
    A. His Core Values (v. 10)
    B. His Persecutions (vv. 11, 12)
    C. His Opponents (v. 13)
II. TIMOTHY'S EXPERIENCE IN LEARNING (2 Timothy 3:14-17)
    A. Learning from Mentors (vv. 14, 15)
    B. Learning from Scripture (vv. 16, 17)
    Read the Owner's Manual!
III. TIMOTHY'S CHARGE FROM PAUL (2 Timothy 4:1-8)
    A. Ultimate Evaluation of an Evangelist (v. 1)
    B. Tireless Task of an Evangelist (vv. 2-4)
    C. Hard Work of an Evangelist (v. 5)
    It's Not a Pretty Picture
    D. Final Reward of an Evangelist (vv. 6-8)
CONCLUSION
    A. Mentoring Ministers
    B. Prayer
    C. Thought to Remember

Introduction

A. The Perils of Ministry

From where will the ministers of the future come? Will there be any full-time ministers left in 10 years? Recent research has shown some alarming trends in this regard. One publication recently estimated that 1,000 people were leaving full-time ministry in the United States every week among evangelical churches. A survey of ministers taken by the Institute for Church Growth revealed that 70 percent of ministers did not believe they had a close friend, 80 percent thought that ministry affected their families in a negative way, and 90 percent felt they had inadequate training to cope with the demands of ministry.

The corps of full-time ministers is in an ongoing state of crisis. One survey found that the average length of time spent in career ministry has dropped from 20 years to 14 years. Some believe it is now less than 10 years. Can these trends be reversed? Some ministers self-destruct as a result of immoral or unethical behavior. Others burn out from financial pressures, constant criticism, and lack of guidance and support. Can we do anything to help?

Some answers are found in today's lesson. As we consider Paul's advice to Timothy, we may realize that things haven't really changed that much. Ministry was in crisis in their day too! Young Timothy was facing pressures that threatened to overwhelm him and destroy his ministry. Paul, as his father in the faith and mentor in ministry, understood the danger. In today's text Paul speaks frankly and boldly about what it takes to succeed in ministry in the long term. [See question #1, page 246.]

B. Lesson Background

While 2 Timothy is difficult to date exactly, we usually understand it to have been written by Paul while he was imprisoned in Rome. This was his second Roman imprisonment, not where we find him at the end of the book of Acts. Tradition tells us that Paul was released from that first imprisonment, perhaps because his accusers from Judea never arrived to present their case.

Paul probably returned to Rome in about A.D. 65 or 66. He apparently was caught up in the persecutions by Emperor Nero while there. This second imprisonment would have been relatively brief, ending with Paul's execution in A.D. 66 or 67. This was when he wrote to Timothy a second time. Paul now had given up all hope of release and expected to be put to death (2 Timothy 4:6). His only hope of seeing Timothy again was dependent upon Timothy's coming to Rome (2 Timothy 4:9). We don't know if Timothy made the trip or not. But we do have Paul's letter to him.

I. Paul's Grit in Ministry
(2 Timothy 3:10-13)
A. His Core Values (v. 10)

10. But thou hast fully known my doctrine, manner of life, purpose, faith, long-suffering, charity, patience.

In laying out his ministry before Timothy, Paul gives a list of characteristics. [See question #2, page 246.] Some today would identify these characteristics as Paul's core values—the guiding principles by which he is identified. While the items in this list are well known to Timothy, the terms are significant and merit our attention.

By *my doctrine* Paul means the body of teaching that he has presented consistently throughout his ministry. For Paul this teaching is always in harmony with Scripture (see 1 Corinthians 15:3, 4). This teaching is always consistent with what Jesus taught (Acts 20:35). Paul's teachings could tackle heady theological issues (see Philippians 2:5-11) or be very practical (see 2 Thessalonians 3:10). Paul's *manner of life* is his public and private behavior, which is in harmony with what he teaches. Paul never implies, "Do what I say, not as I do." He always demands, "Judge my teaching by my actions."

Paul's *purpose* is his fundamental goal in life. It implies a persistent plan that guides one's actions as used in God's design (see Romans 8:28). That goal for Paul is to be used by God to preach the gospel.

The *faith* of which Paul speaks is more than the sum total of his doctrine. It is Paul's ongoing drive to answer the call of God, despite many reasons to abandon this calling. This is coupled with Paul's *long-suffering*. Paul strives faithfully and doggedly toward the goal that is not visible to his earthly eyes. He does so without losing heart or giving up (see 2 Corinthians 4:1; Galatians 6:9). His patience has lasted a lifetime.

All of Paul's actions are characterized by love *(charity)*. This is unselfishness. He always has wanted the best for his children in the faith with little regard for himself. Finally, Timothy is advised to remember Paul's *patience* or endurance. Paul runs the race until the end. He never retires from ministry (2 Timothy 4:7).

B. His Persecutions (vv. 11, 12)

11, 12. Persecutions, afflictions, which came unto me at Antioch, at Iconium, at Lystra; what persecutions I endured: but out of them all the Lord delivered me. Yea, and all that will live godly in Christ Jesus shall suffer persecution.

Paul also reminds Timothy of some things that were not Paul's choice: the constant physical traumas he suffered in ministry. He was beaten up. In Timothy's hometown of Lystra, Paul's Jewish opponents stoned him and left him for dead (Acts 14:19). It is likely that this caused permanent damage to his body that left him somewhat disabled even after healing. Yet Paul does not regret this. From it he draws out a simple truism for ministry: In our world, you *shall suffer persecution* for godly living.

Without doubt, godly living is at best an unnoticed lifestyle. At worst, it is ridiculed and punished. Why is this? The reason is that those of the world do not submit to the lordship of Jesus, and naturally they feel threatened by those who do. We should note that by *live godly in Christ* Paul is not speaking of the belligerent, defiant "standing up for what's right" attitude that some Christians seem to take so much pleasure in today. He is talking about the quiet, simple life that is patterned after Jesus (compare 1 Thessalonians 4:11).

C. His Opponents (v. 13)

13. But evil men and seducers shall wax worse and worse, deceiving, and being deceived.

Paul's observations here could be drawn from any century of human history. *Evil* and sin rarely diminish in our world. They seem to grow in intensity on a daily basis. The word *seducers* does not have a sexual meaning here. Rather, it refers to those who are like false miracle workers, driving their duped followers to new depths of evil.

Paul gives the underlying cause of all of this: those who are *deceiving* are themselves *deceived*. One day there will be no more possibility of deception for all spiritual fraud will be exposed. Everyone will bow in reverence to the

---

How to Say It

ANTIOCH. *An*-tee-ock.
CORINTHIANS. Ko-*rin*-thee-unz (*th* as in *thin*).
GALATIANS. Guh-*lay*-shunz.
ICONIUM. Eye-*ko*-nee-um.
LYSTRA. *Liss*-truh.
PHILIPPIANS. Fih-*lip*-ee-unz.

lordship of Jesus (Philippians 2:10, 11). That doesn't mean that everyone will accept Jesus as Savior. Rather, it means that people will have no choice but to acknowledge the truth about Jesus.

II. Timothy's Experience in Learning (2 Timothy 3:14-17)

A. Learning from Mentors (vv. 14, 15)

14, 15. But continue thou in the things which thou hast learned and hast been assured of, knowing of whom thou hast learned them; and that from a child thou hast known the holy Scriptures, which are able to make thee wise unto salvation through faith which is in Christ Jesus.

As time moves on, Timothy probably will outlive his older teachers. Without their presence, what will sustain him then? Paul offers him two pillars of faith strength: the credibility of the lives of his teachers and the foundation of *the holy Scriptures.*

Many parents today seek to give their children future advantages through specialized education. This may be music lessons, computer classes, foreign language instruction, or private schools. Yet true success in life will never depend upon such knowledge. There is no more important source of learning than the Bible. A parent who helps his or her children hide God's Word in their hearts (Psalm 119:11) has given them sustaining, life-giving values that never will go out of date.

Paul gives a theological reason for this: Scripture can make us *wise unto salvation.* But this does not happen automatically or accidentally. People find salvation in the Bible only through faith in Jesus. Outside of that faith, the Bible will seem as myths, religious stories, and optional moral teachings. With faith, we meet Jesus and recognize Him as Lord and Savior. With faith, we understand God's plan to save us from the eternal death that our sin has earned.

B. Learning from Scripture (vv. 16, 17)

16, 17. All Scripture is given by inspiration of God, and is profitable for doctrine, for reproof, for correction, for instruction in righteousness: that the man of God may be perfect, thoroughly furnished unto all good works.

This is the most important text in the Bible concerning the nature of the Bible itself. It should be admitted that Paul has our Old Testa-

Point to this visual as you discuss how the Bible is our pathway to greater godliness.

Visual for Lessons 8, 12

ment in mind as he speaks of *all Scripture.* This is because the New Testament is not yet compiled and some of its books are not even in existence as Paul writes. Even so, the principles hold for our entire Bible today.

Paul outlines three major reasons why Scripture must be held in high esteem by any Christian. First, it is *given by inspiration of God.* Literally, it is God-breathed. When God breathes into something, He gives it life (see Genesis 2:7). When God inspires Scripture, He makes it alive. It becomes a living, active, powerful Word (see Hebrews 4:12).

Second, Scripture is *profitable.* Think of its uses! It may be used for *doctrine* (teaching), *reproof* (pointing out wrong behavior), *correction* (showing the way to right behavior), and *instruction in righteousness* (training to be godly).

Third, Scripture is a complete resource to bring believers to proficiency for ministry and life. We don't need to explore the writings of Buddhists or Muslims in order to learn how to live. Books on how to be successful in business do not tell Christians how to be Christian. The Bible has everything we need for that; we can (and do) spend our entire lifetimes just living up to its standards. [See question #3, page 246.]

READ THE OWNER'S MANUAL!

Very rarely do I buy a new car. The high price and the deep depreciation after driving the car off the lot make it seem like a waste of good money. So I buy used cars. But one thing that always bothers me about doing that is that, more times than not, the owner's manual is missing.

It's hard to understand why someone would remove the manual from the car. What good is an owner's manual sitting on a coffee table or in a closet at home? You need the manual with the car to answer questions as they arise. But for some reason, people don't return them to their rightful place in the car's glove box.

Unfortunately for many Christians, the owner's manual—the Bible—is often missing. It is missing from both their hands and hearts. Some churches regularly put Scripture texts on an overhead projection system or print them in a program. This can add to the problem of people neglecting their own time in the Word.

Use of preprinted texts on PowerPoint® slides or in programs is not all wrong, of course. But preachers and teachers can encourage the people to turn to a passage of Scripture and read along during the course of a sermon or lesson. Biblical illiteracy is rampant. This is a starting point for curing this problem. —A. E. A.

III. Timothy's Charge from Paul (2 Timothy 4:1-8)

A. Ultimate Evaluation of an Evangelist (v. 1)

1. I charge thee therefore before God, and the Lord Jesus Christ, who shall judge the quick and the dead at his appearing and his kingdom.

Elsewhere Paul teaches that Jesus is not only Savior but also judge (Acts 17:31). Jesus' first coming was to bring salvation, not judgment (John 12:47). But His second coming will be to render verdicts on all, both the *quick* (living) and the *dead*. Christians should never fear for the loss of their salvation. Instead, all Christians must remember that there is an ongoing, eternal evaluation being made of their ministries.

B. Tireless Task of an Evangelist (vv. 2-4)

2-4. Preach the word; be instant in season, out of season; reprove, rebuke, exhort with all long-suffering and doctrine. For the time will come when they will not endure sound doctrine; but after their own lusts shall they heap to themselves teachers, having itching ears; and they shall turn away their ears from the truth, and shall be turned unto fables.

The number one task of the preacher is the ministry of *the word*. It must be preached faithfully whether it is popular or unpopular, whether it is received gladly or soundly rejected. Notice that there is a great deal of overlap between what Timothy is to do and the list of the Bible's uses in 2 Timothy 3:16, above.

Alas, much preaching today has little to do with the Bible. We hear sermons on social causes, self-help issues, or theological speculations. While entertaining, such preaching has little value in the long run. If preachers wrestle with Scripture deeply, their preaching will be of lasting consequence to their hearers. The Bible text must first be read carefully, then understood fully, then believed deeply, then proclaimed boldly. Preaching the great doctrines of the Bible will never go out of style and never needs an apology. [See question #4, page 246.]

C. Hard Work of an Evangelist (v. 5)

5. But watch thou in all things, endure afflictions, do the work of an evangelist, make full proof of thy ministry.

Being a minister is hard work! God does not reward laziness in *ministry*, although there are lazy ministers. God does not bless slothfulness in ministry, although there are sloppy, disorganized ministers. God wants ministers who are attentive, who will put up with discomfort, all for the opportunity to *do the work of an evangelist*.

There is some disagreement as to whether or not *evangelist* is a church office parallel to elder or deacon (compare Acts 21:8). The term means "gospel preacher," therefore the work of an evangelist is preaching the gospel (see 2 Timothy 4:2, "preach the word"). The word *evangelist* does not carry the idea of having authority over elders. It makes no sense to say, "I preach the gospel, therefore I get to boss the elders around."

Preaching the gospel always must come first in the many tasks of ministry. Without it, Timothy has no hope of fulfilling his calling. [See question #5, page 246.]

IT'S NOT A PRETTY PICTURE

In a practical ministry course in Bible college, the professor warned the students that things did not always go just right in the work of the ministry. Heartaches, frustrations, and conflicts would arise. Sometimes these would come in droves.

These students had spent much time complaining about the pressures of school and how time seemed so fleeting. They were looking forward to getting out of school so their time would be their own time without those pressures. Then the professor shared notes from recent graduates who were working in full-time ministry. Note after note spoke of the time pressures. One who had complained loudly during school said that time pressures at school did not even come close to equaling those in the ministry.

Some would say that these warnings should not be shared with young people who are excited about going into ministry. Yet as Paul sought to prepare Timothy for the continual work of ministry, he reminded him that those who live for God would suffer. Jesus, in training His disciples for their work, warned them that they would go forth as sheep among wolves (Matthew 10:16).

Care should be taken to help people understand what a call to commitment in Christ involves. The caution is in general for all who would make their initial commitment to Christ and in particular for those thinking of entering full-time ministry. There are eternal benefits, but with these come the trials. Being open about this up front can prepare new Christians—and new preachers—for what lies ahead. But we also stand with Paul in affirming that "it's worth it!" (See Romans 8:18.) —A. E. A.

D. Final Reward of an Evangelist (vv. 6-8)

6-8. For I am now ready to be offered, and the time of my departure is at hand. I have fought a good fight, I have finished my course, I have kept the faith: henceforth there is laid up for me a crown of righteousness, which the Lord, the righteous judge, shall give me at that day: and not to me only, but unto all them also that love his appearing.

Paul does not write these things to give himself a pat on the back. He writes them to encourage Timothy in his discouraging times of ministry. Paul can die with no regrets. He knows the *fight* is nearly over; the race is nearing the finish line. He will be judged by Jesus, but he can face this judgment without fear. His prize will not be punishment but reward: *a crown of righteousness*, which is the reward of eternal life (see James 1:12; Revelation 2:10).

Paul is not speaking of *crown* in the sense of a headpiece that signifies royalty. In the ancient Greek world, the type of crown at issue here is given to the victor in athletic competitions (like the Olympic games). It is symbolic, but carries great prestige and honor. It is something that athletes train their entire lives to win. Paul hopes that his influence on Timothy, even in dying, will encourage the young evangelist to strive for this crown of righteousness as he has.

Conclusion

A. Mentoring Ministers

There is a church in my area that has a reputation for chewing up ministers. What surprises me most is not that this church does this, but that it is able to find anyone to come and be its preacher! Churches earn reputations (as do ministers), and these are often very difficult to overcome. Maybe you know a church like this—a church with sharp-tongued evaluators and unrelenting criticism. Maybe your church is like this. Maybe you have experienced a parade of ministers, all of them run off because of perceived laziness, stubbornness, or inadequate preaching.

There is another church in my area that has a reputation for nurturing young people into full-time ministry. This church has produced dozens of ministers from within its own ranks. It has patiently trained other ministerial greenhorns and then released them to serve. It is not a big church, but its impact is felt around the world.

Some churches are *consumers* of ministers, and others are *producers*. Which kind of church is yours?

One thing that separates these churches is an attitude of gentle mentoring. At the first church, ministers are expected to fail and their critics wait eagerly. At the second church, ministers are allowed to fail, and leaders are there to pick them up and help them learn from their mistakes. The hapless ministers of the first

---

Home Daily Bible Readings

Monday, Feb. 13—Treasure God's Word in Your Heart (Psalm 119:9-16)

Tuesday, Feb. 14—Turn Your Heart to God's Statutes (Psalm 119:33-40)

Wednesday, Feb. 15—An Example to Imitate (2 Thessalonians 3:6-13)

Thursday, Feb. 16—Avoid Godless People (2 Timothy 3:1-9)

Friday, Feb. 17—Continue in the Things You Have Learned (2 Timothy 3:10-17)

Saturday, Feb. 18—Carry Out Your Ministry Fully (2 Timothy 4:1-8)

Sunday, Feb. 19—Final Instructions (2 Timothy 4:9-22)

church have no one within the congregation whom they feel they can trust or talk to. The fortunate ministers of the second church have leaders who befriend and encourage them from day one.

Now think of your minister (or one of them). Is this individual (as seen through human eyes) a pathetic, hopeless kind of person who seemingly does not belong in ministry? Maybe. Are you willing to risk yourself to speak sincere words of encouragement, to look out for his welfare, to pay loving attention to his family? Are you willing to allow for blunders and push him for excellence and faithfulness? Are you willing to give him opportunities for further education in the richness of God's Word? Do you pray for him daily? If so, you have begun to catch the vision that Paul has presented in today's lesson.

B. Prayer

Great God our teacher, as You have given to us of Your mighty treasures of wisdom and grace, may we find others to pass these riches to. May we appreciate our teachers. May we continue to follow their examples. May we leave behind children and grandchildren in the faith who love You as dearly as we do. We pray this in the name of Your Son, Jesus, amen.

C. Thought to Remember

Spiritual investment in the life of another is expected from every believer.

Learning by Doing

This section contains an alternative lesson plan emphasizing learning activities. Classes desiring such student involvement will find these suggestions helpful.

Learning Goals

After participating in this lesson, each student will be able to:

1. List some examples that Paul set as Timothy's mentor.
2. Explain how godly mentoring works and why it's important.
3. Take specific steps to have a mentor or be a mentor to someone.

Into the Lesson

Before the lesson, make a brief video of one or more of your church ministers speaking. The purpose of the video is to provide examples of how mentoring may be helpful to a minister or to any believer in Jesus. Ask the minister to open the video by completing the statement below. Then the minister is to share an example of someone who was (or is) an encourager or mentor.

The minister will begin with this statement: "Ministry is filled with joy. It is also packed with frustration and hurt. I am so thankful for people who have provided encouragement to me and who have been examples as I serve the Lord. One of those people was (or is) . . ."

Before playing the video, open the class by mentioning the alarming statistics about evangelical ministers as cited in today's lesson Introduction. Then play the video you have recorded.

Make the transition to Bible study by explaining that mentoring is guidance of a less experienced person by someone with more wisdom. Say, "Mentoring has been a wonderful blessing to some in our churches. Today's text not only encourages mature believers to become mentors for younger believers but also gives clues to ways we can do this effectively."

Into the Word

Explain that the class will be looking at today's printed text with two sets of eyes. Say, "As we read of Paul's model in mentoring Timothy, one set of eyes will focus on lessons about mentoring ministers. The other set will seek to discover how to mentor any believer."

The following activity may be done in small groups or by the entire class. Print the following instructions and questions to be distributed to the entire class or to small-group leaders.

Focus #1: Mentoring Ministers. Read 2 Timothy 3:10–4:8 and answer the following:

a. What does this text imply the primary task of a minister or senior minister to be? *(4:1, 2)*

b. What are some other tasks given to these church leaders?

c. What are some personal traits or qualities the minister should cultivate?

d. Paul and Timothy faced problems in ministry. What were a few of those challenges?

Focus #2: Mentoring Other Believers. Read 2 Timothy 3:10–4:8 and answer the following questions. We are looking for principles or tips on how to mentor other believers effectively.

a. What clues do you find in this text about when or in what circumstances mentoring or encouragement would be helpful?

b. What are the goals for mentoring believers?

c. What clues are there about how to be a mentor? Add to that list other methods you think may work in today's church.

d. When should you seek out someone to be a mentor to you?

Allow groups (if used) to present their findings to the class. Make the transition to application by reminding everyone that there are two lessons to apply in this passage: helping young ministers in addition to mentoring young believers.

Into Life

Next, do both of the activities below.

Activity #1. Display a poster board with the heading "I commit myself to becoming a mentor to another believer." Then say, "This is an opportunity to commit to following Paul's model as a mentor. But who should take the initiative in forming a mentoring relationship, the mentor or the one being mentored (the protégé)? Why?"

After discussion, offer the chance to sign the poster after class. Leave the poster up for a few weeks to allow others to sign up for this responsibility after having a chance to think it over.

Activity #2. Write a note to a minister. The notes may express thanks, promise continuing prayer support, etc. Distribute inexpensive note cards and envelopes for this task. Play soft music while people write. If there is not enough time, ask students to take the cards home for completion. Encourage use of pen and paper rather than e-mail.

Let's Talk It Over

These questions are designed to promote discussion of the lesson. The answers here are only discussion starters. Let your class talk it over from there.

1. How can we reverse the present crisis in vocational ministry? Be specific!

One way to begin to reverse the rate of ministerial dropouts is through the use of accountability partners. Some kings in the Old Testament had prophets to redirect them when they got off track. King Saul had Samuel (1 Samuel 13) and King David had Nathan (2 Samuel 12). Apparently King Solomon had no prophetic voice of confrontation, to his detriment! Ministers can be encouraged to find accountability partners who will speak frank (but kind) words of caution when necessary.

Another idea is to have the church's board of elders act as a kind of buffer zone between the minister and his critics. This idea can be worked out in different ways. But a key concept is to prevent the minister from feeling as if he's "going it alone" when dealing with a critic.

2. Following question #1, what characteristics are required of accountability partners? How are those qualities the same as or different from what would be expected of mentors?

Ministers need friends who can be trusted with confidences; encouragers who look beyond his faults to see needs; counselors who listen well; advisers with common sense; supporters who are loyal; buddies who share common interests beyond church matters; associates who will point out shortcomings in private; advocates who will speak highly of him at every opportunity.

Some of these traits are more appropriate for accountability partners and some are more suited for mentors. Accountability partners are usually thought of as being roughly "equals" in experience, education, etc. Mentors, on the other hand, are experienced or highly trained persons exercising oversight of those who are less experienced. This was the case with Paul and Timothy. When we keep that distinction is mind, we should be able to see fairly easily what traits are needed in each relationship.

3. Someone says, "Since only the Bible is inspired by God, we don't need commentaries to muddy the water and bring in people's opinions." How do you respond?

First of all, the person saying this has just given you his or her *own* commentary! If commentaries and opinions have no value, then what the person has just said is of no value either.

Reference books can be real time-savers. Concordances, Bible dictionaries, maps of the Holy Land, and commentaries on Old and New Testament books can enrich our Bible study. Think about the commentary you're using right now and how helpful it is! We use study aids, of course, with due regard for the possibility of error.

4. Which style of preaching is best? Which is the worst? Why?

The only *wrong* style of preaching is the style that a minister *always* uses. There are many styles, and people can benefit from hearing a variety. Textual, topical, and expository preaching methods are classic designations. Sermons also can be inductive, deductive, confessional, first person, etc. Use of arts such as drama, video clips, and storytelling can be valuable enhancements to preaching.

Helpful messages almost always will be based upon Scripture. Effective preaching is passionate, clear, and relevant. It engages the mind, emotions, and will—as Peter's sermon did at Pentecost. All sermons, no matter the style, should answer two questions: "What's so?" and "So what?"

5. Should *specific* expectations be included in ministerial job descriptions? Or do the *general* expectations of 2 Timothy 4:2-5 give us all the job description that ministers need? Explain.

A detailed description of ministerial duties can be useful in addressing unique needs of particular churches. Larger churches often have very specialized ministry staff positions, and detailed job descriptions for those can help achieve a "meeting of the minds" on expectations.

Even so, contracts with ministers should also be based on mutual trust. We can express this trust by listing expectations in general terms. This allows a leader to minister in ways that seem best to him personally, through Holy Spirit guidance. Overly specific job descriptions can be seen as controlling and unreasonable.

Live and Teach the Truth

February 26
Lesson 13

Devotional Reading: Ephesians 4:11-16.

Background Scripture: Titus 2.

Printed Text: Titus 2.

Titus 2:1-15

1 But speak thou the things which become sound doctrine:

2 That the aged men be sober, grave, temperate, sound in faith, in charity, in patience.

3 The aged women likewise, that they be in behavior as becometh holiness, not false accusers, not given to much wine, teachers of good things;

4 That they may teach the young women to be sober, to love their husbands, to love their children,

5 To be discreet, chaste, keepers at home, good, obedient to their own husbands, that the word of God be not blasphemed.

6 Young men likewise exhort to be soberminded.

7 In all things showing thyself a pattern of good works: in doctrine showing uncorruptness, gravity, sincerity,

8 Sound speech, that cannot be condemned; that he that is of the contrary part may be ashamed, having no evil thing to say of you.

9 Exhort servants to be obedient unto their own masters, and to please them well in all things; not answering again;

10 Not purloining, but showing all good fidelity; that they may adorn the doctrine of God our Saviour in all things.

11 For the grace of God that bringeth salvation hath appeared to all men,

12 Teaching us that, denying ungodliness and worldly lusts, we should live soberly, righteously, and godly, in this present world;

13 Looking for that blessed hope, and the glorious appearing of the great God and our Saviour Jesus Christ;

14 Who gave himself for us, that he might redeem us from all iniquity, and purify unto himself a peculiar people, zealous of good works.

15 These things speak, and exhort, and rebuke with all authority. Let no man despise thee.

Golden Text: In all things showing thyself a pattern of good works: in doctrine showing uncorruptness, gravity, sincerity, sound speech, that cannot be condemned; that he that is of the contrary part may be ashamed, having no evil thing to say of you.—Titus 2:7, 8.

> *God's Commitment—Our Response*
> Unit 3: Faithful Followers, Faithful Leaders
> (Lessons 10-13)

Lesson Aims

After participating in this lesson, each student will be able to:

1. List the behaviors that must be taught to various age groups.
2. Explain why sound doctrine is necessary as a background to right behavior.
3. Participate in the teaching ministry of the church as both a learner and a teacher.

Lesson Outline

INTRODUCTION
    A. Bible Literacy Today
    B. Lesson Background
I. TEACHING SOUND DOCTRINE (Titus 2:1)
II. TEACHING SENIOR MEMBERS (Titus 2:2, 3)
    A. Teaching Older Men (v. 2)
    B. Teaching Older Women (v. 3)
III. TEACHING YOUNGER MEMBERS (Titus 2:4-10)
    A. Teaching Younger Women (vv. 4, 5)
        It's Time to Grow Up
    B. Teaching Younger Men (vv. 6-8)
    C. Teaching Slaves (vv. 9, 10)
IV. TRAINING A PECULIAR PEOPLE (Titus 2:11-15)
    A. Living Our Salvation (vv. 11, 12)
        Where Are You Now, Really?
    B. Waiting for Jesus (vv. 13, 14)
    C. Being Above Reproach (v. 15)
CONCLUSION
    A. Is the Sunday School Dead?
    B. Lifetime Learners
    C. Prayer
    D. Thought to Remember

Introduction

A. Bible Literacy Today

On a recent late-night talk show, the host moved through the audience asking basic questions about the Bible. "Name one of the Ten Commandments," he requested. One brave soul answered, "God helps those who help themselves." The host then asked, "Name one of the 12 apostles." No one could. Finally, the audience was asked, "Name the Beatles." Quickly, the crowd responded, "John, Paul, George, and Ringo."

Knowledge of the Bible in historically "Christian nations" seems to be at an all-time low. A national survey published in 1989 revealed that less than half of those who identified themselves as Christians could name the original preacher of the Sermon on the Mount. In the 17 years that have passed since that survey, things certainly haven't gotten any better!

Those who teach in Bible colleges often swap stories about astounding Bible ignorance among incoming students. The most extreme example I can cite is the student who didn't understand the difference between the Old and New Testaments. Not only did this student not understand the difference, he didn't even know that such a division existed! And this was a young man whose family attended church regularly!

Yet the church has long taught that knowing Bible content and Bible principles is essential for godly living. Today's lesson reminds us that this is an ongoing, lifelong process. We never fully arrive at perfect knowledge of the Bible. Applying the Bible to our lives in an absolute manner is a goal that no one seems able reach. Education in godliness is crucial for young people, but older people can gain from it too. Christians are called to be both teachers and learners of the Word.

B. Lesson Background

The book of Titus involves events after the close of the book of Acts, but we have no exact knowledge of the sequence. Paul apparently was released from his imprisonment in Rome (where we leave him at the end of Acts), and he did more traveling. One of the places he visited was the island of Crete, where he evangelized successfully and started some churches. It is likely, however, that the gospel already had reached Crete many years earlier through unnamed believers (see Acts 2:11).

Paul was accompanied on Crete by one of his most trusted associates, Titus. Titus was a Gentile believer (Galatians 2:3). Titus is not mentioned in the book of Acts, but he figures prominently in the letters of Paul. In 2 Corinthians he is named (in Greek) nine times (example: 2 Corinthians 8:23). Paul wrote his letter, in about A.D. 65, to Titus after departing from the island. Paul had left Titus behind to correct a

Post this visual and ask "What could happen to the church if this imperative is ignored?"

Visual for lesson 13

chaotic situation in the Cretan churches. Titus especially needed to get an eldership in place in each congregation (Titus 1:5).

Crete was famous in antiquity as a source of culture and religion. The Cretan people, however, were not highly esteemed in the Roman world. In Titus 1:12, Paul quotes a native Cretan "prophet" who describes his own people as "always liars, evil beasts, slow bellies." While Paul does not name this person, he can be identified as Epimenides, a famous Cretan author who lived about 600 B.C. This statement has been called the Cretan Paradox, because if all Cretans are liars, and Epimenides was a Cretan, then was he lying when he made the statement?

Yet assuming some truth to that statement (as Paul himself claims in Titus 1:13), can you imagine trying to bring order to a church made up of lying, brutal, pleasure-seekers? You couldn't trust their word. You would be afraid they might turn on you. You would feel pressure to entertain and feed them. This sounds surprisingly contemporary!

Part of Paul's solution to this difficult situation is to institute an ongoing educational program within the congregation to train the believers in godliness (see Titus 1:1). Today's lesson, Titus 2, is the heart of this instructional program. This is the nitty-gritty of helping believers mature into godly men and women.

I. Teaching Sound Doctrine (Titus 2:1)

1. But speak thou the things which become sound doctrine.

The word translated *sound* is a medical term from which we get our English word *hygiene*.

We could say that Paul wants *healthy doctrine*. Such teaching helps us maintain spiritual health.

There are many in churches today who suffer from general spiritual malaise, from a sickness of the soul. They live as victims of church conflicts, in fear that personal problems will be made public, or with serious doubts about the validity of their faith. Spiritual healing ultimately comes from God (Romans 8:26). Spiritual health may be achieved by serious, rigorous training in the ways of godliness.

II. Teaching Senior Members (Titus 2:2, 3)

A. Teaching Older Men (v. 2)

2. That the aged men be sober, grave, temperate, sound in faith, in charity, in patience.

Paul begins to speak about the groups that make up the Cretan churches. Everyone is included, but he begins with the older *men*. Then he works his way down the social pecking order of the ancient world. Older men and women generally are those whose children (if they have any) are grown.

Paul asks Titus to give attention to four specific areas for the older men. First, they are reminded to be *sober*. This implies that some of the older men, who should be church leaders, have drinking problems. Alcoholism among seniors is a hidden problem today. We may think *that would never happen in my church*, but it can and does. The men are expected to lead with clear and sober minds, not through an alcoholic haze.

Second, Paul demands that the older men be *grave*. While it is good for older people to remain "young at heart," it is important that they present an example that brings respect, not derision.

Third, Paul points out that older men need to be *temperate*. We already discussed alcohol with regard to being sober, and the idea here is one of self-control. Our world today seems to encourage impulsiveness. It lionizes those who are the most conspicuous consumers. Self-control, however, is essential in church leaders, who are called to make decisions with far-reaching implications.

Fourth, Paul wants older men to be *sound* (or "healthy") in three areas: *faith, charity* (meaning love), and *patience*. Churches need leaders who have a tested, deep faith, and who abound in patient love for those less mature than they. Yet in many churches the older leaders are crabby, sharp tongued, and in a state of constant complaining. Paul's guidelines still speak today.

B. Teaching Older Women (v. 3)

3. The aged women likewise, that they be in behavior as becometh holiness, not false accusers, not given to much wine, teachers of good things.

Likewise, the older *women* are to lead by example of their *behavior*. They are to act their age, a lifestyle one would expect from mature believers. Paul will give a specific rationale for this in verse 4: the older women are to be teachers of the younger women. The young are always looking for examples. Isn't it better if the younger women find examples of strong, confident women in their churches and thereby avoid the horrid examples of our celebrity-worshiping media world?

For Paul, two things characterize mature behavior: what you say and how much you drink. The older women are to be leaders in the way they talk about others. They should not be *false accusers*, fabricating or perpetuating rumors that damage the reputation of others. A war of words often leaves no winners, only casualties.

As with the older men, the women must not give in to heavy drinking *(much wine)*. Ancient society was comfortable with drinking diluted wine at meals in small amounts. This often amounted to little more than a flavored beverage and did not cause drunkenness. Young women hardly would be attracted to the life example of an older woman who spent most of her day intoxicated! It is a life of good behavior that allows a platform for the older women to teach good things, especially to the younger women.

III. Teaching Younger Members (Titus 2:4-10)

A. Teaching Younger Women (vv. 4, 5)

4, 5. That they may teach the young women to be sober, to love their husbands, to love their children, to be discreet, chaste, keepers at home, good, obedient to their own husbands, that the word of God be not blasphemed.

> **How to Say It**
> CRETAN. *Cree*-tun.
> CRETE. Creet.
> EPHESIANS. Ee-*fee*-zhunz.
> EPIMENIDES. Ep-ih-*men*-ih-deez.
> TITUS. *Ty*-tus.

Paul knows that the most effective teachers of *young women* are older women. He does not expect Titus to be their primary teacher in one-on-one situations. A young minister who spends much time with the young women of the church is asking for disaster. Paul's way is the better way.

The model for a young wife and mother that Paul presents may not fit our modern lifestyles exactly. But the foundational principles are sound. The young mother has the huge responsibility of ensuring that the home is a happy, secure place. She does this by loving her children and husband dearly, and by staying *chaste* or sexually pure at all times. The pressures of life bombard us outside the home. At home we need a refuge. [See question #1, page 255.]

IT'S TIME TO GROW UP

Proverbs 16:31 says, "The hoary head is a crown of glory." With the graying of hair comes growth and maturity, or at least that's the ideal. In that sense, gray hair is something to be honored. But you would not think that to be the case given all the hair-care products to counteract the graying process! The illusion is that taking away the gray counteracts aging. Do it and stay young!

Trying to be what one is not can create problems. Young men want to have the perks that go with increased age. Older men buy sports cars and have illicit affairs with younger women in order to create the illusion of being "young again." Such is the pattern of the world.

The church, however, must be different. Younger people don't need the older people as "pals" who try to be youthful in clothing, musical tastes, etc. The younger people need examples and mentors! The challenge is for those who are older to bring the young toward spiritual maturity. But when older people don't realize this responsibility, the result is immature churches.

Faith is passed on to succeeding generations by those who are older and, hopefully, more spiritually wise. The church needs those whose spiritual maturity matches or outpaces their maturity in years. Set a goal to be one of those. —A. E. A.

B. Teaching Younger Men (vv. 6-8)

6-8. Young men likewise exhort to be soberminded. In all things showing thyself a pattern of good works: in doctrine showing uncorruptness, gravity, sincerity, sound speech, that cannot be condemned; that he that is of the contrary part may be ashamed, having no evil thing to say of you.

Titus has an obligation to instruct the older men and women in the paths of godliness. The older women are to be the teachers of the younger women. The younger men, though, are to be taught by Titus. They will be observing, of course, the example of his life. Paul describes this under the broad category of *a pattern of good works*.

People are looking for consistency in leaders, aren't they? They expect teachers to measure up to what they teach. If we teach others to live by faith, our lives should have evidence of living confidently for Jesus. If we teach the necessity of sacrificial giving, we should be leaders in contributing our time and money. If we teach the importance of godly speech, we should guard our words and not be found using questionable language or slander. [See question #2, page 255.] Sin of church leaders made public has a huge impact on those who are new believers (and old).

It has been said that the greatest stumbling block for young people in the church is perceived hypocrisy of the leaders. Jesus said that if our hypocrisy causes the children of the flock to sin and fall away, it would be better to have a great stone tied to our necks and be drowned in the depths of the ocean (Mark 9:42). Paul then lays a great responsibility at the door of Titus. He is to live in such a way that his observers cannot doubt his commitment to godliness.

C. Teaching Slaves (vv. 9, 10)

9, 10. Exhort servants to be obedient unto their own masters, and to please them well in all things; not answering again; not purloining, but showing all good fidelity; that they may adorn the doctrine of God our Saviour in all things.

It is dangerous to apply this passage to anything in our modern situation, because we who live in Western democracies no longer have the institution of slavery that was widespread in the Roman world. Yet those of us who are employees and work for a living can find some principles here. We should be good employees so that our work habits show that we are serving a higher master. We should work diligently, not talking back *(answering again)* or stealing *(purloining)* from our employer. We are respectful. Again, there is the possibility that our actions are being monitored carefully by someone who reaches conclusions about Jesus by viewing us.

IV. Training a Peculiar People (Titus 2:11-15)

A. Living Our Salvation (vv. 11, 12)

11, 12. For the grace of God that bringeth salvation hath appeared to all men, teaching us that, denying ungodliness and worldly lusts, we should live soberly, righteously, and godly, in this present world.

Paul sums up all of this teaching by saying that we should live as saved people. God did not save us to continue to wallow in the filth of sin. God saves us *from* sin.

Forgiveness is also deliverance. Paul knows that in his day godly living goes against the grain. Nothing is really different in that regard today. We are called to live in contrast to the values of *this present world,* which are controlled by *worldly lusts*—namely, self-interest, self-gratification, and general selfishness.

WHERE ARE YOU NOW, REALLY?

The United States Army adopted a slogan a few years ago that tempted potential recruits to sign up and become "An Army of One." The statement is a contradiction in terms if you think about it. An army, by definition, is a large, organized body of soldiers. The recruiting idea thus seems to be something like, "Leave the civilian world behind as you come and join our team where individuality is more important than teamwork." Whew!

A somewhat similar mix-up of concepts is found in the pages of Christian history. Centuries ago, some Christians sought to separate themselves from "the world" by joining together with others who wanted to do the same. These individuals were known as *monks;* this comes from the Greek *monos,* meaning "alone" or "solitary." These monks lived together in *monasteries,* which has the meaning of "to live alone"!

Yet Christians never were called to live alone, separated from the culture, whether individually or as a group. Christians live in this present world as active participants in culture and society (compare 1 Corinthians 5:10). Jesus, as He prayed for His followers, said to the Father, "I pray not that thou shouldest take them out of the world, but that thou shouldest keep them from the evil" (John 17:15).

Churches, along with individual Christians, constantly must find ways in which to engage this present world in order to be an influence of godliness. In this way we live *in* this world but not *of* this world until Christ returns. —A. E. A.

B. Waiting for Jesus (vv. 13, 14)

13, 14. Looking for that blessed hope, and the glorious appearing of the great God and our Saviour Jesus Christ; who gave himself for us, that he might redeem us from all iniquity, and purify unto himself a peculiar people, zealous of good works.

In the antique English of the *King James Version,* the word translated *peculiar* doesn't mean "odd" or "eccentric." Rather, it conveys a deep sense of ownership. (See also 1 Peter 2:9, although a different Greek word is used there.) *Christ* has saved us and purified us, or made us holy. Paul is confident that Jesus has not forgotten us. He will return and claim His possession, His bride, the church (Revelation 19:7, 8). [See question #3, page 255.]

C. Being Above Reproach (v. 15)

15. These things speak, and exhort, and rebuke with all authority. Let no man despise thee.

This concluding verse underlines the urgency of what Paul commands Titus to do. Titus must gain a hearing for what he is to say. Titus must exercise the *authority* he has from Paul and from the moral imperative that teaching godly behavior requires. Paul demands that Titus *Let no man despise thee* in this effort. Teaching how to live the godly life is an essential task of church leadership.

Conclusion

A. Is the Sunday School Dead?

Many churches today have abandoned the traditional Sunday morning Bible school hour. In some cases, all efforts are concentrated on the worship service, which often has been expanded. An emphasis is put on fellowship groups that meet in homes for prayer and support. Is there any place for Sunday school today? [See question #4, page 255.] Is there a place for regular, systematic instruction in godly living?

If you are using this lesson series, you have answered *yes* to at least the second question. While "delivery systems" may change over the years, there will always be a place for godly, dedicated teachers instructing children, young people, and older people in the ways of our Lord.

Such instruction should lift up the timeless principles found throughout Scripture. It should also study the lives of the godly men and women in the Bible who practiced these principles. It always should include a modeling of this lifestyle by the teacher. We cannot lead where we have not been or are unwilling to go. [See question #5, page 255.] In this regard, not all are fit to be teachers. (See James 3:1.)

I have never ministered with a church that had a surplus of teachers. Has God called you to this ministry? Are you willing to study His Word carefully, prepare lessons, and live up to the

---

Home Daily Bible Readings

Monday, Feb. 20—Speak the Truth in Love (Ephesians 4:11-16)

Tuesday, Feb. 21—Be Established in the Truth (2 Peter 1:3-12)

Wednesday, Feb. 22—Walk in the Light of Truth (1 John 1:5-10)

Thursday, Feb. 23—Support All Believers in the Truth (3 John 2-8)

Friday, Feb. 24—Teaching Older Men and Women (Titus 2:1-5)

Saturday, Feb. 25—Teaching Younger Men and Servants (Titus 2:6-10)

Sunday, Feb. 26—Teach What God Expects of Believers (Titus 2:11-15)

principles you teach? The responsibility is great, but the rewards are eternal.

B. Lifetime Learners

Do we ever progress to the point where the Bible has nothing left to teach us? Do we ever get to the place where we think we've heard it all before? The truth is that some people have spent decades in weekly Bible study, and the material may seem repetitive at times. However, some of the greatest scholars in the history of the church have never tired of studying the Bible.

John Locke (1632–1704) was one of the greatest thinkers of his day. He is credited with being the primary influence in the British Enlightenment, of finally overcoming the antiquated thinking of the medieval period. Locke's writings still influence people today. Some of his essays on government helped begin the era of democracy and end the era of kings and queens. Yet at the end of his life, Locke had some regrets. His was one of the most powerful minds in the history of the world, but he was not content. He once stated that if he had it all to do over again, he would spend more time studying the Bible and learning its truths.

The Bible as the Word of God is an inexhaustible source of wisdom, inspiration, and knowledge. These things are available for everyone who is willing to study it.

C. Prayer

Holy God our Father, renew our love for Your mighty Bible. May we dedicate ourselves more fully to learning Your Word and to teaching it faithfully to others. Help us set our priorities to include digging deeply into the Word of life. Please, we ask, continue to bless us as we let Your Word transform us. We pray in the name of the living Word, Your Son, Jesus Christ, amen.

D. Thought to Remember

We never should be too old or too young, too busy or too preoccupied for the serious study of the Bible's principles for living.

Learning by Doing

This section contains an alternative lesson plan emphasizing learning activities. Classes desiring such student involvement will find these suggestions helpful.

Learning Goals

After participating in this lesson, each student will be able to:

1. List some behaviors that must be taught to various age groups.
2. Explain why sound doctrine is necessary as a background to right behavior.
3. Participate in the teaching ministry of the church as both a learner and a teacher.

Into the Lesson

Display a banner that reads, "We Learn from Our (and Others') Misteaks!" (The irony of the misspelling should provoke laughter.) Begin by asking students to share incidents from their childhood years when an admired adult disappointed them by inappropriate conduct or words. This may be done in small groups.

Make the transition to Bible study by saying, "We may learn several lessons from such experiences. We learn about disappointment, human imperfections, and the power of a model in behavior. Today's study teaches how believers in Christ are to behave in a world that watches."

Into the Word

Use the Lesson Background to prepare and deliver a brief lecture on the problems and culture on Crete. Emphasize the challenges facing Titus.

Prior to class, prepare the following four signs and affix them in the corners of the room:

1. Senior Members (Titus 2:2-4)
2. Younger Members (Titus 2:4-8)
3. Lessons from Servanthood (Titus 2:9, 10)
4. A Peculiar People (Titus 2:11-15)

Also prepare a task sheet with the following instructions for the study teams:

Team #1: Paul suggests some "behavior biggies" for older members of the church. List these on the poster board and discuss why these are so important in Christianity. Then list a few practical ways today's church can encourage these traits in its older adults.

Team #2: Paul suggests some "behavior biggies" for younger members of the church. List these on the poster board and discuss why these are so important in Christianity. Then list a few practical ways today's church can encourage these traits in its younger adults.

Team #3: While those who live in Western democracies no longer experience slavery in church or culture, we do learn lessons from this passage that can be applied to Christian employees. List the lessons you learn from this passage about Christian behavior in that regard. Why are these traits so important for believers?

Team #4: Verses 11-15 cite some "behavior biggies" for Christians living in a watching world. List these traits or qualities on the poster board. Discuss why these behaviors or traits are so important to us and to the kingdom of God.

Say, "We are going to discover behavioral traits and challenges that face Christians. Paul teaches us about older adults, younger adults, the church in general, and even lessons from slavery." Ask students to take chairs and move to one of the signs you've posted. In order to keep the groups somewhat balanced, you may place a limit on the number of people allowed for each task. Give each group a copy of the task sheet, a piece of poster board, and a marker.

After the groups reach conclusions, allow time for them to report their discoveries to the class as a whole. Then make the transition to application by saying, "These lists of behaviors or values are not complete. We could add many other values or characteristics that are important as people watch us living out our faith."

Into Life

Ask the teams to turn their poster boards over and write the letters of the word *Christlike* vertically. The teams are to compose a prayer expressing the traits or behaviors suggested in today's text. Post the following example:

I am thankful, Lord, You

  Call me to
  Hear and obey the
 tRuths of Your Word.
  I know my
  Speech and
ac**T**ions will bring either
 g**L**ory or dishonor to You.
  I, therefore,
  Know I must commit myself to be an
  Example for Your glory. Amen.

Close with a prayer for Christlikeness.

Let's Talk It Over

These questions are designed to promote discussion of the lesson. The answers here are only discussion starters. Let your class talk it over from there.

1. Titus 2:5 speaks of young women being "keepers at home." How do we apply this to modern culture while not violating Paul's intent?

This is a difficult question, and the discussion can become heated if you're not careful! Start by considering what Paul may be speaking *against*. In 1 Timothy 5:11-15, Paul notes the young widows' tendency "to be idle, wandering about from house to house." Nothing good can come of this, even today. Putting that passage alongside Titus 2:5 lets us conclude that the focus should be on one's own home instead of the homes of others.

This focus can take various forms. Those who are able financially to be stay-at-home moms are privileged and blessed. (So are the kids!) Some find homeschooling to be an ideal option, good for both mother and children. The home should be a safe place emotionally, physically, and spiritually for all members of the family. Wives and mothers play a key role in making it so.

2. What type of vocabulary should be classified as "sound speech"? How has postmodern society blurred the distinction between sound and unsound speech?

Unfortunately, the general public today hardly recognizes the distinction between acceptable and unacceptable language. Television parades vulgarity before us daily. Society doesn't seem to mind, with one key exception: anything that may be labeled "hate speech." Postmodern culture vigorously condemns that, often as a response to those preaching the gospel!

Some experts say that language should evolve from common usage. Those who disagree are labeled disparagingly as "guardians of the language." *Sound speech* in the context of our lesson is, at the very least, not profane or vulgar. Christ was clear when He warned, "By thy words thou shalt be justified, and by thy words thou shalt be condemned" (Matthew 12:37). Perhaps Paul had that warning in mind when he added that Christians should engage in "neither filthiness, nor foolish talking, nor jesting" (Ephesians 5:4).

3. How can you, as one of the "peculiar" people, influence the lives of "popular" people?

In a general sense, it starts as being the salt and light of the world as noted in Matthew 5:13-16. This should lead us to ask ourselves what we've done this past week to make that happen within our circles of acquaintances. Having a friendship with an unbeliever provides an open door. You can speak plainly and seriously to someone who has become your friend. Sincere, friendly relationships generate mutual trust. It may take a while to establish such friendships, but eventually you will have opportunities to witness to eternal truths through word and deed.

4. Has Sunday school outlived its usefulness in the twenty-first century? Why, or why not?

Sunday school has served for decades as a primary way to teach Bible content. If Sunday school is eliminated, what will take its place for the specific teaching of Scripture? Small-group fellowships undoubtedly serve a vitally important role in building relationships among Christians. But by design, many such fellowships emphasize things other than Bible study. A recent magazine article offered 10 commandments for making small groups "work," but did not list teaching Bible content within those ten!

People without knowledge of Bible content can fall back only on their worldly knowledge and experiences. Until a satisfactory replacement is found, Sunday school remains one of the best methods for imparting Bible knowledge.

5. Do you agree with the lesson writer's axiom, "We cannot lead where we have not been or are unwilling to go"? Why, or why not?

The apostle Paul knew that great teaching required both knowledgeable words and godly living. Having *knowledgeable words* requires prior study to gain that wisdom, and teachers definitely are trying to lead students down that same path.

The *godly living* part of the equation shows the student both the credibility of the teacher and the natural result of applying the knowledgeable words to one's life. These ideas are consistent with the lesson writer's axiom, which can be restated as, "You cannot teach what you do not know; you cannot lead where you will not go."

Quarter Review

Use this page to form questions for the class to answer and discuss. Then provide the information as a handout to summarize the lessons of the past quarter.

Lesson 1: Justice for All

The quarter begins with one of the "Servant Songs" of Isaiah. It is a beautiful picture of the Messiah—Jesus—revealed some 700 years before His birth. The anticipated blessing to the Gentiles is also seen here in clear and unmistakable terms.

Lesson 2: Strength for the Weary

The Servant is uniquely qualified to give "strength to the weary." He himself has been sustained in a time of distress. This prophecy foretells Jesus' humiliation at the crucifixion. Then it promises to sustain those who believe in Him!

Lesson 3: Hope for the Suffering

Isaiah says the Servant is despised and rejected. That was not what was uppermost in Mary's mind, however, when she learned she would bear the Messiah. Joy and sorrow are mixed in the Messiah's life and in the lives of His followers.

Lesson 4: Good News for the World

The "Christmas" looks at the birth of Christ from the Gospel of Luke. Angels reveal to shepherds "good tidings of great joy." Our understanding of that good news is enhanced by the Servant's "mission statement" from Isaiah 61.

Lesson 5: Rely on God's Strength

In this first lesson from the Pastoral Epistles, Paul recalls his own past and the terrible life from which he was delivered. This he uses as a charge to the young evangelist Timothy to hold fast to his faith and to pass it on to others.

Lesson 6: Pray for Everyone

Paul urges prayer for all people. Specifically mentioned is prayer for government leaders, but the injunction goes well beyond them. At the heart of Paul's concern is the salvation of the lost. That must be central in our prayer requests.

Lesson 7: Call Godly Leaders

The third chapter of 1 Timothy is vital in the consideration of leadership of the local church. What qualities are needed? While not an exhaustive list, the one in this chapter paints a picture of sterling character. Who would want less?

Lesson 8: Teach for Godliness

Paul is very much concerned with sound doctrine. What leaders teach in the church is vital to the success of the church. Warning timothy of opposition to come, Paul urges his son in the faith to continue to teach what is right and true.

Lesson 9: Practice Justice and Mercy

How do we relate to others in the church? Using the images of family, Paul tells Timothy how best to get along with and to encourage others in the church. Of special importance are the elders, and special instructions are given for them.

Lesson 10: Be True to Your Christian Heritage

As Paul nears the end of his life, he writes again to Timothy. Paul is concerned that Timothy leave a legacy. It's a legacy that Timothy inherited—not from Paul, but from his own faithful mother and grandmother!

Lesson 11: Develop Christian Character

Good character is developed by doing some things and not doing others. Paul addresses both as he writes his final letter to Timothy, and Timothy must address both in his own ministry. And so must the church today.

Lesson 12: Follow a Good Mentor

Last words are always significant. This lesson draws from the last known words written by the apostle Paul. They include a charge for Timothy to live as Paul lived, preaching the Word, standing up for truth, keeping the faith.

Lesson 13: Live and Teach the Truth

The book of Titus is a good place to finish the quarter, In it, Paul summarizes much of the same information he gave Timothy in the two letters he wrote to him. Doing right and teaching right remain Paul's focus. Are they ours?

Copyright © 2005. STANDARD PUBLISHING, Cincinnati, Ohio. Permission is granted to reproduce this page for ministry purposes only. Not for resale.

Spring Quarter 2006

Living in and as God's Creation

Special Features

	Page
Quarterly Quiz	258
Repair and Prepare (Essay Feature) .... J. Michael Shannon	259
Solomon and Jesus (Chart Feature)	261
Living in and as God's Creation (Chart Feature)	262
Putting the Em´·pha·sis on the Right Syl´·la·ble (Teacher Tips) .... Ronald G. Davis	263
How to Say It	266
Quarterly Review	384

Lessons

Unit 1: The Glory of God's Creation

March	5	God Made Us Special .... *Psalm 8:1-9*	267
	12	God Created Wonderful Things .... *Psalm 104:1-13*	276
	19	God Created and Knows Us .... *Psalm 139:1-3, 7-14, 23, 24*	285
	26	Sing Praise to the Creator .... *Psalm 145:1-13*	294

Unit 2: Living with Creation's Uncertainty

April	2	Responding to Tragedy .... *Job 1:14-22; 3:1-3, 11*	303
	9	Searching for Hope .... *Job 14:1, 2, 11-17; 32:6, 8; 34:12; 37:14, 22*	312
	16	God Gives Life .... *Job 38:1, 4, 16, 17; 42:1, 2, 5; Mark 16:1-14, 20*	321
	23	Finding Life's Meaning .... *Ecclesiastes 1:1-9; John 20:19-23*	330
	30	Living in God's Time .... *Ecclesiastes 3:1-8, 14, 15*	339

Unit 3: Lessons in Living

May	7	Seek Wisdom .... *Proverbs 2:1-5; 3:1-6, 13-18*	348
	14	Accept Wisdom's Invitation .... *Proverbs 8:1-5, 22-32*	357
	21	Follow the Path of Integrity .... *Proverbs 11:1-14*	366
	28	Living Out Wisdom .... *Proverbs 31:8-14, 25-30*	375

About These Lessons

Those who live in technologically advanced countries are always on the lookout for "the next big thing" as yesterday's gadgets become boring. In the spiritual life, however, the next big thing comes to us ever new from a source in the ancient past: the wisdom in God's unchanging Word. This wisdom is priceless. It serves us into eternity. It is our subject this quarter.

Quarterly Quiz

This quiz can be used to preview the lessons, to review at the end of the quarter, or as a review after each lesson. The quiz may be copied and distributed to students. **The answers are on page 264.**

Lesson 1
1. To whom is Psalm 8 addressed? (David's enemies, the Lord, Israel?) *Psalm 8:1*
2. God gave us dominion over the earth. T/F *Psalm 8:6*

Lesson 2
1. In Psalm 104 David specifically repeats God's promise to Noah that the earth will be covered again by a flood. T/F *Psalm 104:9*
2. In Psalm 104 God himself is a flaming fire. T/F *Psalm 104:4*

Lesson 3
1. When David appeals to God to examine him closely, he includes what? (heart and thoughts, feet and eyes, arms and legs?) *Psalm 139:23*
2. At the end of Psalm 139, David asks to be led in what kind of "way"? (everlasting, of safety, of wisdom?) *Psalm 139:24*

Lesson 4
1. What three words are used at the beginning of Psalm 145 as ways we honor God with our words? (exalt/honor/magnify, lift/glorify/exalt, extol/bless/praise)? *Psalm 145:1, 2*
2. In addition to praising God for who He is, David thought it appropriate to speak of God's power. T/F *Psalm 145:10-13*

Lesson 5
1. The text says that Job's enemies also plugged up his wells. T/F *Job 1:14-22*
2. How many oxen did Job lose? (500, 1,000, 3,000?) *Job 1:3, 14, 15*

Lesson 6
1. Job does not compare life to what? (rainbow, flower, shadow?) *Job 14:2*
2. The fourth friend who came to console and question Job is named what? (Berechah, Elihu, Lemuel?) *Job 32:2*

Lesson 7
1. When God confronted Job, He allowed Job to have a glimpse of Heaven. T/F *Job 38:1, 4, 16, 17*
2. As soon as Mary Magdalene told other disciples of the empty tomb, those disciples believed her. T/F *Mark 16:11*

Lesson 8
1. What three-word phrase does Solomon use to characterize earthly existence? (vanity of vanities, under the moon, hope of eternity?) *Ecclesiastes 1:2*
2. What one word of encouragement does Jesus give to His fearful disciples? (hope, peace, come?) *John 20:19, 21*

Lesson 9
1. How many pairs of contrasts does Solomon use in his "a time for" list? (9, 12, 14?) *Ecclesiastes 3:2-8*
2. "A time to sleep and a time to awaken" is one of Solomon's contrasts. T/F *Ecclesiastes 3:2-8*

Lesson 10
1. In Proverbs 2 and 3, wisdom is likened to gold and what two other valuable assets? (beryl/turquoise, sapphire/topaz, silver/rubies?) *Proverbs 2:4; 3:15*
2. Solomon uses "tree of life" as a figure for discussing wisdom. T/F *Proverbs 3:18*

Lesson 11
1. The first thing that understanding does in Proverbs 8 is to put forth her _____. *Proverbs 8:1*
2. Proverbs 8 characterizes wisdom as being quietly hidden, waiting for the diligent to find her. T/F *Proverbs 8:1-3*

Lesson 12
1. The opposite of "false balance" is what? (just weight, idolatry, praise?) *Proverbs 11:1*
2. Riches will be of no value/profit in the day of (victory, wrath, rain?) *Proverbs 11:4*

Lesson 13
1. The virtuous woman of Proverbs 31 does not eat the bread of what? (God's Sabbath, her children, idleness?) *Proverbs 31:27*
2. Social justice is one of the themes of Proverbs 31. T/F *Proverbs 31:8, 9*

Repair and Prepare
by J. Michael Shannon

THE LATE STEVE ALLEN told of a lady named Liz who had been hurt in an automobile accident. A lawyer came to visit her and said, "I've come to assist you in getting damages." Liz replied, "I got all the damages I want. What I need is repairs." This is true of many hurting people we come in contact with every day. The church in general and we in particular are to assist people in making repairs to their lives. The world we live in is imperfect. It is a mixture of great beauty and ugliness, of triumphs and tragedies. The lessons this quarter will help us deal with the damages and make the repairs.

Yet at the same time let us not overlook the repairs that we ourselves are in need of. These repairs begin when we remember that we are part of the fabric of God's creation even as we live within that creation. Even though we recognize that God is the author of all creation, we often still live at odds with creation. Part of God's repair for our lives is to learn how to live in this world that God has created. This quarter's lessons will help.

Our studies primarily examine parts of what is called *the wisdom literature* of the Old Testament. Such literature very often is poetic. Some of our selected passages from Job, Psalms, Proverbs, and Ecclesiastes are widely read, while others often are avoided. We will see why as we allow those texts to assist us in understanding and living in this world even as we prepare ourselves for the next.

Unit 1: March
The Glory of God's Creation

The first unit offers us selections from the psalms. This is one of the books most precious to us because of its poetic beauty and frequent frankness. The book of Psalms is the Hebrew hymn book. The chapters are separate songs that speak to a variety of situations. These songs sing of God's power, creativity, and mighty acts. When we reach the end of this unit, we will be puzzled that people could look at the world around them and not believe in God.

Lesson 1: God Made Us Special. This lesson from Psalm 8 emphasizes how human beings are a glorious act of God's creation. This has profound implications concerning how we view ourselves and how we view God.

Lesson 2: God Created Wonderful Things. This lesson from Psalm 104 examines the more traditional elements of God's created order. It helps us express a sense of awe concerning the one who could make such beauty.

Lesson 3: God Created and Knows Us. This Sunday features an examination of Psalm 139 as our attention turns to the character of the creator himself. How completely He knows us and is ever present in our lives! We may look at ourselves a bit differently at the end of this lesson, even with regard to our physical forms. We are God's crowning act of creation.

Lesson 4: Sing Praise to the Creator. The final session in this unit, taken from Psalm 145, celebrates the God of creation. As such, it leads us into acts of worship. We will learn that praise has inner and outer aspects: our feelings and our actions.

Unit 2: April
Living with Creation's Uncertainty

The lessons for April deal with material that is more difficult. How do we respond when the entire created order, even the creator himself, seems to be against us? Sometimes there appear to be no answers. Here we will deal with a problem that is age old, yet as current as this morning's newspaper: the problem of tragedy. For these lessons we will examine primarily Job and Ecclesiastes. Both books are rather dark. Both seem to yearn for answers. We will find answers by looking at selected New Testament passages from the Gospels of Mark and John.

The book of Job begins with a scene in Heaven. There Satan charges that Job loves God only because that man has had life so easy. Life then becomes anything *but* easy for Job! Much of the book then features an ongoing discussion between Job and his friends concerning why all Job's tragedies have happened. In the end Job does not get complete answers, but he does get an audience with God.

Ecclesiastes, for its part, is a book of musings about the meaning of life. Most of the book sets a despairing and rather hopeless tone. Nevertheless, by the end of the book we are drawn inevitably back to God.

Lesson 5: Responding to Tragedy. The first lesson in this unit, taken from chapters 1 through 3 of Job, show us why Job's testing happened in the first place. It also examines Job's feelings of grief.

Lesson 6: Searching for Hope. For Palm Sunday, we will look at selected verses from Job 14, 32, 34, and 37. These passages follow some of Job's discussions with his friends. Those friends accuse Job of not being as good as he says. Yet Job maintains his innocence. This lesson deals specifically with the longing for eternal life.

Lesson 7: God Gives Life. The Easter lesson begins in Job 38 and 42. But we finish by visiting the Gospel of Mark to see how the resurrection of Jesus comes to bear on the questions raised in Job. Job believed he had a redeemer. We now know him as Jesus of Nazareth.

Lesson 8: Finding Life's Meaning. This lesson has its foundation in Ecclesiastes 1. Since this Sunday takes us to the afterglow of Easter, our lesson also finds us in the Gospel of John and one of the postresurrection appearances of Jesus. The writer of Ecclesiastes wonders about a sense of purpose. This lesson shows how Jesus provides just what we need in that regard.

Lesson 9: Living in God's Time. The last lesson in this unit takes us back to Ecclesiastes. This time we're in chapter 3. There we will ponder the meaning of time and history in one of the most well-known, yet hard to decipher, passages in the Bible.

When we come to the end of this unit, we may breathe a bit of a sigh, because we have dealt with many of the most perplexing and difficult issues of life. Yet we hope to come out with a new perspective!

Think about the issue of perspective. When you look at a field of dandelions, you probably see just weeds. When Peter A. Gail looks at it, he sees lunch! Dr. Gail, an ethno-botanist who is called "the wizard of weeds," eats many dandelions every day. He claims that the dandelion is both healthy and flavorful. Much of our enthusiasm in life is related to our perspective, isn't it?

Unit 3: May
Lessons in Living

Our final unit of the quarter teaches us how to conduct our lives in this fallen world. For these lessons we draw from the book of Proverbs. Most of this book consists of a collection of wise sayings written by, collected by, and in honor of King Solomon.

Certain themes are discussed repeatedly in Proverbs. Specifically, wisdom, industry, self-control, honesty, and humility are encouraged. While the book of Proverbs is part of the Old Testament's wisdom literature, it cannot magically provide wisdom. We must study these passages thoroughly, ask God's help earnestly, and apply them diligently. Wisdom is developed with God's blessing. Without that blessing all we have is the world's "whatever works" wisdom.

Lesson 10: Seek Wisdom. The first lesson in this unit focuses on selected verses from Proverbs 2 and 3. There wisdom and its acquisition are praised. The distinction between secular and spiritual wisdom is vital to know.

Lesson 11: Accept Wisdom's Invitation. This lesson from Proverbs 8 portrays wisdom as a person calling out for those who desire her. The fact that wisdom really is attainable is a great encouragement of this study.

Lesson 12: Follow the Path of Integrity. This session from Proverbs 11 explores the matter of integrity in work and personal life. Integrity carries spiritual rewards. Since integrity is important to God, it should be important to us as well.

Lesson 13: Living Out Wisdom. The final lesson in this quarter, taken from Proverbs 31, provides a profile of the honorable wife and mother. She is no shrinking violet! The ancient challenges are quite relevant to today. Men will gain wisdom as well as they explore ways to honor the godly and diligent women in their lives.

Wisdom Calls!

Wisdom does indeed call, but not everyone answers. How sad to see so many settle for worldly "street smarts"! In his book *A Wee Bit of Irish Wisdom*, Jim Gallery records this old Irish blessing: "May you have the hindsight to know where you have been, the foresight to know where you are going, and the insight to know when you are going too far." May God grant you this blessing as well through this quarter's lessons.

Solomon and Jesus

Solomon	Jesus
Wisest on Earth 1 Kings 4:29-34	**Wiser than Solomon** Luke 11:31
Life of Splendor and Self-Indulgence 1 Kings 11:3; Ecclesiastes 2:3-10	**Life of Sorrow and Self-Denial** Isaiah 53:2-5
Built Earthly Temple 1 Kings 6	**Rebuilt Bodily Temple** John 2:19-22
Accepted as King 1 Chronicles 29:22	**Hailed then Rejected as King** John 12:13; 19:15
Embraced a Kingship 1 Kings 1:30	**Refused a Kingship** John 6:15
Had Wisdom from God 1 Kings 4:29	**Was Wisdom from God** 1 Corinthians 1:30
Lost Focus; Sinned 1 Kings 11	**Stayed Focused; Never Sinned** Hebrews 4:15; 1 Peter 2:22

Living in and as God's Creation

The Glory of God's Creation	Living with Creation's Uncertainty	Lessons in Living
God Made Us Special: Crowned with Honor Psalm 8	Responding to Tragedy: Loss and Grief Job 1, 3	Seek Wisdom: Path of Happiness Proverbs 2, 3
God Created Wonderful Things: Heaven and Earth Psalm 104	Searching for Hope: Change is Coming Job 14, 32, 34, 37	Accept Wisdom's Invitation: God's Delight Proverbs 8
God Created and Knows Us: Marvelous Works Psalm 139	God Gives Life: Resurrection Job 38, 42 Mark 16	Follow the Path of Integrity: God's Right Way Proverbs 11
Sing Praise to the Creator: Worship Psalm 145	Finding Life's Meaning: Peace in God Ecclesiastes 1 John 20	Living Out Wisdom: A Noble Woman Proverbs 31
	Living in God's Time: A Season for Everything Ecclesiastes 3	

Teacher Tips

Putting the Em´•pha•sis on the Right Syl´•la•ble

by Ronald G. Davis

EMPHASIS. That is what writer and speaker strive for. God's Spirit certainly knows emphasis. So, much of God's Word is written in emphatic form and style. Poetic style, in which much of the Bible is presented (including all of this quarter's texts), is always emphatic.

In poetry there is the emphasis of repetition. This is especially true of Hebrew poetry's emphatic parallelism. But there is also the emphasis of figurative language that manages to say something twice with one set of words. The figurative stirs a thought of recognition and application.

A Christian teacher of adults will at times wisely choose poetry and poetic activity to follow in the Spirit's train. And every such teacher wants the educational emphasis of ideas that such choices allow. Several planning pages in the lesson developments suggest learning activities related to figurative language, parallelism, and poetry. But consider others given here.

A Favorite Poem

To get class members involved, establish a display board for verses the students bring that are related to the studies. Put the title of this article as the title of your display. At the first study, or even a week or two before, give your class members a list of the primary themes of the quarter. Say, "You probably have one or more favorite poetic verses that relate to our coming studies. I have put up this board for a display. Bring them in week to week, and we will all enjoy them."

Next distribute this list of themes: "The Glory of God's Creation," "Living with Creation's Uncertainties," and "Lessons in Living"—the quarter's unit titles. You can add key phrases such as *Praise, God's Presence, Hope, Resurrection, Meaning, Times and Seasons, Wisdom and Success, Integrity and Shame,* and *Godly Women and Family.* Suggest sources such as hymn and chorus lyrics, classic poems from school curriculum, greeting cards, and even class members' own compositions.

You may wish to post a few samples to get the activity started. Consider the following two, one a silly rhyme about dying, the second a traditional song about the sadness and futility of life without God and Jesus.

In Boxes
Birthday presents tied with bows,
Christmas gifts of wrapped up clothes,
Securely locked deposit box,
Assorted candies—creams and chocs—
Rectangular cartons filled with glee;
But the last thing I want in a box . . .
Is me!

How Tedious and Tasteless
How tedious and tasteless, the hours
When Jesus I no longer see;
Sweet prospects, sweet birds, and sweet flowers,
Have all lost their sweetness to me.
. . . .
O drive these dark clouds from the sky,
Thy soul cheering presence restore;
Or take me to thee up on high,
Where winter and clouds are no more.

The former might be used in either Lesson 5 or 6, where Job's tragedies elicit death wishes from him. The latter will work well in Lesson 8 in which Solomon bemoans the futility and discouragement of life "under the sun."

A simple poem such as Emily Dickinson's "I'm Nobody! Who Are You?" could well reflect an attitude in contrast with David's expression of Psalm 8:4: What is man, that You, God, are even mindful of him? Such a poem as E. E. Cummings's "i thank you God for most this amazing" is a beautiful expression of praise, certainly appropriate for Lesson 2.

Further, one can hardly hear Job's humble acknowledgement of God's sovereignty and care in Lesson 7 and not remember the powerful confession of Civilla Martin's words: "Why should I feel discouraged, why should the shadows come, / Why should my heart be lonely, and long for heaven and home, / When Jesus is my portion? My constant Friend is He: / His eye is on the sparrow, and I know He watches me." And the hymnal is also a certain source of poems extolling the resurrection and its power for Lessons 7 and 8.

Just a Couplet

Two-line poetic expressions are among the first that children learn to chant, and they still intrigue the adult. Because several of this quarter's studies are written in the parallelism that is common to Hebrew writers, encouraging your adults to express themselves similarly is a worthy goal.

Lesson 1 has Psalm 8 for its text, each verse a typical example of an expression followed by a related expression—sometimes a simple restatement in other words. For such a lesson, consider asking your students to complete the first expression with a second of their own composition. Verse one begins, "O Lord our Lord, how excellent is thy name in all the earth!" The couplet could be completed with an expression such as, "May your name be praised by all," etc.

Consider selecting a first expression from verses such as the following and asking class members to complete them: Lesson 1—Psalm 8:6a; Lesson 2—Psalm 104:5a; Lesson 3—Psalm 139:7a; Lesson 4—Psalm 145:13a; Lesson 5—Job 1:21b; Lesson 6—Job 32:8; Lesson 7—Job 42:2a; Lesson 8—Ecclesiastes 1:4a; Lesson 9—Ecclesiastes 3:14a; Lesson 10—Proverbs 3:5a; Lesson 11—Proverbs 8:5a; Lesson 12—Proverbs 11:12a; Lesson 13—Proverbs 31:26a. This exercise could be the assignment as students arrive or could be the homework for a lesson to come. Later comparisons and contrasts with the Bible text will emphasize the truth of the selected verses.

It Figures

An important part of poetic expression is the careful choice of figures of speech. Just as Robert Frost emphasized the importance of simple decisions in the course of life in "The Road Not Taken" by using the figure of a fork in the road; just as the proverb writer personifies wisdom (Proverbs 8:1); just as Job compares a life to a flower (Job 14:2)—the comparative device of figurative language must be used fully.

The teacher's device can be as simple as beginning a comparison and letting class members complete it. For example, for Lesson 1 try "Man is like a . . . " Such similes allow not only a discussion of similarities but also demand a discussion of differences, such as the psalmist does when he says, "made him a little lower than the angels" (Psalm 8:5). In Lesson 13, the writer says of the godly woman that "strength and honor" are her clothing. Having the students examine the text for other articles of her "clothing" that would prove profitable. For example, do not several verses speak of her skill in household crafts? Does not verse 20 show generosity and kindness hanging in her "wardrobe"? Let your adults think creatively of her whole "closet of finery."

Child's Play

Involving children in the adult classroom offers real interest and variety. A class member's child or grandchild presenting a short and simple children's poem to the adult class can provoke true discussion of the significant themes of this quarter's lessons.

Though one might think children's poems are all fluff and nonsense, the great children's poets tackle the real issues of a child's life: feelings, hopes, life, and death. In the collections of such children's poets as David McCord, Aileen Fisher, Karla Kuskin, John Ciardi, Arnold Adoff, Jack Prelutsky, Shel Silverstein, and others, deep thoughts are expressed in humor and in deep sensitivity. (If you have an elementary school teacher or former one in your class, that person may relish finding "just the right poem" and inviting "just the right child" to read or say it to your class.)

In only 32 words Langston Hughes calls vividly for the hope only "Dreams" can sustain and which Lesson 6 promises. Christina Rossetti

---

Answers to Quarterly Quiz on page 258

Lesson 1—1. the Lord. 2. true. **Lesson 2**—1. false. 2. false. **Lesson 3**—1. heart/thoughts. 2. everlasting. **Lesson 4**—1. extol/bless/praise. 2. true. **Lesson 5**—1. false. 2. 1,000 (which equals 500 yoke). **Lesson 6**—1. rainbow. 2. Elihu. **Lesson 7**—1. false. 2. false. **Lesson 8**—1. vanity of vanities. 2. peace. **Lesson 9**—1. 14. 2. false. **Lesson 10**—1. silver/rubies. 2. true. **Lesson 11**—1. voice. 2. false. **Lesson 12**—1. just (accurate) weight. 2. wrath. **Lesson 13**—1. idleness. 2. true.

(1830–1894) captures the wonder of creation that the psalmist extols in Lesson 2; hear her "Who Has Seen the Wind?":

> Who has seen the wind?
>   Neither I nor you:
> But when the leaves hang trembling,
>   The wind is passing through.
> Who has seen the wind?
>   Neither you nor I:
> But when the trees bow down their heads,
>   The wind is passing by.

Such expressions are reminiscent also of God's challenges to Job in Lesson 7. For Lesson 12, "Follow the Path of Integrity," a reading/saying of the stanzas "I Would Be True" by Howard A. Walter can add impact at application time. Having two alternating readers/speakers will add impact. For Lesson 2, a child reading Calvin Miller's "Catherine Caterpillar" from his book of children's poems *When the Aardvark Parked on the Ark* can emphasize the marvel of God's plans for each of His creatures. (Note: poems and stanzas not reproduced here can often be found on the Internet.)

Wax Poetic

God's Spirit often waxed poetic when He wanted to reveal God and His will. The beauty, the emphasis, the thought-provoking value of those expressions in the Word are a strong challenge to the teacher of Christian adults: how can I follow in His example? Give poetry a chance, and it will weave its web of power over your students.

How to Say It

Use this list to help you pronounce the names and hard to pronounce words in the lessons of the spring quarter.

A

AGUR. *Ay*-gur.
AHAB. *Ay*-hab.
AL-QAEDA. Al *Kai*-duh.
ARABIA. Uh-*ray*-bee-uh.

B

BARACHEL. *Bar*-uh-kel.
BATHSHEBA. Bath-*she*-buh.
BETHLEHEM. *Beth*-lih-hem.
BILDAD. *Bill*-dad.
BUZITE. *Bew*-zyet.

C

CAPERNAUM. Kuh-*per*-nay-um.
CASSINI-HUYGENS. Kuh-*see*-nee *Hoi*-genz.
CAVEAT EMPTOR (Latin). *ka*-vee-at *emp*-ter.
CLEOPAS. *Clee*-uh-pass.
CORINTHIANS. Ko-*rin*-thee-unz (*th* as in *thin*).

D

DEUTERONOMY. Due-ter-*ahn*-uh-me.
DIETRICH BONHOEFFER. *Dee*-trick *Bon*-huh-fur.

E

ECCLESIASTES. Ik-*leez*-ee-*as*-teez (strong accent on *as*).
EDOMITES. *Ee*-dum-ites.
ELIHU. Ih-*lye*-hew.
ELIJAH. Ee-*lye*-juh.
ELIPHAZ. *El*-ih-faz.
EMMAUS. Em-*may*-us.
EPHESIANS. Ee-*fee*-zhunz.
EUNICE. U-*nye*-see or *U*-nis.
EZEKIEL. Ee-*zeek*-ee-ul or Ee-*zeek*-yul.

G

GALILEE. *Gal*-uh-lee.
GOLIATH. Go-*lye*-uth.

H

HANNAH. *Han*-uh.
HEBREWS. *Hee*-brews.
HEZEKIAH. Hez-ih-*kye*-uh.
HOSEA. Ho-*zay*-uh.

I

IMMANUEL. Ih-*man*-you-el.
ISAIAH. Eye-*zay*-uh.

J

JEREMIAH. Jair-uh-*my*-uh.
JERUSALEM. Juh-*roo*-suh-lem.
JOCHEBED. *Jock*-eh-bed.
JONAH. *Jo*-nuh.
JOSES. *Jo*-sez.

L

LEMUEL. *Lem*-you-el.
LEVITICUS. Leh-*vit*-ih-kus.
LUCIUS ANNAEUS SENECA. *Loo*-shuss Uh-*nee*-us *Sen*-uh-kuh.

M

MACHIAVELLI. *Ma*-key-uh-*veh*-lee (strong accent on *Ma*).
MAGDALENE. *Mag*-duh-leen or Mag-duh-*lee*-nee.
MALACHI. *Mal*-uh-kye.
MAO TSE-TUNG. Mau dzuh-*dung*.

N

NAPOLEON BONAPARTE. Nuh-*pol*-yuhn *Bo*-nuh-*part* (strong accent on *part*).
NAZARETH. *Naz*-uh-reth.
NEBUCHADNEZZAR. *Neb*-yuh-kud-*nez*-er (strong accent on *nez*).
NEHEMIAH. Nee-huh-*my*-uh (strong accent on *my*).

O

ONESIMUS. O-*ness*-ih-muss.

P

PHARAOH AKHENATON. *Fair*-o (or *Fay*-roe) Ock-*naw*-tun.
PHILEMON. Fih-*lee*-mun or Fye-*lee*-mun.

S

SABEANS. Suh-*be*-unz.
SALOME. Suh-*lo*-me.
SANHEDRIN. *San*-huh-drun or San-*heed*-run.
SATAN. *Say*-tun.
SHALOM (Hebrew). shah-*lome*.
SHEBA. *She*-buh.
SHEKEL. *sheh*-kul.
SOLOMON. *Sol*-o-mun.
SØREN KIERKEGAARD. *So*-ren *Kir*-kuh-gard.

Z

ZEBEDEE. *Zeb*-eh-dee.
ZECHARIAH. Zek-uh-*rye*-uh (strong accent on *rye*).
ZOPHAR. *Zo*-far.

God Made Us Special

March 5
Lesson 1

DEVOTIONAL READING: Genesis 1:26-31.

BACKGROUND SCRIPTURE: Psalm 8.

PRINTED TEXT: Psalm 8:1-9.

Psalm 8:1-9

1 O LORD our Lord, how excellent is thy name in all the earth! who hast set thy glory above the heavens.

2 Out of the mouth of babes and sucklings hast thou ordained strength because of thine enemies, that thou mightest still the enemy and the avenger.

3 When I consider thy heavens, the work of thy fingers, the moon and the stars, which thou hast ordained;

4 What is man, that thou art mindful of him? and the son of man, that thou visitest him?

5 For thou hast made him a little lower than the angels, and hast crowned him with glory and honor.

6 Thou madest him to have dominion over the works of thy hands; thou hast put all things under his feet:

7 All sheep and oxen, yea, and the beasts of the field;

8 The fowl of the air, and the fish of the sea, and whatsoever passeth through the paths of the seas.

9 O LORD our Lord, how excellent is thy name in all the earth!

GOLDEN TEXT: What is man, that thou art mindful of him? and the son of man, that thou visitest him? For thou hast made him a little lower than the angels, and hast crowned him with glory and honor.—Psalm 8:4, 5.

> *Living in and as God's Creation*
> Unit 1: The Glory of God's Creation
> (Lessons 1-4)

Lesson Aims

After participating in this lesson, each student will be able to:

1. Describe the position of human beings in creation.
2. Explain how knowledge of humanity's place in creation enhances his or her self-worth and gives life meaning.
3. Sing a song praising God as creator or complete a self-worth chart based on truths from the lesson.

Lesson Outline

INTRODUCTION
    A. Our Big Rocks
    B. Lesson Background
I. CREATOR PRAISE, PART 1 (Psalm 8:1, 2)
    A. Excellent Name, Revealed Glory (v. 1)
    B. Ordained Strength, Stilled Enemy (v. 2)
        An Excellent Reputation
II. CREATION PRIORITIES (Psalm 8:3-8)
    A. Heavens and Humanity (vv. 3, 4)
    B. Angels and Humanity (v. 5)
    C. Other Works and Humanity (vv. 6-8)
        Care for the Creation
III. CREATOR PRAISE, PART 2 (Psalm 8:9)
CONCLUSION
    A. The Order of Creation
    B. Prayer
    C. Thought to Remember

Introduction

A. Our Big Rocks

There is a standard object lesson for children that requires two jars of the same size, several large rocks, some gravel, and some sand. Into the first jar the teacher pours several cups of sand. Then the gravel is dumped in. Finally, the teacher asks the children, "Can we fit the rocks into this jar?" By then, there is no way that the rocks can possibly get into the jar.

In the second jar, the teacher begins with the rocks. Gravel is then gradually added, with care taken to distribute it throughout the jar. Finally, the sand is poured in. If done correctly, the jar easily contains all of the material, even though the same number of objects did not come close to fitting into the other jar.

The point of that object lesson for children is *prioritization:* take care of the big things first and the smaller things will fit into place. That is a lesson that many of us adults need to relearn as well!

Today we see that this is a vital part of Psalm 8's message for us. When our priorities are correct, everything fits together. Those universal priorities are quite straightforward, though that does not make them easy to accept. Most Christians understand intellectually that God is first. It is living out that reality, truly putting Him in first place, that we struggle with. Saying that *God is Number 1* is easy. Most of us, though, can relate with the lament of the orchestra conductor who noted that the hardest position to fill in any symphony was the position of second fiddle.

B. Lesson Background

King David, who lived about a thousand years before Christ, wrote Psalm 8. We are not entirely sure of its historical context; its address "to the chief Musician" is tantalizingly brief.

I. Creator Praise, Part 1 (Psalm 8:1, 2)

A. Excellent Name, Revealed Glory (v. 1)

1. O LORD our Lord, how excellent is thy name in all the earth! who hast set thy glory above the heavens.

The psalms are the music of faith. Many are intended to be sung or chanted as part of worship. When they are sung they can express the heart of the individual worshiper and the collective heart of the community of believers. The psalms accomplish this by pointing in each of the directions we face while worshiping. The main direction is upward (toward God). But we also face inward (personal reflection), sideways (toward other worshipers), and outward (toward unbelievers and nonworshipers).

The opening of Psalm 8 is decisively upward toward God. One Christian writer has noted that even though God is your Father, He is not your "old man." We may want so much to have a personal relationship with God that we may lose sight of God's transcendence (that is, His "otherness"). God the redeemer is also God the creator. That means we are accountable to Him, and not He to us. God is love—but that love in no way diminishes the fact that God is God and we are not. [See question #1, page 275.]

Even so, when David writes *O Lord . . . how excellent,* he is not writing to appease an unknowable, distant tyrant. David is writing in delight of a knowable, personal God. David is in awe of the God whom he knows, the God who can be known, the God who wants to be known. His *name* is excellent *in all the earth* not only because of its power but also because of its "knowability." God is worth knowing because it is His presence that gives value to everything and everyone. God's excellent name makes the earth a better place because of the association. How could it be otherwise?

Even so, this close association should not cause us to ignore or minimize the power and majesty of God. We've all heard the old saying "familiarity breeds contempt," and there is a certain danger here. Our association with God does not mean that we are to see Him as a pal or a buddy. It is His *glory* that is *above the heavens,* and not our own.

God has set His glory above the heavens because it is natural for Him to do so. My son likes to jump and touch the ceiling simply because he can—it shows he is growing and is able to do something he couldn't before. By contrast, God places His glory in the highest place not merely because He is able to do so, but because there is nowhere else that is more appropriate. The fact that a seven-foot-tall basketball player can reach the top shelf of a cupboard surprises no one. That is an expression of the person's height—a natural and expected by-product of his physical nature. The fact that God's glory is above the heavens is an expected result of His transcendence.

VISUALS FOR THESE LESSONS

The visual pictured in each lesson (for example, page 272) is a small reproduction of a large, full-color poster included in the *Adult Resources* packet for the Spring Quarter. The packet is available from your supplier. Order No. 392.

As awe-inspiring as that is, what is even more remarkable is the fact that Jesus "who, being in the form of God, thought it not robbery to be equal with God: but made himself of no reputation, and took upon him the form of a servant, and was made in the likeness of men: and being found in fashion as a man, he humbled himself, and became obedient unto death, even the death of the cross" (Philippians 2:6-8). The transcendent God not only has a name that is excellent in all the earth, He actually walked upon the earth —and more.

B. Ordained Strength, Stilled Enemy (v. 2)

2. Out of the mouth of babes and sucklings hast thou ordained strength because of thine enemies, that thou mightest still the enemy and the avenger.

Despite the power and greatness of God, His name can be enjoyed and celebrated by the youngest. No one can ever fully know how great God is. However, even a child can have some level of appreciation of God.

No tyrant can ever remove awareness of God from the creation. As part of the creation, we also have a fundamental appreciation for the creator. We may ignore that appreciation, deny its source, flaunt its implications, reject its conclusions, or pretend to be unaware of it altogether. However, we cannot escape ultimate accountability (Romans 1:18-20). Echoes of the creator are heard in the creation; His fingerprints are all over the firmament (compare Psalm 19).

We will see David explore more of the conclusions posed by this reality as Psalm 8 continues. Before moving on to consider that, we should not forget that Jesus quoted part of this psalm to His enemies in response to their complaint that children were praising Him (Matthew 21:15, 16).

An Excellent Reputation

A woman living in southern California was looking for a home with a view of the Pacific Ocean. She spent $1.2 million on a home with the view she wanted, but it needed a larger kitchen and two more bedrooms to meet her ideal of what the home should be. So she hired a friend to remodel the house. He assured her of his professional qualifications and promised her that he could do the architectural plans as well as the construction work.

Six months and more than $100,000 later, her La Jolla house had been reduced to a concrete slab. The owner was forced to hire another builder and construct a new house from the ground up. A state investigator said the site was the worst case she had ever seen. The owner discovered to her chagrin that the "friend" had no architect's license, his professional reputation was seriously clouded by a string of lawsuits that he had lost, and he had avoided paying the judgments against him in those suits.

What a contrast to God's reputation! The glories of the creation speak of God's power, but there is more: the power of God eventually will silence the foes of goodness and righteousness. That process began on the cross and will be completed in God's time when the Lord returns for those who trust Him. —C. R. B.

II. Creation Priorities
(Psalm 8:3-8)

A. Heavens and Humanity (vv. 3, 4)

3, 4. When I consider thy heavens, the work of thy fingers, the moon and the stars, which thou hast ordained; what is man, that thou art mindful of him? and the son of man, that thou visitest him?

At this point David celebrates the faith of the child who looks upward and asks, "Daddy, who made the stars?" Lost in the modern conflict between faith and science is the fact that all exploration of the universe is driven by a common wonder. Each of us shares a desire to know more about our origin. Where did we come from? The same question drives both the astronomer and the theologian. Physics and faith are both vehicles for the curious and the intellectually adventurous. We should not be surprised that many of the greatest scientific minds belonged—and even today yet belong—to people of profound faith.

Theologians describe two ways that God communicates with us. *Special revelation* occurs when God speaks through prophecy, miracles, etc. (compare Hebrews 1:1, 2). *General revelation* is much less precise, though vitally important in reflecting the character and nature of God. Creation itself is general revelation: principles evident in nature reflect the handiwork of the creator. Romans 1:19, 20 expresses it this way: "that which may be known of God is manifest in them; for God hath showed it unto them. For the invisible things of him from the creation of the world are clearly seen, being understood by the things that are made, even his eternal power and Godhead; so that they are without excuse." [See question #2, page 275.]

As David considers the power and care evident in the creation, his thoughts turn to the vast differences between created objects. Traveling through space, governed by physical laws that we are only beginning to understand, the moon and the stars reveal the awe-inspiring power of God's creative hand. Even with modern technology we cannot begin to approach the power that spoke the worlds into being. Speaking into the darkness, "God said, Let there be light: and there was light" (Genesis 1:3). Many of us cannot get our own children to listen well enough to flip a light switch on or off!

The parallels between humans and celestial objects go back to Genesis. In Genesis 1, God created the sun and *moon* to govern day and night, whereas humans were granted authority to rule the earth (Genesis 1:14-18, 28). Given the similarity between these verses of Psalm 8 and selected parts of Genesis 1, this parallelism is almost certainly intentional on David's part.

As David considers the grandeur of the heavens, the apparent insignificance of humanity stands out. Rather than being awe-inspiring physical objects, having an observable presence and noticeable influence through the eons and across the light years, we are frail creatures of dust. Our lives are short. At first glance, nothing about us seems to compare favorably with those other parts of creation.

Yet one thing about us stands out to David: God's special care for us. Unique among creation, humanity is in the image of God (Genesis 1:26, 27). Alone among all the physical creations, humans communicate with God, provoke emotions in God, influence God's decisions and actions, exist in relationship with God, even reject God and engage in rebellion against Him. No other physical creation of God rejects Him (John 1:11) and denies His very existence (again, Romans 1). (Only the nonphysical angels—the next beings considered in verse 5, below—are at all like us in these ways.) Yet God continues to

---

How to Say It

CORINTHIANS. Ko-*rin*-thee-unz (*th* as in *thin*).
HEBREWS. *Hee*-brews.
ISAIAH. Eye-*zay*-uh.

love us passionately and to remain deeply involved in our lives.

Before we move on, we should note that many students believe that this verse has two layers of interpretation: David, in speaking of *man* in the strictly human sense, may at the same time be speaking prophetically of the Messiah to come. Note the phrase *son of man,* which Jesus will later use to describe himself. Hebrews 2:6-8 quotes from Psalm 8 in a context that many commentators and translators believe applies to Jesus. Others think, however, that Psalm 8:4-6 as used in Hebrews 2 applies to us mortals instead—so we see the two potential layers of interpretation in the New Testament as well.

B. Angels and Humanity (v. 5)

5. For thou hast made him a little lower than the angels, and hast crowned him with glory and honor.

David continues his meditations on the amazing priorities within the creation by commenting on the relationship between humans and angels. A first-glance view of the relative differences between humans and angels reflects very poorly on us. We humans seem to be bound by time and space. Our bodies present more limitations than they do opportunities. None of these physical limitations affects angels. Thus David's conclusion that we are *a little lower than the angels.*

But let's look deeper. True, we may not have some of the abilities or natural empowerments of angels, stars, or animals. But value does not come from comparisons such as these. Our value comes because we have been crowned with *glory and honor.* This is tied in with being created in God's image—something that is not said of angels. Our status of being *a little lower than the angels* is temporary. Ultimately, we will sit in judgment on angels (1 Corinthians 6:3).

C. Other Works and Humanity (vv. 6-8)

6. Thou madest him to have dominion over the works of thy hands; thou hast put all things under his feet.

David's words reflect the priorities of creation. They show the hierarchy of God's attention and intention. Certainly, God gave humans *dominion* over the earth, and we exercise that dominion (both wisely and not so wisely) every day. That is not to say that we rule over every aspect of existence on earth. No one can predict the exact

---

Home Daily Bible Readings

Monday, Feb. 27—God Creates Humankind (Genesis 1:26-31)
Tuesday, Feb. 28—God Creates Man and Woman (Genesis 2:7, 15-25)
Wednesday, Mar. 1—God Establishes a Covenant with Noah (Genesis 9:8-17)
Thursday, Mar. 2—God Is Our Help and Strength (Psalm 63:1-8)
Friday, Mar. 3—God Is Our Guide and Refuge (Psalm 73:21-28)
Saturday, Mar. 4—God Leaves Nothing Outside Our Jurisdiction (Hebrews 2:5-10)
Sunday, Mar. 5—Created a Little Lower Than the Angels (Psalm 8)

---

course of a hurricane or the time of the next earthquake, let alone control them. Being the dominant species on earth has not resulted in the defeat of AIDS or even the common cold. Dominion has limitations.

Having dominion also has implications for ecology. Although the environmental movement often errs on the side of fanaticism, we still have a responsibility for stewardship. That responsibility is a clear reflection of our mandate to have dominion over all the earth. Rulers bear responsibility in the eyes of God for that which they rule. As we rule the earth, we will answer to God for our deeds (or lack of deeds) in that role.

Acknowledging that God puts more value on humans than on other elements of creation does not negate the value of the rest of creation. Our concern for the creation is driven by our love for the creator. We look forward to the day when the ideal of Psalm 8 and Genesis 1:26 will be realized fully (compare Revelation 21:4, 5). [See question #3, page 275.]

7, 8. All sheep and oxen, yea, and the beasts of the field; the fowl of the air, and the fish of the sea, and whatsoever passeth through the paths of the seas.

David now describes the extent of human dominion. Obviously, domestic animals (sheep and oxen) are ruled by people. There is no question about that. But what about the other creatures listed?

Birds, fish, and sea creatures in David's time are not particularly subject to humans in any practical sense. Apart from limited hunting and fishing techniques, ancient people have little impact upon such creatures. Perhaps David's confidence is a kind of prophetic hint—a God-given awareness that humanity's future reach would extend to the depths of the ocean and beyond the heights of the atmosphere. Thus David's faith allows him to affirm that God has given humanity dominion over those creatures. Adding specifics to the general statement about dominion in verse 6 makes the psalm more beautiful and more memorable. We can almost hear the Hebrew children pleading, "Sing the one about the birds and fish again!"

When we think of the idea of dominion, we should remember that David is well acquainted with the reach and limitations of human power. Years before he became king himself, he was a regular in King Saul's presence. David knows that kings may rule countries, but their personal impact on the day-to-day lives of their subjects is often quite limited. Many of a king's subjects will live their lives without ever seeing the king. Yet a king's influence can be felt profoundly through taxation, conscription into military service, etc. The king's dominion is extensive, but also has certain limits.

We may draw a similar parallel concerning our dominion over the earth and her creatures. We do not influence directly the daily lives of every bottle-nosed porpoise, sparrow hawk, or giant anteater. Yet human ability that is exercised improperly can result in eventual extinction of various species. As those with dominion over creation, we need to use extra care.

CARE FOR THE CREATION

The story of "Dr. Dolittle" has captured the fancy of children for nearly a century. The story began somewhere in France during the First World War. Captain Hugh Lofting (1886–1947) was writing home to his wife and children. Knowing that censorship of soldiers' letters was strict, he decided to tell his children a story.

Lofting had been thinking about the many horses in military use that were injured in combat. He wished they could be given medical treatment such as the soldiers received. But, Lofting reasoned, that would require learning "horse language." Thus was born the legend of Dr. Dolittle, a kindly, eccentric veterinarian who could talk to the animals. Lofting's wife suggested he write more stories for the children. Eventually they were collected into a series of about a dozen books and, more recently, several movies.

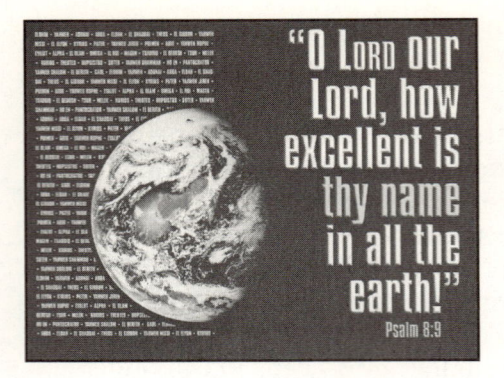

Visual for lesson 1

Refer to this visual as you ask, "How will you lift the glory of God's name in your own corner of the earth this coming week?"

Who cannot relate to such compassion, even if it is fictional? However, concern for animals late in the twentieth century expanded into thinking of them as the equal of human beings. Reforms in the way animals were used for research certainly were needed. But some activists for "animal rights" ignored the significant scriptural difference that exists between humans and animals. However, the dominion that God gave us over the lower creatures implies that we are to exercise care and discretion in how we treat His creation.   —C. R. B.

III. Creator Praise, Part 2 (Psalm 8:9)

9. O LORD our Lord, how excellent is thy name in all the earth!

David returns to the main thrust of Psalm 8. It is the *Lord our Lord* whose *name* is *excellent*. Our value comes from Him. Our authority comes from Him. Our unique place in all creation comes from Him. Our very being results from the creator's decision, and only the creator deserves praise as a result. The Bible reminds us of this often (compare Isaiah 42:8). [See question #4, page 275.]

Conclusion

A. The Order of Creation

The ideal order of creation can be set forth this way: God (who is uncreated) is first, humanity is second, and everything else is third. Humans got themselves into big trouble when they tried to move up a notch (see Genesis 3:4-6). As a result, we often have to struggle against creation in trying to exercise our dominion over it (Genesis 3:17-19). Never again should we confuse our intended role within creation with God's unique role as creator! Again, it is His name that is excellent, not ours. [See question #5, page 275.]

If you ever need a reminder of God's excellent name, just look skyward on a starry night! When Job challenged God, God pointed him back to His creation to show just how much He cared and was in control. Job responded with humility and awe. The special revelation (God's conversation with Job) in that case was a bonus—Job really just needed to look around! Our relationship with God will be strengthened if we do the same.

B. Prayer

Father, Your name is indeed excellent. May our lives be dedicated to glorifying and praising Your excellent name. As we consider Your works, may we always be mindful of the hand behind them. Guide us in fulfilling our role within Your creative plan. In Jesus' name we pray, amen.

C. Thought to Remember

Acknowledge your place and role in creation.

Learning by Doing

This section contains an alternative lesson plan emphasizing learning activities. Classes desiring such student involvement will find these suggestions helpful.

Learning Goals

After this lesson, each student will be able to:
1. Describe the position of human beings in creation.
2. Explain how knowledge of humanity's place in creation enhances his or her self-worth and gives life meaning.
3. Sing a song praising God as creator or complete a self-worth chart based on truths from the lesson.

Into the Lesson

Distribute copies of the following agree/disagree exercise. (This is also printed in the student book.) Allow two minutes to complete the exercise, then discuss responses. Information to help in the discussion is in parentheses.

1. Humans and apes are basically the same animals because they have nearly identical genes. Agree/Disagree? *(Human DNA is 95 percent to 98.5 percent identical to chimpanzee DNA. However, even a difference of only 1.5 percent means a difference of millions of DNA base pairs.)*

2. Humans and apes have similar brains. Agree/Disagree? *(A human brain is much larger than an ape's.)*

3. Until about age 2, humans and apes develop at the same rate. Agree/Disagree? *(An ape's brain is half its adult weight at birth. A human's is only one-third its mature weight. Apes are more developed at birth, but by age 1 humans are quickly surpassing apes.)*

4. If apes could talk, they could learn to speak human languages as well as humans do. Agree/Disagree? *(Many scientists believe that language is unique to humans because only humans have the inborn intellectual capacity for something so difficult. Even the most primitive human tribes speak very complex languages! Yet children learn these languages very easily compared with efforts to teach apes rudimentary sign language.)*

After discussing students' responses to the survey, say, "Today's lesson deals with our unique place in God's creation."

Into the Word

Divide your class into small groups of three or four. Assign half of the groups *Exercise #1* and the other half *Exercise #2* (also in the student books).

Exercise #1—Position: Use Psalm 8 and Genesis 1:26, 27 to answer these questions and determine our position in God's creation order: (1) How do you understand David's statement that we were made "a little lower than the angels"? (2) How are we "crowned" with "glory and honor"? (3) What does it mean to be made in God's image? (4) What is significant about the fact that humans were the last of God's earthly creations?

Exercise #2—Purpose: Use Psalm 8 and Genesis 1:28-31; 2:15 to answer these questions and determine what our purpose is in God's creation: (1) What commands did God give to the first humans after He created them? (2) How are we to exercise dominion over nature? (3) What was/is involved in subduing the earth? (4) What function did humans serve in the Garden of Eden?

Using your lesson commentary as a guide, discuss each group's answers.

Into Life

Make a transition by saying, "As you know, not everyone agrees with these conclusions about our position and purpose. Let's take a look at some of their arguments." Then distribute copies of the statements below, omitting the material in parentheses (or direct students to this activity in the student books if you're using them). Ask your class to provide a biblical response to the key doctrines of the secular view of nature.

The Secular View of Nature vs. The Biblical View of Creation

1. Nature is all that exists. *(God exists and has created the entire natural realm; Psalm 8:3.)*

2. Humans are just highly evolved animals, produced by natural selection. *(Humans are made by God; Psalm 8:5.)*

3. Because humans are the product of nature, we have no right to claim dominion over nature. *(God created us to have dominion over nature, to be stewards of nature for God's glory; Psalm 8:6.)*

4. Ethical values evolved in order to preserve the human species. *(Ethical values stem from the very nature of God and are unchangeable. Obeying them glorifies God.)*

Discuss responses and then ask volunteers to summarize how the Bible views the worth of each person. What effect should that have on the way we view and treat each other? (See James 3:9.)

Let's Talk It Over

These questions are designed to promote discussion of the lesson. The answers here are only discussion starters. Let your class talk it over from there.

1. Comparing our lives with the majesty of our heavenly Father could give us an inferiority complex! List events from your life that have encouraged you to consider your worth in God's eyes. How can you stay focused on your worth to Him?

We sometimes read about controlling persons who scar others emotionally or physically as they use self-proclaimed power to intimidate. These despots may use fear as a way to maintain their positions of power. God isn't like that. He is who He is. He has no inadequacies.

God uses His power to lift us, not put us down. Various events and times of our lives demonstrate the truth of this, as they did for David in Psalm 40:1-3. God lifts us so we can act as holy children who exalt His name. We reflect His glory as we act more like Him. Holy living gives us value and Him honor (1 Peter 1:15, 16). We need not (and must not) think that we can overcome any perceived inferiority by attempting to become gods ourselves, as some propose.

2. How can we use the realities of special and general revelation to confront and defeat the postmodern worldview?

A key postmodern idea is that there is no objective truth that exists "out there." The result is an individualistic, whatever-works-for-you mentality. Yet the laws of nature apply to everyone without exception! Would any sane postmodernist dare say, for example, "The law of gravity doesn't work for me, so I'll ignore it," and then be willing to step out of a third-story window?

History is rich with examples of the foolishness of trying to make human beings the measure of truth. What postmodernist would say that the Nazis were OK because they were only doing "what worked for them"? The alternative is to recognize God as the measure of truth. Scripture records numerous times when He used events and words to communicate objective truth to His servants. His power and care, demonstrated through general revelation, have no reasonable basis apart from the existence of a creator God.

3. David seemed amazed that God would entrust us to have dominion over His creation. How can we take this responsibility seriously today? What are some extremist positions to avoid, and why?

Often Christians are guilty of overreacting—or of not reacting at all! While there are certainly examples of how environmental extremists place favorite projects above the welfare of humanity, Christians can be charged occasionally with neglecting or abusing the creation that God has given. This is especially true in cultures whose fabric is one of waste and greed. Persons from third-world countries and missionaries sometimes call this to our attention. We must become more sensitive caretakers of God's creations.

4. The vision statements of many businesses include a commitment to excellence. With the excellence of the Lord's name as our own banner, what are some qualities of excellence for which we should strive? What would be the result if we neglect these?

Webster describes *excellence* as "superiority; surpassing goodness." In the Christian life, excellence relates strongly to spiritual maturity. God, who possesses surpassing goodness in perfection, is our reference point (Matthew 5:48).

Christians can display excellence for the Lord in many situations, so expect a wide-ranging discussion. One important area for excellence is in the strength and boldness of our witness. Paul discussed this with Timothy (2 Timothy 1:7). Lack of boldness is fearfulness and cowardice, and this has dire consequences (Revelation 21:8).

5. How will you use Psalm 8 this week to deepen your appreciation of God?

Our relationship with God is both objective and subjective. It is objective because He is what He is. The many names of God speak of this. At the same time, a dialogue about God includes personal (subjective) stories that relate how He has worked in our lives. We can use this psalm (and many other psalms as well) to praise God for those times. Proper use of Psalm 8 will help us avoid two pitfalls. One is to treat God too casually. The other is to assume that God is too distant to be concerned about our decisions or personal lives.

March 12
Lesson 2

God Created Wonderful Things

DEVOTIONAL READING: Psalm 104:31-35.

BACKGROUND SCRIPTURE: Psalm 104.

PRINTED TEXT: Psalm 104:1-13.

Psalm 104:1-13

1 Bless the LORD, O my soul. O LORD my God, thou art very great; thou art clothed with honor and majesty:

2 Who coverest thyself with light as with a garment: who stretchest out the heavens like a curtain:

3 Who layeth the beams of his chambers in the waters: who maketh the clouds his chariot: who walketh upon the wings of the wind:

4 Who maketh his angels spirits; his ministers a flaming fire:

5 Who laid the foundations of the earth, that it should not be removed for ever.

6 Thou coveredst it with the deep as with a garment: the waters stood above the mountains.

7 At thy rebuke they fled; at the voice of thy thunder they hasted away.

8 They go up by the mountains; they go down by the valleys unto the place which thou hast founded for them.

9 Thou hast set a bound that they may not pass over; that they turn not again to cover the earth.

10 He sendeth the springs into the valleys, which run among the hills.

11 They give drink to every beast of the field: the wild asses quench their thirst.

12 By them shall the fowls of the heaven have their habitation, which sing among the branches.

13 He watereth the hills from his chambers: the earth is satisfied with the fruit of thy works.

GOLDEN TEXT: Bless the LORD, O my soul. O LORD my God, thou art very great; thou art clothed with honor and majesty.—Psalm 104:1.

> *Living in and as God's Creation*
> Unit 1: The Glory of God's Creation
> (Lessons 1-4)

Lesson Aims

After participating in this lesson, each student will be able to:
1. Describe some ways that God controls the forces of nature.
2. Contrast our attempts to control the forces of nature with God's ability.
3. Dramatize Psalm 104.

Lesson Outline

INTRODUCTION
    A. Worship Privilege, Worship Style
    B. Lesson Background
I. GREATNESS OF GOD (Psalm 104:1-4)
    A. God Himself (vv. 1, 2a)
        Identity Crisis
    B. God's Creation (vv. 2b-4)
II. GRANDNESS OF THE EARTH (Psalm 104:5-9)
    A. God's Handiwork (vv. 5, 6)
    B. God's Control (vv. 7-9)
III. GRANTING OF HABITAT (Psalm 104:10-13)
    A. Specific Examples (vv. 10-12)
        "Water, Water Everywhere..."
    B. Earth as a Whole (v. 13)
        Tadpoles, Flamingos, and Other Creatures
CONCLUSION
    A. The God of Creation
    B. Prayer
    C. Thought to Remember

Introduction

A. Worship Privilege, Worship Style

Worship is a marvelous privilege, isn't it? Participating in various styles of worship can enrich our Christian experience. Sadly, however, Christians have been known to quarrel over worship styles. Someone may go so far as to label a certain worship style as "worldly."

Too often lost in this kind of bickering is the realization that God's people frequently have borrowed stylistically from the surrounding culture. For example, some of your church's youth may go to Christian summer camp and sing Christian lyrics that are set to the music of familiar secular compositions. The songs of the church frequently echo the songs of the marketplace. We fool ourselves if we think otherwise.

We also fool ourselves if we think the form and style of our own worship should transplant easily into faraway cultures. Most of us instinctively realize that the music of organ and piano translates poorly into the rhythm instruments and reed pipes of African and Amazonian jungles. It is admittedly difficult for many of us to accept the similar task of remolding a worship style of the 1950s into the multimedia experience of Western pop culture. Perhaps some biblical perspective would help a little!

B. Lesson Background

Our text for today is Psalm 104, a beautiful recapitulation of the creation. Although we cannot consider the entire psalm today, take some time this week to read it through while keeping your finger in Genesis 1. The parallels are obvious, and the writer's intent may be to set Genesis 1 to music. If so, then Psalm 104 is an interpretative celebration of Genesis 1.

The original concept for the psalm, though, apparently came from a pagan source. Within Egyptian mythology of the fourteenth century B.C. is found Pharaoh Akhenaton's Great Hymn to the Sun, a hymn to a fictitious sun god. The fact that the pagan sun hymn came first means that the writer of Psalm 104 would be the borrower. Yet the two are not identical! Their conclusions, the focus of their tribute, and Psalm 104's dependence on Genesis 1 assured the ancient Hebrew that there would be no confusion between the two compositions.

Obviously, the writer of Psalm 104 wanted to communicate something. Don't all writers want to do that? So perhaps he decided to borrow from the Egyptian sun hymn because his culture was already familiar with it. In the process the psalmist changed that hymn's glorification of

> **How to Say It**
> BETHLEHEM. *Beth*-lih-hem.
> CASSINI-HUYGENS. Kuh-*see*-nee *Hoi*-genz.
> EZEKIEL. Ee-*zeek*-ee-ul or Ee-*zeek*-yul.
> PHARAOH AKHENATON. *Fair*-o (or *Fay*-roe) Ock-*naw*-tun.

the sun (a part of the creation) into a glorification of the true God (the creator). We should not find this procedure surprising. The apostle Paul, for his part, was able to use pagan thoughts and philosophy in his sermons and letters to uphold Christ (see Acts 17:28; 1 Corinthians 15:33; and Titus 1:12).

I. Greatness of God (Psalm 104:1-4)

A. God Himself (vv. 1, 2a)

1. Bless the Lord, O my soul. O Lord my God, thou art very great; thou art clothed with honor and majesty.

The phrases *bless the Lord* and "praise the Lord" appear dozens of times in the Bible. The majority of these occurrences are in the psalms. The idea is to give God the honor and respect that is due Him. Occasionally, the same Hebrew verb is used to show God's blessing or favor on people (as in Genesis 24:1; 39:5; 2 Samuel 6:11; Job 42:12, etc.). God has come to our level to bless us so many times! In the Garden of Eden, God came to walk with us. In the manger of Bethlehem, the Son of God came to live with us. And on the cross of Calvary, the Son came to die for us. God's goal always has been for us to walk with Him and live with Him, never to die.

The psalmist, of course, does not know of the accomplishments of the manger and the cross. Even so, we feel his exuberance as the words leap off the page! The God before whom we kneel today, the God who clothes himself *with honor and majesty,* is also the psalmist's God—*O Lord my God.* [See question #1, page 284.]

The *very great* God is also the God who wants a close relationship with us. It's easy to forget one or the other of these two aspects. If we focus on how God is personal to us, we may forget that He is also awe-inspiring. If we focus on God's transcendence, we may forget that He is available to us personally. Both facets are essential to a proper relationship with God.

IDENTITY CRISIS

Ransom E. Olds produced the first Oldsmobile in 1897. It would become a well-regarded brand, its sales boosted by popular culture, innovative engineering, and the advance of science. "In My Merry Oldsmobile," a song written in 1905, may well have been the most popular song ever written about a car.

Oldsmobiles were distinctive, with chrome plating in 1926 and the first fully automatic transmission in 1939. After World War II, Oldsmobile's *Eighty Eight* model with "Futuramic" styling appealed to buyers' interest in a bold new world of science. Other cutting-edge advances included turbo-charged fuel-injected engines in 1962, front-wheel drive in 1966, and air bags in 1974.

However, Oldsmobile eventually had trouble coping with changes in consumer tastes. The company tried to appeal to younger buyers with slogans such as "Not your father's Oldsmobile," but young adults bought neither the slogan nor the cars. At the end of the 2004 model run, Oldsmobile ceased production; America's oldest automotive brand name was unable to maintain an identity.

Identity is important, isn't it? We establish our identity when we understand our proper relationship to God. As the psalmist says, God is God. In that light we need to be cautious of thinking of God as just our big, friendly, cosmic buddy. He is our loving Father, but He is also the great and glorious creator, as the psalmist reminds us. God has no identity crisis. Do we?   —C. R. B.

2a. Who coverest thyself with light as with a garment.

In sharp contrast to the pagan Great Hymn to the Sun, Psalm 104 distinguishes the creator from His creation. The sun as the source of light was god for Pharaoh Akhenaton. For the psalmist, on the other hand, God uses *light* as *a garment.* What a majestic, poetic expression!

B. God's Creation (vv. 2b-4)

2b. who stretchest out the heavens like a curtain.

Although today's text does not include the entire psalm, it is worth noting again the parallelism between Psalm 104 and Genesis 1. Day one of creation brought forth the light, light evoked by verse 2a, above. Day two divided *the heavens* and the earth. The second half of verse 2 makes oblique reference to this same creative act. The psalmist develops this reference more fully in the verse that follows.

3. Who layeth the beams of his chambers in the waters: who maketh the clouds his chariot: who walketh upon the wings of the wind.

The psalmist obviously takes tremendous joy in his creator. God's power is something in which to take great delight. Of course we should not push the imagery too far since God has no need of a *chariot* of any sort. The figure of speech is one of majesty. The writer invites us to share his delight in the power of the creator, as exhibited in the greatness of the creation. God made the heavens and the earth, including the seas, the skies, *the clouds,* and *the wind.* All of that power belongs to "O Lord my God," the intimate and personal sovereign.

4. Who maketh his angels spirits; his ministers a flaming fire.

This verse is difficult to translate because some of the Hebrew words can be understood in different ways. The Hebrew word for *angels* can also be translated "messengers" (examples: it is translated "angels" in Genesis 19:1 and "messengers" in Ezekiel 23:16). The Hebrew word for *spirits,* for its part, can also be translated as "winds" (examples: it is "spirits" in Numbers 16:22 and "winds" in Ezekiel 5:10). In any case, verse 4 continues the song of praise for the creator's power. Hebrews 1:7 quotes this passage to examine the superiority of Jesus to the angels.

II. Grandness of the Earth (Psalm 104:5-9)

A. God's Handiwork (vv. 5, 6)

5, 6. Who laid the foundations of the earth, that it should not be removed for ever. Thou coveredst it with the deep as with a garment: the waters stood above the mountains.

The writer continues his poetic retelling of Genesis 1. The description now includes the earth being covered by *the deep* (probably the oceans) *as with a garment.* The psalmist sees the creative artistry of God at work. How often do we pause to think of God by means of the marvel of His creation? [See question #2, page 284.]

At the conclusion of today's lesson, we will turn our attention to the occasional conflicts between faith and science. It is worth noting here, though, that the entire premise of this psalm rests upon the reality of the creation. Every point the psalmist makes about creation depends upon God being the one who made the heavens and the earth. Any worldview that tries to explain the universe's existence apart from God as creator is inadequate. Without that foundational understanding, life has no ultimate meaning.

B. God's Control (vv. 7-9)

7-9. At thy rebuke they fled; at the voice of thy thunder they hasted away. They go up by the mountains; they go down by the valleys unto the place which thou hast founded for them. Thou hast set a bound that they may not pass over; that they turn not again to cover the earth.

The psalmist's thoughts offer a direct contrast to pagan religious beliefs. There is no possibility that a god of the sea exists to battle against a god of the land or some such (compare 1 Kings 20:23, 28). There is one God, and He is able to command His creation in any way He so chooses. God simply gives His command: *At thy rebuke they* [the waters] *fled.* [See question #3, page 284.]

The psalmist may be reminding us of another truth as well. The Lord had chosen to devastate the earth with water in the days of Noah. That great flood wiped every living thing from the face of the earth except for that which was in the ark. At the conclusion of that flood, God sent the waters back to their places and promised never to destroy the earth again through a flood (Genesis 9:15). The psalmist perhaps echoes that promise in verse 9: *they turn not again to cover the earth.* This reminds us both of God's promise and of God's power to keep that promise. [See question #4, page 284.] We note again the psalmist's genuine delight in the marvel of God's hand in creation.

III. Granting of Habitat (Psalm 104:10-13)

A. Specific Examples (vv. 10-12)

10. He sendeth the springs into the valleys, which run among the hills.

The psalmist now partially explores the water cycle. Modern science gives us much more precise knowledge of how this cycle works. Does this mean that we have a greater appreciation of the creator who stands behind it?

"WATER, WATER EVERYWHERE..."

Chemicals at one time so polluted the Cuyahoga River in Ohio that it actually caught fire!

That was in June 1969. Until then, Americans had given little thought to the long-term effects of the way they used (or abused) the water supply. After all, how could we ever run out of a resource that covers more than 70 percent of the earth's surface? Yet only 1 percent of that resource is readily available fresh water. One estimate predicts that two-thirds of the world's population may lack adequate, clean water by the year 2025 if current trends continue.

Nations around the globe are already beginning to feel the pinch. For example, the water levels in Lakes Powell and Mead in North America have declined sharply in recent years. Manufacturing and agriculture requirements along with expansive lawns in desert environments compete with health and hygiene needs to stretch this vital resource to the limit. The lament of Samuel Coleridge's mythical ancient mariner is coming true for landlubbers:

> Water, water, everywhere,
> Nor any drop to drink.

Our God is the Lord of the deep and has created the earth's cycle of weather and water. How we use or abuse this grand system will determine the quality of human life in the near future. We are learning that there is a price to be paid for violating the principles of God's creation in both the physical and spiritual realms!

—C. R. B.

11. They give drink to every beast of the field: the wild asses quench their thirst.

The psalmist now makes a transition from water itself to the creatures that rely upon that water. The psalmist's thoughts never stray from the creator, however. It is God who sends the springs into the valleys (v. 10), thus providing for the creatures nearby.

Although Psalm 104 celebrates each day of creation, it does not follow the exact pattern of Genesis 1. Rather than directly moving from day three (formation of dry ground) to day four (creation of celestial objects), the psalmist spends some time foreshadowing the creation of the animals (day six) and of the birds (day five) as well as provisions for them (Genesis 1:30).

12. By them shall the fowls of the heaven have their habitation, which sing among the branches.

Birds have entered the poetry, but again the focus is on the creator. He is the one who put *their habitation* into place. Because He did this, birds can flourish in the wild places of the earth. One can almost hear the psalmist inviting the birds to sing with him the praises of their creator.

My children love to watch nature shows on TV. One of my sons fervently dreams of being another "Crocodile Hunter." His goal is to study exotic species. I love that dream, and part of me hopes to see him pursue it someday.

Part of me is quite concerned, though. The education required to attain a position like that almost requires one to disengage faith from science. Secular evolutionary theory allows no room for a creator. What a shame that in our eagerness to explore the world around us we have drifted away from the one truth that puts everything into context.

B. Earth as a Whole (v. 13)

13. He watereth the hills from his chambers: the earth is satisfied with the fruit of thy works.

Rather than allow our study of the earth to pull us away from God, our response should be the same as the psalmist's. Examination of the earth leads that writer to conclude two things. First, the fact that the creator *watereth the hills from his chambers* means that He is personally involved in the inner workings of His creation. Second, the fact that *the earth is satisfied with the fruit of thy works* means that creation depends upon that involvement.

Examination of the natural world should be a profoundly spiritual act. As David wrote in Psalm 19:1, "The heavens declare the glory of God; and the firmament showeth his handiwork." As this lesson is being finalized in July 2004, the Cassini-Huygens spacecraft is send-

Visual for lesson 2

Note to your students that this montage is just a start. Ask them to bring in additional pictures to place around the edge.

ing back close-up pictures of Saturn's rings. The ancient psalmist could not have dreamed of seeing such glorious images! These images should cause us to stand in even greater awe of the creator rather than be arrogant at human scientific accomplishment. [See question #5, page 284.]

TADPOLES, FLAMINGOS, AND OTHER CREATURES

How are tadpoles, basking sharks, flamingos, mallards, and blue whales alike? Think about that for a moment, but first note how we humans enjoy the water the psalmist speaks about. Along the various seashores of the world, a trip to the beach is a popular holiday event, whether for swimming, wading, surfing, or just sitting and staring out to sea. Farther inland, a day at the lake or on the river or beside a thundering waterfall can provide a restoration of the human spirit.

Perhaps our psalm today says so much about water in order to remind us of the glory of the creation. The psalmist mentions the beasts and birds on the land, but the sea creatures show God's creative genius as well.

Now, back to that question about tadpoles, flamingos, whales, etc. What they and other creatures have in common is that God has designed them to feed on small organisms suspended in the water. For example, each day a 30-foot basking shark will eat 140 gallons of zooplankton—tiny creatures only one millimeter long—filtering them out of thousands of gallons of water per hour.

The glory of God's creatures is amazing in its own right, but the important message from this is that it speaks more specifically to the glory of God. Here is the question for us: Since God's other creatures testify to His glory, do our lives speak that way as well? —C. R. B.

Conclusion

A. The God of Creation

Science and faith should not be at loggerheads. Both are means of exploring God's relationship with His creation, especially His relationship with us. Unfortunately, though, they do conflict at times. When that conflict occurs, both Christians and non-Christians can make the same mistake in deferring to ever-changing science over never-changing Scripture.

Certainly, committed Christians can and do disagree over the specifics of the creation. What cannot be avoided, though, is the clear foundation laid by those simple words from Genesis 1:1: "In the beginning God created the heaven and the earth." Any explanation of the origins of the heaven and the earth that omits the presence of the creator is fatally flawed at the outset; it has no value.

As our text today makes quite clear, the implications of removing God from creation are far-reaching. The very God praised by the psalmist is the creator God, the God who laid the foundations of the earth, the God of eternity past. If God is not the creator of the heaven and the earth, then very real questions about who He is—and indeed *if* He is—must be asked. Also, we note that the Bible does not recognize a god who is part of creation; rather, any god that is part of the creation is an idol that has its origins in human thought.

But what about those disagreements between science and Scripture? When such conflict arises, wise students will step back and ask themselves some questions. First, is this truly a disagreement, or is it merely two perspectives of the same issue? The Bible is not a scientific textbook. We can affirm its accuracy while at the same time acknowledging that occasionally the Bible uses figures of speech and poetic imagery to make a point.

Second, is the issue at hand a matter of fact or one of speculation on the part of science? The nuclear "cold fusion" claims of the year 1989 is an example of a scientific mistake. That

---

Home Daily Bible Readings

Monday, Mar. 6—The Firmament Proclaims God's Handiwork (Psalm 19:1-6)

Tuesday, Mar. 7—Make a Joyful Noise to God (Psalm 66:1-9)

Wednesday, Mar. 8—God's Steadfast Love Endures Forever (Psalm 136:1-9)

Thursday, Mar. 9—God, the Great Creator (Psalm 104:1-13)

Friday, Mar. 10—God's Creation Is Balanced and Orderly (Psalm 104:14-23)

Saturday, Mar. 11—Manifold Are God's Works (Psalm 104:24-30)

Sunday, Mar. 12—Rejoice in the Lord (Psalm 104:31-35)

is not to say that all scientists, or even those particular scientists, deliberately mislead or misinform people. They are human, though, and as well as occasionally being wrong, they suffer from the very human desire to prove themselves. That can lead to excesses, mistakes, and overreaching. (To be fair we should also ask whether an issue at hand is a matter of fact or speculation on the part of the person who is reading Scripture.)

Scripture and science should be understood together. When they disagree, though, the biblical worldview must take precedence. Science, after all, is humanity's attempt to understand creation—created beings analyzing creation. Scripture, however, is God's perspective. It is the creator speaking directly to us. Given our limited perspective, we should kneel before the one who made Heaven and earth! Only with His guidance can we understand the creation and our role within it.

B. Prayer

Lord, forgive us for those times when we have let the "wisdom of the wise" pull us away from the wisdom of the ages. Forgive us for those times when we have let the credentials of universities distract us from the creator of the universe. As we consider the earth, the seas, and all contained within them, remind us again of Your hand behind the scenes. Thank You for leaving Your fingerprints all over creation. May the psalmist's joy be ours. In Jesus' name, amen.

C. Thought to Remember

"The fear of the Lord is the beginning of knowledge" (Proverbs 1:7).

Learning by Doing

This section contains an alternative lesson plan emphasizing learning activities. Classes desiring such student involvement will find these suggestions helpful.

Learning Goals

After this lesson, each student will be able to:
1. Describe some ways that God controls the forces of nature.
2. Contrast our attempts to control the forces of nature with God's ability.
3. Dramatize Psalm 104.

Into the Lesson

Distribute the following quiz concerning the earth's environment. (If your class uses the student books, you will find the quiz there.) If you wish, you can put these in your students' chairs to give them something to work on and talk about as they arrive.

From answers *a–d* select the correct answers for questions 1–4. (1) If the earth were closer to the sun, which of the following would be true of the earth's atmosphere? (2) If the earth were farther from the sun, which would be true? (3) If the earth's gravity were stronger, which would be true? (4) If the earth's gravity were weaker, which would be true? *(a) It would be full of lethal ammonia and methane. (b) It would be too cool to maintain a stable water cycle (water evaporates from the oceans, forms rain clouds, falls as rain, flows back to the oceans). (c) It would be too warm to maintain a stable water cycle. (d) It would lose too much water into space.* (Bonus: Name planets in the solar system as examples.)

From *e–h* below, select the correct answers for questions 5–8. (5) It the earth took longer than 24 hours to rotate, which of the following would be true? (6) If the earth were not tilted on its axis, which would be true? (7) If the ozone level in the upper atmosphere were lower, which would be true? (8) If the ozone level in the upper atmosphere were higher, which would be true? *(e) There would be no seasons of the year. (f) Temperatures would be warmer in the day and cooler at night. (g) Both daytime and nighttime temperatures would be much higher. (h) Both daytime and nighttime temperatures would be much lower.* [Answers: 1c; 2b; 3a; 4d; 5f; 6e; 7g; 8h.]

After your students complete the quiz and you have graded it together, ask them what conclusions they can draw from their answers. The key answer you should look for is that this world is just the way it ought to be to maintain life as we know it. Make a transition to the lesson by saying, "Today's lesson will explore the greatness of God, who created and controls this amazing world."

Into the Word

To explore today's text, students will work in pairs to complete two activities based on Psalm 104. Allow pairs several minutes to complete the first activity, then discuss their conclusions as a class. Follow the same procedure for the second activity (both printed in the student books).

Activity #1: Read Psalm 104:1-4, answer the following questions, and discuss with your partner what *the psalmist* tells us about God. (1) What does the statement "Bless the Lord, O my soul" suggest about worship? (2) How is God "clothed with honor and majesty"? (3) What do the various imageries of God suggest about His control of nature? (4) Why did God create angels?

Activity #2: Read Psalm 104:5-13, answer the following questions, and discuss with your partner what *nature* tells us about God. (1) What does the imagery of the permanent "foundations of the earth" suggest about God? (2) How does setting boundaries illustrate His power? (3) How does God provide for animals? (4) What is the result of God's care of the earth?

Into Life

Say, "Our lesson writer suggests several principles that will help us to better understand God's relationship to His creation." Then offer these statements for consideration: (1) Any explanation of the origins of the universe that omits its creator is fatally flawed. (2) We must distinguish between matters of fact and matters of opinion in our interpretation of Scripture. (3) In science also we must distinguish between matters of fact and testable theories on the one hand and unsupported speculation on the other.

Using these principles, discuss possible solutions to the following hypothetical situations:

1. Dave is a college biology major whose faith is being challenged by his study of Darwinism. How can you help him resolve this spiritual crisis?

2. Rachel believes that all scientists are agents of Satan. She wants to homeschool her children so they won't be exposed to that "brainwashing." How would you counsel her?

Let's Talk It Over

These questions are designed to promote discussion of the lesson. The answers here are only discussion starters. Let your class talk it over from there.

1. David is probably kneeling as he acknowledges the Lord (compare 1 Kings 8:54; Psalm 95:6). Customs showing respect vary with time and culture. What ways do we show our respect for God? Why may it be difficult to teach some of these to our children or grandchildren?

David may also have removed his shoes when worshiping. While this is not Western practice today, the way we dress, remove our hats, or bow our heads during prayer may indicate a similar level of respect. Today's youth do not always use the same means. Before we are critical, we must be careful that we are consistent in how we show respect for God (see Matthew 7:3-5). The most important thing is that children learn that there really is a difference between *respect* and *disrespect*, although how these are displayed may vary from culture to culture and era to era.

2. Psalm 104:5 alludes to the permanence of the earth. How is this significant to our understanding of God's intentions toward us?

While earthquakes and other natural disasters may chip away at local landscapes, God's intent was to build a world in which enduring balance and boundaries were part of the design. If rocks, dirt, and water are to endure, then how much more should we as well!

Even so, the God who created is also the God who can destroy (Matthew 10:28; 24:29). Yet destruction is not His pleasure (Ezekiel 18:23). God is preparing a permanent home for us (Revelation 21). That is comfort in the here and now!

3. Which truths of the creation story give you a hope that is not offered by secular or pagan theory regarding the formation of the earth?

Answers to this question can be highly personal, so expect a variety of answers. You may wish to point out that ancient mythology is filled with stories that contradict the Bible's presentation of God as complete maker and master of all that is. Today some scientists still struggle to disprove that a master designer had complete control over forming the earth and its inhabitants. Romans 1:18-23 notes that those who engage in these futile exercises do so in willful disregard of the truth. The reliability and intricacy of God's cycles of nature give us hope that we too were part of His thinking even before we were formed. We are not God's afterthought.

4. How does our belief that God can still intervene in the courses of nature speak to our trust in Him? How can we demonstrate that trust?

Logic tells us that if God can create things to begin with, then He can also intervene in His creation anytime He so chooses. The evidence of history establishes that He has done just that.

In the midst of his distress, the prophet Jeremiah was one who acknowledged God's continuing abilities in this regard. "Ah Lord God! behold, thou hast made the heaven and the earth by thy great power and stretched out arm, and there is nothing too hard for thee" (Jeremiah 32:17). God's response is interesting: "Behold, I am the Lord, the God of all flesh: is there any thing too hard for me?" (32:27). Considering the entire context, it is as if God is saying, "I heard what you said about me, Jeremiah, but do you *really* believe it to be true?"

It is important that we consider whether we do indeed believe that God is involved continually with His creation and in our lives. Otherwise, why would we go to God in prayer when we face difficulties? But as we express our belief verbally, we may expect events that challenge us to live out our belief in tangible ways.

5. The existence of Saturn's rings shows us God's command of the dynamics of science as well as His flair for the beautiful. What are some other examples? How do you use these to draw closer to God?

What a blessing we receive when we meditate on God's handiwork! While discussing the importance of the water cycle, we may also talk about the incredible beauty of water as it forms a powerful waterfall. A speleologist could talk about the majesty of stalactites formed from calcite deposits in the depths of a cave. The entomologist marvels at the metamorphosis of a butterfly. The biologist wonders at the way cells repair damaged tissue. You can draw closer to God by keeping nearby a picture of beauty in creation.

God Created and Knows Us

March 19
Lesson 3

DEVOTIONAL READING: Psalm 100.

BACKGROUND SCRIPTURE: Psalm 139.

PRINTED TEXT: Psalm 139:1-3, 7-14, 23, 24.

Psalm 139:1-3, 7-14, 23, 24

1 O LORD, thou hast searched me, and known me.

2 Thou knowest my downsitting and mine uprising; thou understandest my thought afar off.

3 Thou compassest my path and my lying down, and art acquainted with all my ways.

. . . .

7 Whither shall I go from thy Spirit? Or whither shall I flee from thy presence?

8 If I ascend up into heaven, thou art there: if I make my bed in hell, behold, thou art there.

9 If I take the wings of the morning, and dwell in the uttermost parts of the sea;

10 Even there shall thy hand lead me, and thy right hand shall hold me.

11 If I say, Surely the darkness shall cover me; even the night shall be light about me.

12 Yea, the darkness hideth not from thee; but the night shineth as the day: the darkness and the light are both alike to thee.

13 For thou hast possessed my reins: thou hast covered me in my mother's womb.

14 I will praise thee; for I am fearfully and wonderfully made: marvelous are thy works; and that my soul knoweth right well.

. . . .

23 Search me, O God, and know my heart: try me, and know my thoughts:

24 And see if there be any wicked way in me, and lead me in the way everlasting.

GOLDEN TEXT: I will praise thee; for I am fearfully and wonderfully made: marvelous are thy works; and that my soul knoweth right well.—Psalm 139:14.

> *Living in and as God's Creation*
> Unit 1: The Glory of God's Creation
> (Lessons 1-4)

Lesson Aims

After participating in this lesson, each student will be able to:

1. Cite various ways that God knows and watches over him or her.
2. Give reasons why God's continuous presence should provide comfort, not concern.
3. Write a sentence or brief paragraph that will remind him or her daily of God's presence.

Lesson Outline

INTRODUCTION
    A. As If He Owned the Place
    B. Lesson Background
I. GOD KNOWS ME (Psalm 139:1-3, 7-14)
    A. My Now Is Known (vv. 1-3)
        He Knows His Children
    B. My Flight Is Futile (vv. 7-12)
        No Darkness Dark Enough . . .
    C. My Creation Is Key (vv. 13, 14)
II. GOD'S SAVES ME (Psalm 139:23, 24)
        "The Genocidal Killer in the Mirror"
CONCLUSION
    A. God with Us
    B. Prayer
    C. Thought to Remember

Introduction

A. As If He Owned the Place

Some years ago a news item caught my attention. Two people entered a home and surprised a man taking a shower. The man in the shower was not nearly as surprised, though, as were the "intruders"—a father and son—who were the residents of the house!

When the father and son arrived home, they heard the sound of running water. Checking out the noise, they found a stranger in their bathroom. They confronted the man, who then began to unscrew the showerhead, claiming that he was a plumber who had come to fix the shower.

When the father and son withdrew to call the police, the man fled—leaving his clothes behind! Police found him in a neighboring yard, knocking on the back door of another house. They took him into custody for a psychological evaluation. It seems safe to assume that he had some kind of confusion that affected his behavior.

I wonder if we are sometimes as confused as this man was. We wander around God's creation acting as though we own the place. We behave as though no one is watching us, as though no one cares about what we are doing. Then, when we realize that God is indeed watching us, we quickly try to cover up or justify our actions (compare 1 Samuel 15:19-21). We may even flee, hoping somehow to escape His attention.

B. Lesson Background

True wisdom requires that we acknowledge God's ability to know everything. We cannot hide from Him. Psalm 139 captures the futility of hiding from God, as we shall see.

More than being unable to hide from God, though, David—who was the author of Psalm 139—affirms the positive aspect of this truth: we never can be lost from His sight. David was one who knew both truths! (See Psalm 69:5.) Ecclesiastes 12:14 reveals that his son Solomon knew it as well. We may be uncomfortable with God's total knowledge during those times when we are disobedient. Even so, there is incredible comfort in the awareness that we are always under the watchful eye of our loving heavenly Father (Psalms 33:18; 34:15; Proverbs 15:3).

I. God Knows Me
(Psalm 139:1-3, 7-14)

A. My Now Is Known (vv. 1-3)

1. O LORD, thou hast searched me, and known me.

David, the author, begins with a simple declaration. We could rephrase it by saying, "God, You know all about me." This knowledge includes David's faults and his strengths, his sin and his nobility. God knows all about David—and about each of us. No part of our psyche, no piece of our personal history, no secret longing, hidden sin, or private behavior escapes the awareness of God. His knowledge is total, complete, and comprehensive.

This truth is explored more fully later in the psalm, but it is implicit in the personal address David uses: *O Lord, thou.* David is not lamenting

God's knowledge or fearing God's involvement. David is simply recognizing a fact and addressing the God of all knowledge. "You," David says, "know me."

Does that fact sink into our thoughts as well? Many people fear that if God really knew what they were like, He would not want anything to do with them. These people recognize their sin and understand that God hates sin. What they fail to understand, however, is that God already knows all about their sin. He knows everything about us. We are not a mystery to Him. Nothing we do surprises Him. Certainly, He often is disappointed, even angry, about our behavior. But never is He surprised.

The morning before I wrote this lesson, I was getting my sons ready for school. As I finished a few tasks, two of them disappeared. They were supposed to be in the car, buckling up and preparing for the ride to school. When I went to the car, though, they were not there.

Now I know my sons. I knew exactly where they were. They had gone downstairs and turned on the TV. We have strict rules in our house about the TV. Among those rules is this one: no TV before school in the morning. They know this rule. They understand the consequences of being caught watching TV against the rules. Yet they were downstairs watching *Animal Planet.*

Although I was disappointed, I was not surprised. Children will do things they should not do. Part of my job as a loving father is to teach them right from wrong, and part of that lesson is meting out appropriate consequences for wrong behavior. Never, though, do those consequences involve any less love from me for them. I love my children deeply, and nothing they do will make me love them any less.

Far more than I am capable of loving my children, God loves us. "God is love" (1 John 4:16). Far more than I am able to know my children, God knows us. God knows all of our secrets and all of our sins. It is "He that searcheth the hearts" (Romans 8:27). With all of that knowledge, God never abandons us, rejects us, or gives up on us. Rather, God loves us just as deeply and intimately as He knows us. In His knowledge He disciplines us for our good (Deuteronomy 8:5; Job 5:17; Proverbs 3:12; Hebrews 12:5-11).

2. Thou knowest my downsitting and mine uprising; thou understandest my thought afar off.

David expands upon his initial statement that God knows us. Even in the mundane, ordinary business of living, God is aware and involved. Sitting and standing are hardly worth noting. Yet no movement we make can escape the attention of God.

Similarly, our thoughts do not escape His awareness. We may try to hide our feelings and fail to express our emotions. We may lock our mouths shut, keeping our thoughts to ourselves. But God knows what we feel and think. He is more aware of our motives and passions, our jealousies and pettiness, our selfishness and our unselfishness, than even we ourselves are aware of.

The ancient Israelites sometimes bowed down to physical, visible idols, and sometimes they bowed down to idols in their hearts (Ezekiel 14:1-8). God knew about their idols, and He knows about ours!

3. Thou compassest my path and my lying down, and art acquainted with all my ways.

The word *compassest* translates an intriguing word. The idea in modern English is "to measure." In other contexts the Hebrew verb being translated refers to the threshing process; see the translations "winnoweth" or "winnowed" in Ruth 3:2 and Isaiah 30:24. Here, though, the concept focuses more on God's knowledge than on God's actions. He knows it all: *my path, my lying down,* and *all my ways.* In other words, nothing I do is too insignificant for God's attention.

Even after nearly 20 years of marriage, I must admit that the light in the room seems to brighten when my wife enters. In a room full of people, she still captures my attention simply by smiling. Her voice, though soft, is the one I hear above all other voices. When she laughs, my heart leaps. I cannot say I am the most observant person in the world—I have no idea how long she has owned any dress in her closet!—but I

How to Say It

ELIHU. Ih-*lye*-hew.
EZEKIEL. Ee-*zeek*-ee-ul or Ee-*zeek*-yul.
HEBREWS. *Hee*-brews.
IMMANUEL. Ih-*man*-you-el.
JONAH. *Jo*-nuh.
ONESIMUS. O-*ness*-ih-muss.
PHILEMON. Fih-*lee*-mun or Fye-*lee*-mun.

am much more aware of her than I am of anyone else.

She captures my attention because I love her. Far more than the attention I give to my wife is the attention God gives to me and to every other person. His attention is limitless, His awareness is total, and His love is comprehensive. We capture His attention because He loves us.

He Knows His Children

A 6-year-old girl vanished in 1986 while playing hide-and-seek in the yard of her home. Seventeen years later, a woman called the little girl's parents, saying that she was the long-lost daughter. Of course, the parents' hopes for a joyful reunion skyrocketed. Over the next few days the "lost daughter" talked to the police and news media, sometimes pretending that she was yet another person corroborating the story.

Then the story fell apart, shattering the parents' hopes. The perpetrator of the hoax admitted her guilt, but pleaded mental illness and was sentenced to 18 months in prison. During the trial, her mental condition was described as predisposing her to a compulsion to perpetrate "grand hoaxes" for the attention these would gain her. It turned out that her list of previous illegal activities in several states included crank calls, false fire alarms, bad checks, bomb threats, and stolen credit cards.

In this tragic case evil people (not the daughter herself) inflicted the pain of loss not once but twice. In our case it is we who inflict the pain of loss on God each time we accept the enemy's enticements and run away from Him. But God knows His children. If they wander, He still knows who they are, why they are gone, and where they are. If we try to return to Him in pretense, He is not fooled. But neither is His love for us dimmed when we return in complete repentance. What a steadfast love! —C. R. B.

B. My Flight Is Futile (vv. 7-12)

7. Whither shall I go from thy Spirit? Or whither shall I flee from thy presence?

David's questions here are rhetorical. The answers are obvious: there is no place to hide from the scrutiny of God. David understands that space and time do not constrict God. His presence is not limited to one area, nor must His actions follow linear time as we know it. God is not following us around like a private investigator. Rather, He already has arrived anywhere we may wish to go long before we get there.

When my children were babies, we would play a certain game. They would begin crawling away from me, possibly even into another room. I would tiptoe around and over them, out of their line of sight. Then I would stand directly in front of them. From their perspective, I suddenly appeared from nowhere. They were trying to escape from me, but there I was ahead of them! I would giggle, they would squeal, and then we would do it again.

In our childishness, foolishness, or ignorance, we may believe that we can crawl out of our Father's sight. We cannot. Never does His attention waver; never does His stamina wane. We may attempt to flee from Him only to realize that He has moved in front of us. Jonah discovered that the hard way!

8. If I ascend up into heaven, thou art there: if I make my bed in hell, behold, thou art there.

Although we should not limit God's comprehension and presence to the physical realm, this verse should be understood in the context of the earth. David is not referring to *heaven* and *hell* in the spiritual sense as the places of eternal reward or eternal punishment. Rather, David is referring to heaven in the sense of "the skies" and hell in the sense of "the depths of the earth."

We could paraphrase by saying "from the highest mountain to the deepest part of the ocean" or "from the clouds to the caves." We are probably not stretching David's meaning of the word *heaven* too far to view it "as reaching to the stars."

9, 10. If I take the wings of the morning, and dwell in the uttermost parts of the sea; even there shall thy hand lead me, and thy right hand shall hold me.

The poetry again focuses on the physical realm. The *wings of the morning* is a reference to the east, which is the direction of the sunrise. The *uttermost parts of the sea* refers to the west, which is the direction of the Mediterranean Sea from Israel. Poetically, David is saying "from the east to the west You are with me." So once again David is emphasizing how comprehensive God's presence is. Go as far to the east or to the west as you wish. Regardless of how far you travel, God is there.

This presence, though, is not one of concern and fright to David. Rather, it is one of comfort. Even after traveling as far as possible, God's

Home Daily Bible Readings
Monday, Mar. 13—We Belong to God (Psalm 100)
Tuesday, Mar. 14—Our Help Comes from the Lord (Psalm 121)
Wednesday, Mar. 15—Our God Watches over All (Psalm 146)
Thursday, Mar. 16—God Is Acquainted with My Ways (Psalm 139:1-6)
Friday, Mar. 17—God, You Are Always with Me (Psalm 139:7-12)
Saturday, Mar. 18—Fearfully and Wonderfully Made (Psalm 139:13-18)
Sunday, Mar. 19—Search Me, O God (Psalm 139:19-24)

hand is there to lead and to hold. We cannot elude His attention, which means we cannot escape from His protection. Nor should we wish to escape from His protection. His presence is there because He is God, but the fact that He is there results in benefit to those who love Him.

Make no mistake: God is not there because of us. He is there because of who He is. Part of God's nature is His ability to be present everywhere. God is not every*thing* in the sense that some false viewpoints hold. Nevertheless, God is every*where*. And the fact that He is present everywhere is good for us. [See question #1, page 293.]

11, 12. If I say, Surely the darkness shall cover me; even the night shall be light about me. Yea, the darkness hideth not from thee; but the night shineth as the day: the darkness and the light are both alike to thee.

Shadows obscure our vision. Darkness hides what light reveals to us. This is especially true in an ancient culture that does not have streetlights or night-vision goggles. But God is not limited by human senses. Presence and absence of light mean nothing to Him who looks at the heart. Compare the words of these two verses with the words of Elihu in Job 34:22: "There is no darkness, nor shadow of death, where the workers of iniquity may hide themselves." [See question #2, page 293.]

NO DARKNESS DARK ENOUGH . . .

H. G. Wells (1866–1946) wrote a famous story entitled *The Invisible Man*. It's about the temptation we would face if we could hide our identities (in effect, becoming invisible). The story is fantasy; the premise behind it is not. From time immemorial people have gone to "the big city" to become lost in the crowd—invisible to those who knew them before and unknown to people in their new surroundings. That may be the reason Onesimus (see Paul's letter to Philemon) went to Rome, where he was "found" by Paul and converted to Christ.

The 1997 movie *Face/Off* also toys with the idea of hidden identity. An FBI agent fighting a terrorist puts the criminal into a coma. Surgery results in having their faces switched. The agent, with his true identity and motives hidden, then can go into the prison where the terrorist's brother is in order to discover the details of a terrorist plot. When the terrorist comes out of his coma, he escapes to pose as the agent.

Fantastic? *Yes!* But no more in the realm of fantasy than the attempts many people make to escape the view of God so they can sin with impunity. We may be able to hide our sins from others, but we cannot hide from God (see Isaiah 29:15). As our text today says, we cannot find a darkness so dark that the light of God's purity cannot penetrate.
—C. R. B.

C. My Creation Is Key (vv. 13, 14)

13. For thou hast possessed my reins: thou hast covered me in my mother's womb.

The *King James Version* uses an interesting word picture when it says *For thou hast possessed my reins*. The Hebrew word translated *reins* means "kidneys." Ancient people see certain internal organs as the seat of emotions and the will. While they may think of the kidneys, bowels, or heart in this way, most of us simply prefer to speak of the heart. Scientifically, we know that emotions are seated in the brain. Figuratively, though, most of us would prefer to be loved with a person's heart. Most Western cultures consider the heart to be the symbolic home for emotions, feelings, and will.

Whatever we prefer to think of as the seat of our emotions, will, and being, God is the one who creates and possesses it. The psalmist (David) has no doubt of this fact. God's ownership of our lives begins from the moment of conception. That's what David means when he says *thou hast covered me in my mother's womb*. [See question #3, page 293.]

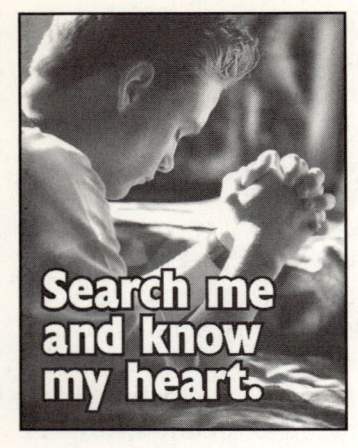

Point to this visual as you ask, "Who among us is willing to invite God to do this today?"

Visual for lesson 3

14. I will praise thee; for I am fearfully and wonderfully made: marvelous are thy works; and that my soul knoweth right well.

Staying focused on David's main point, we celebrate with him the fact that God's presence in our lives blesses us tremendously. God is present with us because He is God—it is His nature. That presence, though, cannot help but benefit those who love Him.

The phrase *fearfully and wonderfully made* affirms the value of human life. God's handiwork in our lives extends back to the point of conception, as noted above. Unfortunately, many assume that life and individuality begin at some undefined, subjective point after conception. This viewpoint is what allows abortion, embryonic stem-cell research, and a host of other dehumanizing procedures. This dehumanization is also seen at the other end of human life. One politician spoke of a "duty to die" for elderly and terminally ill people. A nursing home attendant convicted of murdering elderly patients said that they were "useless eaters."

Interestingly, those whose lives often are defined as having little or no value—preborn children, those with mental disabilities, those with terminal illnesses, etc.—also have little or no political power. Could it be that we define the value of someone's life in terms of that which is useful to me or to society rather than to God?

When someone's life becomes a burden or an inconvenience, that's when many see life as ceasing to be valuable. Some wonder how long God will delay His judgment on cultures that travel this path. Perhaps God also will judge the silence of His church in these matters.

God is the God of the living and the dead; He is the God of the widow and the orphan; He is the God of the preborn, the disabled, and the aged. Regardless of our physical health or social status, we are indeed *fearfully and wonderfully made*. We must remain fully aware of that truth. [See question #4, page 293.]

II. God Saves Me (Psalm 139:23, 24)

23, 24. Search me, O God, and know my heart: try me, and know my thoughts: and see if there be any wicked way in me, and lead me in the way everlasting.

Psalm 139 invites God to do within us that which He wishes. He searches us anyway. That is part of His nature. He knows our thoughts and our intentions. Our sins do not escape His notice (see Hebrews 4:13). How could it be otherwise?

But it is only by invitation that He comes in and cleanses us. God will not impose himself on anyone in this regard. If we desire His direction, though, He will lead us into *the way everlasting*. When that happens, we can rejoice with David, "For as the heaven is high above the earth, so great is his mercy toward them that fear him" (Psalm 103:11). [See question #5, page 293.]

"THE GENOCIDAL KILLER IN THE MIRROR"

With startling frequency we hear of the systematic killing of masses of people. They become victims due to race, ethnicity, religion, or nationality. The 1940s saw the Nazis try to destroy the Jews; in the 1970s it was the infamous Cambodian killing fields; in the 1990s Rwandan Hutus slaughtered the Tutsis. In the twenty-first century, religious extremists attempt to gain access to weapons of mass destruction daily.

Perhaps it is not so much *governments* that commit these atrocities as it is *individuals* who get caught up in their own passions when they are inflamed by demagogic leaders. Some students of psychology see several factors at work: (1) blind deference to authority, (2) response to social consensus, (3) stereotyping people in groups, and (4) willingness to make moral compromises to protect the security of one's own group. As one social commentator has said, there is a "genocidal killer in the mirror" if we look closely.

Given the right circumstances (and except for the grace of God), each of us is capable of sinful acts that horrify us when we see others committing them. This is why the psalmist's prayer in these verses is so significant and why it ought to be the daily prayer of every Christian.
—C. R. B.

Conclusion

A. God with Us

What David knew in part, Jesus revealed in full. "The way everlasting" is the "new and living way" (Hebrews 10:20) created for us by Jesus. He is the one who bridged the chasm between us and God—the chasm of sin. The total presence that David celebrated became Immanuel, "God with us."

The promise of God's presence continues today with the indwelling of the Holy Spirit. May we allow Him to continue to lead us in that everlasting path!

B. Prayer

Father, when Elijah felt alone, You sent him a storm, an earthquake, and a fire. But You were not present in these. Instead, You came to Elijah in a whisper. People have looked for You in the midst of the awe-inspiring and the incredible. Even today, though, You are present in our midst, dwelling in our hearts, speaking through Your Word. Help us to recognize Your presence in the silences, in the quietness, when we are alone. In the name of Jesus, who came into our presence in the softness of a baby's cry, we pray, amen.

C. Thought to Remember

"Reputation is what others think about you. Character is what God knows about you."

Learning by Doing

This section contains an alternative lesson plan emphasizing learning activities. Classes desiring such student involvement will find these suggestions helpful.

Learning Goals

After participating in this lesson, each student will be able to:

1. Cite the various ways that God knows and watches over him or her.
2. Give reasons why God's continuous presence should provide comfort, not concern.
3. Write a sentence or brief paragraph that will remind him or her daily of God's presence.

Into the Lesson

To begin the class, reproduce and distribute these questions to no more than three couples (married or dating) or to pairs of good friends. You may wish to ask for volunteers in order to preserve the good-natured aspect of this exercise. (The questionnaire is also printed in the student books.)

Be sure that both parties are present to fill out the questionnaire and that they do not collaborate on their answers. Say, "So that those not filling out questionnaires won't get bored, your time limit is two minutes."

How Well Do You Know Him/Her?

Working independently, answer the following questions about yourself and your spouse or friend:

1. What is his/her favorite color?
2. What is his/her favorite dessert?
3. What is his/her favorite TV program?
4. What is the last book he/she read for enjoyment?
5. When is his/her birthday?
6. What is his/her dream vacation?
7. What is your favorite color?
8. What is your favorite dessert?
9. What is your favorite TV program?
10. What is the last book you read for enjoyment?
11. When is your birthday?
12. What is your dream vacation?

When all the pairs have completed the questions, ask volunteers to reveal their answers to see how well they really know their spouses or friends. The results can be humorous, but do not allow this exercise to drag out. Make a transition by saying, "Today's lesson deals with God's intimate knowledge of our deepest secrets."

Into the Word

Divide your class into small groups of two or three. Half of the groups will do *Study #1* regarding God's ability to know everything. The other half will do *Study #2* regarding God's ability to be everywhere. (If your class uses the student books, space is provided there for this activity; otherwise, copy the activities below and provide one for each group.)

After the groups finish, discuss findings with the class as a whole. Use the lesson commentary to guide your discussion.

Study #1—God's Ability to Know Everything: Read Psalm 139:1-4, 13, 14, 23, 24. Together with your group members, write a paraphrase of these verses in the space provided, restating the verses in your own words. Next, write a brief paragraph to explain why these verses should bring comfort to the believer who reads them.

Paraphrase of verses 1-4, 13, 14, 23, 24:
    [Provide several blank lines for writing.]
These verses give us comfort because:
    [Provide several blank lines for writing.]

Study #2—God's Ability to Be Everywhere: Read Psalm 139:7-12. Together with your group members, write a paraphrase of these verses in the space provided, restating the verses in your own words. Next, write a brief paragraph to explain why these verses should bring comfort to the believer who reads them.

Paraphrase of verses 7-12:
    [Provide several blank lines for writing.]
These verses give us comfort because:
    [Provide several blank lines for writing.]

Into Life

Make a transition by saying, "One way to draw closer to God is to write our own psalms. Although we should not pretend that we are writing Scripture, God will be pleased when we pour out our hearts to Him."

Then ask students each to create a brief psalm. It is to remind themselves daily that God is ever-present in their lives. Provide paper for this exercise or refer your class to the student books, where space is provided. Ask volunteers to share their work and then close with prayer, thanking God for knowing our hearts. If time is too limited, suggest this activity as homework.

Let's Talk It Over

These questions are designed to promote discussion of the lesson. The answers here are only discussion starters. Let your class talk it over from there.

1. Many of us have been irritated by the persistent salesman who follows us around the store. When have you felt the same way about God? In what ways are you both concerned and thankful for His ever-present, watchful eyes?

Obviously, there are those moments we may wish that God had not seen where we were or what we had done. When that happens our conscience may begin to bother us. But Titus 1:15 reminds us that we can't always depend upon our conscience. Some people live their whole lives trying to outwit God. Their consciences have been seared (1 Timothy 4:2). They have lost the benefit of knowing that God's watchful eye is there to bring us life more abundant.

2. In verses 11, 12, David notes differences between how light and darkness affect us vs. how they affect God. Why are these perspectives so different? How does this matter in your daily life?

If physical darkness separates us from others or puts us in danger, we panic and try to correct the situation. But amazingly some folks who avoid physical darkness for that reason will deliberately choose to live in spiritual darkness that separates them from God and puts them in danger of Hell! Many Scriptures talk about this from various angles, but the book of 1 John is particularly rich in *light* vs. *dark* imagery.

We should also note that some people apparently believe that by avoiding the gaze and judgment of humanity (which is possible at times) they can also do the same with God (which is never possible). Perhaps they think this way because they "haven't been caught so far" or that a loving God will cut them a break on judgment day. The result is a tragic, misguided belief that God's delay in judgment means that He doesn't see or care. Instead, the delay is to allow time for repentance (2 Peter 3:8, 9).

3. Some may resist Christianity because they are afraid of being controlled. How would you respond to someone who expressed such a reservation?

One who creates something is naturally thought to be the owner of that which was created. God is our maker; His ownership of our lives in that regard cannot be escaped.

Concerning matters of the will, a distinctive characteristic of humanity is that we have been given the ability to make decisions—even those that may be harmful. Obviously, David was not referring to us as being puppets on a string. In contrast David seems to be indicating that he is, by his own will, choosing to give God control of his life. Can anyone really take comfort in the idea that it would be better to be in absolute, personal control of one's own life rather than allow God to be the one in control?

4. Scientists are now able to clone life or at least control certain characteristics by tinkering with the DNA structure. Does this mean that the declaration that we are the products of God's design is losing its value? Why, or why not?

The strides that science has made in understanding our genetic makeup are amazing! The ability to correct genetic defects is a blessing. At the same time, however, scientists must admit that they cannot create life or characteristics from nothing. Neither can they create a soul. Life is more than the convergence of matter.

5. We are sometimes reluctant to share our secrets with others because of potentially damaging results. David, however, invited God to do a thorough search of his innermost thoughts and actions. How can we do the same while maintaining right motives?

God's examination of our thoughts, motives, and deeds is potentially more devastating than the wagging tongues of disloyal friends! God makes judgments that determine eternal destinies.

Just the same, we are better off to ask for His candid review. We can do so with confidence if we go to Him having first evaluated ourselves against His standards. We need to remember that He wants us to open ourselves to Him for our own good, not because He wants to harm us. But if our invitation is something like "Dear God: Come and take a look at how good I am," then we exhibit a lack of humility. Motives are important to God (compare Matthew 6:2).

March 26
Lesson 4

Sing Praise to the Creator

DEVOTIONAL READING: Psalm 150.

BACKGROUND SCRIPTURE: Psalm 145.

PRINTED TEXT: Psalm 145:1-13.

Psalm 145:1-13

1 I will extol thee, my God, O King; and I will bless thy name for ever and ever.

2 Every day will I bless thee; and I will praise thy name for ever and ever.

3 Great is the LORD, and greatly to be praised; and his greatness is unsearchable.

4 One generation shall praise thy works to another, and shall declare thy mighty acts.

5 I will speak of the glorious honor of thy majesty, and of thy wondrous works.

6 And men shall speak of the might of thy terrible acts: and I will declare thy greatness.

7 They shall abundantly utter the memory of thy great goodness, and shall sing of thy righteousness.

8 The LORD is gracious, and full of compassion; slow to anger, and of great mercy.

9 The LORD is good to all: and his tender mercies are over all his works.

10 All thy works shall praise thee, O LORD; and thy saints shall bless thee.

11 They shall speak of the glory of thy kingdom, and talk of thy power;

12 To make known to the sons of men his mighty acts, and the glorious majesty of his kingdom.

13 Thy kingdom is an everlasting kingdom, and thy dominion endureth throughout all generations.

GOLDEN TEXT: The LORD is gracious, and full of compassion; slow to anger, and of great mercy.— Psalm 145:8.

Living in and as God's Creation
Unit 1: The Glory of God's Creation
(Lessons 1-4)

Lesson Aims

After participating in this lesson, each student will be able to:

1. Review the reasons the psalmist gives for praising God.
2. Describe various ways to praise God.
3. Create a plan for one generation to express God's praise to a different generation.

Lesson Outline

INTRODUCTION
    A. Preferences and Passions
    B. Lesson Background
I. MY PRAISE OF GOD (Psalm 145:1-3)
    A. His Name (vv. 1, 2)
    B. His Greatness (v. 3)
    Pink Margarine and the Worship of God
II. OTHERS' PRAISE OF GOD (Psalm 145:4-7)
    A. His Deeds and Majesty (vv. 4-6)
    The Object of Our Praise
    B. His Goodness and Righteousness (v. 7)
III. WORTHINESS OF GOD (Psalm 145:8-10)
    A. Lord's Attributes (vv. 8, 9)
    B. Double Praise (v. 10)
IV. KINGDOM OF GOD (Psalm 145:11-13)
    A. Glorious Majesty (vv. 11, 12)
    B. Enduring Dominion (v. 13)
CONCLUSION
    A. Our Kingdom Responsibilities
    B. Prayer
    C. Thought to Remember

Introduction

A. Preferences and Passions

One can gain an appreciation for the differences in people by watching a youth soccer game. Parents approach the games with very different mind-sets. Some of them are totally focused on the experience, shouting out "Good job, sweetie" as their daughter falls in the mud for the sixth time. Others emphasize the team skills more, cheering on every good pass or other quality team play while paying little attention to individual efforts. Still others are just the opposite: "Pass it to my son!" "That's my boy!" etc.

Some parents shout until they are hoarse. Others will call out a couple of times to let their child know they are present but will not get too enthusiastic or passionate. There are always some who go all out, wearing the team's colors and chasing their team up and down the field to show their support. And, sadly, a few do not understand the goals of youth sports and focus solely on winning or on negativity. Styles!

We can see similar differences in stylistic approaches to worship, from very expressive to very subdued and reverent. Some worshipers raise their hands, while others prefer not to, etc. The different ways that people cheer at youth soccer games reflect cultural background, social mores, emotional temperament, and personal values. This is true in worship as well. Yet God is the same God, whether we worship Him in exuberant celebration or in stately reflection. We are the ones who differ.

Too often people let those superficial differences divide them. I may not paint my face blue or wear the latest fad in team apparel at sporting events. That does not mean that I am any less committed to my team than those who are more expressive. In worship I may lift my hands or sit serenely. I may worship with guitars or with pipe organs or with voices only. I may pray in English or Spanish or Swahili, but if I am worshiping the one true God, then it does not matter. Differences in worship style do not change the fact that God is the same yesterday, today, and forever.

B. Lesson Background

King David was a man who knew all about the ups and downs of life. His victory over Goliath, being chased by Saul, selection to be king, adultery with Bathsheba—so many experiences on both the spiritual mountaintop and in the spiritual valley! Probably it was both types of experiences that drove David to greater praise and worship.

I. My Praise of God
(Psalm 145:1-3)

A. His Name (vv. 1, 2)

1. I will extol thee, my God, O King; and I will bless thy name for ever and ever.

Notice the words *extol*, *bless*, and *praise* in the first two verses of Psalm 145. Each word has the same essential meaning: to lift high, to give honor publicly and openly, and to promote. David makes very clear from the outset what this psalm is about. He intends to promote God publicly and vigorously.

Although David addresses God directly, the intended action is for others to notice. David wants to make sure that the fame of God is spread everywhere. No one should fail to know or understand how great God is, and David will make sure that God's greatness is unmistakable and undeniable.

2. Every day will I bless thee; and I will praise thy name for ever and ever.

David intends to promote God over two time periods. The first is daily. The promise *Every day will I bless thee* is a promise to be consistent in doing so. Rather than remembering to speak about God only occasionally or merely on the Sabbath, David plans to promote Him day by day. [See question #1, page 302.]

Sometimes we fool ourselves into thinking that we will do great things for God "someday." That usually is neither necessary nor valuable. Daily consistency in small things will win out in the long run. Daily prayer is a start. Following that, we may make it our goal to speak to one person today about Jesus Christ. This could be very low key—perhaps a comment like, "I am grateful to God for my family." Such conversation starters may not seem like much, but God can use them to do great things. Do not let another day go by without publicly praising and blessing the name of God.

The second time period that David refers to is *for ever and ever*. Eternity will not be too long a "time" to sing the praises of God. Indeed, that will be our main task (compare Revelation 19:1-8). Those of us who know God will find new things about His deeds, His creativity, His character, etc., for which to praise Him constantly.

B. His Greatness (v. 3)

3. Great is the LORD, and greatly to be praised; and his greatness is unsearchable.

The *greatness* of God is inexhaustible. The more we know Him, the more we want to praise Him. The idea of praise is so important that it is repeated in Psalms 48:1 and 96:4, among others.

I spent four years in Bible college. During that time, I met some of the best people in the world. I learned some of the most exciting and dynamic concepts and facts that I will ever encounter. I could go on and on describing the value and the quality of my alma mater, not to mention the debt I owe to her for giving me so many critical relationships, especially my relationship to my wife. If Bible college can give me such rich material with which to sing praises, imagine what a lifetime spent knowing God will provide! We will begin entirely new symphonies of praise after our time on earth is finished.

PINK MARGARINE AND THE WORSHIP OF GOD

In some places in America a half-century ago, one could not buy yellow margarine. The dairy industry was protecting its butter production. Margarine was sold in an unappetizing white form with a pouch of yellow food coloring. Thus yellow margarine was a do-it-yourself project.

Actually, the story starts much earlier. In the late 1890s, New Hampshire law required that margarine be colored *pink!* The theory was that pink is not a color most people are attracted to in food—except, perhaps, for strawberry ice cream. In 1898 the New Hampshire Supreme Court struck down the law. Eventually margarine became accepted as a substitute for butter.

How silly! Yet don't we see some Christians going to curious lengths to protect their favorite style of worship? They act as if all other forms of worship are to be rigorously rejected, resented, and prevented. They try to protect their only-true-butter by seeing all else to be pink margarine.

Many who resist changes in worship would reject the worship of medieval times with its very different styles of music and preaching. But God is not locked into any one culture, time, or place. As time passes, culture changes and people need culturally acceptable, yet still *scriptural*, ways to worship God. We should praise God when each new generation of Christians finds meaningful ways to worship, even if those ways are not particularly helpful to us!
—C. R. B.

II. Others' Praise of God (Psalm 145:4-7)

A. His Deeds and Majesty (vv. 4-6)

4. One generation shall praise thy works to another, and shall declare thy mighty acts.

Communication of God's greatness must cross from *generation* to generation. Moses recognized how important this task was in his own day (see Deuteronomy 4:7-9; 11:18-21).

Visual for lesson 4

Have your students repeat these verses together. Then ask for examples of how one generation witnesses to the next.

5. I will speak of the glorious honor of thy majesty, and of thy wondrous works.

There is a bit of uncertainty about some of the Hebrew words in this verse regarding who is to *speak*. Is it "I" or "they"? Verses 1 and 2 stress "I" (meaning David), while verses 4, 6, and 7 have "generations," "men," and "they" offering praise. Surely it is everyone who is to tell *of the glorious honor of thy majesty!* Not only must we teach about God to each succeeding generation, we also must model our awe of God to our children and grandchildren. Knowing God's Word without knowing God's *works* is incomplete: the works lend power and credence to the words.

Obviously, we are responsible for sharing the gospel with others of our own generation. The reality, though, is that most evangelism occurs from parent to child. Thus we exert every effort to bridge the gap between generations. One of the challenges is to prevent personal feelings and stylistic choices from interfering.

I visited a very contemporary church one weekend where a smiling couple, who appeared to be in their 70s, greeted me at the door. As we took our seats, I asked them about their church. "Actually," the wife said, "I hate the music! Oh, they play it very well but it is not to my taste. But I will never go to another church. This church brought my grandchildren to Christ. If they can do that, they can play any kind of music they want to!" [See question #2, page 302.]

6. And men shall speak of the might of thy terrible acts: and I will declare thy greatness.

The *terrible acts* of which David speaks should be thought of as "things that terrify," "things that cause fear," or "things that inspire awe." Such acts witness to a power of God that is far beyond our comprehension. David's son Solomon rightly tells us "the fear of the Lord is the beginning of knowledge" (Proverbs 1:7; also see Job 28:28; Psalm 111:10; Proverbs 9:10).

Declaring the *greatness* of God is parallel to speaking of His acts that cause terror or fear. On the night the angel of the Lord appeared to the shepherds, they were quite afraid (Luke 2:9). After recovering from their fear and seeing the baby Jesus, they spread the good news and praised God (Luke 2:17, 20). That's one example of what it means to stand in awe of God's deeds and *declare* His greatness. [See question #3, page 302.]

The Object of Our Praise

"Pastor's acquittal praised, scorned" read a headline of the *San Diego Union-Tribune* on March 22, 2004. At issue was the ordination of a "self-avowed, practicing" lesbian. A church court had determined that she had done nothing wrong according to the denomination's *Book of Discipline*, even though one section reads that "the practice of homosexuality is incompatible with Christian teaching, [thus] self-avowed practicing homosexuals are not to be accepted as candidates, ordained as ministers, or appointed to serve."

Many praised the decision as being compassionate, forward-looking, and in touch with the times. Those who objected to the church court's verdict found it to be hypocritical, heretical, and out of touch with Scripture.

We live in a time when much that is sinful is praised in the media and advocated by the noisy opinion makers of Western culture. In recent years laws have been proposed in Canada, Sweden, and other nations that would make churches guilty of "hate speech" if they quoted biblical prohibitions against the homosexual lifestyle. On this and many other issues the church today thus is faced with the question "Who or what is to be the object of our praise?" Will it be God? Or will it be the sinful customs of an irreligious and increasingly pagan culture?
—C. R. B.

B. His Goodness and Righteousness (v. 7)

7. They shall abundantly utter the memory of thy great goodness, and shall sing of thy righteousness.

The Bible speaks of God's *goodness* and *righteousness* in dozens of passages. But this is a

> **How to Say It**
>
> AHAB. *Ay*-hab.
> BATHSHEBA. Bath-*she*-buh.
> ELIJAH. Ee-*lye*-juh.
> GOLIATH. Go-*lye*-uth.
> NEBUCHADNEZZAR. *Neb*-yuh-kud-*nez*-er (strong accent on *nez*).
> NEHEMIAH. *Nee*-huh-*my*-uh (strong accent on *my*).

rare case in which these two exact words stand side by side. God extends His goodness especially to those whose hearts are clean and pure (Psalm 73:1). Even so, He offers some of His goodness to the unrighteous people as well (Matthew 5:45).

The concept of righteousness, for its part, is the same as justice when applied to God. It means that God always does the right thing. This is the very foundation of God's throne (Psalms 89:14; 97:2). What kind of heart is it that never can ponder the goodness or righteousness of God?

III. Worthiness of God (Psalm 145:8-10)

A. Lord's Attributes (vv. 8, 9)

8. The LORD is gracious, and full of compassion; slow to anger, and of great mercy.

David makes a transition from praise to God for what He has done to a more general praise to God for His character. Some commentators have tried to argue that the God we see in the Old Testament is very different from the God revealed in the New Testament. According to this line of thinking, the God of the Old Testament is an angry, vengeful God while the God of the New Testament is one of love and grace. This distinction is far from the truth!

Although David knows the wrath of God from firsthand experience, David also knows God as *gracious* and compassionate. This is the same God that Moses knew hundreds of years before David's time: "The Lord, The Lord God, merciful and gracious, long-suffering, and abundant in goodness" (Exodus 34:6).

God does indeed administer corrective punishment from time to time. He may do this in calling us to repentance, to restoration of the covenant relationship that we break. God has done this even when people have rejected and despised Him repeatedly. (See also Numbers 14:18; Nehemiah 9:17; Psalms 86:15; 103:8; Joel 2:13; and Jonah 4:2.)

9. The LORD is good to all: and his tender mercies are over all his works.

We may refer back to our comments on verse 7 that God's goodness extends to both just and unjust. He is truly *good to all!* One example of this that we see in Scripture is the prayer of Elijah that restored rain to Israel. God used drought to punish the country for sin, especially for the sin of King Ahab. For years Ahab and the people sinned grievously. But Elijah prayed, and God restored the rain. The number of righteous people in Israel seemed to be very small, with only 7,000 who had not worshiped Baal. But God blessed everyone with rain nonetheless (1 Kings 17:1; 16:29-33; 18:41-45; 19:18).

Earlier in Israel's history, Aaron led the people to create an idol of gold and worship it. God's initial response was to destroy the people and begin afresh with Moses as the father of a new nation. Through Moses' prayer, however, God granted mercy on the people even though their own sin made them worthy of death (Exodus 32). God is good!

B. Double Praise (v. 10)

10. All thy works shall praise thee, O LORD; and thy saints shall bless thee.

Jesus said that people could be evaluated by their works or fruit (Matthew 7:15-20). God's own *works* speak volumes about His nature (Psalm 19:1; Romans 1:20). The truest praise we can give to God is to discover His character and His will, then align our own character and will with them. Thus we as His *saints* honor and *bless* Him.

In one sense the rest of the creation is better equipped to give praise to God than we are since the rest of creation is less affected by the fall. All creation suffered from humanity's sin (see Romans 8:20-22), but no part of creation suffered as much as humanity—though certainly that suffering is self-inflicted. For our own part we are both ill-equipped and well-equipped to praise God. The quagmire of sin mutes our praise; sin weakens our ability and desire to glorify Him. We have gone further from God than any other part of creation, except perhaps Satan and the fallen angels.

Because of the grace of Christ, though, we are also the best equipped to praise Him. No other part of creation has been so singularly blessed, nothing else has been made in God's image and likeness. Our voices should sound the loudest symphony of praise in all creation! [See question #4, page 302.]

IV. Kingdom of God (Psalm 145:11-13)

A. Glorious Majesty (vv. 11, 12)

11, 12. They shall speak of the glory of thy kingdom, and talk of thy power; to make known to the sons of men his mighty acts, and the glorious majesty of his kingdom.

Praise to God is valuable for its own sake. Praise also benefits the one doing the praising. But a third reason to praise has a testimonial purpose: praising God is part of sharing His good news with others.

Churches that ignore this aspect of worship fail to take full advantage of one of the best tools for witness and outreach. When we truly worship, praise, and exalt the God who is living and active and involved in our lives, the church is at its most inviting. Many people are drawn to true worship. Worship is an attractive, beautiful activity. When that worship declares the glory of God and His kingdom, seekers may catch a glimpse of whom and what they have been seeking all along. [See question #5, page 302.]

B. Enduring Dominion (v. 13)

13. Thy kingdom is an everlasting kingdom, and thy dominion endureth throughout all generations.

King Nebuchadnezzar was another who acknowledged the fact of God's enduring *kingdom* (Daniel 4:3, 34). The simple truth is that God is going to do His will. We will be happiest and most fulfilled when we align ourselves with that will. This is essentially what David is saying here in speaking of an *everlasting* kingdom and God's enduring *dominion.* God does not need our cooperation. God invites us to choose to be part of His movement, part of His kingdom. Operating on our own is self-destructive.

Conclusion

A. Our Kingdom Responsibilities

For several months I worked in retail sales while my wife attended graduate school. One of my job requirements was to sell extended warranties on products. I learned very quickly that this area of sales was not a strength of mine. Sometimes I would stumble over the words. Other times I would rush through the pitch too quickly. Communicating the features and benefits of the products came quite easily to me, but I struggled throughout my brief sales career with the more speculative features and benefits of this form of product insurance.

Similarly, selling credit cards never came easily to me. I am a firm believer in the principle that less debt is better than more debt. Since I do not like credit cards, I had a hard time investing myself in offering them. Although my employer used a carrot-and-stick approach—the carrot being commissions and financial incentives—I struggled for months to achieve even rudimentary results in promoting these things.

My personal desires and giftedness, though, were irrelevant to my employer. Part of my job was to sell those products! For as long as I worked in that company, selling those products was required. My evaluations were based in large measure on my success in those areas. The one time I was written up negatively was when a customer reported (erroneously) that I failed to offer him a credit card. Although I was not skilled in those areas, they were part of the job. Eventually, I mastered the skill enough to attain a measure of success, yet without compromising my integrity.

There are certain tasks in the Christian life that we sometimes try to assign only to those who are spiritually gifted in those areas.

Home Daily Bible Readings

Monday, Mar. 20—Glory in God's Holy Name (Psalm 105:1-11)

Tuesday, Mar. 21—I Sing Your Praise (Psalm 138)

Wednesday, Mar. 22—Sing to God a New Song (Psalm 149)

Thursday, Mar. 23—Praise the Lord! (Psalm 150)

Friday, Mar. 24—I Will Extol You, O God (Psalm 145:1-7)

Saturday, Mar. 25—Your Kingdom Is an Everlasting Kingdom (Psalm 145:8-13a)

Sunday, Mar. 26—God Is Faithful (Psalm 145:13b-21)

"Evangelism is the preacher's job," we may say, or, "The worship leader takes care of the praise in worship." Such excuses may comfort us for a while. But Bible study will convince us that all Christians are called by God to share the good news. All of us are called by God to praise His name. Whether we are skilled or gifted or equipped, we are responsible to do our part.

The challenge is to recognize that these are God's expectations. We also need to recognize, though, that the benefits to us are staggering. There is no feeling in the world like that of leading someone to know Christ. Baptizing someone is a great privilege! Worship and praise do much more for me than they do for God—although I am praising His name, He graciously blesses me more than I am capable of blessing Him.

B. Prayer

Father, we lift Your name on high. We exalt Your name. May those in our families, in our neighborhoods, at our jobs, at our schools, and in our communities see You lifted high. May they be attracted to Your presence by our worship. In Christ's name we pray, amen.

C. Thought to Remember

God—and only God—is worthy of worship.

Learning by Doing

This section contains an alternative lesson plan emphasizing learning activities. Classes desiring such student involvement will find these suggestions helpful.

Learning Goals

After lesson each student will be able to:

1. Review the reasons the psalmist gives for praising God.
2. Describe various ways to praise God.
3. Create a plan for one generation to express God's praise to a different generation.

Into the Lesson

Write the following open-ended statements on the board:

    I like to praise God by . . .
    I praise God because . . .

Ask students to write down as many responses to each statement as they can generate in a minute or two, and then call on volunteers to share their answers with the class. Say, "Today's lesson deals with the *hows* and *whys* of worshiping God in the twenty-first century."

Into the Word

Divide your class in half. One half will study Psalm 145:1-7 to identify the different *methods* that David used to praise God. The other half will study Psalm 145:8-13 to look for *reasons* why David praised God.

Instruct each group to use the questions below (also printed in the student books) to help them complete their studies. Within the two large groups, you may have your students work independently, in pairs, or in small groups depending on class size, seating arrangements, and available space.

Encourage students to refer to the additional Scriptures listed below for background information. You will want to study them yourself in advance to see how they illustrate David's teaching in Psalm 145.

Methods Group (Psalm 145:1-7):
How did David praise God?

1. How often did David praise God (v. 2)?
2. How is it possible to praise God "for ever" (vv. 1, 2)?
3. How is recognizing God's greatness a specific type of praise (v. 3)?
4. How can one generation praise God's works to another (v. 4)? What techniques did the Jews use to do this? (See Deuteronomy 11:18-21.)
5. What is involved in declaring the "mighty acts" of God (v. 4)? (See Exodus 15.)
6. In what ways could David and other Jews have spoken of God's greatness, majesty, and works (vv. 4-6)? (See 2 Samuel 6.)
7. How would the ancient Jews have sung of God's righteousness (v. 7)? (See Psalm 33:1-3.)

Reasons Group (Psalm 145:8-13):
Why did David praise God?

1. What do the terms *gracious, full of compassion, slow to anger,* and *of great mercy* suggest about the nature of God (v. 8)?

2. How did God show His mercy and compassion to David? (See 1 Samuel 16; 2 Samuel 22.)

3. How does God demonstrate His goodness to all people? (See Matthew 5:45.)

4. How do God's works praise Him (v. 10)?

5. What are some examples from the Old Testament of how the ancient Jews testified of God's glory, kingdom, and mighty acts (vv. 10, 11)? (See 1 Kings 10:1-13; Isaiah 52.)

6. Why would the eternal nature of God's kingdom be a reason to praise God (v. 13)? In our present age, what would be involved in testifying to the world about God's kingdom?

Allow 10 to 15 minutes, then have groups discuss their findings with the entire class. Use the lesson commentary to guide the discussion. Emphasize, in particular, the relationship between *how* we praise God and *why*. Ask students to suggest ways to praise God specifically for one of His traits (for example, the trait of mercy).

Into Life

Make a transition by saying, "Now let's think about applying our hows to various groups within the church." Divide your class into small groups of three or four. Provide each group with a paper that is blank except for these three headings: *Adults, Teens, Children.* (Space is also provided for this exercise in the student books.)

Ask each group to take one of God's traits as discussed in the previous activity and spend several minutes brainstorming ways for each of the generational groups to praise God for that attribute. Remind your students that adults, teens, and children may not prefer the same styles of music, sermons, or other worship activities. Discuss each group's answers.

Let's Talk It Over

These questions are designed to promote discussion of the lesson. The answers here are only discussion starters. Let your class talk it over from there.

1. Sunday worship is important, but how we live each weekday is really a better overall measure of our relationship with our Lord. What are some ways that you continue to worship God throughout the week?

This question speaks to our daily spiritual disciplines. Naturally, answers will vary depending on the individual student's personality, level of spiritual maturity, and life situation. For David's part, his love for music likely persisted throughout his life and may have formed a part of his daily recommitment to God. How blessed we are today to have access to recorded music that David never dreamed of! The psalms that David wrote may, in a sense, be thought of as his prayer journal. Perhaps some of your students find journaling to be spiritually beneficial as well.

2. What have you found that improves communication when teaching teens about their need for God?

Parents easily can focus on what is wrong with their children. A much better approach is to take stock of what is most important. For instance, the decibel level of the music may not be as important (up to a point) as its content. Asking questions, knowing our children's likes and dislikes, knowing their friends, offering appropriate praise—all of these can lead to positive relationships that allow us to teach our children (or our friends!) about God with much less resistance. Good communication with teens has its foundations in developing communication in the preteen years.

3. There are many Old Testament passages where God's vengeance is mentioned. Yet David's own life events could allow him to stress God's greatness and kindness. How can you add David's life events to your own to allow you to see God's greatness and kindness today?

David lived a life that seemed to be packed with events that were both good and bad. The incidents involving Goliath, Saul, Jonathan, Bathsheba, and Absalom come to mind. While David wasn't perfect, he did seem to have a strong desire to do what God wanted him to do most of the time. First Timothy 1:8, 9 reminds us that laws are given to control "the lawless and disobedient," not those who are acting properly in the first place. David certainly was one who knew both sides of that equation! David knew the reality of God's forgiveness.

To live such a life means that one need not fear God's wrath. Rather, we accept the wonder of His grace. Our daily wonder should be greater than David's because we have the reality of the risen Christ—something David didn't have. Even so, our accountability to God is greater than that of David because we have more of God's revelation than David had.

4. While all creation may praise God, we humans have very distinct reasons for doing so. What could be some reasons why our praise would be different from the songs of the angels? How will your praise differ from theirs this week?

What a blessing God gave to us when He placed the earth and its creatures under our control! (See Genesis 1:28, 29.) In doing so He was declaring His great love for us. No other created being enjoys this kind of blessing. No other being is said to be made in God's own image.

We can enjoy these blessings using every sense. Furthermore, even when we go astray, God wants to bring us back into relationship with Him. We can praise God for His offer of forgiveness to us through Christ. The Bible says nothing about God making forgiveness available to fallen angels. What wonder!

5. You may or may not have the poetic flair of a David. Still, we all are called to praise God. If you were called upon to declare your personal testimony in the worship of God, where would you begin and what would you say?

While there are many blessings we share in common, God has poured out individual blessings for us. We need to share these with one another. They are encouraging and inspiring. Perhaps your class would benefit from sharing even one-sentence praises. For instance, "When I was going through the personal distress of ____, God provided me with a friend to give me the godly encouragement I needed."

Responding to Tragedy

April 2
Lesson 5

DEVOTIONAL READING: Psalm 22:1-11.

BACKGROUND SCRIPTURE: Job 1–3.

PRINTED TEXT: Job 1:14-22; 3:1-3, 11.

Job 1:14-22

14 And there came a messenger unto Job, and said, The oxen were plowing, and the asses feeding beside them:

15 And the Sabeans fell upon them, and took them away; yea, they have slain the servants with the edge of the sword; and I only am escaped alone to tell thee.

16 While he was yet speaking, there came also another, and said, The fire of God is fallen from heaven, and hath burned up the sheep, and the servants, and consumed them; and I only am escaped alone to tell thee.

17 While he was yet speaking, there came also another, and said, The Chaldeans made out three bands, and fell upon the camels, and have carried them away, yea, and slain the servants with the edge of the sword; and I only am escaped alone to tell thee.

18 While he was yet speaking, there came also another, and said, Thy sons and thy daughters were eating and drinking wine in their eldest brother's house:

19 And, behold, there came a great wind from the wilderness, and smote the four corners of the house, and it fell upon the young men, and they are dead; and I only am escaped alone to tell thee.

20 Then Job arose, and rent his mantle, and shaved his head, and fell down upon the ground, and worshipped,

21 And said, Naked came I out of my mother's womb, and naked shall I return thither: the LORD gave, and the LORD hath taken away; blessed be the name of the LORD.

22 In all this Job sinned not, nor charged God foolishly.

Job 3:1-3, 11

1 After this opened Job his mouth, and cursed his day.

2 And Job spake, and said,

3 Let the day perish wherein I was born, and the night in which it was said, There is a man child conceived.

. . . .

11 Why died I not from the womb? Why did I not give up the ghost when I came out of the belly?

GOLDEN TEXT: What? shall we receive good at the hand of God, and shall we not receive evil? In all this did not Job sin with his lips.—Job 2:10.

> *Living in and as God's Creation*
> Unit 2: Living with Creation's Uncertainty
> (Lessons 5-9)

Lesson Aims

After participating in this lesson, each student will be able to:

1. Recite the fundamental facts about the person and book of Job.
2. Discuss the nature of grief and right ways to respond to it.
3. Make a plan to worship God when personal grief comes.

Lesson Outline

INTRODUCTION
    A. Age-Old Problem
    B. Lesson Background
I. JOB'S LOSSES (Job 1:14-19)
    A. By the Sabeans (vv. 14, 15)
    B. By the Fire of God (v. 16)
    C. By the Chaldeans (v. 17)
    D. By a Great Wind (vv. 18, 19)
II. JOB'S REACTION, PART 1 (Job 1:20-22)
    A. Grief and Worship (v. 20)
    B. Praise and Integrity (vv. 21, 22)
        In the Face of Death
III. JOB'S REACTION, PART 2 (Job 3:1-3, 11)
    A. Desire to Turn Back Time (vv. 1-3)
    B. Desire to Turn Back Life (v. 11)
        Anxious, Troubled, Distressed?
CONCLUSION
    A. One of Christianity's Greatest Challenges
    B. When Life Tumbles In
    C. Prayer
    D. Thought to Remember

Introduction

A. Age-Old Problem

The tragic element of life is painfully obvious. We need look no further than this morning's newspaper or our own experience to know that tragedy is everywhere. This is not just a concern of the modern world. The book of Job, which is the basis for our next three lessons, is an ancient book. There the author explores the meaning of suffering, particularly unjustified suffering. Admittedly, some suffering comes from our own poor decisions. At other times we suffer because of the poor decisions of other people. Some suffering, however, is inexplicable, and we must turn to God for answers.

Some believe that the issue of suffering is Christianity's greatest problem. They ask, "Why would a good God allow the suffering of innocent people?" But it is not just a problem for Christianity. Every religion and philosophy must address the problem of suffering. The author of Job takes these themes quite seriously.

B. Lesson Background

The book of Job is the subject of countless opinions. Scholars disagree about the author. Some say Job himself wrote it. Others try to make a case for Moses or even Elihu, a friend of Job who appears near the end of the book. Since no author is given, we cannot know for sure. Its value comes from the fact that the book is inspired by God; the value is not dependent on knowing the identity of the human author.

Scholars also differ as to the date. Their estimates range from Job's being one of the earliest Old Testament books to one of the last. Even the language is hard to translate. That would be an indication of its being a very old book. A good guess is that Job himself lived sometime in the age of the patriarchs, between 2000 and 1500 B.C. It is possible that the time period of Job himself and the time of the writing of the book are not the same.

Scholars also offer different opinions about the man Job. Was he an Israelite or not? We don't know. We are certain, however, that Job was not a fictitious character (see Ezekiel 14:14, 20; James 5:11). He is described as being from Uz (Job 1:1). This is in the territory of the Edomites, south of Palestine (Lamentations 4:21).

The book of Job depicts Job as a righteous man. He feared God. He turned away from evil. He was good to his neighbors. He worshiped God and offered sacrifices. God himself declared Job to be "a perfect and an upright man, one that feareth God, and escheweth evil" (Job 1:8). That will be important to remember as we explore this book. The book of Job is more than just the story of a man with patience. It forces us to wrestle with our understanding of, and our response to, suffering.

After chapter 1 introduces us to Job, we move quickly to an assembly in Heaven. God is there, and standing in His presence are the "sons of God" (Job 1:6). These are probably angels (see also Job 38:7), although they are definitely not "sons of God" in the same sense as Jesus (see Hebrews 1:5).

Among the angels is one called Satan, which means "adversary" or "accuser." (It is more of a title than a name.) God brags about Job, but Satan accuses God of taking it easy on that man. Satan tells God that Job's faithfulness is understandable considering all the material blessings God has given him. Satan then proclaims that Job will curse God to His face if God makes Job's life difficult (Job 1:11). Consequently, the Lord grants Satan permission to oppress Job. "Behold, all that he hath is in thy power; only upon himself put not forth thine hand" (Job 1:12). [See question #1, page 311.]

I. Job's Losses
(Job 1:14-19)

Our text begins in the middle of chapter 1 as we see Satan beginning his assault on Job.

A. By the Sabeans (vv. 14, 15)

14. And there came a messenger unto Job, and said, The oxen were plowing, and the asses feeding beside them.

The first attack is on Job's possessions. As our text unfolds, we see a pattern as each disaster is followed by one surviving *messenger* bringing the bad news to *Job*. The first disaster falls upon the domesticated farm animals, the *oxen* and donkeys. Job has "seven thousand sheep, and three thousand camels, and five hundred yoke of oxen, and five hundred she asses, and a very great household" (1:3), so a lot is at stake here! [See question #2, page 311.]

15. And the Sabeans fell upon them, and took them away; yea, they have slain the servants with the edge of the sword; and I only am escaped alone to tell thee.

The first attack involves human villains, namely *the Sabeans.* They engage in brazen theft and murder. The Sabeans can be found in several areas in the ancient world. Some are associated with an area in southern Arabia we know as Sheba (Isaiah 60:6; Jeremiah 6:20). The queen of Sheba will visit Solomon (1 Kings 10:1-13).

Some think that these particular Sabeans are associated with Tema in northern Arabia (Job 6:19). In any case the amount of loss to Job is incredible, even at this early stage.

B. By the Fire of God (v. 16)

16. While he was yet speaking, there came also another, and said, The fire of God is fallen from heaven, and hath burned up the sheep, and the servants, and consumed them; and I only am escaped alone to tell thee.

The tragic drama is underscored by the appearance of *another* messenger while Job is still talking with the first. This second calamity appears to be a kind of natural disaster. The *fire of God* is most likely a lightning strike, although it also may refer to something like a volcanic eruption (compare 2 Kings 1:10, 12, 14). The amount of *sheep* lost is 7,000, since Job 1:3 says that that's what Job owns. Immeasurably more tragic is the loss of human life.

C. By the Chaldeans (v. 17)

17. While he was yet speaking, there came also another, and said, The Chaldeans made out three bands, and fell upon the camels, and have carried them away, yea, and slain the servants with the edge of the sword; and I only am escaped alone to tell thee.

The sad pattern repeats. Another messenger arrives on the heels of the others to report a third disaster. This one is at the hands of *the Chaldeans.* Again we see theft and murder.

We don't know exactly how many *servants* are slain. Job's 3,000 *camels,* for their part, are now the property of bandits. Camels are of great value to nomads in the ancient world. Their ability to carry loads and adapt to the desert heat is prized even today.

D. By a Great Wind (vv. 18, 19)

18, 19. While he was yet speaking, there came also another, and said, Thy sons and thy daughters were eating and drinking wine in their eldest brother's house: and, behold, there came a great wind from the wilderness, and smote the four corners of the house, and it fell upon the young men, and they are dead; and I only am escaped alone to tell thee.

Job has seven *sons* and three *daughters* (Job 1:2). He has lost animals and servants to this point, but now the tragedies strike much more personally. The problem occurs at the home of

> **How to Say It**
> AL-QAEDA. Al *Kai*-duh.
> ARABIA. Uh-*ray*-bee-uh.
> EDOMITES. *Ee*-dum-ites.
> ELIHU. Ih-*lye*-hew.
> EZEKIEL. Ee-*zeek*-ee-ul or Ee-*zeek*-yul.
> ISAIAH. Eye-*zay*-uh.
> JEREMIAH. Jair-uh-*my*-uh.
> SABEANS. Suh-*be*-unz.
> SATAN. *Say*-tun.
> SHEBA. *She*-buh.
> SOLOMON. *Sol*-o-mun.

Job's oldest son. This feast he is hosting may be a birthday celebration, or the 10 children simply may socialize together from time to time. Each of the seven sons takes a turn hosting the periodic gathering (Job 1:4). It is Job's custom to offer sacrifices for his children afterward (1:5).

Job 1:13 says much of what Job 1:18 says. This reinforces the fact that all these disasters happen on the same day. This fourth disaster happens when a *great wind* topples *the house* on those gathered for the meal. These winds, called sirocco winds, are common problems for nomadic peoples (compare Jeremiah 4:11).

II. Job's Reaction, Part 1 (Job 1:20-22)

None of these tragic circumstances is necessarily rare in the desert. But the accumulation of all these in such a short time attests to the unusual nature of these trials. They can't be happening by mere chance.

A. Grief and Worship (v. 20)

20. Then Job arose, and rent his mantle, and shaved his head, and fell down upon the ground, and worshipped.

The fact that *Job* rises means that he has been sitting to this point. He expresses his grief in a way that is normal for his time and place as he tears his outer garment and shaves *his head*. The tearing of garments can been seen in numerous passages, including Genesis 37:34; Joshua 7:6; Ezra 9:3, 5; and Acts 14:14. The tearing and the shaving indicate profound grief of the heart. We also see a connection of shaved heads with mourning in Jeremiah 16:5-7; 47:5; and 48:36-38, to name just a few. [See question #3, page 311.]

In spite of his grief, *Job* still worships God. Sometimes people are prone to stop attending church and to stop their personal devotions when grief comes. A newlywed couple had just started coming to church, but stopped when they found out that the wife had contracted AIDS from a previous, immoral situation. They lost faith. What a great mistake to close ourselves off from the one who can help us in our pain!

B. Praise and Integrity (vv. 21, 22)

21. And said, Naked came I out of my mother's womb, and naked shall I return thither: the LORD gave, and the LORD hath taken away; blessed be the name of the LORD.

In the midst of grief, Job makes a rather philosophical statement in this verse. He points out—correctly—that he came into the world with nothing and will leave with nothing anyway (compare Ecclesiastes 5:15). Job sees all his possessions, as well as his family, as a blessing from God. Ultimately they all belong to the Lord.

What may be troublesome to us is that God is named as being responsible for taking away the lives of Job's family. In what sense is that true? Since God has given each of us the breath of life, ultimately He can take us back to himself whenever and wherever He wishes. That is His right. But what is going on in this case? Job is not aware of what is happening behind the scenes. It is Satan who has taken away Job's children. This does not completely solve our problem, because the Lord gave Satan permission to do it.

In technical language we say that while it was not God's *prescriptive* will, it was definitely His *permissive* will. That means that while God did not prescribe for the tragedies to happen, He definitely permitted them. Such a distinction undoubtedly is of little use to Job in the midst of his profound distress. To Job, it is all from God. Job may not even be aware of the existence of Satan.

22. In all this Job sinned not, nor charged God foolishly.

Looking at the situation from a worldly viewpoint, we may say that Job has every reason to curse *God*. Job's wife even suggested it (Job 2:9). But he never does. The book of Job tells us that Job does not sin throughout this ordeal. He never charges God with any sin.

It's not that Job does not question God. Job will ask some tough questions of the Lord. Some of these questions will irritate God (see Job 38:2; 40:2). Even so, in the final analysis it is Job and not his friends who speaks what is right of God (Job 42:7).

Some people assume that a faith that questions is a weak faith. [See question #4, page 311.] To the contrary, it is through respectful questioning that we learn and our faith deepens.

In the Face of Death

Daniel Pearl was beheaded in Pakistan in 2002—the first of a grisly string of murders by Islamic militants that would continue for years. Most victims were civilians from the nations in the coalition of forces trying to break up al-Qaeda, the Islamic terrorist group. Pearl was a news reporter; others were business people helping Iraq rebuild after the war. In many cases Islamic television and Web sites showed pictures of the extremists committing their atrocities.

The poignancy of these murders was due partly to the fact that we saw the victims' family members pleading for the lives of the hostages. The scenes we saw on television moved us to empathize with their feelings of helplessness. Job, for his part, didn't get any advance warning. The fact that all of his children died in a natural disaster rather than by human barbarity scarcely made it easier to take.

Death is heart-wrenching. We all hope that the lives of our loved ones will run their full courses. When life is cut short, we fall back on our spiritual resources. In this Job set the example: he did not blame God for his loss, but instead found his strength in God. Like Job we realize that God is our only source of hope when we are faced with our own death or of those we love.

—C. R. B.

III. Job's Reaction, Part 2 (Job 3:1-3, 11)

Several things happen in the intervening verses that are not in today's text. For one, Satan makes another visit to Heaven to argue with God. Satan admits that Job has done well, but points out that Job himself has not been stricken. Thus Satan proposes to harm Job physically. Job then is afflicted with painful boils all over his body. Satan believes this will cause Job to curse God.

Some have supposed that Satan has overplayed his hand. He already has done his worst with Job's family. It is quite probable that Job cares more about his family than about his own health. Thus the additional problems in Job 2:7 are less important to Job than the losses he has already suffered. Nevertheless, the pain is great.

Interestingly, Satan does not appear after chapter 2. He is defeated, so there is no reason for him to reappear. The focus shifts to discussions between Job and his friends. They make some attempt to comfort Job. They offer their most valuable comfort in Job 2:13 as they sit with him without saying a word. Simply being there is so important. But then things go downhill after they open their mouths to speak. Their attempts to help come after Job speaks first.

A. Desire to Turn Back Time (vv. 1-3)

1. After this opened Job his mouth, and cursed his day.

Job does not curse God, but he does express his great grief. When the text says that Job *cursed his day,* it refers to the day of his birth. Job is sorry he was ever born! As fruitless as it is to try to change the past, many spend much time and energy reliving the past or wishing things had been different. While Job's curse is understandable in the midst of his pain, the wish not to be born is fruitless. We are here, and we have to deal with the hard realities. At this point Job cannot see any beauty or good in his life.

2, 3. And Job spake, and said, Let the day perish wherein I was born, and the night in

Visual for lesson 5

"The Lord gave, and the Lord hath taken away; blessed be the name of the Lord" (Job 1:21).

Use this poster as a discussion starter as you ask, "In what other ways does the Lord give and take away?"

which it was said, There is a man child conceived.

Verse 1 announced Job's curse. Now verses 2 and 3 tell us the words of the curse as we see Job cursing even his birth announcement! Yet Job does not curse God. The closest he comes is in cursing the day of his birth. This is very similar to something the prophet Jeremiah said in Jeremiah 20:14, 15.

In Job's day male children are particularly celebrated. They will be the ones to take leadership of the family in a patriarchal society. There now appears to be nothing left for Job to live for in this regard.

B. Desire to Turn Back Life (v. 11)

11. Why died I not from the womb? Why did I not give up the ghost when I came out of the belly?

Verses 4-10 (not in our text for today) continue Job's curse against the day of his birth. Now in verse 11 Job even begins to wish that he had not survived birth. He wishes he had been stillborn. If not that, then he wishes he had died as a newborn infant. This indicates severe emotional trauma. The curse against the very beginning of his life continues in verses 12 and following. [See question #5, page 311.]

ANXIOUS, TROUBLED, DEPRESSED?

"When the Lord sends tribulations, I think He expects me to 'tribulate.'" Those are the sentiments attributed to a (probably) imaginary Christian. Most of us know the feeling,

---

Home Daily Bible Readings

Monday, Mar. 27—Job, a Blameless and Upright Man (Job 1:1-5)

Tuesday, Mar. 28—Satan Determines to Strike Job (Job 1:6-12)

Wednesday, Mar. 29—Job Loses All, but Remains Faithful (Job 1:13-22)

Thursday, Mar. 30—Job Falls Ill, but Praises God (Job 2:1-10)

Friday, Mar. 31—Job Curses His Day of Birth (Job 3:1-10)

Saturday, Apr. 1—Job Wishes for Death (Job 3:11-19)

Sunday, Apr. 2—Job Questions God's Benevolence (Job 3:20-26)

---

don't we? When troubles come to us, even if not to the extent that they did to Job, we feel *troubled!*

Scientists have discovered that the human brain is "hardwired" for fear; it helps us respond quickly to danger so that we can take the necessary steps to avoid serious harm. When the driver in the lane next to us is using the cell phone with one hand, is eating a hamburger with the other, and then suddenly crosses over into our lane, it is our fear that makes us able to take the necessary evasive action. Along with fear, the emotions of stress, apprehension, and depression are common (and normal) reactions to a world that sometimes seems to be spinning out of control.

As we examine how we react to the unsettling circumstances of our world—even when they don't affect us directly—we can hardly blame Job for the thoughts he expresses in our text today. Who *wouldn't* be depressed after experiencing all the bad things that happened to Job? Take heart: next week we will see what we can learn from Job's response to his troubles.   —C. R. B.

Conclusion

A. One of Christianity's Greatest Challenges

Job brings us face-to-face with one of Christianity's greatest challenges: If God is good, then why does He allow the innocent to suffer? It was not God who brought the problems into Job's life—but neither did God interfere with Satan as he oppressed Job.

Sometimes suffering comes about as a direct consequence of the personal choices that people make (example: contracting a sexually transmitted infection through immoral behavior). Sometimes God himself inflicts suffering because of sin (example: Ezekiel 32:1-15). But at other times, as with Job, the suffering is unexplainable from an earthly point of view. God may have a bigger plan in mind that we can't see. (In Job's case we can see it but he can't.) In such instances we continue to trust God above all else (Job 13:15; 19:25). Job thought the solution to his problem was more knowledge (see Job 13:23; 23:5). But that was not God's viewpoint.

We should notice in passing that Satan is limited. He cannot do anything that God will not allow him to do. In the end even the devil must honor God's sovereignty. Satan has tried to put

God down through Job. But ultimately it is Satan who is proven wrong.

B. When Life Tumbles In

Even though Job eventually passes his tests, this lesson does not end on a high note. We will have to wait for the next two lessons to have a more satisfactory conclusion. Still, our lesson displays the great faith of Job. Even in despair he does not make foolish statements nor does he take foolish actions.

Many do not follow Job's example, but some do. Arthur John Gossip was the preacher at Beechgrove church in Aberdeen, Scotland. In 1927 he lost his wife quite suddenly. His congregation was curious as to what he would say on his first day back in the pulpit. His sermon title was "When Life Tumbles In—What Then?" That sermon has become a classic. It appears in many sermon collections and frequently is studied in seminaries. While that sermon displays an extraordinary use of language and organization, it is a classic because it deals with fresh grief.

Arthur John Gossip communicated that when all is lost, we must turn to God. Gossip said, "I do not understand this life of ours. But still less can I comprehend how people in trouble and loss and bereavement can fling away peevishly from the Christian faith. In God's name, fling to what? Have we not lost enough without losing that too?"

C. Prayer

Dear Lord, like Your servant Job we often do not understand. Like Job we struggle with the whys of life. When tragedy comes, may it draw us near to You that we may overcome. In the name of Jesus, who also suffered unjustly, amen.

D. Thought to Remember

The ultimate loss is to reject God.

Learning by Doing

This section contains an alternative lesson plan emphasizing learning activities. Classes desiring such student involvement will find these suggestions helpful.

Learning Goals

After participating in this lesson, each student will be able to:

1. Recite the fundamental facts about the person and book of Job.
2. Discuss the nature of grief and right ways to respond to it.
3. Make a plan to worship God when personal grief comes.

Into the Lesson

Give each student a sheet of paper and pen. Direct everyone to draw a 12-block chart—three columns and four rows. Tell students to write *J, O, B* in the top row of three boxes.

Next, say, "We are going to play a game of Job by the Numbers. I am going to say both a category related to the book of Job and give the answer that goes with that category. All the answers will be numbers. You are to choose 9 of the 12 categories that I read. Write them down in your chart—1 category per box. Do **not** write down the answers/numbers, only the category."

Use the following categories or others of your own composition. Remember to state the answers/numbers, but remind the class not to write down the answers/numbers: (A) number of chapters in the book of Job—*42;* (B) number of friends who came to comfort and console Job—*4;* (C) number of Job's family members referred to in the book—*21* (10 children killed, 10 children born later, plus his wife); (D) number of the chapter in which God finally confronts Job—*38;* (E) number of chapters that dominate in poetic format—*39;* (F) number of occasions Satan speaks to God about Job—*2;* (G) number of messengers who brought Job news of disaster—*4;* (H) number of times Job spoke with a monologue of affirmation or defense—*10;* (I) number of enemy nations said to have taken Job's livestock—*2;* (J) the number of animals Job lost—*11,500;* (K) number of chapters containing God's challenge to Job—*3;* (L) number of people mentioned by name in the book—*5.*

Before class, write all answers/numbers on slips of paper and put these in a bag or box. After reading the categories and the answers/numbers, say, "Next I'm going to pull out the slips one at a time and read them. Write the answer/number down in the matching category on your charts. When you have three in a row, call out 'Job!' and we will declare you the winner."

Pull out numbers and read them until someone wins. Verify the winner's responses.

Into the Word

Say, "Most of us know something of the book of Job, but perhaps we need some familiarization with the various elements of that story." Assign the following roles for the reading of the text by distributing to students slips of paper with the following words (one word per slip): *messenger, oxen, Sabeans, servants, sheep, Chaldeans, camels, sons, daughters, Job*. Repeat any of the words (except *Job*) as necessary to give a role to each student.

An alternate use of these assigned roles involves selecting one person to stand, identify his or her role, and call for any others to stand with him or her if the roles are somehow related in the text. For example if a "sheep" stands, other related roles would be "servants" and "messenger," for the servants would have been keeping the sheep, and one servant would have been the messenger who ran to Job regarding the sheep's being stolen. Continue until each student has stood and joined a group at least once. Save the word *Job* until last, and all can stand.

Into Life

Make a transition by saying, "We've had a bit of fun so far, but the book of Job is serious business. When we examine the life of Job, we must become introspective. We must ask, 'How would my faith hold up in similar circumstances?'"

Then give your students a copy of the following list (also found in the student book). Ask each to respond honestly and personally to the following circumstances using this rating scale: 1 (=doubt would overwhelm) to 5 (=faith would grow).

"How would you fare if..."

1. A flood destroys your property?
2. An adversary steals an idea you had and profits from it?
3. Criminals break into your home and steal your family's valuables?
4. Your spouse gives up on God and encourages you to do so as well?

Discuss as time allows.

Let's Talk It Over

These questions are designed to promote discussion of the lesson. The answers here are only discussion starters. Let your class talk it over from there.

1. Where do most people seem to put the blame for evil? How would you respond to them?

Some experts suggest that evil behavior is rooted in genetics or in the way people are brought up. This is the old *nature* vs. *nurture* (or *heredity* vs. *environment*) debate. Either side of the debate allows blame for evil behavior to be placed somewhere other than on the perpetrator.

Rather than quoting the Bible, you could show where this kind of thinking leads. If people aren't responsible for their own actions, isn't it unfair to have prisons? Once the other person sees the folly of explaining (and perhaps excusing) evil behavior through either nature or nurture, then he or she may be open to thinking about what the Bible has to say. See 1 Thessalonians 3:5 and James 1:13.

2. How important are your earthly possessions to your faith in God?

This may be a question we can answer only after *losing* our possessions! Possessions can be lost either voluntarily or involuntarily. Jesus once asked a man to give up all his possessions, with a sad result when the man refused (Luke 18:18-30). Undoubtedly, Jesus tailored His request to that individual's specific problem.

Involuntary loss of possessions can come from job layoffs, natural disasters, etc. Many faithful Christians around the world live in poverty not of their own choosing. But many still exhibit joy in their faith. If having less ultimately would give us a deeper faith, perhaps we should pray that God would take away some of our possessions!

3. Cultures around the world have varying traditions regarding expressions of grief and sorrow. What are some examples? In what ways are these helpful or harmful spiritually?

Grief is a God-given emotion. From wearing black clothing, to the sprinkling of ashes on the head, to singing and dancing—cultures throughout the world have ways of expressing grief. God himself is said to have grieved (Genesis 6:6).

For many Americans today, customs that express grief have been dramatically de-emphasized. Funerals often are not well attended. The wearing of traditional black clothing has been abandoned in some places. Some think an absence of tears to be a "good witness" or a sign that people are "handling it well." Yet the Bible does not support the suppression of mourning (John 11:35; Acts 8:2; 20:36-38; Romans 12:15).

Traditions that allow uninhibited emotions show a higher rate of emotional recovery. Grief expressions may be harmful spiritually if they pull us into blaming God for something. The apostle Paul expressed concern on one occasion that an outpouring of grief on his behalf should not dissuade him from his duty (Acts 21:12-14).

4. What was an occasion when you felt confused or disappointed with God? What hard questions did you desperately want God to answer? How did this affect you spiritually?

Spend a few hours in the waiting room of a surgical intensive-care unit and you will be confronted with questions such as "Why is this happening?" "How could God let this occur?" "Why doesn't God answer my prayer?" These questions are being asked thousands of times every day. When your world is crashing in, the hurt, disappointment, and confusion seem both unique and completely overwhelming.

Yet many Christians emerge from their long dark valleys with faith intact or even stronger. One reason could be that they had a godly friend to walk with them through that valley. Job's friends were on the right path when they "sat down with him . . . and none spake a word" (Job 2:13). It's when they opened their mouths that their helping became counterproductive (Job 13:4; 16:1-5).

5. What would you do if you heard someone say, "I wish I had never been born"?

Such a question may indicate suicidal tendencies. As with Job, there may be moments when the pain of living one more day seems overwhelming. Suicide is a taboo subject, rarely discussed among Christians. Such silence may mean that proper help is not offered. Or if a suicide occurs, the lack of dialogue may inhibit appropriate grief and healing among loved ones. Take every indication of suicidal tendencies seriously. Safeguard the person and get help!

April 9
Lesson 6

Searching for Hope

DEVOTIONAL READING: Job 36:24-33.

BACKGROUND SCRIPTURE: Job 14; 32:1-8; 34:10-15; 37:14-24.

PRINTED TEXT: Job 14:1, 2, 11-17; 32:6, 8; 34:12; 37:14, 22.

Job 14:1, 2, 11-17

1 Man that is born of a woman is of few days, and full of trouble.

2 He cometh forth like a flower, and is cut down: he fleeth also as a shadow, and continueth not.

. . . .

11 As the waters fail from the sea, and the flood decayeth and drieth up;

12 So man lieth down, and riseth not: till the heavens be no more, they shall not awake, nor be raised out of their sleep.

13 Oh that thou wouldest hide me in the grave, that thou wouldest keep me secret, until thy wrath be past, that thou wouldest appoint me a set time, and remember me!

14 If a man die, shall he live again? All the days of my appointed time will I wait, till my change come.

15 Thou shalt call, and I will answer thee: thou wilt have a desire to the work of thine hands.

16 For now thou numberest my steps: dost thou not watch over my sin?

17 My transgression is sealed up in a bag, and thou sewest up mine iniquity.

Job 32:6, 8

6 And Elihu the son of Barachel the Buzite answered and said, I am young, and ye are very old; wherefore I was afraid, and durst not show you mine opinion.

. . . .

8 But there is a spirit in man: and the inspiration of the Almighty giveth them understanding.

Job 34:12

12 Yea, surely God will not do wickedly, neither will the Almighty pervert judgment.

Job 37:14, 22

14 Hearken unto this, O Job: stand still, and consider the wondrous works of God.

. . . .

22 Fair weather cometh out of the north: with God is terrible majesty.

GOLDEN TEXT: If a man die, shall he live again? All the days of my appointed time will I wait, till my change come.—Job 14:14.

> *Living in and as God's Creation*
> Unit 2: Living with Creation's Uncertainty
> (Lessons 5-9)

Lesson Aims

After this lesson each student will be able to:
1. Articulate the reasons why Job felt his life situation was so hopeless.
2. Identify those beliefs that can give a person both earthly and eternal hope.
3. Write a prayer that expresses hope for the current life and the life to come.

Lesson Outline

INTRODUCTION
    A. Unwelcome Subject
    B. Lesson Background
 I. REALITY OF DEATH (Job 14:1, 2, 11, 12)
    A. Are Our Lives Brief and Troubled? (v. 1)
    B. Are We Like Flowers and Shadows? (v. 2)
    C. Are We Like Rivers? (vv. 11, 12)
 II. DESIRE FOR LIFE (Job 14:13-17)
    A. Will God Remember Us? (v. 13)
    B. Will We Live Again? (vv. 14, 15)
    Mummies, Pyramids, and Other Strange Ideas
    C. Will God Forgive Us? (vv. 16, 17)
 III. RELIABILITY OF GOD (Job 32:6, 8; 34:12; 37:14, 22)
    A. God Gives Wisdom (32:6, 8)
    B. God Does What Is Right (34:12)
    C. God Does Marvelous Things (37:14, 22)
    God's Amazing Works
CONCLUSION
    A. How Shall We Live?
    B. Prayer
    C. Thought to Remember

Introduction

A. Unwelcome Subject

Death is an unwelcome visitor. We don't even like to read about it, much less experience it. We don't want to see it happen to our family and friends, and we sometimes (or often) fear the day we must face it ourselves.

Death is an unwelcome subject. It's not talked about in polite society. Sometimes the only opportunity to deal with the subject of death is when it has happened, while the hurt is still fresh and the mind still confused.

There is a sense in which we are touched by death every day. We see stories about it in the newspaper or on TV. Or we hear about a friend of a friend who has died. There also come those tragic moments when death hits home to us. Death indeed is a subject we need to talk about.

Since God's Word meets our deepest needs, it certainly will have much to say to us on the subject of death. So let's force ourselves to look at death. It is not so bad to speak of this subject at this particular season of the year. In the next seven days we will deal with both death and life. We already know that life will win out. But for now let us put ourselves in the shoes of people who have no hope, or at least people like Job who struggle.

In some ways you would think that we would get used to death. After all, everything that lives a physical existence dies. Even the tiniest plant that is given the privilege of life must die. The small microorganisms die. The animals die. The most difficult concept of all, of course, is to realize that we are going to die.

Death comes at various times. Sometimes the newborn is subject to death. Other times death waits until the summertime of life when someone is in his or her teens. We all are touched by the tragedy when death takes one away in middle age, often when there is still family to take care of. Even when death waits until old age, we are never quite ready for it.

Death comes in various ways. We are certain we don't want to experience any of them. Death may come through accident, sickness, or old age.

Though it comes in various ways at various times, the inescapable fact is that death comes to all. No one can bargain his or her way out of it. There will be no escape. It happens to the good and the bad, the successful and unsuccessful, the attractive and the plain. It happens to the religious and irreligious, young and old, intelligent and ignorant.

Even though we know death will happen to us, we still try to avoid the ramifications in our emotional life. Indeed, it probably would be quite unsettling if we had to think of death every day. Still, we know that death will come. We see it as the common experience of all, yet there is something within us that says this should not be so. [See question #1, page 320.]

> **How to Say It**
> BARACHEL. *Bar*-uh-kel.
> BILDAD. *Bill*-dad.
> BUZITE. *Bew*-zyet.
> ELIHU. Ih-*lye*-hew.
> ELIPHAZ. *El*-ih-faz.
> ZOPHAR. *Zo*-far.

B. Lesson Background

Last week we looked at Job's initial response to tragedy. This week we examine Job's musings on life and death. To Job, this is not idle chit-chat. He is discussing these issues in depth with his friends, with grief still in his heart and scabs still on his body.

Throughout this book Job goes back and forth in his thinking. This polar swing is normal for grieving people. Chapter 14 seems to return to the despair of Job expressed earlier in the book. Our lesson picks up at the end of the first cycle of dialogues with Eliphaz, Bildad, and Zophar. Some evaluate Job's responses to these three men as being almost totally negative and fatalistic. Others see in his words hints of hope.

It is important for us to take the ride with Job. What he says in this section is not to be taken as the last word. He is not sharing final conclusions or convictions. He is engaged in a give-and-take where he answers some questions but raises others. We must engage in the discussion with Job and his friends.

I. Reality of Death (Job 14:1, 2, 11, 12)

A. Are Our Lives Brief and Troubled? (v. 1)

1. Man that is born of a woman is of few days, and full of trouble.

Job ponders the length and quality of life. To a young person, time seems like it lasts forever. To those in middle years, time seems short as they begin to note that there are more years behind them than ahead of them. The elderly ponder how it all happened so fast. No matter how much time we have, it is in some sense short.

Not only are our days brief, in Job's view, they are also *full of trouble*. Jacob also was one who noted the brevity and difficulty of life when he said "few and evil have the days of the years of my life been" (Genesis 47:9)—and he was age 130 when he said it! We should recall that Job was a wealthy and blessed man most of his life. No doubt Job had experienced many good days. But a state of grief often colors one's perceptions. [See question #2, page 320.]

B. Are We Like Flowers and Shadows? (v. 2)

2. He cometh forth like a flower, and is cut down: he fleeth also as a shadow, and continueth not.

In beautiful but sad words, Job compares human life first to *a flower*. How short is a flower's beautiful life! Flowers bring great joy due to their radiance and fragrance. But soon their petals are dropping, they lose their color, and they smell like dirt itself. The Bible writers often compare the brevity of life to that of flowers (see Psalm 103:15, 16; Isaiah 28:1, 4; James 1:10, 11; 1 Peter 1:24).

Job also compares human life to a *shadow*. Is there anything more transitory than that? Shadows come and go with the sun and clouds as well as our movement. They appear for a moment and then are gone (compare 1 Chronicles 29:15; Job 8:9; Psalms 102:11; 109:23; 144:4; Ecclesiastes 6:12).

Job's thoughts on the brevity of life in verses 1 and 2 here lead up to his question in verse 3 (which is not in today's text). Paraphrased, that question is something like "Lord, why do You even bother paying attention to creatures like us whose lives are so fleeting?" This is part of Job's agony: the Lord has (in Job's view) singled out one of His creatures—a creature with a vanishingly short life span—to punish. That creature is Job himself.

C. Are We Like Rivers? (vv. 11, 12)

11, 12. As the waters fail from the sea, and the flood decayeth and drieth up; so man lieth down, and riseth not: till the heavens be no more, they shall not awake, nor be raised out of their sleep.

In the intervening verses Job contrasts humans with a dried up tree stump and tree root that may still hope to spring forth with new life (vv. 7-9). Unlike that tree, "man dieth, and wasteth away" (v. 10). A stump may bring new life—that's hope. But is there any hope for humanity?

Job's words come from strong emotion. His mood seems to swing a bit in comparing humans to *waters* that evaporate. A similar use of water evaporation also is found in Isaiah 19:5.

There we see a prediction of Egypt's downfall. Water evaporates. So do people and nations.

But is that evaporation permanent? A lake may dry up, but with time the drought ends and the waters may return. By saying that we *riseth not: till the heavens be no more*, there is the possibility that Job may be thinking that humans can have life again after the heavens undergo some kind of turmoil. After the prediction of disaster on Egypt in Isaiah 19:5, that prophet predicts restoration of that country (Isaiah 19:19-25). The thoughts of Job and Isaiah on evaporation and restoration are interesting to compare!

We should pause to remember that Job does not have a full revelation about life after death. He does not have the revealed promises of Christ or the New Testament testimony of resurrection. Still, Job longs and dreams for something more that his current earthly life.

Some have argued that the Old Testament saints do not believe in an afterlife. Others convincingly argue that life after death is indeed affirmed in the ancient texts (see Daniel 12:2). Today we still don't understand everything about life after death, but the New Testament does bring this idea into sharper focus.

In both Old and New Testament eras, God gives His people all they need to know on this subject. Probing further than what God has revealed is dangerous (see Revelation 22:18). Even so, we note that Jesus declared that His return would be connected with the disruption of the heavens (Matthew 24:29-31; Mark 13:24-27; Luke 21:25-27; Revelation 6:12-14).

II. Desire for Life
(Job 14:13-17)

A. Will God Remember Us? (v. 13)

13. Oh that thou wouldest hide me in the grave, that thou wouldest keep me secret, until thy wrath be past, that thou wouldest appoint me a set time, and remember me!

A faint hint of life after death is noted in this verse. Job wants to have a final word with God. Job has assumed all along that his troubles are happening because God is angry with him. He wants a restored relationship. Above all else, he wants God to *remember* him. When God does remember him, he wants it to be when God's *wrath* has passed.

B. Will We Live Again? (vv. 14, 15)

14. If a man die, shall he live again? All the days of my appointed time will I wait, till my change come.

This is one of the most famous verses in the book of Job. *If a man die, shall he live again?* is a question often asked yet today. Job has no proof of life after death, only a hunch. As one preacher pondered, "Would God go to all the trouble of creating great personalities only to see them utterly destroyed? That would be like a crazy artist who paints paintings, only to tear them up."

There are several theories about what *change* Job is talking about when he speaks of his change to *come*. One is that Job is speaking of a change in his relationship with God—that God will pardon him and be angry with him no more. Another theory proposes that Job is merely saying that he will have to wait to find out what happens when his life changes—that is, when he dies. A third theory says that Job is not speaking of death as such, but of a mortal or terminal illness; his change would then refer to his healing from that illness. Finally there is the theory that Job is holding out hope for life after death. The change would refer to his change from death to new life beyond the grave.

All of these explanations have some credence. But in light of the question the verse begins with, we should favor the last theory. Even though Job has no detailed revelation about life after death, he still hopes for it. See the next verse.

15. Thou shalt call, and I will answer thee: thou wilt have a desire to the work of thine hands.

Job believes, quite logically, that the creator will long for what He has made—that He will call

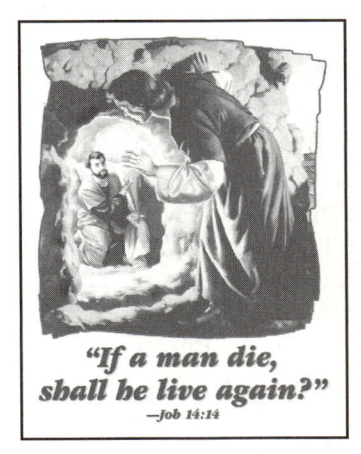

Use this visual to illustrate how Jesus provides the answer to Job's question.

Visual for lessons 6 & 7

him forth from the grave. What kind of god would create, but then take no interest in his creation? That doesn't make sense! Job believes that God will indeed take interest in what He has taken so much care to create. In Job's case that will happen when God *shalt call* and Job *will answer.* To Job it doesn't work the other way around.

MUMMIES, PYRAMIDS, AND OTHER STRANGE IDEAS

For "only" $74,000 you can become a mummy! Sitting in the pyramid in the front yard of his Salt Lake City home, Corky Ra, a former Mormon missionary, is promoting a patented system for preserving the dead. To sell his system he uses the image of a moth wrapping itself in silk. He guarantees that "You will stay like this for eternity. There will be no decomposition" (*Los Angeles Times,* June 21, 2003).

This is all a part of the beliefs of the church that Ra founded, based on ancient Egyptian religious ideas (as you probably already have guessed). Oh, that $74,000 fee? Easily covered by life insurance policies taken out by the customers in favor of Ra's company. So far Ra has convinced more than 1,400 people to take advantage of his mummification services. (One may wonder, of course, who it is being taken advantage of!)

Isn't it interesting how anxious people are to preserve these mortal bodies? This is true even of people who believe there is no life beyond this one. (But perhaps it makes more sense for them, since the decaying body would be all that remained of them if their beliefs were true.) However, Job's faith—even without the validation that Christians find in Christ's resurrection—is solid: God will keep Job safe in the grave. At the appointed time God will call him forth from the dead. Christ *proved* it! —C. R. B.

C. Will God Forgive Us? (vv. 16, 17)

16. For now thou numberest my steps: dost thou not watch over my sin?

By using the word *now,* is Job referring to his present situation, or is he referring to his hoped-for situation of verse 15? The second idea fits the context better. This strengthens the idea that Job believes in (or at least yearns for) life after death.

God knows what is going on in Job's life—and Job knows that God knows. God numbers Job's *steps* (compare Job 31:4, 37). He also knows all of Job's *sins* (Job 7:20; 10:14). The type of relationship that Job wants with God is one in which Job will not be fearful of God analyzing Job's steps and sins. That idea is extended in the next verse.

17. My transgression is sealed up in a bag, and thou sewest up mine iniquity.

The picture here is that God will collect Job's sins *in a bag* and then seal the bag so that the sin is never seen again. Thus Job expresses a confidence in God's grace, an idea that will find fuller treatment in the New Testament.

III. Reliability of God (Job 32:6, 8; 34:12; 37:14, 22)

A. God Gives Wisdom (32:6, 8)

6. And Elihu the son of Barachel the Buzite answered and said, I am young, and ye are very old; wherefore I was afraid, and durst not show you mine opinion.

Elihu is a fourth friend of Job who speaks up after all the others have had their say. Interestingly, Elihu's name means "He is my God."

Elihu sums up and counters the arguments of the others. His analysis is closest to the truth, but it comes with an attitude. Not all students appreciate the contributions of Elihu. One commentator describes him as a man who is confident that he has a message but is in fact a "pompous bore."

Some have described Elihu as an angry and impatient young man. Readers are free to draw their own conclusions. Just remember that Elihu begins his remarks with customary deference to his elders. Also, his words may sound harsher to modern ears than they do to ancient ones. [See question #3, page 320.]

8. But there is a spirit in man: and the inspiration of the Almighty giveth them understanding.

Elihu makes his case for entering the debate. Although he admits to being relatively young, he reminds the others that wisdom does not always come from those who are older. He contends that it is *the inspiration of the Almighty* that grants *understanding.*

B. God Does What Is Right (34:12)

12. Yea, surely God will not do wickedly, neither will the Almighty pervert judgment.

One thing that Elihu is steadfast about is his belief that *God* cannot do wrong. Whatever question we may ask, we must assume that a holy God will always do what is right. [See question #4, page 320.] In the *King James Version*, the word *judgment* often means the same thing as *justice*.

C. God Does Marvelous Things (37:14, 22)

14. Hearken unto this, O Job: stand still, and consider the wondrous works of God.

In the verse before us, Elihu confronts and questions *Job* directly. Elihu's questions are similar to those that God will ask of Job in chapter 38. This verse appears in the middle of a discussion of God's rule over nature. Elihu speaks of the chill of winter and the fierceness of storms. However problematic these storms may be, they have their place in the rhythms of nature.

22. Fair weather cometh out of the north: with God is terrible majesty.

This verse is Elihu's conclusion of his poetic tribute to God's work in nature. As we saw with Psalm 145:6 in Lesson 4, this is an older use of the word *terrible*. This word originally meant "that which produces terror." Thus Elihu simply is talking of the awe-inspiring nature of God. Perhaps Elihu also is suggesting that God will reveal himself in *majesty* to Job. Despite the storms of Job's life, God is still there. [See question #5, page 320.]

GOD'S AMAZING WORKS

Racetrack Playa is a dry lake bed in Death Valley National Park. It is so flat that the north end is only two inches higher in elevation than its south end, nearly three miles away! Dozens of rocks—ranging in size up to several hundreds of pounds—are on the clay surface, having tumbled there from the nearby mountains. But the amazing thing about them is that they move on this perfectly flat surface!

The trails that the rocks make vary from perfectly straight to angular to circular. Geologists have been trying for more than 50 years to come up with the reason for this strange phenomenon. But so far all they have are theories, none of them proven. Some scientists theorize that wind is behind the movement. Others believe winter rains that freeze at night may "float" the rocks enough to be blown by the wind. But no one has ever seen the rocks move.

The phenomenon of the erratically moving rocks of Death Valley is just one of many strange and wonderful facets of God's marvelous creation. In chapters 36 and 37 of the book of Job, Elihu calls Job's attention to many of God's wonders.

> **Home Daily Bible Readings**
> **Monday, Apr. 3**—Job Pleads for Respite Before Death (Job 14:1-6)
> **Tuesday, Apr. 4**—Job Petitions the Grave as Refuge (Job 14:7-17)
> **Wednesday, Apr. 5**—Mortality Finally Overcomes Life (Job 14:18-22)
> **Thursday, Apr. 6**—God's Spirit Makes for Understanding (Job 32:1-10)
> **Friday, Apr. 7**—God Repays According to Our Deeds (Job 34:11-15)
> **Saturday, Apr. 8**—Elihu Proclaims God's Majesty (Job 36:24-33)
> **Sunday, Apr. 9**—Around God Is Awesome Majesty (Job 37:14-24)

This is good for us to consider as well. We all have found that life can bring some violent storms, but Elihu advises us to remember that after the storm—and sometimes even in the midst of it—God shows His grace by sending evidence of the sunshine of His love. —C. R. B.

Conclusion

A. How Shall We Live?

What should our attitude be as we ride out the storms of life? Should we cozy up to death as just a natural part of living? Everyone dies, after all. Even the most respectable people do. On the other hand, should we cower in fear over this universal experience?

When an official of the Episcopal Church spoke at a certain historic church, he noted that some thought he desired to be buried in that church's graveyard. "That's nonsense," he responded as he expressed his desire not to be buried *anywhere!* None of us particularly wants to face death. Even if we are at peace with God and totally prepared, it is still a new experience, and there is always some anxiety associated with mystery. Death is God's penalty for sin (Genesis 2:17), and it is not to be embraced as a "friend."

We also must admit that it is not so easy to think of eternity when our feet are still planted firmly on the surface of the earth. We can scarcely do better than to have the attitude of the apostle Paul: "For I am in a strait betwixt two, having a desire to depart, and to be with Christ; which is far better: nevertheless to abide in the flesh is more needful for you" (Philippians 1:23, 24).

We should not waste any of our moments fearing the time of death. Every moment spent on fear robs us of a moment to dwell on our hope in Christ. The brevity of our life should motivate us to devote it to something worthwhile and important. Indeed, the fact that death is coming ought to drive us to Jesus Christ. He is the one who forgives, renews, and has gone to prepare a place for us. In the meantime let us remember the words of James S. Stewart, the Scottish preacher and university professor: "Let us live as people preparing to die so that we might die as people preparing to live."

B. Prayer

Dear Father of life, Your servant Paul described death as an enemy, but a defeated enemy. Help us to have that same perspective. Help us neither to welcome death as a friend nor to fear it as an enemy. Thanks to Your Son, death becomes a doorway not a dead-end street. Through Christ who gives us eternal hope, amen.

C. Thought to Remember

"One short sleep past, we wake eternally,
And death shall be no more;
death, thou shalt die."
—John Donne (1572–1631)

Learning by Doing

This section contains an alternative lesson plan emphasizing learning activities. Classes desiring such student involvement will find these suggestions helpful.

Learning Goals

After this lesson each student will be able to:

1. Articulate the reasons why Job felt his life situation was so hopeless.
2. Identify those beliefs that can give a person both earthly and eternal hope.
3. Write a prayer that expresses hope for the current life and the life to come.

Into the Lesson

Divide the class into small groups of three or four. Give each group one or more "similes on life" from the list that follows (or those of your own creation). The number of similes you give each group will determine how much time is spent on this activity.

You may decide also to give groups the same similes or not. Without explanation, simply say, "Please finish these thoughts." (If you like to give your students something to work on individually as they arrive, place a copy of one or more of the similes in each chair ahead of time.)

   1. Life is like a river because . . .
   2. Life is like a rubber band because . . .
   3. Life is like a bowl of cherries because . . .
   4. Life is like a round-trip flight because . . .
   5. Life is like a candle because . . .
   6. Life is like a jack-in-the-box because . . .
   7. Life is like a birthday present because . . .
   8. Life is like a box of chocolates because . . .

After 10 minutes have groups share their answers with the class. Secretly keep count of how often the concept *hope* comes up. At the conclusion of the discussion, say, "I noticed that *hope* was mentioned _____ times. What does this say about our outlook?"

For an alternate introductory activity emphasizing the title of the lesson, hand each person a card bearing one of these letters: *H, O, P, E*. Give the following directions: "Circulate and find three people with letters that you do not have. With your four letters, a key word can be made. When the four of you have formed your group, bring your cards to me and be seated. Do not talk during this exercise."

If the total number of students in your class is an exact multiple of four (not including yourself), give yourself a letter to ensure that there will be one or more "leftover" students at the end. Once all the groups have been formed, say, "Well, [fill in name(s) of those who were unable to form the word *hope*], I guess there's no hope for you!"

After either activity, introduce today's texts and lesson title. Say, "To discuss hope, we have two distinguished guests with us today. They are Job and Elihu."

Into the Word

Prior to today's lesson, invite two class members to deliver monologues on behalf of Job and Elihu, using the verses of today's text. Give your two orators a copy of relevant verses and suggest that the monologues be memorized and delivered emphatically. (If necessary, reading the texts will suffice.)

"Job" will deliver Job 14:1, 2, 11-17 (about 175 words); "Elihu" will give Job 32:6b, 8; 34:12; 37:14, 22 (about 75 words). Have the two actors wear large name tags labeled *JOB* and *ELIHU*.

After the monologues make a transition to the Into Life segment by saying, "People of all eras search for hope and meaning. This was as true of Job and Elihu as it is of us."

Into Life

Ask your class to identify Bible verses that reveal the hope that Christians share. Give as examples biblical truths such as "The Lord is my shepherd; I shall not want" (Psalm 23:1), or "In my Father's house are many mansions; . . . I go to prepare a place for you" (John 14:2).

Write their examples on the board. Then distribute blank-inside note cards to each student. (Such cards often can be found in multiple packs at dollar stores.) Suggest that each person "send a little hope" this week to someone they know who is tired and discouraged. Have them write the following on the inside: "Searching for hope? Remember what the Spirit says"; then add one of the verses and references from the list that is on the board or another of their choice.

This exercise will be most effective in spreading hope if the cards don't sound preachy and/or don't pretend to give pat answers. Cards that the sender delivers personally will have the most positive effect. Discourage use of e-mail.

Let's Talk It Over

These questions are designed to promote discussion of the lesson. The answers here are only discussion starters. Let your class talk it over from there.

1. What are the different ways that people view the idea of *death*? Which are most and least biblical? Why is it important to sort this out?

Non-Christians have numerous viewpoints, from death being nothingness to death being endless reincarnations. Christians who assert that death is something good (at least for the believer in Christ) will point out that death "is gain" (Philippians 1:21). Our spirits groan to be rid of our current bodies—"our earthly house of this tabernacle"—and to be in Heaven with God (2 Corinthians 5:1, 2). It is indeed blessed to die in the Lord (Revelation 14:13). Others rightly point out that death is God's penalty for sin (Genesis 2:17; 3:3; Ezekiel 18:20; Romans 6:23; James 1:15). The last enemy that Christ overcomes is death (1 Corinthians 15:26; Revelation 1:18; 20:14).

Both of the viewpoints that Christians hold are correct in their proper senses. We must stress that death is not an inherently good thing. Death can take on a sense of goodness only when it is seen as that which brings about our transition into the presence of Christ. Failure to understand the true meaning of death can mean that a person won't see a need for Christ.

2. Why is it difficult for many people to express despair at church? What can be done about this?

One oddity of the Western church is the unspoken rule that everyone should look happy. But many who sit in the pews this Sunday are going through times of despair. The challenge is for the church to remain a place for joyful celebration of God while still being a place where discouraged people are free to express openly their feelings. Compare Psalm 42:3-6 with 69:1-3.

One solution is to recruit a small number of people who have good listening skills and can empathize. They will be able to recognize those on Sunday morning who need the comfort that a fellow Christian can provide.

3. Is Elihu right? If so, does his attitude get in the way? Or is he just the young well-intentioned friend who gets it wrong? Defend your answer.

It is worth the time to try and figure out what to make of this late-arriver to the dialogue. Some see Elihu as just another guy, like Job's three other friends, trying to put a human spin on Job's suffering. Others point out that God's own words (chapters 38–41) seem to confirm and expand on the insights of Elihu. Read Elihu's advice (chapters 32–37) before drawing your conclusion.

Many assume that younger Christians don't really have much insight for older Christians; thus God gave oversight of the church to *presbyters,* a Greek word that refers to older men as elders (1 Timothy 5:17). On the other hand, the apostle Paul commanded a younger man, Timothy, to teach and guide the church at Ephesus (1 Timothy 4:6-14). All can agree that spiritual maturity counts for more than physical maturity.

4. Someone asks, "If your God is so good and powerful, how can there be suffering and evil in the world?" How do you answer?

This question always pops up after tragedy strikes. The newspapers and airwaves were filled with this question in the aftermath of 9/11. The ideas behind the question are that suffering exists either because (1) God is good but is not powerful enough to stop tragedies or (2) God is all-powerful but doesn't have a character of goodness strong enough to make Him want to stop tragedies.

You can answer with a few questions of your own: "What would it be like if God had made a world without any suffering? Suppose someone falls out of a third-story window and—what happens next? A giant safety net magically appears? What kind of world would that be?" When the time is right, you may be able to discuss Luke 13:1-5; Revelation 6:9-11; 21:4.

5. A popular Christian song, drawing on Matthew 8:26, claims that God may indeed calm the storms of life, but at other times He calms His child while the storms continue to rage. What other options does God have? How has God dealt with you during your own storms?

There is at least one additional option: sometimes God reprimands His child. We see examples of this in Job 38:2; Jeremiah 12:5; and Habakkuk 2:20. Expect a wide-ranging discussion of personal experiences.

God Gives Life

April 16
Lesson 7

DEVOTIONAL READING: Luke 24:1-9.

BACKGROUND SCRIPTURE: Job 38:1-4, 16, 17; 42:1-6; Mark 16.

PRINTED TEXT: Job 38:1, 4, 16, 17; 42:1, 2, 5; Mark 16:1-14, 20.

Job 38:1, 4, 16, 17

1 Then the LORD answered Job out of the whirlwind, and said,

. . . .

4 Where wast thou when I laid the foundations of the earth? Declare, if thou hast understanding.

. . . .

16 Hast thou entered into the springs of the sea? Or hast thou walked in the search of the depth?

17 Have the gates of death been opened unto thee? Or hast thou seen the doors of the shadow of death?

Job 42:1, 2, 5

1 Then Job answered the LORD, and said,

2 I know that thou canst do every thing, and that no thought can be withholden from thee.

. . . .

5 I have heard of thee by the hearing of the ear; but now mine eye seeth thee.

Mark 16:1-14, 20

1 And when the sabbath was past, Mary Magdalene, and Mary the mother of James, and Salome, had bought sweet spices, that they might come and anoint him.

2 And very early in the morning, the first day of the week, they came unto the sepulchre at the rising of the sun.

3 And they said among themselves, Who shall roll us away the stone from the door of the sepulchre?

4 And when they looked, they saw that the stone was rolled away: for it was very great.

5 And entering into the sepulchre, they saw a young man sitting on the right side, clothed in a long white garment; and they were affrighted.

6 And he saith unto them, Be not affrighted: ye seek Jesus of Nazareth, which was crucified: he is risen; he is not here: behold the place where they laid him.

7 But go your way, tell his disciples and Peter that he goeth before you into Galilee: there shall ye see him, as he said unto you.

8 And they went out quickly, and fled from the sepulchre; for they trembled and were amazed: neither said they any thing to any man; for they were afraid.

9 Now when Jesus was risen early the first day of the week, he appeared first to Mary Magdalene, out of whom he had cast seven devils.

10 And she went and told them that had been with him, as they mourned and wept.

11 And they, when they had heard that he was alive, and had been seen of her, believed not.

12 After that he appeared in another form unto two of them, as they walked, and went into the country.

13 And they went and told it unto the residue: neither believed they them.

14 Afterward he appeared unto the eleven as they sat at meat, and upbraided them with their unbelief and hardness of heart, because they believed not them which had seen him after he was risen.

. . . .

20 And they went forth, and preached every where, the Lord working with them, and confirming the word with signs following. Amen.

Living in and as God's Creation
Unit 2: Living with Creation's Uncertainty
(Lessons 5-9)

Lesson Aims

After participating in this lesson, each student will be able to:

1. Tell how the texts from Job and Mark affirm God's power over life and death.
2. Explain how Job's hope is realized in the resurrection of Christ.
3. Express confidence that he or she can deal with all circumstances in life without anxiety because of the resurrection.

Lesson Outline

INTRODUCTION
    A. "I Want Answers!"
    B. Lesson Background
I. GOD UNDERSTANDS LIFE (Job 38:1, 4, 16, 17; 42:1, 2, 5)
    A. God Speaks to Job (38:1, 4, 16, 17)
        What Is the Shape of Pie?
    B. Job Responds to God (42:1, 2, 5)
II. GOD BESTOWS LIFE (Mark 16:1-14, 20)
    A. Risen Christ Appears (vv. 1-7)
        The Meaning of the Stones
    B. Startled Followers Respond (vv. 8-14, 20)
CONCLUSION
    A. "What Does Easter Mean to You?"
    B. Prayer
    C. Thought to Remember

Introduction

A. "I Want Answers!"

Those who want definitive answers will find the passages we discuss today virtually unsatisfactory. Those who are willing to trust will find that when human understanding fails, God is still there. In biblical research there is an area of study called apologetics. Apologetics seeks to defend the truth of Christianity by finding answers to perplexing questions. Apologetics has its place. Many have found it comforting to know that Christianity is intellectually respectable. You don't have to check your brain at the door when you go to church. Many are heartened when they find out there are explanations for the things they have been told were contradictions.

Still, there are elements of faith that depend on trust. Our understanding may well be built on what we can reason through and be convinced of, but the human mind cannot comprehend all that God knows. Parents often discover that their children ask questions that the parents cannot answer satisfactorily. The parents may indeed know the answer. But the reason that the parents can't fully respond to the questions is that their children do not yet have the intellectual ability to grasp the answers. So parents try to answer as simply and as honestly as they can—hoping that the children will trust them when the answers seem incomprehensible.

In today's lesson we will see that Job is satisfied with God's response, even though He does not get answers to all his questions. Hundreds of years later Jesus' disciples will preach the gospel everywhere. They will do this with incomplete knowledge of God's future plans (see Acts 1:7). But they will have enough knowledge to trust God and obey.

B. Lesson Background

This lesson sets two passages of Scripture in counterpoint: one from Job and the other from Mark. The passage in the book of Job offers a personal encounter between God and Job. The section from Mark deals with a personal encounter between the risen Christ and His disciples.

How do these two passages fit together? They both deal with difficult issues. They both deal with the need to trust. Both passages provide tangible reasons to trust. In the first passage God appears to Job and honors his request for a personal meeting. Many of Job's questions go unanswered. But Job is content in fellowship with God. Job is content to trust in the God who gives life.

Some of Job's unanswered questions are dealt with in the passage from Mark and elsewhere in the New Testament. Job wondered about life after death. Jesus' crucifixion and resurrection settle the issue. Job wondered why the good suffer. Jesus was perfect, yet He faced horrific suffering. The disciples had something in common with Job: personal encounter with God caused them to trust God for what was not clear.

I. God Understands Life
(Job 38:1, 4, 16, 17; 42:1, 2, 5)

Back in Job 13:3, Job asked for an audience with God (see also 9:14-19; 31:35). God now answers that bold request. There is an old cliché: "Be careful what you ask for, because you just may get it!" Job is about to "get it."

A. God Speaks to Job (38:1, 4, 16, 17)

1. Then the LORD answered Job out of the whirlwind, and said.

Isn't it interesting that God speaks through a *whirlwind* or storm? It would seem that Job has had enough storms. After all, it was a windstorm that killed his children (Job 1:19). His friends had accused him of uttering words that amounted to nothing more than strong wind (8:2; 15:2).

This storm is different however. This storm announces the presence of God. God's presence occasionally is associated with storms elsewhere in the Old Testament (compare Jeremiah 23:19; 30:23; Ezekiel 1:4; Nahum 1:3; Zechariah 9:14; contrast 1 Kings 19:11, 12). But none of those associations is quite like this one!

4. Where wast thou when I laid the foundations of the earth? Declare, if thou hast understanding.

Using a particular teaching method, God answers Job's questions with questions of His own. The questions are rhetorical—they don't really need an audible answer from Job because both God and Job know what the point of the questions is.

Through His questions God reminds Job that he was not there when the *earth* was planned. God was the one there at creation, not Job. This passage also reinforces the idea that the world is not here by accident. God designed it.

16. Hast thou entered into the springs of the sea? Or hast thou walked in the search of the depth?

Modern underwater explorers such as Jack Ballard can take us to the depths *of the sea*. But Job has not been there. He does not understand its secrets. The sea is a fearful and mysterious place to ancient Middle Eastern peoples. Job's people and those around him probably are not seafarers.

Even those today who know the ocean well are stunned by its mystery. In some ways it still remains a great mystery, having been called the earth's last frontier. Our increased knowledge of the sea today should cause us to walk in even greater humility before the creator of that sea.

17. Have the gates of death been opened unto thee? Or hast thou seen the doors of the shadow of death?

As Job has not been to the depths of the sea, neither has he seen beyond *the gates of death*. He has not seen what lies beyond this life. None of us will be able to have a practice or trial run *death*. No movie or book can prepare us for what will happen. Medical science cannot answer all the unknowns. *Death* is still in the hands of God.

WHAT IS THE SHAPE OF PIE?

You may have heard about the backwoods fellow who sent his son off to college to get some "book l'arnin'." When the son came home at Christmas break, the father said, "Son, tell us somethin' in 'rithmetic." The son thought back to his course in geometry and replied "Pi r². " (Pronounced "pie are squared," this is the formula for calculating the area of a circle.) Embarrassed, the father rebuked the young man: "Son, everyone knows pie are round; corn bread are square."

Despite his bad grammar, that backwoods father was correct in his conclusions. The problem was that the limits of his knowledge didn't allow him to see what his son was really talking about. And when we compare our knowledge and perspective with that of God, this can be our problem too. To help Job see his place in the overall scheme of things, God asks dozens of questions. No matter how smart we are, compared with God we are like the backwoods father. We have ample reason to be humble about our ignorance.

We also do well to remember that more knowledge doesn't always lead to greater wisdom. Think again on the issue of Pi. Most of us

---

GOLDEN TEXT: Ye seek Jesus of Nazareth, which was crucified: he is risen; he is not here: behold the place where they laid him.—Mark 16:6.

learned its mathematical value to be 3.14, or perhaps we learned it to a few more decimal places. Not satisfied with this, a certain college professor used a computer to calculate Pi out to 1.24 *trillion* places! This is definitely greater knowledge, but is it greater wisdom?

Job's response to God, which we will see next, shows us spiritual wisdom. If it ever comes down to having to choose between greater knowledge or greater wisdom, the path is clear. —C. R. B.

B. Job Responds to God (42:1, 2, 5)

1, 2. Then Job answered the Lord, and said, I know that thou canst do every thing, and that no thought can be withholden from thee.

We now reach the climax of the book. Job admits his limitations and testifies to God's absolute power. Job also confesses the ability of God to know. We often forget that God knows our hearts—our very thoughts (see especially Psalm 139:1-4). We can react in one of two ways: shrink back in horror or open ourselves to Him.

5. I have heard of thee by the hearing of the ear; but now mine eye seeth thee.

How is it that Job has *heard* of God? At the time there may not be much (if any) of the Old Testament even written! Even so, Job says that he has heard of God. All of us depend to some extent on what others tell us of their spiritual pilgrimages. Job's faith is no longer a hearsay faith. Now, his *eye seeth*. He does not mean to say that he literally has seen God (compare Exodus 33:20). Rather, he means that his faith is now personal and experiential. The hope of Job 19:27 is realized. The presence of God is better than intellectual answers. [See question #1, page 329.] Grieving people often will state that the most helpful thing another person can do is just to be there. [See question #2, page 329.]

How to Say It

CAPERNAUM. Kuh-*per*-nay-um.
CLEOPAS. *Clee*-uh-pass.
EMMAUS. Em-*may*-us.
GALILEE. *Gal*-uh-lee.
JOSES. *Jo*-sez.
MAGDALENE. *Mag*-duh-leen or Mag-duh-*lee*-nee.
NAZARETH. *Naz*-uh-reth.
SALOME. Suh-*lo*-me.
ZEBEDEE. *Zeb*-eh-dee.

II. God Bestows Life (Mark 16:1-14, 20)

We come now to the New Testament part of our lesson. Here in the Gospel of Mark we can find more complete answers to the dilemma that Job faced. As we begin we find ourselves with the women who struggled with the unfair and seemingly meaningless death of Christ.

A. Risen Christ Appears (vv. 1-7)

1. And when the sabbath was past, Mary Magdalene, and Mary the mother of James, and Salome, had bought sweet spices, that they might come and anoint him.

Jesus' body had been taken down from the cross in a hurry because a special *sabbath* approached (John 19:31). Some of the women now come to finish the burial preparation. *Mary Magdalene* is part of the delegation. Jesus had delivered her from great spiritual oppression (Mark 16:9; Luke 8:2). The second *Mary,* who is *the mother of James* (and Joses; see Mark 15:40), is unknown to us. *Salome* is the mother of James and John (combine Matthew 4:21 with 27:56).

The first to witness the resurrection are not priests, the Romans, or even Jesus' closest 11 disciples. Rather, He reveals himself to a group of women who had supported His ministry and had been blessed by Him (Mark 15:40, 41). [See question #3, page 329.]

2. And very early in the morning, the first day of the week, they came unto the sepulchre at the rising of the sun.

The first day of the week is, of course, Sunday. The Jews worship on Saturday according to Sabbath regulations (Exodus 20:8). Before Christ's resurrection there is no particular significance to the first day of the week. This is a normal workday to these women.

They arrive at the tomb at about dawn. This is just a simple historical detail, but it also has some poetic meaning for us. It is surely the dawn of a new era when Jesus rises from the dead.

3. And they said among themselves, Who shall roll us away the stone from the door of the sepulchre?

Burial places often are carved into the sides of hills in ancient Palestine. There may be several burial spots grouped together in one room. The entrance would be covered by a large *stone*.

The concern of the women is the removal of that stone. No doubt such an effort will take several strong hands. The women apparently are in such a rush that they don't remember this important fact until they are almost there.

4. And when they looked, they saw that the stone was rolled away: for it was very great.

To their surprise the *stone* is *rolled away* already. This means that they now have full access to Jesus' body inside. At least two of these women had seen the tomb and its stone previously (Mark 15:46, 47). They know where to go and what to look for.

THE MEANING OF THE STONES

"How did they *get* there?" The question is a common reaction from people upon first seeing the circle of monoliths at Stonehenge in England. The upright stones weigh up to 40 tons! How the prehistoric builders could raise the stones, and how they could put the horizontal "caps" in place, is still a source of speculation.

An equally relevant question is *"why* did they get there?" Stonehenge is just one of several similar arrangements of stones spread across the Salisbury Plain of England. It was once theorized that the monuments were prehistoric astronomical observatories. More recently, researchers have found evidence that the complexes were ancient burial grounds and crude temples for the worship of Druidic deities. People flock to the sites yet today to conduct pagan worship.

Compare those stones with the one that blocked the entrance to Jesus' tomb. That stone may still exist—somewhere. Or it may have been broken down into smaller rocks centuries ago and scattered. We don't care! That stone existed to be cast aside by the power of God so Jesus' followers could see that the tomb was empty.

The continued presence of Stonehenge serves as mute testimony to the futility of idolatry. The absence of the stone that sealed Jesus' tomb serves as evidence for the truth of the Christian faith. That stone is missing for our benefit. —C. R. B.

5. And entering into the sepulchre, they saw a young man sitting on the right side, clothed in a long white garment; and they were affrighted.

Inside the tomb the women see what Mark describes as a *young man*. He appears seated beside the shelf that had contained the body of Jesus. We are not meant to understand this man as a normal human being. Putting all the Gospel accounts together, it is clear this is an angel (Matthew 28:2-5). The women understandably are gripped with fear *(affrighted)*.

6. And he saith unto them, Be not affrighted: ye seek Jesus of Nazareth, which was crucified: he is risen; he is not here: behold the place where they laid him.

Without even asking the angel knows whom they *seek*. He informs them that they will not find *Jesus* in the tomb, but that *he is risen*. As partial proof the angel even allows them to look at *the place* where Jesus' body had been. Full proof will come when they see their risen Lord.

7. But go your way, tell his disciples and Peter that he goeth before you into Galilee: there shall ye see him, as he said unto you.

The women are given a mission: remind the disciples that Jesus had promised to meet them in *Galilee*. That area, particularly its city of Capernaum, had been Jesus' base of operations. Most of His disciples are from Galilee. The Gospel of John relates Jesus meeting His disciples by the Sea of Galilee, having breakfast with them, and teaching them after His resurrection (John 21).

B. Startled Followers Respond (vv. 8-14, 20)

8. And they went out quickly, and fled from the sepulchre; for they trembled and were amazed: neither said they any thing to any man; for they were afraid.

The scene at the tomb prompts several actions on the part of the women. First, they leave *quickly*. The angel had told the women in verse 7 to "tell his disciples," but at least for a while the women seem to be too frightened to say *any*

Use this visual to continue last week's discussion on how Jesus' resurrection answers Job's question.

Visual for lessons 6 & 7

thing to any man. Their fear is coupled understandably with amazement. After calming down the women speak freely (Mark 16:10; Luke 24:9).

9. Now when Jesus was risen early the first day of the week, he appeared first to Mary Magdalene, out of whom he had cast seven devils.

Even though *Jesus* appears to these women briefly (Matthew 28:9, 10), He has a specific meeting with *Mary Magdalene.* See John 20:11-17. It was Mary Magdalene who was last at the cross and first at the tomb.

10, 11. And she went and told them that had been with him, as they mourned and wept. And they, when they had heard that he was alive, and had been seen of her, believed not.

Mary's dramatic announcement comes as Jesus' followers express grief over the death of Jesus. It must be quite frustrating for Mary when, at first, they do not believe her (Luke 24:11). Others will soon have the same experience that Mary had. [See question #4, page 329.]

An important part of the Christian message is that the first reports of Jesus' resurrection are met with skepticism by His closest followers. They aren't expecting it. They are not out preaching confidently, "Just wait a few days—you'll see!" Rather, they are cowering behind locked doors (John 20:19).

12. After that he appeared in another form unto two of them, as they walked, and went into the country.

This refers to the encounter that Jesus has with the *two* disciples on the road to Emmaus. This story is told more fully in Luke 24:13-35.

Home Daily Bible Readings

Monday, Apr. 10—Where Were You During the Creation? (Job 38:1-7)

Tuesday, Apr. 11—Do You Understand My Creation? (Job 38:8-18)

Wednesday, Apr. 12—I Know You, and I Repent (Job 42:1-6)

Thursday, Apr. 13—Job's Fortunes Are Restored Twofold (Job 42:10-17)

Friday, Apr. 14—He Is Not Here (Mark 16:1-8)

Saturday, Apr. 15—Jesus Appears to His Followers (Mark 16:9-14)

Sunday, Apr. 16—Go and Proclaim the Good News (Mark 16:15-20)

Two disciples—one named Cleopas, the other not named—travel with Jesus as they journey away from Jerusalem. They have conversations about the Messiah and the death of Christ, but they do not recognize Jesus.

As night approaches, they invite Jesus to stay with them. Eventually they recognize Him. We know there were many appearances of Jesus after His resurrection; this one is particularly sweet.

13. And they went and told it unto the residue: neither believed they them.

Like Mary, the disciples on the road also face skepticism. This counters the claim of some critics that the story of Jesus' resurrection was the product of some psychological wish-fulfillment. It is claimed that the disciples' desire to see Him alive produces the belief that He indeed is alive. The Bible, however, portrays the disciples as quite slow to accept the news that Jesus is risen.

14. Afterward he appeared unto the eleven as they sat at meat, and upbraided them with their unbelief and hardness of heart, because they believed not them which had seen him after he was risen.

The appearances of Jesus in the body are very mysterious to us. He does not have to obey the laws of nature—laws that He created. But He is no mere phantom either (see Luke 24:36-42; John 20:19-29). He can eat food and does so.

On the occasion mentioned here, Jesus has to speak sternly to *the eleven* because of their lack of faith and discernment. This is *hardness of heart* (also Mark 3:5; 6:52; 8:17). The phrase *because they believed not them which had seen him after he was risen* means that Jesus expects us to believe credible testimony about Him. Very few people have had the privilege of seeing the risen Jesus personally. But Jesus still expects belief.

20. And they went forth, and preached every where, the Lord working with them, and confirming the word with signs following. Amen.

This is a summary statement of all that happens in the earliest church. Above all, *the word* is preached. It is obvious that the Lord blesses the efforts as the disciples are able to do the things that Jesus himself did.

Conclusion

A. "What Does Easter Mean to You?"

God did not explain the meaning of suffering in the book of Job. But Job was satisfied with God's presence. After Jesus' ascension the disciples were satisfied too because they knew they eventually would be in Jesus' presence for eternity.

Do you eagerly await the personal presence of God? Like Job who stood humbly before the Father, we stand humbly before Mark's account and admit that there is much we don't understand. Like Job, we may think that more knowledge is what we really need. Yet the Gospel accounts of the resurrection, as brief as they are, are what the Father has decided we should have. They are enough to assure us of God's presence both now and in the age to come.

A Sunday school teacher once asked, "What does Easter mean to you?" One boy answered honestly, "Egg salad sandwiches for the next three weeks." We all know that Easter is more than eggs, bunnies, and flowers. Still, many do not contemplate the absolute changes it signifies. If Jesus is risen, then He is who He claimed to be. If He is risen, then the truth-claims of the Bible are validated. If He is risen, then there is life after death that is only hinted at in Job 14:14; 19:25.

The death and resurrection of Jesus change everything. [See question #5, page 329.] Because He died, our sin penalty is paid and we can come into the presence of God. Because Jesus rose again He defeated death. This allows us to be in God's presence for all eternity (Revelation 1:18).

B. Prayer

Dear Lord, I thank You that our redeemer does live and that we shall live again. Help us to be ready to experience new life as well as to live well in this one. Through the risen Christ, amen.

C. Thought to Remember

The presence of the Lord is better than answers.

Learning by Doing

This section contains an alternative lesson plan emphasizing learning activities. Classes desiring such student involvement will find these suggestions helpful.

Learning Goals

After this lesson each student will be able to:

1. Tell how the texts from Job and Mark both affirm God's power over life and death.

2. Explain how Job's hope is realized in the resurrection of Christ.

3. Express confidence that he or she can deal with all circumstances in life without anxiety because of the resurrection.

Into the Lesson

As students arrive hand each a piece of paper (about 4" x 6") that has a large question mark printed on one side. When class begins, say, "This is a lesson of hard questions. What would you say are some of life's hardest questions?" Pause for responses and discussion. When you're ready for a transition, say, "Life is full of hard questions. We may begin to answer some of these in today's study."

As an alternative activity say, "Our texts today are records of people meeting God in different settings. See if you can identify the people who met God as represented by the following short monologues." At this point give the following monologues to volunteers to read. (Make sure that the volunteers don't accidentally read the answers!)

1. "God spoke to me in the strangest place. I even had to take off my shoes! I suppose if one can stand in God's presence, one can stand before the most powerful man on earth." *(Moses)*

2. "I was certainly in no mood to meet God like I did. Even though I thought I was doing His work, I discovered otherwise. You may say that I 'saw the light.'" *(Saul/Paul)*

3. "I came into God's eternal presence when I was very old. Though my island home was very beautiful, God was more so." *(the apostle John)*

Make a transition by saying, "Given a choice, we all would prefer to meet God as the apostle John did, right? But that is not necessarily God's plan in all cases, as we shall see."

Move into a study of today's Old and New Testament texts, using the commentary as an aid. Make sure to compare and contrast the two sets of texts. Do not study either without observing how it relates with the other.

Into the Word

After you have familiarized your students with the Old and New Testament texts for today, use the following Hard Questions activity. You can read the questions to the class for discussion as a whole or make copies of the questions for small-group study. Ask students to decide which verses of today's texts give insight to the question at hand. (Verses are given in parentheses after each question. Do not print these on the handout.)

1. What knowledge do we still lack regarding the origins of the universe? Why is it important to realize what we don't know? *(Job 38:4)*

2. If God would grant you a question and answer session with Him just for the asking, would you accept it? What would you ask? *(Job 38:4)*

3. In what way(s) is it possible to "see" God today? How have people gone astray with their imaginations in this regard? *(Job 42:5)*

4. What kind of evidence do you need to believe that Jesus died and rose again? *(Mark 16:6)*

5. Why is it possible to hear the gospel account from credible witnesses and still reject it? *(Mark 16:10, 11)*

6. Can a loving God become impatient and irritated with humans? What about your life would make Him irritated with you? *(Mark 16:14)*

Into Life

Make a transition by saying, "A key line of thought in today's lesson has been that of life, death, and rebirth. Let's do some further thinking about that." Buy a package of large seeds ahead of time. Place seeds in small, unsealed envelopes, one seed each. Ask one of your students who enjoys crafts to stamp the following words on each envelope: "Dead or Alive?"

Distribute one envelope to each student and ask all to look inside. Some questions to ask as they look are "Is it dead or alive?" "In what sense does God give it life?" "What is its potential?" "What is its destiny?" "In what ways do you resemble the seed?"

At some point, be sure to mention (if a student doesn't point it out first) 1 Corinthians 15:37 and the surrounding verses. Allow time for discussion. Then suggest that students carry their envelopes in a pocket or purse for a time to recall the great truth of future resurrection.

Let's Talk It Over

These questions are designed to promote discussion of the lesson. The answers here are only discussion starters. Let your class talk it over from there.

1. How would you react if God responded to you as He did to Job? In the end would you, like Job, be satisfied with God's response? Why, or why not?

Many readers may expect God to step gently onto the scene in Job's case, pat him sympathetically on the head, and say something like, "There there, now. Let me explain why these terrible things happened to you." Instead, God explodes onto the scene, barraging Job with dozens of unanswerable questions (many more than are printed in the lesson today). This should lead us to exercise caution when questioning God's ways! Baruch, who served as Jeremiah's scribe, received a rebuke from God after complaining about his status while doing the Lord's work (see Jeremiah 45).

2. How does just "being there" help someone who is suffering? What was a time when someone helped you just by being present?

Many people feel awkward visiting someone who is dying or has just lost a loved one to death. This hesitation may be because they think they do not know what to say—they do not have any real answers. Yet, experts in grief therapy affirm what the commentary asserts: often the most helpful thing you can do is just to be there. Too much talking can make matters worse.

Hurting people often raise questions that have no simple answers. Like Job, though, getting an answer may not be as important as knowing someone was really listening to the question. Listening, even to the same stories over and over, can be an act of love and mercy. God will listen to your despair even if He does not immediately answer your questions and pleadings. Listening is a ministry of comfort from God. When you listen to others, you can offer that same comfort (2 Corinthians 1:3-5).

3. Are there times when being first in line to serve means you end up being first in line to be blessed? How can we guard our motives in this regard?

The Gospels make it clear that the first witnesses to, and heralds of, the resurrected Christ were the women. Several of them were present at Calvary throughout the crucifixion (Matthew 27:55; Mark 15:40; Luke 23:55; John 19:25). The blessing and privilege they received took them by complete surprise! They certainly weren't thinking, "If we just hang in there through all this and make it to the tomb first, we will be first in line to talk to Jesus after His resurrection." They simply were ministering out of servants' hearts. So must we.

4. Often we should remain in dialogue with people who don't believe what we have to say about Christ. There are other times, however, when it's better to back off for a while. How do we know when to do which?

Jesus never chased after people who decided not to accept His message. He never pleaded or begged anyone to follow Him. He was patient, however, with those who were "slow of heart to believe" (Luke 24:25). Some people just need a bit more time. But if your time investment in witnessing to one unbeliever reaches the point where you might have had positive responses with two others instead, then it may be time to reevaluate. Backing off your verbal witness for a while doesn't mean you stop praying for that person, however.

5. Someone says to you, "I believe in Jesus, but belief in a literal resurrection is not essential for a person to be a Christian." Why would a person think this way? How do you respond?

Some believers think that they are doing Christianity a favor by minimizing certain gospel ideas such as Jesus' bodily resurrection. Stripping away this difficult doctrine makes Christianity more believable, so they think. But it is exactly the opposite that is true. The resurrection of Jesus, as supported by credible evidence, establishes Christianity as the only true religion.

If the skeptic is open to Bible teaching, you can respond by pointing out Paul's conclusions in 1 Corinthians 15:12-19. If the skeptic is not open to hearing what the Bible has to say, you can try an approach based on logic. One good question is, "Since God gives people life to begin with, doesn't it stand to reason that He could also grant life again to someone who died?"

April 23
Lesson 8

Finding Life's Meaning

DEVOTIONAL READING: Luke 24:36-48.

BACKGROUND SCRIPTURE: Ecclesiastes 1:1-11; John 20:19-23.

PRINTED TEXT: Ecclesiastes 1:1-9; John 20:19-23.

Ecclesiastes 1:1-9

1 The words of the Preacher, the son of David, king in Jerusalem.

2 Vanity of vanities, saith the Preacher, vanity of vanities; all is vanity.

3 What profit hath a man of all his labor which he taketh under the sun?

4 One generation passeth away, and another generation cometh: but the earth abideth for ever.

5 The sun also ariseth, and the sun goeth down, and hasteth to his place where he arose.

6 The wind goeth toward the south, and turneth about unto the north; it whirleth about continually, and the wind returneth again according to his circuits.

7 All the rivers run into the sea; yet the sea is not full: unto the place from whence the rivers come, thither they return again.

8 All things are full of labor; man cannot utter it: the eye is not satisfied with seeing, nor the ear filled with hearing.

9 The thing that hath been, it is that which shall be; and that which is done is that which shall be done: and there is no new thing under the sun.

John 20:19-23

19 Then the same day at evening, being the first day of the week, when the doors were shut where the disciples were assembled for fear of the Jews, came Jesus and stood in the midst, and saith unto them, Peace be unto you.

20 And when he had so said, he showed unto them his hands and his side. Then were the disciples glad, when they saw the Lord.

21 Then said Jesus to them again, Peace be unto you: as my Father hath sent me, even so send I you.

22 And when he had said this, he breathed on them, and saith unto them, Receive ye the Holy Ghost:

23 Whosesoever sins ye remit, they are remitted unto them; and whosesoever sins ye retain, they are retained.

GOLDEN TEXT: Then said Jesus to them again, Peace be unto you: as my Father hath sent me, even so send I you.—John 20:21.

> *Living in and as God's Creation*
> Unit 2: Living with Creation's Uncertainty
> (Lessons 5-9)

Lesson Aims

After participating in this lesson, each student will be able to:

1. Articulate the basic features and purpose of the book of Ecclesiastes.

2. Explain how Solomon's quest for meaning finds fulfillment in the resurrected Christ.

3. Write a vision statement for his or her life that is based in Jesus' concept of peace.

Lesson Outline

INTRODUCTION
    A. Any Despair Out There?
    B. Lesson Background
I. PROBLEM OF HOPELESSNESS (Ecclesiastes 1:1-9)
    A. Declared by the Preacher (vv. 1, 2)
    B. Illustrated in Nature (vv. 3-7)
        The Cycles of Nature
    C. Illustrated by Human Endeavor (vv. 8, 9)
II. PROVIDER OF HOPE (John 20:19-23)
    A. Peace Given (v. 19)
    B. Proof Given (v. 20)
    C. Purpose Given (v. 21)
        Peace with a Purpose
    D. Power Given (vv. 22, 23)
CONCLUSION
    A. Empty Tomb, Meaningful World
    B. Prayer
    C. Thought to Remember

Introduction

A. Any Despair Out There?

During the past week have you met someone who is in despair? Chances are you have. Such folks keep hospitals, police, bookstores, counselors, and churches very busy. Maybe you need look no further than your own home or heart to find someone in despair. Like Solomon of old, people look to relieve their despair in a variety of unproductive and even destructive ways. People try to make their lives more enjoyable by giving in to excesses in food, alcohol, sex, pursuit of fame, pursuit of wealth, etc.

Some finally sit down and, with the ultimate shrug of the shoulders, declare "There is no meaning." Are they right? The author of our first text today might well have felt at home with them. But at the end of his book, he judges that to fear God and keep His commandments form enough purpose for anyone. If we take Solomon's words out of context, we may feel better *before* we read his words than *after!*

As ancient as the book of Ecclesiastes is, it is in a sense contemporary. People are still trying to discover the meaning of life. They still experiment with power, possessions, and pleasure. And they still find such things as fruitless as Solomon did. People today have an advantage here. Not only can we learn from Solomon's mistakes, we also have Jesus and the New Testament to give us redemptive insights.

B. Lesson Background

Today's lesson comes from the unusual Old Testament book of Ecclesiastes and the New Testament Gospel of John. The name *Ecclesiastes* means something like "assemblyman" (see comment on Ecclesiastes 1:1, below). This fact does not really tell us what Ecclesiastes is about. We have to read the book to discover that. When we do we see that it is a book of musings on the nature of life "under the sun." The author uses that expression more than two dozen times, and it appears nowhere else in the Bible. This expression refers to a life focused on this present world and its values. This helps us make more sense of this book, since it can be depressing in many ways. It is particularly depressing if we do not read all the way through to the end.

The other book we find ourselves exploring today is the Gospel of John. This Gospel account is different from the other three Gospels (Matthew, Mark, and Luke) in paying greater attention to Jesus' ministry south of Galilee—in Judea and Samaria. It features much of Jesus' personal teachings to the disciples.

Today we are looking at a postresurrection appearance of Jesus. All four Gospels give great attention to the last week of Jesus' life, including the crucifixion and the resurrection. The most complete account of Jesus' life presents itself when we compare all four Gospels. Just as a reminder, we recall that the Gospel of John was written by the disciple John, son of Zebedee (Mark 3:17).

Today's passages will let Solomon pose some problems then let Jesus propose some solutions. Our teachers will be the wisest man on the face of the earth (1 Kings 4:29-34) and God's own Son, whose wisdom surpasses even that of Solomon (Luke 11:31).

I. Problem of Hopelessness (Ecclesiastes 1:1-9)

A. Declared by the Preacher (vv. 1, 2)

1. The words of the Preacher, the son of David, king in Jerusalem.

Students debate the identity of the author of this book. But the opening words surely make Solomon the most obvious choice, even though he is not mentioned by name. In fact we would be hard pressed to make the words point to anyone other than Solomon. He is attributed also as the author, or primary author, of Proverbs and Song of Solomon (also called Song of Songs).

You will recall Solomon's role as the third *king* of Israel. He was a *son of David* and Bathsheba. Many students believe that the book of Ecclesiastes represents Solomon's musings in old age. These are the words of a man who has tried it all and is weary of his attempts to understand any meaning in life.

When Solomon is described as *the Preacher*, it is not exactly a preacher as we think of it today. The idea is more of "assemblyman" or "one who addresses an assembly." *Teacher* is also a good translation in this regard. In the ancient world there may not be much difference between preaching and teaching (see Luke 20:1, where both tasks describe Jesus' activities).

Solomon is one who had great opportunity to try all the various roads to happiness. He was known also as a man of great wisdom. We yet can learn much from both his successes and his failures.

2. Vanity of vanities, saith the Preacher, vanity of vanities; all is vanity.

We are hit by the writer's dark mood right at the outset. His opening musings project a sense of hopelessness or at least resignation. By using the expression *vanity of vanities*, he underlines just how hopeless he thinks it all is. It is as if he has said "utter emptiness." He has tried everything. Instead of bringing happiness, his attempts have brought the opposite. Remember: the Preacher (Solomon) has had more money, lovers, wisdom, and fame than we can imagine (1 Kings 3:1-15; 4:20-34; 11:1-3, etc.). But he declares *all is vanity.*

B. Illustrated in Nature (vv. 3-7)

3. What profit hath a man of all his labor which he taketh under the sun?

The Preacher (Solomon) is someone who can see the results of *labor*. Over the course of 20 years, he had built two magnificent structures: the temple and his own palace (1 Kings 9:10). Essentially, Solomon built whatever he wanted to build (examples: 1 Kings 9:17-19, 26).

Even after all this, however, Solomon can wonder what it all really amounts to. We may be prone to assume that his answer would be "nothing" by the way he asks the question. But Solomon takes a leisurely journey to his conclusion.

4. One generation passeth away, and another generation cometh: but the earth abideth for ever.

The Preacher (Solomon) begins to recite a list of things that he has noticed are repetitive. Generations of people come and go. That pattern never changes. [See question #1, page 338.] *The earth*, for its part, doesn't come and go but seems to abide *for ever*. The earth certainly is more stable than the people on it. But that stability also is as predictable as the succession of generations.

We know now from the New Testament that the *earth*, as we are familiar with it, will not remain forever (Luke 21:25; Revelation 21:1). In Solomon's day, the *earth* is a symbol of permanence. He has more to say about the earth in Proverbs 8:29.

5. The sun also ariseth, and the sun goeth down, and hasteth to his place where he arose.

The Preacher (Solomon) begins to speak of the various cycles of nature. The *sun* is repetitive and predictable in moving in its order day after day. Some have tried to criticize the Bible because it

---

How to Say It

BATHSHEBA. Bath-*she*-buh.
JERUSALEM. Juh-*roo*-suh-lem.
SANHEDRIN. San-huh-drun or San-*heed*-run.
SHALOM (Hebrew). shah-*lome*.
SOLOMON. *Sol*-o-mun.
ZEBEDEE. *Zeb*-eh-dee.

says that the sun *ariseth* and *goeth down* when the scientific truth is that the earth goes around the sun. This criticism doesn't take into account the fact that the Bible uses phenomenological language. That is, it speaks from the standpoint of how we experience life. We do not think it unusual when the evening news report tells us what times the sun will rise and set tomorrow. From our perspective it does rise and set. That's how we view the phenomena of dawn and dusk.

Solomon may also be describing the brevity of life in noting that the sun *hasteth to his place where he arose*. In other words Solomon depicts a day as happening quickly. Think of how true that is!

6. The wind goeth toward the south, and turneth about unto the north; it whirleth about continually, and the wind returneth again according to his circuits.

The *wind* may seem to be aimless, but it is not. The *wind goeth* and *turneth about* according to natural laws. It has its *circuits,* and they seem to be repetitive.

7. All the rivers run into the sea; yet the sea is not full: unto the place from whence the rivers come, thither they return again.

This is an illustration from the water cycle. *Rivers run into the sea,* yet the sea level remains relatively constant. Water continues to go back into the sky, fall to the ground again, make rivers, and run into the sea. Again, the process seems repetitive.

THE CYCLE OF NATURE

Almanacs have a long history. Benjamin Franklin's *Poor Richard's Almanac* is one of the best-known examples. It is famed for its proverbs, such as "Would you live with ease, do what you ought, and not what you please." That one from the 1734 edition sounds almost biblical, doesn't it? Another almanac—this one still in publication—is the *Old Farmer's Almanac.* Since we live in the Information Age, you can of course access it on the Internet. Do you want a planting guide to help you in your gardening? long-range weather forecasts? consumer trends? recipes? interesting facts? It's there!

But that's not all. Phases of the moon, times for the rising and setting of sun and moon, tide tables, etc., also are covered by these books. Many generations past considered them to be essential in the same way we think of The Weather Channel® today.

In our text the Preacher (Solomon) takes a look at the same cycles of nature, but from a philosophical perspective. We may not be used to such an approach. And although we may find his (apparent) fatalism to be uncomfortable, we must agree with him that humans always have been at the mercy of the weather and the seasons. This is all the more reason to be on good speaking terms with God, who created and controls them! —C. R. B.

C. Illustrated by Human Endeavor (vv. 8, 9)

8. All things are full of labor; man cannot utter it: the eye is not satisfied with seeing, nor the ear filled with hearing.

The first idea that the Preacher (Solomon) is proposing here is that we cannot explain the meaning of our *labor.* The second idea is that humans cannot see or hear enough to satisfy themselves. As people in Solomon's day experience the "latest and greatest" things, they want even more new experiences of *seeing* and *hearing.* Sound familiar?

9. The thing that hath been, it is that which shall be; and that which is done is that which shall be done: and there is no new thing under the sun.

Solomon looks for something *new,* but everything finds reference in the past. He despairs of finding anything novel. The past just keeps repeating itself. [See question #2, page 338.] As we move from the book of Ecclesiastes to the book of John, we will see God take action to reverse that problem. Jesus will give us something to live for.

Perhaps what Solomon is experiencing is the problem of sin that subjects creation "to vanity" and "the bondage of corruption" (Romans 8:20, 21). While nature has its cycles, it does not mean that they are meaningless cycles. History is going somewhere. History is moving toward a goal. Satan tried to derail that goal in the Garden of Eden. But Jesus is the one who corrected the problem, as we shall see.

II. Provider of Hope
(John 20:19-23)

A. Peace Given (v. 19)

19. Then the same day at evening, being the first day of the week, when the doors were shut where the disciples were assembled for fear of

the Jews, came Jesus and stood in the midst, and saith unto them, Peace be unto you.**

We now shift forward in time more than nine centuries. The incident at hand happens the same day as Jesus' resurrection, *being the first day of the week*, which is Sunday.

The disciples are *assembled* in secret because they are understandably afraid of the ruling authorities. John uses the phrase *the Jews* to identify those who brought *fear* to the disciples. John uses that phrase in his Gospel not to refer to Jewish people in general but to identify the Jewish leaders. After all, *Jesus* and His disciples are Jewish. The particular group John has in mind probably consists of the chief priests and their associates on the Sanhedrin, which is the Jewish ruling council.

We may safely assume that these disciples are of the original 12 apostles. But only 10 are present since Judas is dead (Matthew 27:1-5) and Thomas is absent (John 20:24). Somehow, moving past or through the *doors*, the resurrected Jesus appears to them. Jesus' resurrection body does not appear to have the same limitations as our normal human bodies. Jesus can appear without having to open the door. Remember that even before the resurrection, Jesus could defy the laws of nature. Walking on water is a good example of this (Matthew 14:25).

Still, Jesus is no ghost or phantom. He can be touched and He can eat (Luke 24:36-43). As we will see in the next verse, there is a certain continuity between His preresurrection body and His postresurrection body.

The first word Jesus utters is *peace*. That is what He offers a group of discouraged disciples not once but three times (here and vv. 21, 26). In some ways we may see this as a simple greeting. (Modern Jews still greet each other with the word *shalom*, the Hebrew word for *peace*.) Yet after the resurrection we surely can see this as stronger than a mere greeting! Before the crucifixion Jesus had promised to bestow peace (John 14:27; 16:33). Jesus' payment of sin's penalty on the cross has now brought true peace—it is a peace with God.

B. Proof Given (v. 20)

20. And when he had so said, he showed unto them his hands and his side. Then were the disciples glad, when they saw the Lord.

It is important to prove that the one who died on the cross is the same one who rose from the

Visual for lesson 8

Refer to this visual as you ask, "In what ways can we experience the peace of Jesus in the twenty-first century?"

dead. That is why Jesus' resurrected body still bears the marks of the crucifixion. The scars prove He is the same person. Christianity always has claimed to be a historical religion with verifiable truth claims. Jesus has kept His promise to turn their grief into joy (John 16:20). He does this by showing *them his hands and his side*.

C. Purpose Given (v. 21)

21. Then said Jesus to them again, Peace be unto you: as my Father hath sent me, even so send I you.

See the commentary on verse 19 concerning Jesus' *peace*. Along with this peace Jesus gives *them* a directive: *so send I you*. This is a foretaste of the Great Commission, which He will give before His ascension (Matthew 28:19, 20). Jesus was sent to earth with the gospel. In His absence the apostles must carry on the task (John 17:18). The task seems daunting to us who read about it today; it may have seemed impossible to those who first heard it. [See question #3, page 338.]

We can only wonder what the disciples would have done if they had not witnessed the risen Lord. They are not meeting in the secret room to plot church growth strategies! Rather, they are there to figure out how to save their own skins. The proof of Jesus' resurrection changes the whole course of their lives—and the direction of history.

PEACE WITH A PURPOSE

Jet Propulsion Laboratory is a corporate success story—a company that has played a leading role in the exploration of space over the last half-century. But one of its founders—John Whiteside Parsons—is an example of how even successful people may find no peace in life.

In spite of having dropped out of college, Parsons became a highly respected scientist. His private life was something else, however, as he entered into pursuits that would eventually destroy him. He got involved in Satanism and the occult, calling himself antichrist. Hallucinogenic drugs became part of his unfulfilled quest for peace. In his own words, he had a "madness that burns at the heart." Parsons died in 1952 at the young age of 38 in an explosion that was either suicide, murder, or a drug-related accident.

How greatly Parson's life contrasts with those of the apostles! Jesus offered them a peace with God that would empower them for a great mission. Although they faced extreme hardships, this peace gave meaning to their lives. Those who commit themselves to Christ and His mission can know that same peace today. —C. R. B.

D. Power Given (vv. 22, 23)

22. And when he had said this, he breathed on them, and saith unto them, Receive ye the Holy Ghost.

By breathing on the disciples, Jesus seems to convey *the Holy Ghost* to them. This verse causes us to wonder what the link is to Acts 1:4-8. There Jesus asks them to remain in Jerusalem until they receive the Holy Spirit. Since that is indeed what happens on Pentecost (Acts 2), then what do they experience here?

There are several theories. One idea is that the first granting of the Spirit here in John 20:22 is a "sprinkling" while the second granting of the Spirit in Acts 2 is a "saturation." Another theory is that the first bestowal of the Spirit grants power for new life to the disciples while the second bestowal grants them power for ministry.

These are just two possible answers among many proposals! The best answer is that when Jesus breathes, it is symbolic of what happens when the Holy Spirit later descends dramatically on the Day of Pentecost. What is crucial to recognize is that Jesus does not give them their mission without also promising them the power to succeed. [See question #4, page 338.]

23. Whosoever sins ye remit, they are remitted unto them; and whosoever sins ye retain, they are retained.

This verse has troubled some people, but it need not be a problem. Jesus is speaking to His chosen apostles. They will become His personal representatives in this world. As Jesus came to deal with the problem of sin, the apostles will also continue this ministry of liberation.

As the apostles share the message of the gospel, they can, under Christ's authority, assure those who listen and accept the message that they are forgiven. The use of the passive voice *they are remitted* points to God as being the one who does the forgiving. It does not mean that if the apostles forgive someone, then God is obligated to forgive them. It means that the apostles are to announce the forgiveness that God already offers—that's the preaching of the gospel. When people hear the gospel, they either accept it or reject it. Accepting the gospel means forgiveness of sin. Rejecting the gospel means the opposite. This is God's plan. [See question #5, page 338.]

We should not forget that the assurance that God forgives us is the greatest truth we shall ever know. There is freedom in the knowledge that God will not count our sins against us. He let Jesus take care of them on the cross. That is a message to embrace and to share.

Conclusion

A. Empty Tomb, Meaningful World

We frequently speak of the empty tomb as being a sign of the resurrection of Jesus. That is true enough, but there is much more. Also highly significant are the postresurrection appearances of Jesus. The disciples had more than a month to interact with the risen Lord (Acts 1:3). It was His very presence that convinced them that the resurrection was real. If He had risen from the dead only to return to Heaven

---

Home Daily Bible Readings

Monday, Apr. 17—Nothing New Under the Sun (Ecclesiastes 1:1-11)

Tuesday, Apr. 18—The Futility of Seeking Wisdom (Ecclesiastes 1:12-18)

Wednesday, Apr. 19—The Futility of Self-Indulgence (Ecclesiastes 2:1-11)

Thursday, Apr. 20—All Is Vanity (Ecclesiastes 2:12-17)

Friday, Apr. 21—Of What Good Is Our Toil? (Ecclesiastes 2:18-26)

Saturday, Apr. 22—Jesus Gives the Disciples a Mission (Luke 24:36-48)

Sunday, Apr. 23—Receive the Holy Spirit (John 20:19-23)

immediately and secretly, then they would always doubt. Jesus made postresurrection appearances not only to convince the disciples that He was alive but also to give them their marching orders.

In the end we see quite a contrast between the lives of Solomon and Jesus. Jesus proclaimed of himself that one greater than Solomon had arrived (Luke 11:31). Jesus did not live the kind of royal lifestyle Solomon did. Jesus did not engage in all the experimentation. In his dark moments, Solomon wondered if life "under the sun" had any meaning. We may sympathize with Solomon as we echo Paul's words "what advantageth it me, if the dead rise not? let us eat and drink; for tomorrow we die" (1 Corinthians 15:32).

But Christ has indeed been raised! And it is "life under the Son" that gives "life under the sun" ultimate meaning. This is meaning that Solomon could only long for and catch a glimpse of (see Ecclesiastes 12:13).

B. Prayer

Dear God, we are eternally grateful that You came into this world and brought us meaning. We sometimes fail to recognize it, but thanks to Jesus we always have meaning. We thank You for our mission and Your indwelling Spirit whom You gave us to complete it. It is in Jesus' name we pray, amen.

C. Thought to Remember

History, in Jesus, is going somewhere.

Learning by Doing

This section contains an alternative lesson plan emphasizing learning activities. Classes desiring such student involvement will find these suggestions helpful.

Learning Goals

After this lesson each student will be able to:
1. Articulate the basic features and purpose of the book of Ecclesiastes.
2. Explain how Solomon's quest for meaning finds fulfillment in the resurrected Christ.
3. Write a vision statement for his or her life that is based in Jesus' concept of peace.

Into the Lesson

Prepare two copies of the word bank and puzzle that follow. *Word Bank:* behold, here, queen, Solomon, south, wisdom. *Puzzle:* "The ___ of the ___ . . . came . . . to hear the ___ of Solomon; and, ___, a greater than ___ is ___" (Matthew 12:42).

Divide the class into two teams. Give one copy of the word bank and puzzle to each team. Say, "At my signal, fill in the blanks of this Scripture quotation about the wisdom of Solomon and Jesus as quickly as you can."

Have the team that finishes first read the completed quote to the rest of the class. Make a transition to Bible study by saying, "Solomon's wisdom is famous. But the wisdom of Jesus far exceeds that of Solomon. In the words of the Father about His Son, 'Hear ye him.' We will discuss both Solomon and Jesus today."

Into the Word

Pass out paper and pencils. Say, "Solomon's musings on life and reality paint a black-and-white, universal-truth existence. Everything is . . . or nothing is. Number from 1 to 10 on the paper. Then, based on your knowledge of the New Testament, answer *agree* or *disagree*, for the following 10 statements Solomon makes." Read:

1. Everything is meaningless.
2. Work gains one nothing.
3. One generation lives, then another.
4. The earth lasts forever.
5. The sun rises and sets predictably.
6. Wind follows relatively predictable paths.
7. Though rivers all run into the sea, the sea does not overflow.
8. As long as the eye can see, it sees; as long as the ear hears, it hears.
9. The same things occur over and over.
10. There is nothing new under the sun.

After reading all the statements and allowing time for responses, go back through the list and ask for class decisions. Ask for explanations where appropriate. Make a transition by saying, "Solomon saw things as cut-and-dried, black-and-white. When Jesus was killed, however, the disciples may not have viewed the world that way in the midst of their pain."

Next, divide the class into small "huddle" groups. Students are to sit as closely together as comfortably possible. Say, "After Jesus was crucified and buried, the disciples fearfully huddled in a small room. For this activity we will assume the role of the disciples. Each group will be given an assignment, and then you are to huddle up and respond!"

Hand out the following assignments:

Group #1: You are afraid. What are some of the fears you are sensing?

Group #2: Someone says, "If only Jesus were here . . ." How would your group be different if Jesus were there?

Group #3: Someone says, "I remember what our Lord said." What specific sayings of Jesus would be recalled in this setting?

Group #4: Now that Jesus has died, what is your group planning to do? When are you planning to do it?

Group #5: As you gathered in fear, Jesus appeared and offered you peace. What did He mean? (If you have more than five groups, give duplicate assignments. If you have fewer than five groups, select the assignments you believe will elicit the most responses.)

Give the huddle groups time to work, then ask for reports. For a more dramatic effect, ask the group reporters to use a stage whisper appropriate to their hiding-place atmosphere.

Into Life

Bring the lesson to application by continuing to focus on Group 5's response. Say, "Each of us is now going to write a vision statement for life that is based on Jesus' concept of peace." Stress that vision statements should be short, to the point, and easy to remember. A sample would be, "I will demonstrate godliness—anytime, any place." Ask for volunteers to share their vision statements.

Let's Talk It Over

These questions are designed to promote discussion of the lesson. The answers here are only discussion starters. Let your class talk it over from there.

1. How often do you think about your own mortality? Do you think about it too much or too little? What value is there in thinking about it?

Ecclesiastes is a favorite book of many poets and philosophers. Accepting its unflinching analysis of how brief and fleeting life "under the sun" really is, many are determined not to put off important decisions about personal direction in life. An astute observer once noted that America, for its part, had changed from a death defying to a death denying culture. This means that many simply avoid thinking about the unpleasant issue of their own mortality. But it is our mortality that should give us a sense of urgency.

When we're in the midst of a stressful situation, the fact of our mortality can also help us ask "Years from now, how much of this will matter?" Sometimes a long slow walk through a cemetery can make you listen for birds singing and children laughing. More importantly, such a walk can give you new perspective and urgency regarding your work in the kingdom of God.

2. In what sense is it still true that there is nothing new under the sun? How does this fact help you serve Christ better?

Microchips, microphones, microwaves, and microbiology are all relatively new on the timeline of history. Yet in terms of human nature, Solomon is exactly right—there is nothing really new.

Our usual focus is on how everything in the world is changing, and changing fast! But Solomon wants to remind us that the world we live in is the same as it was in his day in all the most important ways. New modes of transportation or medical technology aren't all that important when compared with the need for meaning, longing for wisdom, and, of course, longing for God.

3. In what ways is the mission of Jesus one that believers share? In what ways was His mission unique to Him? How do you make sure you keep these two questions separate?

Jesus stands alone in history in so many ways! He alone is the fulfillment of prophecy of a Messiah. He alone is the virgin-conceived Son of God. He alone came to die for the sins of the world. Such things cannot (and need not) be said of His disciples in any era.

In thinking about how we share in His mission, it is important that we focus on what Jesus said that we should be doing (example: Matthew 28:19, 20). It is easy, sometimes, to turn our eyes too quickly to what we think is wrong with our church, its leaders, etc. This is necessary at times, but faultfinding as a primary mission won't win the world for Christ!

4. How does the Holy Spirit help us in ways that are both similar to and different from the way the Spirit helped the apostles in the first century? Why is this question important?

Sorting out what the Spirit does for all Christians everywhere compared to what the Spirit did only for the first-century apostles is a difficult and controversial task. Many books have been written and many churches have split over this subject! Some benefits that the Holy Spirit brings for all believers of the entire Christian era can be seen clearly in Romans 5:5; 8:26; 1 John 4:13.

One problem to avoid is the tendency to think of the Holy Spirit solely in terms of self-benefit. "He can give me peace." "He can empower my life." "He can enrich my praise." All of these are true, but we must not lose sight of the Spirit's continuing role in evangelism—a task that occurs only through us.

5. Jesus included both the idea of forgiveness *given* and forgiveness *withheld* in His promise to the apostles. In what ways should your church reflect both ideas? What improvements can your church make?

Some Christians preach "easy believism" instead of the entirety of the gospel. A one-sided emphasis on grace can end up creating the impression that sin is not that bad and that holiness is more of an option than a demand (1 Peter 1:15, 16; 1 John 3:6). On the other hand, a one-sided emphasis on the need for personal holiness can end up clouding the idea of salvation as a gracious gift of God (Romans 3:21-26; Ephesians 2:8-10). Both the Bible's promises of forgiveness and condemnations of sin must be preached.

Living in God's Time

April 30
Lesson 9

DEVOTIONAL READING: Psalm 34:1-8.

BACKGROUND SCRIPTURE: Ecclesiastes 3.

PRINTED TEXT: Ecclesiastes 3:1-8, 14, 15.

Ecclesiastes 3:1-8, 14, 15

1 To every thing there is a season, and a time to every purpose under the heaven:

2 A time to be born, and a time to die; a time to plant, and a time to pluck up that which is planted;

3 A time to kill, and a time to heal; a time to break down, and a time to build up;

4 A time to weep, and a time to laugh; a time to mourn, and a time to dance;

5 A time to cast away stones, and a time to gather stones together; a time to embrace, and a time to refrain from embracing;

6 A time to get, and a time to lose; a time to keep, and a time to cast away;

7 A time to rend, and a time to sew; a time to keep silence, and a time to speak;

8 A time to love, and a time to hate; a time of war, and a time of peace.

. . . .

14 I know that, whatsoever God doeth, it shall be for ever: nothing can be put to it, nor any thing taken from it: and God doeth it, that men should fear before him.

15 That which hath been is now; and that which is to be hath already been; and God requireth that which is past.

GOLDEN TEXT: To every thing there is a season, and a time to every purpose under the heaven.—Ecclesiastes 3:1.

> *Living in and as God's Creation*
> Unit 2: Living with Creation's Uncertainty
> (Lessons 5-9)

Lesson Aims

After participating in this lesson, each student will be able to:

1. Recite the rhythms of life as Solomon understood them.
2. Illustrate Solomon's rhythms of life with modern examples.
3. Explain to an unbeliever or new Christian how history is "going somewhere" even as the rhythms of life continue.

Lesson Outline

INTRODUCTION
  A. Time Management?
  B. Lesson Background
I. SEASONS OF PHYSICAL LIFE (Ecclesiastes 3:1-3)
  A. Time and Purpose (v. 1)
  B. Living and Dying (v. 2a)
  C. Planting and Harvesting (v. 2b)
  D. Killing and Healing (v. 3a)
  E. Breaking and Building (v. 3b)
II. SEASONS OF EMOTIONAL LIFE (Ecclesiastes 3: 4, 5)
  A. Laughing and Crying (v. 4a)
  B. Mourning and Celebrating (v. 4b)
  C. Scattering and Gathering (v. 5a)
  D. Embracing and Refraining (v. 5b)
  A Delicate Balance
III. SEASONS OF BUSINESS LIFE (Ecclesiastes 3: 6, 7a)
  A. Gaining and Losing (v. 6a)
  B. Saving and Discarding (v. 6b)
  C. Tearing and Sewing (v. 7a)
IV. SEASONS OF SOCIAL LIFE (Ecclesiastes 3:7b, 8)
  A. Keeping Silent and Speaking (v. 7b)
  Family Time
  B. Loving and Hating (v. 8a)
  C. Warring and Peacemaking (v. 8b)
V. SEASONS IN PERSPECTIVE (Ecclesiastes 3: 14, 15)
  A. God Does Good Work (v. 14)
  B. God Rules Past, Present, and Future (v. 15)
CONCLUSION
  A. What Will You Do with Your Time?
  B. Prayer
  C. Thought to Remember

Introduction

A. Time Management?

Take a trip to your local bookstore and discover how many best-sellers have been produced that deal with the subject of time management. Whole industries have been built around helping people to manage time. Executives keep buying each new book, hoping it will contain an insight that will forever enable them to make the best use of time. We are interested in time, but we don't really manage it. We can only manage ourselves. Time continues at a regular pace for everyone; the only difference is how we fill up those years, months, weeks, days, hours, minutes, and seconds.

As interested as we are in time, its definition is slippery and elusive. Think of the many ways we use the word *time*. We say "I don't have time to go" or "It's time for a new car." We may say "Time to get up" or "Time's up." There are other uses such as "What time is our meeting?" or "I think it's time for me to reevaluate my life." There are so many uses of the word *time!*

These various uses demonstrate that there are different kinds of time. There is clock time, which focuses on minutes and hours. There is also seasonal time, which means the right or appointed time for something. For example, there is a time for snow and a time for sun. The seasons of the year reflect the design of the creator. It is this kind of time Solomon is interested in when he says that for everything there is a season.

B. Lesson Background

Last week we considered Solomon's musing on the apparent emptiness of life "under the sun." We must admit that little if any meaning can be constructed out of life without God.

Today's text is a section containing a poem that describes the many seasons or cycles we will face in life. These seasons are ordained and controlled by God. This passage contains a list of 14 pairs of opposites that describe our lives. One of the big questions scholars discuss is whether this passage is to be taken positively or negatively. Is it praising the divine order of nature and God's control over it, or is it bemoaning the circular, unrelenting regularity of life?

It is possible that we may take it as neither positive nor negative. There is a middle position: Solomon simply may be stating facts. We can either accept those facts or rebel against them. That these comments should not be taken as completely negative is seen in the Preacher's (Solomon's) statement that God makes all things "beautiful in his time" (Ecclesiastes 3:11). In that same verse, Solomon says that God has "set the world in their heart." Many students believe that the Hebrew word translated *world* in this context refers to eternity. If that idea is correct, then we see that in spite of frustration concerning the unending cycles of life, God still directs us to look to the future, to eternity.

The pairs of contrasts have a fairly consistent pattern. Interestingly, we see the positive activity mentioned first about half the time with the negative coming first the other half. These items are polar opposites. As such they seem to be mutually exclusive. That is, one side of a pair cannot happen at the same time as the other side.

This passage defies an attempt to determine a definitive outline. You don't just outline a poem! That would be like dissecting a flower and then complaining that it had lost its beauty. For the purpose of teaching, however, we can isolate some very general categories for the seasons and times. These categories involve physical life, emotional life, business life, and social life.

I. Seasons of Physical Life (Ecclesiastes 3:1-3)

A. Time and Purpose (v. 1)

1. To every thing there is a season, and a time to every purpose under the heaven.

This verse opens what is probably the most familiar passage in the book of Ecclesiastes. This passage even inspired a famous rock song in the 1960s. The next few lines list a wide range of human activity. They do not cover every single activity *under the heaven*, but they do cover the landscape of human endeavor in a big-picture kind of way.

B. Living and Dying (v. 2a)

2a. A time to be born, and a time to die.

The Preacher (Solomon) begins with the most basic cycle of life—two seasons that mark the beginning and the end of earthly existence. *A time to be born, and a time to die* are the two bookends of life. Birth and death—each is a great mystery, even today. Scientists and ethicists still ponder the meaning and proper responses to these two milestones. Under normal circumstances, neither is under our control. Ultimately only God can (and should) control the conditions for life and death. [See question #1, page 347.]

C. Planting and Harvesting (v. 2b)

2b. A time to plant, and a time to pluck up that which is planted.

Solomon also uses the figure of speech of seedtime and harvest, a vital concept in an agricultural society. This makes the point that God has ordained various activities for various times.

It is true, literally, that there would be no fruit, vegetables, and grain if we did not have *a time to plant, and a time to pluck up that which is planted*. But the law of the farm may be applied to many other human activities. When it comes to the most important things of life, we sow in one season and reap in another. Education, health, spiritual growth, church growth, and countless other things operate by this law of sowing and reaping. See Jeremiah 1:10; 4:3 and Matthew 13:24-30 for sowing and reaping in a nonagricultural sense.

D. Killing and Healing (v. 3a)

3a. A time to kill, and a time to heal.

When the Preacher (Solomon) says that there is *a time to kill*, he does not mean murder. Instead, Solomon may be describing self-defense, war, or capital punishment. Ethicists and theologians debate the circumstances when the taking of life may be appropriate (compare Genesis 9:6; Exodus 19:13; Acts 25:11).

We have often found time for killing. We must take *time to heal*—a much more difficult job. A life may be taken with ease in a moment, but healing can take much skill and patience.

E. Breaking and Building (v. 3b)

3b. A time to break down, and a time to build up.

The phrases *break down* and *build up* are quite general but probably refer to constructing a house or tearing one down. Think how much emotion is associated with those acts. With the destruction of a house comes the strong emotion associated with the many memories that are attached to it. There is also the excitement of moving into a newer and bigger house.

II. Seasons of Emotional Life (Ecclesiastes 3:4, 5)

A. Laughing and Crying (v. 4a)

4a. A time to weep, and a time to laugh.

People often apologize when they cry, but there is indeed *a time to weep* in sorrow (compare James 4:9). Crying can be a very cleansing experience for the soul. Tears may have been created to lubricate the eyes, but how quickly they are used to express deep emotion and grief.

Our faith should inform us that there is also *a time to laugh*. We don't prove we are Christians by continual gloomy expressions. Have you ever noticed how close together weeping and laughing are? We may hear a person tell an emotional story and sum up "I didn't know whether to laugh or cry." (Compare Ezra 3:11-13.) A Christian needs to do both. If we do one but not the other (or do neither), we may be bottling up our emotions to our detriment. [See question #2, page 347.]

B. Mourning and Celebrating (v. 4b)

4b. A time to mourn, and a time to dance.

Mourning (here) and weeping (in v. 4a) seem very much the same thing, don't they? The distinction may come down to private emotions (v. 4a) vs. public emotions (v. 4b). Sharing the emotions of others is important. "Rejoice with them that do rejoice, and weep with them that weep" (Romans 12:15). The Preacher (Solomon) undoubtedly had heard of the time when his father David danced publicly (2 Samuel 6:14). Mourning over a death could include professional, public mourners (Matthew 9:23, 24).

C. Scattering and Gathering (v. 5a)

5a. A time to cast away stones, and a time to gather stones together.

Students disagree as to the meaning of this couplet. What may be in mind here is *to cast away stones* into an enemy's field to make it unusable for harvest (2 Kings 3:19, 25). The casting away of stones in this respect would be done in anger.

To gather stones together may refer to the opposite: to restore a field to usefulness. This could be an act of civic kindness. Not only does gathering stones make a field useful, the stones themselves can be used to build something—perhaps a fence. Neighbors helping one another do such things from that sense of kindness. Thus we see that this discussion of stones does have to do with the emotional seasons of life, but it is not obvious at first glance.

How to Say It

CORINTHIANS. Ko-*rin*-thee-unz (*th* as in *thin*).
ISAIAH. Eye-*zay*-uh.
MALACHI. *Mal*-uh-kye.
SOLOMON. *Sol*-o-mun.

D. Embracing and Refraining (v. 5b)

5b. A time to embrace, and a time to refrain from embracing.

Some scholars believe that this has to do with romantic love. Others say that it is more general and can refer to any kind of love. It is certainly true that there are limits and boundaries to all human intimacy, especially sexual intimacy. Sex is not evil, but it is so powerful that it must be regulated. What is holy and healthy in marriage can be quite destructive outside of it.

A DELICATE BALANCE

A man we'll call Mr. B was changed by the power of the gospel from a fighting, drinking, angry man to one who raised his children in the peaceable way of Christ. The church fellowship in which he found the Lord had a strongly rationalistic approach to interpreting the Bible; this fact reinforced the rational side of Mr. B's own personality.

There was another side to Mr. B: a deep undercurrent of emotion that probably was *repressed* in the way his faith was *expressed*. This emotional side would show, for example, when family members who lived at a distance would come for a visit. Later, as they were preparing to leave, Mr. B would disappear until after they had gone. In a time when men were not supposed to show their feelings, this was a way for Mr. B to weep without getting caught. (Perhaps some of us can relate to that!) And yet he reared a family that greatly enjoyed laughing; family get-togethers were filled with hilarity. In short there was a marvelous balance to their emotional lives that mirrored the sentiments of this part of today's text.

Many church fellowships fail to find a proper balance in expressing the faith, with traditionalism, emotionalism, and rationalism all vying for supremacy. What dangers do you see in overemphasizing any of these? —C. R. B.

III. Seasons of Business Life (Ecclesiastes 3:6, 7a)

A. Gaining and Losing (v. 6a)

6a. A time to get, and a time to lose.

There is an appropriate manner and time in which one may acquire wealth. The half-verse before us seems to apply to many situations beyond one's control. Success often requires hard work, but we all know that outside factors can intervene.

B. Saving and Discarding (v. 6b)

6b. A time to keep, and a time to cast away.

This second half of verse 6 may apply to conditions under which one consciously makes decisions. Some possessions should be kept; others can safely be *cast away*. Isn't this often a difficult decision? We have a hard time deciding which mementos *to keep*. We wonder if things in our basement really could be useful in the future. Wisdom tells us that some things need to be saved, while others need to be discarded. [See question #3, page 347.]

C. Tearing and Sewing (v. 7a)

7a. A time to rend, and a time to sew.

Some say that this verse refers to tearing one's garment during a period of mourning (as in Esther 4:1). It is more likely that it refers to common household practices: sometimes we tear *(rend)* clothing into rags; at other times we *sew* and repair our clothing or even make new clothing altogether. Rending has applications beyond mere clothing (compare Joel 2:13).

IV. Seasons of Social Life (Ecclesiastes 3:7b, 8)

A. Keeping Silent and Speaking (v. 7b)

7b. A time to keep silence, and a time to speak.

Many have learned this truth by hard experience. Have you ever spoken up and later realized that you should have kept your *silence?* (Compare Job 13:5; Psalm 4:4; Amos 5:13.) Have you ever kept silent and later realized that you should have taken advantage of the *time to speak?* (Compare Esther 4:12-14; Isaiah 62:1; Matthew 28:19, 20.) When we are prone to speak out of anger, malice, or selfish interest, then perhaps we should keep quiet. If an injustice is at issue and our motives are good, then maybe we should *speak* up.

FAMILY TIME

A certain family court judge in Las Vegas is a good man and highly respected—a good judge who tries to help families whose children are in trouble. But he has a major problem in his own family.

Once his home was a place of pleasant conversation; now it often knows only a sullen silence. There was a time when his home was a place of love between the man and his daughter; now it knows, if not hate, at least feelings of extreme ambivalence. At one time his home was a place of peace; now it is, if not a battleground, at least a place where lines are drawn in the sand. Father and daughter are each firmly entrenched on opposite sides of a deep emotional divide (source: www.nytimes.com, June 1, 2004).

The judge and his family are not unique. The scenario is replicated tens of thousands of times across the continent. Like the judge, many parents find their own children have fallen into sin and a pattern of self-destruction. The parents may have contributed to the problems by not knowing when to speak and when to keep silence. As a sad result, parents and children—Christian or not—often find cold silence an easier choice than hot words. How can *our*

This image is a reminder of the seasons of life. Use it to introduce the Learning by Doing activities.

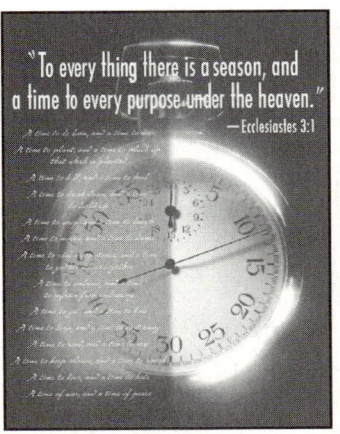

Visual for lesson 9

church help them find reconciliation with each other and with God? —C. R. B.

B. Loving and Hating (v. 8a)

8a. A time to love, and a time to hate.

It may bother some that the Preacher (Solomon) says that there is *a time to hate*. But are we not to hate evil? (See Psalm 97:10; Romans 12:9; Revelation 2:6.) A good rule of thumb is that we should hate what God hates; we find possibilities in this regard in Proverbs 6:16-19; Isaiah 61:8; Malachi 2:16. Jesus offers us an important caution in Matthew 5:43, 44.

C. Warring and Peacemaking (v. 8b)

8b. A time of war, and a time of peace.

War should always be a last resort. To a certain extent, we all would like to be pacifists, wouldn't we? Yet there are occasions when a just war is needed to correct an unjust peace (Romans 13:4). [See question #4, page 347.]

V. Seasons in Perspective (Ecclesiastes 3:14, 15)

A. God Does Good Work (v. 14)

14. I know that, whatsoever God doeth, it shall be for ever: nothing can be put to it, nor any thing taken from it: and God doeth it, that men should fear before him.

Verses 11-13 (not in today's text) show us the optimistic side of the Preacher (Solomon). He describes God's timing as "beautiful." He also counsels that we should learn to enjoy life, particularly simple pleasures.

Solomon then says in the verse before us that God's works are permanent, for *whatsoever God doeth, it shall be for ever*. By this Solomon does not mean that all God's works must last eternally. We know of God's promise of "a new heaven and a new earth" (Revelation 21:1). Solomon means that compared with those things that inhabit it, the earth appears to last forever. We remember that Genesis 8:22 says, "While the earth remaineth, seedtime and harvest, and cold and heat, and summer and winter, and day and night shall not cease."

Further, Solomon says that the earth is just fine the way it is. *Nothing can be put to it, nor any thing taken from it*. Therefore, we human beings must stand in *fear before him*.

B. God Rules Past, Present, and Future (v. 15)

15. That which hath been is now; and that which is to be hath already been; and God requireth that which is past.

This verse reminds us of one of Solomon's themes: there is nothing really new (Ecclesiastes 1:9, 10). This is vitally true in terms of human nature. People keep making the same mistakes. We keep seeing the same old sins over and over. Admittedly there are new technologies, but people (and what motivates them) stay pretty much the same. [See question #5, page 347.]

When Solomon states that *God requireth that which is past*, he simply may be saying that nothing escapes the rule of God. God is the one who is in a position to judge what happened in the past. God is the one who calls all of history to account.

Conclusion

A. What Will You Do with Your Time?

We accept the fact that the seasons of life are only partially within our control. We cannot stop the progression of time. We can, however, control our attitude as we face each season. Every season has some kind of lesson to teach us if we are willing to learn. Time marches on, and we must decide how we fill our days.

There is the story of an army private who was loafing when he should have been working. When his sergeant asked what he was doing, he decided that since he had been caught red-handed he may as well just be honest. "I'm procrastinating, Sergeant," he said.

Home Daily Bible Readings

Monday, Apr. 24—The Lord Is Good (Psalm 34:1-8)

Tuesday, Apr. 25—Use Moderation and Respect God's Authority (Ecclesiastes 7:15-22)

Wednesday, Apr. 26—Every Matter Has Its Time (Ecclesiastes 8:2-8a)

Thursday, Apr. 27—Life Is in God's Hands (Ecclesiastes 9:1-12)

Friday, Apr. 28—For Everything There Is a Season (Ecclesiastes 3:1-8)

Saturday, Apr. 29—Whatever God Does Endures Forever (Ecclesiastes 3:9-15)

Sunday, Apr. 30—Judgment and Future Belong to God (Ecclesiastes 3:16-22)

"All right," said the sergeant after carefully considering the response, "as long as you're busy." Many people are "busy procrastinating" while time hurries along!

Most of the seasons mentioned in today's lesson have some seed of joy in them. This does not mean that every event is joyous or positive in and of itself. But since each cycle has a purpose in God's cosmic design, we can be happy we are part of a universe on purpose.

Our priority can be to make the most out of the seasons of life. We can compare this a bit with the rhythms of the individual calendar week. The first day of the week, Sunday, brings us together for worship. This is a time of spiritual reflection. Monday takes us back to the reality of the workaday world. Wednesday has a feeling, for many, of being "over the hump" toward the weekend. Friday night and Saturday offer opportunities to unwind.

Each day can bring its joys and challenges. This depends on the rhythm of the week and our own mind-sets. Keeping an eternal perspective through it all is our challenge.

B. Prayer

Dear Father, just as You have a design for Your creation, I believe You have designed me with a sense of purpose. I thank You for the miracle of life and pray that You would help me respond properly to the seasons of life. Through Christ the Lord, amen.

C. Thought to Remember

The cycles and seasons of life
have lessons to teach us.

Learning by Doing

*This section contains an alternative lesson plan emphasizing learning activities.
Classes desiring such student involvement will find these suggestions helpful.*

Learning Goals

After participating in this lesson, each student will be able to:

1. Recite the rhythms of life as Solomon understood them.
2. Illustrate Solomon's rhythms of life with modern examples.
3. Explain to an unbeliever or new Christian how history is "going somewhere" even as the rhythms of life continue.

Into the Lesson

Divide your class into four brainstorming groups. Give each group one category based on the lesson writer's outline of today's text: *Seasons of Physical Life*, *Seasons of Emotional Life*, *Seasons of Business Life*, or *Seasons of Social Life*. Ask each group to write other "a time for . . ." statements based on their assigned season of life.

Provide groups with the following examples. For the *Seasons of Physical Life* group: "a time to rue aging and its consequences and a time to rejoice in the wisdom of age." For the *Seasons of Emotional Life* group: "a time to share your great disappointments and a time to keep quiet." For the *Seasons of Business Life* group: "a time to raise prices and a time to mark prices down." For the *Seasons of Social Life* group: "a time to forgive and a time to demand justice."

After 10 or 12 minutes, let groups share their work with the class. Ask them to comment on the godly wisdom and truthfulness of each statement. Say, "Now let's compare your ideas with Solomon's."

Into the Word

Assign each of the contrasts from Ecclesiastes 3:1-8 to a pair of volunteers to pantomime. (If you have two class members who are good at drama, they could do all the pantomimes.) Have the pantomimes performed in a random order. As each pantomime is completed, ask other class members to identify the contrast and the verse number that pantomime represents. Before class, print up the pantomime directions that follow, but tell your volunteers to feel free to improvise.

1. One actor shows the motions of cradling and carrying a baby; the other lies down, closes eyes, and folds arms across the chest (v. 2a).

2. One actor walks like a sower scattering seed from a pouch at his or her waist; the other follows behind as if picking ears of corn, pulling husks back, and gnawing across the ear (v. 2b).

3. One actor marches, as if a sentry carrying a gun—suddenly ducking and looking afraid; then he stands, aims his gun, fires, and then nods approvingly. The other examines the first actor's shoulder, wipes it, and applies a bandage (v. 3a).

4. One actor, as if wearing goggles and a hard hat, wields a sledgehammer against a brick wall; the other mimes putting mortar into place and setting bricks one on top of another (v. 3b).

5. One actor pulls out, as it were, a large handkerchief and puts it to his or her eyes, occasionally putting it down to show a sad, sobbing face; the other looks, points, and then doubles over all to simulate a large laugh (v. 4a).

6. One actor, with a sad but otherwise expressionless face, leans as if over a casket, shakes his head, and turns away in tears; the other simply does a jig of joy (v. 4b).

7. One actor bends over as if picking up a rock, straightens, throws the object, and repeats; the other moves around, showing the effort of picking up something heavy, and makes an invisible pile (v. 5a).

8. The two actors walk toward each other, hug each other with smiles, and then pass on by. They reverse directions, frown as they approach, fold their arms, and deliberately pass each other by (v. 5b).

9. [Provide two paper bags (one with a hole cut in the bottom) and a dollar.] One actor hands the other the money from his bag; the wide-eyed recipient crams the money into his/her bag (the bag with the hole in it). They walk on, as money falls out of the bottom of the bag with a hole (v. 6a).

Create additional pantomimes for the remaining contrasts, to use as time allows.

Into Life

Say to your class, "Ephesians 5:16 speaks about the importance of 'redeeming the time, because the days are evil.' What are you doing in obedience to this instruction?" Suggest that students memorize this brief phrase as a defense against the devil's challenge to waste time in worthless or less significant activities.

Let's Talk It Over

These questions are designed to promote discussion of the lesson. The answers here are only discussion starters. Let your class talk it over from there.

1. Many deaths are caused by people doing sinful things such as drunk driving. How does that fact fit with the lesson writer's claim that "ultimately only God can (and should) control the conditions for life and death"? Why is it important for you to sort through this issue personally?

There is a big difference between the words *cause* and *control*. *Cause* means "to bring about" while *control* means "to have power over." The fact that God is sovereign means that nothing escapes His control. In exercising His sovereign control, He may permit things to happen that He himself does not cause. All sinful actions would fit into this category (James 1:13).

This distinction will help us avoid a sense of fatalism or "what will be, will be." The fact that God knows in advance what will happen does not mean that He is the one who causes it.

2. In what ways does (or should) the life of your church reflect the cycles of life and death, laughter and tears, up and downs—of life here "under the sun"?

Solomon writes that life *under the sun* involves seasons: births and deaths, weeping and laughing, ups and downs. In churches, though, many want every gathering to be upbeat. People want one spiritual mountaintop experience after another, even though it keeps getting harder to top whatever was last week.

To balance the cycles, some churches have conducted solemn assemblies (Joel 1:14; 2:15) as well as Maundy Thursday and Good Friday services. Each has a somber theme due to its nature. Naturally, your church's leadership would have to sort through doctrinal issues as well as local sensitivities before implementing any of these.

3. How do you decide when it is time to save and when it is time to discard?

Have you ever decided you needed something, only to remember that you threw it away? Have you ever looked at a box of stuff and muttered, "What was I thinking when I decided to keep this junk?" A humorist once said that the definition of *junk* is "something you keep for 20 years, then throw out two weeks before you need it."

In some ways our thoughts serve (for good or for ill) as storage closets. We sometimes hang on to emotional and spiritual junk that we should have thrown away long ago. Sometimes we discard things that we should remember and treasure. Making godly decisions in this regard is a matter of spiritual growth.

4. What are some circumstances where reasons for conducting a *just war* would outweigh the reasons for enduring an *unjust peace*?

Some great Christian leaders of the eighteenth, nineteenth, and twentieth centuries were pacifists. They believed the Bible to be the Word of God, and they were aware of Solomon's words. Many also believed, however, that Christ set a new standard when He said "love your enemies" (Matthew 5:44). In their view no Christian should take up arms against another human being, much less another Christian. There are many Bible-believing leaders and groups today that continue to hold this view.

However, Augustine (A.D. 354–430) and a number of other Christian thinkers have shown that war may be warranted and morally acceptable in some circumstances. They point to passages such as Ecclesiastes 3:8 and to the use of the sword by governing authorities under God's divine plan as noted in Romans 13:4. A law enforcement officer may have to take the life of a criminal in order to save the life of an innocent victim or hostage. The "just war theory" fits this idea.

5. What kinds of things can (or should) be learned from history? What kinds of things cannot (or should not) be learned? Why is it important to know the difference?

In order to pull Israel out of idolatry, God reminded that nation of His providential care many times. The phrase "out of Egypt" in reference to the exodus under Moses is used dozens of times in the Old Testament as one of those reminders. Israel failed to remember the lessons of its history. Those who occupy themselves with studying trivia, etc., to the neglect of studying God's movement through history will find their spiritual lives to be shallow indeed!

348

May 7
Lesson 10

Seek Wisdom

DEVOTIONAL READING: Proverbs 2:6-15.

BACKGROUND SCRIPTURE: Proverbs 2, 3.

PRINTED TEXT: Proverbs 2:1-5; 3:1-6, 13-18.

Proverbs 2:1-5

1 My son, if thou wilt receive my words, and hide my commandments with thee;

2 So that thou incline thine ear unto wisdom, and apply thine heart to understanding;

3 Yea, if thou criest after knowledge, and liftest up thy voice for understanding;

4 If thou seekest her as silver, and searchest for her as for hid treasures;

5 Then shalt thou understand the fear of the LORD, and find the knowledge of God.

Proverbs 3:1-6, 13-18

1 My son, forget not my law; but let thine heart keep my commandments:

2 For length of days, and long life, and peace, shall they add to thee.

3 Let not mercy and truth forsake thee: bind them about thy neck; write them upon the table of thine heart:

4 So shalt thou find favor and good understanding in the sight of God and man.

5 Trust in the LORD with all thine heart; and lean not unto thine own understanding.

6 In all thy ways acknowledge him, and he shall direct thy paths.

. . . .

13 Happy is the man that findeth wisdom, and the man that getteth understanding:

14 For the merchandise of it is better than the merchandise of silver, and the gain thereof than fine gold.

15 She is more precious than rubies: and all the things thou canst desire are not to be compared unto her.

16 Length of days is in her right hand; and in her left hand riches and honor.

17 Her ways are ways of pleasantness, and all her paths are peace.

18 She is a tree of life to them that lay hold upon her: and happy is every one that retaineth her.

GOLDEN TEXT: Happy is the man that findeth wisdom, and the man that getteth understanding.—Proverbs 3:13.

LESSON 10

> *Living in and as God's Creation*
> Unit 3: Lessons in Living
> (Lessons 10-13)

Lesson Aims

After participating in this lesson, each student will be able to:

1. List the blessings that can come from acquiring godly wisdom.
2. Suggest ways that obedience to God can result from having wisdom.
3. Make a plan to change one thing in his or her life in order to better reflect godly wisdom.

Lesson Outline

INTRODUCTION
    A. Poor Choices, Wise Choices
    B. Lesson Background
 I. LISTENING FOR WISDOM (Proverbs 2:1-5)
    A. Wanting to be Wise (vv. 1, 2)
    B. Seeking Wisdom Obsessively (vv. 3, 4)
    C. Finding the Treasure of Wisdom (v. 5)
    Avoiding Spiritual Altitude Sickness
 II. TRUSTING IN GOD (Proverbs 3:1-6)
    A. Lifelong Obedience (vv. 1, 2)
    B. Lifelong Mercy (vv. 3, 4)
    C. Lifelong Trust (vv. 5, 6)
 III. ENJOYING WISDOM'S REWARDS (Proverbs 3: 13-18)
    A. Wisdom's Profits (vv. 13, 14)
    B. Wisdom's Riches (vv. 15-17)
    C. Wisdom's Blessings (v. 18)
    A Colossal Hoax
CONCLUSION
    A. Risky Faith: Trusting and Doubting
    B. Tragedy and Godliness
    C. Prayer
    D. Thought to Remember

Introduction

A. Poor Choices, Wise Choices

Today the headlines are filled with stories of people who have made incredibly poor choices. A soldier at a nearby Army base recently was arrested for participating in Internet chat rooms in which he offered to help Islamic terrorist groups. What was he thinking? On another front the media reported the bankruptcy of a famous athlete, despite enormous cash flow. This former heavyweight champion is estimated to have earned $300 million in his boxing career, but is now broke. Where did those mega-millions go? Some of this may be explained by reckless spending such as a $410,000 bill for his birthday party a few years ago. What was he thinking when he made such poor choices? Proverbs 17:16 says, "Wherefore is there a price in the hand of a fool to get wisdom, seeing he hath no heart to it?"

Life is a series of choices. As adults we are required to make dozens of choices every day. Some are mundane: What clothes should I wear today? What should I eat for lunch? What TV shows will I watch this week? But other, far more important choices confront us on a regular basis: Should I quit my lousy job and look for another? Should I honor my marriage commitment when someone else entices me? Should I tell the truth when I find myself in a tight spot?

Parents are expected to help their children learn how to make good choices. Young adults need to know how to handle money, how to decide which friends are safe and good influences, and to understand the benefits of being a hard-working, dependable employee.

In an increasingly chaotic society, however, what standards do we use to make our decisions? Do we follow the hedonistic advice, "If it feels good, do it"? Do we fall back on the cult of irresponsibility's quick answer to everything, "It's not my fault; I didn't do anything wrong." Or should we use the survivalist approach of making it up as we go, rolling with the punches in order to adapt, survive, and find out "what works" in the various situations in which we may find ourselves? [See question #1, page 356.]

The book of Proverbs has a better way. It lays out many guidelines for our lives. These guidelines have served the people of God well for 3,000 years. It is to this book that we now turn for the next four lessons.

B. Lesson Background

What is the difference between a wise person and a foolish person? In the book of Proverbs, this usually has nothing to do with education. Many of us can name someone with a college degree who acts the fool on a regular basis. We may be able also to point to a person who never graduated from high school, yet stands as a source of quiet, reliable wisdom.

In Proverbs wisdom is a matter of how one responds to the will of God. The wise person is the one who knows what is right and wrong from God's perspective and chooses to do the right thing. The foolish person is the one who knows what is right or wrong from God's perspective and chooses to do the wrong thing. Foolishness, then, is not a matter of ignorance. Conversely, wisdom is not a matter of education. Both the wise and the foolish are assumed to be educated in the ways of God, knowing what is right from wrong. The fools consistently disregard God's standards and freely do the wrong thing (sin).

Central to the message of Proverbs, however, is that foolish behavior is more than just displeasing to God. The life of the fool is also self-destructive. When we shun God's standards to follow our own desires, we will be frustrated, unhappy, and without hope. "The way of a fool is right in his own eyes: but he that hearkeneth unto counsel is wise" (Proverbs 12:15).

The book of Proverbs in general is attributed to King Solomon (see Proverbs 1:1). Solomon's wisdom was given to him by God (1 Kings 4:29). This wisdom was legendary even during Solomon's own lifetime (1 Kings 10:24). We know that some of the proverbs of Solomon were compiled several hundred years later by the advisers of King Hezekiah (Proverbs 25:1). Apparently, this compilation process included a few authors beyond Solomon. The book also contains proverbs that are attributed to Agur (Proverbs 30:1) and Lemuel (Proverbs 31:1), although we know nothing about these men.

I. Listening for Wisdom (Proverbs 2:1-5)

A. Wanting to be Wise (vv. 1, 2)

1, 2. My son, if thou wilt receive my words, and hide my commandments with thee; so that thou incline thine ear unto wisdom, and apply thine heart to understanding.

Proverbs often uses a form of Hebrew poetry called *parallelism*. This means that there are two or more lines of text that make the same basic point using different words. This is seen twice in these verses. In other words, *receive my words* is equal to *hide my commandments* while *incline thine ear unto wisdom* is equal to *apply thine heart to understanding*. In fact all four of these lines are similar in meaning—so much so that we can think of *my words* and *my commandments* and *wisdom* and *understanding* all as parallel concepts for Solomon.

Proverbs 9:10 teaches that wisdom begins with the "the fear of the Lord." Does this mean that the wisest person is the one who most cowers in terror before God? Not exactly. It means that the wise person is the one who fears or respects God to the point of obedience. We are on the path of *wisdom* when we listen for God's directions for our lives. This is the path that Solomon desperately wants his hearers to find and follow.

B. Seeking Wisdom Obsessively (vv. 3, 4)

3, 4. Yea, if thou criest after knowledge, and liftest up thy voice for understanding; if thou seekest her as silver, and searchest for her as for hid treasures.

Again, Solomon uses a couple of vivid metaphors to describe the necessary quest *for understanding*. We holler for it, crying out and lifting our voices. We also go on a treasure hunt for it, seeking and searching. The point is that wisdom is available, but still must be sought. We are not born wise. Wisdom is not intuitive. In fact the wisdom of God is sometimes counter-intuitive because it goes against our impulses of self-preservation, self-importance, and greediness. [See question #2, page 356.]

C. Finding the Treasure of Wisdom (v. 5)

5. Then shalt thou understand the fear of the Lord, and find the knowledge of God.

The quest for wisdom is not an impossible, idealistic dream walk. It is very much within our grasp if we turn to God. Our search is governed by our respect for God and His ways. Our goal is to know God and His ways more fully so that we may better follow them. This is a happy, joyous journey, the lifelong pursuit of godliness. [See question #3, page 356.]

Avoiding Spiritual Altitude Sickness

Altitude sickness is an ailment that affects you when you exert yourself in such activities as climbing high mountains. It can make you violently ill even at a relatively low 8,000 to 10,000 feet if you have not conditioned your body for the climb. (Sitting in the pressurized

> **How to Say It**
> AGUR. *Ay*-gur.
> DIETRICH BONHOEFFER. *Dee*-trick *Bon*-huh-fur.
> HEZEKIAH. Hez-ih-*kye*-uh.
> LEMUEL. *Lem*-you-el.
> LUCIUS ANNAEUS SENECA. *Loo*-shuss Uh-*nee*-us *Sen*-uh-kuh.
> SOLOMON. *Sol*-o-mun.
> SØREN KIERKEGAARD. *So*-ren *Kir*-kuh-gard.

environment of a commercial airliner at 35,000 feet doesn't count as conditioning!)

The best way to avoid altitude sickness when mountain climbing is to train for the activity at intermediate altitudes. Spending a few days at those heights will help your body get adjusted before tackling the bigger peaks. Many amateur climbers get into trouble when they try to cram as much activity into their vacation time as possible and are not patient until their bodies adjust to the higher elevation.

Gaining wisdom is somewhat like mountain climbing. We all would like to "get to the top" as soon as possible without the struggle of conditioning and preparation that is required to do it correctly. Getting a bit of wisdom *may* come occasionally by what some would call blind luck. More frequently it will come, as our text says, because we actively listen, apply ourselves to understanding what is going on, call out (pray) for insight, and seek wisdom as if it were the greatest of treasures. If we try to attain life's heights by shortcuts, we may experience the spiritual sickness that lack of divine wisdom brings. —C. R. B.

II. Trusting in God
(Proverbs 3:1-6)

A. Lifelong Obedience (vv. 1, 2)

1, 2. My son, forget not my law; but let thine heart keep my commandments: for length of days, and long life, and peace, shall they add to thee.

In this chapter we begin to see some of the rewards for the one who seeks to live wisely: *long life, and peace*. The word translated *peace* is the Hebrew word *shalom*. It has a much richer meaning than simply peace in the sense of a quiet life with no trouble. Peace in the Old Testament also includes the idea of prospering emotionally and even materially.

We are thus confronted with a great paradox. If we seek God and shun the quest for material prosperity, God will cause us to be prosperous and satisfied. This pattern was seen in the life of Solomon himself, who asked God for wisdom and was given both wisdom and wealth (see 2 Chronicles 1:11, 12).

B. Lifelong Mercy (vv. 3, 4)

3, 4. Let not mercy and truth forsake thee: bind them about thy neck; write them upon the table of thine heart: so shalt thou find favor and good understanding in the sight of God and man.

The ethical keys to godly behavior are given here: *mercy and truth*. The person who lives a merciful and truthful life will be honored by God and people. The word translated *mercy* is one of the key words in all the Old Testament. It is a rich word and can also be translated "lovingkindness" (as it is in Jeremiah 9:24).

This concept of showing mercy to others is central to godly behavior. To behave like God is not to be cruel or mean-spirited, yet many Christians (even church leaders) have fallen into this sinful pattern. The Lord requires that His people are to "love mercy" (Micah 6:8). This is not a legalistic regulation as in "Aw, do I have to be merciful *again*?" Rather, it is a pattern of life that should come naturally and joyfully.

C. Lifelong Trust (vv. 5, 6)

5, 6. Trust in the LORD with all thine heart; and lean not unto thine own understanding. In all thy ways acknowledge him, and he shall direct thy paths.

One of the most famous pieces of advice in the history of the world is found here: *trust* your life to God and you will not be disappointed. It was true in Solomon's day, and it is still true today. God is our creator, and He has not abandoned us to find our own way in a confusing world. He has given us patterns for successful living. But living a flourishing life begins with our acknowledgement of God in the proper way. He is great and we are small. He is powerful and we are weak. He consistently loves and we are fickle. No matter how smart, educated, or experienced we are, we will fail repeatedly in life if we ignore God and try to make our own way.

Why don't we trust God more? Just as children must often learn life's lessons the hard way, we want to be independent. We want to be responsible for our own success and not share the credit. We are fiercely proud, and pride is the opposite of trust. Faith in God requires humility, and nothing in modern culture celebrates humility. But the promise is sure: if we humble ourselves and trust God, no matter how painful it may be, He will reward us with a richness of life beyond our dreams.

III. Enjoying Wisdom's Rewards (Proverbs 3:13-18)

A. Wisdom's Profits (vv. 13, 14)

13, 14. Happy is the man that findeth wisdom, and the man that getteth understanding: for the merchandise of it is better than the merchandise of silver, and the gain thereof than fine gold.

The story is told of a very wealthy man who lay sick and near death. His daughter asked him if he wanted anything. In a moment of lucid candor, the sick man replied, "Two things: a clear conscience and a good night's sleep." He had accumulated the riches of the world but died miserably.

Proverbs teaches us that *wisdom* and *understanding* will ultimately be more rewarding than wealth. This does not mean that wealth and wisdom are incompatible. We can be wise, wealthy, and happy. We can be wise, poor, and happy. But we cannot be foolish, wealthy, and happy.

B. Wisdom's Riches (vv. 15-17)

15-17. She is more precious than rubies: and all the things thou canst desire are not to be compared unto her. Length of days is in her right hand; and in her left hand riches and honor. Her ways are ways of pleasantness, and all her paths are peace.

Wisdom can never be purchased because no one can fix a price for it. Its value is beyond any monetary standard. We must work to be wise, but we do not earn wisdom. Wisdom is gained by obeying God's instructions for our lives; God does not charge us anything but obedience. [See question #4, page 356.]

Proverbs emphasizes that the ways of godliness are *ways of pleasantness*. This is not a tedious, joyless path. Truly godly people are both

Use this provocative question to help your class examine both the sources and the types of wisdom.

Visual for lesson 10

wise and happy, and yet the world does not understand this. People of faith often are portrayed as narrow bigots who are missing the best things in life. When the apostle Paul confronted the Roman governor Festus with the wisdom of the gospel of Christ, Festus concluded that Paul was insane (Acts 26:24). Yet Paul knew that he wasn't crazy. He was satisfied with his life of the pursuit of godliness and obedience to God's will. He faced death secure in the knowledge that he had chosen well and that God's rewards awaited him (2 Timothy 4:8).

C. Wisdom's Blessings (v. 18)

18. She is a tree of life to them that lay hold upon her: and happy is every one that retaineth her.

Solomon offers a striking description of wisdom as *a tree of life*. This image comes from the Genesis account of creation in which the tree of life is in the center of the Garden of Eden. Eating its fruit apparently could give Adam and Eve immortality.

The Bible mentions this tree in three places: Genesis (original paradise), Revelation (restored paradise), and four times in Proverbs. In the text before us, it is equivalent to personal happiness. It also is a product of righteousness (Proverbs 11:30), the hope a faithful person has (Proverbs 13:12), and wholesome speech (Proverbs 15:4). The version of the tree of life in Proverbs is not something in the future, but a present blessing in the life of the wise, godly person.

In the book of Genesis, Adam and Eve were barred from access to the tree of life after they sinned (Genesis 3:24). In the book of Revelation, access is regained. The Revelation version of the tree of life has 12 kinds of fruit, and its leaves produce a healing balm (Revelation 22:2). Why, then, does Proverbs see wisdom as a tree of life? It is because the wise life brings us back into a relationship of obedience with God, a relationship first broken by Adam and Eve. We will not have paradise restored completely until the end of time. But we can have our own personal paradise of peace and contentment in the present life if we trust and obey God. [See question #5, page 356.]

A Colossal Hoax

Have you seen the satellite pictures of North and South Korea taken at night? If you have, you have noticed that the Korean peninsula is as starkly divided visually at the 38th parallel as it is divided politically. The satellite picture shows the north almost totally dark, while the south blazes with the lights of prosperous cities.

The government of North Korea tries to hide its dismal performance. One of the ways it does so can be seen in the village of Kijongdong, on the border of the demilitarized zone between the two Koreas. From the south, one can see impressive apartment buildings designed to lure South Koreans northward to the supposed good life in the "people's paradise." But no one lives in the village; the apartments are two-dimensional façades like those built for Wild West movies. The whole thing is a colossal hoax.

The message of Proverbs alerts us: the so-called "good life" the world promises, with all its baubles and beauty, is also a colossal hoax. It is worth nothing compared to the precious jewel of the wisdom that comes from God. Do we want something more substantial that the proverbial 15 minutes of fame that this life offers? We'll find that "something more" in the wisdom of God.

—C. R. B.

Conclusion

A. Risky Faith: Trusting and Doubting

The Danish Christian writer Søren Kierkegaard (1813–1855) wrote "without risk, no faith." This outlook has many implications for the man or woman trying to live a godly life. Believers must trust that God, their creator and master, knows what is best for them. God's instructions for living are not designed to deprive us of enjoyment. The moral guidelines found in Scripture are not legalistic attempts to ruin everybody's fun. Instead, the Bible teaches us how we should live if we are to get the most out of life.

Often, though, we think we know better. The Bible teaches that there should be no sex outside of marriage. We think we know better. The Bible teaches that we always should tell the truth. We think we know better. The Bible teaches that we should not be greedy for luxury possessions. We think we know better. Ignoring the Bible's rules for living always invites disaster: children born without the support of fathers, a career destroyed for being caught in a lie, and overextended credit and financial ruin.

Trusting in God's ways is risky from a human perspective. Does God's advice always work? Aren't there loopholes and exceptions? Don't we need *new* moral guidelines for this century? Such questions of doubt are normal, given our human frailty and limitations. But one of the central promises of Scripture is that God's way is a better way, that we can trust Him with our lives. As the German martyr Dietrich Bonhoeffer (1906–1945) wrote from his Nazi prison, we must "throw ourselves completely into the arms of God." That means trusting that His way is superior even if we don't understand it completely.

We are strange creatures in which faith and doubt reside side by side. May we allow the doubts to grow weaker as we live by faith, trusting God's Word as a pattern for our living.

B. Tragedy and Godliness

Proverbs seems to be giving a blanket promise that the wise, godly life will be a long happy life. Why, then, do some of God's finest

---

Home Daily Bible Readings

Monday, May 1—Seek Wisdom (Proverbs 2:1-5)

Tuesday, May 2—Wisdom Brings Knowledge, Prudence, and Understanding (Proverbs 2:6-15)

Wednesday, May 3—Follow the Way of the Good (Proverbs 2:16-22)

Thursday, May 4—Trust and Honor God (Proverbs 3:1-12)

Friday, May 5—Wisdom Is Precious (Proverbs 3:13-20)

Saturday, May 6—Wisdom Brings Security (Proverbs 3:21-30)

Sunday, May 7—Do What Is Right (Proverbs 3:31-35)

people tragically die early? Why would God allow a faithful, young Christian mother to die and leave her small children behind?

As I write this lesson, I am in prayer for one of my college's graduates who suddenly fell into a coma last week while alone at his church's office. Without a powerful miracle, he will soon die and leave behind his ministry and his young family. He is a fine, godly man who rejected worldly success for the call of God to preach. Why does it seem that he will die so young?

It is impossible to answer that question because we can never totally understand it from God's perspective. But I know that this young man recently had won a great victory. After many years of prayer and discussion, he finally had led his brother-in-law to the Lord. Maybe that was the most important thing he could ever do. Perhaps in God's eyes his faithful life already has been long and pleasant and successful. And maybe part of wisdom is not fighting or resenting God when He calls a faithful servant home, but trusting that He knows best in everything.

C. Prayer

Great God, the wise and the true, grant to us the strength to find reward by trusting Your Word in faith and obedience. May we not revert to trusting our own wisdom but always rely on Your guidance for our lives. May we never look upon You as a strict taskmaster who deprives us of fun, but rather as a loving creator who has given life to us. We pray this in the name of our Savior, Jesus Christ, amen.

D. Thought to Remember

A wise person trusts God and His Word to show the best way to live.

Learning by Doing

This section contains an alternative lesson plan emphasizing learning activities. Classes desiring such student involvement will find these suggestions helpful.

Learning Goals

After participating in this lesson, each student will be able to:

1. List the blessings that can come from acquiring godly wisdom.
2. Suggest ways that obedience to God can result from having wisdom.
3. Make a plan to change one thing in his or her life in order to better reflect godly wisdom.

Into the Lesson

As your students arrive, distribute copies of the following quotes about wisdom (or direct their attention to the student books, where these quotations are printed). Ask students to read these quotations about wisdom, and then to write their own definition or description of wisdom.

Wisdom quotations: "It's so simple to be wise. Just think of something stupid to say and say the opposite" (Sam Levinson). "Wisdom consists of the anticipation of consequences" (Norman Cousins). "The perfection of wisdom and the end of true philosophy is to proportion our wants to our possessions, our ambitions to our capacities; we will then be a happy and a virtuous people" (Mark Twain). "Science is organized knowledge. Wisdom is organized life" (Immanuel Kant).

After students have had time to complete their definitions, ask several volunteers to share their conclusions. Then tell the class that today's lesson will deal with the nature of true wisdom as defined by the book of Proverbs.

Into the Word

Before completing the following exercise, ask three volunteers to read aloud one of the three passages from today's text: Proverbs 2:1-5; 3:1-6; 13-18. Next, ask your students to study these three passages independently and complete a true/false quiz. (This quiz is reprinted in the student books.) Correct answers are in parentheses.

T F 1. Proverbs 2 makes wisdom and understanding parallel ideas. *(True)*

T F 2. To receive wisdom, one must search for it. *(True)*

T F 3. According to Proverbs 2, our fear of the Lord depends on our knowledge of God. *(False*

Verse 5 has it the other way around: the fear of the Lord leads to the knowledge of God.)

T F 4. Proverbs 3 says keeping God's commandments will contribute to peace and long life. *(True)*

T F 5. Proverbs 3 says we should inscribe the words *mercy* and *truth* on our doorposts so that won't forget them. *(False. They are to be written on the heart.)*

T F 6. If we practice mercy and truth, we will find favor with both God and people. *(True)*

T F 7. Proverbs 3 says that if we trust God rather than relying on our own wisdom, He will give us direction in life. *(True)*

T F 8. According to Proverbs 3, wisdom is better than diamonds. *(False. Proverbs 3 says it is better than silver, gold, or rubies.)*

T F 9. Proverbs 3 says that wisdom holds riches and honor in her right hand. *(False. In her right hand is length of days. Riches and honor are in her left hand.)*

T F 10. Proverbs 3 compares wisdom to a tree of life. *(True)*

As you correct the quizzes together, use this time to discuss the meaning of the text with your class.

Into Life

Lucius Annaeus Seneca, a Roman philosopher and playwright who was born about the time that Jesus was, said of wisdom, "If wisdom were offered me with this restriction, that I should keep it close and not communicate it, I would refuse the gift." Read this quote to your class. Next, ask students to brainstorm some ways that they could communicate godly wisdom to others, both Christians and non-Christians, without coming across as arrogant or as wise guys.

After you have discussed possible ways to share godly wisdom with others, ask students to return to the definitions they wrote for the Into the Lesson exercise. Incorporating what they have learned about wisdom from today's lesson, students should rewrite their first definitions. Ask volunteers to read both versions of their definitions. What changes did they make and why?

Close with a prayer for your students that each would desire to live a wise and godly life pleasing to God. Pray that each would change one thing in his or her life in order to better reflect godly wisdom to others.

Let's Talk It Over

These questions are designed to promote discussion of the lesson. The answers here are only discussion starters. Let your class talk it over from there.

1. What was a time in your life when you had the godly wisdom necessary to make the right decision, but you voluntarily chose to make your decision based on ungodly "wisdom"? What was the outcome?

Some answers may be silly, some serious, but all will point out consequences when we ignore God's wisdom. Participants should recognize that although they may have gained godly wisdom through the years, they still must apply it. Solomon himself was an example of someone who had godly wisdom but didn't apply it (see 1 Kings 11:1-8).

2. Think of the differences between *knowledge, understanding,* and *wisdom.* How do you relate each of these to your service for Christ?

In Proverbs 2:1-3 there is a certain parallelism and overlap between the meanings of these three words. But if we were to push for distinctions we could say that (1) *knowledge* is merely the awareness of some fact, (2) *understanding* deals with how certain facts relate to other facts, and (3) *wisdom* is the ability to live out the principles of life. The three words are placed alongside one another in Proverbs 2:6; 9:10; Isaiah 11:2; and Colossians 1:9.

Knowing the facts of the Bible is important. "My people are destroyed for lack of knowledge" (Hosea 4:6). See also Romans 10:2, which talks about the danger of having zeal without knowledge. But having knowledge by itself isn't enough. James 2:19 speaks of demons who have a knowledge of God without gaining any benefit thereby.

Having understanding is better, but this is still not wisdom in the fullest sense. Spiritual wisdom comes from the Lord. The best source of wisdom is, of course, His Word. We also gain wisdom indirectly through spiritual leaders and through our own mistakes. We can wonder if Hymeneus and Alexander, whom Paul "delivered unto Satan, that they may learn not to blaspheme" (1 Timothy 1:20), gained any wisdom as a result!

Knowledge without wisdom is dangerous, as 1 Corinthians 8 establishes. If time allows, you can introduce the idea of *discernment* to the discussion. See 1 Kings 3:9; Ecclesiastes 8:5.

3. Where are you most likely to search for wisdom—in the Scriptures themselves, in the words of preachers and teachers (or perhaps their books you read), or in the counsel of godly friends and mentors? What advantage does each of these sources hold for you?

Since Christians are wired differently from one another, we naturally gain wisdom in a variety of ways. It is OK for Christians to lean more heavily on one method than another. It is *not* OK to neglect the Scriptures or to use only one method. If we eagerly seek wisdom, we will seek it on several paths (example: Proverbs 27:17). You should make it clear that the Bible is the most stable source for God's wisdom. Wisdom gained through preachers, teachers, friends, and mentors must itself have the Bible as its ultimate source.

4. Make a list of the advantages of wisdom—how it truly makes life better. Which advantages do you crave most in your life right now? Why?

The text lists several advantages of wisdom: long life, peace, favor with others, direction for your path in life. But there are more, such as good relationships with parents, avoiding errors in parenting, a healthy marriage, balanced priorities, etc. Help the class see the multiple and practical benefits of wisdom.

5. What kinds of things compete with a quest for wisdom? Why is it significant that items of high monetary value are mentioned several times in Proverbs 3:13-18? How does our pursuit of wealth frequently hinder gaining wisdom?

Often we are too busy for wisdom, which requires time for meditation, reflection, and listening. We get trapped in the pursuit of things that do not really make us happy. So why are we still so enamored with worldly pursuits? With this question we are trying to break the spell of worldly allures so that the grandeur of wisdom can shine brightly. We should remember that the church of Laodicea (Revelation 3:14-22), in their materialistic self-reliance, is the only church of seven in Revelation 2 and 3 about which Jesus had nothing good to say. She is the church that looks most like that of the Western world.

Accept Wisdom's Invitation

May 14
Lesson 11

DEVOTIONAL READING: Proverbs 8:10-21.

BACKGROUND SCRIPTURE: Proverbs 8, 9.

PRINTED TEXT: Proverbs 8:1-5, 22-32.

Proverbs 8:1-5, 22-32

1 Doth not wisdom cry? and understanding put forth her voice?

2 She standeth in the top of high places, by the way in the places of the paths.

3 She crieth at the gates, at the entry of the city, at the coming in at the doors:

4 Unto you, O men, I call; and my voice is to the sons of man.

5 O ye simple, understand wisdom: and, ye fools, be ye of an understanding heart.

. . . .

22 The LORD possessed me in the beginning of his way, before his works of old.

23 I was set up from everlasting, from the beginning, or ever the earth was.

24 When there were no depths, I was brought forth; when there were no fountains abounding with water.

25 Before the mountains were settled, before the hills was I brought forth:

26 While as yet he had not made the earth, nor the fields, nor the highest part of the dust of the world.

27 When he prepared the heavens, I was there: when he set a compass upon the face of the depth:

28 When he established the clouds above: when he strengthened the fountains of the deep:

29 When he gave to the sea his decree, that the waters should not pass his commandment: when he appointed the foundations of the earth:

30 Then I was by him, as one brought up with him: and I was daily his delight, rejoicing always before him;

31 Rejoicing in the habitable part of his earth; and my delights were with the sons of men.

32 Now therefore hearken unto me, O ye children: for blessed are they that keep my ways.

GOLDEN TEXT: Doth not wisdom cry? and understanding put forth her voice?
—Proverbs 8:1.

> *Living in and as God's Creation*
> Unit 3: Lessons in Living
> (Lessons 10-13)

Lesson Aims

After participating in this lesson, each student will be able to:

1. Identify imagery the writer uses to give human qualities to wisdom.
2. Tell how godly wisdom is seen in a person's actions.
3. Use Scripture in a case study format to help someone make a wise decision.

Lesson Outline

INTRODUCTION
    A. The Unaccepted Invitation
    B. Nation of Fools
    C. Lesson Background
I. INVITATION TO WISDOM (Proverbs 8:1-5)
    A. Wisdom's Call to Us (vv. 1-3)
    B. Wisdom's Challenge to Us (vv. 4, 5)
II. ORIGINS AND PURPOSE OF WISDOM (Proverbs 8:22-32)
    A. Wisdom Created (v. 22)
    B. Wisdom at Creation (vv. 23-29)
        Wisdom in the Heavens
    C. Wisdom as a Delight to God (vv. 30, 31)
        Why We Don't Find (or Cause) Delight
    D. Wisdom as a Blessing to Us (v. 32)
CONCLUSION
    A. Confident, Godly Living
    B. Jesus Christ as the Wisdom of God
    C. Prayer
    D. Thought to Remember

Introduction

A. The Unaccepted Invitation

Many years ago I was involved in a state math competition for high school students. Surprisingly I came in second and was awarded a scholarship to attend the local university. The scholarship, however, required that I be a math major. This was not my interest, so I turned the offer down and let it go to the third-place student.

I have wondered, though, how different my life would have been had I accepted this offer. Would I have made a contribution to the field of mathematics? Would I have become a high school or college math teacher? Would I have met people at that university who influenced my life and pointed me in other directions? There is no way to know these things. But whenever we reject an invitation, we make a choice that has an effect on our future.

Today's lesson invites us to join the people of God in the path of wisdom. It is an invitation that comes from God himself. He invites us to wisdom because He knows this is the best course for us to follow. The wise life is the life for which God created us.

B. Nation of Fools

In the book of Proverbs, knowledge is a clear understanding of what is right and wrong from God's perspective. The wise person is the one who has this knowledge and chooses to do the right thing. The fool is the one who knows what God has ordained as right and wrong, but chooses to do the wrong thing, the thing that is displeasing to God. Thus there is a direct correlation between wisdom and righteousness and between foolishness and sin (see Psalm 37:30; Proverbs 24:9). [See question #1, page 365.]

Recently an American state court ruled that an abstinence-based sex education course could not be taught in public schools. The ruling stated that such a course promoted a particular type of morality, and the state must be morally neutral. This illustrates the confusion between religious neutrality and moral neutrality. It is ridiculous to expect a government to be morally neutral. This confusion has led courts to define acceptable morality as that which is not promoted by any religious group. Thus, governments often have promoted the views of a minority of citizens. National and local governments and court systems are on a course of losing any sense of morality, any sense of virtue.

The Bible teaches that the divine purpose for government is to reward good and punish wrong (1 Peter 2:14). Governments that cease to do this will not endure. If truth is excluded from public discussion, there will be no morality. If there can be no sense of absolute truth, there can be no guiding principles of morality.

Increasingly we live in a culture that has little regard for God's standards of morality. It was recently revealed that the president of my state's largest university (40,000+ students) was having an extramarital affair with one of his staff members. This relationship was an "open secret" among many on the campus, but no one spoke up to condemn it. This issue of a powerful person's disregard for traditional standards of moral behavior was seen as a private matter, and no one else had the right to criticize this man.

Today's culture retains a basic understanding of God's standards for behavior because of the Bible's enormous influence on Western civilization across the centuries. But while the culture has this knowledge, it increasingly disregards these standards and chooses to accept and normalize immoral behavior. The verdict of Proverbs, then, is that while education levels may be at an all-time high, we live in a nation of fools. Our TV shows are written by fools. Our legal system is controlled by fools. Our educational system listens carefully to fools.

It does not have to be this way. In today's lesson, wisdom is calling us, inviting us to join her in partnership with God. We don't have to join the stampede toward foolishness that is engulfing our culture. The ancient, timeless ways of righteousness and godliness will bring blessings to us and to our children and grandchildren.

C. Lesson Background

Proverbs 8 uses an exciting literary technique called *personification* to portray wisdom. This means that wisdom is not presented as an abstract, doctrinal item that can be reduced to a list of dos and don'ts. Instead, wisdom takes a personality and becomes the companion of God in creating Heaven and earth. Wisdom is also the channel of God's blessing.

I. Invitation to Wisdom (Proverbs 8:1-5)

A. Wisdom's Call to Us (vv. 1-3)

1-3. Doth not wisdom cry? and understanding put forth her voice? She standeth in the top of high places, by the way in the places of the paths. She crieth at the gates, at the entry of the city, at the coming in at the doors.

A common cartoon situation depicts someone scaling a tall mountain to talk to a person on the top. This person is assumed to be a fount of wisdom, able to answer any and all human questions. The cartoon punch line is often based on the fact that such isolated hermits have little insight and give ridiculous advice.

The Bible does not portray *wisdom* this way. Wisdom calls to us. Wisdom is presented as making this invitation at the most public places of the ancient city: from the towers or *top of high places,* at the most trafficked *paths,* at the city's entrance *gates,* at the *doors* to all the homes. Wisdom does not play hide-and-seek with us. We can find wisdom and understanding in the pages of Scripture if we approach them with faith and willing obedience.

Last week in our study of Proverbs 2, we saw the use of a poetic technique called *parallelism.* Here it is again! *Wisdom* and *understanding* are parallel with one another; their meanings tend to overlap. The same is true of *cry* and *put forth her voice.* We can note in passing that the Hebrew words for *wisdom* and *understanding* are both feminine. This is what leads the writer of Proverbs to use the feminine pronouns *she* and *her* in personifying wisdom.

B. Wisdom's Challenge to Us (vv. 4, 5)

4, 5. Unto you, O men, I call; and my voice is to the sons of man. O ye simple, understand wisdom: and, ye fools, be ye of an understanding heart.

Wisdom submits a universal challenge: Get me! [See question #2, page 365.] There is no elitism here. Wisdom is not restricted to highly intelligent or deeply spiritual people. The most foolish among us can reverse course and begin to incorporate godliness in his or her life. Likewise, the wisest, most godly people can be even

---

Home Daily Bible Readings

Monday, May 8—Learn Prudence and Acquire Wisdom (Proverbs 8:1-9)

Tuesday, May 9—Receive Advice, Wisdom, Insight, and Strength (Proverbs 8:10-21)

Wednesday, May 10—Wisdom Participated in Creation (Proverbs 8:22-31)

Thursday, May 11—Listen to Wisdom's Instruction (Proverbs 8:32-36)

Friday, May 12—Wisdom Extends an Invitation (Proverbs 9:1-6)

Saturday, May 13—Wisdom Multiplies Our Days (Proverbs 9:7-12)

Sunday, May 14—Folly Extends an Invitation (Proverbs 9:13-18)

wiser and more consistently righteous in their choices. No one is ever beyond hope for wisdom, nor is anyone above the need for becoming wiser still.

It is never too late or too early to begin to live wisely. I have crossed paths with many young people who are sold out to living for God and make careful, prayerful choices. I have also known people who have come to faith late in life and begin to make consistent, godly choices for the first time. This does not mean that the effects of all their bad choices instantly disappear, but error is no longer compounded by additional error. Things do get better, even in the most chaotic of lives. [See question #3, page 365.]

II. Origins and Purpose of Wisdom (Proverbs 8:22-32)

A. Wisdom is Created (v. 22)

22. The LORD possessed me in the beginning of his way, before his works of old.

In the antique English of the *King James Version,* the word *possessed* is not used in the sense of "ownership" but in the sense of "creation." See Genesis 4:1 where this same Hebrew verb is used in the sense of "giving birth to." Thus God is the possessor of wisdom with the implication that He is the creator of wisdom.

Proverbs does not present wisdom as something uncreated, then. Wisdom is the initial creation of God. In the Genesis account, the first thing created is light (Genesis 1:3). In some ways, wisdom is indeed light—the enlightenment of humans as to the ways of God. (See the parallel between wisdom and light in Ecclesiastes 2:13.)

In other ways wisdom is the foundation of creation. God does not create wisdom after designing the universe. The universe is not self-explanatory. God's wisdom is shown in every aspect of creation: material, spiritual, and ethical. "The heavens shall declare his righteousness" (Psalm 50:6).

B. Wisdom at Creation (vv. 23-29)

23-26. I was set up from everlasting, from the beginning, or ever the earth was. When there were no depths, I was brought forth; when there were no fountains abounding with water. Before the mountains were settled, before the hills was I brought forth: while as yet he had not made the earth, nor the fields, nor the highest part of the dust of the world.

This text emphatically states that wisdom precedes any aspect of material creation. Even the most spectacular geographical features of our planet—the heights of the *mountains* and the *depths* of the oceans—came after the creation of wisdom. Wisdom takes second place to nothing in the created *world*.

Those who study the natural world are repeatedly amazed by the complexity they find. Single mountains comprise entire ecosystems of stunning interdependence. When fields such as cell biology and quantum mechanics cease to search for naturalistic explanations for life, their discoveries are breathtaking in their depth. It is estimated that human cells have 3.5 billion genetic bases, allowing for almost infinite genetic variety. Each human being is made up of billions of such cells. Each cell contains billions of lines of genetic code. [See question #4, page 365.]

When these findings are put under the perspective of faith in a creator, we stand in awe. The raw intellectual power behind all of this is far beyond our comprehension (Jeremiah 10:12). Yet the Bible does not speak of God's intelligence, but of His wisdom. God's wisdom permeates every aspect of the created universe. We will never be able to comprehend that wisdom fully.

27, 28a. When he prepared the heavens, I was there: when he set a compass upon the face of the depth: when he established the clouds above.

How to Say It

CORINTHIANS. Ko-*rin*-thee-unz (*th* as in *thin*).
ECCLESIASTES. Ik-*leez*-ee-*as*-teez (strong accent on *as*).
EPHESIANS. Ee-*fee*-zhunz.
HOSEA. Ho-*zay*-uh.
MACHIAVELLI. *Ma*-key-uh-*veh*-lee (strong accent on *Ma*).
MAO TSE-TUNG. Mau dzuh-*dung*.
NAPOLEON BONAPARTE. Nuh-*pol*-yuhn Bo-nuh-*part* (strong accent on *part*).
SOLOMON. *Sol*-o-mun.
ZECHARIAH. *Zek*-uh-*rye*-uh (strong accent on *rye*).

The author now describes wisdom's presence at the creation of *the heavens*. For those in the ancient world, the heavens are everything above the landmass of the earth. This would include both the sky (where birds fly) and the place of spiritual residence for God and the angels. The spiritual world was also created by God according to His pattern of wisdom. It is neither chaotic nor contradictory, but exists as a part of God's orderly creation.

Some people believe that spiritual principles are unscientific and illogical. Proverbs will not stand for this line of argument. Just as God created an orderly and brilliant material world, He created a spiritual world intended to conform to His patterns of wisdom. The fact that sin exists on the spiritual level is a testimony to the reality that created beings have been able to choose against God's mandates and thus play the spiritual fool.

WISDOM IN THE HEAVENS

Quick, now: what is the outermost planet in the solar system? You're right: it's Pluto—or maybe not! Since Pluto was discovered in 1930, astronomers have debated its status. All the other planets orbit in the same plane; Pluto's orbit is tilted 17 degrees. The four inner planets are rocky bodies while the next four are gas giants; Pluto, for its part, is a tiny ball of ice. One scientist says it is merely a comet; others say there are many other planets that are not counted.

First estimates of Pluto's size were that it was the size of the Earth. But now we know that its icy brilliance confused those who made those guesses. Next, we discovered the early estimates also were fooled by including the brightness of Pluto's large moon. In the 1990s the situation became even more complex when hundreds of icy planetary bodies similar to Pluto were discovered orbiting the sun beyond Neptune. To make matters more complicated, the innermost planet, Mercury, is not a planet by some definitions!

Perhaps the one thing we can be sure of in all of this is what Proverbs says: when God prepared the heavens, His wisdom was at work. Our own wisdom—or perhaps we should say our mere *knowledge*—regarding the universe is finite. We need to be reminded of that occasionally!
—C. R. B.

28b, 29. When he strengthened the fountains of the deep: when he gave to the sea his decree, that the waters should not pass his commandment: when he appointed the foundations of the earth.

The vast seas are very mysterious and majestic to people in both the ancient and modern worlds. While we know more about the oceans today, they still remain untamed. They are ruthless to those who disregard their vast power.

Yet as with the rest of creation, the oceans are subject to the laws of God. God has not created something that He cannot control. The mammoth might of the oceans is a part of the master plan of the wise creator.

C. Wisdom as a Delight to God (vv. 30, 31)

30, 31. Then I was by him, as one brought up with him: and I was daily his delight, rejoicing always before him; rejoicing in the habitable part of his earth; and my delights were with the sons of men.

The personification of wisdom takes a new twist here. God has not only created wisdom and used it to design the rest of creation, He also takes special delight in wisdom. Likewise, wisdom rejoices at being with God. We see here echoes of God's judgment at the end of creation: "God saw every thing that he had made, and, behold, it was very good" (Genesis 1:31).

As we find elsewhere in the Bible, the crown of God's creation is humanity itself (Psalm 8:5). God created us in His image, to be in fellowship with Him. This brings a *delight* to God that we cannot fully understand but only appreciate. This appreciation, however, helps us understand why God wants us to behave wisely. When we choose sin and act as fools, we take away God's delight and joy and cause Him grief (Genesis 6:5, 6; 1 Samuel 15:11, 35; Ephesians 4:30).

WHY WE DON'T FIND (OR CAUSE) DELIGHT

Dave Barry has a weekly humor column that appears in many newspapers. In one column he describes what he calls Male Genetic Dirt Blindness, a factor at the heart of many husband-wife problems. There is scientific evidence that the male brain takes in less sensory detail than the female brain. This is one reason why many wives cannot take delight in their husbands as much as they both would like—men simply do not "see" dirt the way women do. As Barry quotes one household conversation, "What snow tires in the dining room? Oh, 'those' snow tires in the dining room."

We probably shouldn't risk the peace of the class today by pressing the matter any further! But the fact is that differences in people (of either gender) can create problems in relationships. Wisdom is the daily delight of God, and that's what He wants us to be to Him as well. But part of bringing delight to God involves our use of wisdom in dealing with differences between people. Improper relationships between family members can result in relationship problems between us and God, as 1 Peter 3:7 establishes.

Our problem is that we often have neither sought wisdom nor invited her into our lives in this regard. The result is that we sometimes do not bring delight to the God who created us.

—C. R. B.

D. Wisdom as a Blessing to Us (v. 32)

32. Now therefore hearken unto me, O ye children: for blessed are they that keep my ways.

The invitation to wisdom is repeated, now with the promise of a blessing to those who heed her. This invitation is a win-win situation. We win because we begin to make wise, moral choices that will be honored by God and will avoid the chaos and self-inflicted pain of the foolish life. God wins because His lost children have come home. His delight is restored.

What a motivation to make wise choices, to live lives of godliness! May we not do this as a way of earning a reward. May we do this, rather, out of the realization that God, our creator, has shown us how to live, even in our culture of moral confusion and relativity.

Conclusion

A. Confident, Godly Living

My great-grandfather, who spoke German much better than English, used to say, "Da proplem is dat we be too soon olt and too late schmaht." (Translation: The problem is that we are too soon old and too late smart.) That rings true for many of us. How we wish we knew then what we know now!

Yet old age is no guarantee of wisdom. Older people are not necessarily wise people. Experience can be a hard taskmaster, a brutal teacher. Even so, adults who are mature in years often make incredibly foolish decisions. Both old people and young people make unwise decisions with money, selfish decisions

Visual for lesson 11

This question reminds your students that they will be listening to something this week—but exactly what is their choice.

with relationships, and destructive decisions with spiritual matters.

If we depend on our own resources, wise decisions always will be a matter of chance rather than choice. If we depend on God's instructions for living as found in His Word, we can confidently choose the right thing, knowing that God will never lie to us or mislead us. God created us to enjoy life and live it to the full as we glorify Him. But this can happen only if we study His Word and model our lives after His patterns.

The greatest example of this is found in the life of Jesus, God's Son. Studying His teachings and actions is a reliable way to godly living. But Jesus is not available to us in the flesh as a life example to see with our own eyeballs. Paul understood this when he urged his readers to "be ye followers of me, even as I also am of Christ" (1 Corinthians 11:1). We all need godly examples to pattern our lives after, people we know and love. One of the central elements of wise living is to pattern our lives after truly godly people. When we find these people, we can learn from them as they have learned from God's Word and from other godly people. We can live the godly life with confidence, not waiting on old age for wisdom.

B. Jesus Christ as the Wisdom of God

Proverbs 8:22-32 personifies wisdom and finds her dwelling with God. This passage also pictures wisdom as the agent of God in creation (see also Proverbs 3:19).

The Gospels, for their part, portray Jesus as being a manifestation of superior wisdom. Luke depicts Jesus' childhood years as a time of being "filled with wisdom" (Luke 2:40; see also v. 52). Jesus answered His critics by mentioning wisdom in an obvious reference to himself (Matthew 11:19). He claimed superiority over the wisdom of Solomon, the wisest person in history (Matthew 12:42). The great wisdom of Jesus was astounding to those He encountered (Mark 6:2). Jesus promised to impart wisdom to His followers in times of trials (Luke 21:15).

In Paul's great discussion of the inadequacy of human wisdom (1 Corinthians 1:18–2:5), he is not shy about identifying Jesus as "the wisdom of God" (1 Corinthians 1:24) and "who of God is made unto us wisdom" (1 Corinthians 1:30). Thus, the Old Testament's invitation to wisdom is continued in the New Testament's invitation to Jesus. If wisdom is a matter of correct choices, we can make no wiser choice than choosing to believe in Him. [See question #5, page 365.]

C. Prayer

God, our creator, You have formed the heavens and the earth according to Your master plan. This plan is too marvelous for us ever to understand fully. You have given us access also to the knowledge of right and wrong. Help us understand this fully, knowing right from wrong according to Your will.

Help us to make wise choices for the right and reject the foolish choices for the wrong. May we be granted the blessings of wisdom from Your hand. We pray these things in the name of Jesus, Your Son, amen.

D. Thought to Remember

The life-changing invitation to wisdom is open to all, and its promises are sure.

Learning by Doing

This section contains an alternative lesson plan emphasizing learning activities. Classes desiring such student involvement will find these suggestions helpful.

Learning Goals

After this lesson each student will be able to:
1. Identify imagery the writer uses to give human qualities to wisdom.
2. Tell how godly wisdom is seen in a person's actions.
3. Use Scripture in a case study format to help someone make a wise decision.

Into the Lesson

To begin today's lesson, ask your students to write down several examples of well-known sayings that reflect worldly wisdom. (Provide paper and pencils or direct your class to the student books, where this activity is printed). Such expressions could include common sense advice like "change your oil every 3,000 miles." Or they could reflect a worldly view of life, such as "it's a dog-eat-dog world."

After several minutes call on volunteers to share their work. Ask them to decide which sayings are truly wise and which are actually foolish or flawed in some way. Then tell your class that today's lesson will help them recognize the difference between genuine, godly wisdom and the worldly imitation.

Into the Word

A popular teaching technique used by ancient philosophers was the dialogue. For today's lesson text, ask your class to pretend that wisdom is a person, as in Proverbs 8. Imagine that wisdom is having a dialogue with a seeker who is trying to uncover wisdom's true nature.

Below are the questions the seeker asks. Distribute copies of these questions (but not the answers in brackets). Then instruct students to supply the answers given by wisdom in Proverbs 8:1-5, 22-32. (This exercise is in the student books also.) After students complete the exercise, discuss their answers with the aid of the lesson commentary.

Seeker: Where can you be found? From where do you call to us?

Wisdom: *[Everywhere! On the top of the high places, on the paths, at the gates, in the doors of the city; vv. 1-3.]*

Seeker: What is your challenge to us?

Wisdom: *[Get me! Gain an understanding heart; vv. 4, 5.]*

Seeker: Where do you come from? When did you come into being?

Wisdom: *[I am of the Lord, from eternity before He created the universe; vv. 22-26.]*

Seeker: How were you involved in creation?

Wisdom: [*God showed His wisdom in the creation of the heavens, the oceans, and the earth; vv. 27-29.*]

Seeker: What do you think of the world in general and people in particular?

Wisdom: [*I rejoice in the world and take great delight in humanity; vv. 30, 31.*]

Seeker: What is the promise to those who follow God's wisdom?

Wisdom: [*They will be blessed; v. 32.*]

Into Life

Below are quotations that reflect a worldly point of view. Make a transition by saying, "Now let's look at wisdom from a different angle." Ask students to respond to each quote with an appropriate Scripture passage that indicates God's wisdom on the subject. Discuss their responses in light of today's lesson. Some suggested Scriptures are indicated following each quotation. (These quotations are also in the student books).

1. "Religion is the opium of the masses."—Karl Marx [*John 8:31-36; 1 Corinthians 1:18-25*]

2. "Political power grows out of the barrel of a gun."—Mao Tse-tung [*Romans 13:1-5*]

3. "If you wish to be a success in the world, promise everything, deliver nothing."—Napoleon Bonaparte [*Zechariah 8:16, 17; Matthew 5:33-37*]

4. "You can get much farther with a kind word and a gun than you can with a kind word alone." —Al Capone [*Matthew 5:38-47; Romans 12:17-21*]

5. "Christ died for our sins. Dare we make his martyrdom meaningless by not committing them?"—Jules Feiffer [*Romans 6:1-7*]

6. "I am free of all prejudices. I hate everyone equally."—W. C. Fields [*Matthew 5:43-46*]

7. "Under capitalism man exploits man; under socialism the reverse is true."—Polish proverb [*Philippians 2:1-4*]

8. "Success is the sole earthly judge of right and wrong."—Adolf Hitler [*Proverbs 21:2, 3; Hosea 14:9; Micah 6:6-8*]

Let's Talk It Over

These questions are designed to promote discussion of the lesson. The answers here are only discussion starters. Let your class talk it over from there.

1. If foolishness and sin mean the same thing in Proverbs, then modern culture demonstrates a monumental lack of wisdom! What are some specific behavioral examples that show the foolishness of the world? Defend your choices.

To give your students a jump start on this question, you can bring in a magazine, newspaper, and/or page from a Web browser so they can see some examples of absolute foolishness. You can expect students to mention a wide range of topics such as legalization of gay marriages, terrorism, biased sex education in public schools, governmental funding of immoral art, or abortion. Point out that such lack of wisdom is inevitable when God's voice is ignored or suppressed (Romans 1:18-23).

2. What would it mean for you to respond to wisdom's invitation today? How would your life be different in your schedule, finances, and family relationships?

The invitation to come to wisdom is an invitation to behavioral change. So let's get specific! For improvements to our schedules, some possibilities include spending time reading God's Word and carving out time for quiet reflection. An improvement in how we handle finances could include sacrificial giving to promote God's priorities. Leading family devotions may be a way to improve family relationships.

But adding any of the above improvements almost always must mean subtracting or sacrificing something else to make room. Examples could include less TV watching, making the old car last another year, and limiting the children's involvement in extracurricular activities. Ultimately this question should lead to confession and accountability within your small group or class.

3. Who is the wisest person you have ever known? What made him or her wise? What did that look like in practical terms of how he or she talked, spent time and money, and carried himself or herself publicly?

Although Proverbs 8:1-5 describes some characteristics of wisdom, most of us could also use a tangible role model to help us become wise. The purpose of this question is to draw a portrait of just such a person. In turn, the types of people mentioned may help us understand the kind of role model we need to be. Should we be strong, outgoing leaders or quiet, meditative mentors? Do we need to be gentle or firm? Should we mention our own mistakes in life as a don't-do-what-I-did teaching tool, or should we keep quiet about a sinful past? Explore as time allows.

4. The apostle Paul notes in disparaging terms that "the Greeks seek after wisdom" (1 Corinthians 1:22). If he were to restate this for the twenty-first century by saying "secular scientists seek after wisdom," what would he mean? Give some examples.

Secular science's insistence on godless explanations in physics, biology, etc., would be the overall framework. Within that framework your students may list many examples. Some possibilities are the use of evolutionary theory to make sense of biology, the presumption that matter has existed eternally, and the use of statistical projections to assume that beings of greater intelligence "must" exist on planets elsewhere in the universe. First Corinthians 1:18-31 can enrich this discussion.

5. What similarities and differences do you see between the invitation to get wisdom and the invitation to follow Jesus? How do you apply these similarities and differences in your own life?

Both invitations require a behavioral change. You cannot come to either Jesus or wisdom and carry on as before. We become slaves to wisdom's call as well as to Christ's. Wisdom leads us to greater holiness, as does obedience to Christ.

A person can live a life of wisdom by applying carefully the knowledge of God that is available through general revelation (Romans 1:19, 20). But a knowledge of Jesus and His work is available only through special revelation (Romans 3:21, 22; Hebrews 1:1, 2). Accepting Solomon's invitation to follow wisdom should lead us to accepting Jesus. That's what a truly wise person will do! Accepting Jesus involves recognizing that He died on a cross, was buried, and rose again—things that cannot be said of the concept of wisdom itself.

May 21
Lesson 12

Follow the Path of Integrity

DEVOTIONAL READING: Proverbs 10:27-32.

BACKGROUND SCRIPTURE: Proverbs 11.

PRINTED TEXT: Proverbs 11:1-14.

Proverbs 11:1-14

1 A false balance is abomination to the LORD: but a just weight is his delight.

2 When pride cometh, then cometh shame: but with the lowly is wisdom.

3 The integrity of the upright shall guide them: but the perverseness of transgressors shall destroy them.

4 Riches profit not in the day of wrath: but righteousness delivereth from death.

5 The righteousness of the perfect shall direct his way: but the wicked shall fall by his own wickedness.

6 The righteousness of the upright shall deliver them: but transgressors shall be taken in their own naughtiness.

7 When a wicked man dieth, his expectation shall perish: and the hope of unjust men perisheth.

8 The righteous is delivered out of trouble, and the wicked cometh in his stead.

9 A hypocrite with his mouth destroyeth his neighbor: but through knowledge shall the just be delivered.

10 When it goeth well with the righteous, the city rejoiceth: and when the wicked perish, there is shouting.

11 By the blessing of the upright the city is exalted: but it is overthrown by the mouth of the wicked.

12 He that is void of wisdom despiseth his neighbor: but a man of understanding holdeth his peace.

13 A talebearer revealeth secrets: but he that is of a faithful spirit concealeth the matter.

14 Where no counsel is, the people fall: but in the multitude of counselors there is safety.

GOLDEN TEXT: The integrity of the upright shall guide them: but the perverseness of transgressors shall destroy them.—Proverbs 11:3.

> *Living in and as God's Creation*
> Unit 3: Lessons in Living
> (Lessons 10-13)

Lesson Aims

After participating in this lesson, each student will be able to:
1. Contrast the actions of a righteous person with those of one who is dishonest.
2. Explain how personal integrity can be destroyed by pride and dishonesty.
3. Perform an integrity checkup in his or her life.

Lesson Outline

INTRODUCTION
  A. "I Always Tell the Truth, Lois"
  B. Lesson Background
I. INTEGRITY OF A PERSON (Proverbs 11:1-9)
  A. Integrity in Business (v. 1)
    Know Any Christian "Music Men"?
  B. Integrity and Humility (vv. 2, 3)
  C. Integrity and God's Judgment (vv. 4-6)
  D. Integrity and God's Deliverance (vv. 7-9)
II. INTEGRITY OF A COMMUNITY (Proverbs 11:10-14)
  A. City Celebrates (vv. 10, 11)
    Communal Integrity
  B. Damage of Careless Accusals (vv. 12, 13)
  C. Nation Adrift (v. 14)
CONCLUSION
  A. Satan Hates Integrity
  B. The Hard Choice for Integrity
  C. Prayer
  D. Thought to Remember

Introduction

A. "I Always Tell the Truth, Lois"

A great fantasy hero of the twentieth century was Superman, "the man of steel." The Superman story arose out of the hard times of the Great Depression and served as an inspiration during the years of World War II.

Superman was touted as fighting for "truth, justice, and the American way." Some would dismiss this motto today as being too simplistic and too focused on America. Yet this childhood hero of many was more than a superb athlete—strong, fast, and able to fly. Superman was always portrayed as a man of great moral strength, a man of integrity.

In the motion picture version of the Superman saga, there is a scene in which the man of steel meets with the skeptical Lois Lane for the first time. During this encounter in her rooftop garden, there comes a point where Lois questions whether or not Superman is lying to her. In perfect sincerity, without a trace of guile, Superman says, "I always tell the truth, Lois."

I always tell the truth. How wonderful it would be if we all could say this! We are confronted dozens of times every day with situations that demand that we be either truthful or deceitful. Truth is an absolute value. In matters of integrity, there is no gray area. We either tell the truth, or we don't. We all know that we are lied to constantly in our culture. We are lied to by advertisers. We are lied to by politicians. We are lied to by employers. We are lied to by employees. Tragically, we are sometimes lied to by church leaders, family members, and even spouses. [See question #1, page 374.]

A basic definition of integrity is doing what you say you will do. For example, a person who refuses to help and, in fact, does not help has not violated integrity. But the person who promises to help and then refuses (or denies making the original promise) has compromised integrity. This week's lesson hits us where we live: the daily decisions of telling the truth and keeping our commitments. [See question #2, page 374.]

B. Lesson Background

It is helpful to review the concepts of knowledge and wisdom as presented in the book of Proverbs. Knowledge is knowing what God expects us to do, recognizing His standards of right and wrong. Wisdom is discerning these standards and choosing to obey God. Foolishness is knowing the expectations of God but choosing to do the wrong thing. In the realm of integrity, the Bible teaches that our integrity is never for sale and never to be sacrificed. Wisdom, therefore, is keeping one's word, no matter what the consequences. The fool is the person who breaks his or her word for money or other selfish reasons that are within his or her control.

A vivid illustration of the importance of integrity is found in Job 2:9, 10. Job is a righteous,

God-fearing man who has experienced every type of personal tragedy imaginable. At the height of his suffering, Job's wife berates him for maintaining his integrity—that is, his trust in God. She pushes him to "curse God and die." Job refuses to do this and preserves his integrity. He will not abandon his obedient relationship with God. Significantly, Job calls his wife a foolish woman. As in Proverbs the fool is the one who concedes integrity in difficult situations. The verdict of the text for Job's decision is that by not giving up his integrity, Job did not sin.

The Hebrew word translated *integrity* in Proverbs 11:3 (below) has several related words with various shades of meaning in the Old Testament. It can have the sense of *perfect* (Job 1:1). It can also mean *simplicity* in the sense of *innocence* (2 Samuel 15:11). The "perfect" person (the person of integrity) may be a target of attack by the wicked (Psalm 64:4). Integrity can have a protective function (Psalm 25:21). Most importantly, God is a protective shield to those who "walk uprightly" (Proverbs 2:7).

> **How to Say It**
> CAVEAT EMPTOR (Latin). *ka*-vee-at *emp*-ter.
> ECCLESIASTES. Ik-*leez*-ee-*as*-teez (strong accent on *as*).
> SHEKEL. *sheh*-kul.

I. Integrity of a Person (Proverbs 11:1-9)

A. Integrity in Business (v. 1)

1. A false balance is abomination to the LORD: but a just weight is his delight.

Nothing is prepackaged in the ancient world. Basic items are bought and sold based on *weight,* quantity, or volume. Merchants measure at the time of sale. This is done using a beam-balance scale with dishes on either end. Such scales are dependent upon standardized weights being used on one side.

Commodities such as spices or incense are weighed out on the merchant's scale using his set of stone weights. The basic unit of weight measurement in Old Testament times is the shekel (Ezekiel 4:10; 45:12). It weighs about four-tenths of an ounce (11.5 grams, or about the weight of two U.S. quarter dollars). Stone weights are sized in fractions and multiples of shekels.

If payment is being made in gold or silver, the customer's metal also will be weighed because there are no absolute standards. A dishonest merchant might keep two sets of weights. One would be lighter, thus favoring him when weighing his commodity. The other would be heavier, thus penalizing the customer when weighing the money. The Bible teaches that such dishonesty is more than bad business practice; it is offensive to God himself (see Deuteronomy 25:13-16; Proverbs 20:10; Amos 8:4, 5; Micah 6:11).

Consumers today are warned by the Latin phrase *caveat emptor:* "Let the buyer beware!" Although modern government standards require truth in packaging, such packaging often is misleading anyway. The people of God should have no part in this business philosophy. A business with integrity builds a loyal customer base because the merchant treats the customers fairly. Deception and lack of integrity may build short-term profits but will lead to collapse in the long run. Think of the Enron scandal.

KNOW ANY CHRISTIAN "MUSIC MEN"?

Not quite a century ago, a very entertaining (fictitious) con man—"Professor" Harold Hill by name—got off the train in River City, Iowa. Who doesn't remember that story from the stage play and film *The Music Man*? Although Hill had no musical talent, he was a mesmerizing salesman. He convinced the citizens of River City that the recent addition of a pool table to their community would lead to the degradation of their youth. His solution? A boys' marching band would "keep the young ones moral after school."

His plan to skip town after collecting the money for mail-order instruments and uniforms went awry when he fell in love with Marian, the town librarian. Of course it all ended well, with the uniforms magically fitting and the "76 trombones" and other instruments miraculously hitting all the right notes in the hands of the untutored, juvenile musicians.

We all know that real life doesn't work out so nicely. Too often the dishonest salesman gets the money, and the victim realizes the deception too late. Technology has provided substitutes for dishonest scales in the form of Internet scams, telemarketing frauds, etc. Times change and the means of cheating may change, but the

Lord still abhors dishonesty. Christians, of all people, are to be known for integrity in business dealings. —C. R. B.

B. Integrity and Humility (vv. 2, 3)

2, 3. When pride cometh, then cometh shame: but with the lowly is wisdom. The integrity of the upright shall guide them: but the perverseness of transgressors shall destroy them.

There is a direct correlation between boastful pride and lack of *integrity*. When we inflate and tout our accomplishments and virtues, credibility and integrity evaporate. Sometimes it feels good to be able to say we are the smartest, the richest, or the cleverest in a given situation.

The wise person realizes that *pride* is fleeting, that false claims will be found out. It is better to live in humility and simplicity, not seeking the acclaim of others. While this kind of life may not seem as exciting, it will safeguard the wise person from the social embarrassment that inevitably comes to the boastful, exaggerating individual.

C. Integrity and God's Judgment (vv. 4-6)

4-6. Riches profit not in the day of wrath: but righteousness delivereth from death. The righteousness of the perfect shall direct his way: but the wicked shall fall by his own wickedness. The righteousness of the upright shall deliver them: but transgressors shall be taken in their own naughtiness.

There are some things that money cannot buy (compare Proverbs 11:28). Money cannot buy a happy, stable home and family. Money cannot buy a happy marriage.

Neither can money buy the satisfaction that comes from a task well done. Money cannot buy friends who will stick with you when there is no money (the prodigal son in Jesus' parable found this out). Money cannot buy a fulfilling and satisfying relationship with God. Money cannot buy a faithful church. In fact, when we consider the most important things in life, money can buy none of them.

Greek mythology tells the story of King Midas, who was given the power to turn everything he touched into gold. His greed caused him to be delighted with this ability until mealtime came. Then Midas found that all food and drink became gold before he could eat or drink. He learned that great wealth is not life's greatest blessing.

In the book of Proverbs, wisdom is the realization that money is to be used, not worshiped. The wise use money for godly purposes. Foolishness, therefore, is to trust wealth for salvation or happiness. Money can never buy integrity.

D. Integrity and God's Deliverance (vv. 7-9)

7-9. When a wicked man dieth, his expectation shall perish: and the hope of unjust men perisheth. The righteous is delivered out of trouble, and the wicked cometh in his stead. A hypocrite with his mouth destroyeth his neighbor: but through knowledge shall the just be delivered.

Is the life of integrity one in which we have no problems, trials, or trouble? God does not promise this. To the contrary, the Bible is full of stories of people who suffer because of their personal stand for integrity. Daniel was committed to praying to God every day. When his enemies conspired to have a law made that required prayer be made only to the king, Daniel did not sacrifice his integrity. He opened his windows and continued to pray to God (Daniel 6:10), knowing full well that he was putting his life on the line.

Proverbs teaches that righteous people, those who walk in integrity, have the blessing and the protection of God (see Proverbs 28:18). This does not mean that righteous people never suffer or that the way of integrity is easy. It means that God ultimately will vindicate us and reward our intentions to live lives of integrity and righteousness (compare Revelation 6:9-11). To some degree, righteousness is its own reward.

Home Daily Bible Readings

Monday, May 15—God's Way Is a Stronghold (Proverbs 10:27-32)

Tuesday, May 16—Wisdom, Not Pride (Proverbs 11:1-5)

Wednesday, May 17—Righteousness, Not Treachery (Proverbs 11:6-10)

Thursday, May 18—The Importance of Guidance and Counsel (Proverbs 11:11-15)

Friday, May 19—Blameless Ways, Not Wickedness (Proverbs 11:16-21)

Saturday, May 20—Generosity, Not Stinginess (Proverbs 11:22-26)

Sunday, May 21—Goodness, Not Evil (Proverbs 11:27-31)

But the Bible promises more than this. God notices our efforts. He smiles upon those who choose integrity. [See question #3, page 374.]

II. Integrity of a Community (Proverbs 11:10-14)

A. City Celebrates (vv. 10, 11)

10, 11. When it goeth well with the righteous, the city rejoiceth: and when the wicked perish, there is shouting. By the blessing of the upright the city is exalted: but it is overthrown by the mouth of the wicked.

Proverbs throws in an unexpected twist at this point and focuses on a community's integrity rather than an individual's. Communities take pride in the integrity of their leaders. There is reason to celebrate when a community achieves a reputation for integrity. On the other hand, a city that tolerates dishonesty and corruption among its officials will earn a bad reputation.

I once lived in a large city that was having an election for prosecuting attorney between two men of very questionable reputation. Both men were under indictment by federal grand juries for corruption. Remarkably, though, the political parties could find no better candidates. When the campaign mudslinging began, the message for each candidate was basically "my indictment is not as serious as my opponent's indictment." What an embarrassment to that city!

It is doubly embarrassing if Christians run for office, are elected, and then fall because of corruption and dishonesty. It is an embarrassment to *the city*, to the church, and to our Lord. We should encourage believers to be involved in civic affairs. But the battle for integrity will be ongoing and intense. How joyous it is when a person retires from office with a long and distinguished career marked by both accomplishment and integrity!

COMMUNAL INTEGRITY

Missionaries in third-world countries sometimes have to deal with corruption on the part of government officials. One missionary, for example, found himself frustrated time and again by officials looking for a "dash," as bribes were called. When mission business required a government permit, officials created numerous delays in hopes of eliciting a bribe. Policemen often expected a bribe as the price of overlooking an imaginary traffic offense.

After several such incidents, the missionary was reaching the proverbial boiling point. It was then that he recalled the many cities in his home country that had similar problems. Back home the wheels of government often were greased with kickbacks, payoffs, and favors of various kinds.

Such failures of communal integrity (wherever they may take place) are an indication that the common people accept the situation as normal and nothing to be concerned about. Of course in some cases it may be impossible for "the little guy" to have any influence on entrenched governmental corruption. But in democracies, where the people have a voice, Christians ought to be in the front ranks of those who demand that their leaders conduct themselves with integrity. A community or nation will destroy itself if it lacks such godly counsel.
—C. R. B.

B. Damage of Careless Accusals (vv. 12, 13)

12, 13. He that is void of wisdom despiseth his neighbor: but a man of understanding holdeth his peace. A talebearer revealeth secrets: but he that is of a faithful spirit concealeth the matter.

In the movie *Bambi*, little Thumper the rabbit is taught by his father, "If you can't say something nice, don't say nothin' at all." There are times when we must stand up for righteousness and be vocal. But what about the times when our criticisms are little more than attempts at self-righteousness? The way of wisdom is often marked by holding our tongues (Ecclesiastes 3:7).

Holding our tongues naturally involves prudence in dealing with *secrets*. Those who have been leaders in the church for many years often know awkward things about many people. What do we do with this knowledge? First, we cannot and should not feel obligated to deny or alter the facts. But second, we also must trust that people grow and change.

When we see that a person has abandoned a sinful behavior, we serve no purpose by bringing up past problems. Instead, we rejoice that God has changed a person for the better. When we are entrusted with a secret, our integrity is being put to the test. Will we use this knowledge as power to hurt or destroy someone unnecessarily? Or will we keep our word by keeping the secret? [See question #4, page 374.]

We all have done things in the past that we are not particularly proud of. Let's let those things die as we live for the future as servants of our gracious Lord. This does not mean, however, that we become silent facilitators for criminal behavior. It's always dangerous to give a blanket *yes* answer in advance to someone who says "I need to talk to you about something, but you have to promise not to tell anyone." The person may be about to divulge information that involves the safety of others. When in doubt about issues of confidentiality, consult someone who is spiritually mature in this area.

C. Nation Adrift (v. 14)

14. Where no counsel is, the people fall: but in the multitude of counselors there is safety.

The proposition in the first half of this verse is that lack of integrity among national leaders will have widespread implications. There is no such thing as a morally neutral society. We have every right to demand integrity and honesty from public officials. We should not stand for the conventional wisdom that says a campaign promise equals a lie to help get the candidate elected.

A nation that ignores foundational issues of truth and justice will not be blessed by God. Wisdom should extend into the civic arena. We should desire leaders who are wise by God's standards, not fools. A look at who is serving as a leader's *counselors* can be very revealing! (See 1 Kings 12:8-11.) [See question #5, page 374.]

Conclusion

A. Satan Hates Integrity

The book of Job has a lot to say about integrity. In the conversation between God and Satan at the beginning, God points to Job as a shining example of this characteristic (Job 2:3). Satan thinks that Job's integrity will crack under pressure and proceeds to test him mightily. Satan is always looking to attack the people of God in the area of integrity.

There is a practical side of this for Christians. In the book of Titus, Paul instructs his apprentice to appoint church leaders who are "blameless" or men of integrity (Titus 1:6, 7). Titus himself is to be a model of integrity or incorruptness (Titus 2:7; see Lesson 13 from winter).

Why is this? The underlying principle is that church leaders need to be seen as people of integrity in the community so that unbelievers will not be offended. The church is open to all who believe, even those who struggle with matters of integrity. But leadership must be restricted to those who have proven themselves to be people of honesty and truth. Otherwise the reputation of the church will be damaged, and our Lord Jesus will suffer undue disgrace.

Point to this visual as you ask, "What are some life-path choices that you will face this week?"

Visual for lesson 12

Satan would like nothing better than to besmirch the name of Jesus and His followers. May we have the strength to resist giving Satan that victory.

B. The Hard Choice for Integrity

Sir Thomas More (1478–1535) was a prominent statesman during the reign of Henry VIII, king of England. More was a man of great principle. Although he wanted to see young Henry succeed, More was unwilling to sacrifice his integrity. Eventually More was accused of treason and imprisoned because of his unwillingness to yield to the king's demand to be recognized as the lawful head of the Church of England.

While in prison More's daughter Margaret visited and implored him to take the oath that would save his life. She reasoned that he could say the oath but think otherwise in his heart. For More, though, this was a matter of integrity. He cupped his hands as if holding water and told her that when a man makes an oath, he is holding his own self in his hands. More then opened his fingers to show Margaret that when an oath is false, the man will lose himself like the water that would slip away. Then there would be nothing left.

More was executed for his refusal to take the oath. Today, however, he is celebrated and honored as one of the greatest examples of integrity in all of history. He was nicknamed by a friend as the "man for all seasons." For More, integrity was worth dying for!

For most of us, decisions of integrity are not matters of life and death. A little lie here, a little cheating there, who will ever know? Shouldn't people look out for themselves? Think of your own life. Do you have limits to your integrity? If a cashier incorrectly gives you back extra money, do you see this as good luck or as an opportunity to act with integrity? How much would you need to be paid to lie for your employer? Would you do it for $100,000? What value makes something worth stealing? Would you steal something worth $10,000 if there were little risk of being caught?

The Bible teaches that no monetary value can be assigned to our integrity. Honesty applies in things little or big. As Proverbs 28:6 says, "Better is the poor that walketh in his uprightness, than he that is perverse in his ways, though he be rich." Faithfulness applies to things small and big (Luke 16:10). May we learn to live wisely and to walk with integrity in everything we do.

C. Prayer

God of truth, we ask that You help us follow Your examples. You always tell the truth. You always keep Your promises. You are the ultimate and perfect model of integrity. Make us people of truth and integrity. We pray this in the name of Your Son Jesus, the full embodiment of truth, amen.

D. Thought to Remember

Sacrificing integrity for temporary benefit is a long-term disaster.

Learning by Doing

This section contains an alternative lesson plan emphasizing learning activities. Classes desiring such student involvement will find these suggestions helpful.

Learning Goals

After participating in this lesson, each student will be able to:
1. Contrast the actions of a righteous person with those of one who is dishonest.
2. Explain how personal integrity can be destroyed by pride and dishonesty.
3. Perform an integrity checkup in his or her life.

Into the Lesson

For each scenario below, your class should decide what advice to give the central character. The scenarios are also printed in the student books.

Scenario #1. Martha has joined with several other investors to purchase some real estate they hope to develop into a residential community. However, Martha has learned from a friend on the zoning commission that the property has drainage problems that will be very costly to correct. Unaware of the problems, another investor wants to buy Martha's share of the land. Should she tell him about the problems?

Scenario #2. Ken owned a thriving gas station and convenience mart. He invited his friends and employees to invest in his expanding business and many did. Now, however, new competition has hurt his business. Ken has enough money to sell out, take a loss, and start over elsewhere. But many others will lose their jobs and/or their investments. What should he do?

Scenario #3. Arthur is an accountant for a local cell phone provider. He knows the company is headed toward bankruptcy. But the owner has offered him a bonus to keep that information secret so the other employees and customers won't go elsewhere. What should Arthur do?

Discuss your students' responses to each scenario. Then tell your class that today's lesson concerns issues of personal and community integrity.

Into the Word

Lead your class in a discussion of today's text, Proverbs 11:1-14, using the lesson commentary and the following discussion questions:

1. How should we apply the standard of an honest "balance" (v. 1) to our business practices today?

2. What is the relation between integrity and humility (vv. 2, 3)?

3. Why is integrity better than wealth in the Day of Judgment (vv. 4-9)?

4. What does integrity have to do with the well-being of a community (vv. 10, 11)?

5. What can happen to a community beset by dishonesty (vv. 12-14)?

Return to the three scenarios from the Into the Lesson activity. Say, "Based on today's study so far, what would you now say to Martha, Ken, and Arthur?"

Into Life

To close today's lesson, make and distribute copies of the self-evaluation activity below. (This exercise also is printed in the student book.) Tell students that they can be completely honest since they will not be asked to share their responses.

Integrity Self-Check

How trustworthy are you? To grade your own sense of integrity, circle the number corresponding to your likely response to each question below.

A. Would you return a wallet full of money you found in a parking lot? *1. Never; 2. Maybe; 3. For a reward; 4. Probably; 5. Absolutely.*

B. Would you break the rules to win a game or improve your golf score? *1. Of course; 2. Probably; 3. If it were important; 4. Doubtful; 5. Never.*

C. Would you cheat on your taxes to save $500? *1. Sure; 2. Probably; 3. Only for $1,000 or more; 4. No, I'd fear an audit; 5. Never.*

D. Would you lie to get out of a difficult situation? *1. Why not? 2. Define lying; 3. Depends on the situation; 4. Rarely; 5. Never.*

E. Would you obey a stop sign on a deserted road? *1. What stop sign? 2. Not unless a cop is nearby; 3. Usually, unless I'm running late; 4. Normally, unless it's an emergency; 5. Of course.*

Now figure your IQ ("Integrity Quotient") by adding the scores for all five responses. Here are possible results:

- 22–25 Habitually honorable
- 17–21 Generally trustworthy
- 13–16 Dubiously reliable
- 9–12 Ethically challenged
- 5–8   Morally bankrupt

Copyright © 2005. STANDARD PUBLISHING, Cincinnati, Ohio. Permission is granted to reproduce this page for ministry purposes only. Not for resale.

Let's Talk It Over

These questions are designed to promote discussion of the lesson. The answers here are only discussion starters. Let your class talk it over from there.

1. What are some times that people think it is OK to lie? How do we guard against methods or philosophies that excuse lying?

People often lie outright in business transactions. Those who are more sophisticated at this use small print, legalese, or half-truths. Such deceit is frequently profitable. News reporters hide their biases behind selective use of facts and emotional images. Politicians master the spin even to the point of asking what the definition of *is* is. All this is even worse in Hollywood, where so-called reality TV is based on deception.

One big problem is that postmodern culture has abandoned the notion of absolute truth. Mainstream sociologists have gone so far as to suggest that we, not God, create our realities.

2. How has living a life of integrity benefited you? What was a time when the temptation to compromise integrity could have helped you in a way that the world considers profitable?

Honest businesses often survive longer since their customers or clients trust them and give them referrals. Owners of such businesses do everything they can to avoid declarations of bankruptcy, which can be viewed as a government sanctioned way to avoid paying legitimate debts (also known as stealing). Businesses of integrity tend to survive attacks of slander, governmental audits, and unscrupulous competitors.

Individuals who are honest make better employees. They don't spend time and energy lying and covering lies with other lies. They have healthier relationships with coworkers and family members. They avoid office politics. There are real and tangible benefits to integrity! But even if there were no earthly benefits, God would still expect us to honor Him in this way.

3. What are some words in Proverbs 11:7-9 that speak strongly to your life right now? Explain.

Expect a wide open discussion. Your class could easily turn into a counseling session for those who focus on painful words such as *delivered* and *trouble*. You may note some features of many proverbs that force us to face reality while creating hope. First, they often set forth a parallelism of thought as good is contrasted with bad. We all know that those two exist side by side in this fallen world (Matthew 13:30)—get used to it. Second, many proverbs show how the wicked ultimately are thwarted and the righteous are justified—expect it!

4. What was a time that someone revealed a secret that ended up hurting you? Have you ever done that to someone else? Why do you think people are so prone to gossip?

By sharing our personal experiences we can "feel the weight" of this proverb. It is not merely an academic issue but a very personal one. When we talk too much, there are serious consequences.

If the consequences are so damaging, then why do we so easily gossip? It seems that there is power in knowing juicy tidbits about others. It gives us a feeling of superiority. If we "know" something it must mean that we are important, and if someone else has sinned it must mean that we are better than they. But think about the reality. There is (for good or for bad) power in knowing personal information about others. But the moment you spill it, you lose that power as well as much of your personal integrity.

5. Some people easily and frequently seek the counsel of trusted individuals, while other people almost never do so. Why is that? What can we do to increase godly counsel in our lives?

Many in the Western world live in contexts that are based on *individualism*. We tend to move away from parents and grandparents, losing God's initial community of wisdom in our lives. We also have been taught from our earliest days that dependence on others is weakness. "We should stand on our own and rely on ourselves" is the message.

Our challenge is to overcome this attitude of self-reliance. That has to happen before we will be able to surround ourselves with godly counsel. Churches can help by reevaluating their programs that tend to be better at gathering crowds than they are at creating a community. Lots of people attend church in isolation and really don't know how to make a connection with mentors who could provide spiritual guidance.

Living Out Wisdom

May 28
Lesson 13

DEVOTIONAL READING: Proverbs 4:10-15.

BACKGROUND SCRIPTURE: Proverbs 31.

PRINTED TEXT: Proverbs 31:8-14, 25-30.

Proverbs 31:8-14, 25-30

8 Open thy mouth for the dumb in the cause of all such as are appointed to destruction.

9 Open thy mouth, judge righteously, and plead the cause of the poor and needy.

10 Who can find a virtuous woman? For her price is far above rubies.

11 The heart of her husband doth safely trust in her, so that he shall have no need of spoil.

12 She will do him good and not evil all the days of her life.

13 She seeketh wool, and flax, and worketh willingly with her hands.

14 She is like the merchants' ships; she bringeth her food from afar.

. . . .

25 Strength and honor are her clothing; and she shall rejoice in time to come.

26 She openeth her mouth with wisdom; and in her tongue is the law of kindness.

27 She looketh well to the ways of her household, and eateth not the bread of idleness.

28 Her children arise up, and call her blessed; her husband also, and he praiseth her.

29 Many daughters have done virtuously, but thou excellest them all.

30 Favor is deceitful, and beauty is vain: but a woman that feareth the LORD, she shall be praised.

GOLDEN TEXT: Favor is deceitful, and beauty is vain: but a woman that feareth the LORD, she shall be praised.—Proverbs 31:30.

Living in and as God's Creation
Unit 3: Lessons in Living
(Lessons 10-13)

Lesson Aims

After participating in this lesson, each student will be able to:

1. Describe the Old Testament ideal for wives and mothers.
2. Explain why principles of justice and character are best learned first in the home.
3. Write a thank-you letter to a woman who has been a godly influence in his or her life.

Lesson Outline

INTRODUCTION
   A. Godly Mothers and Wives
   B. Lesson Background
I. PLEADING FOR JUSTICE (Proverbs 31:8, 9)
   A. Defending the Silent (v. 8)
   B. Defending the Destitute (v. 9)
II. RECOGNIZING A NOBLE WOMAN (Proverbs 31:10-14)
   A. Worthy of Trust (vv. 10, 11)
   B. Brings Good (v. 12)
   C. Works Hard (vv. 13, 14)
     True Nobility
III. APPRECIATING A STRONG WOMAN (Proverbs 31:25-30)
   A. Honorable (v. 25)
   B. Wise (vv. 26, 27)
   C. Grateful Children (vv. 28, 29)
   D. Inner Beauty (v. 30)
     Hidden Treasures
CONCLUSION
   A. Superlative Womanhood
   B. Prayer
   C. Thought to Remember

Introduction

A. Godly Mothers and Wives

Traditional motherhood is under attack as never before. One of the current complaints of Generation X (those born between 1965 and 1980) is that they often were reared in very unstable family situations. Their parents (members of the Baby-Boomer Generation, born between 1946 and 1964) had divorces, substance abuse problems, and financial catastrophes. It is not uncommon to hear stories of Gen Xers who, in effect, became the parent, the responsible adult, in their households during their teenage years. Some tell stories of mothers who dragged them from marriage to marriage, boyfriend to boyfriend, nightmare to nightmare. They tell tales of abusive or absent fathers.

The Bible teaches us that it does not have to be this way. While all parties in a successful family are important, the book of Proverbs lifts up the essential nature of a stable wife and mother. Proverbs portrays a woman who gives selflessly to her children and to her husband. Such a woman is acting in a godly manner. The children of this kind of godly woman will "arise up, and call her blessed" (Proverbs 31:28).

The Bible is full of accounts about godly mothers. Think of Jochebed (mother of Moses), Hannah (mother of Samuel), Ruth (great-grandmother of David), Eunice (mother of Timothy), Mary (mother of Jesus), and others. Not all had stable or ideal situations. Hannah had a rival who tormented her (1 Samuel 1:6, 7). Ruth's husband and brother-in-law died (Ruth 1:3-5). Eunice probably had no help from her husband in young Timothy's spiritual upbringing (Acts 16:1; 2 Timothy 1:5; 3:14, 15).

Yet one thing these mothers had in common was their devotion to family. They loved unconditionally and unselfishly and are still remembered because of it. William Ross Wallace (1819–1881) wrote "the hand that rocks the cradle is the hand that rules the world." Let us never undervalue the call of God for godly mothers. [See question #1, page 383.]

B. Lesson Background

There is no question but that the household and family life reflected in the book of Proverbs is quite different from what we see in the modern, industrialized world. Our world of machines has made many household tasks quicker and simpler. In the ancient household, meal preparation was ongoing, almost throughout the day. Such preparations could require a trip to the market for items such as oil or meat. The household garden, which provided produce and spices, had to be tended.

Preparations also required the frequent baking of bread, perhaps made from flour that had been ground at the village mill (or by hand). Cooking was done using an open fire, and this required constant procurement of adequate fuel. Water had to be toted from the well, whether for drinking or for washing. Other household tasks were repetitive and numerous.

The idea of a woman having a job or career outside the home would have seemed impossible. There was no time! Stay-at-home wives were not women of leisure. They worked hard from dawn until dusk just keeping their households functioning.

Our modern world may have eliminated some of the work involved in managing a household. Yet this same world of conveniences has brought onto women new pressures that were undreamed of in the ancient world. Women in ancient times were not confronted with all the stresses of employment. Their children were less independent and less likely to be corrupted by bad influences outside the home. Divorce in the ancient world was uncommon. Even less common would have been the stresses of a blended household, where children from two families are brought together and expected to get along.

Few would want to go back to the grinding labor of the ancient household. Yet the modern home presents a complex series of challenges for wives and mothers. This week's lesson pictures the woman of Old Testament times, but we will find many principles that still apply today.

Proverbs 31 was not written by King Solomon, but rather by King Lemuel. In fact Proverbs 31:1 indicates that Lemuel's mother is the original source for this chapter. The name *Lemuel* means "one devoted to God." Outside of his name, we know nothing about this king. Some have suggested that Lemuel may be a nickname for Solomon himself, since he was characterized by his devotion to God early in life. If this is true, then the mother mentioned in Proverbs 31:1 was Bathsheba.

At any rate, it is amazing to see that the mother of the king knew the value of a woman who managed the household well. Even at the royal, wealthy level—where there are many servants—there was a need for a faithful wife and mother. Such a person was to be honored.

I. Pleading for Justice (Proverbs 31:8, 9)

A. Defending the Silent (v. 8)

8. Open thy mouth for the dumb in the cause of all such as are appointed to destruction.

Our first section deals with general issues of social justice. A constant theme in the Old Testament is the call for a fair society, where all people can have their basic needs met and live life with dignity. This is part of "Living Out Wisdom," our lesson title. God loves justice (Proverbs 21:3).

The word *dumb* refers to those who have no voice that matters. They have no political clout. They must suffer injustice without effective protest. They are further pictured as having been *appointed to destruction*. The most vivid example of a person in this condition comes in Isaiah's prophecy of the Messiah. He will be a suffering servant, comparable to the sheep that is silent before its shearers (Isaiah 53:7). Jesus fulfills this prophecy as an innocent man unjustly accused and executed, one who will not speak in His own defense.

Jesus suffered silently for our sins, but this is no excuse for letting the powerless in our communities endure injustice quietly. In democratic societies the citizens have voices that are heard if they are used. We who are able must speak up for the homeless, the poor, the weak, the sick, and the disabled. Jesus loved these people, and so must we.

B. Defending the Destitute (v. 9)

9. Open thy mouth, judge righteously, and plead the cause of the poor and needy.

The phrase *judge righteously* reveals an outstanding concept in the Old Testament. The concept of fair and impartial justice was a hallmark of Jewish law. This ideal stood opposed to

---

How to Say It

BATHSHEBA. Bath-*she*-buh.
DEUTERONOMY. Due-ter-*ahn*-uh-me.
EUNICE. U-*nye*-see or *U*-nis.
HANNAH. *Han*-uh.
ISAIAH. Eye-*zay*-uh.
JEREMIAH. Jair-uh-*my*-uh.
JOCHEBED. *Jock*-eh-bed.
LEMUEL. *Lem*-you-el.
LEVITICUS. Leh-*vit*-ih-kus.
SOLOMON. *Sol*-o-mun.

the all-too-often practice of awarding judgment based on a bribe.

Justice should never be for sale. Consistent justice for all parties is very difficult, but both the *poor* and the rich are entitled to justice in the Hebrew courts (Leviticus 19:15). Similarly, both citizens and resident aliens were to be given equal justice (Deuteronomy 1:16). Kings were appointed by God in order to judge righteously among the people (2 Chronicles 9:8). Ultimate justice, however, is to come with the Messiah (Jeremiah 23:5).

One wonders, however, what this has to do with the picture of the virtuous woman, the focus of Lemuel's proverbs. This is not entirely clear, but it makes sense to assume that Lemuel thinks that justice begins in the home. We learn our lessons of right and wrong, of fairness and unfairness, from our mothers. Mothers are naturally inclined to love all their children and not favor one over another. They have an innate sense of justice. This attitude serves anyone well who is called to render judgments.

II. Recognizing a Noble Woman (Proverbs 31:10-14)

A. Worthy of Trust (vv. 10, 11)

10, 11. Who can find a virtuous woman? For her price is far above rubies. The heart of her husband doth safely trust in her, so that he shall have no need of spoil.

Just as wisdom is better than rubies (Proverbs 3:15; 8:11), so is the *virtuous woman*. She cannot be bought. She is truly priceless. "A virtuous woman is a crown to her husband" (Proverbs 12:4). The essential idea behind *virtuous* is that of strong moral character. The virtuous person is not necessarily blessed with great physical beauty or strength. She displays her beauty in her life (compare 1 Peter 3:3, 4).

Lemuel knows that such a person may be overlooked when young men are seeking wives. They will be attracted to women of beauty. The wise man, however, realizes that a woman of integrity and moral strength is a great treasure. [See question #2, page 383.] If he can have such a woman for a wife, he has chosen most wisely. The result is that *he shall have no need of spoil,* meaning that he will then lack nothing of worth.

B. Brings Good (v. 12)

12. She will do him good and not evil all the days of her life.

Do him good has the sense here of repayment. The man who wisely chooses a virtuous wife will reap the reward many times over. She will be faithful to him *all the days of her life.*

How sad when marriages fall apart because of mistrust and selfishness. Lifelong commitment has become so rare that it surprises us when we encounter it. Sometimes a marriage fails because one or both of the partners is not virtuous. She is unfaithful to her husband, or he is unfaithful to his wife. Other times, however, marriages crash and burn because the partners do not esteem the faithfulness of their spouses. They mistake loyalty for boringness and take fidelity for granted. The relationship is neglected and loses the key ingredient of mutual respect.

This is not the course of the wise; it is the path of fools. Much later the apostle Paul will advise, "Husbands, love your wives, and be not bitter against them" (Colossians 3:19).

C. Works Hard (vv. 13, 14)

13, 14. She seeketh wool, and flax, and worketh willingly with her hands. She is like the merchants' ships; she bringeth her food from afar.

The manager of the ancient household works hard to provide for her family. She procures *wool* and *flax,* raw materials of clothing, so that she can provide garments for her family. She shops in unusual places to bring a variety of tasty meals to the family table. None of these things are done to earn the adoration of her children and husband, to earn "mother of the year"

This visual can be a backdrop to your question "How can we encourage godly motherhood?"

Visual for lesson 13

honors. She simply does these things because she loves her family.

True Nobility

Once upon a time (as the saying goes), nobility was a cherished virtue. *Nobility* conjures up the image of brave knights of old, rewarded by their king or queen with a title such as the fabled Sir Lancelot.

Yet it appears that nowadays the notion of nobility has been watered down considerably. Perhaps no society feels this more than the British. Just a few years ago, a committee of parliamentarians recommended doing away with the nobility system. Their report said that "Increasingly, titles appear to be an embarrassment rather than a cause for celebration."

The reason for this embarrassment is that the titles of nobility are given at the rate of some 3,000 per year, and not just to people who have made great contributions to British society. Recipients are more likely to include rock stars and lower-level bureaucrats who just happen to be good friends of members of parliament. As a result, some who really deserve recognition for their contributions refuse their titles in embarrassment.

But truly virtuous people aren't in it for the title anyway. The noble, virtuous woman of Proverbs 31 does her work because she treasures the blessings that come from God to those who exercise wisdom. She does not do it for the acclaim of some government bureau. Even so, she need not be embarrassed at any praise she receives, for it is a recognition of her godly virtue.
—C. R. B.

III. Appreciating a Strong Woman (Proverbs 31:25-30)

A. Honorable (v. 25)

25. Strength and honor are her clothing; and she shall rejoice in time to come.

Again, the virtuous woman is pictured as a person of great moral character. She is so confident that *she shall rejoice in time to come*. This is not cockiness or arrogance. It is because she does not fear the future. She knows that her children love her, her husband trusts and respects her, and that she is serving God by caring for her family. Of course she is confident! Why shouldn't she be? She is prepared for the days ahead.

B. Wise (vv. 26, 27)

26, 27. She openeth her mouth with wisdom; and in her tongue is the law of kindness. She looketh well to the ways of her household, and eateth not the bread of idleness.

The vast majority of women in the ancient world have little influence in community or national affairs. Yet Lemuel sees the virtuous woman as a source of *wisdom*. Her restricted sphere of influence does not limit her effectiveness. [See question #3, page 383.]

This wisdom is characterized three ways. First, she follows a *law of kindness*. The Hebrew word for *kindness* is one of the great words of the Old Testament. The word is variously translated *mercy* (Genesis 19:19), *loving-kindness* (Psalm 17:7), *kindness* (Joshua 2:12), etc. It is an eternal, essential quality of God. One reason we give thanks to God is that we know "his mercy endureth for ever" (Psalm 136:1). The virtuous woman is godly because she embodies this.

Second, the virtuous woman has set her priorities so that the efficient and happy operation of her household is her number one job. She doesn't let outside interests intrude at the expense of her husband and children. This is what it means when she *looketh well to the ways of her household*.

Third, she has no time for *idleness*. Ancient households may not have soap operas to watch, but there are temptations to idleness nonetheless (see 1 Timothy 5:13). She keeps herself busy. This is not for the sake of busyness or because she is a workaholic, but because she loves her family and takes great joy in serving them. [See question #4, page 383.]

C. Grateful Children (vv. 28, 29)

28, 29. Her children arise up, and call her blessed; her husband also, and he praiseth her. Many daughters have done virtuously, but thou excellest them all.

Too often conflicts come between a mother and her children in late childhood. Her strong love is mistaken for overprotectiveness. Her diligence is misunderstood as prying. Her steadiness is seen as boring and restrictive. The promise of this text, though, is that wise children will grow in their appreciation for a godly mother. They will grow up and join with their father to bless and praise this woman.

Lemuel departs from generalities and moves to the praise of a virtuous woman who is well

> **Home Daily Bible Readings**
>
> **Monday, May 22**—Advice for Children (Proverbs 4:1-9)
>
> **Tuesday, May 23**—Keep on the Right Path (Proverbs 4:10-15)
>
> **Wednesday, May 24**—Wise People Value Wise Conduct (Proverbs 10:18-23)
>
> **Thursday, May 25**—Advice from a Mother (Proverbs 31:1-9)
>
> **Friday, May 26**—Portrait of a Capable Wife (Proverbs 31:10-15)
>
> **Saturday, May 27**—What an Ideal Wife Is Like (Proverbs 31:16-23)
>
> **Sunday, May 28**—A Good Wife and Mother (Proverbs 31:24-31)

known to him—a real person. We do not know who this is. It may be his own mother (see Proverbs 31:1). It may be his wife. At any rate, some of us could disagree with him about the identity of the virtuous woman he describes throughout this chapter: we want to argue for our own mothers or wives as the most excellent of all virtuous women! If so, how blessed we are.

D. Inner Beauty (v. 30)

30. Favor is deceitful, and beauty is vain: but a woman that feareth the Lord, she shall be praised.

The central aspect of the virtuous woman's beauty is finally revealed: she *feareth the Lord*. This is not terror but rather obedient respect. With this verse, Proverbs has come full circle. Fear of the Lord was the beginning of knowledge and wisdom (Proverbs 1:7). Fear of the Lord is also the end of wisdom and worthy of praise.

This connection between fear and praise is found elsewhere in the Bible. Praise for God is expected from all who fear him (Psalm 22:23; Revelation 19:5). Yet in this verse it is the virtuous woman rather than God being praised. What is going on?

It's true that we never praise any human in the sense of worship. Worship is reserved only for God. But here we are called to praise this servant of God for her godly character. This is an honest expression of gratitude for someone who may not expect it but who richly deserves it.

I myself am the son of a truly virtuous woman who was tragically killed in an accident nearly 20 years ago. Fortunately I did tell her many times how much I appreciated her love for me and all she did to try and bring me up to be a man of God. I will always be in her debt, as will my children and grandchildren.

Hidden Treasures

Through the years the Philadelphia public school system had been given more than a thousand works of art of the previous two centuries. These included paintings, sculptures, and murals. After being on display for a while, they were put away in basements, boiler rooms, and closets throughout the system's 264 school buildings.

In 2004 school officials discovered that they had a treasure on their hands worth millions of dollars! Art experts said that over 100 of the pieces were "very important" works of art. Then came the question "What shall we do with it all?" The school system was in financial peril, so some wanted to sell the art. But the school system's chief of staff declared that the works should be kept to teach students the value of the arts.

Secular voices have concluded that the only place for a woman of value is in the world of business. To those who hold this view, only a woman with no talent, skill, or drive to succeed would be content to stay at home with her children. But such a judgment mirrors the school system's ignorance of its hidden treasures. Women who spend full time rearing their children with godly wisdom are true "works of art." Women who use God's gifts in the public square deserve honor too, but we must not overlook those who spend full time training the next generation in the ways of God. —C. R. B.

Conclusion

A. Superlative Womanhood

I recently read of a radio talk-show host who was running a contest to find the best all-around mother in his city. A young girl called in and spoke in such glowing terms about her mother that the host announced she was the prizewinner. Then the host asked, "What does she do?" Expecting to learn of some challenging career position, he was taken off guard when the little girl said, "She just stays at home to be my mom." The outraged host rudely withdrew the prize and hung up on the child.

Society has developed a certain contempt for the traditional role of devoted wife and mother. Economic pressures have forced many mothers into the labor force. Some women manage to juggle the demands of job and family very well, often by gaining the help of husband and children. Others realize that the growing-up years of their children are irreplaceable, so they sacrifice in other ways to stay at home with their families. Both models of motherhood can be successful, given the right motivations and circumstances.

The lesson of Proverbs, however, is that the woman who concentrates on household management should not be looked down upon or disrespected. A virtuous woman is identified by her devotion to godliness and to her family. This does not mean, by the way, that single women cannot be godly. If they are virtuous they too will find ways to serve church and family. [See question #5, page 383.]

B. Prayer

Holy and righteous Father, we thank You for providing us with mothers and the institution of motherhood. Help us to appreciate our mothers and our wives and to have the courage to express this appreciation to them. We pray for our mothers and our wives to have a proper fear for You that leads them to a wise and satisfying life. In the name of Your only Son, Jesus Christ, amen.

C. Thought to Remember

"I regard no man as poor
who has a godly mother."
—Abraham Lincoln

Learning by Doing

This section contains an alternative lesson plan emphasizing learning activities. Classes desiring such student involvement will find these suggestions helpful.

Learning Goals

After participating in this lesson, each student will be able to:
1. Describe the Old Testament ideal for wives and mothers.
2. Explain why principles of justice and character are best learned first in the home.
3. Write a thank-you letter to a woman who has been a godly influence in his or her life.

Into the Lesson

For this activity provide your class with colored pencils/markers and paper. (Space for this activity is also provided in the student books.) Ask students to draw a picture of an ideal wife or mother. The picture may be realistic, abstract, or even a stick figure, depending on the skill of the artist. The important thing is to show the qualities represented by their ideal wife or mother.

Allow several minutes for your class to finish their drawings. Then ask volunteers to share their work, indicating which features were most important to them. Make a list of those characteristics on the board. Then tell your class that this lesson will analyze the qualities of a godly woman as discussed in Proverbs 31.

Into the Word

Begin this portion of the lesson by using the lesson commentary to explain the meaning of Proverbs 31:8, 9. Point out that King Lemuel was taught these principles of justice by his mother, as indicated by the first verse of the chapter. The rest of the chapter is a tribute to a wife of noble character or a virtuous woman.

After you finish your lecture, divide your class into several small groups. Half of the groups will do the three activities in *Exercise One*. The other half will complete the three activities in *Exercise Two*. If your class does not use the student books, you will need to provide copies of the exercise activities for each group. Allow 10 minutes for groups to complete the exercise activities. Then ask each group to report its findings to the entire class.

Exercise One

Activity A: Have a volunteer read aloud Proverbs 31:10-14. Identify what you think is the theme of this passage.

Activity B: Work as a group to paraphrase these verses. Since this passage was written in ancient times, you may need to modernize some of the tasks for which the virtuous woman is praised.

Activity C: Discuss the following questions about the text:

1. How important to a healthy marriage is mutual trust between husband and wife?
2. Our society says marital fidelity is optional. How would King Lemuel respond to that?
3. In King Lemuel's day, most wives stayed home and managed the household. Today, many wives have to work outside the home to supplement the family income. How are verses 13 and 14 still relevant today?

Exercise Two

Activity A: Have a volunteer read aloud Proverbs 31:25-30. Identify what you think is the theme of this passage.

Activity B: Work as a group to paraphrase these verses. Since this passage was written in ancient times, you may need to modernize some of the tasks for which the virtuous woman is praised.

Activity C: Discuss the following questions about the text:

1. How does strong moral character help a person to face the uncertainties of the future?
2. What is "the law of kindness"?
3. What kind of example does a virtuous woman set for her children that causes her husband and children to praise her?
4. What is the ultimate source of her wisdom?

Into Life

To close today's lesson, provide paper and pens for students to write thank-you notes to godly women who have influenced their lives. Such women could include students' mothers, sisters, or Bible school teachers—any woman who has made a spiritual impact on them. The notes should explain briefly why these women have been positive influences and indicate some of their godly traits that most affected the note writers' lives.

After several minutes of writing, have volunteers read their thank-you notes to the class. Encourage students to mail their notes.

Let's Talk It Over

These questions are designed to promote discussion of the lesson. The answers here are only discussion starters. Let your class talk it over from there.

1. If you were to submit your own mother as "mother of the year" (even if she is deceased), what would you say about her? What did she do that blessed your life?

This should be an easy question to answer. Perhaps it would be best to have each person participate if the class is of such a size as to make that possible. This will help the class to think along the same lines: What makes a woman godly and worthy of honor? Encourage students to keep their answers short and limited to one or two characteristics or behaviors.

2. How is a virtuous woman like a treasure? What benefits can she bring to her husband or potential future husband? How can her husband show his gratitude for all she does?

First of all, the question "Who can find a virtuous woman?" does not necessarily mean that virtuous women are hard to find. In the poetic imagery, such a woman is being compared to rubies. The point is that she is valuable, not that she is rarely seen.

The second question isn't meant to ignore single women, but it recognizes that the vast majority of women will be married at some point in their lives. Some benefits she brings to her husband are obvious; some are less obvious. She works hard, increasing the value of the home. She offers valuable input on financial priorities. She honors the distinction in gender roles that God has established. She exercises godly discretion in many ways. The list goes on!

3. What do you think are the most important things a woman can communicate to her children and her husband? What are the benefits of such communication?

A woman can and should communicate to her children that they are loved unconditionally. She is a model of unselfish labor (as is the husband) for the benefit of the family as a whole. Her children see in her an example of faithfulness to her husband. Most of all, she communicates Christlikeness that her children may follow the Lord.

With regard to her husband, she can communicate love, faithfulness, and devotion in various ways. None of her words or deeds give anyone a hint that he is not supported, respected, and cherished in her eyes. This honors God.

4. In the twenty-first century, what's the difference between *rest* and *idleness?* Why is it important to draw a distinction?

God himself established the concept of rest (Exodus 16:23; 31:15). Although we do not observe the Sabbath in the New Testament era, we still need times to recharge. God never intended us to operate 24/7/365. The concept of periodic rest has its foundation in the fact that God rested from His labors after creating the heavens and the earth (Genesis 2:2). If He needed to rest, who are we to think that we don't?

A chaplain had this saying as the screensaver on his computer: "Thank God it's Monday!" He, like most others, looked forward to some down time after a week of work. But he also knew the value of getting back to work after recharging. Those who live lives of aimless distraction in an entertainment-oriented culture may find that viewpoint baffling. They are often guilty of idleness (Proverbs 19:15; Ecclesiastes 10:18).

5. What can our church do to empower women to fulfill their giftedness to the glory of God? What do the women of our church need in order to become the godly women they were intended to be?

The answer to this question will vary depending on the ministries the church already has in place as well as its cultural and geographic setting. Nonetheless, most churches would benefit from an organized women's ministry where women can communicate, encourage, and train one another to exercise their spiritual gifts.

Most churches would also benefit from marriage retreats that help women find satisfaction and joy in their primary relationships. And most churches could use a healthy dose of doctrinal preaching on the biblical role of women in all its multifaceted diversity.

Care should be exercised so that this becomes neither a gripe session nor a merely academic exercise. Listen as women tell how we can help them best serve God and the body of Christ.

Quarter Review

Use this page to form questions for the class to answer and discuss. Then provide the information as a handout to summarize the lessons of the past quarter.

Lesson 1: God Made Us Special

The familiar eighth chapter of Psalms provides the basis for this study. It acknowledges the seeming insignificance of people in comparison to the vast creation. At the same time it heralds the unique privilege of man: God is mindful of him!

Lesson 2: God Created Wonderful Things

Lesson 1 noted the special place of people in God's creation. This is a good sequel, as it notes that all of creation is marvelous. It's most important feature may be that it moves—or ought to move—each person to worship the creator.

Lesson 3: God Created and Knows Us

This lesson returns to the special place of people in God's creation. God did not simply create the world and then step back to watch from afar. He knows us intimately. He personally formed each one. We are never far from His loving care.

Lesson 4: Sing Praise to the Creator

Summing up the unit on creation, this lesson describes our response: praise. We praise God for His creation, but we praise Him for very much more—for His works, but also for His nature, for what He does and for who He is.

Lesson 5: Responding to Tragedy

The name Job is well known to Bible students, but most know little of the book that bears his name. Lessons 5-7 will summarize his plight. The key for today is that Job did not speak evil of God when bad things happened to him.

Lesson 6: Searching for Hope

Job's story is longer than can be covered in detail in five lessons, so we take samplings from the book. This text contains an excerpt from chapter 14, a thrilling Old Testament affirmation of life beyond the grave!

Lesson 7: God Gives Life

What Job could only vaguely anticipate we know from historical evidence: resurrection! This lesson puts God's question to Job, "Have you seen the gates of death?" side by side with the account of Jesus' tearing down those gates!

Lesson 8: Finding Life's Meaning

The "Preacher's" dreary assessment of life "under the sun," as presented in Ecclesiastes, begs the question of how to find meaning in life. Jesus' appearances to His disciples, after His resurrection, provide more than sufficient answers.

Lesson 9: Living in God's Time

Time is the only commodity given in equal amounts to everyone: 24 hours a day. Ecclesiastes reminds us that our time is valuable and must be prioritized. God gives us "a time for everything" that He wants done in His world.

Lesson 10: Seek Wisdom

The final four lessons of the quarter come from Proverbs, which may well be titled with the title of this lesson: Seek Wisdom. This lesson especially zeroes in on this quest, including the familiar verses 5 and 6 of chapter 3.

Lesson 11: Accept Wisdom's Invitation

Wisdom is sometimes portrayed as hidden treasure, something to be searched for with diligence. In this lesson wisdom is seeking, calling out. If we have failed to "find" wisdom, we simply have refused her open invitation.

Lesson 12: Follow the Path of Integrity

Sometimes the dishonest think themselves clever, skillfully outwitting others to their own advantage. Such cleverness is not true wisdom. Wisdom is known by righteousness and justice. To be wise in God's sight demands integrity.

Lesson 13: Living Out Wisdom

We all need examples to help us understand precepts, and Proverbs 31 gives us one. The "virtuous woman" is not a lesson on how to be a good wife or how to find a good wife. She is a model for all who would live a life of wisdom.

Copyright © 2005. STANDARD PUBLISHING, Cincinnati, Ohio. Permission is granted to reproduce this page for ministry purposes only. Not for resale.

Summer Quarter, 2006

Called to Be a Christian Community

(1 & 2 Corinthians)

Special Features

	Page
Quarterly Quiz	386
The Old and the New .... Tom Thatcher	387
Paul and the Corinthians (map)	389
Called to be a Christian Community [Chart Feature]	390
The Teacher's Dilemma: "What's Next?" [Teacher Tips]	391
Quarter Review	393
How to Say It	394

Lessons

Unit 1: Servants of God

June	4	Serving in Unity .... 1 Corinthians 1:10-17	395
	11	Serving with Spiritual Wisdom .... 1 Corinthians 2	404
	18	Serving Together .... 1 Corinthians 3:1-15	413
	25	Serving Faithfully .... 1 Corinthians 4:1-13	422

Unit 2: Called to Obedience

July	2	Called to Relationships .... 1 Corinthians 7:1-15	431
	9	Called to Help the Weak .... 1 Corinthians 8	440
	16	Called to Win the Race .... 1 Corinthians 9:24–10:13	449
	23	Called to the Common Good .... 1 Corinthians 12:1-13	458
	30	Called to Love .... 1 Corinthians 13	467

Unit 3: The Spirit of Giving

August	6	Giving Forgiveness .... 2 Corinthians 2:5-11; 7:2-15	476
	13	Giving Generously .... 2 Corinthians 8:1-15	485
	20	Giving Is a Witness .... 2 Corinthians 9:3-15	494
	27	Giving Sufficient Grace .... 2 Corinthians 12:1-10	503

About These Lessons

One definition of *community* is "a unified body of individuals who have a set of common interests." So far, so good! But what exactly are those common interests for Christians? This quarter's lessons provide answers.

Quarterly Quiz

This quiz can be used to preview the lessons, to review at the end of the quarter, or as a review after each lesson. The quiz may be copied and distributed to students. **The answers are on page 392.**

Lesson 1
1. Some from Chloe's house reported that a faction in the Corinthian church was following John. T/F. *1 Corinthians 1:10, 11*
2. Paul was grateful for having had the opportunity to baptize at Corinth. T/F. *1 Corinthians 1:14*

Lesson 2
1. Paul visited the Corinthians with fear, trembling, and what? (weakness, paralysis, blindness?) *1 Corinthians 2:3*
2. Paul spoke the wisdom of God in a what? (dream, mystery, panic?) *1 Corinthians 2:7*

Lesson 3
1. Paul planted, _____ watered, and God gave the increase. *1 Corinthians 3:6*
2. Paul considered the Corinthians to be co-laborers. T/F. *1 Corinthians 3:9*

Lesson 4
1. Paul's role in relation to the mysteries of God was that of what? (priest, referee, steward?) *1 Corinthians 4:1*
2. Paul's reaction to being reviled was to what? (run, bless, pray?) *1 Corinthians 4:12*

Lesson 5
1. A valid reason to get married is to avoid fornication. T/F. *1 Corinthians 7:2*
2. Paul says that it is never a good idea to remain single. T/F. *1 Corinthians 7:8*
3. A Christian woman should divorce her non-Christian husband. T/F. *1 Corinthians 7:13*

Lesson 6
1. Paul discussed the problem of _____ that had been sacrificed to idols. *1 Corinthians 8*
2. Knowledge has a tendency to make a person arrogant. T/F. *1 Corinthians 8:1*

Lesson 7
1. Paul used illustrations of what two kinds of athlete? (runner/boxer, swimmer/runner, boxer/weight lifter?) *1 Corinthians 9:24-27*
2. God won't let us be tempted beyond what we can bear. T/F. *1 Corinthians 10:13*

Lesson 8
1. There are diversities of spiritual gifts, but the same Spirit. T/F. *1 Corinthians 12:4*
2. We were all baptized into one what? (body, conscience, spiritual gift?) *1 Corinthians 12:13*

Lesson 9
1. Without charity (love), tongues are no better than sounding _____. *1 Corinthians 13:1*
2. What three things abide? (belief/faith/trust, faith/hope/charity, thinking/believing/speaking?) *1 Corinthians 13:13*

Lesson 10
1. Paul freely confessed that he was ignorant of Satan's devices. T/F. *2 Corinthians 2:11*
2. Paul asked forgiveness for wronging, corrupting, and defrauding some people accidentally. T/F. *2 Corinthians 7:2*
3. Godly sorrow can lead to repentance. T/F. *2 Corinthians 7:10*

Lesson 11
1. Paul does not mention tithing in 2 Corinthians 8. T/F.
2. Paul used the churches of what province as an example to the Corinthians? (Achaia, Pontus, Macedonia?) *2 Corinthians 8:1*
3. Paul did not use his authority as an apostle to command the Corinthians to give. T/F. *2 Corinthians 8:8*

Lesson 12
1. To sow sparingly will result in reaping _____. *2 Corinthians 9:6*
2. The Corinthians' generous gift would not only supply a need but result in what? (greater business opportunities, thanksgivings, a tax deduction?) *2 Corinthians 9:12*

Lesson 13
1. Which heaven was Paul caught up to in his vision? (seventh heaven, third heaven, first and only heaven?) *2 Corinthians 12:2*
2. Paul's thorn was a what of Satan? (affliction, deception, messenger?) *2 Corinthians 12:7*

The Old and the New

by Tom Thatcher

IN 1864 U.S. President Abraham Lincoln and General Ulysses S. Grant were determined to end the American Civil War. One key element in their strategy was for General George Sherman to capture the city of Atlanta.

After protracted fighting with heavy casualties on both sides, the mayor of Atlanta finally surrendered the city. Little remained to be handed over, however, since much of the city and the surrounding region had been destroyed. Yet this short-term devastation did not reduce Atlanta's long-term status as a cultural and economic center. Today, Atlanta is one of the most modern American cities.

The ancient city of Corinth, home of a church that received two of the apostle Paul's epistles, was much like Atlanta in this regard. Corinth was a center of Greek commerce and culture until Roman forces destroyed the city in 146 B.C. After lying in ruins for a century, Julius Caesar rebuilt Corinth in 44 B.C. The city quickly became large and wealthy.

When Paul arrived there in the early A.D. 50s, Corinth was a center of business, culture, and pagan religion; often those three overlapped to a great degree. In a world where many cities were so old that they could not trace their history, everything in Corinth was relatively new and developing.

The Corinthian church that received Paul's letters was also new and developing. Paul founded the church there in about A.D. 52 and wrote the church two letters five years later. These letters reveal that the new believers were struggling to escape from their old way of life, being divided over a variety of issues. They were constantly tempted by the surrounding culture of material wealth. First and 2 Corinthians remain relevant because they speak to so many aspects of our own battle to remain true to the gospel.

Unit 1: June
Servants of God

Paul opens 1 Corinthians by noting reports of division within the church (1:10, 11) and spends the first four chapters of that book addressing this serious problem. A divided church cannot even hope to provide the mutual support and encouragement that believers need to resist the world, much less proclaim the gospel.

Lesson 1 establishes the basis for Christian unity. Paul insists that unity is not optional, then exposes the Corinthians' partisan spirit. The believers seem to have split into factions centered on their favorite teachers. But Paul reminds them that Christ is undivided. A church focused on Christ can work together effectively to reach a lost world.

Lesson 2 highlights the unity of the gospel by emphasizing its source. While God provides the church with gifted leaders and teachers, true spiritual wisdom does not originate with any of these people. It does not even originate with Paul. True wisdom comes from God's Spirit alone. True teachers will point people to this fact rather than cause division by pointing to themselves.

In **Lesson 3** Paul demonstrates that the church's growth and development is a team effort. That growth does not depend on the brilliance of individuals but rather on the diverse gifts of many people working together.

Paul uses himself as an illustration of this principle in **Lesson 4**. God is aware of each person's work and the motives behind it. He expects us to do what we are called to do. Paul is only a servant himself. His humble position makes it ridiculous to think that the church would be divided between himself, Apollos, and other leaders. All of them are servants of God, and all of them point others to serve with similar humility.

Unit 2: July
Called to Obedience

Having addressed the general problem of division, Paul turns to a series of specific issues that were facing the church. As young believers, the Corinthians were daily enticed to return to the immoral lifestyle of the surrounding culture. Underlying all these problems was a basic misunderstanding of the nature of Christian relationships. Selfless love for others is one of the greatest commandments. It is essential to Christian morality.

Lesson 5 lays out the foundation for sexual purity. Believers are not obligated to get married but must understand that any and all sexual activity outside the bond of marriage is sinful. Marriage is a sacred union, one that should not be entered into lightly, because adultery and divorce are not options for Christians. What a change in mind-set the Corinthians needed!

Lesson 6 addresses the serious problem of moral "gray areas." These are activities that are not specifically forbidden by God but that may become faith issues for some believers. The Corinthians were confronted with the problem of whether to eat meat offered to idols, similar to our modern debates over whether to watch certain types of movies.

In theory, Paul says, the meat/idols issue is not a problem. In practice it touches on a larger, and ultimately much more important, question: How do our actions affect other people? If our example hurts another person's faith or hinders the cause of the gospel, then we choose to abstain even when the Scripture would grant us liberty.

In **Lesson 7** Paul calls us to lives of preparation and self-discipline. Temptations are inevitable, but failure is not. Using examples from sports and the Israelites' wandering in the desert, Paul urges his readers to be ready for their own inevitable challenges. These will be times of temptation. Sometimes temptation feels overwhelming. But God will not allow any tests to come our way that we are not able to pass.

While we often think of temptation in terms of "big ticket" sins such as adultery or stealing, **Lesson 8** touches on one of our most significant challenges: pride. God has blessed Christians with a variety of spiritual gifts in order to equip the church for effective ministry. All these gifts proceed from the same Lord and are intended to serve the common good. Yet it is easy to get caught up in the glamour of certain skills, especially those that place us in the public eye. Paul reminds us that we are all members of one body, each called to fulfill God's purpose.

Lesson 9 explores one of the most beautiful, and most familiar, passages of the Bible. Commonly called the Love Chapter, 1 Corinthians 13 provides a central thesis for this letter: love never fails. But love is not primarily a feeling or an emotion; it is, rather, an observable pattern of behavior. It is actions that we do and do not do to and for others. All the spiritual gifts over which the Corinthian church divided itself would one day fade into oblivion, but love lasts forever. Love is greater than any spiritual gift that we may possess.

Unit 3: August
The Spirit of Giving

Unit 3 focuses on several passages from 2 Corinthians. Written within several months of the first epistle, 2 Corinthians highlights the theme of giving. Giving includes not only tangible things such as money and possessions but also the vitally important intangible of forgiveness.

Lesson 10 offers what may be the sequel to 1 Corinthians 5. Paul had been shocked to learn that the church was tolerating a member who was sexually involved with his stepmother. Such a person was to be removed from fellowship until he repented. Whether 2 Corinthians 2:5-11 deals with that case or some other, Paul's earlier exhortations led to an unforgiving attitude. But that was not what Paul intended. While the church must remain pure, it must also remain generous in forgiveness upon repentance.

Lessons 11 and 12 urge us to be generous with our material resources as well. Sharing is not just the responsibility of the rich but is rather an inherent aspect of Christian fellowship. God often answers the prayers of others through our helping hand. When we give we imitate the unspeakable gift that comes from God through Christ.

Lesson 13 closes the unit by emphasizing God's grace. The Corinthians were beset with many challenges—so many that they could have felt overwhelmed. Paul's own "thorn in the flesh" demonstrates that we are often strongest at our weakest moments, because at these times we are forced to rely solely on God's power.

A World of Change

We are living in a world that changes constantly. New problems and temptations come our way daily, challenging us to abandon the ancient faith. Like the Corinthians, we must confront these challenges with a sharp awareness that we are to be different. No matter the circumstances, we are to live lives of love for others. We do that by relying on the Spirit's strength and always following the voice of Christ. What a community!

Paul and the Corinthians
BLACK SEA
ADRIATIC SEA
MEDITERRANEAN SEA
ITALY
MACEDONIA
THRACIA
ACHAIA
ASIA
CRETE
Philippi
Thessalonica
Berea
Athens
Corinth
Troas
Ephesus
Miletus
Laodicea
Rhodes
In Macedonia, Paul received an encouraging report about the Corinthians from Titus. 2 Corinthians 7:5-7
Paul was in Ephesus (A.D. 55/56) when he wrote 1 Corinthians. 1 Corinthians 16:8, 9
Paul established the church at Corinth in A.D. 50. Acts 18

Called to Be a Christian Community

Unit 1: Servants of God
- Live in unity
- Find wisdom
- Build wisdom
- Serve responsibly

Unit 2: Called to Obedience
- Build relationships
- Help others
- Run the race
- Commit to the common good
- Love as God loves

Unit 3: The Spirit of Giving
- Offers forgiveness
- Gives generously
- Witnesses to others
- Rejoices in God's grace

Teacher Tips

The Teacher's Dilemma: "What's next?"

EVERY FEW WEEKS, Sunday school classes must begin a new study. The question, "What should we study next?" makes us cringe because it comes up so often! Frequently, the study will be that of the teacher's own choice, and the focus may be limited to one of a half dozen favorite themes. Some classes decide by taking a vote, and the result is a curriculum with little structure and no plan for systematic Bible study.

Many teachers have discovered that the best solution to this problem lies in using a teaching commentary that offers International Sunday School Lessons (ISSL) from the Uniform Lesson Series. But how do you go about choosing a good teaching commentary? Five key factors may help you decide.

High View

First and foremost, a good teaching commentary must display a high view of Scripture. "All Scripture is God-breathed and is useful for teaching, rebuking, correcting and training in righteousness, so that the man of God may be thoroughly equipped for every good work" (2 Timothy 3:16, 17). A good teaching commentary starts from that premise. Its writers and editors are committed to that truth; it's the reason they do what they do.

A high view of Scripture recognizes that the message of the Bible is both timeless and timely. It is eternal (Revelation 14:6)—it applies to all people of all time. Yet it is relevant and personal. The good teaching commentary will find ways to make personal application of these eternal truths.

Comprehensive Coverage

From the first point naturally flows the second: the commentary should offer comprehensive Bible coverage. The Bible in its entirety is God's Word, so a good teaching commentary will present lessons from every portion of the Word. It will balance New Testament and Old Testament studies. It will present those favorite passages we all like to read, but it will also delve into more difficult or obscure passages. One of the most important features will be an attempt to cover the whole breadth of Scripture within a reasonable period of time. The best teaching commentaries that are based on the ISSL format do just that. Within a brief cycle of years, adults gain a good overview of the message of the Bible. The cycles that follow do not simply repeat the previous ones but shift to different passages. The treatment is fresh each time.

Relevant to Culture

Cultural relevance concerns the ability of the lesson to connect the eternal, inspired truth of Scripture to people in the here and now. Many lessons stop when the text has been explored and the students informed of what the text meant in its original context, the historical background, and the cultural practices of the past. Better lessons will help the students to apply the principles to today's culture. Students do not leave the classroom wondering, "So what?"

Effective Communication

Closely related to cultural relevance is the ability of the lesson commentary to communicate effectively. The Bible is an ancient book, written in ancient languages scarcely even spoken today. To bring those ancient languages to life requires more than mere translation into English. The English translation may contain words or phrases that, even in English, sound strange to modern ears. These terms must be explained or even illustrated. A helpful feature in some books is a pronunciation guide for those biblical names or other hard-to-pronounce terms.

Unfortunately, some teaching commentaries make the mistake of trying to communicate too academically in such explanations. The mere fact that the students are adults and can understand

> **Answers to Quarterly Quiz on page 386**
>
> **Lesson 1**—1. false. 2. false. **Lesson 2**—1. weakness. 2. mystery. **Lesson 3**—1. Apollos. 2. true. **Lesson 4**—1. steward. 2. bless. **Lesson 5**—1. true. 2. false. 3. false. **Lesson 6**—1. meat. 2. true. **Lesson 7**—1. runner/boxer. 2. true. **Lesson 8**—1. true 2. body. **Lesson 9**—1. brass. 2. faith/hope/charity. **Lesson 10**—1. false. 2. false. 3. true. **Lesson 11**—1. true. 2. Macedonia. 3. true. **Lesson 12**—1. sparingly. 2. thanksgivings. **Lesson 13**—1. third heaven. 2. messenger.

complicated text does not mean they want to communicate at that level. Instead, many prefer to communicate through story. The better teaching commentaries use verbal illustrations to help reach these learners. That fact leads to the fifth key.

Variety of Methods

A good teaching commentary takes into account a variety of teaching methods and learning styles. How do you like to teach? How do your students best get involved in the learning process? The teaching commentary must facilitate these methods. Some commentaries provide little more than lecture material because that is the easiest kind of material to provide. But while lecture has its place—face it, adults who attend church are used to it!—it is not always the best method. Adults love to talk and discuss issues. The best teaching commentaryies must provide an opportunity for them to answer the question, "What do you think?"

On the other hand, some adults are more kinetic in their learning style. They love learning activities: crossword puzzles, word search exercises, journaling, drama, problem-solving, case studies—all these are helpful in reaching specific learning styles of specific learners. The better teaching commentaries provide these.

Beyond having versatile teaching methods, a teachable commentary provides a variety of teaching aids. Visualization of biblical themes has been part of the Christian tradition since the first century, when believers used to sketch a fish in the dust to represent their faith in "Jesus Christ, God's Son, Savior." Today's better teaching commentaries will provide maps, charts, Bible art, and other visual aids.

With some there are additional resources, such as large, colorful posters that display the maps, charts, and other visual aids cited in the commentary. In an age in which computers are taking a greater and greater role, some publishers are offering CD's that include Bible study helps, reproducible student handouts, and projectable helps like maps, visual aids, or even whole PowerPoint® slide presentations.

The *Standard Lesson Commentary*

The commentary you are holding in your hands right now meets your teaching needs in all five areas. Coupled with the quarterly *Adult Resources* (containing the visuals pictured in each week's lesson plus a variety of helps on a CD) or available electronically (as the *Standard Lesson eCommentary*), the *Standard Lesson Commentary* measures up to the highest standards of a teaching commentary. It offers the finest study outline (the International Sunday School Lessons), an unabashedly high view of Scripture, comprehensive Bible coverage, cultural relevance, the ability to communicate effectively, and a variety of sound teaching methods. With the *Standard Lesson Commentary*, you will never again have to ask, "What's next?"

Quarter Review

Use this page to form questions for the class to answer and discuss. Then provide the information as a handout to summarize the lessons of the summer quarter.

Lesson 1: Serving in Unity

Paul's first letter to the Corinthians was written to a divided church. As such it will find a great timeliness for study today. Paul's solution is still the best: unity in Christ alone. As some have more recently stated it: "No creed but Christ."

Lesson 2: Serving with Spiritual Wisdom

We live in an age of spectacular advances in technology—and a corresponding arrogance in man's wisdom. This lesson counters that with the truth that only spiritual wisdom offers the answers to the eternal questions of life.

Lesson 3: Serving Together

With marvelous word pictures drawn from agriculture and construction, Paul makes a case for unity. We are but tools in God's hands, he says, fellow workers in God's enterprise. All reason for pride and division evaporate in that light.

Lesson 4: Serving Faithfully

With the fourth chapter of 1 Corinthians, Paul wraps up his discussion of unity. Since we serve in God's enterprise and not our own (chapter 3), then we are but stewards of the grace of God. Our task is to be faithful to His charge!

Lesson 5: Called to Relationships

Once again the text seems especially timely, as Paul addresses the theme of marriages between Christians and non-Christians. Not surprisingly, faith love is the rule. Even one Christian in the marriage ought to make that relationship better!

Lesson 6: Called to Help the Weak

Like many other good things, Christian liberty can be abused. Paul cites a specific example in Corinth in which some were pushing the bounds of liberty beyond the measure of Christian love. That was wrong, he said. And it still is.

Lesson 7: Called to Win the Race

Today's text is one of the passages that cause many to believe that Paul was a sports fan. Whether or not he was a fan, he recognized the similarities between a race and the Christian life. Both require focus, exertion, and endurance.

Lesson 8: Called to the Common Good

Spiritual gifts were a hot topic in Paul's day even as they are today. What Paul told the Corinthians holds true for miraculous and non-miraculous gifts, ancient and modern: the gifts are to help others, not to exalt the gifted!

Lesson 9: Called to Love

Squarely in the middle of Paul's discussion of spiritual gifts is the marvelous "love chapter" of the Bible. What the apostle says here puts spiritual gifts, and every other kind of service, in perspective. Without love, they are all worthless!

Lesson 10: Giving Forgiveness

Following a lesson on love with one on forgiveness seems a natural link. Our texts, however, are separated by several months and much activity. The result was that sinners had come to repentance, and forgiveness was in order!

Lesson 11: Giving Generously

When Paul earlier visited Corinth, the church had promised to help the poor saints in Judea. Here Paul follows up on their promise, cites the Macedonians' example, and gives us timeless principles for giving.

Lesson 12: Giving Is a Witness

We've heard it often, and it applies in so many arenas of life: a man reaps what he sows. Here the application is to our giving, and it seems paradoxical. The more you give, the more you have? In God's economy, that's it exactly.

Lesson 13: Giving Sufficient Grace

What was Paul's "thorn in the flesh"? Many suggestions have been offered, but no one really knows. It's not important. The grace sufficient to overcome the weakness of the thorn is what is important. It was for Paul, and it is for us.

Copyright © 2005. STANDARD PUBLISHING, Cincinnati, Ohio. Permission is granted to reproduce this page for ministry purposes only. Not for resale.

How to Say It

Use this list to help you pronounce the names and hard-to-pronounce words in the lessons of the summer quarter.

A
ACHAIA. Uh-*kay*-uh.
AESOP. *Ee*-sup.
APOLLO. Uh-*pah*-low.
APOLLOS. Uh-*pahl*-us.
ATHENS. *Ath*-unz.

B
BAAL PEOR. Bay-al-*pe*-or.
BARNABAS. *Bar*-nuh-bus.
BEREA. Buh-*ree*-uh.

C
CARTHAGE. *Car*-thij.
CEPHAS. *See*-fus.
CHLOE. *Klo*-ee.
COLOSSIANS. Kuh-*losh*-unz.
CORINTH. *Kor*-inth.
CRISPUS. *Kris*-pus.

D
DAMASCUS. Duh-*mass*-kus.
DELPHI. *Del*-fi.
DIONYSIUS. Die-oh-*nish*-ih-us.

E
EGYPT. *Ee*-jipt.
EPHESIANS. Ee-*fee*-zhunz.
EPHESUS. *Ef*-uh-sus.

F
FORNICATION. for-neh-*kay*-shun.

G
GAIUS. *Gay*-us.
GALATIA. Guh-*lay*-shuh.
GENTILES. *Jen*-tiles.

H
HEBREWS. *Hee*-brews.
HOSEA. Ho-*zay*-uh.

I
ISAIAH. Eye-*zay*-uh.
ISTHMIAN. *Is*-me-unh.

J
JEREMIAH. Jair-uh-*my*-uh.
JERUSALEM. Juh-*roo*-suh-lem.

K
KOINONIA (Greek). koy-no-*nee*-uh.
KORAH. *Ko*-rah.

L
LAMENTATIONS. Lam-en-*tay*-shunz.
LEVITICUS. Leh-*vit*-ih-kus.

M
MACEDONIA. Mass-eh-*doe*-nee-uh.
MALACHI. *Mal*-uh-kye.
MOABITE. *Mo*-ub-ite.
MOSAIC. Mo-*zay*-ik.
MOSES. *Mo*-zes or *Mo*-zez.

N
NIEBUHR. *Nee*-burr.

P
PHARAOH. *Fair*-o or *Fay*-roe.
PHILIPPI. Fih-*lip*-pie or *Fil*-ih-pie.
POTIPHAR. *Pot*-ih-far.

S
SANHEDRIN. *San*-huh-drun or San-*heed*-run.
STEPHANAS. *Stef*-uh-nass.
SYNAGOGUE. *sin*-uh-gog.

T
THESSALONIANS. *Thess*-uh-*lo*-nee-unz (strong accent on *lo*; th as in *thin*).
THESSALONICA. *Thess*-uh-lo-*nye*-kuh (strong accent on *nye*; th as in *thin*).
TITUS. *Ty*-tus.
TROAS. *Tro*-az.
TROPHIMUS. *Troff*-ih-muss.

Z
ZECHARIAH. *Zek*-uh-*rye*-uh (strong accent on *rye*).
ZEUS. Zoose.

Serving in Unity

395

June 4
Lesson 1

Devotional Reading: 1 Corinthians 1:2-9.

Background Scripture: 1 Corinthians 1:10-17.

Printed Text: 1 Corinthians 1:10-17.

1 Corinthians 1:10-17

10 Now I beseech you, brethren, by the name of our Lord Jesus Christ, that ye all speak the same thing, and that there be no divisions among you; but that ye be perfectly joined together in the same mind and in the same judgment.

11 For it hath been declared unto me of you, my brethren, by them which are of the house of Chloe, that there are contentions among you.

12 Now this I say, that every one of you saith, I am of Paul; and I of Apollos; and I of Cephas; and I of Christ.

13 Is Christ divided? was Paul crucified for you? or were ye baptized in the name of Paul?

14 I thank God that I baptized none of you, but Crispus and Gaius;

15 Lest any should say that I had baptized in mine own name.

16 And I baptized also the household of Stephanas: besides, I know not whether I baptized any other.

17 For Christ sent me not to baptize, but to preach the gospel: not with wisdom of words, lest the cross of Christ should be made of none effect.

Golden Text: I beseech you, brethren, by the name of our Lord Jesus Christ, that ye all speak the same thing, and that there be no divisions among you; but that ye be perfectly joined together in the same mind and in the same judgment.
—1 Corinthians 1:10.

> *Called to Be a Christian Community*
> Unit 1: Servants of God
> (Lessons 1-4)

Lesson Aims

After participating in this lesson, each student will be able to:

1. Retell how the church at Corinth fractured.
2. Explain how interpersonal loyalties and insistence on personal preferences can cause division within the church.
3. Tell one way that he or she can give up a personal preference for the sake of church unity.

Lesson Outline

INTRODUCTION
    A. Does Unity Really Matter?
    B. Lesson Background
I. APPEAL FOR UNITY (1 Corinthians 1:10)
    A. Authority of the Appeal (v. 10a)
    B. Aim of the Appeal (v. 10b)
        A Perfect Fit
II. LACK OF UNITY (1 Corinthians 1:11, 12)
    A. Exposed by Quarrels (v. 11)
    B. Evidenced in Divisions (v. 12)
        Follow the Leader
III. BASIS OF UNITY (1 Corinthians 1:13-17)
    A. Unity in Christ (v. 13)
    B. Unity in Baptism (vv. 14-16)
    C. Unity in the Gospel (v. 17)
CONCLUSION
    A. Cost of Disunity
    B. Cure for Disunity
    C. Prayer
    D. Thought to Remember

Introduction

A. Does Unity Really Matter?

One of the ancient fables of Aesop (620–560 B.C.) was about a hungry lion and four oxen. The lion often tried to find a way to attack the four oxen as they stood together in a field. But the lion was no match for all four together.

Then one day the oxen had a quarrel and separated. When the lion came, he found them standing as far away from one another as they could get. Now it became an easy matter for the lion to pick them off one by one. Aesop's moral to the story was this: "United we stand, divided we fall."

As Paul's opening chapter to the church in Corinth shows, God's will is for His people to serve in unity. In the 2,000 years since Christ, the church has divided into so many different faith expressions that it is virtually impossible to list them all. These divisions have existed for so long that they seem to be almost normal, right, and unchangeable. In this light the question must be asked: Does unity really matter? The answer must be yes for three reasons.

First, unity matters because division denies Jesus' prayer. On the night before He died, Jesus prayed earnestly for the unity of His followers (see John 17:20-26). Sincere followers of Christ simply must not ignore that solemn prayer.

Second, unity matters because division exposes us as carnal. Division is a work of the flesh (see 1 Corinthians 3:3, 4; Galatians 5:20). When the church divides because of power struggles and personality conflicts, it thinks and acts like the world.

Third, unity matters because division destroys our witness. Jesus said the world would recognize His disciples by their sincere love for one another (John 13:35). The reverse of this is also true. Many people are content to ignore Christ and the call of the gospel because they are repulsed by the confusion of so many different churches competing for their souls.

B. Lesson Background

The church in Corinth was founded by Paul himself (Acts 18:1-21). Despite the wickedness that pervaded this city, many people came to Christ in response to Paul's preaching. Apollos and others stepped in to help lead after Paul left the city to continue on his missionary journeys (Acts 18:24–19:1).

However, serious problems developed in Paul's absence. When Paul heard what was happening some four or five years later (about A.D. 55/56), he found it necessary to write to the Corinthians to correct the situation. Foremost among the problems in Corinth was the way the church had divided itself into factions. As the lesson text will show, the Corinthian Christians were aligning themselves with various leaders. Paul would have none of it. Their duty was to serve God—together!

I. Appeal for Unity
(1 Corinthians 1:10)

A. Authority of the Appeal (v. 10a)

10a. Now I beseech you, brethren, by the name of our Lord Jesus Christ.

In his opening greeting (vv. 1-3), Paul reminded his readers of his position as an apostle. Now, as a spokesman for the *Lord,* he presents an authoritative exhortation. To *beseech* is to deliver an impassioned plea, to issue a call for action.

Paul addresses his readers as *brethren,* a reminder that he and they are part of God's family. Paul addresses them in this way numerous times. The Corinthians have many problems, but they are still Paul's brothers and sisters in Christ. Together they have been called into a great fellowship (v. 9). [See question #1, page 403.]

It is important to notice that Paul's appeal for unity does not come merely as a recommendation. Neither is it just his take-it-or-leave-it opinion of the way things ought to be. The appeal is a strong exhortation that comes *by the name of our Lord Jesus Christ.* Any apostolic instruction that comes in His name must be followed!

B. Aim of the Appeal (v. 10b)

10b. That ye all speak the same thing, and that there be no divisions among you; but that ye be perfectly joined together in the same mind and in the same judgment.

To *speak the same thing* does not mean that Christians must have identical opinions (compare Romans 14:5). Rather, it means that they must stand together in their core doctrinal beliefs. [See question #2, page 403.] They must stand ready to give a united testimony to the watching world. In order to present this united testimony, there must be *no divisions* within the church. The body of Christ is not divided; it is one. Paul has more to say about divisions in Romans 16:17; 1 Corinthians 3:3; 11:18.

Furthermore, unity must be more than a matter of external appearances. It must arise from the inward harmony of people who believe in the same God, obey the same Lord, and share the same Spirit. Such people are *perfectly joined together.* They share *the same mind,* attitude, and way of thinking. They share *the same judgment,* ultimate conclusion, and intended purpose. The aim of Paul's appeal is that God's people live and serve in unity. See also Ephesians 4:3, 13; Philippians 2:2.

A Perfect Fit

My wife enjoys working on jigsaw puzzles. It seems at times the more pieces the better for her. One of the more original puzzles she has done was called "Hay in a Needle Stack." It was a 1,000-piece puzzle that featured a pile of sewing needles with a small piece of hay in the center. The color on most of the pieces is the same, to say the least! This meant that the puzzle could be completed only by matching the edges of the interlocking pieces. Finding those perfect fits was a time-consuming task.

In a way the church is like a jigsaw puzzle. There are many pieces that need to be joined together to complete the whole picture. As a jigsaw puzzle does not come already put together, so the church is not complete from its inception. It takes time, effort, and meticulous attention to detail to come up with the final "product."

One difference from the jigsaw puzzle, though, is that a puzzle consists of a preset number of pieces while the church does not. The numbers, types, and opinions of people in the church who must fit together are always changing. As a result, the puzzle is never finished but is a continual work in progress.

This extraordinary complexity means that no matter how hard we try to fit the puzzle of the church together, we are always at a loss to do it by our own knowledge and power. This is why we must allow the Spirit of God to work in and through us to move this task forward. —A. E. A.

II. Lack of Unity
(1 Corinthians 1:11, 12)

A. Exposed by Quarrels (v. 11)

11. For it hath been declared unto me of you, my brethren, by them which are of the house of Chloe, that there are contentions among you.

Paul's strong appeal is necessary because of what has *been declared* or revealed to him

---

VISUALS FOR THESE LESSONS

The visual pictured in each lesson (for example, page 399) is a small reproduction of a large, full-color poster included in the *Adult Resources* packet for the Summer Quarter. The packet is available from your supplier. Order No. 492.

about the *brethren* in the Corinthian church. Family members or servants of *the house of* a certain *Chloe* have either sent a letter to Paul or visited him in person, exposing the problem of disunity that has arisen. Their communication to Paul may have also included information about the other problems that Paul will address in 1 Corinthians. The number one problem, however, appears to be division. [See question #3, page 403.]

The lack of unity among the Corinthian Christians is caused and exposed by the *contentions* that exist among them. What Paul means by *contentions* is the kind of strife that exists where people do not get along with one another for various reasons (compare 2 Corinthians 12:20; Galatians 5:20; 1 Timothy 6:4; Titus 3:9). When people quarrel and wrangle, they expose their failure to be the undivided body of Christ.

B. Evidenced in Divisions (v. 12)

12. Now this I say, that every one of you saith, I am of Paul; and I of Apollos; and I of Cephas; and I of Christ.

The specific problem that exists in Corinth is a childish act of choosing up sides. This problem apparently is not limited to just a few people! Their man-made divisions and cliques threaten to undo all of Paul's work in founding that church.

The divisions appear to be at least four in number. Some say, "We are *of Paul*." Such people probably think they are honoring the apostle in this way as the founder of their church (see Acts 18). Others say, "We are *of Apollos*." This group in some sense rejects Paul, with his weak public image (see 1 Corinthians 2:1-4); they prefer the powerful oratory of the leader who followed after him (Acts 18:24-28).

Still others say, "We are *of Cephas*," the Aramaic form of Simon Peter's name (John 1:42). This faction pledges allegiance to a man who was an apostle even before Paul and who has a focused ministry to those of Jewish heritage (Galatians 2:7-9). Each party is guilty of exalting a man, thus minimizing everyone who does not join them. [See question #4, page 403.]

Members of a fourth group are reported to be saying, "We are *of Christ*. What they mean by this is open to question. Perhaps they sincerely want to follow the Lord, so they correctly refuse to align themselves with any mere man. On the other hand they may think they have found a way to make their group superior to the others. ("You may follow Peter or Paul, but *we* follow Christ!") They may even be claiming that they are the *only* ones who are of Christ.

Significantly, Paul does not commend any of the groups, even the one claiming to be of Christ. By listing all four on the same basis, he makes them all guilty of dividing the body. Their petty cliques are tearing apart the fabric of unity. They should feel shame, not pride, for what they have achieved. [See question #5, page 403.]

FOLLOW THE LEADER

In many childhood team games, two children serve as captains and then take turns choosing teams. Each child has his or her favorite captain and will do all they can to get the attention of that captain in order to be chosen. In the world of politics, people line up behind certain leaders and question the motives of anyone who would follow any other. We choose our favorite ball team or player and feel that that team or person is always right.

Unfortunately, people in the church are guilty of the same. It began early in the life of the church with this lining up of the Christians behind their favorite leader. Yet the problem goes back even further. Old Testament Israel experienced problems on several occasions because of the exaltation of certain men and their ideas over the will of God.

Much of this problem in the church is based upon the principle of "what's in it for me." The

---

How to Say It

ACHAIA. Uh-*kay*-uh.
AESOP. *Ee*-sup.
APOLLOS. Uh-*pahl*-us.
CEPHAS. *See*-fus.
CHLOE. *Klo*-ee.
CORINTH. *Kor*-inth.
CORINTHIANS. Ko-*rin*-thee-unz (*th* as in *thin*).
CRISPUS. *Kris*-pus.
EPHESIANS. Ee-*fee*-zhunz.
GAIUS. *Gay*-us.
PHILIPPIANS. Fih-*lip*-ee-unz.
STEPHANAS. *Stef*-uh-nass.
TITUS. *Ty*-tus.
ZECHARIAH. *Zek*-uh-*rye*-uh (strong accent on *rye*).

leader who will provide what I want, agree with what I believe, hold to the traditions I want to hold to, or make the changes I want to see made is the one who is followed. Too often these decisions are not based on God's will. So before we criticize the speck in the eye of the cult-hero worshipers in the realms of celebrities and politicians, we do well to see if there is a beam in our own eye in the way we follow church leaders. —A. E. A.

III. Basis of Unity
(1 Corinthians 1:13-17)

A. Unity in Christ (v. 13)

13. Is Christ divided? was Paul crucified for you? or were ye baptized in the name of Paul?

The Corinthians need to learn what the nature of the church really is. Their divisions serve to cut themselves off from other believers; they have, in effect, expelled the others from membership in the body. To teach them the true basis of unity, *Paul* asks several questions—each with an obvious answer. These questions show that the basis of unity is Christ.

Paul first asks, *Is Christ divided?* The obvious answer is no. God does not divide Him; "God is one" (Galatians 3:20). Neither does Jesus divide himself (compare Matthew 12:25). If the Corinthians in their day—or we in ours—try to divide Christ, then the intent of God is being opposed.

Second, when Paul asks, *Was Paul crucified for you?* he shows himself to be unworthy of a group's devotion. The question implies the same about Apollos and Peter. Neither Paul nor Apollos nor Peter can give his life in atonement for anyone. Only Christ was worthy to carry our sins on that tree.

The third question, *Were ye baptized in the name of Paul?* is significant in that baptism is to be done in the name of the Father and the Son and the Holy Spirit (Matthew 28:19) or, by abbreviation, in the name of Jesus (Acts 2:38; 8:16; 10:48; 19:5). Baptism is certainly not in the name of any mortal man.

B. Unity in Baptism (vv. 14-16)

14. I thank God that I baptized none of you, but Crispus and Gaius.

The Corinthians, as other Christians, have the baptismal experience in common. Their oneness or unity should find expression in "one body,

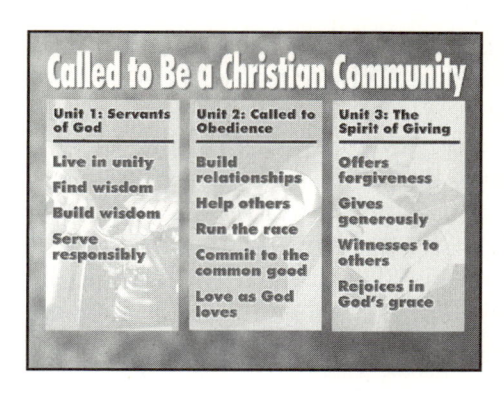

Visual for lesson 1

Use this outline of the quarter to remind your students of the multi-faceted nature of the Christian community (the church).

and one Spirit, . . . one hope . . . one Lord, one faith, one baptism, one God and Father of all" (Ephesians 4:4-6). As Paul considers the situation, he is aware that some are placing false importance on the person who does the baptizing. When Paul says, *I thank God I baptized none of you,* his desire is to remove that false view of baptism that contributes to disunity. As such, this statement serves to deemphasize the importance of the person performing the baptism.

The focus instead is to be on Christ, into whose name we are baptized. Paul does not minimize the importance of being baptized—that's not the issue here. Rather, Paul wants to remove himself from the spotlight. By implication he is also removing from the spotlight anyone else who performs baptisms.

Almost as an afterthought, Paul adds, *but Crispus and Gaius.* Paul did baptize a few people personally. But he thinks that fact to be of little consequence as the next verse makes clear.

15. Lest any should say that I had baptized in mine own name.

Paul knows that people are quick to take pride in the wrong things. The very reason that he leaves the act of baptizing to others is *lest any should say* they were *baptized* in Paul's *own name.* They may think that to be baptized that way carries some kind of merit or special virtue.

Certainly Paul never baptizes anyone in (or into) his own name! Neither does he ever take any credit for anyone's conversion as though he were hanging scalps from his belt or putting notches on his gun. As Paul elsewhere explains, baptism is "into Jesus Christ" (Romans 6:3). The focus of baptism must be on Christ, not on any mere man.

16. And I baptized also the household of Stephanas: besides, I know not whether I baptized any other.

As Paul reviews his work in Corinth, he also remembers that he baptized *the household of Stephanas*. Paul hastens to add these people to his very short list, apparently in order to be completely honest. Other than the people he now has named, Paul simply does not remember if he *baptized any other*. It is obviously not a matter of any importance to Paul whether new believers are *baptized* by him or by someone else.

We should note that the household of Stephanas constituted Paul's first converts in Achaia, the province that includes the city of Corinth (1 Corinthians 16:15). This group would include both members of the family and servants in the home. Following their conversion, they devoted themselves to "the ministry of the saints." Since they were the first converts in the area, who else would have baptized them except Paul or a traveling companion?

C. Unity in the Gospel (v. 17)

17. For Christ sent me not to baptize, but to preach the gospel: not with wisdom of words, lest the cross of Christ should be made of none effect.

Paul's statement that Christ sent him *not to baptize, but to preach the gospel* can be easily misunderstood. Paul is not intending to exclude baptism, for the Great Commission given by Jesus specifically includes it (Matthew 28:18-20).

Home Daily Bible Readings

Monday, May 29—Jesus Is Lord of All (Romans 10:9-13)

Tuesday, May 30—We Are Reconciled in Christ (Colossians 1:15-20)

Wednesday, May 31—One Body and One Spirit (Ephesians 4:1-6)

Thursday, June 1—Called Together in Christ (1 Corinthians 1:1-9)

Friday, June 2—Be United in Christ (1 Corinthians 1:10-17)

Saturday, June 3—We Proclaim Christ Crucified to All (1 Corinthians 1:18-25)

Sunday, June 4—God Brings Us to Christ (1 Corinthians 1:26-31)

Neither is Paul minimizing baptism, given the importance he places on it in his other letters (Romans 6:1-4; Galatians 3:27; Ephesians 4:5; Colossians 2:12).

Rather, Paul's point is that his primary job is to do the preaching that leads people to accept Christ and submit to baptism. If Paul preaches and someone else baptizes, all is well.

Paul certainly feels the weight of his commission to preach the gospel. That is the central purpose of his life. He knows that he has been *sent* by no less than Christ himself, so he must stay true to this mission. Furthermore, Paul knows that he will not fulfill his task by trying to do it with his own power and with his own clever *wisdom of words*. (Perhaps he is thinking of Zechariah 4:6 as he writes this!) Paul's task is to tell the good news that Jesus has died for our sins. That is why Paul resolves "not to know any thing . . . save Jesus Christ, and him crucified" when he preached in Corinth (1 Corinthians 2:2; see next week's lesson).

Without "excellency of speech or of wisdom" (1 Corinthians 2:1), Paul had preached the simple gospel facts to these people. The message of *the cross of Christ* has pierced their hearts (compare Acts 2:37) and has drawn them to accept Jesus as Lord. Had Paul chosen to rely on his own forcefulness or powers of persuasion rather than the facts of the gospel, then the death of Jesus on the cross would have been *made of none effect*. The power of the gospel lies in the historical facts of the cross and the empty tomb, not the force of the preacher.

Paul goes on in 1:19-22 (not in today's text) to warn further of mere human wisdom. Human wisdom divorced from God's Word will only divide. True unity in the gospel is found in the wisdom of God (1 Corinthians 1:24).

Conclusion

A. Cost of Disunity

Lack of unity in the church is a costly problem, one that lies at the root of many other problems. Lack of unity prevented the Corinthians from coming together to confront an immoral brother (1 Corinthians 5:1-5). Lack of unity led them to take each other to court before pagan judges (6:1-6). Lack of unity drove a wedge between those who ate certain foods and those who did not (8:1-12). Lack of unity even corrupted their observance of the Lord's Supper, which should have been central to their oneness (10:14-17; 11:18-22). Lack of unity produced the situation where members were in competition with each other to show off their spiritual gifts (chapters 12–14). None of these problems in Corinth could be resolved as long as disunity existed.

B. Cure for Disunity

Disunity can be cured! In the opening chapter of this letter, Paul noted how divided Christians can come together: we must set Christ, the Son of God, above any other loyalty. Loyalty that places anyone else above Christ for any reason can only result in defeat.

Unity will never happen as long as we insist that everyone else has to come and join our group. Unity will happen only when we come together at the foot of the cross. God's Spirit can make us one—but only if we are willing. The way we respond to Paul's plea will determine whether or not we will be found serving in unity.

C. Prayer

Father, forgive us for promoting divisive squabbles. Help us to find the ways to resolve them. Show us how to serve You in true and loving unity. In the name of Jesus, amen.

D. Thought to Remember

Service *for* Christ begins with unity *in* Christ.

Learning by Doing

This section contains an alternative lesson plan emphasizing learning activities. Classes desiring such student involvement will find these suggestions helpful.

Learning Goals

After this lesson, each student will be able to:
1. Retell how the church at Corinth fractured.
2. Explain how interpersonal loyalties and insistence on personal preferences can cause division within the church.
3. Tell one way that he or she can give up a personal preference for the sake of church unity.

Into the Lesson

Place two or three pieces of poster board on different walls of the classroom. Divide the class into the same number of groups as you have poster boards. (If you have a large class, create more groups and provide more poster board.) Appoint a "scribe" for each group. Groups are to stand by their assigned poster boards and list as many Christian faith groups that they can think of within three minutes.

When time is up, acknowledge the group with the longest list. Ask: "What are some of the reasons for so many groups?" List answers on the board. Then ask: "Does unity in the church really matter? Why is unity better than having so many divisions in Christ's church?"

Make the transition to the Bible study by saying (paraphrased from the Lesson Introduction), "The church has been divided into so many 'pieces' that it is virtually impossible to list them all. Such divisions have existed for so long that they seem almost normal and right. Unfortunately, these are not the only divisions experienced in Christianity. Local congregations themselves often experience division and disharmony. The apostle Paul addresses this problem when he writes to the church at Corinth."

Into the Word

Prepare a brief lecture using the background information in the commentary. Illustrate the lecture with a map showing Corinth, if available. Following the lecture, read aloud today's printed text. Use the questions that follow to stimulate purposeful discussion. The questions may be asked of the whole class or may be assigned to small groups for discussion.

1. "What is the significance of the words 'by the name of our Lord Jesus Christ' in verse 10? Why does Paul include this phrase in his letter?" *(The authority for this teaching is in Jesus, not in Paul's own feelings. This plea is more than just a recommendation or opinion. It is an exhortation from our Lord.)*

2. "What is the source of division in the Corinthian church? See verses 11 and 12." *(Church members are quarreling as they form groups claiming allegiance to different leaders. The result is disunity and contentions.)*

3. "Some Corinthians claimed to follow Paul, some Apollos, some Cephas, and some said they were of Christ. What do you think the last group may have meant when they said they followed Christ? Do you think this was a good claim or just another way to divide the church?" *(Perhaps they were sincerely following Jesus alone as their master. Or they may have been trying to make themselves sound superior to the other groups. They may even be thinking they were the only real Christians in the church. We do not know their motivation.)*

4. "Paul speaks at length about baptism, using it as an illustration of division and unity. Baptism is to be a basis of unity in the Lord's body (Ephesians 4:5). Tragically, baptism in the contemporary church still divides but in different ways. What are some ways that different views of baptism divide the church today?" *(What it does and does not result in, when to perform it, how to perform it, etc.)*

Into Life

Ask students to brainstorm issues that are not listed in today's text that cause division in the local church. Write these on the board. Have the class discuss the negative impact of disunity in the local church. Review the sources of disunity compiled by your class.

Ask each person to identify a potential problem in his or her life, such as insisting on a particular style of music in the worship service. Encourage each person to make a commitment during the prayer time to resist becoming divisive over his or her particular issue. After a time of prayer, close the lesson by having the class sing "Bind Us Together, Lord" or another familiar song that calls for unity and fellowship in the church.

Let's Talk It Over

These questions are designed to promote discussion of the lesson. The answers here are only discussion starters. Let your class talk it over from there.

1. How does Paul's description of Christians as family (brethren) help us understand and live out Christian unity today?

"Family language" shows us that what bonds us together is more significant than our differences. This imagery reinforces the fact that our faith, although personal, is not isolated. Our identity is not shaped simply by who we are as individuals but also by the spiritual family in which God has placed us.

This view of ourselves and others helps us desire and demonstrate Christian unity. Such unity is for God's glory (John 17:20-26).

2. A focus on Christ is understood by some believers to mean that doctrine should be de-emphasized since, as they claim, "doctrine divides." How should we respond?

As Paul indicates here, God intends for doctrine—our beliefs about the nature of Christ, His work, His church, etc.—to function as a unifying influence among His people. Sound doctrine should be a source of encouragement (Titus 1:9).

The extent to which doctrinal controversies have divided virtually every generation of Christians is a tragic irony. Devoting more attention to doctrine will help us mirror God's own perspective regarding what is foundational to the unity of His people. Failure to do so heightens the possibility of our making secondary that which God views as primary (and vice versa). Right doctrine is Paul's solution to the problems in Corinth! See also 1 Timothy 4:16; Titus 2:1.

3. Paul was informed by church members of the problems in Corinth. Why is this report itself not equally quarrelsome and divisive? After all, "Nobody likes a tattletale!"

Perhaps those who made the report to Paul realized that failing to address the situation would have been more harmful than reporting it. Churches sometimes attempt to avoid internal problems by creating an outward impression that all is well. Such efforts to avoid confrontation often are self-defeating and only delay the inevitable.

We should also note that these believers informed someone who had a responsibility to address such issues, namely the apostle Paul. Also, the report was true. Thus the report was not an expression of slander or gossip (compare Ephesians 4:31). Even informing the right person can produce sin if our motivation for doing so is prideful or malicious. Such was apparently not the case with the report to Paul.

4. What are some ways that Christians today intentionally or inadvertently demonstrate a greater allegiance to leaders than to Christ? How do we avoid this problem?

Defending the sinful behavior of church staff members or elders simply because of their roles is one example. We must be gracious while also remembering that Scripture calls church leaders to high moral, doctrinal, and relational standards (1 Timothy 3:1-7). While we should respect gifted preachers, we must also evaluate their teaching in light of Scripture (Acts 17:11).

Another problem is identifying our church fellowship based on the vocational ministers. For example, the statement "I attend where _____ preaches" may indicate an overemphasis on human leadership. This is determined by the speaker's mind-set, however, as the speaker simply may be trying to distinguish between two congregations that could otherwise be confused.

5. What are some factors that indicate whether a group of people within a congregation is a positive or a negative influence?

Groups that form around common interests or causes are unavoidable and often desirable. For example, Sunday school classes often form based on age (the seniors class) or life situation (the young couples class). In such classes people can discuss common problems and find mutual support.

On the other hand, some groups can inhibit church health. Self-absorbed attitudes among group members may produce a mind-set that shuns potential new members and refuses diversity of opinion. Competitiveness between groups may produce quarrels over financial resources or classroom scheduling. A commitment to groups within the congregation must not transcend a commitment to the health of the congregation.

June 11
Lesson 2

Serving with Spiritual Wisdom

DEVOTIONAL READING: Ephesians 1:15-21.

BACKGROUND SCRIPTURE: 1 Corinthians 2.

PRINTED TEXT: 1 Corinthians 2:1-16.

1 Corinthians 2:1-16

1 And I, brethren, when I came to you, came not with excellency of speech or of wisdom, declaring unto you the testimony of God.

2 For I determined not to know any thing among you, save Jesus Christ, and him crucified.

3 And I was with you in weakness, and in fear, and in much trembling.

4 And my speech and my preaching was not with enticing words of man's wisdom, but in demonstration of the Spirit and of power:

5 That your faith should not stand in the wisdom of men, but in the power of God.

6 Howbeit we speak wisdom among them that are perfect: yet not the wisdom of this world, nor of the princes of this world, that come to nought:

7 But we speak the wisdom of God in a mystery, even the hidden wisdom, which God ordained before the world unto our glory;

8 Which none of the princes of this world knew: for had they known it, they would not have crucified the Lord of glory.

9 But as it is written, Eye hath not seen, nor ear heard, neither have entered into the heart of man, the things which God hath prepared for them that love him.

10 But God hath revealed them unto us by his Spirit: for the Spirit searcheth all things, yea, the deep things of God.

11 For what man knoweth the things of a man, save the spirit of man which is in him? even so the things of God knoweth no man, but the Spirit of God.

12 Now we have received, not the spirit of the world, but the Spirit which is of God; that we might know the things that are freely given to us of God.

13 Which things also we speak, not in the words which man's wisdom teacheth, but which the Holy Ghost teacheth; comparing spiritual things with spiritual.

14 But the natural man receiveth not the things of the Spirit of God: for they are foolishness unto him: neither can he know them, because they are spiritually discerned.

15 But he that is spiritual judgeth all things, yet he himself is judged of no man.

16 For who hath known the mind of the Lord, that he may instruct him? But we have the mind of Christ.

GOLDEN TEXT: We speak, not in the words which man's wisdom teacheth, but which the Holy Ghost teacheth; comparing spiritual things with spiritual.
—1 Corinthians 2:13.

> *Called to Be a Christian Community*
> Unit 1: Servants of God
> (Lessons 1-4)

Lesson Aims

After this lesson each student will be able to:
1. State what Paul said was the primary content of his preaching.
2. List some differences between human wisdom and spiritual wisdom.
3. Apply spiritual wisdom to one area of life.

Lesson Outline

INTRODUCTION
  A. The Source of True Wisdom
  B. Lesson Background
I. OUR WEAK WISDOM (1 Corinthians 2:1-5)
  A. Paul's Action, Part 1 (vv. 1, 2)
  B. Paul's Confession (v. 3)
  C. Paul's Action, Part 2 (vv. 4, 5)
II. GOD'S CONCEALED WISDOM (1 Corinthians 2:6-9)
  A. Hidden Since the Beginning (vv. 6, 7)
  B. Missed by Rulers (v. 8)
    No Mulligan for Satan
  C. Prepared for God's People (v. 9)
III. SPIRIT'S REVEALED WISDOM (1 Corinthians 2:10-16)
  A. The Spirit's Knowledge (vv. 10, 11)
  B. The Spirit's Teaching (vv. 12, 13)
  C. The Spirit's Help (vv. 14-16)
    Misunderstood Riches
CONCLUSION
  A. Recognizing Spiritual Wisdom
  B. Serving with Spiritual Wisdom
  C. Prayer
  D. Thought to Remember

Introduction

A. The Source of True Wisdom

Terrence was born in Carthage in about 195 B.C. As a young man he was brought to Rome as a slave. He lived only a short life, dying in his mid-thirties. Despite this he still had time to become a famous writer. One of his observations is well worth remembering: "What a difference there is between a wise person and a fool!"

Everyone would rather be known as wise than as foolish. No one enjoys being ridiculed or called stupid. This is why the average person tries hard to make the right impression on others. Even a teenager in outlandish garb is trying to show his or her peer group a degree of worldly wisdom.

But where can we find true wisdom? Is it from humans or from God? And what shall we do if following God's wisdom makes us look foolish in the eyes of the world? These were the issues that Paul faced in his counsel to the Corinthians, and they are the same issues that we must face today.

B. Lesson Background

Before Paul reached Corinth on his second missionary journey, he suffered repeated rejection. He was beaten and jailed in Philippi, chased out of Thessalonica by a riot, forced to flee Berea, and laughed off of Mars' hill by the philosophers in Athens (see Acts 16, 17). When he came to Corinth (Acts 18), he probably was out of money and out of friends. Paul had left his various coworkers along the way to help lead the new churches (Acts 17:14). In Corinth Paul worked daily as a tentmaker (Acts 18:3) and tried to present the message of Christ in the synagogue every Sabbath (Acts 18:4). Eventually he had to leave that place as well (Acts 18:5-7).

Since Paul faced so much opposition, what should he do? Should he adjust his message to make it less offensive? Should he use more eloquent oratory? Should he try to impress people with his education or his wisdom? It was a crucial point in Paul's ministry. As Paul writes his first letter to the Corinthians, he carefully reminds them which choice he made.

I. Our Weak Wisdom (1 Corinthians 2:1-5)

A. Paul's Action, Part 1 (vv. 1, 2)

1. And I, brethren, when I came to you, came not with excellency of speech or of wisdom, declaring unto you the testimony of God.

Paul wants his *brethren* in the church in Corinth to think back a few years to the time when they first met him. He had come with a difficult task: to preach the gospel in a city that was notoriously wicked and worldly. They should well remember that Paul does not make a very impressive appearance (compare 2 Corinthians 10:10).

Apparently, Paul's lack of *excellency of speech* stands in contrast to the eloquence of Apollos, who ministered in Corinth after Paul left (Acts 18:24-28). Good speaking skills serve many preachers well. But ultimately the *testimony of God* requires neither eloquence nor *wisdom* to shine through. [See question #1, page 412.] The wisdom that Paul refers to is human wisdom that is divorced from God's wisdom. Paul will make this distinction between the two wisdoms clearer in verses 5-7, 13 (below).

2. For I determined not to know any thing among you, save Jesus Christ, and him crucified.

As Paul preached in Corinth, he was aware that the message of the cross was a stumbling block to Jews and foolishness to Gentiles (1 Corinthians 1:23). After all, the cross is an ugly, horrible means of execution. Under Roman law only the worst criminals are subject to crucifixion.

Yet Paul also knows that the cross represents the power and wisdom of God. Despite opposition everywhere, Paul refuses to abandon this core belief. Nothing and no one except *Jesus Christ* can save people. It is not Jesus' exemplary life or fascinating parables that can save, as valuable as those are; rather, it is the fact that He was *crucified* (Romans 3:25, 26). Thus, Paul refuses to be ashamed of the gospel (Romans 1:16).

B. Paul's Confession (v. 3)

3. And I was with you in weakness, and in fear, and in much trembling.

Paul readily admits that his public oratory had not been impressive. In fact he had stood before them in noticeable *weakness*. This weakness may have been his own inadequacy, or it may have been a physical ailment such as he had in Galatia (Galatians 4:13). However, as Paul would later write to the Corinthians, God's strength is made perfect in weakness (2 Corinthians 12:9).

Paul's preaching in Corinth with *fear and in much trembling* (compare 2 Corinthians 10:1) does not mean that Paul had been afraid of the people or the authorities. Rather, it was that Paul knew that the eternal destinies of his listeners hung in the balance. Paul had the same kind of reverent awe for his task that he encouraged the Philippians to have in regard to working out their salvation "with fear and trembling" (Philippians 2:12). [See question #2, page 412.]

C. Paul's Action, Part 2 (vv. 4, 5)

4. And my speech and my preaching was not with enticing words of man's wisdom, but in demonstration of the Spirit and of power.

Paul's *preaching* had been, above all, a proclamation of the gospel of Christ. Paul knows that the power is in the gospel message itself (again, Romans 1:16); therefore, he makes no effort to embellish or "contextualize" the gospel *with enticing words of man's wisdom*. Worldly philosophical arguments may have wider appeal, but Paul rejects that approach. There is nothing wrong with philosophy as such. But one must always be on the alert to philosophy that is rooted in the human mind rather than God's mind (Colossians 2:8). [See question #3, page 412.]

Paul's *preaching* in Corinth had been a *demonstration of the Spirit and of* God's *power*, not a display of human wisdom (see also 1 Thessalonians 1:5). The gospel message puts God's Spirit, not God's spokesman, on display. When the clear facts of the gospel had pierced the hearts of Paul's hearers, the Spirit moved to bring them under conviction (compare John 16:8). Thus was exhibited God's great power, not the feeble power of Paul.

5. That your faith should not stand in the wisdom of men, but in the power of God.

If Paul had impressed the Corinthians with his own communication skills, they could well have become "Paul-ites" instead of Christians. Perhaps it was the oratorical skills of Apollos that had led some to become "Apollos-ites" (1 Corinthians 1:12). But no person—whether Paul or Apollos or anyone else—deserves our allegiance more than *God* does. When the Corinthians make sure that their faith does *not stand*

How to Say It

BEREA. Buh-*ree*-uh.
CARTHAGE. *Car*-thij.
COLOSSIANS. Kuh-*losh*-unz.
CORINTH. *Kor*-inth.
CORINTHIANS. Ko-*rin*-thee-unz (*th* as in *thin*).
GALATIA. Guh-*lay*-shuh.
GALATIANS. Guh-*lay*-shunz.
PHILIPPI. Fih-*lip*-pie or *Fil*-ih-pie.
PHILIPPIANS. Fih-*lip*-ee-unz.
THESSALONIANS. *Thess*-uh-*lo*-nee-unz (strong accent on *lo*; *th* as in *thin*).
THESSALONICA. *Thess*-uh-lo-*nye*-kuh (strong accent on *nye*; *th* as in *thin*).

in the wisdom of men, but in the power of God, they will make no mistake in this regard.

II. God's Concealed Wisdom (1 Corinthians 2:6-9)

A. Hidden Since the Beginning (vv. 6, 7)

6. Howbeit we speak wisdom among them that are perfect: yet not the wisdom of this world, nor of the princes of this world, that come to nought.

When Paul said that he did not speak in words of wisdom (vv. 1, 4), he was referring to human wisdom. He now makes plain that he does indeed *speak wisdom* but with two qualifications. First, he speaks wisdom *among them that are perfect.* This refers to mature believers. Unbelievers do not understand it, and "baby believers" are ready only for the "milk," not "meat," of the Word (1 Corinthians 3:2, next week's lesson). Only the mature can appreciate fully how wise God's message is (see Ephesians 4:13, 14).

Second, the wisdom that Paul speaks is *not the wisdom of this world* or of its *princes.* The world and its leaders eventually will come to nothing; all earthly powers will pass away. But Paul speaks with a type of wisdom that does not originate within the world and is not recognized by the world. [See question #4, page 412.]

7. But we speak the wisdom of God in a mystery, even the hidden wisdom, which God ordained before the world unto our glory.

Paul rejects human wisdom so that he may proclaim *the wisdom of God.* God has given this *hidden wisdom* as a kind of *mystery.* Paul's message from God is not a mystery because it is complicated or difficult to understand, but because it was kept secret until God was ready to reveal it.

In the distant past, *before the world* was even created, God was already preparing for our salvation. He ordained that salvation would not come by human merit but by the atoning death of His own Son. This great plan for salvation was for our benefit and *unto our glory.* How privileged we are to have this mystery revealed to us!

B. Missed by Rulers (v. 8)

8. Which none of the princes of this world knew: for had they known it, they would not have crucified the Lord of glory.

The *princes of this world,* such as the Roman officials and the Jewish chief priests, do not understand God's wisdom. Nothing about Jesus makes any sense to them. If they had *known* Jesus' true identity, would they have dared to crucify *the Lord of glory?* All the evidence was there, but they ignored it. But their self-inflicted blindness resulted in Jesus' death for our sin according to God's plan (see Acts 4:25-28).

In one sense even Satan can be included in the reference to *princes of this world* (see John 14:30). Just like the human rulers, Satan was unaware of God's real plan. If Satan had known that Jesus would defeat him at the cross, would he have moved the heart of Judas to betray the Lord?

No Mulligan for Satan

"If I had known then what I know now, I would have done things a lot differently." People often would like to have an opportunity to do something over in the hope of getting it right the second time around. Some circumstances do allow a "do over." For example an actor may retape a scene until it's just right. In golf a "do over" is called a mulligan. Mulligans are used to make up for errant shots. There never seem to be enough mulligans in real life as we would like!

Although it's safe to say that we would all like more mulligans, we can rejoice that God did not allow Satan to have one at Calvary. Sometimes Christians wish that Satan had not temporarily "succeeded" in the way that he did. But if things had gone differently, then the sacrifice for our sins would not have been established.

We can thank God that Satan did not get a mulligan; we can also thank God that we *do* get one. And not just one, but many. Each new day, each new minute, we get a "do over" in our relationship with Christ. If we confess our sins, God is faithful to forgive us (1 John 1:9). In this we have a perpetual clean slate. Praise God!

—A. E. A.

C. Prepared for God's People (v. 9)

9. But as it is written, Eye hath not seen, nor ear heard, neither have entered into the heart of man, the things which God hath prepared for them that love him.

Paul reminds his readers, in a general way, of what is written in Isaiah 64:4. In that context *God,* unlike false idols, actually steps into history to take action on behalf of those who wait on

Him. Yet even the prophet Isaiah himself did not know what the entire plan would be; he only knew that something wonderful was coming.

We who live on this side of the cross can marvel at the great sacrifice Jesus made, but even we have not yet seen the end of it. When we try to imagine the unseen joys of Heaven, or hear the distant praise, or conceive of the place that is *prepared for* us, our minds simply are too small.

III. Spirit's Revealed Wisdom (1 Corinthians 2:10-16)

A. The Spirit's Knowledge (vv. 10, 11)

10. But God hath revealed them unto us by his Spirit: for the Spirit searcheth all things, yea, the deep things of God.

The world and its rulers did not know God's secrets, but now He has *revealed them* to Paul and the other inspired writers of the New Testament. Paul does not want his readers to overlook the importance of sharing in this revealed wisdom. What *God* has revealed to His divinely appointed spokesmen is for the church. As with the holy men of old, who spoke and wrote "as they were moved by the Holy Ghost" (2 Peter 1:21), the Spirit can reveal these things because of His intimate connection with the mind and will of *God* the Father. The Spirit continues to work in ways involving *the deep things of God* in the lives of Christians (Ephesians 1:17-19; 3:16-19).

11. For what man knoweth the things of a man, save the spirit of man which is in him? even so the things of God knoweth no man, but the Spirit of God.

It is reasonable that only *the Spirit of God* can know the mind of God. After all, who can possibly know the inner things of *a man* except the *spirit* that is in that man? A man can know his own mind, but no one else (other than the creator) can know it without that man revealing it. So if anyone wants to know what is on God's mind, he or she must turn to what God's Spirit has said. Only the Spirit—and those to whom the Spirit chooses to reveal things—can know the deep things of God.

B. The Spirit's Teaching (vv. 12, 13)

12. Now we have received, not the spirit of the world, but the Spirit which is of God; that we might know the things that are freely given to us of God.

In a unique way Paul and certain others have been prepared by *the Spirit* to be spokesmen of God's truth (John 14:26). They do not speak a human message, as though they have received merely a *spirit of the world.* Rather, they speak a revealed message that was freely given to them from God by means of *the Spirit which is of God.*

The New Testament writers, then, have conveyed to us the truth that was taught to them by God's Spirit. As a result, all believers can say, in a sense, that *we have received* divinely revealed truth. It is wrong, however, for later believers to put themselves on the same level with the first-century apostles in claiming to speak authoritatively for God. [See question #5, page 412.]

13. Which things also we speak, not in the words which man's wisdom teacheth, but which the Holy Ghost teacheth; comparing spiritual things with spiritual.

Paul makes a bold claim: the very words that he and the other apostles speak have been taught to them by the *Holy Ghost.* This is in sharp contrast to *the words which man's wisdom teacheth.*

Yet we should caution that Paul does not mean that the Holy Spirit has used him as a kind of computer keyboard, merely pushing words through Paul's mind and fingers and onto the parchment. Each author's own style and vocabulary show through in Scripture but the message—every word of it—carries the divine stamp of ownership. In this way the divine message comes through with words approved by the Spirit.

C. The Spirit's Help (vv. 14-16)

14. But the natural man receiveth not the things of the Spirit of God: for they are foolishness unto him: neither can he know them, because they are spiritually discerned.

Visual for lesson 2

Point to this visual as you ask, "How do we make sure that any wisdom we gain in this world has God as the ultimate source?"

The natural man is one who acts on his own without God's guidance. As such, he cannot take in the things of the *Spirit*. Divine truths seem mere *foolishness* to him. He cannot *know them;* he cannot understand them; he probably doesn't even want to bother with them. The truths are *spiritually discerned* by those who have given their lives to *God* (compare John 8:47; 14:17).

It was much the same during the earthly ministry of Jesus. When He spoke in parables, He revealed deep truths about God. But the stories seemed to be foolish and pointless to people who refused to follow the Spirit's leading. Jesus said that those who chose to do God's will would know that His doctrine is from God (John 7:17).

MISUNDERSTOOD RICHES

The quest for wealth has been a part of the human condition as long as anyone can remember. Seeking the riches of this world has led to theft, murder, divorce, and war. Sometimes we are astonished at how people are willing to risk life, limb, and reputation in the pursuit of things.

At other times, however, it is our personal ignorance that causes us to look on in astonishment at the price that someone is willing to pay for various items. For example a person may go to a flea market and see some glass products for sale. Having an eye for collectibles, she buys the whole batch. The previous owner thinks he has done well to unload those old hand-me-downs. Unbeknownst to the seller, however, is the fact that the buyer has just ended up with many thousands of dollars worth of rare glassware. She knew what she was doing all along! We see this kind of thing described all the time on *Antiques Roadshow*.

To people of the world, the things that Christians are willing to sacrifice for their faith seems foolish. But the Christian realizes that eternal life is worth any cost of ridicule, discrimination, or persecution that he or she may have to endure. The person of this world thinks the foolish Christian is being duped. But what is foolishness in the eyes of the world is the very wisdom of God.   —A. E. A.

15. But he that is spiritual judgeth all things, yet he himself is judged of no man.

In contrast to the natural person, the *spiritual* person is able to discern that which is spiritual,

---

Home Daily Bible Readings

Monday, June 5—Faith and Wisdom (James 1:2-8)
Tuesday, June 6—Two Kinds of Wisdom (James 3:13-18)
Wednesday, June 7—A Spirit of Wisdom (Ephesians 1:15-21)
Thursday, June 8—Warn and Teach Everyone in Wisdom (Colossians 1:24-29)
Friday, June 9—Faith Not Based on Human Wisdom (1 Corinthians 2:1-5)
Saturday, June 10—We Speak God's Wisdom (1 Corinthians 2:6-10)
Sunday, June 11—Words Not Taught by Human Wisdom (1 Corinthians 2:11-16)

---

not just that which is earthly. The inspired apostles passed on to us the revealed truth of the Spirit, and it is by that light that we are able to discern spiritual things as well as earthly. To be *judged of no man* means that faithful believers do not need to worry what the world thinks of them.

16. For who hath known the mind of the Lord, that he may instruct him? But we have the mind of Christ.

Paul already has said that only the Spirit of God can know the mind of God. Obviously, no mere human can know *the mind of the Lord.* How foolish for a mere human to think that he or she could *instruct* God or teach Him anything He does not already know! (See Isaiah 40:13; Romans 11:34.)

Although no one has *known the mind of the Lord* in terms of being able to instruct him, it is also true that *we have the mind of Christ.* We see this truth in the fact that the writers of the New Testament have Christ as their source of wisdom. The early church is careful to continue faithfully in the apostles' doctrine (Acts 2:42). When we today hold faithfully to this same revealed truth, we also have the mind of Christ.

Conclusion

A. Recognizing Spiritual Wisdom

Our greatest goal is to receive eternal life. But recognizing and following true wisdom comes first. While the wisest philosophers disagree with each other and the greatest scientists are revised by each new generation, the wisdom from above never changes. If we are to reach the goal of true wisdom, we must not be impressed by eloquent oratory or clever intellectualism. We must recognize the power and permanence of spiritual wisdom.

The highlight of God's wisdom is the cross and empty tomb. God's plan was in His mind from the beginning, but what was revealed only partially to the Old Testament prophets becomes known more fully in the life of Jesus and the gospel proclaimed by the apostles. We must see Christ's great sacrifice not as a stumbling block or as foolishness but as a demonstration of divine wisdom and power.

B. Serving with Spiritual Wisdom

Paul and the other apostles revealed the truth that was given to them through the Spirit. The first-century church and its leaders accepted this truth and served God faithfully. Through the centuries the torch has been passed, and now it has come to us. Just as Paul exhorted the believers in Corinth, believers today must rely not on their own strength but on the power and wisdom of God. In that way the message—and not the messenger—will offer the bright beacon of light to a lost world.

C. Prayer

Father, thank You for revealing Your wisdom to us through Your Spirit. Help us to hold to Your truth and to serve You faithfully. In the name of Christ, amen.

D. Thought to Remember

May we allow God's wisdom to be our own.

Learning by Doing

This section contains an alternative lesson plan emphasizing learning activities. Classes desiring such student involvement will find these suggestions helpful.

Learning Goals

After this lesson each student will be able to:
1. State what Paul said was the primary content of his preaching.
2. List some differences between human wisdom and spiritual wisdom.
3. Apply spiritual wisdom to one area of life.

Into the Lesson

Early in the week, ask a class member or guest to prepare a ten-minute introduction on New Age philosophy. This person will probably need time to visit the church library or Christian bookstore for resources. Material you can provide may be the best alternative.

Begin the class by putting up a poster that reads, "New Age Movement & Mysticism." Ask the class to cite illustrations or examples of New Age philosophy and mysticism from movies and television shows. After the exercise, explain that sometimes it's difficult to define New Age philosophy. Introduce the person who will make the presentation mentioned above.

After the presentation, ask: "Why do you think there is such an interest in New Age spirituality and other mystical concepts? What do these imply about our culture?"

Make the transition to Bible study by saying, "Paul wrote to a culture much like ours in certain ways. The people were exploring all kinds of religions and were having trouble sorting out truth. Even many Christians, like some Christians today, were struggling with identifying true wisdom. We'll find wonderful lessons for believers today as we learn from this struggle in the Corinthian church and culture."

Into the Word

Briefly set the stage for the Bible study by summarizing the thoughts from the Lesson Background. Then say, "As long as we are seeking wisdom, we are going to play school and take a test. We will do this in small groups [or pairs]." Distribute separate handouts as below. (Note: a similar activity is included in the student books.)

Group #1. Your portion of the test is to do some creative writing. Read 1 Corinthians 2:13-16. Then paraphrase the passage, making its wisdom speak clearly to our culture. Please note that verse 13 is often considered the key verse of this chapter.

Group #2. Your portion of the test is to write part of a test question. Read 1 Corinthians 2:1-5. Then give four possible answers to the multiple choice question below. Your possible answers should include an absolutely wrong answer, two answers that are partially correct, and an absolutely correct answer. The question: *Why did Paul emphasize his weakness and fear in 1 Corinthians 2:1-5?*

Group #3. Your portion of the test is to do some creative thinking. After reading 1 Corinthians 2, list your conclusions about the difference between human wisdom and God's wisdom.

Group #4. Your portion of the test is a brief essay that cites examples of how to apply the principles taught in 1 Corinthians 2:14.

Allow each group to share its test results.

Into Life

Begin the application segment with two brainstorming exercises. For the first exercise ask, "What are some examples of 'worldly wisdom'—wisdom that is untrue since it does not come from God? These may be huge philosophical positions such as the New Age philosophy or simple statements such as 'Nice guys finish last.'" List the answers on the board.

Make the transition to the second brainstorming exercise by explaining, "The world seeks wisdom, but from the wrong places. Believers also want true wisdom, something that is of eternal significance. Today's text tells us the Holy Spirit offers us that wisdom. In this exercise we want to create a list of tips for allowing the Holy Spirit to give us that precious wisdom. What are some ways we can encourage this?" List the answers on the board. Make sure to stress that the Holy Spirit offers wisdom through God's written Word.

Conclude by reading Solomon's prayer for wisdom in 1 Kings 3:5-14 and God's response. As you close with prayer, tell students you will allow them a quiet moment when they can ask for wisdom for any issue of life. Remind students to remember Solomon's selfless prayer as they make their requests.

Let's Talk It Over

These questions are designed to promote discussion of the lesson. The answers here are only discussion starters. Let your class talk it over from there.

1. What are some things that may cause sincere, committed congregations to slip accidentally into approaches that impress people with the *packaging* of the gospel rather than the *message* of the gospel? How do we avoid this trap?

Churches naturally try to avoid placing barriers between people and the gospel. This is the will of God. However, there is a difference between using culturally relevant approaches to help people *understand* the gospel and approaches that result in trying to *impress* them with the gospel. In trying to do the first, churches can sometimes end up with the second.

Paul's example in Acts 17:16-34 helps to clarify the difference between the two. As he encountered the pagan philosophers, they referred to him as a "babbler." Paul's mannerism wasn't impressive to them! But he used some of their own, familiar terminology to help make a connection—to help them understand the gospel. We can do the same. (See also question #3, below.)

2. What steps can we take to cultivate a mindset like that of Paul, who recognized the eternal stakes involved in proclaiming the gospel?

Our own acceptance of the gospel indicates some awareness, of course. But our appreciation of its impact only grows as we mature. Personal Bible study heightens our sensitivity to the pivotal importance of responding to the gospel. Sermons and lessons that address the reality of Hell and the certainty of judgment can also help.

Regular contemplation of our own mortality personalizes the need for Jesus and helps us appreciate the plight of the lost. Even our efforts to ponder the concept of eternity itself can be of some benefit, since doing so reminds us that our time on this earth is comparatively brief.

3. In light of Paul's statement in verse 4, what is the appropriate role of personality and persuasion in preaching and teaching?

Preachers and teachers cannot help expressing their personalities. People naturally make an effort to persuade others regarding that which they value; how they do so is partly an expression of their God-given personality.

Persuasion and personality get in the way, however, when the dominant impression created by the sermon or lesson has more to do with the messenger than the message. As a wise preacher once observed, "One sermon cannot express both that the preacher is clever and that Christ is mighty to save." Something similar can be said about aspects of a worship service that entertain more than they convict.

4. The lesson contrasts God's wisdom with that of this world. Name some sources and examples of the latter. How do we guard against it?

The world's sources of wisdom include schools, TV programs, films, music, self-help experts, and personal introspection that are not grounded in a Christian worldview. Postmodernism, which locates the source of truth within each person, is a foundation for much of this error.

Two doctrines resulting from such "wisdom" are (1) that self-preservation is of the highest value and (2) that the greatest virtue is tolerance. We guard ourselves by asking the question, "What is the ultimate source of this bit of 'wisdom' that I'm being asked to accept?"

5. Suppose you talk to someone who uses verse 12 to claim that God reveals messages to him today. How do you respond?

Don't respond too quickly! Ask him to explain the types of messages he claims to be receiving and how they are being received. The other person may really be claiming that God has provided him with insight regarding particular *applications* of a text. Further discussion may reveal that the insight is coming through opened and closed doors of opportunity that God may be directing.

A claim that God is revealing a *meaning* of a text, or entirely new texts altogether, is very different. When appropriate, you can point out that adding to or subtracting from Scripture is quite dangerous (Revelation 22:18, 19). You could also suggest a case where two people end up with "messages from God" that are contradictory. Since God is not a God of confusion, what then? Of course a claim by the person to be "hearing voices" may be a sign of mental illness.

Serving Together

June 18
Lesson 3

DEVOTIONAL READING: Matthew 13:3-9.

BACKGROUND SCRIPTURE: 1 Corinthians 3:1-15.

PRINTED TEXT: 1 Corinthians 3:1-15.

1 Corinthians 3:1-15

1 And I, brethren, could not speak unto you as unto spiritual, but as unto carnal, even as unto babes in Christ.

2 I have fed you with milk, and not with meat: for hitherto ye were not able to bear it, neither yet now are ye able.

3 For ye are yet carnal: for whereas there is among you envying, and strife, and divisions, are ye not carnal, and walk as men?

4 For while one saith, I am of Paul; and another, I am of Apollos; are ye not carnal?

5 Who then is Paul, and who is Apollos, but ministers by whom ye believed, even as the Lord gave to every man?

6 I have planted, Apollos watered; but God gave the increase.

7 So then neither is he that planteth any thing, neither he that watereth; but God that giveth the increase.

8 Now he that planteth and he that watereth are one: and every man shall receive his own reward according to his own labor.

9 For we are laborers together with God: ye are God's husbandry, ye are God's building.

10 According to the grace of God which is given unto me, as a wise masterbuilder, I have laid the foundation, and another buildeth thereon. But let every man take heed how he buildeth thereupon.

11 For other foundation can no man lay than that is laid, which is Jesus Christ.

12 Now if any man build upon this foundation gold, silver, precious stones, wood, hay, stubble;

13 Every man's work shall be made manifest: for the day shall declare it, because it shall be revealed by fire; and the fire shall try every man's work of what sort it is.

14 If any man's work abide which he hath built thereupon, he shall receive a reward.

15 If any man's work shall be burned, he shall suffer loss: but he himself shall be saved; yet so as by fire.

GOLDEN TEXT: We are laborers together with God: ye are God's husbandry, ye are God's building.—1 Corinthians 3:9.

> *Called to Be a Christian Community*
> Unit 1: Servants of God
> (Lessons 1-4)

Lesson Aims

After participating in this lesson, each student will be able to:

1. Paraphrase Paul's description of the immaturity of the Corinthian Christians.
2. Explain how a diversity of gifts can help the fulfillment of the church's mission.
3. Make a plan to work cooperatively in a specific area of church ministry.

Lesson Outline

INTRODUCTION
    A. Power of Unity from Diversity
    B. Lesson Background
I. DIVISION IS BAD (1 Corinthians 3:1-4)
    A. Mere Infants (vv. 1, 2)
        Beyond Baby Talk
    B. Mere Men (vv. 3, 4)
II. DIVERSITY IS GOOD (1 Corinthians 3:5-9)
    A. The Lord Assigns Tasks (v. 5)
    B. The Workers Do Their Jobs (v. 6)
        Teamwork
    C. God Blesses and Rewards (vv. 7-9)
III. COOPERATION IS ESSENTIAL (1 Corinthians 3:10-15)
    A. Laying the Foundation (vv. 10, 11)
    B. Choosing the Materials (vv. 12, 13)
    C. Receiving the Reward (vv. 14, 15)
CONCLUSION
    A. Working Together
    B. Winning Together
    C. Prayer
    D. Thought to Remember

Introduction

A. Power of Unity from Diversity

The headline read, "Managers Err If They Limit Their Hiring To People Like Them." The story went on to quote a company's "chief people officer" as saying, "The power of any group of people is the power of the mix" (*The Wall Street Journal,* October 12, 2004). Some will read that conclusion as if it were something new. But the apostle Paul knew and taught this truth some 2,000 years ago. Like the human body itself, strength starts with diversity—with the specialization of body parts (see 1 Corinthians 12:12-31).

Diversity, however, isn't enough by itself. Those diverse parts must work together in unity. Nothing good can happen in the church (the body of Christ) without unity. Unity creates strength because it combines the separate spiritual gifts and abilities of each member. When people are united, their power is far greater than just the sum of their separate strengths.

B. Lesson Background

Paul founded the church in Corinth on his second missionary journey. He continued to work in that city for at least a year and a half (Acts 18:11, 18). Soon after Paul left, Apollos came to Corinth and had a fruitful ministry working with the new church (Acts 18:24-27). As previously discussed in the first chapter of his letter, Paul warned his readers that they must not choose up sides. To align themselves with human leaders such as himself or Apollos or Cephas (Peter) was wrong because it divided the body of Christ (1 Corinthians 1:12, 13).

In this week's lesson we will see Paul expand his argument. While division is a mark of immaturity and worldliness, unity is a beautiful part of God's master plan. If the Corinthians will learn the lesson that Paul is teaching, they will heal the divisions in their church; they will become productive coworkers in the kingdom of God.

I. Division Is Bad (1 Corinthians 3:1-4)

A. Mere Infants (vv. 1, 2)

1, 2. And I, brethren, could not speak unto you as unto spiritual, but as unto carnal, even as unto babes in Christ. I have fed you with milk, and not with meat: for hitherto ye were not able to bear it, neither yet now are ye able.

Paul reveals his feeling of goodwill when he once again addresses the Corinthians as *brethren* (see previously 1 Corinthians 1:10; 2:1). However, this sense of fellowship moves quickly to words of rebuke. The believers in Corinth are indeed brothers—but they are still baby brothers.

When Paul first arrived in Corinth he spoke to audiences that were not *spiritual,* that is, they

LESSON 3   415   JUNE 18

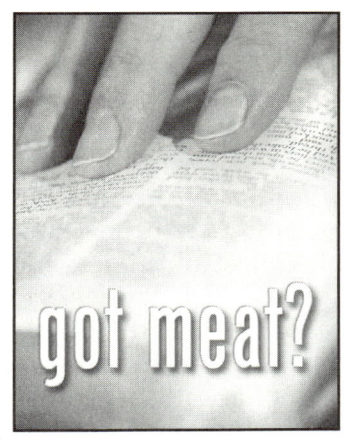

As you begin discussing verses 1, 2, ask if anyone recognizes the tie-in to a famous commercial.

Visual for lesson 3

were not in tune with divine things. The ungodly people were *carnal*; they lived their lives in response to the desires of their flesh. As carnal people they were totally unprepared to receive the deep things of God—the *meat* of the Word. Thus Paul had had to start teaching with the very basics, what he figuratively calls *milk*. (Hebrews 5:11–6:2 gives us a list of some things that are considered "milk.")

Now Paul evaluates their lack of progress toward spiritual maturity. A wise teacher knows how much the students are able to tolerate at any given time (John 16:12). That's why Paul started with "milk." But *yet now*, some four or five years later, they are still unable to digest "meat." This is unacceptable! This refusal to grow to maturity is a root cause of the division in their church. [See question #1, page 421.]

BEYOND BABY TALK

If you've ever been embarrassed when caught making nonsense sounds to an infant, take heart! You actually were doing a good thing. A new study shows that baby talk is ideal for the infant's developing neural system. A researcher noted that "the singsong, drawn-out, exaggerated form of speech has a melody to it. Inside the melody is a tutorial for the baby that contains exceptionally well-informed versions of the building blocks of language" (www.nwrel.org).

While this kind of speech may work in "conversations" with an infant, trying it with your boss could land you in the unemployment line! There is a time to move beyond baby talk. In the spiritual life all Christians should desire to move beyond being spoon-fed their spiritual diet. Teaching Bible stories through cute songs such as "Only a Boy Named David" is fine for youngsters. But to continue that into the Sunday morning worship service would be out of place.

Yet, sadly, many Christians never seem to move beyond the most elementary spiritual truths. We use the description *arrested development* when we notice people holding on to certain emotional patterns from early childhood as they grow physically toward adulthood. Unfortunately, arrested development on a spiritual level is too often considered normal and acceptable. —A. E. A.

B. Mere Men (vv. 3, 4)

3. For ye are yet carnal: for whereas there is among you envying, and strife, and divisions, are ye not carnal, and walk as men?

The statement *ye are yet carnal* is a strong rebuke. *Carnal* is the word that described the Corinthians before they came to Christ (v. 1, above). It is a tragedy that it still describes them four or five years later. The existence of *envying* (jealousy) and *strife* are symptoms of spiritual failure.

Unfortunately, Paul will have to address these same problems again (2 Corinthians 12:20). Paul also warns the churches of Galatia that "strife, seditions, . . . envyings" are products of the flesh, not of the Spirit (Galatians 5:20, 21). The plain fact is that the members of the church at Corinth are not acting as Christians ought.

4. For while one saith, I am of Paul; and another, I am of Apollos; are ye not carnal?

If the Corinthians resist being called *carnal* and immature, Paul is quick to offer proof. When *one* person says *I am of Paul* and *another* proclaims *I am of Apollos*, these very divisions expose their carnal state. As mere humans they split up over the issue of who baptized them (1 Corinthians 1:13-16). As mere humans they turned the observance of the Lord's Supper into class warfare (11:18-22). As mere humans they have a problem with orderly worship (14:26-33). As mere humans they are destroying the body of Christ!

II. Diversity Is Good (1 Corinthians 3:5-9)

A. The Lord Assigns Tasks (v. 5)

5. Who then is Paul, and who is Apollos, but ministers by whom ye believed, even as the Lord gave to every man?

Paul challenges his readers to remember the nature of both his own ministry and that of *Apollos*. Paul, of course, came along first to found their church (Acts 18:1-21). Then Apollos came after Paul. He was "an eloquent man, and mighty in the Scriptures" (Acts 18:24). When he came to Corinth he "helped them much" and "mightily convinced the Jews . . . showing by the scriptures that Jesus was Christ" (Acts 18:27, 28).

So although Paul was the founder, Apollos apparently was more eloquent and in some ways more effective. Their relative merits, however, are not the point. Both are servants of the gospel. As the Lord's servants they carry out the tasks assigned to them. They present the message; the people believe. All of this happens as *the Lord* provides. [See question #2, page 421.]

B. The Workers Do Their Jobs (v. 6)

6. I have planted, Apollos watered; but God gave the increase.

At this point Paul uses familiar agricultural imagery. Neither man should be idolized; they are just workers doing their jobs. The most important role belongs to *God*. He is the one who empowers the church planter; He is the one who gives eloquence and ability to the church builder. All the credit for the growth and *increase* of that which is planted, therefore, belongs to God.

Teamwork

Employers recognize the need for good teamwork. But what about employees who let the team down in various ways? The following are some suggestions for letters of "recommendation" (with double meanings!) for such folks as they seek employment elsewhere. For the chronically absent employee, you could write: "A man like him is hard to find"; for an employee with no ambition: "You would indeed be fortunate to get this person to work for you"; for an employee who is so unproductive that the job is better left unfilled: "I can assure you that no person would be better for the job" (www.crosswalk.com).

The church also has its share of chronically absent, poorly motivated, and unproductive members who let the team down. At the same time there are those who do quite a bit of work but also want others to know how much they have done. This is a bit like the chest thumping and strutting that goes on in sports: the player seeks to draw attention to personal accomplishments while ignoring the contributions of teammates.

Paul calls instead for the church to recognize that ministry is a cooperative effort. It is teamwork. He models this in his own ministry. It is not a matter of who gets the glory, because all the glory belongs to God. The work of the church, the team, is simply to get the work done.
—A. E. A.

C. God Blesses and Rewards (vv. 7-9)

7. So then neither is he that planteth any thing, neither he that watereth; but God that giveth the increase.

The lesson to be learned is reinforced. The Corinthians should not think that *he that planteth* is anything special; neither should they give undue credit to the one that *watereth*. No one can make a plant grow. All the praise and glory must go to God.

Even today, people should not be too quick to give people the credit—or the blame—for the way a church grows. When the workers do their assigned jobs, when every part is working effectively (Ephesians 4:16), and when Christ is honored as the head, then the body exhibits a growth that comes from God. This kind of growth is God's blessing. [See question #3, page 421.]

8. Now he that planteth and he that watereth are one: and every man shall receive his own reward according to his own labor.

There are several truths included in the statement *he that planteth and he that watereth are one*. In terms of necessity both workers are one and the same, because if either is left out no plant will grow. In terms of purpose both workers are one, because they are working to accomplish the same end. In terms of honor in the eyes of humanity, they are the same, for neither worker should be exalted above the other.

God will attend to whatever *reward* a person should receive for his or her work. Paul does not specify at this point what kind of reward that may be. Surely the highest reward any servant

---

How to Say It

APOLLOS. Uh-*pahl*-us.
BARNABAS. *Bar*-nuh-bus.
CEPHAS. *See*-fus.
CORINTH. *Kor*-inth.
CORINTHIANS. Ko-*rin*-thee-unz (*th* as in *thin*).
EPHESIANS. Ee-*fee*-zhunz.
ISAIAH. Eye-*zay*-uh.
THESSALONIANS. *Thess*-uh-*lo*-nee-unz (strong accent on *lo*; *th* as in *thin*).

of God could ever receive will be to hear the master say, "Well done" (Matthew 25:21). [See question #4, page 421.]

9. For we are laborers together with God: ye are God's husbandry, ye are God's building.

Paul and Apollos, as well as other leaders of the church, are co-laborers. They work together on the same team, striving to accomplish the same purpose. Even more importantly, in this endeavor they are also coworkers with God. What a vast thought: they are working side by side with their creator at His invitation! Their joy is seeing their work blessed by God and growing as He gives it increase.

The church is *God's husbandry,* that is, God's cultivated field. The growing church represents a harvest that belongs to God (compare Matthew 13:3-9). Using another type of imagery, Paul says the church is also *God's building.* Each of God's workmen helps to construct it, but the building itself belongs to God. Paul expands on this picture in the next several verses.

III. Cooperation Is Essential (1 Corinthians 3:10-15)

A. Laying the Foundation (vv. 10, 11)

10. According to the grace of God which is given unto me, as a wise masterbuilder, I have laid the foundation, and another buildeth thereon. But let every man take heed how he buildeth thereupon.

In the ancient world the *masterbuilder* has the responsibility of conceiving what a building should look like, setting out the *foundation,* and supervising the workmen. As the masterbuilder of the church in Corinth, Paul laid the spiritual foundation on which the new congregation was built. It was his faithful preaching that called the church there into existence.

Only by the *grace of God* is the man who had once persecuted the church now allowed to become one who lays the foundation of new congregations! Paul accepted his role as the wise masterbuilder of churches in Asia Minor and in Greece, but he never forgot that this role was given to him. He had done nothing to deserve it (compare 1 Corinthians 15:10).

Paul was not the kind of missionary to hang around in any one place too long with any one church. His task was to keep moving and planting new churches (Romans 15:20-24). When

---

Home Daily Bible Readings

Monday, June 12—Spreading God's Word (Matthew 13:3-9)
Tuesday, June 13—Let Both Grow Together (Matthew 13:24-30)
Wednesday, June 14—The Need for Teachers (Hebrews 5:7-14)
Thursday, June 15—Strengthened with Power Through the Spirit (Ephesians 3:14-21)
Friday, June 16—Servants Through Whom You Believe (1 Corinthians 3:1-9)
Saturday, June 17—Building on the Foundation of Christ (1 Corinthians 3:10-15)
Sunday, June 18—Do Not Boast About Human Leaders (1 Corinthians 3:18-23)

God led Paul to continue his missionary journeys, the task of building upon the work in Corinth necessarily fell into other hands. Those who followed Paul had to be aware of this caution: *let every man take heed how he* continues the building project.

11. For other foundation can no man lay than that is laid, which is Jesus Christ.

The most important thing for Paul and for those who follow him is that the church must be built on the right *foundation.* The foundation chosen by God and recognized by Paul is *Jesus Christ.* It is the sovereign decree of God that no one can lay any *other* foundation (Isaiah 28:16; 1 Peter 2:4-6).

Wherever and whenever we may try to establish churches, the foundation must always be Jesus Christ. The truth that He is the Messiah (Matthew 16:16), the reality that He is the Son of God (John 5:17-23), and the fact that He died on the cross and rose from the dead—this is the bedrock upon which Christianity stands.

B. Choosing the Materials (vv. 12, 13)

12. Now if any man build upon this foundation gold, silver, precious stones, wood, hay, stubble.

When a *foundation* has been laid, then each worker has the responsibility to *build upon this foundation* with certain material. The worker may be found adorning the structure with costly materials such as *gold, silver,* or *precious stones* in a given building project. Or perhaps the worker may decide to use ordinary *wood,* or even cheap materials such as *hay* or *stubble*. In each instance the worker chooses the material and then is held responsible for the result.

As we join the ongoing project of building the church of God, we should be careful to use our very best. Our commitment to live in God's truth and our sacrifices for that cause should be as if they were gold, silver, and precious stones. Any lesser effort would be like the wood or even like the hay or stubble. The way we approach our task does make a difference, as the next verse makes clear.

13. Every man's work shall be made manifest: for the day shall declare it, because it shall be revealed by fire; and the fire shall try every man's work of what sort it is.

Poor workmanship with inferior materials will not stand the test on Judgment Day. As one observer said, "Holy shoddy is still shoddy." The test of *the fire* will have different effects on works of gold and works of hay!

In the context of the leaders of the church in Corinth, this means that when they teach the pure truth of God, they make a lasting contribution. On the other hand if they focus on men's doctrines or mere personal opinions, then their work will have no lasting value.

C. Receiving the Reward (vv. 14, 15)

14. If any man's work abide which he hath built thereupon, he shall receive a reward.

Godly people will be the ones who rejoice to see their *work abide*. They did not waste their time on trivial issues; they did not put major emphasis on things of minor importance. They built on the true foundation; they chose to use the most important building materials. Therefore their work will last into eternity.

God will *reward* such faithful workers. The exact nature of this reward is not stated. Part of the reward could be the satisfaction of seeing that their lives had made an eternal difference. Perhaps an additional reward in Heaven is in mind. Paul only assures his readers that there is a reward to be gained. The Bible does teach that there are degrees of reward and punishment (Luke 12:47, 48; 19:11-27).

15. If any man's work shall be burned, he shall suffer loss: but he himself shall be saved; yet so as by fire.

On the other hand the work of certain others will not last. A teacher who does not teach the sure truths of God but wastes his time on insignificant trifles builds a house of straw. Such a person has not necessarily done evil things; rather, this kind of teacher simply has not done the best things. This person works to build something that will not matter in eternity. [See question #5, page 421.]

Paul does not say that such a person will lose eternal salvation. We are not saved, after all, by how much we have contributed to the building of the kingdom. We are saved by the grace of God that is available through the atoning death of Christ that pays the penalty for sin. The kind of person in this context who *shall suffer loss* shall be saved, but the result will be like a person who has lost possessions in a fire.

Conclusion

A. Working Together

Sometimes spiritually mature Christians will "part ways" from one another because of thoughtful, sincere differences of opinion. The split between Paul and Barnabas in Acts 15:36-41 is an example. In that instance good things resulted as two missionary teams went out rather than one.

More often, however, division in the church is a terrible thing when the root is spiritual immaturity. But diversity in the church is a good thing. It happens when God gives each person spiritual gifts, talents, and abilities to be used in building the kingdom.

We should not feel threatened when other people serve God in ways that we ourselves cannot. Instead, we should thank God that He has designed the body of Christ to have such a variety of spiritual gifts. When we each do the work God has given us to do, we can accomplish great things for His glory. Paul was not jealous of Apollos's speaking skills, and Apollos was not jealous of Paul's church-planting skills.

Cooperation is key. We are coworkers with God and with one another. Like Paul and Apollos, we serve God in assigned roles. We cooperate with God by following His instructions; we cooperate with one another by lending mutual support. God does not just want us to serve Him; He wants us to serve Him together.

B. Winning Together

The church that serves together wins together. Following the church's beginning on the Day of Pentecost in Jerusalem, it was no coincidence that victory and unity went hand in hand; believers were solidly united in victorious fashion (Acts 1:14; 2:1, 42-47). By their love for one another and their complete confidence in God, the whole city knew that they were disciples of Jesus Christ.

Winning together is more than just the result of "team spirit" or of "many hands making light work." It is the success that comes from doing what God wants in the way that He directs—and then receiving God's blessing. If we can learn to serve God together with the same spirit that Paul and Apollos had, planting and watering according to our own specific roles, then God will give the increase.

C. Prayer

Holy Father, we ask for Your forgiveness where we have been selfish and separated. Help us to reflect on earth the beautiful unity that You have shown us from Heaven. Help us to have willing hands and loving spirits so that we can serve You together. In Jesus' name, amen.

D. Thought to Remember

United we serve.

Learning by Doing

This section contains an alternative lesson plan emphasizing learning activities. Classes desiring such student involvement will find these suggestions helpful.

Learning Goals

After participating in this lesson, each student will be able to:

1. Paraphrase Paul's description of the immaturity of the Corinthian Christians.
2. Explain how a diversity of gifts can help the fulfillment of the church's mission.
3. Make a plan to work cooperatively in a specific area of church ministry.

Into the Lesson

Display a poster with the old saying, *United We Stand, Divided We Fall.* Say, "This truth illustrates national strength. It is a saying that is also true for the local church." Ask class members to discuss strife that they witnessed in other congregations. (Make sure to stress that the question is about *other* congregations, which should not be named.) What were the issues? How did the contentions surface in church life?

Make the transition to Bible study by reminding the class that divisions and contentions are not new. We have illustrations of contention in the Bible—and advice on how to overcome them.

Into the Word

Ask a volunteer to read aloud today's printed Bible text. Ask students to watch for causes of the divisions and quarrels in the Corinthian church during the reading.

Next, distribute handouts printed with the title and questions that follow; you can display them on the board or on an overhead instead if you wish. (The words in parenthesis are suggested answers to help the teacher; they should not be printed for the students.)

What About Division and Teamwork?

1. What is the evidence of problems in the Corinthian church? *(v. 3: carnality, envy, strife, division; vv. 4, 5: allegiances to different leaders)*

2. What does Paul see as the source of the divisions and quarrels? *(vv. 1, 2: spiritual immaturity, a failure to grow up as Christians)*

3. How does Paul illustrate the importance of teamwork in the church? *(vv. 6-8: an illustration of how leaders have different roles and gifts)*

4. What is Paul saying about the relationship of church leaders and members in verse 9? *(Leaders have different roles to play yet work together for the same purpose. Leaders and members must also work together in building the church.)*

5. What is one of the principles implied in verses 10-15 that we must remember in building a strong church? *(Build the church on a strong foundation.)*

6. What do you think Paul is implying in verse 15? *(God doesn't view all work done for Him to be of equal quality.)*

Divide the class into groups of two or three students. Groups are to review the Bible passage and try to discover the truths about unity and division that Paul teaches. After several minutes, call for answers and responses to each question.

Into Life

Divide the class into four groups. Give each group a piece of poster board, marker, and one of the tasks that follow. After several minutes, allow each group to share its conclusions.

Group #1: Sources of Quarrels and Division! Brainstorm potential sources of quarrels and divisions in churches. The list will be long and will highlight our need to be diligent.

Group #2: How Diversity Works! Use your imagination and list the many different gifts and passions that people bring to the church. Remember, today's Scripture makes it clear that the church is to enjoy and use these gifts, skills, and passions to labor together for the glory of Christ.

Group #3: Diversity in Our Class! Our class enjoys people who have many different spiritual gifts, skills, and passions. Use your imagination and list some of these. Feel free to mention class members' names as you make this list. However, if you do list names, be sure to use everyone's name that is present today.

Group #4: Working Together! Your task is to brainstorm several projects that we as a class could do for our church. Then select one of these projects to propose to the class as a whole. Explain how the project would use the different skills and gifts of class members.

Be sure to make plans to complete Group 4's proposal. It may be necessary to appoint two or three people to complete the planning. Conclude the class with a prayer time of thanks to God for the diversity of gifts He has given to the church leadership and members.

Let's Talk It Over

These questions are designed to promote discussion of the lesson. The answers here are only discussion starters. Let your class talk it over from there.

1. What are some things that you have allowed to hinder your own spiritual growth at times? How do you guard against these?

Hebrews 5:11 provides helpful insight regarding the fundamental reason for this failure. Like these first-century Christians, many contemporary believers are "dull of hearing." This phrase refers to a lack of willingness rather than diminished mental capacity. Simply put, believers often fail to mature because it is not a high priority.

We may complain that we lack time, but we usually find time to do the things that we most value. We may attribute spiritual immaturity to a lack of growth opportunities, but Internet resources, distance learning possibilities, and the availability of small groups through the church indicate otherwise! Ultimately, the extent of our maturity usually shows what we most desire.

2. How should viewing ourselves as servants make a difference in the way we approach our ministries?

When we truly view ourselves as God's servants, we are less likely to grumble about the specific tasks He assigns us. As we mature in this area, we notice certain results: the relative status we assign to various tasks becomes less significant. The way our master decides to use other servants becomes less of a concern. A preoccupation with how God may choose to reward us fades into the background. We focus less on our rights and more on our responsibilities. We focus less on receiving affirmation by others and more on gaining the approval of God. We view ministry as a gracious privilege God gives rather than viewing God as fortunate to have us on His side.

3. Does verse 7 mean that we should not evaluate periodically the effectiveness of our own ministries and those of others? If we do evaluate ministries, how do we balance personal responsibility with God's role in providing the increase?

Our responsibility is to work hard and demonstrate diligence (1 Timothy 4:12b-15), thereby providing a willing vessel through which God can work to accomplish His purposes. This means that we probably should hold vocational ministers more accountable for their work ethic than for the results produced. Even so, a lack of fruitfulness in a given ministry may indicate that a person is not working in an area of primary ministry strength. We can also evaluate the extent to which we (and to some degree others) are providing our master a clean vessel through which to work (2 Timothy 2:21).

4. Paul seems to indicate that God's reward functions as a motivating influence for Christians. How do we serve God without our motivation for service becoming selfish as a result?

Our ultimate motivation must be honoring God, not gaining extra stars in our crowns. Revelation 4:10 seems to depict certain individuals humbly placing their rewards before God as an expression of gratitude and worship.

One way to assess our motivation is to ask, "If the only reward I received for my service was God's pleasure with my life, would I consider my efforts to be worth it?" It is also helpful to resist speculating on the nature of our reward, especially since, as the lesson indicates, Paul doesn't offer details on this subject. This will help us avoid the temptation to view our reward in overly materialistic terms.

5. What was a time when you gave God less than your best effort? Why?

This question can serve as a time of confession for your class. You may hear many say that other matters simply received higher priority. As a result less time was available for ministry, which affected the quality of the result.

For some Christians the reason may have been a lack of concern. This may be due to selfishness. Some churches don't have quality control standards or simply don't expect high quality effort from volunteers. Perhaps many Christians think of God's judging activity purely with regard to their salvation and not in relationship to their service. (Verses 12-15 can help Christians develop a clearer understanding of this last issue.)

The list can go on and on! In order not to leave this subject on a down note, suggest some solutions that are based in accountability.

June 25
Lesson 4

Serving Faithfully

Devotional Reading: Matthew 23:8-12.

Background Scripture: 1 Corinthians 4:1-13.

Printed Text: 1 Corinthians 4:1-13.

1 Corinthians 4:1-13

1 Let a man so account of us, as of the ministers of Christ, and stewards of the mysteries of God.

2 Moreover it is required in stewards, that a man be found faithful.

3 But with me it is a very small thing that I should be judged of you, or of man's judgment: yea, I judge not mine own self.

4 For I know nothing by myself; yet am I not hereby justified: but he that judgeth me is the Lord.

5 Therefore judge nothing before the time, until the Lord come, who both will bring to light the hidden things of darkness, and will make manifest the counsels of the hearts: and then shall every man have praise of God.

6 And these things, brethren, I have in a figure transferred to myself and to Apollos for your sakes; that ye might learn in us not to think of men above that which is written, that no one of you be puffed up for one against another.

7 For who maketh thee to differ from another? and what hast thou that thou didst not receive? now if thou didst receive it, why dost thou glory, as if thou hadst not received it?

8 Now ye are full, now ye are rich, ye have reigned as kings without us: and I would to God ye did reign, that we also might reign with you.

9 For I think that God hath set forth us the apostles last, as it were appointed to death: for we are made a spectacle unto the world, and to angels, and to men.

10 We are fools for Christ's sake, but ye are wise in Christ; we are weak, but ye are strong; ye are honorable, but we are despised.

11 Even unto this present hour we both hunger, and thirst, and are naked, and are buffeted, and have no certain dwelling place;

12 And labor, working with our own hands: being reviled, we bless; being persecuted, we suffer it:

13 Being defamed, we entreat: we are made as the filth of the world, and are the offscouring of all things unto this day.

Golden Text: Let a man so account of us, as of the ministers of Christ, and stewards of the mysteries of God.—1 Corinthians 4:1.

> *Called to Be a Christian Community*
> Unit 1: Servants of God
> (Lessons 1-4)

Lesson Aims

After participating in this lesson, each student will be able to:

1. List the word pictures that Paul uses to describe the ministry of the apostles.

2. Give examples of the demands, costs, and sacrifices often required of faithful stewards.

3. Make a commitment to be a faithful steward in a specific ministry.

Lesson Outline

INTRODUCTION
    A. Hard Lesson to Learn
    B. Lesson Background
I. FAITHFUL STEWARDS (1 Corinthians 4:1-5)
    A. Position of a Steward (v. 1)
    B. Requirement of a Steward (v. 2)
        What Measure of Success?
    C. Evaluation of a Steward (vv. 3-5)
II. UNWORTHY JUDGES (1 Corinthians 4:6-8)
    A. Unwarranted Pride (v. 6)
    B. Undeserved Glory (vv. 7, 8)
III. SUFFERING APOSTLES (1 Corinthians 4:9-13)
    A. Spectacle to the World (v. 9)
    B. Fools for Christ (v. 10)
        Wise Fools
    C. Mistreated by All (vv. 11-13)
CONCLUSION
    A. Help Wanted: Inquire Above
    B. Anticipated Salary?
    C. Prayer
    D. Thought to Remember

Introduction

A. Hard Lesson to Learn

The lesson of humble servanthood is hard to learn. It is a lesson that goes against human nature, against our inner drive to climb to the top of the ladder. That's why the apostles still had not mastered it even after three years with Jesus. They were still competing with each other for the chief seats in the kingdom (see Mark 10:35-41). Even the beauty of the Last Supper was marred by their arguing over who should be regarded as the greatest (see Luke 22:24).

Fortunately, the apostles finally did learn the lesson of humble servanthood. They learned to honor Christ as the head of the church and to see themselves as His servants. As a result, they worked hard in those early years to spread the gospel and to plant churches. They did not waste time worrying over the roles assigned to anyone else. They understood that serving Christ faithfully was the most important thing.

B. Lesson Background

Now Paul has to teach the Corinthians the same lesson. The believers in Corinth were still jockeying for positions, even four or five years after their church had come into existence. They look for ways to set themselves apart as superior to others in the church. Part of the way they tried to gain importance was by lining up behind favorite leaders. When they did this, they exposed their lack of understanding of who those leaders really were.

Paul addresses this problem across four chapters in 1 Corinthians. As he moves to a conclusion, he shows how the believers in Corinth should regard Apollos and himself. More importantly, he will insist that they adopt a new way of regarding themselves. Their pride and divisions will have to be set aside before the church can go forward. They must learn the lesson of serving faithfully as God's stewards.

I. Faithful Stewards (1 Corinthians 4:1-5)

A. Position of a Steward (v. 1)

1. Let a man so account of us, as of the ministers of Christ, and stewards of the mysteries of God.

Paul insists that a person must *account*, or regard, Apollos and himself as nothing more than what they really are. These thoughts follow the stern "Therefore let no man glory in men" admonition of 1 Corinthians 3:21. [See question #1, page 430.] It is no compliment to Paul for any of his supporters to try to put him on a pedestal. It is important for the Corinthians to recognize that men such as Paul and Apollos are fellow *ministers* and *stewards*.

Those two terms bear a closer look. When Paul calls himself and Apollos *ministers,* he does not mean to imply that they are in special positions as clergy. The Greek word that Paul uses carries the idea of an "attendant" or "servant" (as, for instance, in Matthew 26:58).

The word *steward* is also interesting. In ancient times a steward has the responsibility of taking care of something. For instance, it is typical for a trusted slave to be put in charge of running a household. (See Genesis 39:2-19, where Joseph was given this role in Potiphar's household.) Paul and Apollos have been entrusted with the task of proclaiming *the mysteries of God* to the church at Corinth. These mysteries are the divine plan for salvation, a plan that previously had been disclosed only partially (see Luke 10:21, 22). In addition to his functions as minister and steward, Paul has something to say about his role as apostle in verse 9, below.

B. Requirement of a Steward (v. 2)

2. Moreover it is required in stewards, that a man be found faithful.

To be *stewards*, then, does not mean that Paul and Apollos are men of unusual importance. Instead, it means that they have been given a job to do. As stewards with a responsibility in the household of God, they answer to God for how they carry out their tasks. God requires above all that a steward *be found faithful*. This is an important point because to focus on being faithful is a bit different from a focus on being successful.

Since it is God who gives the increase (see 1 Corinthians 3:6), God's steward must not assume credit or blame for success. The Lord warned the prophet Jeremiah that he would not be successful (Jeremiah 7:27). But the Lord expected Jeremiah to be faithful nonetheless.

Visual for lesson 4

Point to this visual as you ask for specific examples of how one generation demonstrates its faithfulness to the next.

The steward who makes success the primary goal may rationalize that the end justifies means. The faithful steward, however, obeys the instructions of the Lord. Unlike King Saul in the Old Testament (see 1 Samuel 15), the faithful steward does not yield to the temptation of thinking that he or she has a better idea than the master. See also Jesus' extended remarks in Luke 12:42-48.

WHAT MEASURE OF SUCCESS?

Dr. Clarence Jordan began Koinonia Farms in Sumter County, Georgia in 1942. The Greek word *koinonia* means "fellowship," and this venture was an attempt to provide an opportunity for the poor, both black and white, to better themselves through farming. By the 1950s, however, "the locals" began to boycott this effort. Businesses would not trade with Koinonia Farms. Koinonia's roadside market was attacked. Shots were fired into Koinonia homes. The Ku Klux Klan held rallies.

On one occasion following a massive attack and destruction by opponents of Koinonia Farms, a local reporter came to interview Jordan. He asked Jordan how successful he felt now that the crops as well as many buildings on Koinonia Farms were destroyed. Jordan's response was, "As successful as the cross."

Think about it: Jesus' crucifixion did not seem like a success at the time. Yet it was the faithfulness of Jesus in going to the cross that paved the way for the ultimate success. So it was faithfulness that kept Koinonia Farms going, even to today (www.koinoniapartners.org).

God's desire for His people is that they remain faithful. Our human definitions of success, however, are often bound up in numbers or "metrics." That can be a trap! Number of Scripture verses memorized, number of services attended, number of Sunday school pins earned, etc., are things that, at their best, *result from* faithfulness. At their worst, they become a basis for salvation by works (Luke 18:9-12).

—A. E. A.

C. Evaluation of a Steward (vv. 3-5)

3. But with me it is a very small thing that I should be judged of you, or of man's judgment: yea, I judge not mine own self.

It is a very small thing to Paul whether the Corinthians praise him or condemn him. Paul has no interest in winning a popularity contest. [See question #2, page 430.] It is God's judgment that matters (v. 5, below).

In a sense not even Paul's own judgment matters. Think about how important that is! If Paul were to judge himself highly, he could become arrogant (Romans 12:3). On the other hand, to judge himself too low may lead to despair; it may lead him to forget about the Spirit as his source of strength.

Thus it is irrelevant whether Paul holds himself in high esteem or in low. The only evaluation of Paul and his ministry that really counts will not come from any human. It will not even come from Paul himself.

4. For I know nothing by myself; yet am I not hereby justified: but he that judgeth me is the Lord.

Paul goes on to strengthen the argument of verse 3. He can say in good conscience that he knows *nothing* against himself. This is the same kind of statement he made to the Sanhedrin in Acts 23:1. Paul thinks that a good conscience is important (see Acts 24:16; Romans 9:1; 2 Corinthians 1:12; etc.). However, a good conscience alone will not make him *justified* or proved right. Paul's self-assessment is not the evaluation that counts.

The one to evaluate Paul is the *Lord*. Paul is a steward of God; therefore God must be the judge who rules on Paul's case. God will do this through Jesus Christ, to whom He has assigned all judgment (see John 5:22).

5. Therefore judge nothing before the time, until the Lord come, who both will bring to light the hidden things of darkness, and will make manifest the counsels of the hearts: and then shall every man have praise of God.

The issue of human judgments is somewhat complicated in the New Testament. In the verse before us, Paul tells the Corinthians to *judge nothing*. But then in chapter 5 he will stress the importance of judging the immoral behavior of a church member. How shall we sort this out?

The solution is the context. Notice that the word *therefore* ties *judge nothing* to what was said in verses 1-3. Thus the Corinthians are not to try to evaluate anything about the ministries of Paul and Apollos *before the time* of the Lord's return. At the proper time all stewards will present their accounts. It is the *Lord* who *will bring to light* even *the hidden things of darkness,* the things that people think that no one else even knows about. The Lord, who knows the *hearts* of all, is the one who *will make manifest* their secret thoughts and *counsels.*

For the faithful steward this future time of judgment need not be feared. Everyone who has faithfully done his or her duty will have the *praise of God.* Even though a person may have been despised by others, even though a person may be unworthy in his or her own eyes, the faithful steward will be rewarded by the master.

II. Unworthy Judges (1 Corinthians 4:6-8)

A. Unwarranted Pride (v. 6)

6. And these things, brethren, I have in a figure transferred to myself and to Apollos for your sakes; that ye might learn in us not to think of men above that which is written, that no one of you be puffed up for one against another.

This verse cements the idea of "judge nothing" in verse 5. Up to this point the Corinthians have been *puffed up for one against another.* This means that when the Corinthians started choosing sides—lining up behind Paul, *Apollos,* etc.—they naturally began to think "our group is more in the right than your group." This kind of arrogance and pride must come to an end.

By seeing that Paul does not desire to be glorified, the Corinthians will learn that no one among their number should seek such glory either. [See question #3, page 430.] Their thinking should be controlled by what Scripture says *(that which is written).* When that happens, they will refrain from giving mere men their allegiance. Thus there are two parts to the issue: mature leaders who wisely know not to accept undue praise and church members who learn not to give it.

B. Undeserved Glory (vv. 7, 8)

7. For who maketh thee to differ from another? and what hast thou that thou didst not receive? now if thou didst receive it, why dost thou glory, as if thou hadst not received it?

Next, Paul challenges his readers to give honest answers to three questions. First, who is it that makes any one of them any different from any other? The necessary answer is "God"; thus unless the Corinthians get out of the judging business they will find themselves judging God's choices! The Corinthians must stop trying to set up a "pecking order" to assign the relative worth of each person (see also 2 Corinthians 10:12).

Second, what does anyone have that was not received as a gift from God? Paul has much more to say about spiritual gifts in Romans 12; 1 Corinthians 12; and Ephesians 4. The bottom line is that every person's position is a stewardship that he or she has received from God.

Third, since it must be admitted that no one has anything that was not a gift from God, then why should anyone *glory* or boast? How can anyone try to pretend that he or she has any good thing that was not a gift? It is a dangerous thing to receive glory from other people, as Herod learned at his death (see Acts 12:23).

8. Now ye are full, now ye are rich, ye have reigned as kings without us: and I would to God ye did reign, that we also might reign with you.

Up to this point the Corinthians apparently have responded incorrectly to the issues of verse 7. So Paul uses irony to rebuke his readers. In their spiritual immaturity they see themselves as *full* and *rich;* since they reign *as kings* in their own minds, they think they do not need Paul and the apostles.

Generously, Paul says he would to *God* that actually the Corinthians *did reign.* If they really did hold positions of power and authority, then they could share the benefits with the church. Paul and the other apostles could reign with them. But surely they see that the lofty positions of their imaginations are false!

III. Suffering Apostles (1 Corinthians 4:9-13)

A. Spectacle to the World (v. 9)

9. For I think that God hath set forth us the apostles last, as it were appointed to death: for we are made a spectacle unto the world, and to angels, and to men.

As an antidote to the sickness of the Corinthians' pride, Paul shows them what God has done with the *apostles* themselves. God has not put them on "church thrones" with special glory and privileges. Rather, He has set forth the apostles as men *appointed to death.* In contrast to the Corinthians' self-importance, Christ's own apostles are treated as though they are condemned criminals. The world gawks at them in derision. The apostles suffer and are put on display while *angels* above and *men* below look on. (See also

---

How to Say It
APOLLOS. Uh-*pahl*-us.
CORINTH. *Kor*-inth.
CORINTHIANS. Ko-*rin*-thee-unz (*th* as in *thin*).
JEREMIAH. Jair-uh-*my*-uh.
KOINONIA (Greek). koy-no-*nee*-uh.
LAMENTATIONS. Lam-en-*tay*-shunz.
POTIPHAR. *Pot*-ih-far.
SANHEDRIN. *San*-huh-drun or San-*heed*-run.
THESSALONIANS. *Thess*-uh-*lo*-nee-unz (strong accent on *lo; th* as in *thin*).

Romans 8:36; Hebrews 10:32-34.) [See question #4, page 430.]

B. Fools for Christ (v. 10)

10. We are fools for Christ's sake, but ye are wise in Christ; we are weak, but ye are strong; ye are honorable, but we are despised.

The irony continues. Paul and the apostles are regarded by the world as *fools,* and they willingly accept that role for *Christ's sake.* By contrast, the proud Corinthians see themselves as *wise in Christ.* Although they are really just babies in their spiritual understanding, they proudly exalt themselves above their teachers. If they are really *wise,* they would not need this harsh lesson!

Pushing the irony yet further, Paul shows how the apostles are willing to be *weak,* but the Corinthians see themselves as *strong.* The Corinthians claim to be *honorable,* even though their original leaders are *despised.* They do not understand the principle of a steward caring only for the approval of his master and disregarding human judgments.

WISE FOOLS

Students in the second year of college or high school are called sophomores. This label actually is not very flattering! It's a combination of two Greek words: *sophos,* meaning "wise," and *moros,* meaning "foolish." Thus a sophomore is a wise fool, a seeming contradiction in terms. Perhaps the idea is that a little knowledge can be dangerous. Some Christians, wise in their own eyes, are rightly called fools by the world because of their immaturity and self-promotion.

Other Christians (like the apostle Paul) are indeed very wise in the knowledge of God, yet they too are called fools by the world. The reason for this is that the world, in its "wisdom," does not understand the things of God (Romans 1:22). True Christian wisdom appears to be foolishness to this world. Sometimes true Christian wisdom even appears to be foolishness to some spiritually immature Christians.

A mark of spiritual maturity is the willingness to be considered foolish by all others, knowing that you are wise toward God (see 1 Corinthians 1:18-31). We could say that the idea is to be a permanent sophomore—a permanent wise fool—in the kingdom of God. Any takers? —A. E. A.

C. Mistreated by All (vv. 11-13)

11. Even unto this present hour we both hunger, and thirst, and are naked, and are buffeted, and have no certain dwelling place.

When Paul lists these sufferings, he is not asking for pity. Rather, he is hoping that the Corinthians can see the folly of their pride. The apostles are not treated like princes of the church; instead, they *hunger and thirst*. See a more graphic list in 2 Corinthians 11:23-28. [See question #5, page 430.]

Although bringing the message of salvation to all, the apostles are mistreated. They accept this as part of the role that God has assigned to them. Living as they do, they show what things are important and what things really are not. Jesus had warned the apostles that it would be like this. He had no place to lay His head (Luke 9:58); He was despised and rejected (Isaiah 53:3). The apostles are not surprised when they don't receive any better treatment than He did (see John 15:20).

12. And labor, working with our own hands: being reviled, we bless; being persecuted, we suffer it.

Rather than living off of the offerings of the people, Paul and the others often *labor* and work with their own *hands* (Acts 18:3; 20:34; 1 Corinthians 9:14, 15; 1 Thessalonians 2:9; 2 Thessalonians 3:8). This is not the pattern of traveling pagan teachers of the day. Do the Corinthians now look down on Paul for lowering himself to manual labor? (See 2 Corinthians 11:7.)

When the apostles are *reviled*, they *bless* and encourage in return. In so doing the apostles are only doing what Jesus himself taught (see Matthew 5:44). When the apostles are *persecuted*, they endure it. They ask for no special treatment.

13. Being defamed, we entreat; we are made as the filth of the world, and are the offscouring of all things unto this day.

This sounds like Lamentations 3:45, which speaks of the condition of the Jews in exile. The apostles serve Christ in unique positions, yet they are treated like *filth* and *offscouring*. They have been made to be no better than the mud people scrape off their feet. But when the apostles are *defamed*, they respond gently *(entreat)*.

If the apostles are willing to be treated like garbage, why should the Christians in Corinth try to climb ladders of self-importance? How can they wallow in their own pride while ignoring greater issues of stewardship and faithfulness to their master? Surely the vivid language of Paul will wake them up and make them see the truth.

Conclusion

A. Help Wanted: Inquire Above

God is hanging out the "Help Wanted" sign in every congregation. He is not looking for more people to serve as critics; there are already too many people who have taken that job. God does not need any self-inflated people who waste their time trying to establish the order of importance of all the members of His family.

The job openings that God has available are for stewards. The people who apply for this position do not need to be highly skilled; neither do they have to have a history of great success. What they really need is a commitment to be faithful. God will place certain job responsibilities in the hands of His stewards, with each job suited to the worker. God will work side by side with His stewards. There al-

---

Home Daily Bible Readings

Monday, June 19—Good Stewards of God's Grace (1 Peter 4:1-11)

Tuesday, June 20—Jesus Washes Peter's Feet (John 13:2-9)

Wednesday, June 21—Serve One Another (John 13:12-17)

Thursday, June 22—Become a Servant (Mark 10:41-45)

Friday, June 23—Stewards of God's Mysteries (1 Corinthians 4:1-7)

Saturday, June 24—We Are Fools for Christ (1 Corinthians 4:8-13)

Sunday, June 25—A Fatherly Admonition on Responsibility (1 Corinthians 4:14-21)

ways will be an opening for the person who is sincerely interested.

B. Anticipated Salary?

The reward for self-appointed critics is minimal. They are making no real contribution to the kingdom; they are not doing anything God has asked them to do. But the reward for stewards is great, even more than they can imagine.

The reward may not be immediate. Like the apostles in the first century, faithful stewards of God may face persecution and suffering. They may endure hunger and thirst; they may be dishonored and homeless. In the eyes of the world they may be as worthless as the garbage scraped from dirty pots and pans. The world may think they are fools.

If the steward is a fool to work for this kind of wage (in the eyes of the world), then he or she is a fool for Christ's sake. This steward is faithful to a heavenly calling, obedient to a worthy Lord. This kind of steward knows of those things that have lasting significance. Most of all, he or she puts all trust in God, believing that God will reward.

C. Prayer

Our Father, thank You for entrusting to each of us a responsibility in Your work. Strengthen us in the face of opposition. Teach us to bless those who revile. Help us to strive, above all else, to be faithful. In the name of Jesus, amen.

D. Thought to Remember

The goal of a steward is to be found faithful.

Learning by Doing

This section contains an alternative lesson plan emphasizing learning activities. Classes desiring such student involvement will find these suggestions helpful.

Learning Goals

After this lesson each student will be able to:

1. List the word pictures that Paul uses to describe the ministry of the apostles.
2. Give examples of the demands, costs, and sacrifices often required of faithful stewards.
3. Make a commitment to be a faithful steward in a specific ministry.

Into the Lesson

Before class begins, display a sign that says, *Valuable Church Leadership Traits and Qualities*. On a nearby table have painter's tape (so walls and paint are not damaged), paper, and markers.

As class members enter the room, ask each to jot on a sheet of paper one characteristic that he or she values in a church leader. Have students tape their completed papers to the wall around the sign you prepared.

Begin the lesson by telling the class, "Today's study obviously has something to do with church leadership. We've already learned from each other what we value in church leaders." Review the characteristics that students posted on the wall. You may want to ask why some of these traits are significant in church leaders.

Tell the class, "Today we'll discover some unexpected traits and characteristics valued by the apostle Paul." Put up signs with the following words: *hungry and thirsty, rags for clothes, persecuted, slandered and cursed, filth of the world*, and *servant*. Say, "This is how Paul described himself as an apostle of Christ. While Paul would not belittle the valuable traits in leadership we've already posted, he has something to teach us about church leadership in today's encounter with the Corinthian church."

Into the Word

Activity #1: A Brief Lecture. Prepare your lecture from the notes in the lesson Introduction, using the following main points: 1. A Hard Lesson; 2. Lessons Learned; 3. A Lesson to Teach. List the outline on the board as you speak.

Make the transition to activity #2 by saying, "Today's Bible text could be confusing at first glance. We must realize that Paul, while sounding like he is filled with praise for the Corinthian church, occasionally writes with sarcasm and irony. In our last study Paul accused the church of failing to grow up. They were still merely babes feeding on milk. Today's text is not one of praise but is laced with irony."

Activity #2: Listing and Lessons. This activity can be done in small groups or completed as a whole class. (This activity can also be found in the student books.)

Prepare handouts (or a visual if the whole class is working together) that have three columns. The left column will have the verse references below. The middle column should have the heading *Paul's Description of Himself.* The right column should have the heading *Lessons from Observing the Corinthians.*

Students are to look up each verse, determine what the passage teaches about Christian leadership, then write what they learned under the two headings. Discussion ideas are listed in parenthesis. Before work begins, remind students that Paul uses irony and sarcasm in verses 8-12. Allow time for students to share their answers.

v. 1a (ministers of Christ); *v. 1b* (stewards of the mysteries of God); *v. 2* (faithful); *vv. 3, 4* (God's judgment matters, not man's); *v. 5* (be careful in judging leaders); *vv. 6, 7* (Paul practices what he preaches); *v. 8* (irony: teaching a false self-sufficiency); *v. 9* (a spectacle unto the world); *v. 10* (irony: the apostles are fools and weak while the Corinthians are wise and strong); *v. 11* (hungry, thirsty, naked, persecuted, homeless); *v. 12* (hard labor, reviled yet blessing the revilers, persecuted); *v. 13* (defamed, filth of the world).

Into Life

Use one or more of the following as time allows:

Activity #1: Ask the class what additional characteristics of church leaders they would add to the signs created at the beginning of the lesson.

Activity #2: Ask the class for names of church leaders who demonstrate positive qualities listed in the previous activity.

Activity #3: Distribute inexpensive thank-you cards to each student. Ask class members to write an appreciation note to a church leader and mail it this week. Better yet, deliver the note with a homemade dessert!

Let's Talk It Over

These questions are designed to promote discussion of the lesson. The answers here are only discussion starters. Let your class talk it over from there.

1. How do you welcome sincere expressions of appreciation without becoming prideful? In what ways do you need continued spiritual growth in this area?

Biblical writers express appreciation to their readers (examples: Romans 1:7, 8; 2 John 4; Revelation 2:2, 3). Thus it must be possible to receive such expressions in humility.

One way we can receive compliments in a godly fashion is by crediting the Lord for our ministry successes (1 Corinthians 3:6, 7). We can do this verbally in response to others, but we can also remind ourselves of this regularly so we don't get carried away by expressions of gratitude. We can also view these moments as affirmations from one of God's fellow servants that we are serving effectively in ways that match our gifts to the ministry we perform.

We should also be careful not to go so far as to shrug off compliments; to do that may undervalue the need of others to express appreciation.

2. The statement, "I'm not concerned about what people think" can appear arrogant. How can we be accountable to other believers without becoming overly focused on human judgments?

Paul defends the credibility of his ministry in 1 and 2 Corinthians, so he was not completely unconcerned about how people viewed his work. Like Paul, however, we are to recognize that only God can perfectly judge our work. Sincere Christians can misevaluate the effectiveness and motivation of others—not to mention themselves.

Therefore, we must treat the assessments of others as a means through which God *may* be working to guide us. We do not assume that every such assessment is directly from God. Maintaining this delicate balance requires both a commitment to God and a recognition that He often guides us through the insights of mature believers. Think of how Moses might have ended up if he had not paid attention to the wise evaluation of his father-in-law! (See Exodus 18:13-26.)

3. What was a time when learning by example helped you develop selflessness in a way that a sermon or lesson may not have?

Sermons and lessons play a crucial role in helping us understand Scripture's call to godly, selfless living. However, effective sermons work best when combined with tangible examples of godly people who put their faith into action. Sermons can be an excellent means of providing God's principles for living; a "live illustration" of someone's godly, selfless behavior becomes a very personal example to us. Jesus and Paul both knew this (see John 13:15; 1 Corinthians 11:1).

4. Was there ever a time when Paul's own experiences of suffering helped you through a time of hardship for Christ? Explain.

Difficulties and persecution can sometimes cause us to wonder if God really cares about us or even if we truly are saved. Paul's experiences show that such trials may be evidence that God is working actively through us; our reaction to trials is often the best evidence that we are living faithfully for God (2 Timothy 3:12). Knowing that Paul suffered great hardship for Christ reminds us that such experiences should not come as a surprise.

Hardship challenges us to make appropriate, godly responses to those who make life difficult for us. Our love for Christ motivates us to respond with kindness and to endure patiently. Paul's example reflects that of Jesus.

5. Paul's criticism contains a fair amount of what can be termed "sanctified sarcasm." What are some benefits and dangers of employing this same strategy ourselves?

Irony or sarcasm is a strategy most safely employed by those who are inspired directly by God to do so. Old Testament prophets (as in Isaiah 44:12-20) and New Testament apostles are examples. Paul's use of irony does show that God may be in favor of its usage at times. It can shock people into recognizing a shortcoming.

Such a strategy must be used carefully, however! We must assess our motivation to make sure we really have others' well-being in mind. It is easy to justify sarcasm when we are really just letting off steam or revealing an angry or cynical spirit. Perhaps we should err on the side of caution when considering the use of sarcasm.

Called to Relationships

July 2
Lesson 5

DEVOTIONAL READING: 1 John 4:7-16.

BACKGROUND SCRIPTURE: 1 Corinthians 7.

PRINTED TEXT: 1 Corinthians 7:1-15.

1 Corinthians 7:1-15

1 Now concerning the things whereof ye wrote unto me: It is good for a man not to touch a woman.

2 Nevertheless, to avoid fornication, let every man have his own wife, and let every woman have her own husband.

3 Let the husband render unto the wife due benevolence: and likewise also the wife unto the husband.

4 The wife hath not power of her own body, but the husband: and likewise also the husband hath not power of his own body, but the wife.

5 Defraud ye not one the other, except it be with consent for a time, that ye may give yourselves to fasting and prayer; and come together again, that Satan tempt you not for your incontinency.

6 But I speak this by permission, and not of commandment.

7 For I would that all men were even as I myself. But every man hath his proper gift of God, one after this manner, and another after that.

8 I say therefore to the unmarried and widows, It is good for them if they abide even as I.

9 But if they cannot contain, let them marry: for it is better to marry than to burn.

10 And unto the married I command, yet not I, but the Lord, Let not the wife depart from her husband:

11 But and if she depart, let her remain unmarried, or be reconciled to her husband: and let not the husband put away his wife.

12 But to the rest speak I, not the Lord: If any brother hath a wife that believeth not, and she be pleased to dwell with him, let him not put her away.

13 And the woman which hath a husband that believeth not, and if he be pleased to dwell with her, let her not leave him.

14 For the unbelieving husband is sanctified by the wife, and the unbelieving wife is sanctified by the husband: else were your children unclean; but now are they holy.

15 But if the unbelieving depart, let him depart. A brother or a sister is not under bondage in such cases: but God hath called us to peace.

GOLDEN TEXT: I would that all men were even as I myself. But every man hath his proper gift of God, one after this manner, and another after that.
—1 Corinthians 7:7.

> *Called to Be a Christian Community*
> Unit 2: Called to Obedience
> (Lessons 5-9)

Lesson Aims

After participating in this lesson, each student will be able to:
1. Summarize Paul's views on singleness, marriage, and divorce.
2. Give examples of how the secular world rejects Paul's views on marriage and divorce.
3. Use scriptural principles to recommend godly conduct on issues or cases of singleness, marriage, and divorce.

Lesson Outline

INTRODUCTION
  A. What Would You Do?
  B. Lesson Background
I. SEXUAL PURITY (1 Corinthians 7:1, 2)
  A. What Is Good, Part 1 (v. 1)
  B. What Is Good, Part 2 (v. 2)
II. SHARED OWNERSHIP (1 Corinthians 7:3-5)
  A. Duty to Fulfill (v. 3)
  B. Temptation to Avoid (vv. 4, 5)
III. STAYING SINGLE (1 Corinthians 7:6-9)
  A. Singleness as a Choice (v. 6)
  B. Single like Paul (vv. 7, 8)
    No Sin in SINgle
  C. Self-Control (v. 9)
IV. TILL DEATH DO US PART (1 Corinthians 7:10-15)
  A. God's Ideal (vv. 10, 11)
  B. Our Responsibilities (vv. 12, 13)
  C. Sanctified Homes (v. 14)
    My Mission, My Mate
  D. Not Under Bondage (v. 15)
CONCLUSION
  A. Not in Bondage
  B. Prayer
  C. Thought to Remember

Introduction

A. What Would You Do?

Ray was a godly man faced with a dilemma. He had been a faithful Christian for almost 30 years and was very active in his church. His wife, Susan, had been raised in a Christian home and was also involved in various types of service. Not surprisingly, Ray eventually was asked to consider serving as a deacon, but he was unsure whether to accept the nomination. When Ray accepted Christ, his first wife left him because she was not interested in religion.

Susan, for her part, had divorced her husband after suffering years of mental and physical abuse; he immediately remarried a nonbeliever. Ray and Susan eventually met through a mutual Christian friend, and they have been married for almost 20 years. Many in the church were not even aware that this was a second marriage for both. Yet Ray still was concerned that his divorce could threaten his credibility as an officer of the church.

Valerie also had a problem. She had lived with a man for 10 years, finally marrying him when she became pregnant. But before the child's first birthday, her husband announced that married life was not for him and dissolved the union. She then began to date a coworker who recently was widowed. Soon after their marriage they accepted Christ together. Valerie knew that her past sins were forgiven but remained plagued with doubt as to whether she should accept certain service opportunities in the church.

Situations such as these often are the norm rather than the exception. They bring with them doubt, guilt, and uncertainty. They were all too common in Corinth, a city known throughout the ancient world for sexual immorality. Paul attempted to address such problems by giving the Corinthians clear instructions for sexuality, marriage, divorce, and remarriage.

B. Lesson Background

As we have seen thus far in our summer lessons, the Corinthian church was troubled with many problems. Paul had received reports of these issues from certain individuals who visited him (1 Corinthians 1:11). They apparently also had brought Paul a letter from the church to request his insights on certain issues (7:1).

At the time Paul wrote his letter, the church in Corinth was no more than five years old. Given the moral climate within that church (see 1 Corinthians 5:1-11) and in that city, Paul sees the need to discuss at some length godly values about sex and marriage.

I. Sexual Purity
(1 Corinthians 7:1, 2)

A. What Is Good, Part 1 (v. 1)

1. Now concerning the things whereof ye wrote unto me: It is good for a man not to touch a woman.

This statement is apparently a summary answer to a specific question that is not indicated in the text. The phrase *whereof ye wrote unto me* indicates that the Corinthian believers had asked Paul whether Christians ought to be married in the first place. Some religions and philosophies of the time teach that the physical body is inherently evil. They therefore advocate strict abstinence from all physical pleasures, including sex. Or perhaps the Corinthians had asked whether Christians must be married in order to be faithful to Christ.

As Paul begins his answer, we should pause to note that the word *touch* in the original Greek is sometimes used as a figurative way of referring to sexual relations. Is Paul, then, saying that people who take a vow of chastity are somehow more spiritual? It is important to stress that the word *good* here could be paraphrased "fine" or "OK." Thus it is valid for a person to remain single if he or she wishes—provided, of course, that such a person is not sexually active. Marriage is the norm (Genesis 2:18), but Christians are not obligated to get married.

B. What Is Good, Part 2 (v. 2)

2. Nevertheless, to avoid fornication, let every man have his own wife, and let every woman have her own husband.

While it's fine to stay single, Paul realizes that most people will seek sexual intimacy. He therefore clarifies two things about God's design for sexuality. First, sex outside of marriage *(fornication)* is wrong. [See question #1, page 439.] Sex between unwed people is a sin, and marriage is God's solution. Being single is fine as long as one can control sexual desires and avoid sexual temptation. Paul's second clarification is in the verse that follows.

II. Shared Ownership
(1 Corinthians 7:3-5)

A. Duty to Fulfill (v. 3)

3. Let the husband render unto the wife due benevolence: and likewise also the wife unto the husband.

Paul now describes the sexual responsibilities inherent in marriage. Sex between married partners is not simply for reproduction. The desire for sexual intimacy with a spouse is a natural and important aspect of marriage, even when it does not result in childbirth.

In the antique English of the *King James Version*, the word *benevolence* should not be understood in the modern sense of taking pity and "doing someone a favor." The idea is more one of *obligation*. The Greek word at issue is translated in terms of "something owed" in numerous places in the *King James Version* (examples: Matthew 18:32; Luke 16:7). In cultures where sexual immorality is rampant, a Christian should protect his or her spouse from temptation by fulfilling the partner's reasonable desires and needs.

Sexual intimacy is thus, in one sense, a duty of Christian marriage. (Some prefer to speak of *marital responsibility* rather than *duty*.) It should go without saying that a Christian should be sensitive to his or her spouse's needs and should not use sexual intimacy as a bargaining chip or a reward. Such conduct can ruin the marriage.

B. Temptation to Avoid (vv. 4, 5)

4. The wife hath not power of her own body, but the husband: and likewise also the husband hath not power of his own body, but the wife.

Verse 4 emphasizes the point in verse 3 by appealing to the principle of Genesis 2:24: *husband* and *wife* are united as one flesh in a bond. The mutual nature of Paul's remarks is encouraging, for in the ancient world women typically are viewed as the property of their husbands, with few rights.

The stress of mutual "ownership" in the marriage relationship should not be taken as a license to be insensitive or inconsiderate. The

---

How to Say It

CORINTH. *Kor*-inth.
CORINTHIANS. Ko-*rin*-thee-unz (*th* as in thin).
DEUTERONOMY. Due-ter-*ahn*-uh-me.
FORNICATION. for-neh-*kay*-shun.
MALACHI. *Mal*-uh-kye.
MOSAIC. Mo-*zay*-ik.

> ### Home Daily Bible Readings
>
> **Monday, June 26**—God Is Love (1 John 4:7-16)
> **Tuesday, June 27**—Instructions for Husbands and Wives (1 Corinthians 7:1-5)
> **Wednesday, June 28**—Advice to the Unmarried and Widows (1 Corinthians 7:6-11)
> **Thursday, June 29**—An Unbelieving Spouse (1 Corinthians 7:12-16)
> **Friday, June 30**—Live as God Called You (1 Corinthians 7:17-24)
> **Saturday, July 1**—Remain as You Are (1 Corinthians 7:25-31)
> **Sunday, July 2**—Unhindered Devotion to the Lord (1 Corinthians 7:32-40)

larger context of Paul's teachings simply won't allow that idea. That larger context speaks of the need to show respect to all, especially members of one's family. If one's spouse is ill or burdened temporarily with stress, it should be assumed that sexual expectations will be set aside for a time.

Further, a spouse's legal rights are to be respected because we are bound to obey the laws of the land (Romans 13:1-7). A spouse is not to be forced into unwanted sexual contact.

5. Defraud ye not one the other, except it be with consent for a time, that ye may give yourselves to fasting and prayer; and come together again, that Satan tempt you not for your incontinency.

In some cases, however, a couple may voluntarily choose to refrain from sexual contact. Such periods must be by mutual agreement and for spiritual purposes. Caution: one cannot use spiritual concerns as an excuse to withhold sexual intimacy, especially in cases where this would *tempt* the spouse to be unfaithful.

III. Staying Single
(1 Corinthians 7:6-9)

A. Singleness as a Choice (v. 6)

6. But I speak this by permission, and not of commandment.

This verse presents us with a slight problem: does the word *this* refer to what Paul has just finished saying, or does it refer to what he's about to say next? The context of *permission, and not of commandment* makes us think that it's what Paul is about to say next regarding the choice to remain single. Sexual intimacy in marriage is expected. But whether or not one gets married in the first place is a matter of personal choice. Paul therefore offers the following comments as good advice, not as an absolute rule that every person must follow.

B. Single like Paul (vv. 7, 8)

7a. For I would that all men were even as I myself.

Very little is known about Paul's pre-Christian life. We are not certain if Paul was ever married, but verses 7, 8 imply that he is single at the time he writes this letter (see also 1 Corinthians 9:5). The fact that he is not responsible for a wife and children allows him greater freedom to pursue his ministry. [See question #2, page 439.]

NO SIN IN SINGLE

Remember the old "Pairs and Spares" Sunday school class name? We should thank the Lord that the insensitive viewpoint expressed by such a designation is largely behind us! Scripture does not consider singleness to be a sin or something that must be "corrected." For those who can resist the sin of fornication, singleness is even praised in the New Testament.

Churches must find ways to minister effectively to singles. Churches should also open doors of opportunities for singles to be involved in the ministry of the church. Both imperatives require churches to be sensitive to the special circumstances in which singles sometimes find themselves. On the occasion of a Christmas dinner in a nice restaurant, a married man sitting next to a single woman suggested that she was better off at this meal since she had to pay only for one. She quickly replied, "Yes, but I have only one income."

Does your church have a deliberate, intentional plan for singles? Or do your church's ministries to and by singles happen pretty much "by accident"? There is no sin in singleness, but there is sin in ignoring this group. —A. E. A.

7b, 8. But every man hath his proper gift of God, one after this manner, and another after that. I say therefore to the unmarried and widows, It is good for them if they abide even as I.

Later Paul will say that believers should serve Christ as well as they can in whatever situation they find themselves (1 Corinthians 7:17-24). Viewed from this perspective, singleness and marriage are both gifts of God, opportunities for service. Those who are single therefore should not feel like second-class citizens. They should not rush into a marriage just because they think that that's what "normal" people do. Paul apparently does not feel compelled to find a wife, even though almost all Jewish men in his culture have families. If you can best serve God by remaining single and celibate, then don't get married.

C. Self-Control (v. 9)

9. But if they cannot contain, let them marry: for it is better to marry than to burn.

The word *contain* refers to controlling one's sexual desires. Some may wish, like Paul, to remain single. Paul advises them to try that lifestyle for a time and see if it suits them; if sexual desires become a distraction or threaten to lead one into sin, then get married. *Burn* does not refer to the fires of Hell but rather to the burning sexual desires that a single person may encounter.

Singleness may open distinct opportunities for service. But if sexual temptation is too much of a distraction, then singleness becomes counterproductive. This same philosophy underlies Paul's remarks in 1 Timothy 5:9-15. [See question #3, page 439.]

IV. Till Death Do Us Part (1 Corinthians 7:10-15)

A. God's Ideal (vv. 10, 11)

10. And unto the married I command, yet not I, but the Lord, Let not the wife depart from her husband.

Paul now turns from the situation of the single believer to that of the *married* Christian. The Corinthians are apparently uncertain about godly standards for divorce and remarriage. As in our culture, divorce is common in the ancient world. Paul's general rule for divorce is simply this: don't do it.

Not I, but the Lord means that Paul is referring back to something that Jesus said about this issue, probably the teaching in Matthew 5:27-32 or 19:3-9 (or both). Jesus taught that *husband* and *wife* are joined together by God. As such, divorce must always be the very last option in marital difficulty. God hates divorce ("putting away"; Malachi 2:16).

Paul also undoubtedly supports Jesus' conclusion that divorce is permissible in cases where one's spouse is guilty of adultery (note: permissible, not required). But since the situation under consideration in these verses does not involve adultery, Paul states the general rule without mentioning Jesus' exception clause.

11. But and if she depart, let her remain unmarried, or be reconciled to her husband: and let not the husband put away his wife.

Paul seems to be touching on a loophole in the Mosaic law about divorce that Jesus also anticipated. Jesus notes in Matthew 5:31 that someone theoretically could get divorced and remarried just to avoid adultery—simply divorce your current *wife*, following Deuteronomy 24:1-4, and then marry the other woman whom you now desire.

To avoid this problem, both Jesus and Paul insist that the divorced person must not remarry. In other words, you cannot divorce your wife and then marry another just so that you can fulfill your sexual desires, even though this technically would avoid the sin of adultery (because you did not have sex with the other person before the divorce). [See question #4, page 439.]

B. Our Responsibilities (vv. 12, 13)

12. But to the rest speak I, not the Lord: If any brother hath a wife that believeth not, and she be pleased to dwell with him, let him not put her away.

I, not the Lord means that Paul now is going to extend Jesus' principle about divorce to a situation where a believer is married to an unbeliever.

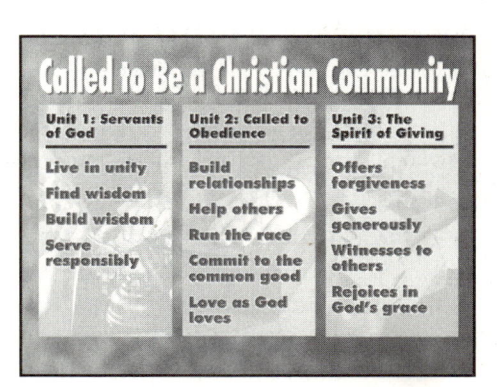

Visual for lesson 5

Refer again to this quarter's outline to remind your students of the multi-faceted nature of the church.

In cities such as Corinth, people would often accept Christ whether their spouses did or not. This means that many Christians were married to people who continued in pagan beliefs and lifestyles.

One might point to Paul's teaching that believers should not be unequally yoked (2 Corinthians 6:14) in order to justify the divorce of an unbelieving spouse and getting remarried to a member of the church. While this would be a more reasonable grounds for divorce than mere lust, it still violates the basic integrity of marriage. Marriage is an institution that is ordained by God even when the marriage partners do not believe in Him.

13. And the woman which hath a husband that believeth not, and if he be pleased to dwell with her, let her not leave him.

The fact that one's husband does not go to church is not sufficient grounds for divorce. In verse 16 (not in today's text), Paul urges Christians who are married to nonbelievers to view their situations as opportunities for evangelism. It is hard to imagine that a man would accept Christ after his wife had left him due to his lack of faith. Paul hopes that over time the witness of a godly wife will gradually win her husband.

C. Sanctified Homes (v. 14)

14. For the unbelieving husband is sanctified by the wife, and the unbelieving wife is sanctified by the husband: else were your children unclean; but now are they holy.

Paul's remarks about *the unbelieving husband* being *sanctified by the wife* reflect the purity language of the Old Testament. The Christian may feel that the unbelieving spouse's influence is unhealthy, leaving her unholy in God's sight. She may fear that her husband's evil influence will corrupt her and her *children*, providing just grounds for divorce. But Paul argues that the presence of the believer will sanctify the household; the believer's influence should pervade the home (compare Romans 11:16). God will not judge the children by the father's unfaithfulness but will rather bless them through their mother's faith.

One may be concerned legitimately about the moral influence of an unbelieving spouse on the family. Yet the fact that an unbeliever presents a threat of moral corruption is not grounds for divorce. It simply means that the believer will have to work that much harder to create a Christian atmosphere in the home.

While Paul hopes that a believing spouse eventually can lead an unbelieving partner to faith, he clearly does not think that the believing partner's faith can save the nonbeliever. Such an interpretation would be entirely inconsistent with Paul's emphasis elsewhere on personal acceptance of God's grace.

My Mission, My Mate

Leslie's wife became a Christian. She desired nothing more than to see her husband come to Christ as well. But Leslie was more involved in things he enjoyed, and church was not one of those things.

Leslie's wife sought to live out a life of faith before her husband. A small group would gather weekly with Leslie's wife to pray for his salvation. Over time Leslie's resistance to the gospel melted away. He became a Christian.

Mac and Jane, a married couple, were both seeking the Lord. They attended church where they heard many sermons and lessons. They participated in home Bible studies as well. Each waited for the other to make the first move.

One Sunday evening during a closing song of commitment, Mac decided it was time to go forward to proclaim to the congregation his desire to commit his life to Christ. Jane was looking at the words in the hymnal, so she did not see Mac go forward. When she looked up and saw Mac standing with the preacher at the front of the auditorium, she stepped out to join her husband. Together they committed their lives to Christ.

Do you have a mate who needs the master? If so, make it your mission to be that influence personally. If you are not in this situation but know someone who is, make a commitment to be a prayer warrior on his or her behalf.

—A. E. A.

D. Not Under Bondage (v. 15)

15. But if the unbelieving depart, let him depart. A brother or a sister is not under bondage in such cases: but God hath called us to peace.

Paul's reference to being *not under bondage* means that we are not responsible for another person's actions. Just as the unbelieving spouse cannot be saved by the faith of the believer, the believer is not responsible if the unbeliever seeks a divorce on his or her own initiative. In this instance, the believer is free to remarry a Christian if desired. [See question #5, page 439.]

Conclusion

A. Not in Bondage

In considering divorce or remarriage, it is important to avoid two extremes. On the one hand, some act as though divorce were the unpardonable sin. There are, in fact, biblical provisions for divorce and remarriage. On the other hand, the fact that Jesus and Paul allow for divorce in some circumstances does not mean that the church can take a lax posture toward that practice. Solid marriages and families are the backbone of a stable society. The church always must protect the integrity and sanctity of marriage as an institution and must denounce every form of sexual sin.

It is also critically important to remember that God forgives through the grace of Jesus. In today's society most people are sexually active before marriage—indeed, before they finish high school. Thus most members of any given congregation have been guilty at some point of sexual immorality. Further, many are divorced, some more than once. Yet sins are erased when we embrace Jesus as Savior. God is not concerned about what we used to do when we were sinners; He is concerned about how we use our bodies now.

B. Prayer

Lord, we live in a world full of temptations. It is a world where sexual sin and divorce are rampant. Please give us strength to resist sin with our bodies and our minds. Help us preserve our homes and our marriages as godly witnesses to Your power and grace. In Jesus' name, amen.

C. Thought to Remember

Don't ruin your relationship with God by ignoring His rules on human relationships.

Learning by Doing

This section contains an alternative lesson plan emphasizing learning activities. Classes desiring such student involvement will find these suggestions helpful.

Learning Goals

After participating in this lesson, each student will be able to:

1. Summarize Paul's views on singleness, marriage, and divorce.
2. Give examples of how the secular world rejects Paul's views on marriage and divorce.
3. Use scriptural principles to recommend godly conduct on issues or cases of singleness, marriage, and divorce.

Into the Lesson

Begin by relating this real-life situation: Rex is a 32-year-old single man. He has grown up in the church and has been active in many roles. He now plays drums for the worship band. However, Rex has been disappointed that he's never been asked to serve in any leadership roles. While his married friends are asked to serve on task forces, committees, and as ministry leaders, Rex is never approached. He knows his singleness has somehow kept church leaders from viewing him as a mature individual.

Assuming that you are able to interact only with Rex and not his church's leadership, what counsel would you offer? Would "giving advice" be appropriate, or should you stick to being a sympathetic listener? Why?

After a bit of discussion, make the transition to the Bible study by saying, "Singleness is an important issue of today's church. In addition to issues of singleness and marriage, Christians wrestle with the ethics of sexuality, divorce, remarriage, and more. Paul speaks to these issues when writing to the Corinthian church."

Into the Word

Introduce the Bible study by sharing information from the Lesson Background. Be sure to stress the loose sexual standards of Corinth.

Read aloud the printed text. Then divide the class into groups of three to five. Provide each group a prepared copy of the work sheet below. Assign each group one of the issues on the work sheet. (Larger classes will have two or more groups working on the same issue.) After groups have finished working, allow each to report its conclusions.

Work sheet: Issues of Sexuality and Marriage

Read the text and jot down some notes about Paul's teaching on the following topics.

Group #1: Singleness (1 Corinthians 7:1, 2, 6-9)
  Paul's preferences:
  Sexual practices:
  The widowed:
  How the world rejects these views:

Group #2: Divorce for Christians (7:10-15)
  Paul's general rule for divorce:
  After divorce:
  Divorce and an unbelieving spouse:
  Explain verse 14:
  How the world rejects these views:

Group #3: Marriage for Christians (7:2, 3-5, 9)
  Some reasons to marry:
  Sexual responsibilities in marriage:
  How the world rejects these views:

Into Life

With students still in their small groups, assign each group one of the scenarios below that you have written out ahead of time. Allow time at the end for groups to share their responses.

Bill and Bev have been married four years. Bill is a believer. Bev is not a Christian and has become increasingly hostile to Bill's faith. Bill has come to you for counsel. He says Bev has threatened to leave him if he continues in what she calls "religious nonsense." How do you respond? How would you know if you needed to refer Bill to someone with more spiritual insight?

Jim and Jean have been living together for two years. They've begun attending your church and want to get married. But the church policy states that couples cannot be living together if they want to have a church wedding. Jim and Jean have come to you wanting to talk about the church's policy and what the Bible says about all this. What would you tell them?

Sue has been married to Fred for three years. Both are Christians. Fred, however, has become sexually abusive to Sue. Sue suspects that Fred has become involved with pornography but isn't sure. Sue has been told by another Christian that she needs to be submissive to her husband. Her counselor, however, says that she needs to leave her husband. Sue is very confused and wants your opinion. What do you say to her?

Let's Talk It Over

These questions are designed to promote discussion of the lesson. The answers here are only discussion starters. Let your class talk it over from there.

1. What are some cultural factors that make it difficult for us to maintain and demonstrate sexual purity? How do we guard against these?

The presence of implied or explicit sexual content in films, magazines, the Internet, etc., comes immediately to mind (which is, of course, part of the problem). Immodest fashion trends, sometimes evident even in church, further contribute to the difficulty. Sexual attractiveness and activity affect many people's sense of personal identity in destructive ways, causing them to express their sexuality in a sinful manner. The extent to which sexual matters are openly discussed in conversations also can contribute to the problem.

Guarding against these dangers may begin simply by avoiding lust-producing images and conversations. See Psalm 101:3a; 1 Corinthians 6:18.

2. Paul makes it clear that single people are whole persons. What are some ways we can affirm unmarried adults in our churches?

One way that many singles like to be affirmed starts simply by not having others "single them out." It is also important to recognize that people are unmarried for a wide variety of reasons. Therefore, we must be careful not to generalize or stereotype the interests and concerns of singles.

We can remind all Christians that godly friendships are a great blessing; following that, we can provide significant opportunities to help unmarried believers develop such relationships. We can also encourage singles to view and use their status as an opportunity for increased Christian service.

3. What are some benefits and dangers of discussing sexual matters as openly as Paul does in this passage?

Since sexuality is discussed so openly in modern culture, there is a sense in which directly stated issues warrant direct responses. If the church fails to respond, God's perspective will be more easily misunderstood or ignored.

And yet, frank discussion about sexual issues also raises some dangers. Open discussion can bring unhealthy or inappropriate thoughts to mind and create a fixation on the subject. Further, there is a sacredness to God-approved sex that is violated when people talk too specifically about such matters (except in counseling contexts). We should not be embarrassed to speak about sexual matters, but we should also resist the temptation to do so constantly.

4. Many people, including some believers, think that Paul's teaching about divorce is outdated and irrelevant. How do you respond?

We must avoid the temptation to embrace only the parts of the Bible that match contemporary cultural practices. God's design for marriage is clear from the first pages of Scripture (Genesis 1, 2).

The foundational reasons that divorce seems desirable haven't changed. The practical and emotional problems that result from divorce haven't changed either. When people suggest God's teaching about divorce is outdated, they often have something personal at stake. It may be a desire to justify a past or contemplated divorce or a concern for loved ones in similar situations. Gently exposing this hidden agenda may be a key. In any case we must not allow our feelings to dwarf our commitment to God's Word.

5. What are some specific ways we can ease the burden on those in our congregations who are married to unbelieving spouses?

We begin by realizing that the main problem in this kind of "blended family" is mixed messages: children hear (or see) one set of ethics and spiritual guidelines from one parent but quite another set from the other. Thus one key task is to provide spiritual insight and assistance that will help the Christian parent rear godly children.

We also can provide a support network of friends. When we have opportunities to interact with the unbelieving spouse, we can provide a consistent godly witness to complement the lifestyle evangelism efforts of the believing spouse. As we strive to minister effectively to Christian brothers and sisters in this position, we should strive to connect them to people of their own gender. This helps them avoid vulnerability to extramarital affairs that may come from a desire to have a spiritually meaningful relationship with a Christian of the opposite gender.

July 9
Lesson 6

Called to Help the Weak

DEVOTIONAL READING: Mark 9:42-48.

BACKGROUND SCRIPTURE: 1 Corinthians 8:1-13.

PRINTED TEXT: 1 Corinthians 8:1-13.

1 Corinthians 8:1-13

1 Now as touching things offered unto idols, we know that we all have knowledge. Knowledge puffeth up, but charity edifieth.

2 And if any man think that he knoweth any thing, he knoweth nothing yet as he ought to know.

3 But if any man love God, the same is known of him.

4 As concerning therefore the eating of those things that are offered in sacrifice unto idols, we know that an idol is nothing in the world, and that there is none other God but one.

5 For though there be that are called gods, whether in heaven or in earth, (as there be gods many, and lords many,)

6 But to us there is but one God, the Father, of whom are all things, and we in him; and one Lord Jesus Christ, by whom are all things, and we by him.

7 Howbeit there is not in every man that knowledge: for some with conscience of the idol unto this hour eat it as a thing offered unto an idol; and their conscience being weak is defiled.

8 But meat commendeth us not to God: for neither, if we eat, are we the better; neither, if we eat not, are we the worse.

9 But take heed lest by any means this liberty of yours become a stumblingblock to them that are weak.

10 For if any man see thee which hast knowledge sit at meat in the idol's temple, shall not the conscience of him which is weak be emboldened to eat those things which are offered to idols;

11 And through thy knowledge shall the weak brother perish, for whom Christ died?

12 But when ye sin so against the brethren, and wound their weak conscience, ye sin against Christ.

13 Wherefore, if meat make my brother to offend, I will eat no flesh while the world standeth, lest I make my brother to offend.

GOLDEN TEXT: Meat commendeth us not to God: for neither, if we eat, are we the better; neither, if we eat not, are we the worse. But take heed lest by any means this liberty of yours become a stumblingblock to them that are weak.
—1 Corinthians 8:8, 9.

LESSON 6 441 JULY 9

> *Called to Be a Christian Community*
> Unit 2: Called to Obedience
> (Lessons 5-9)

Lesson Aims

After participating in this lesson, each student will be able to:

1. Restate the reasons that Paul gives for eating or not eating meat sacrificed to idols.
2. Propose one modern parallel to the first-century issue of eating meat sacrificed to idols.
3. State how he or she has made a sacrifice of personal liberties for the sake of another, or state an area in which he or she will do so in the immediate future.

Lesson Outline

INTRODUCTION
    A. To Eat or Not to Eat?
    B. Lesson Background
I. PROBLEM: WRONG EMPHASIS (1 Corinthians 8:1-3)
    A. Love vs. Arrogance (v. 1)
    B. Knowledge vs. Ignorance (v. 2)
    C. Love and Knowledge of God (v. 3)
II. GROUNDWORK: TRUE GOD (1 Corinthians 8:4-6)
    A. Many "Gods" and "Lords" (vv. 4, 5)
    B. One God and Lord (v. 6)
III. SOLUTION: TEMPERED FREEDOM (1 Corinthians 8:7-13)
    A. Weakness of Conscience (v. 7)
    B. Matters of Opinion (v. 8)
    C. Exercise of Conscience (vv. 9-11)
        Freedom Isn't Free
    D. Restriction of Freedom (vv. 12, 13)
        Offended, Uncomfortable, or . . . ?
CONCLUSION
    A. Freedom, Not Slavery
    B. Prayer
    C. Thought to Remember

Introduction

A. To Eat or Not to Eat?

Not long ago I was talking to a friend in my office, and we decided to go out for lunch together. On the way to the restaurant, he told me about a movie he had seen recently. While I did not say anything to him, I was somewhat surprised by his taste in films and by the frankness of his discussion. I had not seen the movie he mentioned. But I knew from the advertisements and his description that it included scenes that I would consider sexually inappropriate.

As he spoke, I reflected on my own standards for evaluating such issues. I avoid movies with explicit sex scenes but have no difficulty watching films with graphic violence or profanity, because such things do not tempt me. I also generally do not see R-rated films in movie theaters but occasionally watch them on video or cable television at home.

As I thought about my own inconsistencies and my friend's taste in movies, we arrived at the restaurant. I was in the mood for Chinese food, but he hesitated as we got out of the car. He explained that he had been involved deeply in Eastern religions before accepting Christ. The owner of this restaurant displayed statues of Asian gods in the front of the store. He even set out fruits as symbolic offerings to these deities for luck. My friend wondered if I would mind eating somewhere else. He suggested a place where he knew they had specials on draft beer at lunch.

Moral issues relating to drinking in moderation, smoking, dancing, movies, television programs, and styles of clothing are especially difficult simply because there is no precise, clear biblical teaching about the right thing to do in these specific areas. [See question #1, page 448.] Each individual must therefore make a personal choice as to whether or not he or she may participate. A major "gray area" in Paul's time was eating meat that had been sacrificed to idols.

B. Lesson Background

As in Judaism, animal sacrifices were a key feature of most pagan religions in the ancient world. Worshipers typically would bring goats, bulls, doves, or other animals to the pagan priest. These animals would be killed and offered to the deity to appease his anger or in thanksgiving for some blessing.

In most cases, however, only a portion of the animal actually was burned on the altar. For example, the Law of Moses prescribed that priests could keep the hides from burnt offerings and a portion of the ground meal from grain offerings

Jul 9

(Leviticus 7:7-10). The pagan religions had similar stipulations that allowed their "priests" to eat or sell the leftover meat. In large cities such as Corinth, it was common for pagan temples to run butcher shops to sell excess meat.

This created an awkward situation for some newer Christians. Those who had come out of Judaism may view such meat as unholy because of its association with pagan religions; for those Christians who once had been pagans themselves, the food may bring back memories of the old way of life. On the other hand older, more mature Christians who were no longer committed to the Jewish kosher laws or who had not been involved in paganism for many years may have no scruples at all about eating this meat. In fact they might even bring a plate of such meat straight from the butcher shop at the temple of Isis to a church dinner, bragging about the bargain they got.

At least some of the Corinthians apparently were uncertain of how to handle this issue. Perhaps they were aware of the letter of the Jerusalem church to the church at Antioch that encouraged abstaining from eating meat that had been sacrificed to idols (Acts 15:29). Whether or not they were aware of that letter, Paul used their concern to lay down principles for respect and sensitivity as befitting Christians.

I. Problem: Wrong Emphasis (1 Corinthians 8:1-3)

A. Love vs. Arrogance (v. 1)

1. Now as touching things offered unto idols, we know that we all have knowledge. Knowledge puffeth up, but charity edifieth.

Paul begins by establishing some common ground: *we know that we all have knowledge.* Who could disagree with that? Part of this knowledge for believers is that there is only one God; thus idols are nothing (more on this below).

The real issue is in the attitude that Christians adopt toward one another. Some could justify their decision to eat meat *offered unto idols* through elaborate theological arguments. "Being right" can thus become more important than being sensitive to another person's conscience. Knowledge, Paul says, tends to breed arrogance unless it is checked by a genuine love *(charity)* that seeks to build up and edify others. [See question #2, page 448.]

B. Knowledge vs. Ignorance (v. 2)

2. And if any man think that he knoweth any thing, he knoweth nothing yet as he ought to know.

Obviously, Paul is not indifferent to sound doctrine. He does not mean that what one believes or thinks is of no importance. The issue here is not the content of someone's knowledge ("what they know"). Rather, the issue is what Christians do with that knowledge.

Some may use their intellect to justify personal actions or to disregard others. A person who travels this path may indeed *know* a great deal of abstract theology while not understanding a basic teaching of the Christian faith: the need to love one's neighbor as oneself (Leviticus 19:18; Matthew 22:39; 1 Corinthians 10:24). Truly wise people exercise humility, aware of all the things that they don't understand (compare Galatians 6:3). [See question #3, page 448.]

C. Love and Knowledge of God (v. 3)

3. But if any man love God, the same is known of him.

Him refers to *God*. We rightly emphasize knowing Bible facts, but knowing those facts should lead to a greater goal: to *love God* with every fiber of our being (Matthew 22:37). This is a proper response to God, who knows and recognizes us as His children (compare Galatians 4:7, 9).

To love God is the most important commandment; the second most important commandment is love of neighbor (Matthew 22:38, 39). If the "knowledge" that the Corinthians have is not leading them in this path, then they need a change in course!

II. Groundwork: True God (1 Corinthians 8:4-6)

A. Many "Gods" and "Lords" (vv. 4, 5)

4, 5. As concerning therefore the eating of those things that are offered in sacrifice unto idols, we know that an idol is nothing in the world, and that there is none other God but one. For though there be that are called gods, whether in heaven or in earth, (as there be gods many, and lords many,).

With the problem of "knowledge over love" clearly identified, Paul proceeds to lay a groundwork for a solution. He noted in verse 1 that

> **How to Say It**
> APOLLO. Uh-*pah*-low.
> CORINTH. *Kor*-inth.
> CORINTHIANS. Ko-*rin*-thee-unz (*th* as in *thin*).
> DIONYSIUS. Die-oh-*nish*-ih-us.
> ISAIAH. Eye-*zay*-uh.
> LEVITICUS. Leh-*vit*-ih-kus.
> ZEUS. Zoose.

there are certain things about which "we all have knowledge." One of those things is that idols do indeed exist as physical objects. Every house and street and store in Corinth is full of them, just as our *world* today is filled with material objects of misplaced devotion. In this sense the Corinthians are familiar with idols and shrines representing *gods many* and *lords many*—Apollo, Zeus, Dionysius, Isis, just to name a few.

Yet all worship of these amounts to nothing because these "gods" do not, in fact, have any existence beyond their representations in wood, stone, etc. (compare Isaiah 44:6-20). [See question #4, page 448.] The basic fact that there is only one God should be the starting point for any discussion about idolatry. Paul's acknowledgment reflects the truth of Deuteronomy 4:35, 39; 6:4.

B. One God and Lord (v. 6)

6. But to us there is but one God, the Father, of whom are all things, and we in him; and one Lord Jesus Christ, by whom are all things, and we by him.

The *one God* truth of verse 4 now receives fuller expression. The verse before us is based on the formula, "one/all, we/him." While people may make many idols, in truth there is only one God; He is the creator of *all things* in the universe. While people may serve many false deities, there is only *one Lord*, the *Christ* who sustains all things in the universe. Because this is the case, *we* know that we exist and receive salvation only *in Him* and *by Him*.

While verses 4-6 expose the lie of idolatry, they also underline the very point under debate in the Corinthian church. Some believers, whom we can call *Group #1*, can appeal to such knowledge to argue that there can't be any harm in eating food from the altar of idols since pagan gods don't exist in the first place. But others, whom we can call *Group #2*, can point to Deuteronomy 4:35, 39; 6:4 to argue that any participation in or financial support of paganism (through meat that is bought with money) represents support of idolatry. Therefore it should be avoided at all costs. This group may consist of the Corinthian Jews who became Christians (Acts 18:4, 8). Our next verse may reveal a third group.

III. Solution: Tempered Freedom (1 Corinthians 8:7-13)

A. Weakness of Conscience (v. 7)

7. Howbeit there is not in every man that knowledge: for some with conscience of the idol unto this hour eat it as a thing offered unto an idol; and their conscience being weak is defiled.

We sketched two groups at Corinth in considering verse 6. Both groups realize that idols are nothing. But here in verse 7, the phrase *Howbeit there is not in every man that knowledge* may introduce us to *Group #3*. This group would consist of newer Gentile members of the church who are fresh out of paganism. (Note that Paul identifies at least four groups in 1 Corinthians 1:12.)

This particular group would be on the verge of confusion when they see others eat this meat. Those in Group #3 have learned the basics that there is one God and Lord. But their memories are still vivid regarding all the other "gods" and "lords" that they used to worship. In this way *their conscience being weak is defiled*.

Some students think, however, that Paul is still speaking about Group #2. Under this theory this group remains very conscious of the fact that this meat was once the property of an idol, despite their understanding of Deuteronomy 4:35, 39; 6:4. Their knowledge of the truth of those verses has not yet penetrated into their consciences. For some reason they still feel bad about eating this food, even though they know that other gods don't really exist. If this theory is true, it means that their conscience is weak in the sense that their feelings of right and wrong have not yet come fully into line with their knowledge of God's truth. Thus they feel guilty even about something that they are free to do.

Whichever group Paul is thinking about, we must remember that our conscience does not carry an authority comparable to the Word of God. Nevertheless, it is definitely not a good idea to get into the habit of doing things that we feel are wrong, even if we cannot explain logically what is wrong with them (see Romans 14:23). When a person feels bad about something that is not specifically forbidden in the Bible, his or her conscience is defiled in some way (Romans 14:14). [See question #5, page 448.]

B. Matters of Opinion (v. 8)

8. But meat commendeth us not to God: for neither, if we eat, are we the better; neither, if we eat not, are we the worse.

Paul places the question of eating *meat* sacrificed to idols in the category of "matters of opinion." What we *eat* or don't eat doesn't inherently affect our relationship to God. Jesus said that nothing that goes into our mouths can make us unclean, because purity is a matter of the heart (Mark 7:17-23).

Theoretically, then, the meat makes no difference in and of itself. Some would see this as parallel to modern concerns about moderate consumption of alcoholic beverages, clothing styles, body piercing, etc. But it is important to stress both sides of Paul's argument: such activities don't necessarily hurt our faith, but they don't necessarily help it either. We therefore decide whether or not to participate on the basis of other factors. Those other factors include the long-term effects on us or other people.

C. Exercise of Conscience (vv. 9-11)

9. But take heed lest by any means this liberty of yours become a stumblingblock to them that are weak.

This verse is a major thesis statement in this letter. Because eating meat that has been offered to idols is not specifically sinful, Christians have freedom to decide whether they will eat it or not. We do not, however, have freedom to do things that may cause other people to go off track in their faith. If eating meat cannot make my faith stronger (v. 8) but may make someone else's faith weaker, then it's best to choose not to do it.

The opening words *take heed* show us the care that a mature Christian should take in this regard. Our carefulness does not mean, however, that we are enslaved to another person's sensitivities. Later Paul will note that his own freedom should not be subject to the judgment of another person's conscience (1 Corinthians 10:29, 30).

This would be especially true of matters of conscience that have no real biblical basis. At some point the weaker brother or sister must simply grow up in the faith, bringing his or her conscience into line with the facts of Christian freedom. In fact the veteran Christian's example may save the rookie believer from legalism. The mature believer is not obligated to live by another person's sensitivities and may do as he or she pleases as long as personal actions do not harm another (see also Romans 14:13, 15, 21; Galatians 5:13). [See question #6, page 448.]

FREEDOM ISN'T FREE

Those of us who grew up in Western democracies undoubtedly remember singing all those patriotic songs from childhood. Those songs often echoed a common theme: the value and cost of freedom. We know that free nations do not achieve their freedom easily. Wars were fought. Our spiritual, eternal freedom also came at a high cost: the death of the Son of God.

Most everyone also knows that the existence of democratic liberties does not mean we have absolute freedom to do just anything we wish. How many children cannot wait until that eighteenth birthday, graduation, or departure for college as they ponder the freedom they think they will have! Eventually, that young adult realizes that this freedom has continuing price tags attached. One of those tags is lawful behavior.

Spiritual liberty also has continuing price tags, as 1 Corinthians 8:9 demonstrates. Also vital is Galatians 5:13: "For, brethren, ye have been called unto liberty; only use not liberty for an occasion to the flesh, but by love serve one another." When we think of the price that Christ paid, is what He asks in return really so burdensome?
—A. E. A.

This image is a starting point for the question, "How can freedom get us into spiritual trouble?"

Visual for lesson 6

10. For if any man see thee which hast knowledge sit at meat in the idol's temple, shall not the conscience of him which is weak be emboldened to eat those things which are offered to idols?

Paul touches on the responsibility that the more mature believers have for setting a good example. While each person is responsible for his or her own actions, the newer Christian may not be in a position to make the best decision or to understand the implications of the decision.

To *sit at meat in the idol's temple* probably refers to a banquet at a pagan shrine. This is a typical practice of the time, similar to an American business meeting at a local civic club. The mature Christian may freely accept an invitation to such a feast and may even see it as an occasion to evangelize. But the potential gain of such a choice is offset by a greater loss if it leads a weaker, less astute person to conclude that the other Christian is endorsing idolatry.

11. And through thy knowledge shall the weak brother perish, for whom Christ died?

Paul returns to the theme introduced at the beginning. The mature Christian knows that idols represent fictitious gods. But can that Christian really say that he or she understands what is most important when doing something that does not show love for a *weak brother*? If *Christ* was willing to die for this person's salvation, is it too much of a sacrifice for you to choose not to eat a piece of meat to help that same person's faith?

D. Restriction of Freedom (vv. 12, 13)

12. But when ye sin so against the brethren, and wound their weak conscience, ye sin against Christ.

This statement is the flip side of Matthew 25:40. There Jesus says that anything we do "unto one of the least" of His followers is done for Him. In a similar way, anything we do that hurts one of *the brethren* having a *weak conscience* is a *sin against Christ*. This error shows that we have violated Jesus' new commandment to "love one another; as I have loved you" (John 13:34). When spiritual pride clouds our thinking about what is ultimately right and wrong, then we prove that we "knoweth nothing yet as [we] ought to know" (1 Corinthians 8:2, above).

13. Wherefore, if meat make my brother to offend, I will eat no flesh while the world standeth, lest I make my brother to offend.

Paul's conclusion is clear, both here and in Romans 14:21: If it's a matter of choice, choose to do what will help the other person. This may mean that I will abstain from eating *meat* or watching certain movies for as long as necessary. But isn't that a small price to pay to honor Christ?

OFFENDED, UNCOMFORTABLE, OR . . . ?

I do not care for tattoos. Yet my two adult daughters each have one. My son-in-law has more than one. Does that offend me? No. Do I have a weak conscience in this area that makes tattoos a stumbling block to me? No. They do not even make me as uncomfortable as they used to. A flower painted on a foot, a dolphin painted on the back, or a cross painted on the leg do not violate Leviticus 19:28. Those tattoos do nothing to undermine my faith in Christ or my love for my family members who choose to have them.

But you may be different. You may find tattoos, certain kinds of music, etc. to be offensive when I do not. But let's keep our terminology straight: what is "offensive" is not necessarily a "stumbling block" that is traced to a weak conscience. And your discomfort may be the price you pay when someone else is being ministered to by music you don't like.

There are doctrinal lines that should never be crossed. Then there are issues of preference that may be crossed freely as long as they don't lead to sin. It is important to learn the difference. As we do, we also remember to practice

---

Home Daily Bible Readings

Monday, July 3—Called to Life and Light (John 1:1-5)

Tuesday, July 4—Do Not Tempt Others (Mark 9:42-48)

Wednesday, July 5—Love Your Neighbor As Yourself (Mark 12:28-34)

Thursday, July 6—Do Not Make Another Stumble (Romans 14:13-19)

Friday, July 7—We Have One God, One Lord (1 Corinthians 8:1-6)

Saturday, July 8—Do Not Create a Stumbling Block (1 Corinthians 8:7-13)

Sunday, July 9—Do All to God's Glory (1 Corinthians 10:23–11:1)

the grace of humility and kindness. The gospel will move forward in unexpected ways when we do. —A. E. A.

Conclusion

A. Freedom, Not Slavery

In applying this passage to our lives, it is important to stress the type of situation that Paul has in mind. He is not thinking of differences of opinion over comparatively minor issues between two mature Christians. Paul's extreme statement in verse 13 pertains to situations where a person's conscience is jeopardized by our actions, leading him or her to question personal faith and possibly abandon it in confusion.

Every person is responsible for his or her own actions before God, and we are responsible only to God, not to the consciences of other people. At the same time, however, we must remember that love for others and considering the results of our behavior are our responsibilities (compare Luke 17:1). The key issue is not whether we are "right" in questions of Christian liberty; the key issue, rather, is the attitude we exhibit toward others who do not share our views.

B. Prayer

Lord, please give us compassionate hearts. Help us to be sensitive to the conscience of others, and help us to help them remain faithful to You. Please open our eyes to the truth of Your Word, so that our conscience will reflect Your perfect will for our lives. In Jesus' name, amen.

C. Thought to Remember

My freedom takes a back seat to others' faith.

Learning by Doing

This section contains an alternative lesson plan emphasizing learning activities. Classes desiring such student involvement will find these suggestions helpful.

Learning Goals

After this lesson, each student will be able to:

1. Restate the reasons that Paul gives for eating or not eating meat sacrificed to idols.

2. Propose one modern parallel to the first-century issue of eating meat sacrificed to idols.

3. State how he or she has made a sacrifice of personal liberties for the sake of another, or state an area in which he or she will do so in the immediate future.

Into the Lesson

Open the class by reading the illustration "To Eat or Not to Eat?" given in the Introduction of the lesson commentary. Pass out paper and pens and say, "Let's take a sampling of the different views from within our own group. Write *agree* or *disagree* to each of the following statements:"

I will not allow alcohol to be served at social events I host.

I have beer in my refrigerator.

I am offended if I see a Christian smoking.

I go to R-rated movies but hope my minister doesn't see me there.

Ask why there are different answers to the above statements. Then transition to Bible study by saying, "We are not the only believers in who have struggled with the 'gray areas' of Christian behavior. The Christians at Corinth also struggled. The gray area for them was whether or not to eat meat that had been offered to idols."

Continue by saying, "Christians today might read today's passage and think, 'This doesn't apply to us because we don't struggle with eating meat offered to idols.' Those who make such a statement will miss one of the greatest principles in the Bible about behavior and witness."

Into the Word

Prior to class ask a student to prepare a brief presentation (no more than five minutes) summarizing the practice of eating meat sacrificed to idols and the problem it presented for some of the Corinthian Christians. Provide your volunteer with a copy of the Lesson Background as the basis of his or her presentation.

After the presentation thank your presenter. Make the transition to the next activity by telling the class that Paul's teaching about food sacrificed to idols can serve as a model for some of the issues mentioned earlier.

Next, display one poster with the heading, "Arguments to Allow Believers to Eat Meat Offered to Idols" and another poster with the heading, "Why Believers Should *Not* Eat Meat Offered to Idols." Read the printed text for the class. Then divide the class into two groups, assigning one poster to each group. Have groups fill in their posters using today's text for their answers.

Answers for the first poster can be found in verses 4-6 *(idols are not gods; therefore, there is no harm in eating meat sacrificed to them)* and in verse 8 *(what food we eat doesn't matter)*. Answers for the second poster are found in verses 7 and 9 *(we may become a stumbling block)*, verse 12 *(we may sin against our brother or sister in Christ)*, and verse 13 *(Paul's example)*.

Into Life

Use the following two questions as a transition: **1.** What principle does Paul teach in today's text that can be applied to the gray areas of Christian behavior? *(We should realize that our actions, even though not harmful to us spiritually, may be a stumbling block to a weaker Christian. To ignore such a fact and act as we please is to sin.)* **2.** Paul applies the above principle in the context of watching out for weaker Christians. How could this principle be applied in the context of showing concern for nonbelievers?

Next, ask the class to compile a list of gray areas of personal behavior that have potential for becoming gospel hindrances to non-Christians or stumbling blocks to weaker Christians. *(A few ideas: celebrating Halloween, using chewing tobacco, buying lottery tickets, watching certain kinds of movies or TV programs, buying an expensive car, wearing certain styles of clothing, having body piercing or tattoos, missing worship while traveling.)*

After discussion, stress that the key to Christ-honoring behavior is to be aware of those who watch our actions. As we do, we will not knowingly become a stumbling block to another person's faith or potential faith.

Conclude with prayer partners. One person should pray for this awareness. The other person should pray for wisdom to make right choices.

Let's Talk It Over

These questions are designed to promote discussion of the lesson. The answers here are only discussion starters. Let your class talk it over from there.

1. What are some other "gray area" issues that currently create struggles for Christians? How are these similar to or different from those listed in the lesson Introduction?

One irony is the lack of agreement among Christians regarding what issues even fall into this category! Fantasy role-playing games are "no problem" to some Christians but abandoned by others due to frequent (but not automatic) connections to the occult; films such as those in the Harry Potter series may also be in this category. Those who convert to Christ from non-Western religions sometimes face issues that directly parallel the concerns of today's lesson text.

2. How can we show respect and love for those whose opinions differ from ours in areas related to Christian behavior? How can we keep people from manipulating church policy through suspicious claims of having a weak conscience?

In the heat of a discussion, we can sometimes end up acting as if all issues are equally clear-cut or equally important. One way we can demonstrate respect is to begin by acknowledging the other person's commitment to Christ. Talk about common ground—that's it!

Responding graciously begins with listening respectfully. Even a significant difference of opinion does not justify acting in ways that violate the clear teaching of Scripture regarding self-control (compare Colossians 3:8).

Sadly, some resort to "playing the weak conscience card" to influence church decisions when their opinion is in the minority. Asking tactful questions about how he or she is in danger of stumbling in the faith because of the issue at hand can help expose the tactic for what it really is.

3. How should increased knowledge of Scripture make us ever more humble?

The more we learn about God the more we realize how much we pale in comparison to Him. As we come to a clearer recognition of His standards for us, we become more aware of our inability to consistently meet those standards. It is Bible study that teaches us this. As we study, we also discover that not all passages are easily understood (compare 2 Peter 3:16). Our humility deepens as we come to realize this.

4. What are some ways the spiritual climate of Corinth is paralleled in modern society? Why is it important to draw those parallels?

Non-Christians in Corinth did not lack sensitivity to spiritual issues. Folks in that area were, in fact, quite religious (compare Acts 17:16, 22, 23). But they didn't worship the true God. Likewise, "spirituality" is very much in vogue in modern culture. Many people practice New Age meditation, and the link between spiritual and physical health is widely acknowledged. Having "faith" is part of every self-help book, but faith is rarely defined in biblical terms. These are just a few ways for people to be "spiritual" but not Christian.

5. What are some ways to train the conscience so that its prompting is in harmony with God's desires?

Conscience is shaped by behavior and environment. We must adjust those factors in order to train the conscience to be a reliable safeguard. For example an overly strict or overly permissive home environment can dramatically shape the way a conscience functions. When we study Scripture regularly, we refine our conscience. A commitment to Spirit-empowered holiness will help us avoid the development of a calloused conscience (see 1 Timothy 4:2; Titus 1:15).

6. How can we demonstrate a commitment to the spiritual health of others without becoming completely controlled by another person's weakness of conscience?

Submitting ourselves to the complete control of someone else's conscience could result in us becoming "enablers" who further entrench someone's legalistic mind-set. Perhaps two questions can help us maintain balance. First, we can ask ourselves *why* we wish to engage in a particular practice. People can actually become bound by their freedoms if they are unwilling or unable to set them aside! Second, we can evaluate *where*. The distinction between what is done publicly and privately is important.

Called to Win the Race

July 16
Lesson 7

DEVOTIONAL READING: Hebrews 12:1-12.

BACKGROUND SCRIPTURE: 1 Corinthians 9:24–10:13.

PRINTED TEXT: 1 Corinthians 9:24–10:13.

1 Corinthians 9:24-27

24 Know ye not that they which run in a race run all, but one receiveth the prize? So run, that ye may obtain.

25 And every man that striveth for the mastery is temperate in all things. Now they do it to obtain a corruptible crown; but we an incorruptible.

26 I therefore so run, not as uncertainly; so fight I, not as one that beateth the air:

27 But I keep under my body, and bring it into subjection: lest that by any means, when I have preached to others, I myself should be a castaway.

1 Corinthians 10:1-13

1 Moreover, brethren, I would not that ye should be ignorant, how that all our fathers were under the cloud, and all passed through the sea;

2 And were all baptized unto Moses in the cloud and in the sea;

3 And did all eat the same spiritual meat;

4 And did all drink the same spiritual drink; for they drank of that spiritual Rock that followed them: and that Rock was Christ.

5 But with many of them God was not well pleased: for they were overthrown in the wilderness.

6 Now these things were our examples, to the intent we should not lust after evil things, as they also lusted.

7 Neither be ye idolaters, as were some of them; as it is written, The people sat down to eat and drink, and rose up to play.

8 Neither let us commit fornication, as some of them committed, and fell in one day three and twenty thousand.

9 Neither let us tempt Christ, as some of them also tempted, and were destroyed of serpents.

10 Neither murmur ye, as some of them also murmured, and were destroyed of the destroyer.

11 Now all these things happened unto them for ensamples: and they are written for our admonition, upon whom the ends of the world are come.

12 Wherefore let him that thinketh he standeth take heed lest he fall.

13 There hath no temptation taken you but such as is common to man: but God is faithful, who will not suffer you to be tempted above that ye are able; but will with the temptation also make a way to escape, that ye may be able to bear it.

GOLDEN TEXT: Know ye not that they which run in a race run all, but one receiveth the prize? So run, that ye may obtain.—1 Corinthians 9:24.

> *Called to Be a Christian Community*
> Unit 2: Called to Obedience
> (Lessons 5-9)

Lesson Aims

After participating in this lesson, each student will be able to:

1. Restate the positive and negative examples that Paul gives regarding following through to the end.
2. Draw one parallel between the ancient Israelites' experiences in the wilderness and the challenges of modern Christian life.
3. Plan to overcome a specific temptation.

Lesson Outline

INTRODUCTION
    A. Be Ready to Run
    B. Lesson Background
I. OUR EFFORTS (1 Corinthians 9:24-27)
    A. How to Run (v. 24)
    B. How to Train (vv. 25-27)
        The Masters
II. THEIR EXAMPLES (1 Corinthians 10:1-6)
    A. Parallel Blessings (vv. 1-4)
    B. Lost Blessings (vv. 5, 6)
        Warning! Warning!
III. OUR TASK (1 Corinthians 10:7-13)
    A. Learn from Examples (vv. 7-12)
    B. Look to the Future (v. 13)
CONCLUSION
    A. Lost in a Moment
    B. Prayer
    C. Thought to Remember

Introduction

A. Be Ready to Run

In modern auto racing, races are often won by inches, with one car crossing the finish line only tenths of a second ahead of the closest competitor. Crossing the finish line of a race is not the time to read a *How to Race* manual! Similarly, the middle of Round 3 is not the time for a boxer to realize that he should have been hitting the punching bag instead of eating pizza and watching television. Common sense tells us that athletes must train and practice before the event so that they will be ready to compete well when the time comes.

In a similar way, we cannot be successful in our Christian lives if we do not prepare. The middle of a moral dilemma is not the time to realize that we aren't really sure about the right thing to do. Paul therefore insists that we train and discipline ourselves so that we will always be ready for anything that comes our way.

B. Lesson Background

Today's passage falls in the middle of a lengthy discussion about whether or not Christians may eat meat that has been offered to idols. In last week's lesson Paul warned mature believers to respect the sensitivities of weaker consciences. This discussion reminded Paul of the ancient Israelites, who were punished in the wilderness for their participation in idolatrous practices. He therefore takes a bit of a sidetrack to urge his readers to discipline themselves. Our weakness is not an excuse for sin but rather an opportunity for spiritual discipline and training so that we may receive God's full reward.

Paul likes to use illustrations from sports, and he opens the discussion here by comparing the Christian life with running a race. Corinth was the site of a major international athletic festival, the Isthmian Games, which drew participants and tourists from a wide area. The Corinthians would be familiar with many of the best athletes of that time and could relate easily to Paul's analogy.

I. Our Efforts
(1 Corinthians 9:24-27)

A. How to Run (v. 24)

24. Know ye not that they which run in a race run all, but one receiveth the prize? So run, that ye may obtain.

Paul begins with the most basic rule of racing: everyone runs but only one person wins. This is not to suggest that the Christian life is a competition in which we get to Heaven by being better than everyone else (although we may often act that way). The emphasis lies in the second part of the verse: *run* to *obtain* the *prize*. The participants *in a race* cannot control how fast their competitors will run. Each only can run as fast as possible. Christians should be prepared to run the race of faith as hard as they can so that nothing will hinder them (compare Philippians 3:14; 2 Timothy 4:7; Hebrews 12:1).

B. How to Train (vv. 25-27)

25. And every man that striveth for the mastery is temperate in all things. Now they do it to obtain a corruptible crown; but we an incorruptible.

Winning athletes in the ancient Isthmian Games are awarded a *crown*, a wreath made of pine garlands that is worn on the head. We saw a throwback to this in the 2004 Olympic games in Athens, where the modern gold-medal winners received similar wreaths.

The actual value of these crowns is minimal but they symbolize victory. An ancient athlete would practice for a year *(striveth for the mastery)* to compete in the games at Corinth, in hope of wearing one of these perishable, *corruptible* wreaths. How much more valuable is the imperishable, *incorruptible* eternal reward that God gives to those who strive to please Him! There is simply no comparison.

That fact leads to an obvious conclusion: if an athlete is willing to expend every ounce of energy for a fleeting honor, then surely we should be willing to discipline ourselves so that we may win the crown of eternal life (2 Timothy 4:8; James 1:12; 1 Peter 5:4). [See question #1, page 457.]

THE MASTERS

Augusta, Georgia, becomes the focus of the golf world each April. The Masters golf tournament that is held there is one of golf's most prestigious events. Phil Mickelson had this to say about his win there in 2004: "I think that winning this tournament, the reason it's so special, is that now I get to be a part of this great event for the rest of my life. I'll be back here every first week of April" (www.masters.org).

This is a tournament that demonstrates that you are among the great masters of this game, as Mickelson is. To reach this achievement demands countless hours of practice, strict training, and the denial of distracting interests. Poor eating, exercise, and sleeping habits do not produce a Masters' champion. In the Christian life it takes personal discipline in all areas to receive the Master's approval. We recall that we are saved by grace. Even so, poor Bible study habits, inconsistent church attendance, and wrong moral choices do not put a person in position to win the prize.

In addition to money the winner of the Masters golf tournament receives another prize: a green jacket. It is an award that these champions wear proudly—for this life. For those who prevail in the Christian life, there is a white robe to be gained—for eternity (Revelation 7:9-17).

—A. E. A.

26, 27. I therefore so run, not as uncertainly; so fight I, not as one that beateth the air: But I keep under my body, and bring it into subjection: lest that by any means, when I have preached to others, I myself should be a castaway.

Victory requires focused training, not random effort. Olympic runners do not rely on leisurely jogs along the beach! A boxer in training does not use worthless training methods. Instead, he labors in the gym every day under a strict regimen of exercise, diet, and practice sparring.

Both running and boxing require the athlete to train intensively. Similarly, believers are to train to be ready at all times for any spiritual challenge that may arise. We keep our bodies under control so that bad habits and lusts don't weaken us. Such weakness would make us easy prey to the temptations that seem to come when we least expect them. [See question #2, page 457.]

Here, as elsewhere, Paul uses himself as an example. He is not just a fat coach who walks the sidelines. He practices what he preaches! He can say from experience that a constant state of personal discipline is critical to success in one's spiritual life. [See question #3, page 457.]

II. Their Examples (1 Corinthians 10:1-6)

A. Parallel Blessings (vv. 1-4)

1. Moreover, brethren, I would not that ye should be ignorant, how that all our fathers were under the cloud, and all passed through the sea.

Paul now applies the principle of a disciplined life to the problem immediately at hand. Some of the Corinthians are struggling with the temptation to participate in pagan religious practices and the immorality that surrounds them. Paul thus emphasizes the real danger by reminding the Corinthians of what happened to the Israelites.

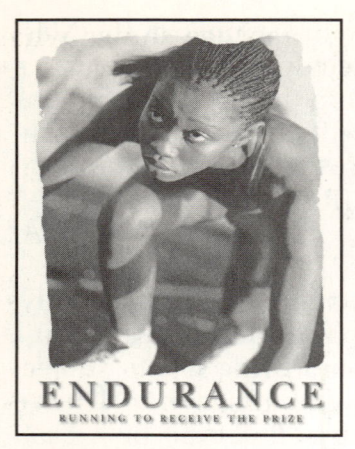

Ask your students to examine this image closely before answering question #2 on page 457.

Visual for lesson 7

The phrase *our fathers* refers to the ancient Jews who came out of Egypt in the exodus under Moses over 14 centuries previously. This analogy sets the tone for the illustration to follow by indicating that Paul is speaking in spiritual terms. Many of the Corinthians are Gentiles by birth. Yet Moses and the Israelites are still their spiritual ancestors in common, godly faith. The ancient Jews' experiences of temptation are similar to those faced by modern Christians. We may see in them an example of the dangers of a careless approach to godly commitment.

Paul begins by describing the blessed state of divine protection and provision that the Israelites enjoyed. Under Moses' leadership, they *passed through the sea* and onto dry land while Pharaoh's pursuing army perished (Exodus 14). God was constantly present, leading the Israelites through the desert in the form of a *cloud* by day and a pillar of fire by night (Exodus 13:21, 22). Such obvious manifestations of God's loving presence should have led them to a deep and abiding appreciation of His salvation and ongoing provision. That appreciation should have expressed itself in loyalty and obedience.

2. And were all baptized unto Moses in the cloud and in the sea.

Paul likens the Israelites' experience to that of Christians. We are baptized "into Jesus Christ" (Romans 6:3, 4), while the ancient Israelites were, in a sense, *baptized unto Moses*. While Moses obviously was not divine as Christ is, Moses did serve as something of a mediator between God and the ancient Jew. The verses that follow draw further parallels. (See also comparisons between Jesus and Moses in Hebrews 3:1-6.)

3, 4. And did all eat the same spiritual meat; and did all drink the same spiritual drink; for they drank of that spiritual Rock that followed them: and that Rock was Christ.

The exodus was not the end of God's care for His people; it was only the beginning. After crossing the sea, they entered a wasteland in which they found themselves homeless and without food or water. God, however, sustained them by miraculous provisions of food (Exodus 16). God also miraculously provided water from a rock when they were thirsty, through Moses' intervention (Exodus 17:1-7). In fact, God provided water in this way twice, in two different locations (see Numbers 20:1-11).

This double blessing led some of the ancient rabbis to suggest that God made the rock that yielded the miraculous water to travel with the Jews through the desert. Thus, as the story goes, they had refreshment whenever needed. Paul may be drawing upon this legend when he discusses the *Rock that followed them: and that Rock was Christ.* More important than the physical food and water that the Israelites enjoyed was God's *spiritual meat* and *spiritual drink*.

Paul's point is that the believers at Corinth enjoy this blessing as well. Do we fail to appreciate how much such blessings are really worth?

B. Lost Blessings (vv. 5, 6)

5. But with many of them God was not well pleased: for they were overthrown in the wilderness.

With all the blessings and advantages described in verses 1-4, it would seem that the Israelites couldn't lose! They had received God's Word directly through Moses, knew God's power when they shook the sand from the floor of the Red Sea off their sandals, felt God's love when they ate quail and drank fresh water in the desert. With all these obvious signs of His favor, how could they possibly fail to remain loyal to Him?

But, as Paul points out, the facts of history show that even the most privileged life can end in tragedy when it is not guided by focused discipline. Of all the Jews who came out of Egypt, only two lived to see the promised land (Numbers 14:26-35). Even Moses faltered in a moment of weakness (Deuteronomy 32:48-52). [See question #4, page 457.]

6. Now these things were our examples, to the intent we should not lust after evil things, as they also lusted.

This verse shows that the fate of the Israelites is not just an interesting story from long ago. It reveals a very significant aspect of God's nature and serves as a warning for all time. God is quick to bless, but He also judges those who disregard His gifts and betray His trust. Despite their many advantages, the Israelites continued to sin and offend God, with dire consequences. Similarly, those Christians who lose focus and do not run the race with discipline are in great danger.

WARNING! WARNING!

Before leaving home this morning, I told my wife that I was going into the kitchen to get some pills that I needed to take at lunchtime. I remember walking up to the kitchen counter, but when lunchtime came I did not have the pills! In the span of just a few seconds, something else occupied my thoughts. So I had forgotten to get them.

We are a forgetful people, aren't we? On more than one occasion I have heard a young person say that he or she will never make the mistake of driving under the influence of alcohol after having lost a friend who did just that. The pain of the recent loss is vivid, a reminder of the fragility of life. But in the matter of a few weeks, those lessons are forgotten. Careless driving, even driving after drinking, returns as a pattern.

As we read through the Old Testament, we are often appalled at the number of times God's people turned their backs on Him. They reform, promising to follow and honor Him. Yet almost in the next breath they are again committing apostasy. We think we would never do such a thing. But it does not take too close of an examination of our lives to see that we are the same.

God has left us the Old Testament as a warning and example of what happens when His way is forsaken. How well are we doing at heeding these warnings? —A. E. A.

III. Our Task
(1 Corinthians 10:7-13)

A. Learn from Examples (vv. 7-12)

7, 8. Neither be ye idolaters, as were some of them; as it is written, The people sat down to eat and drink, and rose up to play. Neither let us commit fornication, as some of them committed, and fell in one day three and twenty thousand.

The example of the Israelites shows what happens when focused discipline is lost. It is imperative for all believers to remain committed to God and ready to resist temptation.

To press home this point, Paul begins with one of the most flagrant acts of treason in history. The quotation in verse 7 comes from Exodus 32:6. The Israelites were worshiping a calf idol made from gold even while Moses was on the mountain receiving commandments from God. *Play* does not refer to checkers or badminton. Rather, it is a figurative way of referring to unholy, pagan festivities.

Essentially, the Jews engaged in the idolatrous worship that they had known about in Egypt. They did this almost immediately after coming out of that country. Their lack of patience is remarkable, especially in view of their incredible experience at the Red Sea only a few weeks earlier. How quickly we forget God's past provision in moments of stress and temptation!

Many more sins followed, and Paul reminds his readers of another occasion when lack of focus led the Israelites into lust and idolatry. Numbers 25 records a situation where Jewish men "began to commit whoredom" with Moabite women. Further, many Israelites began to worship Baal Peor. He punished them by sending a plague that killed 23,000 people.

We should note that Numbers 25:9 in our modern Bibles sets the death toll at 24,000. The difference is most likely due to what is called a textual variant. Paul probably is citing a manuscript that is no longer available to us. The severity of God's judgment remains clear nonetheless (compare Psalm 106:28, 29; Hosea 9:10).

How to Say It

BAAL PEOR. Bay-al-*pe*-or.
CORINTH. *Kor*-inth.
CORINTHIANS. Ko-*rin*-thee-unz (*th* as in *thin*).
DEUTERONOMY. Due-ter-*ahn*-uh-me.
HEBREWS. *Hee*-brews.
HOSEA. Ho-*zay*-uh.
ISTHMIAN. *Is*-me-unh.
KORAH. *Ko*-rah.
MOABITE. *Mo*-ub-ite.
MOSES. *Mo*-zes or *Mo*-zez.
PHARAOH. *Fair*-o or *Fay*-roe.
PHILIPPIANS. Fih-*lip*-ee-unz.

9. Neither let us tempt Christ, as some of them also tempted, and were destroyed of serpents.

Of course, God cannot be *tempted* to sin (James 1:13). But people often do things that test *Christ* in the sense of challenging His authority over their lives. Like a young child who defies his mother's commands in order to see whether she is serious, believers sometimes flagrantly defy God's will. Paul's point is that God is prepared to punish those who act in this way.

One example may be taken from the famous story of the bronze serpent in Numbers 21:4-6. Just before this incident, God had given the Israelites a great military victory; they responded by complaining that they were tired of eating manna. This flagrant defiance resulted in God's defending His own honor by sending a plague of *serpents* into the camp. That punishment was lifted only after the people confessed their sin.

10. Neither murmur ye, as some of them also murmured, and were destroyed of the destroyer.

Some students think that Paul is referring to Korah's rebellion here (Numbers 16). But the verse before us is most likely a general summary statement, for the type of incidents described in verses 7-9 were by no means unique. The Jews' dissatisfaction with God's provision is a running theme in Exodus and Numbers (compare Hebrews 3:7-19). [See question #5, page 457.]

11. Now all these things happened unto them for ensamples: and they are written for our admonition, upon whom the ends of the world are come.

The experiences of the Israelites are *ensamples*, meaning that they function as warnings for future generations. Some may think that God no longer punishes sin because of the grace shown through Christ. But Paul dispels this notion. The *ends of the world* is the Christian era. The time of the fulfillment of God's plan for the Christ is here.

Even now, under the grace available through Christ's blood, we must remain focused and disciplined. Dare we risk losing the ultimate prize of eternal life? (Again, see 1 Corinthians 9:27.)

12. Wherefore let him that thinketh he standeth take heed lest he fall.

Paul now returns to the theme that opened his discussion of meat offered to idols (1 Corinthians 8:1, 2). Many people think they are wise. But their arrogance leads them to miss the obvious and fall into sin. Many people think that they are strong. But this complacency leads them to become careless and undisciplined, leaving them unprepared to resist temptation.

B. Look to the Future (v. 13)

13. There hath no temptation taken you but such as is common to man: but God is faithful, who will not suffer you to be tempted above that ye are able; but will with the temptation also make a way to escape, that ye may be able to bear it.

The closing verse in this section provides both encouragement and warning. When we are *tempted*, we can rest assured that what we are facing is no worse than what other people have faced. And if other people have passed this test, so can we! *God* knows our strengths and weaknesses. He will not allow us to get into situations that cannot be overcome.

Every *temptation* has a built-in escape route. The most common is the fact that we can always simply say *no*. But at the same time, this assurance places all responsibility for sin on our own shoulders, not God's. God's faithfulness is a common Bible theme (Deuteronomy 7:9; 1 Corinthians 1:9; 1 Thessalonians 5:24). Unfortunately, human unfaithfulness is all too real.

Conclusion

A. Lost in a Moment

Several years ago, NASCAR driver Steve Park was involved in a serious accident when his steering wheel came off. The doors on race cars do not open, so drivers must crawl in and out of

---

Home Daily Bible Readings

Monday, July 10—Run the Race with Perseverance (Hebrews 12:1-12)
Tuesday, July 11—Keep Alert and Always Persevere (Ephesians 6:10-20)
Wednesday, July 12—Be Doers, Not Just Hearers (James 1:19-27)
Thursday, July 13—Press On Toward the Goal (Philippians 3:12-16)
Friday, July 14—Run for the Gospel's Sake (1 Corinthians 9:22b-27)
Saturday, July 15—Do Not Follow Our Ancestors (1 Corinthians 10:1-7)
Sunday, July 16—God Will Help You Endure Testing (1 Corinthians 10:8-13)

the vehicle through a window. To make this easier the cars are equipped with removable steering wheels.

Park's accident occurred during a caution period in a race, when the cars move slowly around the track. While he cannot remember exactly what happened, it seems that Park turned his head momentarily as another vehicle approached on his left. In that split second, his steering wheel somehow detached. Park's car veered suddenly and was broadsided by the passing car. Someone at some point had not securely fastened the steering wheel. That momentary loss of focus could have cost Park his life!

When Paul compares the Christian life with a race, he does not mean to encourage a competitive spirit. He means to stress our need to be prepared and vigilant at all times. Unfortunately, we usually do not know when trials and temptations will crop up; they often seem to come when we least expect them or are least prepared to deal with them.

The danger may be greatest when we feel the strongest, because at these moments a false sense of security may lead us to drop our guard. We therefore are on the alert constantly. We discipline ourselves spiritually so that we will be ready for any challenge that comes our way.

B. Prayer

God, please give us the discipline and focus to remain pure in an evil world. Help us to keep focused on the prize ahead, and help us to draw on Your strength to endure temptations. Help us also to understand that You are a holy God and that You have called us to be a holy people for You. In Jesus' name, amen.

C. Thought to Remember

Stay focused and disciplined
to win life's race.

Learning by Doing

This section contains an alternative lesson plan emphasizing learning activities. Classes desiring such student involvement will find these suggestions helpful.

Learning Goals

After participating in this lesson, each student will be able to:

1. Restate the positive and negative examples that Paul gives regarding following through to the end.

2. Draw one parallel between the ancient Israelites' experiences in the wilderness and the challenges of modern Christian life.

3. Plan to overcome a specific temptation.

Into the Lesson

Option #1: Have teams of students list the hurdles or obstacles that racers must overcome in order to win the following kinds of races: NASCAR, 26-mile marathon, Tour de France bicycle race, and hot-air balloon race. Have each team list their answers on poster board.

As teams report, ask what types of qualities racers must possess in order to successfully clear the hurdles and obstacles. When someone mentions *endurance* (or a similar word), tell the class that this quality is also a key to the discipline that Paul teaches about our spiritual lives.

Option #2: Display a list of the following competitions on a poster board: Olympics, bowling, NASCAR, Kentucky Derby, county fair pie-baking contest, ancient Olympic games. Ask the class what prizes are awarded for winning these games or events *(Olympics: medals and wreaths; bowling: trophies; NASCAR: cup; Kentucky Derby: flowers and cup; county fair pie-baking contest: ribbon; ancient Olympic games: wreath crowns.)* Write the answers on the poster board.

Make the transition to the Bible study by saying, "The actual value of many awards is minimal, like the ancient Olympic wreath crowns. The real value of awards is that they symbolize victory. Victory requires lots of discipline and sacrifice. Paul uses sports imagery to teach real lessons about spiritual victory. And the reward is worth more than we could ever imagine."

Into the Word

For this portion of the lesson divide your class into teams of three to five. Give each team a copy of one of the following assignments.

Team #1: Your key word is *prize*. Read 1 Corinthians 9:24-26 and discuss its implications for the Christians in the church at Corinth and for today's believers.

Team #2: Your key word is *hurdles*. Read 1 Corinthians 10:1-11 and discuss the implications of obstacles and failure. How do we keep our focus? What parallel do you see between the experiences of the Corinthians and today's Christians?

Team #3: Your key word is *endurance*. Read 1 Corinthians 10:11-13 and summarize Paul's teaching about endurance and temptation. What assurance comes from these verses?

Allow each team's spokesperson to report. If you have more than one team working on the same task, ask one team to report and others to add to comments already made. Then say, "One thing should be clear: we need a road map to beat temptation!"

Into Life

Prepare a work sheet with three columns. Column headings should read, *Temptations, Helpful Scriptures,* and *Ideas for a Plan*. List the following temptations in the first column: swearing, sexual temptations, worry, greed, not giving, poor worship habits. At the bottom of the chart, print the promise found in 1 Corinthians 10:13.

Divide the class into pairs. Give one work sheet to each pair. Ask pairs to select two of the temptations listed in the first column of the chart and jot down Scriptures and ideas that may be helpful in defeating these temptations. Be sure to have a few Bible concordances available. Allow a couple of pairs to report their findings for each of the temptations listed. (This activity can also be found in the student books.)

To close the session say, "All Christians face temptations. Overcoming these hurdles is a key to running a successful spiritual race." Give each student an index card and a shoestring. Ask them to write the following three words on their cards: *temptation, Scriptures,* and *plan*.

Students can use their cards as reminders to help them identify temptations and the resources to defeat them. The shoestrings can serve as reminder of the need for faithful endurance in the spiritual race. Encourage students to fill out their cards before the end of class. Suggest that they carry their cards and shoestrings in a pocket or a purse for at least one week.

Let's Talk It Over

These questions are designed to promote discussion of the lesson. The answers here are only discussion starters. Let your class talk it over from there.

1. What are some examples of modern "prizes" that we are tempted to pursue that pale in comparison with what is available through Christ? How do we keep a proper focus?

Some people go to great lengths in an effort to become famous or even merely popular. Others pour overwhelming energy into their vocation in an effort to obtain promotions or "self-fulfillment." The pursuit of our culture's status symbols—bigger houses, luxury boats or cars, designer clothing, and the latest electronic gadgets—frequently dominates even the lives of God's people. The pursuit of expertise in various hobbies can essentially become the pursuit of a fading crown. The pursuit of certain relationships can fall into this category.

Perspective is one key to proper focus. For example, the desire for a bigger house can be examined with the prayerful question, "Why do I really think I need a bigger house?" Beware of the danger of rationalizing!

2. What are some additional similarities between the Christian life and athletics that can help us live faithfully for God? Which similarity do you find to be most important? What hidden dangers are there?

One similarity is the single-minded focus required for success. Becoming a world-class athlete in many sports is a full-time job. Similarly, our development as disciples requires that we make spiritual issues the highest of priorities. The physical and mental exertion required to develop athletically is paralleled by the extreme effort required for spiritual maturity. We are sometimes lulled into thinking that Christian maturity can come without great effort. But Paul describes the process as very hard work.

But there is a pitfall: a few people focus so much on being spiritually minded that they no longer are able to "connect with" the unsaved. Shuffling off to join a monastery, either physically or just in one's thoughts, doesn't help!

3. What is the biggest difficulty you face in following Paul's example of setting a positive example? How have you tried to overcome this difficulty?

Answers will be highly personal, of course, but one difficulty in living an exemplary life is the problem of consistency. It is easier to be a positive role model on specific occasions than it is to be so constantly.

When we are consistent, however, we experience many benefits. We find the inner peace that comes from knowing we are the same person publicly and privately. This creates credibility as we share God's truth with others. By setting an example, we demonstrate the practicality of Scripture. Thus we show others how to apply its principles.

4. What modern factors can cause us to take spiritual blessings for granted? How do you guard against these? What will be the result of failure?

Like the Israelites, we may exhibit a selective memory that presents our life prior to conversion as better and more fulfilling than it was (Exodus 16:3). We can also become dissatisfied with how God chooses to provide for us (Numbers 11:4-9).

A modern factor to wrestle with is the prevalence of technology. We can start out using cell phones for God's glory in ministry but end up spending our time complaining about features we wished those phones had! When we are ungrateful we end up with a reduced view of God because we lose sight of His goodness. An "attitude of gratitude" is important.

5. Which do you find more useful in guarding yourself against falling into temptation: God's judgment or God's love? Why?

Emphasizing one factor to the exclusion of the other is a big mistake! Scripture teaches both. Yet often it is God's judgment that gets downplayed. God's just and holy nature should remind us of sin's seriousness. This helps us develop a more consistent recognition of the consequences for violating His will. We tend to think of fear as a "negative" motivation. Healthy fear, however, is central to our overall well-being. We stay away from the edge of a cliff because of fear. We maintain a safe distance from raging fires because of fear. Similarly, fear of sin's consequences is an appropriate weapon in fighting the lure of temptation.

July 23
Lesson 8

Called to the Common Good

Devotional Reading: 1 Corinthians 12:27-31.

Background Scripture: 1 Corinthians 12:1-13.

Printed Text: 1 Corinthians 12:1-13.

1 Corinthians 12:1-13

1 Now concerning spiritual gifts, brethren, I would not have you ignorant.

2 Ye know that ye were Gentiles, carried away unto these dumb idols, even as ye were led.

3 Wherefore I give you to understand, that no man speaking by the Spirit of God calleth Jesus accursed: and that no man can say that Jesus is the Lord, but by the Holy Ghost.

4 Now there are diversities of gifts, but the same Spirit.

5 And there are differences of administrations, but the same Lord.

6 And there are diversities of operations, but it is the same God which worketh all in all.

7 But the manifestation of the Spirit is given to every man to profit withal.

8 For to one is given by the Spirit the word of wisdom; to another the word of knowledge by the same Spirit;

9 To another faith by the same Spirit; to another the gifts of healing by the same Spirit;

10 To another the working of miracles; to another prophecy; to another discerning of spirits; to another divers kinds of tongues; to another the interpretation of tongues:

11 But all these worketh that one and the selfsame Spirit, dividing to every man severally as he will.

12 For as the body is one, and hath many members and all the members of that one body, being many, are one body: so also is Christ.

13 For by one Spirit are we all baptized into one body, whether we be Jews or Gentiles, whether we be bond or free; and have been all made to drink into one Spirit.

Golden Text: The manifestation of the Spirit is given to every man to profit withal.
—1 Corinthians 12:7.

LESSON 8 459 JULY 23

> *Called to Be a Christian Community*
> Unit 2: Called to Obedience
> (Lessons 5-9)

Lesson Aims

After this lesson each student will be able to:

1. Summarize what Paul says about the purpose and function of spiritual gifts.
2. Discuss ways that spiritual gifts can contribute to the common ministry of his or her church.
3. Conduct a spiritual self-examination to determine personal spiritual gifts and suggest a specific ministry in which they can be put to use.

Lesson Outline

INTRODUCTION
    A. The Maker's Mark
    B. Lesson Background
I. SPIRIT'S MARK (1 Corinthians 12:1-3)
    A. Need to Know (vv. 1, 2)
    B. Test of the Spirit (v. 3)
II. SPIRIT'S ONENESS (1 Corinthians 12:4-7)
    A. Differences and Unity (vv. 4-6)
       The Same Thing, Only Different
    B. Common Good (v. 7)
III. SPIRIT'S MANIFESTATIONS (1 Corinthians 12:8-10)
    A. Wisdom and Knowledge (v. 8)
    B. Faith and Healing (v. 9)
    C. Prophecy and Discernment (v. 10a)
    D. Tongues and Interpretations (v. 10b)
IV. SPIRIT'S BLESSINGS (1 Corinthians 12:11-13)
    A. Many Gifts, One Spirit (v. 11)
    B. One Spirit, One Church (vv. 12, 13)
       Pride and Ego
CONCLUSION
    A. A House Divided
    B. Prayer
    C. Thought to Remember

Introduction

A. The Maker's Mark

Several years ago, the Hallmark® greeting card company ran a series of ads that encouraged viewers to look at the back of a card rather than the front. Typically, these commercials would show a young man purchasing a romantic card for his lady friend and presenting it before a date. After opening the envelope, the young woman would immediately turn the card over. If she saw the Hallmark® company logo, the gentlemen was in for a pleasant evening; if she saw another brand name, he could rest assured that she would want to end the evening early.

This ad campaign may or may not have brought grief to well-meaning people who dared to buy other brands of greeting cards. Yet it does illustrate the value that we attribute to a "maker's mark." Companies that take pride in their products generally attempt to display their names or logos prominently, whether it be on a card, an automobile, or a line of clothing. When we see these logos, we are reminded immediately of the quality and reputation of the item.

In today's passage Paul applies this same philosophy to the issue of spiritual gifts that God gives us for service in His church. Because they proceed from God, true spiritual gifts always bear two distinct labels: they always point to doctrinal truth, and they always work toward the common good of the church.

B. Lesson Background

From the founding of the church on the Day of Pentecost (Acts 2), spiritual gifts have been a characteristic feature of Christianity. It is everywhere clear in the New Testament that these gifts represent the power of God working through individuals to benefit the whole church and to advance the gospel. But Paul's extended comments on the gifts in 1 Corinthians 12–14 indicate that they had actually become a source of pride and division in the Corinthian church.

This problem made it necessary for the apostle to lay down strict guidelines on how and for what purposes spiritual gifts should be used. Our lesson today covers the beginning of this discussion in 1 Corinthians 12.

I. Spirit's Mark (1 Corinthians 12:1-3)

A. Need to Know (vv. 1, 2)

1. Now concerning spiritual gifts, brethren, I would not have you ignorant.

The first four chapters of 1 Corinthians reveal that this church is divided along certain lines. The discussion here suggests that a misunderstanding

> **How to Say It**
> CORINTHIANS. Ko-*rin*-thee-unz (*th* as in *thin*).
> DEUTERONOMY. Due-ter-*ahn*-uh-me.
> MOSES. *Mo*-zes or *Mo*-zez.
> TROPHIMUS. *Troff*-ih-muss.

of *spiritual gifts* may be one aspect of that debate. The opening formula for this chapter indicates that the Corinthians had asked Paul to comment on the issue in their letter to him (see also 1 Corinthians 7:1 in Lesson 5).

2. Ye know that ye were Gentiles, carried away unto these dumb idols, even as ye were led.

Many of the Corinthians believers are *Gentiles* rather than Jews. As such, this group has a strong connection to the pagan religious beliefs that they held to prior to becoming Christians (Acts 18:4-8). Before accepting Christ they had worshiped objects of wood, stone, silver, and gold that could say nothing and reveal nothing about God.

Now things are different for all the Corinthian Christians: the true God speaks to the church frequently and powerfully through the Holy Spirit in various ways (vv. 8-10, below). The Corinthians therefore need to be discerning in order to distinguish those who truly speak by the Spirit of God from those who do not. The truth that Paul is about to offer will help them from being *carried away* again into idolatry.

B. Test of the Spirit (v. 3)

3. Wherefore I give you to understand, that no man speaking by the Spirit of God calleth Jesus accursed: and that no man can say that Jesus is the Lord, but by the Holy Ghost.

Sound doctrine is the most basic measure of the Spirit's presence. Like the apostle John, Paul insists that the *Spirit of God* will never inspire anyone to *say* anything false about *Jesus* (compare 1 John 4:1-6). Paul's comments echo Deuteronomy 18:20. There Moses indicates that no true prophet will ever speak in the name of other gods or attempt to lead people into idolatry. Similarly, the Holy Spirit will never lead a Christian away from the truth of Christ. Anyone who claims to speak on behalf of the Spirit while denying biblical doctrine is a liar.

Of course Paul's test *no man can say that Jesus is the Lord, but by the Holy Ghost* would apply only to those professing to be Christians. A nonbeliever obviously can utter the four words "Jesus is the Lord" without conviction; this certainly would not prove that such a person possesses the Spirit. Paul means that those Corinthian believers who are prophesying, teaching, or speaking in a tongue under the Spirit's influence will always say what is true. Correct doctrine is therefore the first and most basic test of the Spirit's presence.

II. Spirit's Oneness (1 Corinthians 12:4-7)

A. Differences and Unity (vv. 4-6)

4-6. Now there are diversities of gifts, but the same Spirit. And there are differences of administrations, but the same Lord. And there are diversities of operations, but it is the same God which worketh all in all.

Unfortunately, people who confess Jesus as *Lord* may still use their gifts in ways that glorify themselves rather than Him. Paul, therefore, stresses that all gifts proceed from a common source. As such they should all work together in harmony for God's purposes.

Paul emphasizes harmony and unity here through a series of contrasts built on the formula, "different but the same." There are different *gifts, but* all come from *the same Spirit*; different *administrations,* but all from *the same Lord*; different *operations,* but all through the power of *the same God*.

At a more subtle level, Paul is relating the diversity and unity of gifts in the church to the diversity and unity of God. These verses contain the most direct statement of the doctrine of the Trinity anywhere in the Bible. The three different personalities of the Trinity—Spirit, Lord (Christ), and God (the Father)—exist and work together in complete harmony. So also should Christians, in a sense, be unified in their use of differing spiritual gifts. [See question #1, page 466.]

It is probably not useful to push for too much of a distinction between the words *gifts, administrations,* and *operations*. Rather than focus on technical shades of meaning among these three, it's much more useful to see Paul's broader point: the Corinthian Christians have no reason to be arrogant. Their gifts, administrations, and operations, whether miraculous or not, are from God. Their use of these should not lead to division.

The Same Thing, Only Different

Remarking on the statement, "It's the same thing, only different," one observer said, "It's commonly used by people who really have no idea what they're talking about. As a phrase, it represents either total ambivalence or total ignorance. Take your pick."

"It's the same thing, only different" does sound like a contradiction in terms, doesn't it? But in the realm of the work of the Holy Spirit, the statement has some validity. The same Holy Spirit works in the lives of all the people of God; yet the Spirit works in different ways. The purpose of the Spirit's work is to accomplish another thing that seems at first glance to be an impossibility: He is seeking to make many into one. Yet the coach of a basketball team has a similar task. So does the army drill sergeant.

Instead of being jealous of the gifts of another person or resentful of the accomplishments of another church, we are to rejoice. We will rejoice when we realize that what they are doing is what we are doing, as we are all one in Christ. We may do it in different ways, we may have different gifts, but in the end it is all the same thing, only different. —A. E. A.

B. Common Good (v. 7)

7. But the manifestation of the Spirit is given to every man to profit withal.

The implications of the phrase *every man* is somewhat controversial. Some argue that Paul means that each individual Christian receives a spiritual gift: every person has received a gift to *profit withal*. This claim may be supported by appeal to Romans 12:6-8 and Ephesians 4:7-13. In those passages Paul includes among the gifts of the Spirit certain general abilities such as teaching, leadership, and generosity.

Others, however, interpret the phrase *every man* more narrowly as a reference to certain people who possess gifts, a limited number within the church. Thus the idea would be that every person who has received such a gift should use it to "profit withal." Those who think this interpretation is the correct one point to the word *manifestation*. They propose that this term suggests miraculous abilities (such as healing) that only certain people possess. [See question #2, page 466.]

In either case, Paul's main point is clear: all spiritual gifts are given for the benefit of the church at large. These gifts are not for the private edification of the person who has been gifted. As Paul indicates in Ephesians 4, the gift is a gift to the church, not to the individual. The individual is simply the vessel through whom God administers the needed skill. [See question #3, page 466.]

III. Spirit's Manifestations (1 Corinthians 12:8-10)

A. Wisdom and Knowledge (v. 8)

8. For to one is given by the Spirit the word of wisdom; to another the word of knowledge by the same Spirit.

In verses 8, 9 Paul lists ways in which the Spirit manifests himself in the church. All are tied together by the repetition of the phrase *by the same Spirit*. The Spirit holds the church together and unites the efforts of individual Christians.

The first listed is *word of wisdom*. This is the ability to apply godly principles to problems of everyday life. The person with this gift is able to interpret situations from the perspective of the gospel of Christ. Such an ability is especially needed in the church in pagan Corinth, for the congregation is only about five years old at the time this letter is written. The leaders of this church, as newer Christians, need the Spirit's help to add maturity to their outlook. The fact that Paul lists wisdom first may indicate that he thinks this is the most important item in this list.

Some think that *word of knowledge* relates to information about spiritual and doctrinal issues and the ability to communicate these to others.

Home Daily Bible Readings

Monday, July 17—Excel in Gifts That Build Up (1 Corinthians 14:6-12)
Tuesday, July 18—Be Rich in Good Works (1 Timothy 6:13-19)
Wednesday, July 19—Varieties of Gifts (1 Corinthians 12:1-6)
Thursday, July 20—All Gifts Activated by the Spirit (1 Corinthians 12:7-11)
Friday, July 21—The Body Consists of Many Members (1 Corinthians 12:12-20)
Saturday, July 22—If One Member Suffers, All Suffer (1 Corinthians 12:21-26)
Sunday, July 23—Strive for the Greater Gifts (1 Corinthians 12:27-31)

Others, however, think *word of knowledge* means pretty much the same thing as *word of wisdom*. If this is the case, it means that Paul is using variety of expression as he does with gifts, administrations, and operations in verses 4-6, above.

B. Faith and Healing (v. 9)

9. To another faith by the same Spirit; to another the gifts of healing by the same Spirit.

Faith, in this context, does not mean "saving faith." Rather, it refers to a supernatural gift of especially effective faith, perhaps relating to prayer. Some students propose that the term should be translated *faithfulness*. This would mean that the person receives a special gift of patience and perseverance to endure hardship and perhaps even martyrdom as a witness to Christ.

The gift of *healing* refers to the ability to cure people of illness miraculously but only as a testimony to God's power for purposes of evangelism. Paul had to leave his friend Trophimus behind sick on one occasion (2 Timothy 4:20), and Timothy was plagued by a persistent stomach problem (1 Timothy 5:23). Thus Paul did not always seem to have the gift of healing as he did in Acts 14:8-10; 28:7-9.

C. Prophecy and Discernment (v. 10a)

10a. To another the working of miracles; to another prophecy; to another discerning of spirits.

In half-verses 10a and 10b, Paul ends his list with four types of gifts that seem to be connected with the most trouble in Corinth. These gifts involve claims about God revealing something through the individual. At the outset we should note that the *working of miracles* is a general term that includes other items on the list.

Prophecy is the first of the four. It refers to the ability to speak on behalf of God, perhaps including predictions of what will happen in the future (see Acts 11:27, 28; 21:10, 11). *Discerning of spirits* is the ability to determine whether someone's words and actions are motivated by genuine desire to please God or by selfish interests or perhaps even by demonic influences. First John 4:1 indicates that all Christians should be able to do this to at least some extent. But Paul seems to be using "discerning of spirits" in a narrower, deeper sense.

D. Tongues and Interpretation (v. 10b)

10b. To another divers kinds of tongues; to another the interpretation of tongues.

Tongues is the ability to speak in languages that one has not studied. The key example is what happened on the Day of Pentecost (Acts 2:1-11; compare 10:46; 11:15; 19:6). This gift apparently is intended to emphasize the universal nature of the gospel by illustrating God's rule over all people groups. Paul's remarks in 1 Corinthians 14 suggest that the content of such utterances is parallel to prophecy in some respects.

Just as in any situation where someone is speaking a language that we do not understand, *interpretation* is needed. The Spirit therefore enables some of the Corinthians to interpret and translate these tongues so that others can benefit from the message (see 1 Corinthians 14:27, 28).

Such gifts can lead to division easily. That division occurs when people lose track of the difference between their own opinions and divine revelations, or when they become more interested in their ability to deliver God's message than in the actual contents of that message. Paul therefore stresses that all these gifts, because they proceed from the same source, should proclaim a unified message that benefits all members of the church. See the next verse.

IV. Spirit's Blessings (1 Corinthians 12:11-13)

A. Many Gifts, One Spirit (v. 11)

11. But all these worketh that one and the selfsame Spirit, dividing to every man severally as he will.

From a human perspective, some gifts are more impressive than others. As such, it is easy for those who possess such gifts to feel

Visual for lesson 8

Point out that the picture on the right is from the 1940s. Then ask, "How has the church improved in making 'many' into 'one'?"

more important than, say, the person who is blessed with a uniquely generous spirit or the ability to encourage others (Romans 12:8). Those who are tempted to rank people based on their gifts should keep in mind the source of all gifts. God chooses which gifts go to which people; they come to the receiver like inherited property—something the receiver had never earned and did nothing to deserve. [See question #4, page 466.]

B. One Spirit, One Church (vv. 12, 13)

12. For as the body is one, and hath many members and all the members of that one body, being many, are one body: so also is Christ.

Earlier, Paul compared the exercise of spiritual gifts with the workings of the Trinity. Now he turns to an analogy of the human *body* as he does in Romans 12:4-8. The parts of the human body are different from one another, with unique functions. Even so, the human body as a whole can function effectively only if each part works properly and in unison with the other parts. Even the simple act of walking across a room involves the coordinated efforts of dozens of bones and muscles.

By analogy, the church can function smoothly and fulfill its mission in the world only when each member uses his or her individual gifts in ways that benefit the common cause of the gospel. God is glorified when that happens.

13. For by one Spirit are we all baptized into one body, whether we be Jews or Gentiles, whether we be bond or free; and have been all made to drink into one Spirit.

When we consider the membership of any given congregation, it is sometimes surprising that churches can be unified at all! People come to Christ from many different backgrounds, and Paul highlights two categories here. Before they entered the church, the Corinthian Christians came from different ethnic and religious environments *(Jews* and *Gentiles)*. They also came from different social classes *(bond* slaves and *free)*.

But the people that they once were took on a new identity in Christian baptism (Romans 6:1-4; Galatians 3:26-29). God brings us back to life as His child in faith. In this way we have a common heritage, a common family, and a common sense of purpose—at least, we should have a common sense of purpose that helps us overcome our differences. [See question #5, page 466.]

The phrase *to drink into one Spirit* may refer to Jesus' description of the Spirit as "living water" that flows to everyone who believes on Jesus (John 7:37-39). On the Day of Pentecost, the gift of the Spirit was associated with baptism (see Acts 2:38). We share a common rebirth as God's children (Galatians 4:1-7). As God's children we all enjoy the privileges of the Spirit's ministry. This being the case, it is an ironic abuse of the Spirit and of our spiritual birthright when we take pride in the gifts God has given us for the common good.

PRIDE AND EGO

Rap singer Queen Latifah was asked about the sin of pride. "Pride is a sin?" she asked. "I wasn't aware of that." Actress Kirstie Alley added, "I don't think pride is a sin. I think some idiot made that up." Rapper Ice-T echoed the same idea: "Pride is mandatory. That's one of the problems of the innercity. Kids don't have enough pride" (source: "MTV," John MacArthur, Jr. via www.biblebb.com).

Our English word *ego* is from the Latin. It has to do with 'I,' the self. It is often used in a negative sense as someone who has "an inflated ego" or "is an egomaniac." When one's ego wins out, he or she becomes the center of his or her universe. It is seen in the strutting, chest-thumping athlete. It is seen in the politician who expects preferential treatment. It is seen in the preacher who leads his congregation with a "holier than thou" attitude. A good acrostic for the word *ego* is *E*asing *G*od *O*ut.

The remedy for human ego is submission to the Holy Spirit. Ego and misdirected pride disappear when we realize that "self" is bound up in the person of Christ and not in our own personhood. Our boasting, as Paul indicates, does not come in our accomplishments but in the cross of Christ (Galatians 6:14). Is pride a sin? It depends on what we are proud of. A good ego check never hurts. —A. E. A.

Conclusion

A. A House Divided

Abraham Lincoln famously said, "A house divided against itself cannot stand." Yet that quote is not original to Lincoln. Jesus said it first (see Luke 11:17). The principle involved is timeless. It is true of every type of organization, from a marriage to a sports team to a large corporation.

The whole group always benefits when everyone works together.

But the church differs from every other organization in one key respect, a fact that Paul underscores in verses 12, 13 in our passage today. When the Christ was in this world, He inhabited a physical body. In that body He prophesied, taught, gave wise counsel, and performed miracles. All this was done to draw attention to the presence of the kingdom of God and to call people to repentance. Now Christ has returned to Heaven, yet He continues His ministry in the world through a different kind of body: the church.

This fact makes unity and harmony in the exercise of gifts vital; it is through the church's message, supported by spiritual gifts, that Christ continues His work of calling the world to a relationship with God. A church divided cannot stand and accomplish this mission.

B. Prayer

Father, please help us to discover the special ways You have gifted us to help Your church. As we use these gifts, give us the humility to be thankful for what You have done. Help us to appreciate others as we work together to fulfill Your mission for our congregation. In Jesus' name, amen.

C. Thought to Remember

Lift the body of Christ with your spiritual gifts.

Learning by Doing

This section contains an alternative lesson plan emphasizing learning activities. Classes desiring such student involvement will find these suggestions helpful.

Learning Goals

After participating in this lesson, each student will be able to:

1. Summarize what Paul says about the purpose and function of spiritual gifts.
2. Discuss ways that spiritual gifts can contribute to the ministry of his or her church.
3. Conduct a spiritual self-examination to determine personal spiritual gifts and suggest a specific ministry in which they can be put to use.

Into the Lesson

Begin the lesson with three mini-skits prepared by a team of four actors. The skits will illustrate the importance of teamwork. The setting for each skit is the construction site of a house. Each skit should last only about 15 seconds.

Skit #1: The actors should wear signs around their necks that read *Foreman*. Each actor, holding a clipboard and pencil, tries to tell the other "foremen" what to do and how to build the house. The result is confusion.

Skit #2: The actors flip their signs over to the other side that reads *Framer*. Actors lay down their clipboards, and each picks up a hammer. Actors try to work framing the house but lack direction. They ask each other for building plans and opinions on how to build the house. Again, the result is confusion.

Skit #3: One actor keeps his hammer and keeps his sign turned to *Framer*. Another actor grabs his clipboard and turns his sign back to *Foreman*. The other two actors put on new signs. One puts on a sign that reads *Plumber* and the other a sign that reads *Electrician*.

The plumber picks up a couple pieces of pipe and the electrician some electrical wire. The foreman gives brief instructions stating that work will be done on the master bathroom today. He then assigns appropriate tasks to each actor. As soon as the actors start pantomiming the building process, lead the class in applause.

Ask: "What is the obvious point of these skits?" Affirm students' answers and then make the transition to the Bible study by saying, "Teamwork in the church is equally important. One of the challenges, however, is discerning what each of our roles on the team is and how we each fit into the overall plan. Paul's letter to the Corinthian church can help us."

Into the Word

Give each student a photocopy of today's printed text, two pencils of different colors, and a regular pencil. Read the entire text to the class and then ask them to do the tasks that follow.

Say, "Use your regular pencil to circle words or phrases in the Bible text that illustrate the diversity or differences in gifts within the church family." After reviewing the answers ask: (1) "What point is Paul trying to drive home to the church with these words and phrases?" (2) "Do you think that the categories of gifts that Paul lists is meant to be all-inclusive? If not, why did he focus on the gifts listed?"

Then say, "Use one of the colored pencils to circle words or phrases that illustrate the unity that we as believers should enjoy—even in our differences." After reviewing the answers ask: (1) "What lesson is Paul teaching in verses 4-6 by using the names *Spirit, Lord,* and *God*?" (2) "Why do you think it is important for us to recognize the various gifts within the church?"

Tell students, "Use the other colored pencil to underline what you think is the key verse in this passage." Students will likely underline either verse 7 or 12. Ask students why they chose their particular verse.

Into Life

Study in advance Paul's descriptions of spiritual gifts (and gifted offices) as found in Romans 12:6-8; 1 Corinthians 12:8-10; and Ephesians 4:11. Make a handout list of those gifts (and gifted offices) that are still in effect today. (Check with your church's leadership if you're in doubt.)

Write your list in a column down the left side of the handout. On the right side of the page, make a list of all your church's ministries. You may want to add some hypothetical ministries; these are ministries that don't yet exist at your church but are possibilities.

Distribute the handout during class. Ask each student to do a self-evaluation by circling his or her own spiritual gifts. Then say, "We are to use our gifts for the common good of the church. With that in mind, match your gifts on the left with ministries on the right." Remind your students of the blessings that a diversity of gifts brings. Close with a prayer to use the gifts wisely.

Let's Talk It Over

These questions are designed to promote discussion of the lesson. The answers here are only discussion starters. Let your class talk it over from there.

1. Paul emphasizes the unity of the Godhead in vv. 4-6. How can our worship services avoid underemphasizing any member of the Trinity?

We can start by making sure that we have some balance in our song selection. That balance will acknowledge, for example, both Jesus' sacrifice on our behalf and the initiative of the Father in sending Him to do so. The centrality of Jesus is important in worship. However, in some churches Jesus is made the focus to the point that God the Father seems neglected by default!

We can also speak openly of our need for the Holy Spirit's ministry within and among us. We can acknowledge the Spirit's movement throughout 2,000 years of church history. Some believers are so careful to avoid overemphasizing the Spirit that they end up undervaluing Him! Over time, a deliberate attempt at balance will help Christians appreciate the important and complex biblical concept of the Trinity.

2. What steps can we take to determine how God has equipped us for service?

Some folks have found it useful to fill out a "spiritual gifts inventory" from a book. But there may be better ways. We can look for parallels between things we already like to do and opportunities for service that are already available. Seeking the counsel of those who know us can provide insight. After sufficient involvement in a particular ministry, we can assess our effectiveness and invite others to do the same.

We can also be alert to how God may guide us through the affirmations of others. In seeking our ideal place of service, however, we must not become persons who help only when the opportunity perfectly matches our preferences. Rather, we should meet needs whenever we can.

3. What are some practical ways we can inspire others to use their ministry gifts?

An enthusiastic attitude toward all Christian service can have a contagious effect. This, in turn, may inspire others to find their areas of greatest effectiveness. We can also make a concentrated effort to express appreciation to those who serve God faithfully and productively. Many Christians are not aware of their effectiveness simply because they are "appreciated from afar."

When fellow believers are discouraged with *all* ministry due to ineffectiveness in a *particular* ministry, we can encourage them to find other avenues for service rather than giving up. In extreme instances we may even gently nudge those who overstate their current effectiveness to move into areas where they will be more productive.

4. What factors may cause Christians to value some ministry abilities over others? How do we guard against this danger?

Often the most public ministry skills are the ones valued most highly. Some examples are preaching, high profile teaching ministries, and certain expressions of administrative gifts. Many people are either highly aware of or are directly affected by such expressions of service. We must be careful, however, not to create an environment in which high-profile believers are elevated as celebrities. Nothing good can come from that.

In other instances people value most highly the ministry skills and spiritual gifts that they themselves possess. This may lead us to think of our particular ministry niche as the most important one. A sense of humility is important.

5. Beyond our use of spiritual gifts, how can viewing the church as "one body" practically affect the way we relate to other Christians?

A "one-body outlook" will show itself as we make an effort to establish relationships with Christians from other ethnic backgrounds. This partly requires appreciating ethnic diversity as an expression of God's creativity. This appreciation won't happen until we fully embrace such brothers and sisters as true family members. An emphasis on overseas missions is part of this.

Joint participation in social ministries and worship may be good places to start. We can also strive to treat all believers equally regardless of social and economic status. In some congregations less wealthy members are not readily welcomed into leadership positions or high-profile ministries. We must consciously reject an attitude of favoritism (compare James 2:1-13).

Called to Love

July 30
Lesson 9

DEVOTIONAL READING: John 3:16-21.

BACKGROUND SCRIPTURE: 1 Corinthians 13.

PRINTED TEXT: 1 Corinthians 13.

1 Corinthians 13

1 Though I speak with the tongues of men and of angels, and have not charity, I am become as sounding brass, or a tinkling cymbal.

2 And though I have the gift of prophecy, and understand all mysteries, and all knowledge; and though I have all faith, so that I could remove mountains, and have not charity, I am nothing.

3 And though I bestow all my goods to feed the poor, and though I give my body to be burned, and have not charity, it profiteth me nothing.

4 Charity suffereth long, and is kind; charity envieth not; charity vaunteth not itself, is not puffed up,

5 Doth not behave itself unseemly, seeketh not her own, is not easily provoked, thinketh no evil;

6 Rejoiceth not in iniquity, but rejoiceth in the truth;

7 Beareth all things, believeth all things, hopeth all things, endureth all things.

8 Charity never faileth: but whether there be prophecies, they shall fail; whether there be tongues, they shall cease; whether there be knowledge, it shall vanish away.

9 For we know in part, and we prophesy in part.

10 But when that which is perfect is come, then that which is in part shall be done away.

11 When I was a child, I spake as a child, I understood as a child, I thought as a child: but when I became a man, I put away childish things.

12 For now we see through a glass, darkly, but then face to face: now I know in part; but then shall I know even as also I am known.

13 And now abideth faith, hope, charity, these three; but the greatest of these is charity.

GOLDEN TEXT: And now abideth faith, hope, charity, these three; but the greatest of these is charity.—1 Corinthians 13:13.

> *Called to Be a Christian Community*
> Unit 2: Called to Obedience
> (Lessons 5-9)

Lesson Aims

After this lesson each student will be able to:
1. List features that characterize Christian love.
2. Contrast the nature of Christian love with the worldly idea of love.
3. Identify a unique, personal way to demonstrate Christian love.

Lesson Outline

INTRODUCTION
    A. Action Love
    B. Lesson Background
I. MATHEMATICS OF LOVE (1 Corinthians 13:1-3)
    A. Spiritual Gifts Minus Love (vv. 1, 2)
    B. Self-Sacrifice Minus Love (v. 3)
    Cheap Talk, Rotten Walk
II. CHARACTERISTICS OF LOVE (1 Corinthians 13:4-7)
    A. What Love Is, Part 1 (v. 4a)
    What Love Does
    B. What Love Isn't (vv. 4b, 5)
    C. What Love Is, Part 2 (vv. 6, 7)
III. GREATNESS OF LOVE (1 Corinthians 13:8-13)
    A. Things That Will End (v. 8)
    B. Why They Will End (vv. 9-12)
    C. What Remains (v. 13)
CONCLUSION
    A. Know Yourself
    B. Prayer
    C. Thought to Remember

Introduction

A. Action Love

"I just don't know," Jane said, "whether we can learn to love each other again." She was speaking to a counselor while Craig, her husband, sat next to her in silence. Several months earlier, Jane had discovered that Craig was having an affair with a woman he had met on a business trip.

Jane responded by forcing Craig to leave their home until he made up his mind. After three weeks in a hotel, he renounced his sinful behavior and begged for forgiveness. She was willing to try but was skeptical about the future. "Could it really ever feel the same?" she asked. "We've been through so much together, but I just don't know if I even love him anymore."

In response the counselor pointed out that love is primarily a sense of commitment rather than an emotion, although we do often have loving feelings. Loving commitment to another manifests itself in a way of living. Love, in other words, is a set of behaviors, a way that we act toward others. Despite her anger, Jane was clearly acting in a loving way by attempting to forgive Craig. The counselor was, therefore, hopeful that the relationship could be healed.

Many of us live in a culture where the word *love* is used so often and so casually that it has become virtually meaningless. We say that we love God, but we also say that we love our family members, chocolate ice cream, and the sales at Wal-Mart®. Paul clarifies that love is not a feeling but rather a mode of living. He stresses that nothing we do can possibly bring glory to God if we do not exhibit a loving spirit.

B. Lesson Background

First Corinthians 13 is a key part of Paul's solution to the problems of a divided church. Up to this point in the letter, he has discussed several serious issues that were points of conflict for the Corinthian church. These ranged from sectarianism, to sexual sin, to lawsuits among believers, to divorce, to Christian liberties, to propriety in worship.

Chapter 12 begins a long section on the pride and arrogance that had entered the church through, ironically, the use of spiritual gifts. That discussion continues into chapter 14, but Paul pauses to give the short answer to all the questions thus far: love. Love for one another, properly understood, will put everything into perspective. Love will unify the church and empower believers to glorify Christ together.

I. Mathematics of Love
(1 Corinthians 13:1-3)

A. Spiritual Gifts Minus Love (vv. 1, 2)

1. Though I speak with the tongues of men and of angels, and have not charity, I am become as sounding brass, or a tinkling cymbal.

The first three verses of today's text establish the importance of love as a guidepost for the

> **How to Say It**
> APOLLO. Uh-*pah*-low.
> ATHENS. *Ath*-unz.
> CORINTHIANS. Ko-*rin*-thee-unz (*th* as in *thin*).
> DELPHI. *Del*-fi.
> MOSES. *Mo*-zes or *Mo*-zez.
> PHILIPPIANS. Fih-*lip*-ee-unz.
> THESSALONIANS. *Thess*-uh-*lo*-nee-unz (strong accent on *lo; th* as in *thin*).

exercise of spiritual gifts. Paul frames his argument with a series of statements based on a formula: "If I do *X*, even if I do *X* to the highest possible degree, but do not have love, then I am nothing." In mathematical terms, this formula may be restated as, *"X minus love equals zero,"* where *X* is any one of the spiritual gifts under discussion. Without love, nothing we do makes any difference in God's sight. (In the antique language of the *King James Version*, the word *charity* refers to "love" rather than the modern idea of "benevolence.") [See question #1, page 475.]

Paul's first example is that of speaking in *tongues*. The miraculous, Spirit-given ability to speak foreign languages is a great thing to the Corinthians. But suppose someone could *speak* not only tongues that other human beings use but also could speak the language used by the *angels* in Heaven (whatever that language may be). This surely would represent the highest form of speaking in tongues!

Yet a person who spoke that angelic language out of selfish motives—to draw attention to self or to demonstrate personal spirituality—would be of no use to anyone. As far as God is concerned, without love even the most elegant speech is like *sounding brass, or a tinkling cymbal*—in other words, just loud noise. Therefore, a tongue that is empowered by the Spirit must also be guided by genuine love.

2. And though I have the gift of prophecy, and understand all mysteries, and all knowledge; and though I have all faith, so that I could remove mountains, and have not charity, I am nothing.

Paul gives more examples. Suppose that someone has *the gift of prophecy*, the ability to speak on God's behalf and perhaps even to predict the future. Also imagine a person who is so endowed with prophetic insight as to have *all knowledge* and to understand *all mysteries*, with a profound awareness of the mind of God. Even such gifts, Paul says, are worthless if not exercised in love.

Faith here is not "saving faith." Rather, it refers to a supernatural gift of especially effective faith (see comment on 1 Corinthians 12:9 from last week's lesson). Jesus once spoke of a kind of faith that was great enough to move a mountain into the sea (Matthew 17:20). Such faith would indeed be impressive to other people! Yet God will be impressed only if the prayer is offered in a spirit of love.

B. Self-Sacrifice Minus Love (v. 3)

3. And though I bestow all my goods to feed the poor, and though I give my body to be burned, and have not charity, it profiteth me nothing.

Generosity is not listed as a manifestation of the Spirit in 1 Corinthians 12, but Paul does include it in the list of gifts in Romans 12:6-8. All Christians are obligated to *give*, but some are specially gifted to give more freely to those in need.

Ultimate giving is found in the phrase *though I give my body to be burned*. This probably refers to some act of Christian martyrdom. It's one thing to give your money *to feed the poor* but much more to sacrifice even your very life for the faith! But even the most extreme self-sacrifice is worth *nothing* in God's sight if it is done without love. [See question #2, page 475.]

CHEAP TALK, ROTTEN WALK

The young man, trying to impress his girlfriend, told her, "I would climb the highest mountain to be with you. I'd walk through a snake-infested jungle to be with you. I would swim the widest river just to be able to be with you." Then, after he kissed her, he said, "I'll see you at church Sunday if it's not raining." There is no limit to the promises some people are willing to make! We call that *cheap talk*.

At other times there is indeed the fulfillment of a noble task but from wrong motives. At a hospital near a town where I once ministered, there was a man who would go into patients' rooms to pray with them. He seemed to be such a loving and kind individual. But it was discovered that he would slip rings from their fingers as he held their hands. On other occasions he would see jewelry or other articles on a surface and pocket them. Love was not the motivation by which he served. What a *rotten walk!*

It is the scoundrel who makes the headline news, but the compassionate ones make the heart new. They are the ones who have answered the call to minister to the poor and downcast through the years. No cheap talk, no rotten walk, just giving themselves day after day to caring for the needs of others. This pleases God. —A. E. A.

II. Characteristics of Love (1 Corinthians 13:4-7)

A. What Love Is, Part 1 (v. 4a)

4a. Charity suffereth long, and is kind.

After stating that no act of service is valuable in God's sight without love, Paul moves on to specify just what love is. *Suffereth long* does not mean that loving always entails suffering (although it often does include that) but rather emphasizes that love is patient. This means that love does not express itself through vengeance, retaliation, or by giving up on people quickly. Instead, love actively extends kindness to others, even those who do not "deserve" our grace.

What Love Does

A man visits his wife in a nursing home. She has Alzheimer's disease. Daily he stops by to see her. He reads to her from the Bible. He tells her how nice the weather is and how the children and grandchildren are doing. He holds her hand and sings some of her favorite hymns to her. After two or three hours he leaves, only to return the next day for the same routine. Only this is not a routine. This is love.

Another man has a wife in the same nursing facility. She too has Alzheimer's. For the first few weeks he visits daily. Then the visits become every other day, then weekly. Then he comes only at Christmas and on his wife's birthday. His thought is, "This is not fair. I've got a life to live."

Both couples had stood before the same minister years ago. They recited vows to each other that said they would love, honor, and cherish each other in sickness and in health until death would separate them. One's man's love suffered long, the other refused to "suffer" for long. One man sought "his own" while the other man served his wife and His Lord. Which choice would you make? —A. E. A.

B. What Love Isn't (vv. 4b, 5)

4b. Charity envieth not; charity vaunteth not itself, is not puffed up.

Paul now emphasizes some things that love is not or does not do. Envy is a desire to obtain what other people have, often accompanied by feelings of bitterness or hatred. Envy and covetousness are never motivated by genuine love.

At the same time, a person who loves does not try to make other people envious by making a display of the things that he or she has. Paul may be thinking here of the pride the Corinthians are taking in their spiritual gifts. All gifts are given by the same Spirit and are of equal importance in God's plan (1 Corinthians 12:4-7, 14-26). Thus it is senseless to boast about them or to envy what someone else has received.

5. Doth not behave itself unseemly, seeketh not her own, is not easily provoked, thinketh no evil.

Neither does love *behave itself unseemly*. That means that love does not lead us to do anything that we would be ashamed of later. In this context Paul probably is thinking especially of envious or prideful things that we may say. Pride and envy are eliminated categorically by the fact that love is not selfish: love always leads us to act in the best interests of the other person (compare Philippians 2:4).

Neither is love compatible with anger toward another person (being *provoked*). Of course we may be angry at the sins that people commit and we may be frustrated by their poor choices. But these feelings should be motivated by genuine concern that the person is doing something harmful to self, others, or the cause of Christ. *Thinketh no evil* means that we should not continue to harbor ill feelings toward those who make us angry. Instead, we should forgive and forget.

C. What Love Is, Part 2 (vv. 6, 7)

6. Rejoiceth not in iniquity, but rejoiceth in the truth.

As we have seen, many of the Corinthian Christians seem to be prideful and arrogant about their spiritual gifts. Others may be angry and resentful toward those individuals. When they feel this way they may delight to see the arrogant ones fall into some sinful behavior *(iniquity)*. But the person who harbors such sentiments is no more loving than the person who constantly boasts about personal abilities. Love always rejoices *in the truth* in the sense that it makes us happy to see other people succeed and do the right thing.

7. Beareth all things, believeth all things, hopeth all things, endureth all things.

These four qualities summarize the way that love responds to other people. The repetition of *all things* emphasizes that we are to act this way despite anything that anyone may do to us.

These qualities do not suggest that love must be naïve but rather that love always remains positive towards others. As such, love does not break under pressure but instead always bears up. The Greek verb for *beareth* can refer to the idea of something remaining watertight, so that no harm comes from the outside. Love always continues to expect and hope for the best from people even when we must wait a long time to see it. [See question #3, page 475.]

III. Greatness of Love (1 Corinthians 13:8-13)

A. Things That Will End (v. 8)

8. Charity never faileth: but whether there be prophecies, they shall fail; whether there be tongues, they shall cease; whether there be knowledge, it shall vanish away.

The Corinthians apparently take great pride in certain spiritual gifts. But a time is coming when they won't need *prophecies, tongues,* and *knowledge.* Even when that time comes, however, love will continue to be the guide. We will always need love, both in this life and the next. For this very reason, Paul opened the discussion in 1 Corinthians 12:31 by calling love "a more excellent way" than the selfish pursuit of spiritual gifts. [See question #4, page 475.]

B. Why They Will End (vv. 9-12)

9. For we know in part, and we prophesy in part.

Through a special gift of knowledge (v. 8), some of the Corinthians have supernatural insight into spiritual matters. This insight can guide their counsel and teachings. Other Corinthians are empowered to *prophesy.* But the Corinthians' knowledge and prophecies of God are

---

Home Daily Bible Readings

Monday, July 24—God So Loved the World (John 3:16-21)
Tuesday, July 25—Conquering Love (Romans 8:31-39)
Wednesday, July 26—Love One Another (John 13:31-35)
Thursday, July 27—Loving One Another Fulfills the Law (Romans 13:8-14)
Friday, July 28—Let Us Love (1 John 3:11-18)
Saturday, July 29—Love Defined (1 Corinthians 13:1-7)
Sunday, July 30—The Greatest Gift Is Love (1 Corinthians 13:8-13)

---

only partial *(in part).* Any person who takes pride in these gifts should realize that he or she doesn't know everything!

10. But when that which is perfect is come, then that which is in part shall be done away.

This verse is not a prediction in the original Greek but rather is a proverb. Paul is, in other words, making a general statement about how things normally work. The word being translated *perfect* can also be understood to mean "mature" or "complete," depending on context (compare Matthew 5:48; 19:21; 1 Corinthians 2:6).

As a rule, something that is partial or incomplete is discarded when the complete thing comes onto the scene. If someone gives me a photocopy of an article from a magazine, I do not need to keep those photocopied pages after I have gone out and bought my own copy of the whole edition. Why this principle is important is the subject of the next verse.

11. When I was a child, I spake as a child, I understood as a child, I thought as a child: but when I became a man, I put away childish things.

Paul now gives an example of the principle he stated in verse 10. A *child* thinks and talks about things according to his or her limited physical and mental capabilities. For this very reason, the *things* that children say and do often amuse us by their simplicity.

But as we grow older, these simplistic ways of thinking are replaced by a more mature perspective. The new perspective is based on a better, more adult understanding of the world around us.

12. For now we see through a glass, darkly, but then face to face: now I know in part; but then shall I know even as also I am known.

Paul now applies the principle of maturity to the use of spiritual gifts. As he noted in verse 9, the revelatory gifts of knowledge, prophecy, and the like are partial and incomplete. They reveal many important things about God and His will, but they don't reveal everything.

Paul compares the knowledge of God that the Corinthians receive through these gifts with a reflection in a mirror. Fine mirrors are manufactured in Corinth at the time, but ancient mirrors are not made of *glass* like ours today. Instead, they are made of polished metal and therefore cannot give a sharp image; the picture they offer is dark, a pale reflection of one's actual features. The gifts, similarly, give us a partial knowledge of God but not the complete picture. This is not due to any lack on the part of the Spirit but rather simply to our inability to comprehend Him fully.

Yet the time will come, Paul says, when the Corinthians' partial knowledge is to be replaced. Scholars are divided on the specific experience to which this verse refers. Some say that Paul is thinking of the second coming of Jesus, a moment when the glorified Christ will reveal himself to the world and all will "see him as he is" (1 John 3:2). Others believe that Paul is referring more generally to our life in Heaven, where we will dwell in God's direct presence and behold His perfect glory. [See question #5, page 475.]

Still others think that this refers to the more complete knowledge that comes to the church as a whole when the New Testament is finished by the end of the first century A.D. Those who hold this theory point to Exodus 33:11 where Moses' "face to face" conversations with God refer to clear communication (since literally seeing God's face meant death; Exodus 33:20).

Whichever theory is true, the point not to be missed is that of all the things that are temporary, love is not one of them! Paul brings this thought home in the next verse.

C. What Remains (v. 13)

13. And now abideth faith, hope, charity, these three; but the greatest of these is charity.

Above all, our thoughts are to be guided by *charity*, or love. Indeed, God is love, and anyone who truly knows anything about God will show godly love to others (1 John 4:7, 8). We have not

Visual for lesson 9

Ask students to fill in this blank: "Love is greater than _____." Use this image to set the tone for the responses.

seen God in this world, and we do not know everything about Him. As such, we must exhibit *faith*, trusting that He knows best because we do not understand all His ways and plans. *Hope* is not wishful thinking but rather the confident assurance that we eventually will be in His eternal presence if we live a faithful life (compare 1 Thessalonians 1:3).

Both faith and hope are critical to our lives *now*. But both of these will, to some extent, become obsolete later on. In Heaven we will have what we now hope for; "hope that is seen is not hope" (Romans 8:24). Our faith will be replaced by complete confidence as we see the reality of God's eternal promises. But love will never be obsolete: it will continue to characterize our relationship with God and other redeemed saints forever.

Love is therefore the greatest of the three in the sense that it never ends. When we exercise our spiritual gifts with love, we are acting with eternity in view.

Conclusion

A. Know Yourself

In Paul's day the great Oracle at Delphi was a major tourist attraction. Legend had it that Delphi, a little over 100 miles northwest of Athens, was the center of the earth. A famous temple to the god Apollo housed a sacred stone marking the spot. Worshipers of Apollo could come to this temple to ask the idol for advice, similar to modern fortune-telling.

Answers came cryptically through a prophetess, who went into a trance and spoke in nonsensical gibberish. These ravings were "interpreted" by priests at the temple to provide the answer to the supplicants' questions.

Despite the obvious flaws of these practices, the oracle at Delphi remained a significant aspect of Greek religion for hundreds of years.

The best advice that pilgrims to Delphi received did not, however, come from a raving prophetess or priest of Apollo. Rather, the best advice came from the famous inscription over the doorway to the temple: *Know Thyself.* Worshipers were, in other words, to reflect on their own motives, weaknesses, and limitations before approaching.

The Corinthians were obsessed with spiritual gifts that offered special insights. As a result, they knew marvelous things about God and His ways, but they obviously did not know their own hearts. For this reason they failed to see that their actions were not truly driven by love or a desire to please God. Without love their greatest efforts could never truly glorify Him.

B. Prayer

Father, we love You and we know that You have called us to love others. Take away our pride and envy, and help us to be truly loving and forgiving people. Give us the wisdom to use the gifts You have given us in humility and for Your glory and honor. In Jesus' name, amen.

C. Thought to Remember

Love lasts forever; implement it now!

Learning by Doing

This section contains an alternative lesson plan emphasizing learning activities. Classes desiring such student involvement will find these suggestions helpful.

Learning Goals

After this lesson each student will be able to:
1. List features that characterize Christian love.
2. Contrast the nature of Christian love with the worldly idea of love.
3. Identify a unique, personal way to demonstrate Christian love.

Into the Lesson

Decorate the classroom with 20 to 24 large hearts affixed to the walls. Using several different colors of hearts will look attractive, but be sure they are light colored so that writing will show.

Open the lesson by dividing the class into small groups of four or five. Within groups students should relate demonstrations of great love that they have experienced. These examples could be from family experiences, church relationships, etc. To get the groups started, give a personal illustration from your life.

After a few minutes of sharing, make the transition to the Bible study by reminding the class that, "Love is manifested in many ways in our everyday lives. The need to be loved never ends. Today's study is a classic text that encourages the deepest love we can ever give or experience. While this passage is often read at weddings, its applications reach every relationship, especially relationships within the church."

Into the Word

Tell the class that they will remain in their small groups throughout today's lesson. Begin the Bible study by reading 1 Corinthians 13 to the class. Then distribute the materials and four small-group assignments listed below.

Group #1: Materials needed: several dark crayons (don't use markers as they may bleed through the paper hearts). Handout narrative: "First Corinthians 13:4-8a is often read at weddings. As time goes on, we discover ways that the characteristics of love found in these verses can be applied to our marriage experiences. Write on the hearts taped to the wall the characteristics from these verses. Be prepared to share an illustration of how each of these characteristics can be demonstrated in a marriage."

Group #2: Materials needed: poster board and a marker. Handout narrative: "Your task is to list the characteristics of love mentioned in 1 Corinthians 13:4-8a. While these characteristics of love are often applied to marriage today, Paul is directing them to personal relationships within the Corinthian church. Beside each of the characteristics listed on your poster board, note a practical way this characteristic can be illustrated in church life today."

Group #3: Handout narrative: "Your task is to read 1 Corinthians 13:4-7 and select two of the characteristics of love to mime for the class. Class members will try to guess the characteristic. Have fun!"

Group #4: Handout narrative: "Your task is to read 1 Corinthians 13 and answer the following questions: (1) Given the quest for power and spiritual gifts in the Corinthian church, what is Paul's point in verses 1-3? What does this say to today's church? (2) In verses 8-12 Paul stresses to the Corinthians that a time would come when spiritual gifts would cease to be relevant but that love endures. Why is that important to know today? (3) Verse 13 is often quoted. Why is love greater than faith and hope?"

Allow Group #3 to present its mimes for the class, and then have the other groups report their findings.

Into Life

Ask students to share, in their small groups, stories about people who embody the characteristics of love Paul mentioned in today's text. After a short time, ask a representative from each group to be prepared to share one of the more creative or unusual stories with the entire class.

Before allowing groups to share their stories, tell the class that you are going to extend a challenge for each person to find a unique way to demonstrate Christian love within the next week. The stories they hear may stimulate an idea.

Then ask each group's representative to share one story with the class. As the stories are being told, walk through the classroom quietly handing each student a piece of heart-shaped candy (or a heart-shaped trinket). Tell the class that the candy is a reminder to find one way to demonstrate Christian love this week.

Let's Talk It Over

These questions are designed to promote discussion of the lesson. The answers here are only discussion starters. Let your class talk it over from there.

1. What are some practical results of inaccurately defining love as a feeling?

Love is often viewed as a mysterious, magical entity that controls us rather than our controlling it. Thus people speak of "falling" into or out of love. Some years ago, a Hollywood celebrity had an inappropriate relationship with his adopted adult daughter. He excused his behavior by claiming that he had fallen in love—he couldn't help himself. Sometimes love is treated as an ideal that exists only in fairy tales and fables.

Inaccurate definitions of love cause people to believe that they can love only a limited number of people. The truth is different: while one can experience deep friendships only with a small number of people, biblical love can be expressed to all. How good it is to know God, who demonstrates and defines true love! (See 1 John 4:7, 8.)

2. What are some ways that expressions of giving come with an unloving attitude? How do we guard against this trap?

Examples are many! Large financial gifts are sometimes given to churches with an accompanying expectation that the giver will inappropriately control the use of the gift. On other occasions similar gifts are provided in efforts to obtain greater leadership influence in the church. Benevolence gifts are offered perhaps for the sake of enhancing one's reputation or as publicity that will advance the giver's business interests.

With a begrudging sigh of exasperation, believers may choose to help a needy person (compare 2 Corinthians 9:5). Offers of apparent kindness can veil thinly an attitude of superiority (compare Luke 18:11, 12). We begin to move toward a solution when we take seriously Jesus' instructions about gifts as found in Matthew 6:1-4.

3. How have you been able to develop a mind-set that sees the worth of people and anticipates their becoming more than they currently are? How can you improve in this area?

Regularly confessing our own sin to God (and, perhaps, to others) helps us to avoid thinking more highly of ourselves than we ought. This, in turn, helps us view others more graciously.

We can also reflect upon the growth we have experienced as we think of those who were gracious to us during times of spiritual immaturity. Remembering how far we have come can help us empathize with those who have the furthest to go. Rereading scriptural accounts of figures like King David reminds us of how easy it is to stumble and how mightily we can struggle. Inspiring conversations with people who have overcome great personal obstacles also help us remain optimistic regarding the potential of others.

4. What are some ways that speaking gifts are used in unloving ways? How can we stay alert to the dangers here?

Using the pulpit or lectern as a forum for attacking those who disagree is an obvious (and hopefully rare) problem. A more subtle problem is what we may call "spiritual manipulation." Truthful, passionate preaching that moves people's hearts to the gospel has God's approval (example: Acts 2:37). Preaching that manipulates people's response through false analogies, false choices, and false assumptions should raise a red flag. The preacher or teacher who slips into these falsehoods may be merely lazy regarding preparation, but people can be harmed nonetheless.

This question is key: "Is this person attempting to present truth in love?" (See Ephesians 4:15.) An answer of "yes, but the problem is a lack of skill or preparation" will require one type of approach. An answer of "no" will require another!

5. How would you respond to a believer who says that Bible study is not very important since someday we will know God more fully anyway?

Passages from both Old and New Testaments affirm the value of Bible study (Psalm 119:105; 2 Timothy 3:16, 17; etc.). Honoring God's commandments is important according to Exodus 20:6; John 14:15; 15:10; but how will we know what those commandments are unless we study?

Nothing makes a greater difference in a Christian's daily life than a proper view of God. Though Scripture's portrait of God is limited in certain ways, it is also accurate—it reflects what God desires us to know at present. So we must study!

August 6
Lesson 10

Giving Forgiveness

Devotional Reading: Matthew 18:21-35.
Background Scripture: 2 Corinthians 2:5-11; 7:2-15.
Printed Text: 2 Corinthians 2:5-11; 7:2-15.

2 Corinthians 2:5-11

5 But if any have caused grief, he hath not grieved me, but in part: that I may not overcharge you all.

6 Sufficient to such a man is this punishment, which was inflicted of many.

7 So that contrariwise ye ought rather to forgive him, and comfort him, lest perhaps such a one should be swallowed up with overmuch sorrow.

8 Wherefore I beseech you that ye would confirm your love toward him.

9 For to this end also did I write, that I might know the proof of you, whether ye be obedient in all things.

10 To whom ye forgive any thing, I forgive also: for if I forgave any thing, to whom I forgave it, for your sakes forgave I it in the person of Christ;

11 Lest Satan should get an advantage of us: for we are not ignorant of his devices.

2 Corinthians 7:2-15

2 Receive us; we have wronged no man, we have corrupted no man, we have defrauded no man.

3 I speak not this to condemn you: for I have said before, that ye are in our hearts to die and live with you.

4 Great is my boldness of speech toward you, great is my glorying of you: I am filled with comfort, I am exceeding joyful in all our tribulation.

5 For, when we were come into Macedonia, our flesh had no rest, but we were troubled on every side; without were fightings, within were fears.

6 Nevertheless God, that comforteth those that are cast down, comforted us by the coming of Titus;

7 And not by his coming only, but by the consolation wherewith he was comforted in you, when he told us your earnest desire, your mourning, your fervent mind toward me; so that I rejoiced the more.

8 For though I made you sorry with a letter, I do not repent, though I did repent: for I perceive that the same epistle hath made you sorry, though it were but for a season.

9 Now I rejoice, not that ye were made sorry, but that ye sorrowed to repentance: for ye were made sorry after a godly manner, that ye might receive damage by us in nothing.

10 For godly sorrow worketh repentance to salvation not to be repented of: but the sorrow of the world worketh death.

11 For behold this selfsame thing, that ye sorrowed after a godly sort, what carefulness it wrought in you, yea, what clearing of yourselves, yea, what indignation, yea, what fear, yea, what vehement desire, yea, what zeal, yea, what revenge! In all things ye have approved yourselves to be clear in this matter.

12 Wherefore, though I wrote unto you, I did it not for his cause that had done the wrong, nor for his cause that suffered wrong, but that our care for you in the sight of God might appear unto you.

13 Therefore we were comforted in your comfort: yea, and exceedingly the more joyed we for the joy of Titus, because his spirit was refreshed by you all.

14 For if I have boasted any thing to him of you, I am not ashamed; but as we spake all things to you in truth, even so our boasting, which I made before Titus, is found a truth.

15 And his inward affection is more abundant toward you, whilst he remembereth the obedience of you all, how with fear and trembling ye received him.

LESSON 10 477 AUGUST 6

> *Called to Be a Christian Community*
> Unit 3: The Spirit of Giving
> (Lessons 10-13)

Lesson Aims

After this lesson each student will be able to:
1. Tell how Paul responded to the evidence of repentance in the Corinthian church and what he urged them to do.
2. Explain why full forgiveness is essential when repentance has taken place.
3. Identify one person to whom he or she needs to extend forgiveness or from whom forgiveness should be asked.

Lesson Outline

INTRODUCTION
    A. Joseph's Attitude
    B. Lesson Background
I. MERCIFUL JUDGMENT (2 Corinthians 2:5-11)
    A. Sufficient Suffering (vv. 5, 6)
    B. Confirming Love (vv. 7, 8)
    C. Unanimous Forgiveness (vv. 9-11)
        Failure Isn't Final
II. PAUL'S COMFORT (2 Corinthians 7:2-7)
    A. Self-Defense (vv. 2, 3)
    B. Encouraging Report (vv. 4-7)
III. GOOD GUILT (2 Corinthians 7:8-15)
    A. Paul's Joy (vv. 8, 9a)
    B. Godly Sorrow (vv. 9b-11)
        Willing to Change?
    C. Mutual Comfort (vv. 12-15)
CONCLUSION
    A. Goal of Discipline
    B. Prayer
    C. Thought to Remember

Introduction

A. Joseph's Attitude

The Old Testament character Joseph models the ability to maintain a gracious spirit in spite of suffering. His divine gifts of wisdom and insight made him Jacob's favorite son but also inspired the resentment of his brothers. In a fit of rage, they sold him into slavery. He eventually wound up in prison in Egypt.

But God remained with him, and after a series of remarkable events, Joseph found himself to be second in command over all Egypt. From this exalted position, he could have exacted vengeance easily. A prime opportunity presented itself when his brothers came to purchase grain during a famine. But, incredibly, Joseph did not condemn them because, as he says in Genesis 45:8, "It was not you that sent me hither, but God."

Joseph was able to maintain this attitude because he saw God's hand at work in the situation (see Genesis 45:4-7). Repairing relationships can be difficult, especially when we have suffered because of another person's actions. The key lies in understanding that God is ultimately in control and that He can work His will in every situation.

B. Lesson Background

From an earlier lesson, we know that Paul founded the church at Corinth as noted in Acts 18:1-18. A few years later, Paul spent a significant amount of time in Ephesus. While there he received a letter from the Corinthians asking for guidance on several difficult issues (1 Corinthians 1:11; 7:1). He responded by sending the letter of 1 Corinthians and also by sending Timothy to assist the struggling church (4:17; 16:5-11).

But these remedies apparently were unsuccessful. After Timothy returned with the bad news, Paul paid them a visit "in heaviness" (2 Corinthians 2:1). This was an unpleasant experience, as Paul apparently had to confront a number of individuals. Paul also suffered slanderous accusations (2 Corinthians 10, 11, 12:11).

After he returned to Ephesus, Paul sent Titus to supervise the situation. Upon hearing no report, he began to worry and decided to return to Corinth. On the way, however, he met Titus coming back to Ephesus over land through Macedonia (Acts 20:1, 2; 2 Corinthians 7:5-7).

Aug 6

Golden Text: Godly sorrow worketh repentance to salvation not to be repented of:
but the sorrow of the world worketh death.—2 Corinthians 7:10.

> **How to Say It**
> CORINTH. *Kor*-inth.
> CORINTHIANS. Ko-*rin*-thee-unz (*th* as in *thin*).
> EGYPT. *Ee*-jipt.
> EPHESUS. *Ef*-uh-sus.
> MACEDONIA. Mass-eh-*doe*-nee-uh.
> TITUS. *Ty*-tus.
> TROAS. *Tro*-az.

Paul was generally pleased with Titus's report, but some issues still needed to be addressed. He therefore sent the letter of 2 Corinthians to prepare the church for his impending return (2 Corinthians 13:1).

I. Merciful Judgment (2 Corinthians 2:5-11)

A. Sufficient Suffering (vv. 5, 6)

5. But if any have caused grief, he hath not grieved me, but in part: that I may not overcharge you all.

While in Ephesus, Paul received word that a member of the church in Corinth was having an affair with his stepmother. Paul recognized that the sin involved demanded that this man be barred from the fellowship until he repented (1 Corinthians 5). The Corinthians were tolerating something that should not be tolerated.

In the text before us, we see the opposite extreme. Apparently the Corinthians refuse to forgive a certain man even after he confesses his sin. (This may or may not be the same man in 1 Corinthians 5.) "To some extent," Paul says, "what this individual said or did grieved all of us, not just me." This sets the tone for the remainder of Paul's remarks.

6. Sufficient to such a man is this punishment, which was inflicted of many.

Disciplinary actions sometimes are needed to underscore the seriousness of sin or false doctrine. By barring the wayward individual from Christian fellowship, the church unites to let him know that he cannot continue to enjoy the company of the redeemed while such behavior continues. The New Testament presents three reasons for disfellowshiping: *doctrinal defection* (Romans 16:17, 18; 1 Timothy 6:3, 4; Titus 1:10-16), *moral defection* (1 Corinthians 5), and *divisiveness* (Romans 16:17, 18; Titus 3:10).

In the case at hand, Paul's advice apparently was too effective! The Corinthians, roused from their complacency, apparently dismissed someone from the church for an appropriate reason. But the punishment the man received is now *sufficient*. The punishment has served its purpose in bringing him back to his senses.

B. Confirming Love (vv. 7, 8)

7. So that contrariwise ye ought rather to forgive him, and comfort him, lest perhaps such a one should be swallowed up with overmuch sorrow.

There are two goals to the extreme action of disfellowshiping. One goal is to protect the church's doctrinal and moral purity. The other goal is to bring about the repentance of the wayward believer. The church is not empowered to punish those who are outside the church; God himself will hand out their punishments in the next life.

The church, instead, is to discipline the backslider who is within the church (1 Corinthians 5:12, 13). A person may be overwhelmed with *sorrow* and grief as a consequence. But if the final result is the person's restoration to a relationship with Christ, then the best possible outcome has been achieved! Godly sorrow leads to repentance (see below).

8. Wherefore I beseech you that ye would confirm your love toward him.

Even though this man has caused considerable grief, *love* must still be the guiding force, not anger and vindictiveness. Paul had reminded the Corinthians in his first letter that love "suffereth long, and is kind" (1 Corinthians 13:4). He now urges them to put this principle into action. Church discipline should have a redemptive purpose (Luke 17:3, 4; 2 Thessalonians 3:14, 15; James 5:19, 20). [See question #1, page 484.]

C. Unanimous Forgiveness (vv. 9-11)

9. For to this end also did I write, that I might know the proof of you, whether ye be obedient in all things.

There is a subtle warning behind this verse. Paul says that he has written as a test of their loyalty to his teaching. Obviously, if they fail to recognize his authority in such matters, then their obedience will again be called into question. As he says in 2 Corinthians 13:1-3, they need to be ready to answer for their actions when he comes on a third visit. [See question #2, page 484.]

10. To whom ye forgive any thing, I forgive also: for if I forgave any thing, to whom I forgave it, for your sakes forgave I it in the person of Christ.

True repentance before *Christ* brings true forgiveness from Christ (1 John 1:9). The man in question probably has already received Christ's forgiveness based on what Paul has just said in verses 7, 8. Will the Corinthians have the mind of Christ by forgiving that man as well?

Failure Isn't Final

It was a typical chapel session on the campus of a certain Bible college. The academic dean was preaching on the ability of God to use even the most difficult moments of life to bring glory to His name. Near the end of his message, he called to the platform—to everyone's surprise—a former professor who had been released from his teaching duties because of a moral failure.

The auditorium fell silent as the young man ascended to the podium. He had been much loved and greatly respected. All who knew his story had been hugely affected by the disclosure of the problems within his life.

The young man began by relating to the student body the nature of his struggles, errors in judgment, and behavior that had so affected his life and ministry. Then he spoke of God's amazing grace working through his own repentance and the loving care and forgiveness of His people.

When he finished there was a keen awareness that we were witnessing the amazing work of God in His ability to use a horrible mistake to bring glory and honor to His name. What an encouragement to realize that God can work even in the midst of our mistakes to bring us back to Him—if we will let Him. —T. B.

11. Lest Satan should get an advantage of us: for we are not ignorant of his devices.

Satan loves to see people fall away from Christ, and he is having a field day with the Corinthians! Their unforgiving spirit is sinful in and of itself. Satan is taking advantage of the situation to keep the penitent backslider away from God for good. Paul hopes that they will see how counterproductive their actions are and that they will evaluate their own motives to be sure they aren't doing more harm than good. [See question #3, page 484.]

II. Paul's Comfort (2 Corinthians 7:2-7)

A. Self-Defense (vv. 2, 3)

2. Receive us; we have wronged no man, we have corrupted no man, we have defrauded no man.

When Paul returned to Corinth earlier, he apparently had been accused of misleading and exploiting the church (see 2 Corinthians 10:1-11). Paul thus sets an example of forgiveness by implying that he harbors no hard feelings in this regard. His motives and actions are always pure. Specifically, Paul never treated anyone disrespectfully, never said anything to encourage moral corruption, and never told the Corinthians what they wanted to hear just to get money (see 1 Corinthians 9:1-12). His actions were always honorable, thus the church is responsible for any hard feelings that ever passed between them.

3. I speak not this to condemn you: for I have said before, that ye are in our hearts to die and live with you.

Although Paul is not responsible for the conflict, he does not lord it over the Corinthians. Even when he uses strong words, Paul's goal is not to *condemn*. Instead, he always acts in their best interests. He models the type of loving forgiveness that he now asks them to demonstrate.

B. Encouraging Report (vv. 4-7)

4, 5. Great is my boldness of speech toward you, great is my glorying of you: I am filled

Visual for lesson 10

Paul's movements are complex. This map will help your students keep a perspective on a segment of one of his journeys.

with comfort, I am exceeding joyful in all our tribulation. For, when we were come into Macedonia, our flesh had no rest, but we were troubled on every side; without were fightings, within were fears.**

Paul begins to review the recent situation. After his confrontational visit, Paul was forced to return quickly to Ephesus to attend to pressing concerns. He therefore sent his disciple Titus to manage the situation in Corinth (see v. 6, next).

The volatility of the situation left Paul plagued with doubts. At that point in time, Paul was making successful inroads in Troas (2 Corinthians 2:12, 13), but his concern for the Corinthians was such a distraction that he set out to visit them once more.

6. Nevertheless God, that comforteth those that are cast down, comforted us by the coming of Titus.

Paul's fears turned to joy, however, when he met *Titus* halfway, in Macedonia. God's comfort is a major theme in 2 Corinthians, and it is notable here that God's comfort came to Paul through the report of Titus. God gave Paul spiritual peace in a difficult situation. But the Corinthians gave him an even deeper peace by resolving the problem (next verse).

7. And not by his coming only, but by the consolation wherewith he was comforted in you, when he told us your earnest desire, your mourning, your fervent mind toward me; so that I rejoiced the more.

Paul wants to make clear that he wasn't just happy to see that Titus had survived (as in "Praise God that those people didn't kill you!"). What truly impressed him was Titus's report that the Corinthians had decided to follow his advice and that they had an *earnest desire* to do so.

III. Good Guilt (2 Corinthians 7:8-15)

A. Paul's Joy (vv. 8, 9a)

8. For though I made you sorry with a letter, I do not repent, though I did repent: for I perceive that the same epistle hath made you sorry, though it were but for a season.

Many of Paul's comments in 1 Corinthians were very strong and could easily cause distress (see 2 Corinthians 2:3, 4). But true love does not seek simply to placate people; it seeks to do what is ultimately best for them. The Corinthians' actions were displeasing to God, and Paul had to make them aware of this fact. Because they eventually responded in the proper way, Paul can look back on the situation and say that he does not really regret his actions. Any sorrow was temporary, and the result was well worth it.

9a. Now I rejoice, not that ye were made sorry, but that ye sorrowed to repentance.

Paul is not happy to have hurt anyone's feelings. He rejoices, rather, that strong words led the Corinthians to repent—to change their minds and take the correct course of action.

B. Godly Sorrow (vv. 9b-11)

9b, 10. For ye were made sorry after a godly manner, that ye might receive damage by us in nothing. For godly sorrow worketh repentance to salvation not to be repented of: but the sorrow of the world worketh death.

Guilt is a powerful force. In our spiritual lives, feelings of guilt can lead to conviction of heart (examples: Psalm 51; Acts 2:37). *Sorrow* of this type reflects what God desires. We should feel ashamed when we sin, but that feeling should lead us to repent. If our feelings of guilt lead to transformation, then it is truly godly in the sense that it helps us to grow in obedience.

WILLING TO CHANGE?

One quiet evening the smiling face of the youngest elder of our church appeared at my office door. I had been waiting because I knew he wanted to discuss something. We always had had an amiable relationship, so I was intrigued by what the nature of this conversation would be.

After exchanging pleasantries, he proceeded to share with me several of my faults. After 45 minutes he had outlined every minor character flaw I had ever possessed and even threw in a few I didn't believe existed! After the ordeal I thanked him for sharing these things with me, and we prayed. He left, no doubt thinking that he had done me a huge favor.

I must admit that my immediate reaction was anger. On the outside I remained calm, but on the inside I was fuming, "Where does he get off thinking he has the right to say these things to me?" I harbored bitterness. I imagined a retaliatory strike.

As the weeks rolled on, however, I began to think. Some of his observations were out of line, but several were right on. I realized I needed to address these areas of my life. Now, nearly 25 years later, I look back on that evening as a key moment in my life. God used it to help me become a more faithful servant.

How we receive discipline is a mark of Christian maturity. God is often waiting for our pride to expire so He can work His will in us. —T. B.

11. For behold this selfsame thing, that ye sorrowed after a godly sort, what carefulness it wrought in you, yea, what clearing of yourselves, yea, what indignation, yea, what fear, yea, what vehement desire, yea, what zeal, yea, what revenge! In all things ye have approved yourselves to be clear in this matter.

The Corinthians' follow-up actions have proved that their sorrow over Paul's rebuke was not simply embarrassment at getting caught. Once he brought the issue to their attention, they realized their error and were motivated to do something about it.

In this context *indignation* means that they became angry with themselves for being lax. *Revenge* does not refer to taking reprisal or retaliation on someone. Rather, it refers to a desire to see that justice is done. Thus Paul is commending the Corinthians for taking proper steps after realizing that they had been tolerant of sinful behavior. [See question #4, page 484.]

C. Mutual Comfort (vv. 12-15)

12. Wherefore, though I wrote unto you, I did it not for his cause that had done the wrong, nor for his cause that suffered wrong, but that our care for you in the sight of God might appear unto you.

The backslidden person's flagrant violation of Paul's teachings, combined with the church's subsequent failure to protect its own purity, was a serious situation. Paul's goal was to assist the church in doing the right thing. He achieved that goal, even though it was painful.

In the process the Corinthians saw how much they really did *care* for Paul. His disciplinary actions actually led to a deeper relationship between them. They, in turn, should take similar steps to restore their fallen brother to full fellowship.

13. Therefore we were comforted in your comfort: yea, and exceedingly the more joyed we for the joy of Titus, because his spirit was refreshed by you all.

Titus not only managed a difficult situation but actually left Corinth *refreshed*. This is a testimony to his pastoral skill. Titus is mentioned most often in the book of 2 Corinthians.

14. For if I have boasted any thing to him of you, I am not ashamed; but as we spake all things to you in truth, even so our boasting, which I made before Titus, is found a truth.

In the ancient world, to be shamed means to lose status in the eyes of another person. Even at their worst, Paul remained confident that the Corinthians would not embarrass him. His hopes were fulfilled by God's providence.

15. And his inward affection is more abundant toward you, whilst he remembereth the obedience of you all, how with fear and trembling ye received him.

Although the Corinthians had received Titus *with fear and trembling,* Paul does not mean that people should fear church leaders. The Corinthians had not been afraid of Titus himself but rather of the implications of his message. They suddenly realized how serious their situation was and how deeply they had offended Paul. [See question #5, page 484.]

But Titus, like Paul, showed true love toward them. Could the Corinthians not extend the same love and forgiveness to a man who repented of a sin, admitting that he had done wrong?

Conclusion

A. Goal of Discipline

Those of us who are parents recall many times when our children made us angry. We go into our son's room after telling him several times to get dressed, only to discover him sitting on the

---

Home Daily Bible Readings

Monday, July 31—Forgive Others Their Trespasses (Matthew 6:9-15)

Tuesday, Aug. 1—Jesus Teaches About Forgiveness (Matthew 18:21-35)

Wednesday, Aug. 2—Forgive, So God May Forgive You (Mark 11:20-25)

Thursday, Aug. 3—You Also Must Forgive (Colossians 3:12-17)

Friday, Aug. 4—Forgive and Console Your Offender (2 Corinthians 2:5-11)

Saturday, Aug. 5—Paul's Pride in the Corinthians (2 Corinthians 7:2-7)

Sunday, Aug. 6—Paul's Joy at the Corinthians' Repentance (2 Corinthians 7:8-16)

floor in his underwear playing with toys. Such offenses make us mad, and we often lash out in frustration. But are such actions intended truly to discipline the child or merely to punish him?

Discipline is an action we take to help another person develop and mature. Discipline may result from some crime but does not focus on the crime. Rather, it focuses on the right things the person should do in the future. Discipline encourages the errant one to do better. When in anger we merely punish our children for jumping on the bed, we are not helping them improve.

God does not empower the church to punish the immoral people of the world. God does, however, call the church to discipline its members. This means to help them become stronger Christians who will make godly, holy choices. Our judgmental feelings of anger and resentment must never get in the way of this objective. Forgiveness is a key.

B. Prayer

Father, we live in a world where people rejoice in the failure of others. Help us to be lights of forgiveness and love. Give us the grace to give others the benefit of the doubt, when called for. Help us to share the forgiveness we have received from You with people who do wrong but repent. In Jesus' name, amen.

C. Thought to Remember

When forgiveness is needed, we must give it.

Learning by Doing

This section contains an alternative lesson plan emphasizing learning activities. Classes desiring such student involvement will find these suggestions helpful.

Learning Goals

After this lesson each student will be able to:

1. Tell how Paul responded to the evidence of repentance in the Corinthian church and what he urged them to do.

2. Explain why full forgiveness is essential when repentance has taken place.

3. Identify one person to whom he or she needs to extend forgiveness or from whom forgiveness should be asked.

Into the Lesson

Prepare four opaque cards, each with a large numeral 4 on one side. Fold each card so that the numeral is on the inside. Hand out the four cards randomly to class members as they arrive. Give the following instruction: "Look at your card but don't let others see what is printed on it."

At the beginning of class, say, "I want those with a card to hand your card to another class member. Be sure to give that person the same directions that I gave you when I handed you the card." Continue in this manner until all have seen a card.

Say, "This activity represents the theme of today's lesson. Who can identify the relationship?" When someone notes that you have been "*four*-giving to others," accept the chuckles and groans, then launch into today's text.

Into the Word

Provide paper for the following agree/disagree activity (or use the activity as it appears in the student book). Say, "As you look at today's text in 2 Corinthians 2:5-11; 7:2-15, decide if you agree or disagree with each of the following statements:

1. A Christian's sin is an affront to those who have taught him or her.

2. Church discipline is designed to make an example of the wayward brother or sister.

3. Correction must come out of a heart of love, not one of vengeance.

4. Obedience is the only sure indication of respect for authority.

5. Satan revels in an unforgiving spirit.

6. Bold speech in the face of sin can elicit a good response.

7. Few things cheer up a parent more than correction received graciously.

8. There is real joy in seeing a sinner repent in tears.

9. Sorrow over sin can have a harmful effect for the sinner.

10. Sometimes the good of the church as a whole is more significant than the good of an individual Christian.

11. Boasting is an appropriate response for one who has met high expectations.

12. True affection for someone will increase as that person acts in obedience to God's truth.

After reading all the statements and allowing time for students to record their answers, say, "Now let's go back and match these statements to the Bible verses in today's text to see whether we should agree or disagree with each one."

Ask a volunteer to read aloud the Golden Text for today, 2 Corinthians 7:10. This verse sharply contrasts godly sorrow and worldly sorrow. Ask, "What are the foundational differences between godly sorrow and worldly sorrow?" Allow for a variety of responses but expect answers to the effect that worldly sorrow remains essentially selfish.

Into Life

Display the following three-word sentences on the board. Ask your class to rank them as to which is most difficult to say: "I was wrong." "Please forgive me." "I forgive you." "We are brothers/sisters." "Christ forgave me." "You were wrong."

Next say, "If one of these statements were on the outside of a greeting card asking for someone's forgiveness, what could the inside of the card say?" If the class needs an example, say, "For the 'We are brothers/sisters' statement, you could write, 'Our love must be greater than my foolishness; please forgive my offense toward you.'"

After brief discussion, hand each class member half of an 8-1/2" by 11" sheet of paper folded to resemble a card. Say, "Write *Forgiveness Card* on the back bottom of this folded sheet. Then create a forgiveness card using one of the six phrases. Someone you know needs your forgiveness. Use this forgiveness card to remind you this week to seek that reconciliation."

Let's Talk It Over

These questions are designed to promote discussion of the lesson. The answers here are only discussion starters. Let your class talk it over from there.

1. When someone is to be restored to full fellowship in the church, what steps may be necessary for the offending individual to feel welcome again? What is necessary for others to accept that person and feel comfortable around him or her?

All parties will be wise to sit together and talk about what has happened in the past and what each would like to achieve in the future. They need to pray together asking God to cleanse and shape their hearts (Psalm 51). Hopes and intentions can be clarified. The members of the church need to invite the restored brother or sister to social events and homes.

Depending on the nature of the offense and the completion of any stipulations the offender has been asked to meet, plans can be made as to the appropriate time frames in which the restored person can take an active role in a position of responsibility. Remember: there is a difference between *forgiveness* and *consequences*. A church treasurer who embezzled funds may be fully forgiven upon repentance (and, if possible, restitution). But that doesn't necessarily mean that he or she will ever be church treasurer again (consequences).

2. Paul had to "sweat it out" about what would happen as someone else took his instructions to the church at Corinth. What practical advice might we gain from looking closely at Paul's approach throughout this process?

Paul agonized over whether to write, what to say, and how it would be taken. But he knew it needed to be done in order to create the right conditions for spiritual growth and changed behavior. His goal was not to condemn or just "tell someone off." His goal was growth and reconciliation.

With that fact in mind, his action steps seemed to follow this order: pray constantly; clarify his goals; write his points very clearly; send someone else as a mediator and teacher; pray through his anxiety; prepare to go personally if necessary; rejoice with those who had chosen to do the right thing; restate the confidence he had in them throughout the process; and praise God for His wisdom and leadership. Depending on the situation today, some of these steps may need to be emphasized more than others.

3. If one person of a group forgives an individual, do all have to forgive? Why, or why not?

Paul trusts the wisdom of the Corinthians in this regard. He is ready to close the chapter on judgment and open a new one on forgiveness and reconciliation if the offending person and congregation are ready to take the next steps.

If some hesitate to forgive after others have done so, there may be good or bad reasons to be investigated. Paul already has forgiven the offender of his past. Now he is waiting on the action taken by the Corinthians before moving into the next phases of full reconciliation.

4. In what practical ways do both the offending person and the church benefit if there is both forgiveness and reconciliation?

The most obvious benefit is that the problem is solved and taken off the "worry list." People can be more at ease with each other and can focus on rebuilding relationships. Other important areas such as evangelism and missions will not be hampered by the energy drain used to deal with disruptive conflicts.

Everyone can be encouraged spiritually as they are reminded that God's way of dealing with these types of problems does indeed work. If the offender and the church really care about whether people are in a right relationship with God, then working through a difficult situation provides the occasion of joy and celebration.

5. Under what circumstances is it wise to send others to help with the "cleanup work" when a messy situation is not improving? What instructions should they receive?

Paul may have recognized that God had given Titus the personality and spiritual gifts suitable to be a mediator. Paul was wise to send someone else who could lead the Corinthians through a very delicate process of dealing with an explosive situation. The Corinthians may have seen Titus as a neutral third party, willing to listen.

Titus was informed of the situation and the goals. He was granted time to complete the task. We will always be wise to send qualified people when a difficult situation must be addressed.

Giving Generously

August 13
Lesson 11

DEVOTIONAL READING: Luke 20:45–21:4.

BACKGROUND SCRIPTURE: 2 Corinthians 8:1-15.

PRINTED TEXT: 2 Corinthians 8:1-15.

2 Corinthians 8:1-15

1 Moreover, brethren, we do you to wit of the grace of God bestowed on the churches of Macedonia;

2 How that in a great trial of affliction, the abundance of their joy and their deep poverty abounded unto the riches of their liberality.

3 For to their power, I bear record, yea, and beyond their power they were willing of themselves;

4 Praying us with much entreaty that we would receive the gift, and take upon us the fellowship of the ministering to the saints.

5 And this they did, not as we hoped, but first gave their own selves to the Lord, and unto us by the will of God.

6 Insomuch that we desired Titus, that as he had begun, so he would also finish in you the same grace also.

7 Therefore, as ye abound in every thing, in faith, and utterance, and knowledge, and in all diligence, and in your love to us, see that ye abound in this grace also.

8 I speak not by commandment, but by occasion of the forwardness of others, and to prove the sincerity of your love.

9 For ye know the grace of our Lord Jesus Christ, that, though he was rich, yet for your sakes he became poor, that ye through his poverty might be rich.

10 And herein I give my advice: for this is expedient for you, who have begun before, not only to do, but also to be forward a year ago.

11 Now therefore perform the doing of it; that as there was a readiness to will, so there may be a performance also out of that which ye have.

12 For if there be first a willing mind, it is accepted according to that a man hath, and not according to that he hath not.

13 For I mean not that other men be eased, and ye burdened:

14 But by an equality, that now at this time your abundance may be a supply for their want, that their abundance also may be a supply for your want; that there may be equality:

15 As it is written, He that had gathered much had nothing over; and he that had gathered little had no lack.

GOLDEN TEXT: Ye know the grace of our Lord Jesus Christ, that, though he was rich, yet for your sakes he became poor, that ye through his poverty might be rich.
—2 Corinthians 8:9.

> *Called to Be a Christian Community*
> Unit 3: The Spirit of Giving
> (Lessons 10-13)

Lesson Aims

After participating in this lesson, each student will be able to:

1. List reasons that Paul cites for why the Corinthians should have felt compelled to give.
2. Explain how a benevolent gift is an appropriate response to God's grace.
3. Examine his or her personal motives for giving or not giving to those in need.

Lesson Outline

INTRODUCTION
    A. Amish Insurance
    B. Lesson Background
I. EXAMPLE OF GIVING (2 Corinthians 8:1-5)
    A. Pain (vv. 1-3)
        Glorious Giving
    B. Privilege (v. 4)
    C. Priorities (v. 5)
        What We Leave Behind
II. GRACE OF SHARING (2 Corinthians 8:6-15)
    A. Corinthians' Start (vv. 6-8)
    B. Christ's Example (v. 9)
    C. Paul's Advice (vv. 10, 11)
    D. Paul's Desire (vv. 12-15)
CONCLUSION
    A. Proving We Exist
    B. Prayer
    C. Thought to Remember

Introduction

A. Amish Insurance

The Amish are a people known for industry and thrift. Their farms and businesses are models of cleanliness and order. They are regarded widely for their ethical business practices and the quality of their workmanship. As a result many Amish families enjoy financial prosperity.

A real estate agent once visited an Amish gentleman to discuss the acquisition of a neighboring piece of land. As they spoke, the agent realized that the man had accumulated a great deal of wealth, with a large farm and several herds of dairy cows. He asked the farmer who provided his insurance. The man replied, "God."

The agent, taken aback, pointed out that even very godly people sometimes lose their properties to theft or disasters. What if the man's barn were struck by fire or a tornado? The farmer explained that God would take care of him in that case, because other members of the community would rebuild the barn for him and help him replace his equipment. That was the kind of insurance he relied on.

This commendable outlook reflects the conditions in Paul's day. Christians could not depend on the government or insurance companies in times of need. They could depend only on God. In our passage for today, Paul discusses God's insurance plan: Christians sharing their wealth to help one another get through tough times.

B. Lesson Background

During his second and third missionary journeys, Paul expended much effort organizing a collection for the needs of the impoverished Christians in Jerusalem. Palestine is a dry region, and during New Testament times there were several major droughts in that area (compare Acts 11:27, 28). Further, there were continual rumblings of rebellion against Rome throughout the A.D. 50s and 60s. These frequently disrupted the economy of the region. (Note that 2 Corinthians was written in A.D. 57.)

Paul saw this situation as a prime opportunity for his congregations, composed primarily of Gentile believers, to extend a gesture of goodwill to the parent church in Judea (see Romans 15:25-27). In our passage for today, Paul instructs the Corinthians on preparations for their gift. In the process he offers the most extended discussion of benevolent giving found anywhere in the Bible.

I. Example of Giving (2 Corinthians 8:1-5)

A. Pain (vv. 1-3)

1, 2. Moreover, brethren, we do you to wit of the grace of God bestowed on the churches of Macedonia; How that in a great trial of affliction, the abundance of their joy and their deep poverty abounded unto the riches of their liberality.

Paul begins with a kind of paradox that sets the tone for the rest of the chapter. Normally, we would think of a *grace* that is *bestowed* as a gift that someone receives. *God*, Paul says, gave the *churches of Macedonia* a gift. But he immediately clarifies that the gift they received was the desire to give something to someone else. What they received from God, then, was a passionate desire to help others.

This fact is especially remarkable in view of their circumstances. Each of the three major churches in Macedonia—namely, Philippi, Thessalonica, and Berea—was born into persecution (Acts 16:16–17:15). These people had suffered adverse circumstances from the day they accepted Christ. Yet, amazingly, this led them to give even more generously. (Corinth itself is part of Achaia, to the south of Macedonia.)

Paul points out two more apparent paradoxes in their situation. First, in a time of great suffering the Macedonians were filled with abundant *joy.* This is certainly not the normal, worldly response to such a situation! Second, their poverty *abounded* in rich generosity. Through God's power they actually were thankful to give from their limited resources to help other Christians who were in need, even people they had never met. [See question #1, page 493.]

3. For to their power, I bear record, yea, and beyond their power they were willing of themselves.

Technically speaking, it is obvious that no one can give more than he or she is able to give since credit cards don't exist in Paul's day. The question is how much we think we can afford to give. That essentially becomes an issue of how much we trust God to provide for us in the future if we give now. The Macedonians not only gave what they could afford, they also gave more than they could afford, to a point where it hurt. In this sense their giving was *beyond their power.* This kind of giving takes faith. This kind of giving hurts!

Glorious Giving

There is an old story of a medieval monk who found a precious jewel and kept it. The monk had taken a vow of poverty, so he had no thought of redeeming the jewel for money. He enjoyed it for its beauty and radiance. It reminded him of the glory of God in creation.

One day the monk met a traveler. As the monk opened his bag to share his provisions, the stranger saw the jewel. Knowing that the monk had taken a vow always to help those in need, he asked the monk to give him the jewel.

The monk asked, "Do you really need the gem, my son?" The stranger replied, "Yes, I do." To the man's astonishment, the monk readily gave him the jewel.

The traveler departed, overjoyed with his unexpected stroke of luck. A few days later, though, he came back in search of the monk. Finding him, he gave him back the precious jewel and made a request: "I want to ask you for something even more precious than this jewel. Please give to me that which enabled you to give me the jewel."

The traveler had discerned a great truth: the ability to give is one of the greatest blessings in life. May God grant to us the joyous ability to be gracious in our giving. —T. B.

B. Privilege (v. 4)

4. Praying us with much entreaty that we would receive the gift, and take upon us the fellowship of the ministering to the saints.

The key concept in this verse, and in this entire chapter, is *fellowship.* This refers to a complete sharing of life with another. Similar terminology is used to describe the earliest life of the church in Acts 2:42-47. There we see the believers constantly worshiping together, sharing meals, and providing for one another's financial needs.

As Jesus said, God has promised to provide for every person who seeks His kingdom (Matthew 6:33). But that provision can come in many different forms. It may come in the form of a new job, an unexpected bonus, or a financial gift. Sometimes God provides for someone else's needs through your prosperity, as you share with them what God has given you. Later on you may be on the receiving end when you are in need.

This sense of communion with other believers allows the Macedonians not only to give money but actually to plead with Paul *(much entreaty)* to be able to share the *gift.* They are confident that the Judean brethren will also help them if the need ever arises.

C. Priorities (v. 5)

5. And this they did, not as we hoped, but first gave their own selves to the Lord, and unto us by the will of God.

Godly stewardship is not just a matter of money but rather is a matter of our very lives. The Macedonians first gave *their own selves* to God in the sense that they placed complete trust in His provision. That was their top priority.

This, in turn, enabled them to share their financial resources to the maximum extent. When we give to help God's people, we are only sharing what belongs to God anyway; literally, we are spending someone else's money—God's.

WHAT WE LEAVE BEHIND

Funerals are a time of reflection in which we remember the most redeeming qualities of those who have departed this life. But what if we heard the following at a funeral?

"This fellow had the finest set of golf clubs that money could buy."

"I will really miss seeing his beautiful, weed-free yard."

"The thing that I will always remember about ol' Bob is the way he could get that extra 10 horsepower out of his car's engine."

"I will always appreciate the fact that he made well over $100,000 a year and that his stocks always performed well."

If we did hear those statements at a funeral, we would pity the shallow lives of the people who made them (not to mention the empty life of the deceased). U.S. President Calvin Coolidge (1872–1933) once said, "No person was ever honored for what he received. Honor has been the reward for what he gave."

Coolidge was giving us a formula for successful living. Yet God is the original source and example of this formula. Giving is inseparably connected to the gracious character of God. We live because God is generous. He gave us His Son. One of the greatest traits of those redeemed by Christ is the ability to become like our heavenly Father in generosity.   —T. B.

II. Grace of Sharing (2 Corinthians 8:6-15)

A. Corinthians' Start (vv. 6-8)

6. Insomuch that we desired Titus, that as he had begun, so he would also finish in you the same grace also.

Paul now turns from the example of the Macedonian churches to urge the Corinthians to prepare a generous gift for the needy in Jerusalem. He begins with a discussion of the ministry of *Titus*.

After delivering a progress report that brought Paul great joy and relief (see 2 Corinthians 7:5-15), Titus is to go to Corinth ahead of Paul. The reason for the return trip possibly is to deliver the letter of 2 Corinthians. Thus Titus will prepare the Corinthians for Paul's arrival. Primary among his list of things to do, Titus is to encourage the Corinthians to have their offering for Jerusalem ready to go. That way Paul can take it along with him (2 Corinthians 9:3-5).

The same grace refers specifically to the financial gifts of the Corinthians. But it also continues the theme of the previous verses and flows into verse 7. God graciously has given many things to His people, including salvation and spiritual gifts; the Corinthians are to exhibit godly graciousness in turn by giving to their needy brethren. God showed favor to us even before we knew Him by sending Christ. The Corinthians should show favor to their brothers and sisters in Judea, even though they have never met them. [See question #2, page 493.]

7. Therefore, as ye abound in every thing, in faith, and utterance, and knowledge, and in all diligence, and in your love to us, see that ye abound in this grace also.

Paul reminds the Corinthians of the spiritual gifts that God had given for their edification and in which they sometimes take too much pride (1 Corinthians 12:14-31). *Faith* as used here is not "saving faith" but rather has the sense of a gift of especially effective faith, perhaps relating to prayer (see 1 Corinthians 12:9; 13:2). *Utterance* refers to spiritual gifts that involve the proclamation of God's will, such as prophecy and tongues. *Knowledge* is the gift of insight into God's nature and plans. The Corinthians, having received such marvelous spiritual gifts, should be motivated in turn to share their material possessions with others.

But their *diligence* in the offering will not show only their appreciation for God's benevolence, it will also demonstrate their *love* for Paul. The Corinthians already have shown their loyalty by

---

How to Say It

ACHAIA. Uh-*kay*-uh.
BEREA. Buh-*ree*-uh.
CORINTH. *Kor*-inth.
CORINTHIANS. Ko-*rin*-thee-unz (*th* as in *thin*).
MACEDONIA. Mass-eh-*doe*-nee-uh.
PHILIPPI. Fih-*lip*-pie or *Fil*-ih-pie.
PHILIPPIANS. Fih-*lip*-ee-unz.
THESSALONICA. *Thess*-uh-lo-*nye*-kuh (strong accent on on *nye*; *th* as in *thin*).

heeding at least some of Paul's warnings (example: 2 Corinthians 7:9). Can he count on them once again? Since they have already received so much, Paul is confident that God will now bestow upon them, like the Macedonians, yet another gracious gift: the willingness to share with those in need.

8. I speak not by commandment, but by occasion of the forwardness of others, and to prove the sincerity of your love.

Giving is the right thing to do. But giving ultimately is a personal expression of faith, a private matter between the giver and God. Paul therefore stresses that he is not ordering them to give. Indeed, such a command could lead to suspicions and accusations about his motives, similar to the skepticism many of us feel toward TV evangelists today.

At the same time, however, Paul makes clear that the Corinthians should feel very ashamed if they fail to give. In the first place they haven't suffered nearly as much as the Macedonians, the *others* who have been so generous. In the second place Paul will have to wonder about the Corinthians' *love* if they don't contribute. It is not clear whether Paul is referring to love for the needy saints in Jerusalem, love for himself as an apostle, or love for Christ who has given them such grace. Perhaps all three are in mind, since a generous gift will help the poor, will validate Paul's confidence in them, and will show trust in God's future provision all at once.

B. Christ's Example (v. 9)

9. For ye know the grace of our Lord Jesus Christ, that, though he was rich, yet for your sakes he became poor, that ye through his poverty might be rich.

Here as elsewhere, Paul appeals to *Christ* as the ultimate example. Christ, as God, was more than *rich* in human terms. He owns everything in the universe! Yet His love for us led Him to give up this privileged position and come to earth in the form of a servant to die for our sins (Philippians 2:5-8). Jesus' suffering led to our blessing—through His *poverty*, we have come to possess all the spiritual riches of salvation. The Corinthians can imitate Christ by sharing.

C. Paul's Advice (vv. 10, 11)

10. And herein I give my advice: for this is expedient for you, who have begun before, not only to do, but also to be forward a year ago.

Point to this visual as you ask, "How can we give in non-monetary ways?"

Visual for lesson 11

Having set the example of Christ before them, Paul now challenges the Corinthians to reflect on their own reputations. They apparently had begun to organize a collection for Jerusalem *a year ago*. As such, they seem to have been one of the first churches to answer Paul's call for aid. But their benevolence program had been sidetracked for some reason.

In the meantime the churches of Macedonia, which probably had fewer resources, had started and completed their giving campaign. Since the Jerusalem offering is a cooperative effort involving many churches in several regions, the Corinthians are in danger of becoming an international spectacle. When someone is absent from a family photo, people will ask why! [See question #3, page 493.]

11. Now therefore perform the doing of it; that as there was a readiness to will, so there may be a performance also out of that which ye have.

Talk is cheap. It is easy to say that we want to help others but quite another thing actually to do something for them. Christ did not save us from our sins by saying that He felt sorry for us; He saved us by dying on the cross. The Corinthians need to finish what they started and actually come up with the money they pledged, lest it become obvious to everyone that their mouths are bigger than their hearts (compare James 2:14-17).

D. Paul's Desire (vv. 12-15)

12. For if there be first a willing mind, it is accepted according to that a man hath, and not according to that he hath not.

On one occasion Jesus and His disciples were watching people drop money into an offering urn in the temple. As people gave their gifts, He noticed one elderly woman who could offer only two small mites—copper coins worth a few pennies. This woman's contribution was greater than all the others because, He said, she had given all that she had. The others had simply shared a small portion of their wealth (Mark 12:41-44).

Paul appeals to this principle to assure the Corinthians that what he has been saying is not intended to make them feel guilty. Perhaps they feel ashamed of the amount they can provide, especially when compared with the Macedonians. [See question #4, page 493.] So Paul clarifies: What is important is not the size of the gift but rather the fulfillment of the pledge to give. God is more concerned with our motives than with the amount of money in our wallets. (See also Proverbs 3:27, 28.)

13, 14. For I mean not that other men be eased, and ye burdened: But by an equality, that now at this time your abundance may be a supply for their want, that their abundance also may be a supply for your want; that there may be equality.

Some could look at Paul's efforts to raise money for Jerusalem and conclude that he cared more for that church than for the Corinthians. Paul therefore assures them that he does not wish to seem unfair. The issue is one of *equality*. Even so, these verses should not be taken as an endorsement of a socialist economic program. Paul never states a plan for a government redistribution of wealth so that everyone has the same amount of money.

The real point is that the Corinthians have been blessed with plenty while those in the Jerusalem church are suffering. Next year the reverse may be true. In that case Paul will expect the Jerusalem believers to be generous in return. This mutual support in times of need will thus create a sort of godly insurance policy. By this all Christians everywhere can be confident that their needs will be met through the generosity of others. [See question #5, page 493.]

15. As it is written, He that had gathered much had nothing over; and he that had gathered little had no lack.

Paul now quotes Exodus 16:18, a passage that is particularly relevant to the topic at hand. It refers to the days when the Israelites wandered in the wilderness for 40 years under Moses. During that period, the Jews did not have a stable source of food from the land about them, so God

---

Home Daily Bible Readings

Monday, Aug. 7—The Widow's Offering (Luke 20:45–21:4)
Tuesday, Aug. 8—Chosen to Serve the Poor (Acts 6:1-6)
Wednesday, Aug. 9—Generosity, a Gift from God (Romans 12:3-8)
Thursday, Aug. 10—The Collection for the Saints (1 Corinthians 15:58–16:4)
Friday, Aug. 11—A Fruit of the Spirit (Galatians 5:16-26)
Saturday, Aug. 12—Excel in Generosity (2 Corinthians 8:1-7)
Sunday, Aug. 13—Rules for Giving (2 Corinthians 8:8-15)

---

sent them bread from Heaven miraculously. Each person was to take a certain amount of manna for the household. And every day, God provided enough for everyone to be satisfied, whether they *gathered* much or little. [See question #6, page 493.]

Conclusion

A. Proving We Exist

People often claim that they cannot believe in God because of the problem of evil. When asked to explain this argument, they often reply that a good God could not let children in Haiti die of starvation. Since there are, in fact, children in Haiti who are dying of starvation, then God must not exist; if He did exist, so the argument goes, then He surely would do something about this problem.

Notably, however, many people who would cite this argument are doing nothing to help these starving children themselves. Does the fact that they are not helping such children also mean that *they* do not exist?

God most certainly exists, and He has provided sufficient material resources to sustain every person who lives on this planet. Even today, with a world population of over six billion, there are more than enough resources for the human race to survive—people simply are not willing to share their wealth. And whether we want to admit it or not, God has provided His people with plenty of money to support one another, His church, and the proclamation of the gospel.

If needs are not being met, it is not because God has not provided; it is because we have not provided. If people judged our existence by whether or not we help with the needs of others, could we prove that we exist? To the person in need, we may as well not exist if we are unwilling to share.

B. Prayer

Heavenly Father, help us to overcome our greed. Lead us to recognize selfishness and not rationalize. Fill us with hearts of compassion, and give us the stewardship to manage the resources You have given us in a way that will please You. In everything we do, help us to imitate the example of Christ. In His name, amen.

C. Thought to Remember

Be the means today by which God provides for someone's need.

Learning by Doing

This section contains an alternative lesson plan emphasizing learning activities. Classes desiring such student involvement will find these suggestions helpful.

Learning Goals

After this lesson, each student will be able to:

1. List reasons that Paul cites for why the Corinthians should have felt compelled to give.
2. Explain how a benevolent gift is an appropriate response to God's grace.
3. Examine his or her personal motives for giving or not giving to those in need.

Into the Lesson

Display the following puzzle for your class.

```
R  I  C  H
__ __ __ __
__ __ __ __
__ __ __ __
P  O  O  R
```

Say, "Today's Golden Text, 2 Corinthians 8:9, reveals the change of status that Jesus willingly chose in order to become our Savior." Have a good reader read this verse aloud. Next say, "Can you change RICH to POOR in this puzzle by changing only one letter per line? The bolded blanks are the letters that need changed."

Allow a few minutes before giving the following clues, row by row: "A covered stack of hay or straw" *(RICK)*; "Another word for a stone" *(ROCK)*; "A type of bird or chess piece" *(ROOK)*; "A library's special loan" *(BOOK)*; "A rude or insensitive person" *(BOOR)*.

Write, "Our Ultimate Example of Generous Giving" on a piece of poster board. Under this title write today's Golden Text. Highlight the following words in the verse: *Jesus Christ/was rich/yet/became poor/that ye.*

Into the Word

Divide the class into small groups of four to six. Say, "Today's text reveals key truths about the money we return to the Lord for the church's work. I want us to meditate on those truths."

If your congregation has a meditation before the offering is collected during the worship service, introduce the following activity. (If there is no such element in your worship service, add the following comments before giving the introduction below: "Many churches have a brief offering meditation before the offering is collected. For this activity let's pretend that this were true of our congregation.")

Introduce this activity by saying: "I am going to give each group member a sheet of paper with a title and a portion of Scripture from today's lesson text printed on it. In your groups you will be writing simple offering meditations based on the titles and Bible passages printed on the top of your sheets. When you get your papers don't do anything, but wait for my instructions."

Ahead of time, print the following offering meditation titles and corresponding Bible references on sheets of paper, one title and Bible reference per sheet. "Poor Man, Rich Man" (vv. 1, 2); "Possible Impossibility" (v. 3); "Reverse Beggars" (v. 4); "First Things First" (v. 5); "Unmerited Giving" (v. 6); "Abundance Begets Abundance"

(v. 7); "Love, Sincerely Yours" (v. 8); "Rich . . . Poor . . . Rich" (v. 9); "Add the Bow and Gift Card" (v. 10); "Talk Is Cheap" (v. 11); "No Less, No More" (v. 12); "Reciprocity" (vv. 13, 14); "Manna" (v. 15).

Give each group member one sheet. Say, "Look at the title and Bible verse at the top of your sheet. Then write the first sentence of an offering meditation based on that title and verse. After you have written your one sentence, stop and wait for further instructions."

Allow a few minutes for students to work and then say, "Now pass your sheet to the person on your right. Once you get a new sheet, look at the title and verse at the top of your sheet and read the one sentence your classmate has written. Continue the mediation by writing a second sentence of your own." Repeat this process four or five times. Then collect all the sheets, shuffle them, and redistribute them to class members.

Allow volunteers to read verses and offering meditations. Include a brief discussion of the meditation titles for each verse.

Into Life

For each student make a list of the offering meditation titles from the preceding activity. Ask students to carry their lists with them or to post them in conspicuous places as daily reminders of the principles of Christian giving. Suggest that they use one title from the list each week as their personal giving guideline for that week.

Let's Talk It Over

These questions are designed to promote discussion of the lesson. The answers here are only discussion starters. Let your class talk it over from there.

1. Paul talked about the Macedonian churches' giving generously even though their circumstances were troubling. Under which condition are we most likely to learn more about giving: while being rich, while living on a tight budget, or while struggling under severe circumstances? Explain.

The Macedonian Christians knew what it was like to live in difficult conditions. Therefore, they could identify with the Christians in Jerusalem who were suffering, perhaps from both persecution and from famine. When we give sacrificially, we can experience the greatest joy.

2. How would a Christian know if he or she really had learned the grace of giving?

No one ever reaches the point of "final arrival" in this regard. Those who think there is no more to learn about giving will stagnate. We learn the most important aspect about the grace of giving when we remember daily and hourly how God has and is giving to us. We cannot outgive God!

3. Some Christians need to be reminded repeatedly to give generously. What are some good ways to encourage all of us in the grace of giving without sounding as if money is the only issue to be discussed?

All of us are susceptible to the constant messages around us to get all we can and spend it quickly on the things we desire. Many who have little understandably can spend time wishing for what they could have. A good approach to the question is to focus on God's ownership of everything and that we are stewards of what He has entrusted to us. Every giving opportunity is to be evaluated in that light. When the emphasis is on grateful stewardship, Christians can experience deep satisfaction in seeing God's work done and the needs of others being met (James 1:27).

4. What temptations do we face while deciding how much to give based on the guideline of "according to our means"? What will help us deal with these temptations?

Ask the class to develop a list of temptations in the area of giving. The temptations would include statements like "don't cheat yourself and give too much," "better be cautious and save for a rainy day," and "since I have so little, my small gift won't be important anyway."

The average Christian probably calculates expenses first and then gives a portion of what is left over. If we would develop an intentional and appropriate giving plan as a first order of business, then we would find it easier to allocate the funds biblically. Ask for testimonies from anyone who has used the "give-first" approach.

5. If members of your congregation needed outside help to be able to live, how easy would it be for your congregation to ask for that help from other churches?

Pride can be a big stumbling block, even for those in great need. God wants to see that our needs are met. God is never embarrassed to help meet that need through the generosity of others. We will grow spiritually both when we help others who are in need and when we accept help when we are the ones in need. Each has something to teach us about God and His church.

6. Some stress that giving must be kept secret according to Jesus' teaching in Matthew 6:3, 4. How does Paul add additional instruction on this topic through his discussion? Why is Paul's instruction not in conflict with what Jesus said?

Jesus did not want individuals openly bragging about how much they gave. Nor was Paul encouraging the churches to brag about their level of giving. Instead, he used the sacrificial giving of one church to stir another congregation to become introspective about their own promises, giving levels, and spiritual motivations.

Paul does not dwell on the comparison between churches. He writes of a higher standard by citing how much Jesus had given in order for the Corinthians to become rich. The last thing Paul would favor would be a failure of the churches to talk about giving because some did not want this subject mentioned when Christians came together. Paul models that it is appropriate to talk about the need, the amounts given by churches as a whole, and the motivation for giving.

August 20
Lesson 12

Giving Is a Witness

Devotional Reading: Psalm 37:16-24.

Background Scripture: 2 Corinthians 9:1-15.

Printed Text: 2 Corinthians 9:3-15.

2 Corinthians 9:3-15

3 Yet have I sent the brethren, lest our boasting of you should be in vain in this behalf; that, as I said, ye may be ready:

4 Lest haply if they of Macedonia come with me, and find you unprepared, we (that we say not, ye) should be ashamed in this same confident boasting.

5 Therefore I thought it necessary to exhort the brethren, that they would go before unto you, and make up beforehand your bounty, whereof ye had notice before, that the same might be ready, as a matter of bounty, and not as of covetousness.

6 But this I say, He which soweth sparingly shall reap also sparingly; and he which soweth bountifully shall reap also bountifully.

7 Every man according as he purposeth in his heart, so let him give; not grudgingly, or of necessity: for God loveth a cheerful giver.

8 And God is able to make all grace abound toward you; that ye, always having all sufficiency in all things, may abound to every good work:

9 (As it is written, He hath dispersed abroad; he hath given to the poor: his righteousness remaineth for ever.

10 Now he that ministereth seed to the sower both minister bread for your food, and multiply your seed sown, and increase the fruits of your righteousness:)

11 Being enriched in every thing to all bountifulness, which causeth through us thanksgiving to God.

12 For the administration of this service not only supplieth the want of the saints, but is abundant also by many thanksgivings unto God;

13 While by the experiment of this ministration they glorify God for your professed subjection unto the gospel of Christ, and for your liberal distribution unto them, and unto all men;

14 And by their prayer for you, which long after you for the exceeding grace of God in you.

15 Thanks be unto God for his unspeakable gift.

Golden Text: And God is able to make all grace abound toward you; that ye, always having all sufficiency in all things, may abound to every good work.
—2 Corinthians 9:8.

> *Called to Be a Christian Community*
> Unit 3: The Spirit of Giving
> (Lessons 10-13)

Lesson Aims

After participating in this lesson, each student will be able to:

1. Restate Paul's reasons for the need of Christians to be generous givers.
2. Explain how God makes it possible to be generous.
3. Make a personal giving plan.

Lesson Outline

INTRODUCTION
    A. Benefits of Sharing
    B. Lesson Background
I. READY AND WILLING? (2 Corinthians 9:3-7)
    A. Paul's Boasting (vv. 3, 4)
    B. Corinthians' Generosity (vv. 5, 6)
    C. Everyone's Choice (v. 7)
        Baptized Pocketbooks
II. SOURCE AND RESULT (2 Corinthians 9:8-15)
    A. God's Provisions (vv. 8, 9)
    B. Corinthians' Fruits (vv. 10, 11)
    C. Others' Thanks (vv. 12-14)
        Liberal Distribution in Disguise
    D. God's Great Gift (v. 15)
CONCLUSION
    A. Happy Ending
    B. Prayer
    C. Thought to Remember

Introduction

A. Benefits of Sharing

For a recent Thanksgiving, my wife and I volunteered to deliver baskets of food from the church to needy families. After spending hours loading and unloading the car and trying to locate addresses on dark houses on a cold evening, we were tired and ready to go home. As we carried our heavy baskets from the car to the last house on our list, I commented wearily that we should perhaps leave this particular service opportunity to others until the time when we did not have two small children to drag around with us.

We knocked on the door and were greeted by a woman in her fifties. With her was a host of children, ranging from infants to girls in high school. She immediately invited us in and asked us to sit. Each child was introduced, and she told us that her eldest daughter had died recently and that another child had moved back in after losing a job. As a result, the lady was working two jobs herself, desperately trying to support her eight children and grandchildren.

We sat speechless, humbled by her testimony and her faith. Before we left she insisted that we all pray together. After we did she burst into tears and thanked us profusely for the food. We told her that she should not thank us; we were only delivering a gift from the church. But as we went out the door, she pressed a letter into our hands expressing deep gratitude for our visit and asking for God's continued blessing on our home. As we walked back to the car, my wife and I decided that perhaps we should volunteer to deliver baskets again next year.

Jesus said, "It is more blessed to give than to receive" (Acts 20:35). This is the case not just because it's better to be able to help than to need help. It is better to give because when we give to meet another's need, we act as God's hand for his sustenance. The food we left at that home was worth perhaps $300; the prayers we took with us were priceless. The benefit of sharing is not a material benefit. The benefit is the chance to participate in God's plan to provide for His people.

B. Lesson Background

As noted in our last lesson, Paul wrote 2 Corinthians at a time when the people of the churches in Judea were suffering through a financial crisis. The Roman government did not have a consistent "federal aid policy" to address such situations. Unemployment insurance did not exist.

> **How to Say It**
> CORINTH. *Kor*-inth.
> CORINTHIANS. Ko-*rin*-thee-unz (*th* as in *thin*).
> GENTILES. *Jen*-tiles.
> ISAIAH. Eye-*zay*-uh.
> JERUSALEM. Juh-*roo*-suh-lem.
> MACEDONIA. Mass-eh-*doe*-nee-uh.
> SYNAGOGUE. *sin*-uh-gog.
> TITUS. *Ty*-tus.

The situation was especially bad for Christians of Jewish descent who were not able to receive support from synagogues. Fortunately, God has a plan to help Christians in need, but it does not involve miraculous provisions of food or money. Manna no longer falls from the sky. Instead, God provides through the generosity of other believers.

I. Ready and Willing? (2 Corinthians 9:3-7)

A. Paul's Boasting (vv. 3, 4)

3. Yet have I sent the brethren, lest our boasting of you should be in vain in this behalf; that, as I said, ye may be ready.

In chapter 8 Paul urged the Corinthians to rise to the example of the Macedonian churches by giving generously to the relief effort for Jerusalem. Paul had sent Titus to Corinth to prepare the church for his own upcoming visit and to collect their offering for the Judean churches (2 Corinthians 8:16-21). But he had also sent along several representatives of the Macedonian churches. They would go with him to Jerusalem as ambassadors of the Gentiles (8:22-24).

Paul's purpose in using this procedure probably is at least twofold. First, it will ensure that the funds will be managed in a proper and ethical way (8:20). [See question #1, page 502.]

Second, it will allow the Jewish Christians in Jerusalem a chance to meet Gentile believers from a variety of different places. These representatives could then report back to their home churches about their experiences in Jerusalem. Hopefully, this will secure a greater sense of unity between the Jewish and Gentile segments of the first-century church.

4. Lest haply if they of Macedonia come with me, and find you unprepared, we (that we say not, ye) should be ashamed in this same confident boasting.

Paul now lays out the first reason why the Corinthians should get serious about preparing their gift. In 2 Corinthians 8:1-5, he bragged about the generosity of the Macedonian churches, but it appears that he also has been bragging about the Corinthians. [See question #2, page 502.] How embarrassed he would be if some of the Macedonian Christians were to travel down to Corinth with him only to discover that the stewardship campaign was in disarray! And not only Paul would be embarrassed—the Corinthians themselves would surely be even more humiliated. Paul therefore urges them to hurry to fulfill their pledges so that his confidence will be confirmed.

B. Corinthians' Generosity (vv. 5, 6)

5. Therefore I thought it necessary to exhort the brethren, that they would go before unto you, and make up beforehand your bounty, whereof ye had notice before, that the same might be ready, as a matter of bounty, and not as of covetousness.

The Corinthians apparently had responded quickly to a previous call for aid. But for some reason almost an entire year passed without any focused efforts to bring this program to a successful conclusion (2 Corinthians 8:10, 11).

Paul assumes that they will be faithful to their pledge. But he goes on to state a key principle about giving: the motive is just as important as the gift. From a financial perspective, money is money; a starving person can buy food with it whether it is given with good motives or poor motives. But giving is intended to benefit not only the recipient but also the giver.

A gift that is well planned and thoughtfully bestowed allows the giver to share in the joy of the fellowship. But a gift that is rushed or given from a sense of guilt does not provide this joy. Instead, it often creates feelings of resentment, either toward the needy (the Jerusalem Christians in this case), toward the one who points out the need, or toward God himself, who calls us to give.

Thoughtful consideration in advance will make giving a blessing to all involved. Paul urges the Corinthians to plan their giving carefully. *Not as of covetousness* speaks of the need to avoid giving a gift that you would really rather keep for yourself.

6. But this I say, He which soweth sparingly shall reap also sparingly; and he which soweth bountifully shall reap also bountifully.

The imagery here is drawn from agriculture: common sense says that a person who plants more seed will reap a larger harvest. But Paul cannot mean that God is more impressed with a larger gift. As we noted last week, Jesus says that the size of the donation makes no difference (Mark 12:41-44).

In this context the terms *sparingly* and *bountifully* are proportionate to an individual's ability to give. God does not expect a person who makes

$30,000 a year to give as much as a person who makes $100,000; He does, however, expect both to be willing to share when others are in need. God is concerned with one's motive for giving. Any gift given without sincere love is worth nothing in God's sight (1 Corinthians 13:3).

With this in mind Paul's reference to reaping probably should be taken to refer to spiritual blessings. Experience teaches us that people who give a lot of money to Christian causes don't automatically become wealthy in a worldly sense. They do, however, enjoy a wealth of peace and satisfaction because they know that they have done the right thing. They know that God will always provide for those who focus on His service. They know that they are rich toward God (Luke 12:21; compare Proverbs 11:24; 22:9).

C. Everyone's Choice (v. 7)

7. Every man according as he purposeth in his heart, so let him give; not grudgingly, or of necessity: for God loveth a cheerful giver.

Giving is not an option, and Paul does not present it as an option to the Corinthians. Some of God's people are clearly in need, and God is going to use the financial resources of the Corinthians to meet that need.

The Corinthians can, however, choose the kind of attitude they will exhibit in fulfilling this obligation. They can give begrudgingly, out of a sense of duty and guilt, or they can give cheerfully, thanking God that they have the means to help other people. God is pleased with such gifts because they reveal a heart that is in line with His own. [See question #3, page 502.]

The amount of money each will give is up to the individual heart (compare Acts 5:4). Even so, Paul is not saying that we can give nothing if we feel like giving nothing. Going back to verse 2, the Corinthians already have pledged to give a certain amount, and Paul seems to be aware of that figure. At least part of the issue is that once we are aware of a need and determine the extent to which we can help, we should not go back on our word.

BAPTIZED POCKETBOOKS

It was a strange statement. But upon reflection, it was quite profound. "Baptized pocketbooks," said the preacher. "That's what we need, more baptized pocketbooks!"

When someone's faith in Jesus leads him or her to respond in Christian baptism, it's natural

Ask, "Why give?" and challenge your students to add to the answers already on this visual.

Visual for lesson 12

for the person to remove all the items that would be ruined by the water. This includes watches, shoes, pens, and wallets. Although it's not useful for wallets to become literally immersed in the waters of baptism, it is essential that our pocketbooks be baptized symbolically. This doesn't mean that we should have some kind of ceremony in that regard. It *does* mean that a Christian's pocketbook is part of his or her Christianity.

Sadly, however, the pocketbooks of many Christians seem to be unbaptized. Often people trust God with every area of their lives except their finances. When a person comes to Christ, every aspect of life is to be brought under the lordship of Christ. Everything from our moral standards to our giving should be a proclamation of the Breastplate of Patrick: "Christ with me / Christ in the front / Christ in the rear / Christ within me / Christ below me / Christ above me / Christ at my right hand / Christ at my left."
—T. B.

II. Source and Result (2 Corinthians 9:8-15)

A. God's Provisions (vv. 8, 9)

8. And God is able to make all grace abound toward you; that ye, always having all sufficiency in all things, may abound to every good work.

Grace in this context does not refer to "saving grace" but rather to God's gracious provision of spiritual gifts (see Romans 12:3-8). As the Corinthians well know, God has blessed them with every spiritual gift that they would ever need to complete the mission, empowering them to abound in doing good works for the gospel. If God can empower a person to prophesy or miraculously heal the sick, should we doubt that He will secure a sufficient income for those choosing to give a little extra money? [See question #4, page 502.]

9. (As it is written, He hath dispersed abroad; he hath given to the poor: his righteousness remaineth for ever.

Paul emphasizes his point by quoting Psalm 112:9. That psalm describes the character of the person who fears the Lord (112:1), noting the blessings that this person enjoys as a result of God's favor. Such a person gives gifts to *the poor* liberally. As a result, God ensures that this person's *righteousness remaineth for ever.*

The Corinthians similarly should demonstrate their righteousness by giving liberally to the needy believers in Judea. God himself has *dispersed* liberally gracious gifts to His church, a testimony to His eternally righteous nature. Those who give generously are thus imitating God.

B. Corinthians' Fruits (vv. 10, 11)

10. Now he that ministereth seed to the sower both minister bread for your food, and multiply your seed sown, and increase the fruits of your righteousness).

Paul now reminds the Corinthians that God provides not only for our spiritual needs but also for our physical needs. Everything comes from Him. The farmer buys *seed* by God's grace; the seed grows by God's grace; the harvest is preserved by God's grace; the *bread* is baked by God's grace; the money we earn to buy the bread is earned by God's grace. Every bite of food that we put into our mouths is thus the final step in a long series of events that reveal God's care.

This physical provision can be a reflection of the abundant spiritual provision that we enjoy in Christ if we allow it to be. Trusting in such care, we should be able to give generously (compare Isaiah 55:10).

11. Being enriched in every thing to all bountifulness, which causeth through us thanksgiving to God.

Every thing refers to both the physical and spiritual blessings mentioned in verse 10. When we give, God promises to provide and to provide abundantly. The Corinthians should therefore have no hesitation about meeting their pledge. If they do meet it, God will be glorified because the Jerusalem Christians will praise Him for providing for their needs in this way. [See question #5, page 502.]

Through us refers specifically to Paul, Titus, and the representatives of the Macedonian churches who are assigned to deliver the gifts to Jerusalem (2 Corinthians 8:16-23; 9:3-5). But in a more general sense, *us* would include the Corinthians as well. God will provide the money to the Corinthians, who will give it to Paul and companions, who will give it to the needy in Jerusalem. The Corinthians will thus be God's hand to the needy, directly causing this *thanksgiving* to take place.

C. Others' Thanks (vv. 12-14)

12. For the administration of this service not only supplieth the want of the saints, but is abundant also by many thanksgivings unto God.

Any benevolent gift to any charitable cause can help meet the needs of a poor person. In this respect it does not make much difference whether we give money to a Christian relief organization or to a secular benevolent group such as the United Way. But a gift given in the name of Christ has a further effect: it brings glory to God because it allows other people to see His hand at work in the world.

This is, ultimately, much more important than the actual physical relief that the gift may bring, for it leads people to a greater trust in God. This has eternal implications. The Corinthians should not give merely as though they are helping some starving people whom they have never met. Rather, they should give as though they are bringing honor to the God who gave them everything they have.

13. While by the experiment of this ministration they glorify God for your professed subjection unto the gospel of Christ, and for your liberal distribution unto them, and unto all men.

Paul notes two things that the Corinthians have done and one thing that other people will do when they see the results. First, they have *professed* their faith in Christ, submitting themselves to Him. Second, they have demonstrated their faith actively by pledging to help the Jerusalem saints. If they are now faithful and live up to their pledge, then others will see Christ at work in them and will *glorify* God for their generosity. In this way a simple act of service—as simple as opening your wallet or writing a check—takes on eternal spiritual significance.

LIBERAL DISTRIBUTION IN DISGUISE

She looked like the cleaning lady from a TV comedy skit. At least that was the first thought that crossed my mind when the director of development at our Bible college introduced me to this humble visitor to our campus. The sweet little lady had arrived to witness the dedication of a new building.

I smiled and introduced myself as one of the professors and made small talk about her home and church family. Then I quickly excused myself to hurry off to my next class. Later that week, I found myself in the school cafeteria and had the opportunity to sit next to my colleague who had introduced me to the older woman.

"Do you remember that nice little lady I introduced you to earlier this week?" she asked.

"Oh, yes," I replied.

"She wasn't very pretentious, was she?"

"No, not at all." And I thought that that was an awfully nice way of putting it. "Very plain and common were the words that would have come to my mind."

"Well, later that day," the director continued, "that very plain and common woman wrote the college a check for $75,000."

Of course, it would have been a great blessing to receive whatever gift she would have generously offered. But God taught me a lesson that day. That very simple lady was one of the most extravagant people I have ever met. Some people choose to live very simple lives in order to be extravagant givers. Only God knows the true nature of each gift. We look on the outer appearance, but God looks upon the heart. —T. B.

14. And by their prayer for you, which long after you for the exceeding grace of God in you.

It is important to stress here that the object of the verb *long after* is *you*, not *grace*. Paul does not mean that the Jerusalem Christians will "long for" the financial blessings that the Corinthians enjoy. Rather, they will return the favor by praying for the Corinthians as they thank God for providing the help.

These prayers are, in a sense, the return on the Corinthians' investment. If such prayers seem to have less worth than the money we give, then we clearly have misunderstood how God operates.

D. God's Great Gift (v. 15)

15. Thanks be unto God for his unspeakable gift.

This verse is foundational to all Christian stewardship. Paul shifts from the narrower discussion of grace as the gifts and financial blessings that the Corinthians have received (v. 14) to a general prayer of thanksgiving. The *gift* of God noted here must be the wonderful grace evident in salvation through Christ. If God loved the world so much that He gave His only Son (John 3:16), then surely we can give a portion of our material blessings to help other believers.

Conclusion

A. Happy Ending

Stewardship is not an optional feature of the Christian life. God has given us many wonderful things—salvation, material blessings, spiritual gifts—and He expects us to use these for His purposes. Thoughtful stewardship not only brings relief to those in need but also ultimately brings glory to God.

Of course, when Paul wrote this letter he had no idea whether the Corinthians would come through with their gift. Perhaps they would back out and embarrass him. But the evidence suggests that they did the right thing. Later in the letter, Paul tells them that he is about to visit them once more to check on their progress (2 Corinthians 12:14; 13:1). Paul did travel to Corinth, and he and the representatives from Macedonia spent the winter with the believers there before going on to Jerusalem (see Acts 20:2, 3).

Home Daily Bible Readings

Monday, Aug. 14—Every Good Gift Is from God (James 1:12-17)

Tuesday, Aug. 15—Give and You Shall Receive (Luke 6:32-38)

Wednesday, Aug. 16—Do Your Giving Quietly (Matthew 6:1-6)

Thursday, Aug. 17—Pleased to Share Their Resources (Romans 15:25-29)

Friday, Aug. 18—Arrangements for the Jerusalem Collection (2 Corinthians 9:1-5)

Saturday, Aug. 19—A Cheerful Giver (2 Corinthians 9:6-10)

Sunday, Aug. 20—Generosity Glorifies God (2 Corinthians 9:11-15)

During this layover, Paul wrote the letter to the Romans. At the end of that epistle, he mentions that the churches in Macedonia and Achaia had made contributions for the needy in Palestine. Achaia is the district in which Corinth was located, suggesting that he found things ready as requested (Romans 15:25-28). When Paul and companions arrived in Jerusalem, the gift was received warmly just as Paul anticipated. Further, also as Paul had predicted, the leaders of the Judean church praised God for the grace given to the Gentiles (Acts 21:17-20a).

The Corinthian church was beset with many serious problems, and it is easy to criticize them for their immorality and immaturity. Yet in this instance the church responded to Paul's warnings. They ultimately did the right thing. As such, they stand as a model not only of generosity but also of willingness to repent.

B. Prayer

God, help us to appreciate the wealth of spiritual and material blessings that You have given us. Help us also to trust Your continuing provision, so that we may give of our time and resources generously as You have called us to do. Let our acts of service always bring glory to You rather than ourselves. In Jesus' name, amen.

C. Thought to Remember
Witness through your giving today!

Learning by Doing

This section contains an alternative lesson plan emphasizing learning activities. Classes desiring such student involvement will find these suggestions helpful.

Learning Goals

After participating in this lesson, each student will be able to:

1. Restate Paul's reasons for the need of Christians to be generous givers.
2. Explain how God makes it possible to be generous.
3. Make a personal giving plan.

Into the Lesson

Write *Why Give?* on the board. Include two columns underneath for answers. Divide the class in half and assign each half one answer column. Alternate back and forth between the two sides of the class as they give their answers and you record them in the appropriate column. Expect responses such as the following: "Because giving is like God," "Because people have needs," "So that the church can do its work." Continue until no additional answers are suggested.

Say, "In today's text, 2 Corinthians 9:3-15, Paul gives reasons why the Christians in Corinth should give generously to the needy churches in Judea." Ask a volunteer to read the Bible text aloud. Say, "Listen to the text and make a mental checklist of the reasons Paul cites for generous giving. How closely does our list compare with Paul's?" After the text has been read, ask, "Which of the reasons in your group's list did you hear represented in the text? What verses correspond?" Let several students respond.

Into the Word

For this activity students will mingle among themselves wearing a name tag with one of the statements about giving listed below. Some of the statements are true and some are false. Direct the class to circulate and greet one another, noting what each other's name tags have to say about giving. After a time direct everyone to be seated. Ask students to turn to today's text to confirm or refute the statements they have read on the lapels.

Use the following statements or others of your own creation. (Additional statements can also be found in the student book in the "Paul Says" activity.) Note: The true statements have Bible verse numbers in parentheses for your reference. Do not write these verse numbers on the name tags.

Statements: *1.* Give because you know that God will make you rich, both in this world and in the next. *2.* Give so that God will give to you. *3.* Selfishness will prove embarrassing to the

Christian (v. 3). *4.* Give to encourage others (v. 4). *5.* Special giving projects that are well planned honor God (v. 5). *6.* Giving helps relieve guilt. *7.* Stingy givers reap few benefits (v. 6). *8.* Gifts that are given grudgingly are no gifts at all (v. 7). *9.* God loves it when people give, regardless of their motives. *10.* God provides abundance so that the receiver can do good works (v. 8). *11.* The origin of all gifts is God (v. 10). *12.* Generosity ultimately brings praise to God (v. 11). *13.* A gift given in the name of Christ brings glory to God (v. 12). *14.* Generous giving is an indication of submission to the gospel (v. 13). *15.* Generous giving elicits prayers for the giver from the recipient (v. 14). *16.* All giving should be in response to God's gift of redemptive grace (v. 15). *17.* God expects us to give a specific amount.

As an alternative activity, introduce students to several ongoing financial needs of people or organizations, such as support for a missionary school, evangelistic training in another culture, or support of a short-term missions team. Ask the class to pick one month-long project to support with a special offering by collecting their spare change and pooling it together for a month. Be sure to give the class weekly reminders.

Into Life

Help your students develop a giving plan with a "treasure hunt" through Matthew. Provide them with a list of the following Scripture references from that book: 6:19-21; 12:35; 13:44; 13:52; 19:21. If you have an artistic class member, ask that person to create a treasure map on parchment paper titled "Matthew's Island" with the Scripture references printed on it. For example, the map could state, "Go five paces to Matthew 6:19."

Suggest to students that they post their list (or map) where they will see it for the next five days, finding one of the "treasures" each day. Tell them that as they read each Scripture they will be discovering real treasure that they can hide in their hearts. Challenge them to think of giving in other than just monetary terms.

Let's Talk It Over

These questions are designed to promote discussion of the lesson. The answers here are only discussion starters. Let your class talk it over from there.

1. To ensure accountability, Paul insisted that individuals from contributing churches travel with the collection. In what ways should we ensure that contributions are handled in order to reduce temptation or suspicion of misuse?

Paul's plan seemed to say, "The more eyes that follow this money and its impact, the better." The specific blessings from Paul's approach are many: this method keeps the local churches interested in the impact of their generosity, it motivates others to give generously, it increases the number who can help distribute the money in Jerusalem, and it gives them personal stories of the level of need and the responses of appreciation to tell when returning home. It also improves the likelihood that the churches will develop a plan for on-going giving to meet the needs of others.

Every church needs accounting procedures, including separation of duties, so that questions concerning integrity will not arise. Most missionaries encourage on-site visits to show where the money is being spent. They gladly accept extra helping hands and welcome enthusiastic first-hand reports going back to the supporting churches.

2. Some may think that Paul's boasting about the Corinthians' intention to give was an attempt to raise a larger offering through guilt. How did Paul guard against the accusation of being manipulative? How can we do the same?

Paul does not obligate the Corinthians to any greater extent than they had previously promised. The Corinthians may have felt guilt for not giving. If they did, the guilt would have been appropriate since their bold talk had not resulted in action. If Paul had obligated them in an arbitrary or authoritarian manner, the guilt would have been on Paul's shoulders.

We must be careful that we do not try to force people to give. Instead, we need to teach consistently the New Testament principles that giving is to be *proportional* to income (1 Corinthians 16:2), *sacrificial* (Mark 12:43), *cheerful* (2 Corinthians 9:7), and *discreet* (Matthew 6:2). The latter has to be balanced at times with the need for giving to be a witness (Matthew 5:16).

3. How will we be affected in the long run if we give grudgingly instead of deciding freely what we want to give?

Paul was aware that some would be tempted to give something just so they had complied (grudgingly or sparingly) with someone's expectations. Paul was also aware that giving to meet another person's expectation does not benefit the giver. God would prefer a giver first decide how much to give based on what he or she has been given, gratitude for God's blessings, the need to follow the example of Jesus in giving out of mercy and love, and how the gifts will bless others. Once the giver has wrestled with this decision, there can be joy (cheerfulness) in the heart.

4. Before an offering is taken, many worship services feature an offering meditation and prayer. How can these help all to see the possibility of giving more than first thought possible?

Perhaps it would be good to pray with boldness and faith, asking God to use our gifts in a powerful way to bring honor to Him. We can pray specifically that our offerings will allow our church to be "salt and light" (Matthew 5:13-16) so the lost can be won and the saved can grow in Christ. There are many other ways to pray: for those who will use our mission offerings that God will grant them wisdom to use these resources in a fruitful way; for health and strength for the ones who will receive aid for their daily needs; for the givers that they will grow in faith and joy as they increase their generosity.

5. Some who preach a "health and wealth" doctrine would use 2 Corinthians 9:6-11 as proof of their belief. How would you respond to them?

The passage does not say directly that givers will have good health or a lot of wealth. God is not a cosmic vending machine—put in a dollar and get blessings. Instead, the giver is expected to be willing to give again if finances get better, perhaps in increasing proportions. God's blessing to the giver may actually be a stronger faith and increased fruits of righteousness (9:10). If finances shrink, the giver can still experience joy in giving according to how God has prospered him or her.

Giving Sufficient Grace

August 27
Lesson 13

DEVOTIONAL READING: James 4:1-10.

BACKGROUND SCRIPTURE: 2 Corinthians 12:1-10.

PRINTED TEXT: 2 Corinthians 12:1-10.

2 Corinthians 12:1-10

1 It is not expedient for me doubtless to glory. I will come to visions and revelations of the Lord.

2 I knew a man in Christ above fourteen years ago, (whether in the body, I cannot tell; or whether out of the body, I cannot tell: God knoweth;) such a one caught up to the third heaven.

3 And I knew such a man, (whether in the body, or out of the body, I cannot tell: God knoweth;)

4 How that he was caught up into paradise, and heard unspeakable words, which it is not lawful for a man to utter.

5 Of such a one will I glory: yet of myself I will not glory, but in mine infirmities.

6 For though I would desire to glory, I shall not be a fool; for I will say the truth: but now I forbear, lest any man should think of me above that which he seeth me to be, or that he heareth of me.

7 And lest I should be exalted above measure through the abundance of the revelations, there was given to me a thorn in the flesh, the messenger of Satan to buffet me, lest I should be exalted above measure.

8 For this thing I besought the Lord thrice, that it might depart from me.

9 And he said unto me, My grace is sufficient for thee: for my strength is made perfect in weakness. Most gladly therefore will I rather glory in my infirmities, that the power of Christ may rest upon me.

10 Therefore I take pleasure in infirmities, in reproaches, in necessities, in persecutions, in distresses for Christ's sake: for when I am weak, then am I strong.

GOLDEN TEXT: He said unto me, My grace is sufficient for thee: for my strength is made perfect in weakness. Most gladly therefore will I rather glory in my infirmities, that the power of Christ may rest upon me.—2 Corinthians 12:9.

> *Called to Be a Christian Community*
> Unit 3: The Spirit of Giving
> (Lessons 10-13)

Lesson Aims

After this lesson each student will be able to:
1. Summarize how Paul's vision relates to his "thorn."
2. Contrast the world's view of power through strength with Paul's view of power through weakness.
3. Commit to God's grace one area of weakness in his or her life, seeking His power to overcome that weakness.

Lesson Outline

INTRODUCTION
    A. Answering the Burning Bush
    B. Lesson Background
I. VISION OF GLORY (2 Corinthians 12:1-4)
    A. Undesired Talking Point (v. 1)
    B. Unexpected Event (vv. 2-4)
        Paul's Vision, Our Vision
II. GLORY OF WEAKNESS (2 Corinthians 12:5-10)
    A. God's Deeds (vv. 5, 6)
    B. Paul's Thorn (vv. 7-9a)
        Strength in Weakness
    C. God's Strength (vv. 9b, 10)
CONCLUSION
    A. Our Limitations
    B. Our Serenity
    C. Prayer
    D. Thought to Remember

Introduction

A. Answering the Burning Bush

Moses and Paul both had remarkable calls to ministry. Paul saw the risen Christ in a flash of light on the road to Damascus; Moses heard the voice of God from a burning bush in the desert. Paul responded to God's calling immediately by setting out to preach the gospel. His Christian life was beset with hardships and persecution from the beginning (see Acts 9:17-26).

Moses, however, responded in a very different way. When God told Moses that He would use him to deliver the Jews from Egypt, Moses balked. He first pointed out that he was a nobody; why should people listen to him? He then demanded some sort of evidence that God had really spoken to him. God replied by empowering him with the ability to do several attesting miracles. Moses then declined the invitation on the basis of his lack of skill in public speaking. He even asked God whether the Jews would know which "god" he was talking about! (See Exodus 3:1–4:17.)

Moses, in other words, resisted God's call by pointing out all of the personal weaknesses that would make it impossible for him to complete the task. Paul, by contrast, refused this path. He too labored under serious personal shortcomings, including the painful "thorn in the flesh" discussed in our passage for today. Yet he was determined to fulfill his calling (as Moses eventually was as well). Paul was confident that God would provide the tools he needed to finish the job.

B. Lesson Background

Paul wrote 2 Corinthians in A.D. 57 at the conclusion of a very tense period between himself and that church. In the letter of 1 Corinthians, Paul had rebuked them sharply for sectarian divisions and a number of serious spiritual and moral failures. But that letter, even though supported by a visit from Timothy, was not as effective as Paul had hoped.

Paul, therefore, left Ephesus to make an emergency visit to Corinth, one characterized by confrontation. The trip was successful, but while there Paul apparently was slandered by some of his enemies. These accusations must have continued after he left (see 2 Corinthians 1:23–2:1; 3:1; 10:1–11:33).

All this placed Paul in a difficult situation. Obviously, he needed to defend his credibility by responding to these attacks. Yet at the same

---

How to Say It
CORINTH. *Kor*-inth.
CORINTHIANS. Ko-*rin*-thee-unz (*th* as in *thin*).
DAMASCUS. Duh-*mass*-kus.
EPHESUS. *Ef*-uh-sus.
GALATIA. Guh-*lay*-shuh.
GALATIANS. Guh-*lay*-shunz.
MOSES. *Mo*-zes or *Mo*-zez.
NIEBUHR. *Nee*-burr.
PHILIPPIANS. Fih-*lip*-ee-unz.

time, he did not want to fall into arrogant boasting about his accomplishments or enter the trap of comparing résumés. He avoided these problems by emphasizing his weaknesses as proof that God was working through him in a unique and powerful way.

I. Vision of Glory (2 Corinthians 12:1-4)

A. Undesired Talking Point (v. 1)

1. It is not expedient for me doubtless to glory. I will come to visions and revelations of the Lord.

Paul begins by stressing that he wishes he didn't have to say any of what he is about to say. Back in 2 Corinthians 10:12-18; 11:5, 6, Paul was clear that he didn't want to rehearse his credentials yet he felt compelled to do so in view of his enemies' slander.

Paul especially feared that the accusations of enemies would lead the Corinthians to doubt the validity of the gospel that he had preached to them (11:4). As such, he determined to boast only about his own weaknesses and thereby emphasize the power of God working through his ministry (11:30). [See question #1, page 511.]

B. Unexpected Event (vv. 2-4)

2. I knew a man in Christ above fourteen years ago, (whether in the body, I cannot tell; or whether out of the body, I cannot tell: God knoweth;) such a one caught up to the third heaven.

The *man* in consideration here is clearly Paul himself. If Paul writes 2 Corinthians in A.D. 57, then *fourteen years ago* would date the experience in question to around A.D. 43. This is near the time of the brief visit to Jerusalem mentioned at Acts 11:27-30; 12:25. It is possible that Paul is referring to a vision that occurred in conjunction with his special commission to preach in Acts 13:1-3.

The biblical Hebrew word for *heaven* actually is plural: heavens (compare Genesis 2:1, 4). In some schools of thought in ancient Judaism, there are seven heavens that make up a complicated scheme. Paul here alludes to a much more basic line of thinking: the first heaven is the sky (where the birds fly), the second heaven is the universe (home to sun, moon, and stars), and the *third heaven* is the realm where God dwells.

The latter is what we call Heaven today. Paul, then, actually was caught up directly into God's own presence on one particular occasion. What an experience!

3. And I knew such a man, (whether in the body, or out of the body, I cannot tell: God knoweth;).

Paul's uncertainty about *the body* emphasizes the spiritual nature of the event. We may conjecture that this event involved a suspension of consciousness. Is it possible for someone to enter God's presence while still in the flesh (Exodus 33:20)? Paul does not know, and it makes no difference to his point.

4. How that he was caught up into paradise, and heard unspeakable words, which it is not lawful for a man to utter.

Paradise, the "third heaven" of verse 2, is the place of God's dwelling (compare Luke 23:43; Revelation 2:7). Paul, in whatever form, had been in God's presence. But he cannot talk about what he heard and saw there for two reasons. In the first place no person is permitted to reveal these things. That probably means that the vision was for Paul and Paul alone. This fact emphasizes the unique nature of Paul's ministry.

In the second place human language cannot express what Paul witnessed—there are no words to describe it. God's glory far exceeds what the human mind can comprehend or what the human tongue can report.

PAUL'S VISION, OUR VISION

Said Alice to the Cheshire Cat, "Would you tell me please, which way I ought to go from here?"

Said the Cat, "That depends a good deal on where you want to get to."

"I don't much care where . . ." said Alice.

"Then," said the Cat, "it doesn't much matter which way you go" (Lewis Carroll, *Through the Looking Glass*).

This humorous little exchange from the realm of "Wonderland" displays the essential nature of having a vision for the future. It also brings to light a certain confusion regarding how we use the word *vision* today *versus* how Paul used that concept in 2 Corinthians.

Paul's vision was miraculous in nature. A modern understanding of vision, however, is more along the lines of "a clear mental image of a preferable future. . . . It is based on an accurate understanding of God, yourself, and your circumstances" (George Barna, *The Power of Vision:*

How You Can Capture and Apply God's Vision for Your Ministry). We should not expect that God will repeat Paul's vision in the lives of Christians today. Even so, every follower of Jesus must have a vision for a preferable future, as controlled by the Word of God.

Paul's vision of the risen Christ on the Damascus Road and subsequent visions of God's will shaped not only his destiny but also the destiny of the church. May God grant us the courage to embrace God's vision for our own lives as it is drawn from His Word daily. —T. B.

II. Glory of Weakness (2 Corinthians 12:5-10)

A. God's Deeds (vv. 5, 6)

5. Of such a one will I glory: yet of myself I will not glory, but in mine infirmities.

Paul now shifts gears to discuss a particularly difficult problem that hinders his ministry. This statement is intentionally ironic, because Paul himself is the very person he has been talking about.

Paul's point is to say that any boasting that he may do will be about things that God has done for him and through him, not about things that he himself has accomplished by personal ability. Specifically, he would defend himself by reminding his detractors that God had given him a vision of Heaven, but he would also remind them that he received this vision as a gracious gift from God. It was not as payment for work Paul had done. If Paul were to speak about things he has accomplished on his own, the discussion would be much less useful.

6. For though I would desire to glory, I shall not be a fool; for I will say the truth: but now I forbear, lest any man should think of me above that which he seeth me to be, or that he heareth of me.

In point of fact, Paul had built an impressive set of credentials by this time in his "career," as both a Jewish and a Christian leader (see 2 Corinthians 11:21b-28). Should it come down to a bragging session, he will not be ashamed (compare 2 Corinthians 10:8; 11:16).

Paul further discusses his credentials in Philippians 3:4b-7, especially those that would impress Jewish Christians. But all these things must be counted as a loss when compared with the glories of knowing and serving Christ. As such, Paul will not be *a fool*, rambling on and on about his own accomplishments. Instead, he will stress the things that God has accomplished through him.

B. Paul's Thorn (vv. 7-9a)

7. And lest I should be exalted above measure through the abundance of the revelations, there was given to me a thorn in the flesh, the messenger of Satan to buffet me, lest I should be exalted above measure.

The flow of this passage suggests that verse 7 is somehow related to the experience described in verses 1-4. Paul's unique vision certainly could make anyone feel special. But his joy was marred by the fact that it was followed by a *thorn in the flesh*. The position of the verb *given* implies that it was God who gave Paul both the miraculous vision and the painful consequence. The purpose of the thorn, Paul says, is to keep him humble. Thus he will not feel undue pride about the special work God has in store for him. [See question #2, page 511.]

The specific identity of Paul's thorn has long been a subject of speculation. The term *thorn* and the references to the buffeting (suffering) in the flesh that it brings suggest that Paul is referring to a chronic physical ailment. Because this vision of Christ, and presumably the thorn also, came to Paul just before the first missionary journey to Galatia, many scholars have sought the key to this puzzle in Galatians 4:13-15. Paul there mentions a serious illness that befell him at that time, one that possibly affected his eyes in some way.

Whether this or some other problem, the thorn threatened Paul's ministry. Although it came from God, he refers to it as a *messenger of Satan* because from a human perspective it hindered his ability to proclaim the gospel. Yet God knows how to turn such things for the good, as the next verses show. (An alternative view is that Satan initiated the thorn, but the thorn is given by God in the sense that God allowed it, as in Job's case of torment.) [See question #3, page 511.]

8. For this thing I besought the Lord thrice, that it might depart from me.

This verse reveals that it took Paul a while to appreciate God's purposes in the thorn. At first, he viewed it only as a burden. On several occasions Paul asked God to relieve him of it. Doubtless Paul prayed about the issue often, but he recalls at least three occasions in particular when he pleaded with God about this troubling issue. Perhaps he accompanied his pleading with fasting.

Paul's example highlights the fact that it's right to ask God for help with our problems. It is acceptable to ask Him for help more than once when we don't receive a clear answer. We remember that Jesus prayed the same prayer several times in the garden (Matthew 26:36-44). [See question #4, page 511.]

9a. And he said unto me, My grace is sufficient for thee: for my strength is made perfect in weakness.

It is unclear whether God said this to Paul after each of his three periods of supplication or only sometime after the third. It is also unclear whether God revealed this insight in yet another vision of some sort or whether Paul gradually came to this conclusion through God's continued rejections of his request.

Either way, the point is clear: no matter how often or how urgently we ask, God reserves the right to say *no.* But He does not say *no* simply because He wants us to suffer and worry. Our weaknesses serve God's purpose, even if that purpose is only that we should remain humble and dependent on Him.

This perspective gives Paul the *strength* to bear his burden without becoming discouraged and to continue to serve despite its limitations. *Perfect* can be understood as "complete." This highlights the contrast between God's power and our *weakness:* where our strength is lacking, Christ still empowers us to serve.

STRENGTH IN WEAKNESS

The life of Joni Eareckson changed forever on July 30, 1967. She was a young girl full of promise and hope for the future. While on a family outing, she dived into the waters of Chesapeake Bay and struck an object hidden just below the surface. She became paralyzed from the neck down.

She had planned to be an artist. She had planned to have a family. She had planned to live a normal life. But all those dreams and plans seemingly ended in the lonely confines of a wheelchair. And yet Joni is one of the most celebrated Christian speakers and writers of our day.

In her autobiography Joni writes of the power of the Lord Jesus Christ to make any life wonderful and exciting. "Jesus is alive and His power is available to you. He proves Himself daily in my life, and what more couldn't He do in your life!" (*Joni,* Zondervan).

Some may argue that had it not been for the debilitating accident, Joni Eareckson Tada would never have become such an international influence for the cause of Christ. Only the Lord knows if this is so. One thing is for certain: Joni allowed the Lord to work through her weaknesses to display His strength and power.

God is able to work though our weaknesses and trials today. He only asks that we approach each hardship with the eyes of faith. That means trusting that "all things work together for good to them that love God, to them who are the called according to his purpose" (Romans 8:28).
—T. B.

C. God's Strength (vv. 9b, 10)

9b. Most gladly therefore will I rather glory in my infirmities, that the power of Christ may rest upon me.

We normally try to hide our shortcomings from other people. Sometimes we try to hide them from ourselves and from God as well. Paul, however, had said earlier that he would boast about his weaknesses (2 Corinthians 11:30). So now he does just that. He can do this because he is confident that God will make up for what he lacks.

When God calls us to a specific task, He does so with full awareness of our inabilities and limitations. In fact He may call us because of those very limitations. That way it will be clear to everyone that His *power* is at work when we succeed, not just our own natural ability.

Paul learned to accept his thorn because he realized that ultimately it could not stop him from accomplishing God's mission. In fact the thorn became the primary evidence of God's

Ask your students to add to this list. Then use this visual to introduce question #5 on page 511.

Visual for lesson 13

power at work in him, because his success makes it clear that he must be empowered by God's support. Paul's thorn, even though it remains painful and embarrassing, reminds him that God provides the strength.

10. Therefore I take pleasure in infirmities, in reproaches, in necessities, in persecutions, in distresses for Christ's sake: for when I am weak, then am I strong.

No one likes to be persecuted or insulted, of course. No one likes to feel inadequate to the task at hand. But Paul delights in these things *for Christ's sake.* That phrase must mean that Paul is willing to suffer, if need be, in order to fulfill God's commission for his life. Paul's Christian life is characterized by hardship (2 Corinthians 11:23-28). It will eventually end with execution (2 Timothy 4:6).

Yet the attacks of his enemies do not stop him because, ironically, he becomes stronger and stronger the more harm they inflict. This is not in the sense that "whatever doesn't kill me makes me stronger." Rather, it is in the sense that God provides him with more and more power the weaker and less capable he feels. [See question #5, page 511.]

Conclusion

A. Our Limitations

We can easily become discouraged in the face of our limitations. So often we feel that we could be much happier and much more effective if God only would resolve certain persistent problems for us.

These thorns can threaten our faith if we allow them to raise questions of God's care for us. At the same time, however, the fact that we are able to keep pressing forward despite these obstacles reveals God's power and sufficient grace working through our inadequacies. Viewed from this angle, we can embrace hardship with the confidence that everything that happens to us can serve a long-term benefit within God's larger plan for our lives. This is part of what it means to live by faith, not by sight.

B. Our Serenity

Reinhold Niebuhr (1892–1971) penned what has become one of the most famous prayers of all time: "God, give us the grace to accept with serenity the things that cannot be changed, courage to change the things which should be changed, and the wisdom to distinguish one from the other."

This simple request is powerful for its combination of faith and resolve. Many difficulties in life are within our power to overcome, and in such cases, we ask God for the courage to fight the battle. He is the one who is able to strengthen us! But we must also realize that some obstacles may never be taken out of our way in this life. Some weaknesses may plague us until we are at home with the Lord.

Things that hinder our bodies must not, however, hinder our faith. We do not abandon God over these struggles. Rather, we ask Him to give us calm in the midst of the storm. The challenge is in the last line of the prayer: learning to know when to fight and when to let go. It is not surprising that the Prayer of Serenity has been adopted by Alcoholics Anonymous and other recovery groups.

Some problems that we face disappear almost before we really have time to worry about them; others last long enough to distract us; some become ongoing struggles that threaten our peace of mind and our faith. Paul underwent many temporary trials, and our passage today reveals that he also labored under the pain of a persistent thorn in the flesh. He makes no bones about the fact that God refused to lift this burden and never planned to do so. Remarkably, that fact did not cripple Paul's progress. It did not stop him from fulfilling his calling. The thorn ultimately made him stronger by forcing him to rely upon God's power.

Sometimes we need to ask God for relief from problems. Sometimes we need to ask God

---

Home Daily Bible Readings

Monday, Aug. 21—Grace Abounds All the More (Romans 5:12-21)

Tuesday, Aug. 22—Grace for the Humble (James 4:1-10)

Wednesday, Aug. 23—The God of Grace Will Restore (1 Peter 5:5-10)

Thursday, Aug. 24—Paul Receives God's Grace (1 Corinthians 15:3-10)

Friday, Aug. 25—Paul Experiences Many Difficulties (2 Corinthians 11:23-29)

Saturday, Aug. 26—Paul's Deep Spiritual Experience (2 Corinthians 12:1-6)

Sunday, Aug. 27—God's Grace Is Sufficient (2 Corinthians 12:7-13)

repeatedly for relief from problems. Sometimes we need His strength to overcome obstacles. Sometimes we need His peace to live with those obstacles. In all circumstances we need the wisdom and faith to trust in His grace. That grace truly is sufficient for us.

C. Prayer

Father, many times we feel weak and inadequate, and we don't understand the problems in our lives. But we know that You understand our problems. You know us better than we know ourselves.

We ask for the faith to trust You no matter what happens. Help us find the strength that only You can provide so that we can always do what You have called us to do. In Jesus' name, amen.

D. Thought to Remember

Allow God's grace
to shine through your weakness.

Learning by Doing

This section contains an alternative lesson plan emphasizing learning activities. Classes desiring such student involvement will find these suggestions helpful.

Learning Goals

After this lesson each student will be able to:
1. Summarize how Paul's vision relates to his "thorn."
2. Contrast the world's view of power through strength with Paul's view of power through weakness.
3. Commit to God's grace one area of weakness in his or her life, seeking His power to overcome that weakness.

Into the Lesson

Prepare eight large cards with letters from the two words *WEAKNESS* and *STRENGTH*. The first card should have the letter *W* written on the front and the letter *S* on the back. The next card should have the letter *E* written on the front and the letter *T* on the back. (The letters on the backside of the cards should be upside down to the letters on the front of the cards.) Continue in like manner for the remaining cards.

Affix the eight cards to the wall using masking tape on the top of each card so that they can be lifted to show the letter on the back. The letters for the word *WEAKNESS* should face outward.

Also prepare 26 small slips of paper in advance. Each slip should contain one letter of the alphabet. Give each class member one of the slips. (Give more than one slip per student if your class is smaller than 26 students.)

Say to the class, "Ask me a question in this manner regarding your letter(s): 'Is an *A* [or whatever letter that you hold] sufficient?' If your letter is not concealed behind the flaps, I will answer: 'No, that letter is not sufficient.' If your letter is one of the concealed letters, I will say, 'Yes, your letter is sufficient, and then I will lift that flap."

Continue until all letters of *STRENGTH* are revealed. Then affirm, "God turns our weakness into strength, and that is the theme today. God's grace is sufficient for our weakness."

Into the Word

A week ahead of time, recruit a volunteer to play the role of Paul for a dramatized interview. Give your volunteer a copy of the questions based on 2 Corinthians 12:1-10 that follow. Ask your volunteer to word his own answers based on the verses. One sample answer is given.

Remind the class that Paul repeatedly expresses his reluctance to talk about himself and his authority and power. Say, "But today Paul has agreed to come and answer questions about his qualifications and ministry."

Randomly hand out the interview questions (without any answers) to members of your class. Have class members ask Paul their questions in numerical order. (The sequence of questions is related to the verses of today's lesson text.) Introduce the apostle Paul to your class with flair, noting your appreciation for his willingness to talk about his God-given authority and power.

Questions: 1. Paul, why do you consider it appropriate to talk about yourself? [*Sample answer:*

"I certainly should not brag. But perhaps you would let me say a few things about special visions that God gave a trusted servant" (v. 1).] 2. Trusted servant, you say? Who is that servant? *(v. 2)* 3. How did this vision come to this Christian brother? *(v. 2)* 4. What was the nature of his vision? What did he see and what did God say? *(vv. 2, 4).* 5. What's this brother's experience got to do with you? *(v. 5)* 6. Don't you ever want to brag a bit about all the things you have done? *(v. 6)* 7. Do all the great spiritual privileges you have been granted ever tempt you to pride? *(v. 7)* 8. Paul, I have often wondered: if you are God's special messenger, why hasn't God taken your disability away? *(vv. 8, 9)* 9. Have you never questioned God's wisdom in this matter? *(v. 9)* 10. Paul, it sounds to me like you're bragging about being weak. Isn't that a strange approach to life and ministry? *(v. 9)* 11. What are the greatest joys of your apostleship? *(v. 10).*

Into Life

Distribute a rose with thorns to each class member or display a large picture of a rose. Say, "Paul's Christian life was occasionally hindered because of his 'thorn in the flesh.' Yet the aroma of his beautiful life 'rose' to God in praise."

Ask the class, "Do thorns deter people from growing roses? Do they deter people from enjoying their aroma? Do they deter people from marveling in their beauty?" Ask students to use their roses as reminders that life in Christ is beautiful in spite of the thorns. Encourage class members to be honest about self-inflicted thorns.

Let's Talk It Over

These questions are designed to promote discussion of the lesson. The answers here are only discussion starters. Let your class talk it over from there.

1. Paul hesitated to resort to boasting. What makes boasting potentially destructive, both in Paul's day and now? Under what circumstances, if any, could boasting be appropriate today?

The one boasting can easily become puffed up and become guilty of pride. Boasting can convince us that we do not need to rely on God because we can rely on ourselves. Our boasting can cause others to revere us too much and displace their awe of God. They may feel so inferior that they will not launch out on faith in their own spiritual journeys. If people put their faith in what a particular person has done, then they could be left leaderless if the revered person dies or reverts to a life of sin.

2. When something significant happens in your life, spiritual or otherwise, what steps do you take to avoid becoming conceited or prideful? What are some thorns that God may give us (or allow us to have) to forestall pride?

By worldly standards, Paul had a right to brag. However, Paul knew that the only commendation that really counted came from the Lord. Life is short, and earthly glory is fleeting. That should be our awareness as well.

Paul reminds us that God can enter the picture in unexpected ways. God may have protected Paul against pride by allowing a balancing influence like a thorn of some type to enter his life. Modern examples of thorns are probably limited only by the imagination.

3. How can we avoid the temptation of drawing false conclusions about God, self, or life when we have to deal continually with a difficult "thorn in the flesh"?

Some people conclude that on-going difficulty means they have done something wrong and God is judging them. They might think, as a result, that they will never be acceptable to God because of something horrible in their past. Others would say they are being tested by God so that they can prove their faithfulness; they then expect God to heal them miraculously. A third group might become bitter at life and want either to give up or to make others suffer to match their own misery.

Paul's answer always focused on the goodness of God. He never assumed he must have special treatment or that life must be good to him. He was willing to work and witness in spite of his suffering. He lived out the words of Jesus that "the servant is not greater than his lord" (John 13:16). Sometimes we are susceptible to false conclusions also when one of our loved ones has to deal with a painful situation for an extended period of time.

4. Some might say that Paul was self-centered by praying for an easier life, thus showing a lack of faith. Why and under what circumstances is it OK for us to pray for ourselves?

We can pray for ourselves as long as we do not pray for things that are nothing more than pleasurable or entertaining distractions (see James 4:3). Paul's motivation was to be healthy in order to reach more people. His "thorn" actually helped Paul preach successfully in at least one circumstance (see Galatians 4:13-15).

As we pray for ourselves, we need to ask God to use His wisdom in the answer. That means, among other things, that we must be willing to accept a *no* answer from God; at the same time we will experience other blessings that God sends instead.

5. What do you do to remain strong when you feel weak?

If we allow Paul's testimony to help us, we can see how God can turn a bad situation into a victory. A blessed part of that arrangement is in realizing how much we are helped in the process.

We must also take to heart the fact that Paul's prayer was not answered quickly. He pleaded with the Lord during three periods of time. Slow answers from God may enable us to realize that we have made it thus far with God's help while awaiting an answer. If He sustained us during the waiting period, then He also can sustain us in the future. Learning to be content (Philippians 4:11) may take longer than we realize. Paul had been a Christian for more than 20 years when he wrote the book of Philippians. Perhaps Paul was describing the same slow learning sequence in today's lesson.

COMPANION DEVOTIONS
for Standard Lesson Commentary® Users

Understand and personalize lessons from the Standard Lesson Commentary with the new **Companion Devotions**.

With daily facts and comments, readers' hearts will be prepared for the coming week's lesson.

Standard PUBLISHING
Bringing The Word to Life™

Available at your local Christian bookstore.